After Hiroshima

By emphasizing the role of nuclear issues, *After Hiroshima* provides a new history of American policy in Asia between the dropping of the atomic bombs on Japan and the escalation of the Vietnam War. Drawing on a wide range of documentary evidence, Matthew Jones charts the development of American nuclear strategy and the foreign policy problems it raised, as the United States both confronted China and attempted to win the friendship of an Asia emerging from colonial domination. In underlining American perceptions that Asian peoples saw the possible repeat use of nuclear weapons as a manifestation of Western attitudes of 'white superiority', he offers new insights into the links between racial sensitivities and the conduct of US policy, and a fresh interpretation of the transition in American strategy from massive retaliation to flexible response in the era spanned by the Korean and Vietnam wars.

MATTHEW JONES is Professor of American Foreign Relations at the University of Nottingham. His previous publications include *Britain, the United States, and the Mediterranean War, 1942–44* (1996) and *Conflict and Confrontation in South East Asia, 1961–1965* (Cambridge, 2002).

After Hiroshima

The United States, Race and Nuclear Weapons in Asia, 1945–1965

Matthew Jones

CAMBRIDGE UNIVERSITY PRESS
Cambridge, New York, Melbourne, Madrid, Cape Town, Singapore,
São Paulo, Delhi

Cambridge University Press
The Edinburgh Building, Cambridge CB2 8RU, UK

Published in the United States of America by Cambridge University Press,
New York

www.cambridge.org
Information on this title: www.cambridge.org/9780521881005

First published 2010

Printed in the United Kingdom at the University Press, Cambridge

A catalogue record for this publication is available from the British Library

ISBN 978-0-521-88100-5 Hardback

For Amir

Contents

Acknowledgements

During the course of compiling what has proved to be a more wide-ranging book than was first anticipated, I have benefited, as always, from the advice and assistance of many individuals. Among the numerous archivists and librarians who have helped with identification of research materials, I would particularly like to thank David Haight, whose immense knowledge automatically makes any trip to the Eisenhower Library productive and fruitful, as well as Regina Greenwill and John Wilson, who proved invaluable guides to the holdings of the Johnson Library. Financial support has come from the Arts and Humanities Research Council, whose excellent research leave scheme made possible the completion of the book, and contributions to travel and expenses from the History Department at Royal Holloway, University of London; the School of American and Canadian Studies at the University of Nottingham; the British Academy; the Lyndon B. Johnson Presidential Library who made a Moody award; the Eccles Centre for North American Studies at the British Library who funded a visiting fellowship; and the Gilder Lehrman Institute of American History who awarded a fellowship allowing work in the Butler Library at Columbia University. Much gratitude is owed to the many friends and colleagues in the academic community in both the United States and Britain who have given support and encouragement, including Richard Aldrich, Kathy Burk, Bill Burr, Steve Casey, Justin Champion, Bob Dallek, Richard Immerman, Joel Isaac, Mark Lawrence, Fred Logevall, Roger Louis, David Milne, Philip Murphy, Jason Parker, Andrew Preston, Brad Simpson, Tony Stockwell, Marc Trachtenberg and Clive Webb. My sincerest thanks go to John Parachini and Hadley Boyd for their incomparable generosity and hospitality on my visits to Washington, DC. Among colleagues at the University of Nottingham, I would particularly like to thank Richard King, Pete Messent, Sharon Monteith, Dave Murray, Judie Newman, Maria Ryan and Bevan Sewell. My editor at Cambridge University Press, Michael Watson, has been immensely supportive since the book's first inception, and guided me through the process of bringing the manuscript to publication with timely advice and comment. I would also like to acknowledge the role played by the anonymous referees who examined and approved the original proposal. I have been exceptionally fortunate to have had Jacqueline French as my copy-editor.

My largest debt of gratitude in the work that follows is, however, owed to my family, who have often had to tolerate the untidy study, moments of absent-mindedness and archival meanderings that have been such a notable feature of the past few years. My morale and confidence have been sustained by seeing my three children, Anya, Alexander and Sofia, growing up around me, and my wife, Amir, has given unwavering support and encouragement. It is to her that this book is lovingly dedicated.

Acronyms

ABCC	Atomic Bomb Casualty Commission
AEC	Atomic Energy Commission
ANZUS	Australia–New Zealand–United States
APAG	Atlantic Policy Advisory Group
CAB	Cabinet
CCP	Chinese Communist Party
CDF	Central Decimal File
CIA	Central Intelligence Agency
CINCFE	Commander-in-Chief, Far East Command
CINCPAC	Commander-in-Chief, Pacific Command
CNO	Chief of Naval Operations
COMSAC	Commander, Strategic Air Command
COS	Chiefs of Staff (British)
CSUSA	Chief of Staff, US Army
DDEL	Dwight D. Eisenhower Library
DDRS	Declassified Documents Reference System
DEFE	Defence
DO	Dominions Office
DRV	Democratic Republic of Vietnam
FEPC	Fair Employment Practices Committee
FO	Foreign Office
FRUS	*Foreign Relations of the United States*
HSTL	Harry S. Truman Library
ICBM	Intercontinental Ballistic Missile
IPR	Institute of Pacific Relations
JCS	Joint Chiefs of Staff (US)
JFKL	John F. Kennedy Library
JIC	Joint Intelligence Committee
JSOP	Joint Strategic Objectives Plan
JSPC	Joint Strategic Plans Committee
JSSC	Joint Strategic Survey Committee
LBJL	Lyndon B. Johnson Library

LC	Library of Congress
LDP	Liberal Democratic Party (Japan)
MAP	Military Assistance Program
MDAP	Mutual Development and Assistance Program
MRBM	Medium-Range Ballistic Missile
NAACP	National Association for the Advancement of Colored People
NARA	National Archives and Records Administration
NATO	North Atlantic Treaty Organization
NIE	National Intelligence Estimate
NSC	National Security Council
NYT	*New York Times*
OCB	Operations Coordinating Board
POLAD	Political Adviser
PPC	Policy Planning Council
PPS	Policy Planning Staff
PRC	People's Republic of China
PREM	Premier
RG	Record Group
SAC	Strategic Air Command
SASAE	Special Assistant to the Secretary of State for Atomic Energy and Outer Space
SEATO	South East Asia Treaty Organization
SIOP	Single Integrated Operational Plan
SNIE	Special National Intelligence Estimate
TNA	The National Archives
TS	Top Secret
UN	United Nations
UNESCO	United Nations Educational, Scientific and Cultural Organization
USIA	United States Information Agency
USIS	United States Information Service
WO	War Office
WP	*Washington Post*

Introduction

Few events of the twentieth century have received as much sustained attention from historians, or been the subject of such enduring controversy, as the atomic bombing of Japan in August 1945. The predominant focus of interest has tended to be on the sequence of events that, along with the motivations of the principal antagonists, led to the attacks that devastated Hiroshima and Nagasaki, with all the terrible human suffering that they involved. Set against repeated efforts to defend the use of the bombs as a means to shorten the war have been accounts which have variously branded the action as needless, in that Japan's surrender was imminent, as a morally reprehensible example of targeting a civilian population for mass destruction, and as partly driven by a political desire to demonstrate American power, not least to intimidate a Soviet Union which was already emerging as a dangerous potential post-war rival to the United States.[1] Many choose, moreover, to look at Hiroshima and Nagasaki either as the coda to a world war of unmatched scope and intensity, or as opening signals for the international tensions, and incipient destructive potential, that would come to characterize the soon to develop Cold War. Virtually all studies recognize that the first operational use of the bomb marked a watershed in conceptions of war and the development of strategic thought. The era of mass, industrialized warfare, with fully mobilized populations primed for prolonged periods of conflict, often attritional in their nature, was now giving way to a technologically driven arms race, where a new vocabulary of deterrence was beginning to take shape, and the awful consequences of nuclear use, and the threat of uncontrollable escalation, would hover over the conduct of international relations.

Less well appreciated though, and one of the important themes of the book that follows, has been the observation – made at the time and subsequently – that the use of the bomb against the Japanese possessed a

---

[1] For the moral critique, see Michael Walzer, *Just and Unjust Wars: A Moral Argument with Historical Illustrations*, 4th edn (New York, 2006), 264–8.

racial dimension. It was alleged, quite simply, that the United States would never have used such terrible weapons on a white population. Americans were, however, accused of being fully prepared to unleash them, in callous and vindictive fashion, on a Far Eastern enemy which bitter wartime prejudice had frequently vilified as subhuman. The atomic attacks were seen as representing but another element of the deep racism that permeated all aspects of American society.[2] This interpretation of American behaviour gained some currency immediately after Hiroshima and Nagasaki, and would be repeated by critics of US policy over many subsequent years, particularly as the prospect of further nuclear use in Asia was suggested by successive administrations in Washington and nuclear testing was undertaken in the Pacific. As far as American officials were concerned, in the competition for political influence in Asia that featured after the emergence of the People's Republic of China (PRC) in 1949, such allegations of racial discrimination, and the wider political problems raised by the presence of nuclear weapons, could do the cause of the United States real and lasting harm. Although not subscribing to the idea that a kind of crude racism informed the American decision to use the bomb in 1945, this book nevertheless endeavours to trace the recurring appearance and operation of this neglected theme, and its impact on American policy, as the Western powers tried to curtail what was seen as the growing threat from Communist China in East and South East Asia, in a process which was to culminate in the escalation of American involvement in the Vietnam War.

In parallel with this aim, this book explores the contours of US nuclear history in the Far East as a whole, and the changing strategic posture adopted by the United States in the era spanned by the wars in Korea and Vietnam, and until the PRC's acquisition of nuclear status. The emphasis throughout has been on the political problems faced by the United States in implementing its evolving nuclear and defence policies in Asia, and how the issue of race could intrude. In this way, it has been possible to use nuclear history as a prism through which to observe the development of American views on their troubled relations with the peoples and states of the region, where anxieties were often expressed over a growing estrangement between the United States – invariably identified with the 'white West' – and an Asia finding its own sense of identity following the end of Western colonial domination.

---

[2] For the argument that a racial undercurrent was at work in the disregard shown by Truman and other senior American officials for the human consequences of nuclear use against Japan, see Ronald Takaki, *Hiroshima: Why America Dropped the Atomic Bomb* (Boston, 1995), 93–100.

Aside from such central preoccupations has been the chance this book offers to present more evidence on the transnational connections that can be drawn between race and US foreign relations after 1945, an area which has been the subject of a growing body of scholarship in recent years.[3] Harold Isaacs, who had worked as a reporter for *Newsweek* in the Far East during the Second World War and moved on to a distinguished post-war academic career as a political scientist, would often point out to the liberal audiences who absorbed his many articles, pamphlets and books on Asia and Africa that American racial discrimination at home had become 'a central fact in our world relations'. To Africans and Asians, this fact served to identify Americans with colonial practices and mentalities: 'they recognize it for what it is and relate it to their own experience. This in turn automatically helps shape their instinctive attitudes toward the United States as a country and toward Americans as a people.'[4] It is a contention of this book that a 'colour consciousness' infused the world-views of senior US policy-makers, making them responsive to the accusation that their actions were underpinned with the racism that then featured in American society, or that they would be seen to be demonstrating indifference towards the lives of 'non-white' Asian peoples. The failure to 'connect' with Asia (particularly with those countries associated with the non-aligned movement) was a constant refrain heard among critical observers of American policy in the Far East in the decade following the 'loss' of China in 1949. If the United States was to win more friends and gather influence in the great arc of states and societies stretching from Japan, around the China periphery across mainland and maritime South East Asia and over to India, then it was widely felt it needed to exhibit sympathy for and understanding of the needs and concerns of local populations, and distance itself from the residual colonial attitudes of the Europeans. This imperative of emotional commitment and empathy was also a notable feature of American middlebrow culture during this period,

---

[3] See, e.g., Mary L. Dudziak, 'Desegregation as a Cold War Imperative', *Stanford Law Review*, 41, November 1988, 61–120; Mary L. Dudziak, *Cold War Civil Rights: Race and the Image of American Democracy* (Princeton, 2000); Azza Salama Layton, *International Politics and Civil Rights Policies in the United States, 1941–1960* (Cambridge, 2000); Brenda Gayle Plummer, *Rising Wind: Black Americans and U.S. Foreign Affairs, 1935–1960* (Chapel Hill, 1996); Penny M. Von Eschen, *Race against Empire: Black Americans and Anticolonialism, 1937–1957* (Ithaca, 1997); Gerald Horne, *Black and Red: W. E. B. Du Bois and the Afro-American Response to the Cold War, 1943–1963* (Albany, 1986); Thomas Borstelmann, *The Cold War and the Color Line: American Race Relations in the Global Arena* (London, 2001); Brenda Gayle Plummer (ed.), *Window on Freedom: Race, Civil Rights, and Foreign Affairs, 1945–1988* (Chapel Hill, 2003).

[4] Harold R. Issacs, *Two-Thirds of the World: Problems of a New Approach to the Peoples of Asia, Africa, and Latin America* (Washington, DC, 1950), 42–3.

as people-to-people narratives and exchanges sought to bridge the gulf between Americans and Asians.[5] So too in the more rarified world of high-level policy advice, many examples can be found of a conscious need to avoid any implication of racial bias in the construction of Cold War policies. The fear that loomed largest, exemplified at the time of the Bandung Conference in 1955, was of a pan-Asian movement mobilized under the leadership of Communist China, with India in cohorts, determined to evict the white West from the area (recalling in striking fashion the Second World War images of Japan leading an 'Asia for the Asians' movement in opposition to Western and white imperialism).[6] While the public discourse of the Cold War was usually conducted in terms of a 'Free World versus Communist' binary, there was also a private and alarmist language of civilizational clashes, often couched in terms of race, that can be discerned in the thinking and attitudes of US officials in the 1940s and 1950s.[7] In September 1960, the retired State Department official Adolf Berle noted how he could see that 'we shall have, pretty soon, not one cold war but two or three: Communist against non-Communist; Negro against White; possibly Asian against them all. The mills of the gods of hatred may grind slowly but they grind terribly.'[8]

Beyond its account of diplomatic history and changing military strategy, therefore, this book argues that the use of the atomic bombs, and the later reliance placed on nuclear weapons in US national security policy, had many complex repercussions for relations between the United States and Asia. It approaches this subject largely from the perspective of American policy-makers, though some illustrative material has been incorporated into what follows in order to give an idea of contemporary Asian views (with a particular emphasis on India and Japan). There has, however, been no intention here to provide a comprehensive and definitive view of the popular and political pulse on the issues surrounding nuclear weapons across the whole of Asia, an undertaking which would

---

[5] See Christina Klein, *Cold War Orientalism: Asia in the Middlebrow Imagination, 1945–1961* (Berkeley, 2003), 27–8 and *passim*.

[6] See the present author's 'A "Segregated" Asia? Race, the Bandung Conference, and Pan-Asianist Fears in American Thought and Policy, 1954–55', *Diplomatic History*, 29, 5, November 2005, 841–68; also Cary Fraser, 'An American Dilemma: Race and Realpolitik in the American Response to the Bandung Conference', in Plummer (ed.), *Window on Freedom*, 115–40.

[7] This is a theme given explicit treatment in Matthew Connelly, 'Taking Off the Cold War Lens: Visions of North–South Conflict during the Algerian War for Independence', *American Historical Review*, 105, 3, June 2000, 739–69; see also Matthew Connelly, *A Diplomatic Revolution: Algeria's Fight for Independence and the Origins of the Post-Cold War Era* (New York, 2002), 91–5, 105–9.

[8] Diary entry for 22 September 1960, Beatrice B. Berle and Travis B. Jacobs (eds.), *Navigating the Rapids, 1918–1971: From the Papers of Adolf A. Berle* (New York, 1973), 717.

require study of an almost overwhelming range and variety of sources across many countries, and where generalization would be inevitable but also arbitrary and hazardous. Readings of 'Asian opinion' ventured at the time tended to be focused on Indian commentary partly because India occupied a special and central place in understandings of Asian nationalist sentiment: as the home of the oldest nationalist movement in the region, the first Asian state to achieve the goal of independence from colonial rule, the most populous non-Communist Asian country, and the pioneering leader of the non-aligned movement in the early post-war years. That said, American observers of the Asian scene also cast their eyes beyond Indian opinion and comment in forming their impressions of the image held by Asians of the United States. In addition, Japanese attitudes and sensitivities regarding nuclear issues, as the only victims of nuclear attack, were of much importance and have been given attention in what follows, especially as Japan was host to key US bases throughout the period and considered the most strategically significant state in the region.

It will be noticed that American officials, along with their British counterparts, made frequent reference during the period covered to 'Asian opinion', as though this were something concrete and tangible. Even providing an acceptable geographical definition of 'Asia', however, is no straightforward task; so vast and complex an area, with a multiplicity of national, ethnic and religious groupings, makes any generalization concerning a shared view or opinion open to numerous objections and qualifications. Yet, often with full awareness of these pitfalls, experienced and knowledgeable officials would fall back on the abstraction. Part of the reason was the understandable human need to simplify and classify a great deal of incoming information from different sources to allow interpretation for policy purposes, but it was also because several Asian opinion-formers and commentators, familiar to Western audiences, themselves employed such generalizations. This was typically to denote the significance of an Asia (the 'new Asia' as it was often styled) that was emerging from colonial rule and Western imperial domination in the period following the defeat of Japan in 1945, when Japan's victories over the Western powers in the years preceding had exploded the myth of European omnipotence. The prime focus of this book remains, therefore, with Western perceptions, attitudes and evaluations, and how they came to influence the formation and conduct of policy. A starting point here is to acknowledge how the use of the atomic bombs in 1945 was seen not just as the culminating event of a war that had witnessed a transformation in the international position of the United States, but as marking the beginning of a new, contested phase of American engagement across the Pacific frontier.

1   In the shadow of Hiroshima: the United States and Asia in the aftermath of Japanese defeat

> After the rain came a wind – the great 'fire wind' – which blew back in towards the centre of the catastrophe, increasing in force as the air over Hiroshima grew hotter and hotter because of the great fires. The wind blew so hard that it uprooted huge trees in the parks where survivors were collecting. Thousands of people were simply fleeing, blindly and without an objective except to get out of the city. Some in the suburbs, seeing them come, thought at first they were Negroes, not Japanese, so blackened were their skins. The refugees could not explain what had burned them. 'We saw the flash,' they said, 'and this is what happened.'[1]

In many respects, the use of the atomic bomb against Japan seemed a fitting climax to the Far Eastern War of 1941–5, a conflict where many Americans exhibited a level of hatred for their Asian adversary that some historians have argued gave the fighting in the Pacific a different quality to that found in the European theatres of war. Racial animosity, fuelled by a desire for revenge, it is maintained, became one of the defining characteristics of the struggle with Japan. Having reared its head several times already since early in the century, anti-Japanese racism in the United States poured forth during the years after Pearl Harbor, with the enemy frequently caricatured in subhuman terms, in some cases fit for little more than extermination. As Japanese forces themselves engaged in widespread atrocities across the areas that came under their control, indulged in their own racial stigmatizing of local peoples, and maltreated allied prisoners of war in a quite appalling fashion, American perceptions of Japanese cruelty, perfidy and fanaticism were recycled and given added credibility.[2]

---

[1] Fletcher Knebel and Charles Bailey, *No High Ground: The Secret History of the Hiroshima Bomb* (London, 1960), 185.
[2] See, e.g., James C. Thomson, Peter W. Stanley and John Curtis Perry, *Sentimental Imperialists: The American Experience in East Asia* (New York, 1981), 205; Christopher Thorne, *The Issue of War: States, Societies, and the Far Eastern Conflict of 1941–1945* (London, 1985), 125–31; Michael S. Sherry, *The Rise of American Air Power: The Creation of Armageddon* (New Haven, 1987), 242–6; John W. Dower, *War without Mercy:*

After reversing the early setbacks of the war, American servicemen felt no compunction to take prisoners as they inched their way forward towards the Japanese home islands, with some even resorting to collecting the body parts of enemy dead. After Pearl Harbor, Japanese-Americans in the United States had their property removed, were physically interned and denied their basic rights as citizens, even as attempts were made to assimilate German-Americans and Italian-Americans into the war effort.[3] To many sections of American public opinion, in fact, incensed by the surprise blows that had been struck in 1941–2, and by tales of the Bataan death march, Japan was their primary opponent in the Second World War, and, notwithstanding the exertions of the British in Burma or the Australians in New Guinea, the Pacific front was where the United States could make its most untrammelled and distinctive contribution to overall victory, largely free from the tiresome requirements of consultation with allies.[4]

Given this context, the bitter fighting during the Pacific island campaigns and then the large-scale conventional aerial bombing of Japan from November 1944 onwards simply paved the way for Hiroshima and Nagasaki: the devastation of the two cities was regarded by most Americans as just retribution for the treacherous attacks in 1941 that had brought the United States into the fighting. It was, moreover, widely considered the only way to end the war without the thousands of casualties a direct invasion was likely to entail.[5] One Gallup poll conducted in late August 1945 found that 85 per cent of those questioned approved of the use of the bomb against Japanese cities.[6] 'I realize the tragic significance of the atomic bomb,' President Harry S. Truman told his radio audience on the evening of the Nagasaki attack. 'Having found the bomb we have used it. We have used it against those who attacked us without warning at Pearl Harbor, against those who have starved and beaten and executed American prisoners of war, against those who have abandoned all

   Race and Power in the Pacific War (New York, 1986), 1–2, 8–9, 36–7, 156–63. The Pulitzer Prize-winning historian Allan Nevins, writing just after the war, affirmed that, 'Probably in all our history, no foe has been detested as were the Japanese', *ibid.*, 33.

[3] Roger Daniels, *Prisoners without Trial: Japanese Americans in World War Two* (New York, 1993).

[4] See Christopher Thorne, *Allied of a Kind: The United States, Britain, and the War against Japan, 1941–1945* (London, 1978), 156, 288.

[5] There is a massive literature on the American use of the bomb in 1945; see, e.g., Michael J. Hogan (ed.), *Hiroshima in History and Memory* (Cambridge, 1996); J. Samuel Walker, *Prompt and Utter Destruction: Truman and the Use of Atomic Bombs against Japan* (Chapel Hill, 1997); Barton J. Bernstein, 'The Atomic Bombings Reconsidered', *Foreign Affairs*, 74, 1, Jan/Feb 1995, 135–52; Martin J. Sherwin, *A World Destroyed: Hiroshima and Its Legacies*, 3rd edn (Stanford, 2003); and for the most recent international history, Tsuyoshi Hasegawa, *Racing the Enemy: Stalin, Truman, and the Surrender of Japan* (Boston, 2005).

[6] See 'The Quarter's Polls', *Public Opinion Quarterly*, 9, 3, Autumn 1945, 385.

pretence of obeying international laws of warfare. We have used it to shorten the agony of young Americans. We shall continue to use it until we completely destroy Japan's power to make war. Only a Japanese surrender will stop us.'[7] The *Chicago Daily Tribune* intoned in one editorial that though the two atomic bombs may have killed thousands of Japanese civilians, 'if they brought Japan to a realization of its condition, they have saved hundreds of thousands of lives, Japanese as well as American. Being merciless, they were merciful ... If the two bombs bring the war to an end, American boys, possibly as many as a million of them, will be restored, in direct consequence, to homes to which they never would have returned, which would have been homes of sorrow ... They were terrible engines of destruction; they were also agents of a greater good.'[8] Many newspapers echoed the commonly held view that having instigated the conflict, Japan was now merely reaping the consequences of its own treachery and rapacious ambitions for Pacific dominance.[9]

Moral doubts about the use of the bomb without warning against a defenceless civilian population did emerge in some (particularly religious) quarters in August 1945, but such voices were drowned out by the immediate celebrations and relief that came with victory. After Hiroshima, an agitated John Foster Dulles, already one of the Republican Party's leading spokesmen on foreign affairs, and who was then chairing the Federal Council of Churches' Commission on a Just and Durable Peace, wanted to see further attacks suspended in order to give Japan a chance to surrender, questioned the moral basis for the bomb's employment against innocent civilians, and called for international controls over atomic energy.[10] The Federal Council of Churches' general secretary, Samuel McCrea Cavert, wrote to Truman on 11 August with a plea that no more bombs be used, only for the President to reply that though disturbed by the destruction, he was even more disturbed by Pearl Harbor and the fate of American prisoners of war who had suffered at Japanese hands: 'The only language they seem to understand is the one we have been using to bombard them. When you have to deal with a

---

[7] Quoted in Herbert Feis, *Japan Subdued* (Princeton, 1961), 118.

[8] 'For This We Fought', *Chicago Daily Tribune*, 11 August 1945.

[9] See Paul Boyer, *By the Bomb's Early Light: American Thought and Culture at the Dawn of the Atomic Age* (New York, 1985), 12–13. See also the recollections of the *Time* war correspondent Theodore White on arriving in Japan in August 1945, in his *In Search of History: A Personal Adventure* (London, 1978), 227–8.

[10] See Neal Rosendorf, 'John Foster Dulles' Nuclear Schizophrenia', in John L. Gaddis, Philip H. Gordon, Ernest R. May and Jonathan Rosenberg (eds.), *Cold War Statesmen Confront the Bomb: Nuclear Diplomacy since 1945* (Oxford, 1999), 64–6.

beast you have to treat him as a beast. It is most regrettable but never-theless true.'[11] In fact Truman, the man on whose shoulders ultimate responsibility for the attacks rested, never seems to have doubted the necessity for using the bomb, a subject on which he was quizzed several times after 1945. For most Americans, perhaps hardly surprisingly, there was no concrete and strong impression of the Japanese as victims of an atomic attack, and no inclination to deflate the exultant flush of victory, where the comforting narrative of a war fought against tyranny whose outcome became an affirmation of American values was already being thoroughly absorbed into cultural and societal memory.[12]

Press and popular comment in the wake of Hiroshima was transfixed by the idea that a new 'atomic age' had now dawned, holding both ominous and beneficent qualities. Delight and pride at American power and achievement was mixed with apprehension about what the revolutionary discovery might mean for post-war peace and security.[13] Officials at the British Embassy in Washington reported that 'stories of the atomic bomb appealed to everything most typical in the American nature. The lurid fantasies of the comic strips seemed suddenly to have come true. Headlines sagged under the weight of the drama and the superlatives they had to carry.'[14] Typical responses, in both the United States and Britain, were to look towards the need for post-war co-operation through world organization, or, as Dulles had anticipated, the international con-trol and safeguarding of atomic energy, if Western societies were to escape the nightmare of nuclear war. The new British Prime Minister, Clement Attlee, expressed his own private concerns in a memorandum of late August 1945, where he argued that 'we must declare that this invention has made it essential to end wars. The new World Order must start now ... Every nation must submit to the rule of law ... All nations ... must look to a peaceful future instead of a warlike past ... This sort of

[11] Quoted in Robert J. Donovan, *Conflict and Crisis: The Presidency of Harry S Truman, 1945–1948* (New York, 1977), 96–7.
[12] On the muted impressions of Hiroshima and Nagasaki, see Lane Fenrich, 'Mass Death in Miniature: How Americans Became Victims of the Bomb', in Laura Hein and Mark Selden (eds.), *Living with the Bomb: American and Japanese Cultural Conflicts in the Nuclear Age* (Armonk, NY, 1997), 123; Sherry, *Rise of American Air Power*, 350–1. The relative insulation of American society from the material effects of the war could also be noted here; as one American put it in 1943, most of his fellow citizens were 'fighting this war on imagination alone'; see John M. Blum, *V Was for Victory: Politics and American Culture during World War Two* (New York, 1976), 16.
[13] See, e.g., Boyer, *By the Bomb's Early Light*, 7–12, 14–24, 29–34, and *passim*; on the concerns of the atomic scientists, see James G. Hershberg, *James B. Conant: Harvard to Hiroshima and the Making of the Atomic Age* (Stanford, 1993), 225–9, 238–45.
[14] Washington (Balfour) to FO, No. 5560, 11 August 1945, AN2433/4/45, FO 371/44537, The National Archives (TNA), Kew.

thing has in the past been considered a Utopian dream. It has become today the essential condition of the survival of civilisation and possibly of life in [*sic*] this planet.'[15] Attlee's first thoughts were echoed across the Atlantic, and American enthusiasts for world government had a tempo-rary field day as people searched for a solution to the contemporary dilemma.[16] As the United States stood poised in 1945 to take up the international responsibilities that many felt it had foolishly shirked after the First World War, the atomic bomb served both as an urgent reminder of the costs of failure and the imperative of involvement.[17] For British observers, the bomb, to their relief, was 'doing more than Pearl Harbour ... to obliterate the last vestiges of the [American] isolationist dream'.[18] A new sense of vulnerability was also apparent, and though there were still hopes that the wartime example of constructive relations with the Soviet Union might be maintained, there was also a growing acceptance, at least in official circles, that the realities of power politics could not be easily avoided and that Russian post-war ambitions might be more extensive than previously anticipated.[19] It was mounting distrust of the Soviet Union, indeed, that helped to turn public and congressional attitudes against forsaking the American nuclear monopoly by yielding control over the bomb to any international authority.[20]

The atomic bomb's use against Japan in 1945 was clearly symbolic of the industrial and technological prowess harnessed by the United States that had contributed so manifestly to victory over the Axis powers.[21] It was in the Far East, moreover, where overwhelming American resources had been on most conspicuous display. In mid-1942 Japan had appeared ascendant throughout the region, from China to the Marshall Islands, and from the Burmese border with India to the South West Pacific, but the Allies had first checked and then reversed the Japanese advance. After its initial setbacks, the US Navy had come to dominate the vast expanses

---

[15] Attlee memorandum, 'The Atomic Bomb', GEN 75/1, 28 August 1945, CAB 130/3, TNA.

[16] See Boyer, *By the Bomb's Early Light*, 7–8, 33–40; and Lawrence S. Wittner, *One World or None: A History of the World Nuclear Disarmament Movement Through 1953* (Stanford, 1993), 66–71, 92–3.

[17] See, e.g., Michael S. Sherry, *In the Shadow of War: The United States since the 1930s* (New Haven, 1995), 114–15.

[18] Washington (Balfour) to FO, No. 5560, 11 August 1945, AN2433/4/45, FO 371/44537, TNA.

[19] See John L. Gaddis, 'The Insecurities of Victory: The United States and the Perception of the Soviet Threat after World War Two', in *The Long Peace: Inquiries into the History of the Cold War* (New York, 1987), 20–47.

[20] See John L. Gaddis, *The United States and the Origins of the Cold War, 1941–1947* (New York, 1972), 256–7.

[21] See, e.g., Melvyn P. Leffler, *A Preponderance of Power: National Security, the Truman Administration and the Cold War* (Stanford, 1992), 2–3.

of the Pacific, its carrier groups roaming the seas near Japan and the China coast. Marine and army units were scattered across numerous islands, and the reoccupation of the Philippines was complete by July 1945.[22] From bases in the Marianas, American aircraft had subjected Japanese cities to a furious degree of bombardment as the time for a final assault on the home islands approached. As well as putting the seal on the victory against Japan, the use of the atomic bomb appeared to underline the position of post-war leadership in Asia that it was now within American capacities to exercise. Holding a newly enhanced sense of expanded security needs, since 1944, the US Joint Chiefs of Staff (JCS) had already begun directing covetous eyes at a network of Pacific island bases that might be brought under permanent American control in the post-war settlement.[23] Though possessing a strong self-image of historic antagonism to colonialism, and having had another opportunity to find fault with the decrepit empires of Britain and France during the war years, many Americans seemed to see little contradiction in their own pursuit of advantage, as if the virtues inherent in the American people could cancel out the practical effects of their actions. The Secretary of the Navy, James V. Forrestal, summed this up with his memorable remark that, 'Power must remain with the people who hate power.'[24] It was in Asia, moreover, where some could see a special role for the unique American experiment opening up, as Japanese militarism was expunged and European colonialism consigned as a failing anachronism. This was certainly the case when it came to an individual such as the vainglorious General Douglas MacArthur, most of whose military career had been spent in the Far East, and who saw a messianic quality to the role of the United States in the area.[25] There was, also, the example of the Philippines to point to, where the United States made good on its pre-war promise of independence in July 1946, in what many Americans regarded as a model of how dependent people should be treated; less conspicuous was the fact that the Philippine economy remained beholden to the American market, and Washington retained the right to maintain military bases.[26] In Japan itself, MacArthur now

[22] See, e.g., Thorne, *Allies*, 407–8, 520–1; White, *In Search of History*, 223.
[23] For American plans to take over the Japanese mandated islands in the Pacific, see Thorne, *Allies*, 490–1.
[24] Forrestal diary, 15–17 April 1945, quoted in Mark A. Stoler, *Allies and Adversaries: The Joint Chiefs of Staff, the Grand Alliance, and U.S. Strategy in World War Two* (Chapel Hill, 2000), 242.
[25] See, e.g., Douglas MacArthur, *Reminiscences* (London, 1964), 32; White, *In Search of History*, 109.
[26] See Stanley Karnow, *In Our Image: America's Empire in the Philippines* (New York, 1989), 330–2; Nick Cullather, *Illusions of Influence: The Political Economy of United States–Philippines Relations, 1942–1960* (Stanford, 1994), 41, 51–9.

stood at the head of an occupation regime which oversaw a process of democratization and demilitarization that, drawing from the New Deal experience (ironically, given MacArthur's Republican proclivities), was intended to reform and reshape the country along liberal, capitalist lines.[27]

Through its victory in 1945, the United States had, on the surface at least, delivered a setback to an Asian challenge to Western domination in the Far East that stretched back into the nineteenth century, as Japan, following the Meiji Restoration, sought to strengthen itself and reverse the unequal treaties imposed after the arrival of Commodore Matthew Perry's black ships.[28] Indeed, Japan had seen fit to cast its war effort in terms of an overall struggle that pitted the white West against an Asia that had at last united under Tokyo's leadership in order to throw off the shackles of colonialism and establish a new order where Asian values might hold centre stage. Although Japanese propaganda regarding 'liberation' from imperialist exploitation had in a great number of cases acted as a cynical cloak for the brutal exploitation of conquered areas, and also increased in volume as allied victories accumulated, the ideological underpinnings of an 'Asia for the Asians' movement were given emphasis at such gatherings as the Greater East Asia Conference that was staged in Tokyo during November 1943, which drew together representatives from Thailand, Burma and the Philippines, as well as officials from the puppet governments in Japanese-occupied China and Manchuria.[29] Looking back on his experience of attendance, the Burmese nationalist leader Ba Maw spoke of it as representing 'a new Asian spirit', and as the war drew to a close, Japanese administrators gave other local nationalist figures the space to assert their own identities while dismantling the old colonial structures.[30] Undergoing Japanese occupation could also, of course, generate resistance, as in the Philippines, Vietnam or Malaya, but this too only hardened the resolve that past patterns of imperial subjugation should not be allowed to reappear.

Japan's defeat in 1945, though it spelt the end of misery and suffering for the many who had suffered at the hands of the Japanese military, also gave an opportunity for the European colonial powers to re-establish their presence in the region, so frustrating the aspirations for independence that

---

[27] See Michael Schaller, *The American Occupation of Japan: The Origins of the Cold War in Asia* (New York, 1985), 20–5; John W. Dower, *Embracing Defeat: Japan in the Wake of World War Two* (New York, 1999), 73–84; and Takemae Eiji, *The Allied Occupation of Japan* (New York, 2002), 235–43.

[28] See, in general, Richard Storry, *Japan and the Decline of the West in Asia* (London, 1979).

[29] Thorne, *Issue of War*, 113–15.

[30] Ba Maw, *Breakthrough in Burma: Memoirs of a Revolution* (London, 1968), 336.

had been fostered in the changed conditions of wartime. This 'second colonial occupation' in South East Asia was, however, to prove relatively short-lived, as the Asian nationalist sentiments unleashed during the war years refused to be subdued. As Japanese authority collapsed across South East Asia in the wake of the atomic attacks and the thrust of Soviet armies into Manchuria, nationalist leaders had made their own bids for power in the interval before the Europeans returned.[31] Amid the chaos and confusion of August 1945, for example, the League for the Independence of Vietnam, or Viet Minh, under the charismatic leadership of Ho Chi Minh, took what David Marr, in his classic study of these events, called the 'opportune moment' and seized control of Hanoi, capitalizing on a long record of resistance to both French colonial rule, and Vietnam's more recent Japanese overlords following their complete takeover from the French in March.[32] Over the next few weeks, the gathering insurrection transformed the patterns of political and social power in Vietnam, as the Viet Minh, moving well beyond their northern base, spread their potent message of liberation through Vietnamese towns and villages; by 2 September 1945, Viet Minh leaders were also in place in government offices in Saigon as crowds listened on their radios to Ho declare, in a ceremony in Hanoi, formal independence and the establishment of the Democratic Republic of Vietnam (DRV), his growing number of adherents determined to resist any attempt to re-establish the old French colonial order. In Indonesia, having spent the final few months of the war working alongside the Japanese administration, Sukarno, the chief exponent of pre-war nationalist sentiment in the archipelago, announced the birth of an independent Republic on 17 August 1945 amid scenes of jubilation and an upsurge of youth mobilization.[33]

Though the specific context was very different, in that the pre-war and long-standing nationalist movement had already wrested important concessions from the colonial power, in British-controlled India the effect of the war and its immediate aftermath was to hasten the preferred timetable of the authorities towards early independence. Owing to the 'psychological effect of revolts in French Indochina and Indonesia', the Viceroy, Lord Wavell, reported, in October 1945, that the situation in India was 'more dangerous' than at any time for ninety years, while in Britain *The Times* opined that 'the entire practice of the rule of one race by another' was now 'discredited'. Improvements to transport links and

---

[31] See J. M. Pluvier, *South-East Asia from Colonialism to Independence* (Kuala Lumpur, 1974), 357–78.
[32] David G. Marr, *Vietnam 1945: The Quest for Power* (Berkeley, 1995), 382–401.
[33] George McT. Kahin, *Nationalism and Revolution in Indonesia* (Ithaca, 1952).

communications were doing much to alter the consciousness of nationalist leaders so that they comprehended shared concerns and enemies, as
well as a crucial sense of the momentous stage of history that had finally
been reached. Having been invited to Indonesia by Sukarno to witness
Britain's use of Indian troops against local nationalist militias, Jawaharlal
Nehru, the leading figure in the Interim Indian Government, informed a
colleague in October 1945 that Jakarta was now only two days by air from
Allahabad, and that if 'there was a need for me there in the interest of
Indonesian freedom' he would go.[34] By August 1947, India had achieved
its independence, along with a Pakistan which was the product of seemingly insurmountable and violent communal tensions. Ceylon gained
similar status early the following year, and influenced by developments
on the nearby subcontinent, but also by the cathartic effects of Japanese
occupation, Burma was quickly propelled on the road to independence in
January 1948, though in a setting still torn by ethnic strife and civil
conflict.

In general terms, and as they had first shown in the war of 1904–5
against the Russians in a victory that had also resonated around Asia, the
Japanese had helped to demonstrate that the white man was not invinci-
ble. In fact the edifice of white supremacy had been dealt a shattering blow
by Japan's initial victories of 1941–2 against the Europeans and
Americans, one from which it was never to recover. In this way, the
challenge mounted to the pre-war order by the Japanese was a racial one
and found a receptive audience as Asian leaders and peoples quickly
moved to assert their independence and the right to control their own
destinies.[35] For Western observers, the overriding and privately expressed
fear was that Japan's wartime successes might be the catalyst for the
formation of a pan-Asian movement that would work to evict Western
influence from the region. After the crushing setbacks to the Western
powers that followed Pearl Harbor, Admiral William D. Leahy, President
Franklin D. Roosevelt's Chief of Staff, worried that 'unless we administer
a defeat to Japan in the near future, that nation will succeed in combining
most of the Asiatic people against the whites'.[36] Stanley Hornbeck, the
long-time State Department adviser on Far Eastern affairs, was led to
conclude by 1943 that the war against Japan had opened up not just 'the
chasm between Occident and Orient' but what he called 'the chasm of

---

[34] See Robin Jeffery (ed.), *Asia: The Winning of Independence* (London, 1981), 2–15. On the
war's fostering of a common sense of 'Asian-ness', see Thorne, *Issue of War*, 169–71.

[35] See Thorne, *Allies*, 5–12, 175, 291, 359; Thorne, *Issue of War*, 144–56; and Thorne,
'Racial Aspects of the Far Eastern War of 1941–1945', *Proceedings of the British Academy*,
66, 1980, 329–77.

[36] Leahy diary, 20 October 1942, quoted in Thorne, *Allies*, 157.

color'.[37] In one conversation held during the month before his death, President Roosevelt expressed his concerns about what he called 'the brown people in the East', saying there were '1,100,000,000 brown people. In many Eastern countries, they are ruled by a handful of whites and they resent it. Our goal must be to help them achieve independence – 1,100,000,000 potential enemies are dangerous.'[38]

This was one reason why China's alignment with the allied war effort in the Far East was so critical to American policy-makers. In May 1942, the Sinophile and popular Nobel Prize-winning writer Pearl S. Buck laid out the relationship between the issue of racial equality and the developing global conflict for the readers of the *New York Times* in an article calling for the barrier of race to be destroyed by the allied nations. Japan's attempt to lead Asia against the West could mean the United States was 'embarked on the bitterest and longest of human wars, the war between the East and the West, and this means the war between the white man and his world and the colored man and his world'. Buck saw the 'crux of the future' as being whether the 'white man and the colored man [can] ever come together in any sort of cooperation'. China's role as an ally in the war with Japan was invaluable to the United States in this context because it undercut Japanese propaganda that the white West could never work with another Asian state on equal terms; at home Americans could also break down the race barrier by treating the 10 per cent of their population who were black as equals. Buck was hopeful that attitudes could be changed 'but only first by unprejudiced information which will lighten our present general dense ignorance about Asia, and then by concentrated determination to hew out our course not according to past lines of race and empire but along new lines of common humanity and cooperative equality'.[39] China, she noted in a later speech, would not 'go on enduring the disadvantages of color prejudice [and] does not want to be dominated by anybody nor does she want to be looked down upon by anybody because her people are Oriental or have yellow skin and black eyes and hair. She wants her people to have a place in the human race equal to that of any other people, and she makes this a principle.'[40] For one State Department

---

[37] Quoted in Thorne, *Issue of War*, 178.   [38] Quoted in Thorne, *Allies*, 594–5.
[39] Pearl S. Buck, 'The Race Barrier "That Must Be Destroyed"', *New York Times* (hereafter *NYT*), 31 May 1942, and for Buck's larger statement on the impact of the Far Eastern war, see her collection of speeches and articles, *American Unity and Asia* (New York, 1942), especially 'Tinder for Tomorrow', 22–33. On Buck, see Dower, *War without Mercy*, 159–60, and 345, n. 17.
[40] Pearl S. Buck, 'China Faces the Future', lecture delivered at the New School for Social Research, New York, 13 October 1942, Pearl S. Buck papers, Butler Library, Columbia University.

official, the importance of the new status of China after Pearl Harbor, and of being aligned with the West in the struggle with Japan, was that it offered the 'best insurance' to prevent the conflict developing into a 'race war'.[41] Thus, in self-congratulatory fashion, the United States in 1943 both renounced its former extraterritorial rights in China and repealed the Chinese exclusion provisions of US immigration law (though setting a miserly admission quota). Roosevelt, moreover, talked of China becoming one of his four global post-war policemen, with an assured permanent seat on what was later to become the United Nations Security Council.[42] These were all actions designed by the Americans to signal to their new Far Eastern ally that the days of unequal treatment were passing. Nevertheless, these were ultimately half-hearted gestures, and the Chinese Nationalist Government was never admitted to the inner sanctum of allied strategic decision-making, despite, for example, the largely symbolic appearance of Chiang Kai-shek at the Cairo Conference in November 1943.[43] There was, moreover, widespread dis-illusionment felt by American officials with China's wartime performance by 1944, as corruption, graft and incompetence came to characterize the Nationalist regime, and Chiang's best forces were held back for the anticipated post-war showdown with the Chinese Communists rather than committed against the Japanese. The limitations of Western policy towards China, which featured also in the whole realm of planning for a post-colonial future, were one indication of how the prime focus of much official attention was still directed towards the European war and subsequent political settlement, and where lack of knowledge and com-mitment to Far Eastern problems was frequently encountered. It was, in addition, a product of the many sharp divisions that arose over how to respond to the growing demands of dependent peoples, with American officials, for example, increasingly concerned about the discord that could arise with European allies over the post-war disposition of colonial territories.[44]

In an outgrowth of the belief that the war had generated disturbing racial tensions, Western observers were anxious that the consequences of Japan's humbling of the white powers would last well beyond her own defeat, and that pan-Asian solidarity might be one unwelcome outcome as the colonial powers attempted to reassert their authority. In May 1945, for example, one can find Joseph Grew, the acting US Secretary of State,

---

[41] See Thorne, *Allies*, 291.   [42] See *ibid.*, 175–8.
[43] See Robert Dallek, *Franklin D. Roosevelt and American Foreign Policy, 1932–1945* (New York, 1979), 424–9.
[44] See Thorne, *Issue of War*, 192–4.

telling Anthony Eden that 'we must always reckon with the future development of an "Asia for the Asiatics" movement'.[45] An anti-colonial Asia-wide revolt, it was recognized, could be exploited by the Soviet Union to its own ends, as local Communist parties in the Far East built support around anti-Western sentiment. At the San Francisco Conference that established the United Nations, Grew was alarmed that the Russian delegation had introduced the idea that the organization should have the power to promote self-government in the colonial world, writing that, 'Although this has been our historic role, Russia, I fear, may appear before the world as the champion of all dependent peoples [and this] move may confirm in the minds of the people of Asia, their already strong suspicion that the Anglo-American powers are not their real champions and [they] will turn to Russia as their more outspoken friend and spokesman.'[46] Pointing to nationalist unrest in Indonesia, Indochina, Korea and India, one column in the *New York Times* noted in early 1946 that 'Japan lost the war, but her slogan "Asia for the Asiatics" appears to have won. What is happening in the Far East is a warning that the oriental peoples, instead of being subdued by the victories of the western powers, are more stirred up than before against occidental domination.'[47] Having undertaken a tour of China, Indonesia and the Philippines, the chief Far Eastern correspondent of that same newspaper reported that the defeats inflicted by the Japanese on the Western powers and the new thinking and activism spawned during the years of occupation meant that the 'white man has lost, probably forever, the superior place he once held by virtue of the power he represented to the Oriental'.[48] One revealing indication of change was the post-war supplanting of the word 'Asiatic' in favour of 'Asian' to denote an inhabitant of the region: 'Asiatic' had often been used in signs and orders in the colonial setting, and rejection of the term came along with the passing of white, European power.[49]

In this kind of overall context, where one of the key effects of the war as a whole was to raise the international profile and transnational significance of issues surrounding race, as well as drawing attention to the structures that underpinned Western dominance, it is therefore not surprising that some Asian commentators saw a racial factor at work in the use of the

---

[45] Grew to Winant, 17 May 1945, *Foreign Relations of the United States* (hereafter *FRUS*), *1945, VI: The British Commonwealth, The Far East* (Washington, DC, 1969), 251.

[46] Grew to Stettinius, 8 May 1945, *FRUS, 1945, I: General: United Nations* (Washington, DC, 1967), 652.

[47] Anne O'Hare McCormick, 'Stormy Passage Toward a Free Asia', *NYT*, 18 February 1946.

[48] Robert Trumbull, 'The West Loses "Face" in the East', *NYT*, 1 December 1946.

[49] See Isaacs, *Two-Thirds of the World*, 30.

atomic bomb by the United States in August 1945. The impression of indifference to Asian lives that the attacks suggested was given special emphasis by Japanese propagandists.[50] On the day of the Nagasaki attack, the *Nippon Times* called the use of the bomb a 'crime against humanity' and an 'act of premeditated wholesale murder, the deliberate snuffing out of the lives of tens of thousands of innocent civilians who had not the slightest chance of protecting themselves'. Soon after, Kiyose Ichiro of the Greater Japan Political Association, and later a defence counsel at the Tokyo War Crimes Tribunal, published a piece in the *Asahi Shinbun*, Tokyo's leading daily newspaper, which highlighted how the bomb had not been used against a 'white' Germany but was reserved for use by the Americans against the Japanese because of 'vengeful racial prejudice'; 'Western opinion,' he had asserted, 'would not allow "this merciless weapon" to be used against a nation of the white race.'[51] Over the final days before the Japanese surrender, radio broadcasts along these lines were beamed out across the Far East. Those sent into India were reported by the British authorities to have been filled with 'an outburst of indignant protest' over the use of the atomic bomb. 'A people who have no regards whatsoever for innocent Japanese women and children,' the broad lines of this propaganda ran, 'will surely have no regard for Indians, if and when the necessity comes to murder them in cold blood.'[52] Within India itself, expressions of Western moral reservations over use of the bomb were also picked up and given wide coverage. The day following the formal Japanese surrender, an editorial in the leading Calcutta newspaper *Amrita Bazar Patrika* was asking,

what were the considerations that weighed with the Allies in not using [the bomb] against the Germans? Is it because that would have shocked "white humanity" all over the world as a barbarity before which the worst stories of Nazi atrocities paled into insignificance? Was the bomb used against the Japanese simply because it was produced at the psychological moment when Japan remained the only enemy to be dealt with? Or was it because there would not be so much of a horror at the atrocity, the victims being mere Asiatics?[53]

---

[50] On the war's role in the internationalization of racial issues, see Frank Furedi, *The Silent War: Imperialism and the Changing Perception of Race* (London, 1998), 160–92; and Hugh Tinker, *Race, Conflict and the International Order: From Empire to United Nations* (London, 1977), 39–50.

[51] See Foreign Office Research Department survey, 'World Reactions to the Atomic Bomb', 4 September 1945, CAB 126/191, TNA; Hein and Selden, *Living with the Bomb*, 7.

[52] Appendix B to Fortnightly Security Intelligence Summary No. 1, 17 August 1945, L/WS/1/1506, India Office records, British Library.

[53] 'How It Ends', *Amrita Bazar Patrika*, 16 August 1945.

The Soviet Union also began to push the line that its own late intervention in the war had been decisive, leading to speculation in September as to why the bomb had been used if Japan was on the brink of surrender in any case.[54] 'The Allies have clearly declared that the aim of using the atomic bomb is to terrorize the Japanese into early surrender,' an editorial in the *Hindustan Times* argued in August 1945, 'but is it to be at any cost to Japanese civilians? International Law recognizes the right to reprisal but the desire for just retribution must be distinguished from the desire for revenge.'[55] When, a few years later, Japanese military leaders were prosecuted at the Tokyo War Crimes trials, Justice Radhabinod Pal of India produced a dissenting opinion which drew attention to the double standards he saw on display and compared the 'indiscriminate destruction of civilian life' through allied use of the atomic bomb to some of the directives issued by Nazi leaders in the war years.[56]

Within the British Foreign Office, the capacity for the atomic attacks to become the long-term focus for Asia-wide resentment was recognized at an early stage. On 9 August 1945, Sir John Sterndale Bennett, the head of the Far East Department of the Foreign Office, writing just after the Hiroshima attack, was highly critical of Washington's decision to use the bomb without warning against a populated city, avowing that 'present tactics in the employment of the bomb seem likely to do the maximum damage to our cause. They are giving a handle to Japanese political warfare in a way likely to cause the most controversy and dissension on the Allied side.' Now that its effects had been demonstrated, Sterndale Bennett hoped that an ultimatum to surrender with a time limit might be delivered to the Japanese Government. Moreover, the story circulating that the decision to use the bomb against Japan had actually been reached

---

[54] *Amrita Bazar Patrika*, 6 September 1945. This was a precursor of the influential argument made by Norman Cousins and Thomas K. Finletter in the *Saturday Review of Literature* in June 1946, and developed by P. M. S. Blackett the following year, that, in the latter's words, 'the dropping of the atomic bombs was not so much the last military act of the second world war, as the first act of the cold diplomatic war with Russia now in progress'; see P. M. S. Blackett, 'The Decision to Drop the Bomb', in Kai Bird and Lawrence Lifschultz (eds.), *Hiroshima's Shadow* (Stony Creek, VA, 1998), 78–89. After the 1960s, it became a staple part of the revisionist view on the use of the bomb that it had been employed partly to pre-empt the entrance of the Soviet Union into the Far Eastern war and as a demonstration of American power designed to intimidate Stalin; see, e.g., Gar Alperovitz, *The Decision to Use the Atomic Bomb* (New York, 1995), and Sherwin, *A World Destroyed*, 222, 226.

[55] *Hindustan Times*, 11 August 1945.

[56] Pal's comments are recorded in B. V. A. Roling and C. F. Ruter (eds.), *The Tokyo Judgement: The International Military Tribunal for the Far East, 29 April 1946–12 November 1948*, Vol. II (Amsterdam, 1977), 982; see also Dower, *War without Mercy*, 37–8.

exactly a year earlier, in August 1944, was, he feared, likely to be 'very damaging by suggesting that we could have used the bomb on the Germans but spared them and kept it for an oriental race'.[57] Sir Robert Bruce Lockhart, the head of the Foreign Office's Political Intelligence Department, was even more explicit:

The fact that the atomic bomb was used for the first time against an Asiatic race so soon after the conclusion of the war in Europe may raise the notion in Asiatic minds that the British and Americans, as Europeans, may well have hesitated to use so devastating a weapon against fellow Europeans while not being averse to employing it against Asiatics when it seemed possible to achieve a quick decision thereby. Some substance would be lent to these suspicions by the sentiments, often expressed in the less respectable sections of the American press and repeated with approval by their British equivalents, that the Japanese are 'sub-human' and thus not to be considered in human terms.[58]

Scattered reflections on the racial themes raised by the atomic attacks can be found among other Western observers. Mackenzie King, the Canadian Prime Minister, confided to his diary on hearing the news of the Hiroshima attack that it was 'fortunate that the use of the bomb should have been upon the Japanese rather than upon the white races of Europe'.[59] In Britain also, as Bruce Lockhart had noted, feelings against the Japanese, fuelled by the brutal treatment accorded to allied prisoners, ran high. Having read the stories of Japanese abuse of British prisoners of war, one Conservative Member of Parliament frothed in his diary over the 'need to punish these beastly creatures [though] short of hanging the Emperor and all his warlords I cannot think of anything calculated to impress the Japanese nation. The only sensible thing to do really would be to drop atomic bombs wholesale over the country and thus to destroy the Japanese race as fully as possible – one cannot see what good service they render to humanity.'[60] In the United States, a poll conducted for *Fortune* magazine in September 1945 indicated that 54 per cent of those questioned approved of the decision to use the two atomic bombs against Japanese cities, but an additional 23 per cent of the same sample opted for the vindictive view that more should have been dropped quickly before the Japanese had been given a chance to surrender.[61]

[57] Sterndale Bennett minute, 9 August 1945, F4953/16/G61, FO 371/46318, TNA.
[58] Bruce Lockhart to Sterndale Bennett, 10 August 1945, F4954/16/G61, FO 371/46318, TNA.
[59] Mackenzie King diary entry, 6 August 1945, www.collectionscanada.gc.ca/databases/king/001059-100.01-e.php, accessed on 27 January 2010.
[60] Entry for 7 September 1945, Stuart Ball (ed.), *Parliament and Politics in the Age of Churchill and Attlee: The Headlam Diaries, 1935–1951* (Cambridge, 1999), 478.
[61] John E. Mueller, *War, Presidents and Public Opinion* (New York, 1973), 172–3.

However, these signs of wartime enmity also need to be put beside evidence that other feelings and calculations were at work. Despite his repeated statements about the need to bomb the Japanese into submission, Truman himself was anxious that the destruction not be prolonged. When Senator Richard Russell telegraphed the President on 7 August urging that Japan should be brought grovelling to her knees by the use of more bombs against her cities, Truman replied that he knew that the Japanese were a 'terribly cruel and uncivilized nation in warfare, but I can't bring myself to believe that, because they are beasts, we should ourselves act in the same manner. For myself, I certainly regret the necessity of wiping out whole populations because of the "pigheadedness" of the leaders of a nation and ... I am not going to do it unless it is absolutely necessary ... My object is to save as many American lives as possible but I also have a humane feeling for the women and children in Japan.'[62] American military planners were prepared to deliver further atomic attacks against Japanese cities once more bombs became available at the end of August, recommending the next bomb be dropped in the 'region of Tokyo' to put even greater pressure on the Japanese leadership.[63] On 9 August, Lieutenant General Albert C. Wedemeyer, the head of all American forces in the China–Burma–India Command, told reporters that the use of atomic bombs was 'very much under consideration in the China Theater wherever military necessity dictates', and mentioned in particular Japanese-occupied Shanghai as a possible military target.[64] But after the receipt of the Japanese surrender proposals, Truman ordered that further planned atomic attacks should cease. As he explained to his Cabinet, 'the thought of wiping out another 100,000 people was too horrible. He didn't like the idea of killing, as he said, "all those kids".'[65]

Of course, the atomic bomb was not developed in time for use before the end of the war in Europe, and there is no indication that 'racial' considerations would have played any part in reluctance to use it against Germany, where the civilian population was already being subjected to the full weight of the allied bomber offensive. Given this background, it is difficult to conceive that the Japanese were somehow being singled out for

---

[62] Quoted in Hasegawa, *Racing the Enemy*, 202.

[63] Richard B. Frank, *Downfall: The End of the Imperial Japanese Empire* (New York, 1999), 303.

[64] 'Wedemeyer Bares Blow to Aid Russia', *NYT*, 10 August 1945. Wedemeyer's claims seem highly dubious coming so soon after the closely held planning for the atomic attacks but accords with his own sense of self-importance.

[65] Entry for 10 August 1945, John Morton Blum (ed.), *The Price of Vision: The Diary of Henry A. Wallace, 1942–1946* (Boston, 1973), 474. Frank makes the point that this was a casualty figure mentioned in a decrypted Japanese Imperial Navy message that Truman had probably seen the previous day; see Frank, *Downfall*, 302.

special treatment because of their notional race, and the terrible toll in lives which came about with the fire-bombing of Japanese cities from March 1945 onwards were but refinements of techniques used over Germany. A more apposite, if prosaic, view is that the demands and exigencies of total war between 1939 and 1945, where whole societies and peoples were seen as vulnerable and legitimate targets for attack, largely as a means to erode industrial-military potential and sap morale and hence will to prosecute war, brutalized the combatants to a degree where previous restraints on behaviour were lifted.[66] Though it could be argued that some of the racially based animosities of the war years made even more unlikely any inclination to check the in-built assumption of the Manhattan Project that once designed and tested the bomb would be used, this is impossible to demonstrate. Apart from the overriding need to prevent further American and allied casualties, there was also the looming Soviet entry into the Far Eastern war to consider, and the desire of the President and his Secretary of War, Henry Stimson, as well as senior figures such as Grew, to hasten a Japanese surrender so that Stalin could not strengthen his position over determining the post-war settlement in the Far East, including the vital matter of claiming a stake in the occupation of defeated Japan. Truman never called a meeting with his advisers to explicitly discuss the issue of whether to use the bomb, and one of the leading historians of the events leading up to the attacks has concluded that the President 'remained primarily concerned with ending the war as soon as possible, and the bomb was the most likely and least risky means to accomplish his objective ... The use of the bomb was not entirely a foregone conclusion; Truman could have decided against it. But he had no compelling reason to do so.'[67]

It is also relevant to note that Truman at least, in sanctioning the attacks, undertook a degree of self-deception by insisting that target selection for the atomic bomb should be justified on military grounds, with mention of industrial plants in cities such as Hiroshima (which also was home to an army headquarters), when it was patently obvious that the large-scale killing of civilians, in order to shock the Japanese leadership into surrender, was the overriding intention.[68] As well as salving

[66] This was a process already under way even before 1939; see Donald Cameron Watt, 'Restraints on War in the Air Before 1945', in Michael Howard (ed.), *Restraints on War: Studies in the Limitation of Armed Conflict* (Oxford, 1979), 57–78. See also Nina Tannenwald, *The Nuclear Taboo: The United States and the Non-Use of Nuclear Weapons since 1945* (Cambridge, 2007), 77–82.
[67] Walker, *Prompt and Utter Destruction*, 60–1.
[68] For excellent discussions, see Sherry, *Rise of American Air Power*, 292–7, 316–22; Frank, *Downfall*, 256–8; Walker, *Prompt and Utter Destruction*, 61–2; Hershberg, *Conant*, 225–7.

individual and national conscience, there was a desire not to be seen to be targeting non-combatants with the atomic bomb because of fears of the bitterness this might produce in a defeated Japanese populace toward a post-war American occupation.[69] Stimson, worried over a possible domestic backlash, suggested on 10 August that bombers should no longer be despatched over Japan, while Forrestal, perhaps looking towards future configurations of power, warned that after Hiroshima 'we must remember that this nation would have to bear the focus of the hatred by the Japanese'.[70] These can best be described as defensive responses from individuals who were beginning to look beyond the moods and demands of wartime towards post-war requirements and how American behaviour would be evaluated in retrospect.

Indeed, after the results of the use of the bomb began to be more widely recognized in the United States, an underlying unease began to be expressed by many contemporary commentators. Stimson was anxious over the 'growing feeling of apprehension and misgiving as to the effect of the atomic bomb even in our own country'.[71] With stories beginning to circulate about the effects of radioactivity and Japanese casualty estimates of 150,000, in the days following the Nagasaki attack the War Department and Office of War Information were becoming concerned by the deluge of anxious telephone calls with which they had to deal. Thus, noted the British Embassy, 'along with the thrill of power and the instinctive pleasure at the thought of Japan cringing in abject surrender, America's deep-rooted humanitarianism has begun to assert itself and this secondary revulsion has been very marked in private conversation although it has not yet appeared in the Press'. British officials detected 'a good deal of heart-searching about the morality of using such a weapon, especially against an enemy already known to be on his last legs'.[72] The influential theologian Reinhold Niebuhr, in September 1945, saw feelings of 'strange disquiet and lack of satisfaction' among soberer sections of the population. This was partly derived, Niebuhr believed, from the question of whether use of the bomb had really been needed when it was known by the authorities in Washington that there was an active peace faction within the leadership in Tokyo.[73] Niebuhr joined twenty other church leaders

---

[69] See Bernstein, 'The Atomic Bombings Reconsidered', 142–7.

[70] Entry for 10 August 1945, James V. Forrestal diaries, box 145, James V. Forrestal papers, Seeley G. Mudd Library, Princeton University.

[71] *Ibid.*

[72] Washington (Balfour) to FO, No. 5560, 11 August 1945, AN2433/4/45, FO 371/44537, TNA.

[73] Reinhold Niebuhr, 'Our Relations with Japan', in *Christianity and Crisis*, 17 September 1945, quoted in Bird and Lifschultz, *Hiroshima's Shadow*, 275–7.

when helping to compile a report in March 1946 for the Federal Council of Churches which condemned the 'indiscriminate, excessive violence' of the 'irresponsible' atomic attacks, which though they may have shortened the war had come at a moral cost which was 'too high'.[74] The influential journalist and writer Walter Lippmann later recalled that 'one of the things I look back on with the greatest regret, as an American, is that we were the ones that first dropped atomic bombs', and considered Truman responsible for failing to negotiate a surrender with Japan before they were used.[75] For Hanson Baldwin, the respected military commentator for the *New York Times*, writing just after Hiroshima, through indiscriminate bombing of civilian areas 'Americans have become a synonym for destruction', and while the atomic bomb might speed Japan's surrender, it could also 'sow the seeds of hate more widely than ever'.[76] Five years later he was warning that use of the bomb, a new and horrible weapon for the 'extermination of man', had been one of the great mistakes of the war that had lost the United States its claim to moral leadership; in a complete inversion of the imagery that Truman had earlier employed, Baldwin felt that 'we are now branded with the mark of the beast'.[77]

Besides these individual reactions, the wider American conscience also seems to have been temporarily disturbed by the reception given to the publication of *Hiroshima*, a book by the Pulitzer Prize-winning journalist John Hersey, which was itself derived from a thirty thousand-word essay which had first appeared in the *New Yorker* magazine in August 1946. Both the article and the book reached a large audience and conveyed in unemotional but vivid prose the horrific experiences of six individual citizens of Hiroshima immediately after the explosion of the bomb.[78] Hersey portrayed the Japanese victims as passive, patient and resigned to their fate. Rather than nurturing prolonged hate towards the Americans who had unleashed the fire storms over Japan's cities in 1945, a picture was offered of docile Asians, even to the point where the anthropologist Ruth Benedict commended the book's presentation of Japanese behaviour, viewing the 'patient fortitude' on display as suggestive of 'sheep without shepherds', and being consistent with a national character

[74] 'Report of Protestant Church Leaders on Atomic Warfare'; 'Japan Atom Bombing Condemned in Federal Church Council Report', *NYT*, 6 March 1946.

[75] Ronald Steel, *Walter Lippmann and the American Century* (London, 1980), 454–5.

[76] See Hanson W. Baldwin, 'The Atomic Weapon', *NYT*, 7 August 1945.

[77] Hanson W. Baldwin, *Great Mistakes of the War* (London, 1950), 94, 99.

[78] See Joseph Luft and W. M. Wheeler, 'Reaction to John Hersey's "Hiroshima"', *Journal of Social Psychology*, 28, August 1948, 135–40; Michael Yavendetti, 'John Hersey and the American Conscience: The Reception of "Hiroshima"', *Pacific Historical Review*, 43, 1, February 1974, 24–49; Robert Jay Lifton and Greg Mitchell, *Hiroshima in America: Fifty Years of Denial* (New York, 1995), 86–91.

'inculcated for centuries'.[79] It was also an account that chimed with American perceptions of the occupation of Japan, where the inhabitants were seen as having proved acquiescent to MacArthur's reform efforts. One effect of *Hiroshima* may have been to effectively expunge whatever feelings of guilt were experienced by some over the decision to use the bomb: if the bomb's Japanese victims did not blame the American perpetrators, then perhaps it was best to accept the world-weary view that such outrages were simply an inevitable result of the ultimate folly of war.[80]

That Americans were now ready to look away from the moral significance of the events of 1945 was also underlined by the fact that with the arrival of Cold War tensions many became convinced that all reservations would have to be laid aside, and reliance placed on the awful destructive power of nuclear weapons as the ultimate deterrent against an implacable and unscrupulous Soviet enemy. Yet Hersey's article and book certainly served to ruffle official feathers, as did emerging theories that the bomb might have been used primarily as a means of forestalling Soviet entry into the war, which, when added to the conclusions of the United States Strategic Bombing Survey that Japan was very close to total collapse and surrender in the summer of 1945, suggested that Hiroshima and Nagasaki were avoidable. The result was the production of an article by Henry Stimson in a February 1947 issue of *Harper's Magazine* that conveyed an official narrative of events leading up to the use of the bombs, designed with the express purpose of refuting some of the doubts that were circulating over the motivations behind the Truman administration's actions and to embed in the American consciousness the firm and factual contention that the atomic attacks had been necessary to save countless lives that would have been lost in any later invasion of Japan. With extracts reprinted in many other newspapers and magazines (the *Washington Post* reproducing it in full), the article became the most widely accepted interpretation, until the appearance of revisionist texts and new archival evidence in the very different political climate of the mid-1960s led scholars to revisit the whole subject.[81]

For Truman himself, though he never recanted on his decision to use the bomb against Japan in the circumstances he confronted, there were many signs that he appreciated the enormity of what had occurred and the qualitative difference between nuclear and all other previous category of

[79] See Boyer, *By the Bomb's Early Light*, 203–9.   [80] *Ibid.*, 210.
[81] See Hershberg, *Conant*, 291–304; Barton Bernstein, 'Seizing the Contested Terrain of Nuclear History: Stimson, Conant and their Allies Explain the Decision to Use the Atomic Bomb', *Diplomatic History*, 17, 1, 1993, 35–72; Lifton and Mitchell, *Hiroshima*, 91–109.

armaments. 'I don't think we ought to use this thing [the atomic bomb] unless we absolutely have to,' he commented in 1948. 'It is a terrible thing to order the use of something that ... is so terribly destructive, destructive beyond anything we have ever had. You have got to understand that this isn't a military weapon ... It is used to wipe out women and children and unarmed people, and not for military uses. So we have got to treat this differently from rifles and cannon and ordinary things like that.' A few months later he was expressing his desire to see the whole US nuclear arsenal dumped into the sea with the thought, 'this isn't just another weapon ... not just another bomb. People make a mistake when they talk that way.'[82] The formation of the Atomic Energy Commission (AEC) in January 1947, following the passage of the Atomic Energy Act the previous August, with its five civilian commissioners appointed by the President, was a further sign that nuclear weapons held a special status in the eyes of both the White House and powerful sections of Congress, where oversight of the legislation was provided by the Joint Congressional Committee on Atomic Energy. However, the principle of civilian control of the American nuclear stockpile represented by the work of the AEC was not without its critics. In July 1948, in the middle of the Berlin Airlift crisis, the Pentagon pressed strongly for an executive order that would transfer custody of the atomic bomb to the military authorities. The head of the AEC, David Lilienthal, objected on the grounds that the atomic bomb 'was not simply another weapon but an instrument of destruction which carried the widest kind of international and diplomatic implications'.[83] On this occasion, Truman acted decisively to rebuff the ambitions of Forrestal, now the Secretary of Defense, asserting the presidential prerogative as Commander-in-Chief and the fact that American political tradition called for civilian authority to stand above the military.[84]

Although overseeing a wholesale expansion of the US inventory of nuclear weapons, and in January 1950 quite prepared to sanction the development of the even more powerful hydrogen bomb, Truman never lost sight of his belief that their indiscriminate and 'mass destruction' nature set them apart, so that any final decisions over their use would need to be made not by a military commander, but by the president

---

[82] Entries for 21 July 1948 and 14 February 1949, *The Journals of David E. Lilienthal*, Vol. II: *The Atomic Energy Years, 1945–1950* (New York, 1964), 391, 474; see also Tannenwald, *Nuclear Taboo*, 98–9.

[83] Entry for 21 July 1948, Walter Millis (ed.), *The Forrestal Diaries* (New York, 1951), 461.

[84] See Michael J. Hogan, *A Cross of Iron: Harry S. Truman and the Origins of the National Security State, 1945–1954* (Cambridge, 1998), 248–50; S. David Brocsious, 'Longing for International Control, Banking on American Superiority: Harry S. Truman's Approach to Nuclear Weapons', in Gaddis *et al.* (eds.), *Cold War Statesmen*, 29–30.

himself. The atomic attacks of 1945 had clearly given nuclear weapons a symbolic standing in domestic and world opinion that meant any future employment would carry serious moral and political repercussions.[85] In September 1948, the National Security Council (NSC), reflecting Truman's thinking, formally instructed the military establishment to proceed with planning that involved the use of nuclear weapons against the Soviet Union but confirmed the key principle that the final word on nuclear use would reside with the Chief Executive; the document that enshrined this position, NSC 30, affirmed that beyond the role of military planners in such areas as target selection, there was an 'additional requirement for blending a political with a military responsibility in order to assure that the conduct of war, to the maximum extent practicable, advances the fundamental and lasting aims of U.S. policy'.[86] Implicit in this statement, crafted at a time when the United States still held a nuclear monopoly, was the notion that the tremendous destructiveness of nuclear weapons might, in some circumstances, undermine the wider goals of the United States, which were not always reducible to the military's capability to overawe any adversary. Furthermore, the President's basic conviction was that the harnessing of nuclear energy held both great promise, for its possible peaceful application, but also great dangers with its capacity to threaten the future of civilization; writing in his diary on the day of the first atomic test in July 1945, he gave vent to the feeling that 'machines are ahead of morals by some centuries'.[87]

Truman's allusions were part of a general perception shared by many observers, both Western and Asian, that the bomb was perhaps the best illustration of the insidious effects of science, technology and 'progress'. From India, Wavell thought the atomic bomb a 'very dangerous scientific development, since I doubt whether man has yet the wisdom to use it wisely. It may end war or it may end civilization. It is not a weapon that any thinking man would willingly have put into the hands of the present-day world. It has shown it cannot be trusted with a box of matches, is it reasonable to think it can play with a Mills grenade and not pull the pin out?'[88] One senior British Foreign Office official ruminated after

[85] See John L. Gaddis, 'The Origins of Self-Deterrence: The United States and the Non-Use of Nuclear Weapons, 1945–1958', in *The Long Peace*, 107–8.
[86] Paragraph 11, 'United States Policy on Atomic Weapons', NSC 30, 10 September 1948, *FRUS, 1948, I, General; The United Nations*, Part 2 (Washington, DC, 1976), 628; see also Steven L. Rearden, *History of the Office of the Secretary of Defense*, Vol. I: *The Formative Years, 1947–1950* (Washington, DC, 1984), 436–8.
[87] Quoted in Brocsious, 'Longing for International Control', 18.
[88] Entry for 7 August 1945, Penderel Moon (ed.), *Wavell: The Viceroy's Journal* (London, 1973), 162.

Hiroshima, 'Well, perhaps after all, nothing mattered. With the arrival of the atomic bomb civilization was finished. It was merely a question of years or even months ...'[89] Some underscored the implications for Western moral standing of the use of such a scientific breakthrough against a civilian population. Alexander Sachs, an economist who had done much to interest Roosevelt in the early development of research into the atomic bomb, was telling the Secretary of Commerce and former Vice-President, Henry Wallace, in October 1945 that 'our moral prestige in the world is very low as a result of the way we used the bomb'.[90] Reporting the outcome of a church conference held at the University of Oxford and attended by African delegates, George Padmore, the Trinidadian intellectual and anti-colonial activist, noted in September 1945, 'whatever has been the military effect of the use of the atomic bomb on a colored Asiatic and non-Christian nation by the two leading Anglo-Saxon Christian Powers, it has certainly lowered their moral standing in the eyes of the dark-skinned peoples of Asia and Africa'.[91]

The use of the bomb as a point of moral friction and debate in the Western relationship with a newly assertive Asia was to become a distinctive feature of the post-war years. In a speech delivered on 16 August 1945, Nehru expressed his concerns over the continuing prevalence of militarism in the world and noted how the atomic bomb was an 'ominous sign' of the 'disastrous way modern civilization is following. No sensitive individual can follow this prospect without dismay.'[92] Indeed for some Indians the bomb showed the continuing validity of concepts such as *ahimsa*, or non-violence, which held an obvious appeal to those who felt it had been the crucial moral key to unlocking British imperial rule in the subcontinent. Writing to Nehru in October 1945, Gandhi expressed his belief that 'if India, and through India the world, is to achieve real freedom, then sooner or later we shall have to go and live in the villages ... I have not the slightest doubt that, but for the pair, truth and non-violence, mankind is doomed. We can have the vision of that truth and non-violence only in the simplicity of the villages.'[93] Asked in early 1946 if the atomic bomb had shaken his belief in truth and non-violence, Gandhi

---

[89] The official was Sir Orme Sargent, Permanent Under-Secretary at the Foreign Office, 1946–49; see entry for 24 August 1945, Kenneth Young (ed.), *The Diaries of Sir Robert Bruce Lockhart, 1939–1965* (London, 1980), 495.
[90] Entry for 24 October 1945, Blum (ed.), *Wallace Diary*, 500.
[91] George Padmore, 'Morals of Whites Dropped with Atom Bomb, Say Africans', *Chicago Defender*, 8 September 1945. On Padmore's influence, see Von Eschen, *Race against Empire*, 11–13.
[92] *Times of India*, 18 August 1945.
[93] Gandhi to Nehru, 5 October 1945, quoted in Thorne, *Issue of War*, 315.

replied it had merely affirmed his faith in them; the two things were wholly different, one being spiritual and moral, the other physical and material, and the one is 'infinitely superior to the other which by its very nature has an end'.[94] In July 1946, Gandhi warned that the atomic bomb had 'deadened the finest feeling that has sustained mankind for ages. There used to be so-called laws of war which made it tolerable. Now we know the naked truth. Wars know no law except that of might. The atom bomb brought an empty victory to the Allied arms, but it resulted for the time being in destroying the soul of Japan. What has happened to the soul of the destroying nation is yet too early to see.'[95] The bomb's ability to bring about the 'wholesale destruction of men, women and children', he recounted, was the most 'diabolical use of science', while non-violence was 'the only thing the atom bomb cannot destroy. I did not move a muscle when I first heard that the atom bomb had wiped out Hiroshima ... I said to myself, "Unless now the world adopts non-violence, it will spell certain suicide for mankind."'[96]

As Asian nationalist sentiment climbed to new heights after 1945, the much-vaunted superiority of 'Western' values began to seem even less worthy of respect as colonialism gave way to self-rule.[97] Having travelled around China, on his return to Calcutta in 1924, the Indian poet and proponent of pan-Asian unity, Rabindranath Tagore, spoke of the need for a new and vibrant Asian civilization based on spiritual values to counteract the materialism of the West:

I feel that Asia must find her own voice. Simply because she has remained silent so long the whole world is suffering. The West has got no voice. She has given us nothing that could save us – that which gives immortality. She has given us science – a great gift no doubt – which has its special value; but nothing that can give us life beyond death. Her cult of power is based on pride and greed and the deliberate cultivation of contempt for other races ... I do feel that if Asia does not find her own voice, humanity will not be saved.[98]

Taken from the perspective of 1945, Tagore's plea can be seen as carrying prophetic layers of meaning, as the supreme achievement of Western science became the destructive potential of nuclear power. In an early

---

[94] 'On Way to Madura', 2 February 1946, *The Collected Works of Mahatma Gandhi*, Vol. 89 (New Delhi, 2001), 345.
[95] Speech at Poona, 1 July 1946, *The Collected Works of Mahatma Gandhi*, Vol. 91 (New Delhi, 2001), 220–1.
[96] 'Talk with an English Journalist', *c.* 24 September 1946, *The Collected Works of Mahatma Gandhi*, Vol. 92 (New Delhi, 2001), 234.
[97] See Thorne, *Issue of War*, 313–15.
[98] Quoted in Stephen N. Hay, *Asian Ideas of East and West: Tagore and His Critics* (Cambridge, MA, 1970), 12.

and unprecedented post-war sign that a distinctly Asian voice might be heard in regional and international affairs, in March–April 1947 the Asian Relations Conference was held in New Delhi under the auspices of the Indian Council on World Affairs, with delegates from over thirty countries invited and an agenda that omitted discussion of contentious defence and security issues, but focussed on unofficial ties and cultural links.[99] To this gathering, Gandhi intoned some of the lessons of the recent past, asserting: 'What I want you to understand is the message of Asia. It is not to be learnt through Western spectacles or by imitating the atom bomb. If you want to give a message to the West, it must be the message of love and the message of truth … Asia has to conquer the West through love [and] truth.'[100] In his own opening speech, Nehru called for Asian unity and regional co-operation, though he was keen to disavow any intention of forming an anti-Western pan-Asian movement; the conference itself generated evidence of the rivalry and divisions which were prevalent between the different national contingents, rather than any overwhelming sense of common purpose.[101]

For Japanese ideologues, transfixed by Japan's wartime mission to exercise leadership in a united Asia, where Asian spiritual values might blossom, it was possible to see the atomic bomb, the key symbol of Western industrial and material strength, as being the principal cause of defeat, rather than any flaw in the nature of the new order that Tokyo had sought to establish.[102] These were all ideas conveyed by the pronouncements of the Japanese Government at the end of the war. After Hiroshima, a formal protest had been delivered to the United States through the Swiss, which called the use of the atomic bomb 'a new crime against humanity and civilization'.[103] The elliptical phrases of Emperor Hirohito's famous imperial rescript formally announcing Japan's surrender on 15 August 1945 had sought to justify this 'unendurable' course as morally necessary given the devastation that had been witnessed in

---

[99] See Tilman Remme, 'Britain, the 1947 Asian Relations Conference, and Regional Co-operation in South-East Asia', in Anthony Gorst, Lewis Johnman and W. Scott Lucas (eds.), *Postwar Britain, 1945–64: Themes and Perspectives* (London, 1989), 109–34.

[100] Speech at Inter-Asian Relations Conference, 2 April 1947, *The Collected Works of Mahatma Gandhi*, Vol. 94 (New Delhi, 2001), 222.

[101] Evelyn Colbert, *Southeast Asia in International Politics, 1941–1956* (Ithaca, 1977), 112–13.

[102] One must not, of course, overlook the fact that Japan had her own atomic bomb programme, rudimentary though it was, during the war years; see John W. Dower, '"NI" and "F": Japan's Wartime Atomic Bomb Research', in *Japan in War and Peace: Essays on History, Race and Culture* (London, 1993), 55–100.

[103] See memorandum from the Swiss Legation to the Department of State, 11 August 1945, *FRUS, 1945, VI*, 473. The American authorities were understandably keen that no publicity should be given to this communication.

Hiroshima and Nagasaki. The Americans had, the Emperor's statement claimed, 'for the first time used cruel bombs to kill and maim extremely large numbers of the innocent', and continuing the war 'could lead in the end not only to the extermination of our race, but also to the destruction of all human civilization'. By offering the surrender as a way to save humanity from further suffering, some of the ignominy attached to this step might be avoided, and the Emperor's aura pre-served.[104] Furthermore, the rescript conveyed the idea that though Japan had been defeated by the material might of the Western powers, the moral and spiritual aspects of its mission in Asia were still valid; the considered view of the British Foreign Office was that the rescript did not show 'repentance for the Japanese entrance into the war or any sense of normal military defeat'.[105] Even before the surrender, Joseph Grew had foreseen the possibility that in their defeat the Japanese would consider that the allies had won 'an unjust victory solely by means of superior material power and that the Japanese cause of "Asia for the Asians" still is a just one'.[106]

Assessing general reactions during the early post-war years to the atomic bomb in Japan is problematic given the distorting effects of the American occupation. It was hardly surprising that in the immediate aftermath of the attacks, anti-American feeling was widespread among the survivors, amounting, as John Hersey put it, to a 'hatred for Americans which nothing could erase'. One doctor noted how there were war crimes trials being held in Tokyo, and that the men who decided to use the bomb should also be tried and hanged for their role in events.[107] The first Western correspondent to enter Hiroshima, the Australian reporter Wilfred Burchett, encountered overt hostility from the patients and their relatives when visiting the shattered city's few remaining hospital wards. Burchett went on to file a famous despatch with the *Daily Express* which not only described the human effects of the bomb and the 'atomic plague' being endured by the residents of the city but went on to claim that, 'From

---

[104] See Dower, *Embracing Defeat*, 36.
[105] Weekly Political Intelligence Summary No. 308, 29 August 1945, in *Great Britain: Foreign Office: Weekly Political Intelligence Summaries*, Vol. XII: *July–December 1945* (London, 1983), 20.
[106] 'An Estimate of Conditions in Asia and the Pacific at the Close of the War in the Far East and the Objectives and Policies of the United States', paper prepared in the Department of State by Grew, 22 June 1945, *FRUS, 1945, VI*, 558–9; one report of October 1945 noted that there was 'little consciousness of war guilt when the occupation forces entered Tokyo', but a wide belief that defeat was 'due solely to industrial and scientific inferiority and the atomic bomb'; quoted in Monica Braw, *The Atomic Bomb Suppressed: American Censorship in Occupied Japan* (Armonk, NY, 1991), 135–6.
[107] John Hersey, *Hiroshima* (London, 1946; rev. edn, 1985), 117.

the moment that this devastation was loosed upon Hiroshima the people who survived have hated the white man.'[108] Mention in the Japanese press of the awful fate of Hiroshima and Nagasaki, along with emerging stories about radiation sickness, were frequent in the immediate aftermath. Just over a month after the surrender, however, MacArthur acted to suspend the publication of *Asahi* which, as well as challenging the stories of Japanese wartime atrocities that the Americans were beginning to disseminate, had published a piece (authored by Ichiro Hatoyama, a future Japanese prime minister) maintaining that if the United States really stood for 'justice and power', then it could not deny that the use of the atomic bomb was a violation of international law.[109] Thereafter a new press code, alongside other reporting restrictions, sharply curtailed discussion and comment, with many Japanese journalists also practising a degree of self-censorship. The view of the occupation authorities was that such stories could become the focus of anti-American feeling and hence posed a threat to 'public tranquillity'. Partial relaxation of some censorship restrictions in 1948 allowed the publication of a few poems and essays, most notably those of Nagai Takashi, whose reflections on surviving Nagasaki achieved enormous popularity, even as he slowly died of radiation poisoning.[110] A Japanese translation of Hersey's work had to wait until 1949, and only with the end of the occupation was publication of scientific and medical accounts of the effects of the bombs allowed. Japanese films of the destruction in Hiroshima and Nagasaki were taken away by the US authorities in 1946, and visual representations of the human impact of the explosions were confined to the work of artists. Photographs of the bombed cities finally began to appear in Japanese magazines in August 1952.[111] That same year also saw the first translation of Justice Pal's dissenting opinion (cited above) at the Tokyo War Crimes Tribunal, much to the pleasure of right-wing Japanese intellectuals as the atomic bomb also became a means to expiate or gloss over completely Japan's own appalling wartime record.[112]

---

[108] See Wilfred Burchett, *Shadows of Hiroshima* (London, 1983), 36, 38.

[109] 'MacArthur Closes Asahi, Tokyo Paper', *NYT*, 19 September 1945. On censorship in Japan, see John W. Dower, 'The Bombed: Hiroshimas and Nagasakis in Japanese Memory', in Hogan (ed.), *Hiroshima*, 116–18; Glenn D. Hook, 'Roots of Nuclearism: Censorship and Reportage of Atomic Damage in Hiroshima and Nagasaki', *Multilingua*, 7, 1/2, 1988, 133–58; and in general Braw, *Atomic Bomb Suppressed*. In a reflection of the anxieties expressed by Grew about possible Japanese sentiment, the national news agency, Domei, had also alleged that Japan might have won the war if the atomic bomb had not been produced; see *ibid.*, 89–90.

[110] Dower, *Embracing Defeat*, 196–8.   [111] *Ibid.*, 414–15.

[112] See Richard H. Minear, *Victor's Justice: The Tokyo War Crimes Trial* (Princeton, 1971), 33, n. 29; and Takemae, *Allied Occupation of Japan*, 250.

Although the authorities had attempted to dissuade any commemoration of the anniversaries of the bombings, peace demonstrations at Hiroshima and Nagasaki became annual events from 1948 onwards.[113] However, the American occupiers never seem to have been subject to sustained resentment because of the events of 1945; one post-war study by the RAND Corporation found that the atomic attacks 'generated very little persistent hostility toward Americans'.[114] As John Dower has highlighted, the particular horror of nuclear attack tended to be absorbed by most Japanese commentary into a revulsion against the cruelty of war in general. While awareness that Japan had slipped into a different category because of the means that had been used to bring about its defeat was always latent beneath the surface of popular opinion, the atomic bombings were to become an essential aspect of what some Japanese regarded as a necessary attitude of atonement or repentance in the decades after 1945. The strong anti-nuclear sentiments that one sees emerging in the 1950s and 1960s were themselves wrapped up in an aversion to war that was part of the reaction against the disastrous path embarked upon by Japan's leaders before 1941.[115]

The Americans themselves helped to keep some of the controversy over the atomic attacks alive in Japan through the formation of the Atomic Bomb Casualty Commission (ABCC) in early 1947.[116] Established through a presidential directive to the National Academy of the Sciences, the ABCC operated with funding support from the AEC and had the long-term task of monitoring the biological and medical effects of the nuclear weapons used against Japan. Accordingly, during the summer of 1947 the ABCC began work in Hiroshima, with a locally based mixture of American and Japanese staff, through conducting epidemiological and genetic studies of the survivors of the atomic bombs and their children. From its inception, the work of the ABCC proved intensely controversial, encapsulated in its 'no treatment' policy.[117] With the commission's brief limited to the study of the health effects of the bombings on the surviving residents of the two cities, it was not intended to offer treatment or advice

---

[113] See Wittner, *One World or None*, 48–9.

[114] Irving L. Janis, *Psychological Effects of the Atomic Attacks on Japan* (Santa Monica, 1950), 65.

[115] See Dower, *Embracing Defeat*, 493–4; Wittner, *One World or None*, 45–54.

[116] The major study here is M. Susan Lindee, *Suffering Made Real: American Science and the Survivors at Hiroshima* (Chicago, 1994).

[117] See John Beatty, 'Genetics in the Atomic Age: The Atomic Bomb Casualty Commission, 1947–1956', in Keith R. Benson, Jane Maienschein and Ronald Rainger (eds.), *The Expansion of American Biology* (New Brunswick, 1991), 284–324; Sue Rabbitt Roff, *Hotspots: The Legacy of Hiroshima and Nagasaki* (London, 1995), 24–7, 59 and *passim*; Monica Braw, 'Hiroshima and Nagasaki: The Voluntary Silence', in Hein and Seldon (eds.), *Living with the Bomb*, 158–9; and Takemae, *Allied Occupation of Japan*, 428–31.

to victims (which might imply guilt or involve an admission of responsibility). There was also an aversion by American officials to attaching any kind of moral opprobrium to the atomic bombing of Hiroshima and Nagasaki by according the survivors any special status. One further contentious issue was that the work of the ABCC with Japanese survivors could be exploited by the US military authorities and the AEC for the knowledge it could provide of radiation effects, and so contribute to the future development and design of nuclear weapons.[118] Many Japanese hence developed a high degree of scorn for the work of the commission, one newspaper editor, for example, remarking that the people of Hiroshima were 'indignant and feel they were treated like guinea pigs – just models for theoretical experiments … We firmly believe that our people were selected to become the first test ground for the effects of A-bombs on human beings.'[119] The co-operation of survivors with the ABCC decreased markedly with the end of the occupation in 1952, as press criticism of the commission also picked up.[120] Accusations that in the eyes of the ABCC Japanese were merely the objects of scientific curiosity were in many respects a progression from the idea that had been spread in 1945 that the Americans were indifferent to the lives and suffering of Asians and that this, moreover, with an underlying source in racism, had played a role in the decision to single out Japan for atomic attack.[121]

In Asia as a whole, the charge that racism lay behind the use of the bomb against Japan gained much credibility as many observers could see a correlation between American attitudes towards their wartime enemy and the race prejudice that was such a pronounced feature of American society itself, whether it be in the form of the outright and pervasive segregation still practised in the South, or the daily de facto discrimination experienced by African Americans living in the urban Northeast or Midwest. Gandhi had already highlighted the interconnected nature of these issues by writing (in the friendliest fashion) to Roosevelt in July 1942, that the 'declaration that the Allies are fighting to make the world safe for freedom of the individual and democracy sounds hollow, so long as India, and for that matter, Africa, are exploited by Great Britain, and America has the Negro problem in her own home'.[122] The whole nature of the 'Negro problem', as Gandhi termed it, was already changing rapidly

---

[118] Beatty, 'Genetics in the Atomic Age', 292–3.   [119] Burchett, *Shadows of Hiroshima*, 58.
[120] Beatty, 'Genetics in the Atomic Age', 288.
[121] See also the reflections on the subliminal racial tensions during these years in Yukiko Koshiro, *Trans-Pacific Racisms and the U.S. Occupation of Japan* (New York, 1999), 49–73.
[122] Gandhi to Roosevelt, 1 July 1942, *FRUS, 1942, I: General; The British Commonwealth; The Far East* (Washington, DC, 1960), 678.

as the war acted to give a huge boost to the nascent civil rights movement, with African Americans being recruited into and volunteering for the armed services, and many finding new, more remunerative, jobs in the expanding war economy, continuing the 'great migration' away from Southern rural poverty that had begun in 1915.[123] With greater economic power than ever before, and emboldened by the rhetoric of freedom that accompanied American war aims, African Americans had rising expectations that their contribution to victory would be rewarded with equality. Membership of the National Association for the Advancement of Colored People (NAACP) had increased from 50,000 to 450,000 during the war years, and black protest had led Roosevelt to concede a modest attempt to secure equal rights over hiring for war industry with the formation of the Fair Employment Practices Committee (FEPC) in 1941. The race riots that broke out in 1943, most notably in Detroit, underlined for many Americans the explosive potential of the issue (in April 1944, *Life* magazine described racial conflict as 'America's No 1 social problem').[124]

The connections between the struggle of African Americans within the United States, and the prevalence of racism and imperialist domination elsewhere in the world, were recognized by many black writers and intellectuals. In the inter-war period black activists had found much to admire in the challenge of Japan to the Western and white-dominated order in the Far East (not least in Tokyo's thwarted desire to see a racial equality clause inserted into the Covenant of the League of Nations), and W. E. B. Du Bois had been a consistent proponent of the idea that domestic racial conditions were a symptom of a wider race-based world order which had to be assailed in parallel with more parochial concerns.[125] Many African Americans had also become accustomed to seeing a racial pattern to world events through the wartime years, as they continued to be denied the democratic freedoms extolled by allied war aims. In a *Chicago Defender* column of August 1945 that mirrored views held elsewhere in Asia, the black poet Langston Hughes used one of his characters to express the belief that atomic bombs had actually been ready before the defeat of Germany, but 'They just did not want to use them on white folks.

---

[123] See, e.g., Richard M. Dalfiume, 'The "Forgotten Years" of the Negro Revolution', *Journal of American History*, 55, 1, June 1968, 90–106; Neil A. Wynn, 'The Impact of the Second World War on the American Negro', *Journal of Contemporary History*, 6, 2, May 1971, 42–54.

[124] See Harvard Sitkoff, 'Racial Militancy and Inter-Racial Violence in the Second World War', *Journal of American History*, 58, 3, December 1971, 661–81.

[125] In general, see Marc Gallicchio, *The African American Encounter with Japan and China: Black Internationalism in Asia, 1895–1945* (Chapel Hill, 2000); for Du Bois in particular, see David Levering Lewis, *W. E. B. Du Bois: The Fight for Equality and the American Century, 1919–1963* (New York, 2000), and Horne, *Black and Red.*

Germans is white. So they wait until the war is all over in Europe to try them out on colored folks. Japs is colored.'[126] Roy Wilkins, editor of the NAACP's journal *The Crisis*, argued that the use of the bomb followed automatically from the racially charged hatred of the Japanese that had been seen during the Pacific Island campaigns.[127]

Among white elites in the United States there was an acute awareness after 1941 that the professed allied war aims of promoting freedom and democracy, as put forward in such seminal documents as the Atlantic Charter, could not easily be reconciled with the denial of basic rights to either fellow citizens, or other humans who could be imagined as part of a wider global community. Officials in the Office of War Information, including its head, Elmer Davis, often expressed their anxiety over the way Axis propaganda latched onto the American record of segregation and discrimination in attempting to expose the hypocrisy of the allied cause in broadcasts to Latin America and Asia, and came to believe that if the United States were to exercise leadership and sell its ideology in a decolonizing world, it would need to reform its own domestic practices in this sensitive area.[128] For some Americans commitment to the war effort meant also embracing a new spirit of liberal internationalism which envisaged a post-war United States acting vigorously to uphold a new conception of world order, where peace, stability and prosperity would, among other things, be assured by the transfer of American notions of liberty and freedom to expectant peoples anxiously waiting to be delivered from their current miseries (including imperialism in its various guises).[129] Defeated as the Republican presidential candidate in 1940, Wendell Willkie embarked upon a global tour in 1942, publishing his experiences as *One World* the following year. In this stirring account, which sold over 1 million copies in 1943, Willkie offered a universalizing picture of a shared human condition where supposed racial distinctions were submerged. Standing in opposition to colonial systems of exploitation and the denial of basic political rights, Willkie presented an image of all peoples, irrespective of religion, nationality or political belief, being united by a common set of needs, hopes and fears; 'we are learning in this war', Willkie averred, 'that it is not racial classifications nor ethnological considerations

[126] Langston Hughes, 'Simple and the Atom Bomb', *Chicago Defender*, 18 August 1945.
[127] See Boyer, *By the Bomb's Early Light*, 199–200, and also Gallicchio, *African American Encounter*, 203–4.
[128] Justin Hart, 'Making Democracy Safe for the World: Race, Propaganda, and the Transformation of U.S. Foreign Policy during World War Two', *Pacific Historical Review*, 73, 1, 2004, 49–84.
[129] Robert A. Divine, *Second Chance: The Triumph of Internationalism in America during World War Two* (New York, 1967).

which bind men together; it is shared concepts and kindred objectives'. To support his outlook, Willkie pointed to the Far East, where Japan was an enemy because of her aggression and treachery, not her race or colour, and China a friend and ally because 'she values liberty': 'Here are two Oriental peoples. One is our enemy; one is our friend. Race and color have nothing to do with what we are fighting for today. Race and color do not determine at whose side we shall fight. These are things the white race is learning through this war. These are things we needed to learn.' Developing his theme, Willkie pointed to China's example of heroic resistance as humbling while America was still developing its full fighting potential. The 'moral atmosphere in which the white race lives' is changing, Willkie claimed, and continued with an attack on what he described as America's own 'race imperialism' at home which replicated the out-moded colonial mentality of the 'white man's burden'.[130] Even Franklin Roosevelt himself, for all his derogatory comments in private about Asian peoples and his curious theories of racial genetics, captured the spirit of the time in October 1942 when he remarked to the Pacific War Council that since 'human beings, given equal opportunities, mix successfully', then in the post-war world, 'racial prejudices, as we know them in the past, will ... probably be subordinated, and the countries of the world will more or less become melting pots'.[131]

Many historians have highlighted how the political, economic and social changes produced by the Second World War, in both the international and domestic settings, helped to precipitate a sea change in American attitudes and responses when it came to the issue of race. The very fact that the United States was engaged in total war with a totalitarian system which had racism at its core, and the extreme violence that societies organized along such lines were capable of, served to discredit ideas of racial hierarchy and prejudice. The genocidal consequences of ideologies of racial supremacy confirmed this viewpoint and the hazards of emphasizing the dividing lines of race.[132] The legitimacy of race thinking and construction of a social hierarchy tiered according to biological difference had also been dealt several hammer blows by developments in physiology and social anthropology in the 1930s and 1940s which discredited 'scientifically' determined 'racial' classifications and placed a stress on group distinctions being a socially constructed phenomenon; in this way, analysing culture became

[130] Wendell L. Willkie, *One World* (New York, 1943), 188–90; and see Robert Dallek, *The American Style of Foreign Policy: Cultural Politics and Foreign Affairs* (New York, 1983), 137–8.
[131] Quoted in Thorne, *Allies*, 158, and see *ibid.*, 158–9, 167–8, for Roosevelt's eccentric ideas on racial crossings.
[132] See Tony Kushner, *The Holocaust and the Liberal Imagination* (Oxford, 1994).

the key means to studying differing human groups.[133] In the United States, this shift in perceptions was complemented by the appearance of Gunnar Myrdal's *An American Dilemma* in January 1944, which carried the authority of social science techniques in its examination of American race relations. Myrdal's work was well received by northern white journalists and intellectuals, and its call for the resolution of the contradiction between the democratic and egalitarian ideals of the American 'creed' and the hard fact of American racism has led one study to argue that it 'played a major role in articulating and shaping a new racial liberalism for postwar America'.[134] By the late 1940s, moreover, the whole notion of 'prejudice' was being placed under the spotlight by social scientists, educators and public policy professionals so that it almost assumed the character of a psychological disorder and was pictured as the product of ignorance, 'irrational' thinking and limited contact and knowledge of other ethnic groups. Under widespread attack in what might be called 'respectable' society outside the South, racial and religious bigotry was condemned by many civic, professional and business groups. In 1946, for example, the Federal Council of Churches denounced segregation as 'a violation of the Gospel of love and human brotherhood' which it pledged to strive to overturn in the Church and society as a whole.[135] In international terms, many scholars point to such shifts as the adoption of the United Nations Declaration of Human Rights in December 1948, and the landmark UNESCO statement of 1950, crafted by Ashley Montagu, that 'mankind is one', as marking the arrival of what Richard King has called a 'consensus position among intellectual and scientific elites in the West' around a 'universalist vision in which the different races were understood to be equal in natural capacities and legal political rights'.[136]

Several major qualifications need to be considered here, before pictures of post-war American racial liberalism become too glowing. Many responses to black demands for equality were inspired by fear of a

---

[133] See Thomas F. Gossett, *Race: The History of an Idea in America* (New York, 1965), 416–30; Philip Gleason, 'Americans All: World War Two and the Shaping of American Identity', *Review of Politics*, 43, October 1981, 483–518, especially 496–500; for the undermining of scientific racism, see Elazar Barkin, *The Retreat of Scientific Racism: Changing Concepts of Race in Britain and the United States between the World Wars* (Cambridge, 1992).

[134] Walter A. Jackson, *Gunnar Myrdal and America's Conscience: Social Engineering as Racial Liberalism, 1938–1987* (Chapel Hill, 1990), 240; see also David W. Southern, *Gunnar Myrdal and Black–White Relations: The Use and Abuse of 'An American Dilemma', 1944–1969* (Baton Rouge, LA, 1987), 74.

[135] See Southern, *Myrdal*, 111; Jackson, *Myrdal*, 279–81.

[136] Richard H. King, *Race, Culture, and the Intellectuals, 1940–1970* (Washington, DC, 2004), 2.

breakdown in societal cohesion and the violence that could ensue, while, as Alan Brinkley notes, 'it would be a mistake to exaggerate the impact of the war on the willingness of Americans to confront the nation's "race problem", not least as Southerners returned from the war determined to defend their own way of life against intrusive federal power'.[137] The limits of the new 'civic nationalism' generated by wartime idealism was also, for example, shown by the widespread hostility that greeted black families trying to move into northern white residential areas in the immediate post-war years.[138] For many African Americans the verbal repudiation of prejudice and discrimination meant little when words were not backed by deeds; the approach of most white liberals was still evolutionary when it came to racial change, while for the cautious majority legal and judicial concessions which might be made over civil rights did not mark any ready acceptance of social equality between groups defined in racial terms. Though the post-war period would see more media attention devoted to the issues of race and bigotry and overt white racism become less socially acceptable, racism 'remained a formidable force' in American society where 'lip service to egalitarian ideals and fair play often did not translate into meaningful action'.[139]

For the purposes of the current analysis, it is necessary to recognize that after 1945 mainstream white attitudes towards race were largely defensive in nature: racism had been rendered morally unacceptable, and though the societal and institutional structures that sustained discrimination in the United States might remain strong, there was a general recognition that change had to occur (albeit at a gradual pace). Indeed, many Americans regarded it as a strength of their democratic system that such change *could* occur. Related to the sense in which American elites had to be defensive about the domestic racial scene were also frequent examples of the way they shared a consciousness of their 'whiteness' on an international stage where many of the new actors emerging as the European empires contracted were 'non-white'.[140] This binary division of states and societies had, of course, a long pedigree, but what was particularly noticeable in the 1930s and 1940s was how white elites in both Britain and the United States saw the rise of race consciousness in overwhelmingly

[137] Alan Brinkley, *Liberalism and Its Discontents* (Cambridge, MA, 1998), 101.
[138] A point made by Gary Gerstle in *American Crucible: Race and Nation in the Twentieth Century* (Princeton, 2001), 234–7; see also Gerstle, 'Race and the Myth of the Liberal Consensus', *Journal of American History*, 82, 2, September 1995, 579–86.
[139] Southern, *Myrdal*, 102–3.
[140] See R.J. Vincent, 'Racial Equality', in Hedley Bull and Adam Watson (eds.), *The Expansion of International Society* (Oxford, 1984), 239–54; Michael H. Hunt, *Ideology and U.S. Foreign Policy* (New Haven, 1987), 46–52.

negative and destructive terms, with race conflict simmering below the surface of international society, and violent anti-white reactions widely anticipated. As Frank Furedi has argued, these often fevered and alarmist notions of anti-white unity and a 'thirst for racial revenge' as driving demands for equality and independence were almost a standard reflex when colonial dominance was challenged, so serving to delegitimize the nationalist cause. In the post-war era, Asian 'racial chauvinism' or 'reverse colour prejudice' were terms frequently used to explain and also to stigmatize the anti-colonial 'revolt against the West'.[141]

In many respects the overt racism of pre-war efforts to classify the behaviour of peoples according to biologically defined characteristics was replaced in the 1940s and 1950s by the new lexicon of development studies or, as it became known, 'modernization theory'. Fortified by the professed objectivity of social science methodology, development theorists and practitioners came to promote Western- and capitalist-orientated economic growth in order to fulfil the Cold War aim of steering newly independent states away from emulation of Soviet-style models. The universalizing currents of this enterprise in nation-building and societal engineering were apparent throughout, as was what Michael Hunt describes as 'an abiding sense of superiority over the dark-skinned peoples of the Third World … these impressive new formulations amounted to little more than a restatement of the old ethnocentric platitudes about uplift and regeneration formerly directed at the Philippines, China, and Mexico'. The overt language of race was in this sense superseded by the new development hierarchy of modernity as opposed to tradition, where 'backwardness' and skin colour did not stand in a direct causal relationship, but through coincidence this link could be inferred by the more privileged observer standing in the transatlantic world.[142] The race consciousness of white American foreign policy-makers was usually manifested in the privately expressed thought that it was essential to avoid any impression that race had entered into the formation of their attitudes, choices and preferences; in this fashion, the conduct of international relations was supposed to adopt the colour-blind features of Myrdal's American creed.

Truman himself was emblematic of the shifting racial mores of the period and how they intersected with political change. As might be expected, with his political and personal background centred on an upper South and segregated state, Truman's pre-war vocabulary was replete with

---

[141] See the discussion in Furedi, *Silent War*, 113–31, 172–5, 202–11.
[142] Hunt, *Ideology*, 159–62; Michael E. Latham, *Modernization as Ideology: American Social Science and 'Nation Building' in the Kennedy Era* (Chapel Hill, 2000), 59–63.

private racist epithets, but after 1946 their recorded appearances drop away very sharply.[143] The political inexpediency of racist language was a consequence of wartime events and sensibilities, but also a signifier of the role of race and the emerging area of civil rights in the agenda of post-war mainstream American liberalism, where Truman found himself, in Barton Bernstein's words, 'slowly prodded by conscience and pushed by politics'.[144] Democratic Party national managers were increasingly drawn to the need to appeal to the enfranchised African Americans who populated many of their urban strongholds in the Northeast and the Midwest, despite the obvious tension this would generate with the Southern segregationist wing of the party. Shocked by a series of brutal racist murders in the South, Truman had responded to the new electoral strength of black Americans, and the changing tenor of the debate around American racism, by establishing his presidential Committee on Civil Rights in late 1946. With no objections from the administration, the committee went well beyond its original remit of examining safeguards against racial violence, by issuing a call for wholesale change in its groundbreaking report of October 1947, *To Secure These Rights*. In this, the committee had stressed that 'we cannot escape the fact that our civil rights record has been an issue in world politics. The world's press and radio are full of it.' This was also the cause of much unease in the State Department, where officials noted the need for the United States to show it was embarked on a course of race relations reform. Indeed, in support of its contentions, the committee had quoted from a letter written in May 1946 to the Chairman of the FEPC by Dean Acheson, then the Under-Secretary of State, but soon-to-be architect of an American-led post-war liberal international order, alerting him to the 'quite obvious' observation that racial discrimination had an 'adverse effect' on US foreign policy, and that the State Department would like to see progress made in this area.[145]

Although not as comprehensive as the recommendations contained in the committee's report, the significant proposals for civil rights legislation that Truman made in his February 1948 special message to Congress, which also included an announcement that discrimination in the armed services would soon be eliminated by executive order, went further than many might have predicted and set the stage for the political struggles to come. The electoral strategy that lay behind some of these initiatives had already been made evident by Clark Clifford, Special Counsel to the

---

[143] Hunt, *Ideology*, 163.
[144] Barton J. Bernstein, 'America in War and Peace: The Test of Liberalism', in Bernstein (ed.), *Towards a New Past: Dissenting Essays in American History* (New York, 1968), 304.
[145] See Dudziak, *Cold War Civil Rights*, 80–1.

President, who had warned in November 1947 that African-American voters who had been attracted to the Democratic ticket by the New Deal could easily be lost back to the Republican Party, but that this might be arrested by Truman's rhetorical endorsement of a civil rights programme. The direct pay-off came exactly a year later, when Truman managed to weather the defection of Strom Thurmond and his hardline segregationist followers and to carve out a winning, if fragile, Democratic coalition in the presidential and congressional elections of 1948.[146] The election outcome had also seen off the challenge of Henry Wallace and the Progressive Party, with its more direct appeals for an instant end to segregation, while African-American international activism was stymied by the support that the NAACP leadership felt compelled to offer Truman in the Cold War, support which helped to isolate the trenchant criticisms of US foreign policy coming from the likes of Du Bois and other 'transnational' black activists.[147] Yet the cynical political calculations that undoubtedly lay behind some of the administration's pronouncements of 1947–8 – Truman was, of course, aware that there was no chance that Congress would pass his proposed civil rights measures, and he had no intention of expending valuable political capital in trying to push them through – must also be set beside the President's recognition that the current dispensation was indefensible for professed liberals, especially in view of the critical international situation. In June 1947, for example, Truman became the first US president to address the annual convention of the NAACP, where he alluded to his concern that the issue of civil rights was beginning to be a factor in the Cold War and was reflected in Soviet propaganda against the United States, affirming 'for these compelling reasons we can no longer afford the luxury of a leisurely attack upon prejudice and discrimination'.[148]

Indeed, from soon after the war, as Mary Dudziak has effectively documented, observers in Africa, Asia, the Middle East and Latin America were casting a critical spotlight on the abundant evidence of racial discrimination and violence still on show in the United States, including the mistreatment of visiting foreign diplomats in the nation's segregated capital. Interest in racial conditions in the United States was, for example, very high in the newly independent states of South Asia: in 1948, the American Embassy in Ceylon was noting stories with these

---

[146] See Harvard Sitkoff, 'Harry Truman and the Election of 1948: The Coming of Age of Civil Rights in American Politics', *Journal of Southern History*, 37, 4, November 1971, 597–616.

[147] On the decline of anti-colonial politics among African Americans in this era, see Von Eschen, *Race against Empire*, 107–9, 114–18.

[148] See Donovan, *Conflict and Crisis*, 333–4.

themes appearing in local newspapers and the 'Asian preoccupation with racial discrimination in the United States'. From the Manila Embassy there was a similar reminder to the State Department that favourable accounts of progress made in race relations would have a beneficial effect on a Filipino audience in 'dispelling or mitigating "color barrier" psychology and its concomitant, the tendency to formation of "color", racial or "Asia for the Asiatics" groupings'.[149] By 1949, State Department officials and US diplomats overseas were commenting in anxious terms about the employment of racial themes in Soviet commentary on the United States, and the way Moscow was beginning to stress this as a key thread in their overall propaganda effort, particularly in Asia.[150] One British official based in South East Asia reported the attraction of the United States in the region was 'one of wealth and power. Their role of the "colony made good" makes an obvious appeal to populations hostile to colonialism. Nevertheless, their callowness, tactlessness, overlavish display and vulgarity are not lost on Far East observers. Their appeal is largely to the rich and well-to-do, who can see in the American way of life a business man's paradise.' One of the advantages of the Soviet Union was, by contrast, that it appeared as 'a "color-less state", which welcomes on terms of equality peoples of all nations and races'.[151] One leading official at the US Embassy in New Delhi wrote in early 1950:

Those who deal with India, either in this country or in the Department, are seldom permitted to forget for any length of time the absorbing interest which Indians have in racial discrimination in other countries, notably South Africa or our own country. The Reuter's News Agency never fails to cable the news of incidents in racial relations back home and these incidents receive attention which is quite surprising in view of the usual paucity of American news in the Indian press. The elimination of racial discrimination along with the termination of Western colonialism are fundamental aspects of Indian foreign policy, which at times seem to take precedence over yet more pressing threats to the independence of peoples, both colored and white ... we here and our opposite numbers in Washington are very thoroughly conditioned to the interest which India takes in our racial problems.[152]

The administration's concerns over the way racial discrimination could tarnish the image of American democracy and harm foreign policy interests was demonstrated by a series of amicus curiae briefs

[149] For these quotations, see Dudziak, *Cold War Civil Rights*, 31, 33.
[150] See *ibid.*, 38–9; also Klein, *Cold War Orientalism*, 39–41.
[151] 'Information Work in the Far East', report by J. A. Pilcher, head of Far East Information Services, 17 March 1948, FO 953/320, TNA.
[152] J. Graham Parsons (First Secretary, US Embassy, Delhi) to the Reverend Anson P. Stokes, 23 February 1950, folder 26, box 1, J. Graham Parsons papers, Georgetown University Library.

that were submitted to the Supreme Court from 1948 onwards in civil rights cases by Justice Department officials, and which highlighted the overseas coverage given to the issue.[153] The intention of policy-makers in the Truman administration was to deflect growing international criticisms of segregation and discrimination by showing the progress that was being made, in an orderly, democratic environment, towards greater racial justice for all American citizens; this in no way required a full frontal assault on the laws and customs of the South but the careful projection of a picture of the harmonious evolution of American society as various landmarks of legal change were reached. The federal author-ities, for example, had worked hard to attempt to moderate the NAACP's petition to the United Nations in 1947, which had high-lighted the contradictions between the values of the UN Charter and the racial practices of the United States.[154] Dean Acheson's own olympian disdain for those he considered of an inferior race, made manifest during the 1960s in his unapologetic support for white minor-ity rule in southern Africa, again indicates that the administration's rhetorical support for civil rights held a strongly instrumental character, rather than deriving from any fundamental moral conviction.[155] For an 'internationalist' Republican such as John Foster Dulles, there was perhaps a deeper sense of the moral issues involved, but a similar unwillingness to contemplate anything other than incremental steps towards a distant goal. In one speech of 1948 to the First Assembly of the World Council of Churches in Amsterdam, where he measured the Soviet danger to the 'free societies' of the West, Dulles went on to highlight that 'the great blot on the escutcheon of the democracies is the discrimination against coloured persons practised by much of the white population of the United States ... the problem is recognised and great efforts are being made to deal with it. It is not possible by legislative fiat to eradicate social prejudices, the origins of which go back hundreds of years. There is, however, a vast change which is in peaceful process.'[156]

[153] For her initial statement of the argument, see Dudziak, 'Desegregation as a Cold War Imperative'.

[154] See Carol Anderson, *Eyes Off the Prize: The United Nations and the African American Struggle for Human Rights, 1944–1955* (Cambridge, 2003), 87–112, 126–9, 141–9.

[155] See Douglas Brinkley, *Dean Acheson: The Cold War Years, 1953–71* (New Haven, 1992), 303–28. In the opinion of Acheson's latest biographer, his interventions over civil rights were 'modest gestures', while the State Department remained virtually silent about racist practices in South Africa or the European colonies; see Robert L. Beisner, *Dean Acheson: A Life in the Cold War* (New York, 2006), 513.

[156] See John Foster Dulles, 'The Christian Citizen in a Changing World', in *The Church and the International Disorder: An Ecumenical Study Prepared Under the Auspices of the World*

This kind of reserved and highly circumspect attitude to change found its international counterpart in the American response to the revolutionary upsurge seen in East and South East Asia in the latter 1940s. Despite an avowed commitment to self-determination, the Truman administration did not intervene as the French in Indochina and the Dutch in Indonesia moved to suppress with force the nationalist movements they confronted after 1945, deferring to the belief that the support and co-operation of their West European allies – when containment and its economic expression, the Marshall Plan, were moving to centre stage – was crucial to meeting the main Soviet challenge, and in the case of Indochina displaying innate hostility to the Viet Minh for its Communist base of leadership and support.[157] Instead, Washington tried to adopt a stance of neutrality and non-involvement, even though its own military assistance and economic aid to the metropolitan powers compromised this position, giving additional opportunities to the French and Dutch to deploy military resources to the Far East. Viewing South East Asia as an area where US interests were not vital, the Truman administration hoped to see the colonial powers undertake measured and orderly steps of reform leading to the eventual concession of self-government to 'responsible' nationalist leaders. Violent outbreaks and insurrections, the Americans tended to increasingly believe, were either instigated by Soviet intrigue or likely to be exploited by local Communist agitators. In Indonesia, only when the 'insurgent' Republican Government had shown its anti-Communist convictions by defeating the Madiun rising in 1948 did American officials begin to adopt a more critical stance towards Dutch policy. When subsequently a second Dutch so-called 'police action' was mounted against the Republic, an outcry was provoked in the United States, particularly in congressional quarters, as previous American and UN backed ceasefire and political agreements were openly flouted. By the spring of 1949, with congressional critics targeting Marshall Plan funds destined for the Netherlands, the State Department finally moved to put decisive pressure on the Dutch to concede independence, a status that was achieved by the end of the year.[158]

Council of Churches (London, 1948), 101. On Dulles and the Amsterdam meeting, see also Mark G. Toulouse, *The Transformation of John Foster Dulles: From Prophet of Realism to Priest of Nationalism* (Macon, GA, 1985), 196–200.

[157] See George McT. Kahin, 'The United States and the Anticolonial Revolutions in Southeast Asia', in Yonosuke Nagai and Akira Iriye (eds.), *The Origins of the Cold War in Asia* (Oxford, 1977), 338–61; Robert J. McMahon, *The Limits of Empire: The United States and Southeast Asia since World War Two* (New York, 1999), 26–8.

[158] Robert J. McMahon, *Colonialism and Cold War: The United States and the Struggle for Indonesian Independence, 1945–49* (Ithaca, 1981), 254–60, 291–6.

The tardy response of the Truman administration to events in Indonesia, and its obvious sympathy for the French campaign against the Viet Minh, won Americans few friends among the emerging nationalist leadership in parts of Asia, where solidarity with the struggle against colonialism was accorded a high value.[159] The initial non-committal stance of the United States after the Dutch launched their second military offensive on Java in December 1948 was, for example, a cause of disquiet and even resentment to the new governments of India, Pakistan and Burma, who had pledged their support to the Indonesians and expected the Americans to follow through on their anti-colonial declarations. With Nehru organizing a conference in New Delhi to discuss recent Dutch policy, some American commentators even saw Communism increasing its appeal to Asian nationalists and that common feelings of anti-imperialism would help forge a disturbing new 'Asiatic bloc' under Indian leadership, employing the Japanese slogan, 'Asia for the Asiatics'.[160] These overplayed fears were typical of the period, and the New Delhi conference on Indonesia held in January 1949 – which included representatives from Australia and New Zealand – merely passed moderate resolutions backing the Republic and UN Security Council negotiations to resolve the conflict. Indeed, Indian criticisms of American policy, and the non-aligned approach that Nehru's Government was starting to promulgate when it came to the Cold War with the Soviet Union, were beginning to attract Washington's general displeasure; Nehru's first visit to Washington, staged in October 1949, was little short of disastrous, with American anti-Communist strictures being met with lofty disdain by the Indian Prime Minister, who preferred to dwell on colonial issues and the simmering Kashmir dispute with Pakistan. Aware of his private suspicions of American economic imperialism, US officials despaired of what they saw as Nehru's naivety and vanity and his disinclination to acknowledge a moral distinction between American and Soviet actions.[161]

With regard to Indochina, Washington's publicly 'neutral' stance began to undergo a subtle but distinct shift during 1948, especially following the outbreak of Communist insurrection in Malaya in June which seemed to

---

[159] See *ibid.*, 252–3.
[160] Robert Trumbull, 'Asiatics May Create a Bloc As Result of Dutch Action', *NYT*, 25 December 1948; see also McMahon, *Colonialism and Cold War*, 268–9. For the New Delhi conference, see Anita Inder Singh, *The Limits of British Influence: South Asia and the Anglo-American Relationship, 1947–1956* (London, 1993), 60; Sarvepalli Gopal, *Jawaharlal Nehru: A Biography*, Vol. II: *1947–1956* (London, 1979), 55.
[161] Robert J. McMahon, *The Cold War on the Periphery: The United States, India, and Pakistan* (New York, 1994), 39–58; Dennis Merrill, *Bread and the Ballot: The United States and India's Economic Development, 1947–1963* (Chapel Hill, 1990), 39–42.

herald a general Communist surge across the region. As a result, American officials gave notice to their French counterparts that concessions to Bao Dai, the pre-war puppet ruler who had now been chosen by Paris as their principal Vietnamese negotiating partner, might lead to more open support for French policy; in March 1949, the French duly signed the Elysée Accords, granting a severely circumscribed autonomy to Vietnam, and three months later the United States formally welcomed the formation of a Bao Dai government, despite its dubious credibility and complete lack of popular backing.[162] To many observers, the anti-colonial credentials of the United States, supposedly bolstered by the granting of independence to the Philippines in 1946, had been significantly tarnished by the attitudes and policies it had chosen to adopt by 1948–9.

The greatest setback to American ambitions for post-war order and stability in Asia was, however, experienced in China, where, following the failure of George C. Marshall's mediation mission, full-scale civil war had resumed in late 1946, with the Nationalist position soon facing steady and inexorable erosion. The collapse of American ambitions for China, as an effective partner and the source of the rich commercial opportunities that dewy-eyed business executives and politicians had discerned in the heady days of wartime, saw Washington switch its attention to Japan as the most viable setting for the preservation of American influence in East Asia. Largely for domestic political reasons, the Truman administration found it necessary to continue aid to the Chinese Nationalists in 1948, but Marshall, by now Secretary of State, and his senior advisers had lost all confidence in Chiang's regime and were already looking to cut American losses on the Asian mainland, just as the strategic analysis of how best to meet the Soviet threat in the Far East was also undergoing new study. Although the JCS would prefer that large-scale military aid to the Nationalists should continue, both they and George F. Kennan's Policy Planning Staff (PPS) at the State Department assigned primacy to the defence of Western Europe, and, given the limitations on available resources, accepted that in the event of global war the Far East would come low on the list of priorities. Following Kennan's discussions in March 1948 with General MacArthur in Tokyo, from where MacArthur held command over all US forces in the Far East, strategic ideas were exchanged involving the need for American forces to concentrate on an offshore island chain of defence extending down through the Aleutians, Midway, the former Japanese-mandated islands, Clark Field in the Philippines and Okinawa in the Ryukyus. This was not so much a line of containment as

---

[162] Mark Atwood Lawrence, *Assuming the Burden: Europe and the American Commitment to Vietnam* (Berkeley, 2005), 217–32.

the minimum series of positions that could be held with available American sea and air capabilities, and was also intended to prevent any hostile force being able to assemble and mount an amphibious operation from any port on the East Asian mainland; accepted, moreover, was Okinawa's key role as a base under undisputed American control from which atomic-equipped US air power might eventually be effectively employed against Soviet targets in the Far East.[163]

Kennan had envisaged Japan as neutralized after the American occupation, and MacArthur too had shared the belief that Japan was not a necessary part of the offshore chain and where retention of American bases would only incite local resentment, omitting it also from the 'island air power' concept. But as the Nationalist armies in China steadily crumbled in the remainder of 1948, Japan's importance as a potential pro-Western bastion of strength multiplied, and both Kennan and MacArthur alike began to see it as an essential part of the emerging defence perimeter, while the 'reverse course' in occupation policy gave this practical expression.[164] For Japanese economic recovery to take root, and so ensure political stability, Kennan also recognized that access to the areas of South East Asia then convulsed by revolutionary change might be essential.[165] Meanwhile, in the autumn of 1947, faced by the intractable problems of effecting a peaceful unification of the Korean peninsula under democratic elections, the State Department and JCS had agreed on a gradual withdrawal of US forces from occupation duties in South Korea. Korea itself was simply not considered an area of cardinal American interest, though the State Department was to remain concerned that the pace of the pull-out should not undermine the viability of Syngman Rhee's right-wing and autocratic Government, which had been established under American auspices in Seoul and was officially recognized by Washington in August 1948. The authority of Rhee's Government was still subject to almost continual question, however, with intense faction-fighting, Communist uprisings in the South and a

---

[163] In July 1948, the Joint Emergency War Plan had identified Okinawa as the only overseas position from which immediate atomic attacks against the Soviet Union could be launched; see Roger Dingman, 'Strategic Planning and the Policy Process: American Plans for War in East Asia, 1945–1950', *Naval War College Review*, 32, November–December 1979, 14.

[164] See Thomas H. Etzold, 'The Far East in American Strategy, 1948–1951', in Etzold (ed.), *Aspects of Sino-American Relations since 1784* (New York, 1978), 110–16; John L. Gaddis, 'Drawing Lines: The Defensive Perimeter Strategy in East Asia, 1947–1951', in *The Long Peace*, 73–5. On the advent of the reverse course, see Takemae, *Allied Occupation of Japan*, 457–68; and Schaller, *American Occupation of Japan*, 122–40.

[165] For a lucid summary, see Leffler, *Preponderance of Power*, 253–9.

military threat from North Korea leading many US officials to fear that it had only a tenuous hold over the populous.[166]

The complete collapse of the Nationalist position in Manchuria in late 1948 underlined the futility of attempting to sustain Chiang through further aid, which was only likely to disappear into the 'rat-hole' (as Truman described it) of the regime's corrupt officialdom or, if in the form of military equipment, fall quickly into Communist hands. When Dean Acheson took over the reins of the State Department from a tiring Marshall at the start of 1949, among his myriad other preoccupations, he thus had to formulate a new policy to China, just as Republicans at home, smarting at their unexpected electoral defeat to Truman the previous November, were beginning to level accusatory fingers at the administration's handling of the Far East. A Europeanist by every inclination (never once visiting Asia while Secretary of State), Acheson preferred to temporize, planning to cut US ties with the doomed Nationalists and eventually build links with a successor regime, provided it demonstrated respectable standards of international behaviour and showed a genuine degree of independence from Moscow.[167] A key point to underline is that few State Department analysts expected China to quickly transform itself into a united and formidable power capable without substantial outside help of threatening American interests, and there were even hopes that a Chinese Communist regime might become a burden to the Soviet Union for the aid it would be expected to provide.[168] Wanting to give the problem in-depth study, Acheson believed he had time to wait, fending off JCS pressure in early 1949 to provide further assistance so that the Nationalists could be sure of retaining Taiwan, and avoiding action which might drive the Chinese Communists towards Moscow (this at a time when Stalin still maintained correct and formal relations with Chiang, and there was no evidence of direct Russian assistance to the Chinese Communist Party (CCP), beyond the handover of captured Japanese weaponry).[169] Yet Acheson's hopes of encouraging 'Titoism' among the leadership of the Chinese Communist Party – shared by several members of the State

[166] *Ibid.*, 251–3; and William Stueck, *The Road to Confrontation: American Policy toward China and Korea, 1947–1950* (Chapel Hill, 1981), 86–8, 106–10.
[167] Nancy B. Tucker, *Patterns in the Dust: Chinese–American Relations and the Recognition Controversy, 1949–1950* (New York, 1983), 1–18; Warren I. Cohen, 'Acheson, His Advisers, and China, 1949–1950', in Dorothy Borg and Waldo Heinrichs (eds.), *Uncertain Years: Chinese–American Relations, 1947–1950* (New York, 1980), 13–52.
[168] See Rosemary Foot, 'Balancing against Threats: The Rise and Fall of the Sino-Soviet Alliance', in *The Practice of Power: U.S. Relations with China since 1949* (New York, 1995), 119–20.
[169] David Allan Mayers, *Cracking the Monolith: U.S. Policy against the Sino-Soviet Alliance, 1949–1955* (Baton Rouge, LA, 1986), 28–31.

Department – were almost certainly manifestations of wishful thinking in this period: Mao Zedong expected nothing but hostility from the Americans, harboured a special resentment at the assistance Washington had provided the Nationalists at the close of the Far Eastern war (when Chiang's troops had been transported back to former Japanese-occupied areas of northern and eastern China, and US Marines held the ring for their return), was suspicious of American efforts to rebuild Japanese strength, and felt clear ideological affinity to the Soviet Union.[170]

When in April 1949 Communist forces crossed the Yangtze and quickly captured Nanjing and Shanghai, it was apparent that complete control of the Chinese mainland was within their reach. Communist successes on the battlefield, combined with the strident anti-American line followed by the CCP – given concrete manifestation since November 1948 by the emotive imprisonment and ill-treatment of US diplomatic staff, most notably Angus Ward, the Consul at Shenyang – narrowed the options available to the Secretary of State, while Truman, though usually prepared to defer to Acheson's judgement, was prone to see Mao as having irretrievably thrown in his lot with Stalin. This latter interpretation was given extra credence in June 1949, when Mao delivered his 'lean to one side' address, avowing that China would align itself with the Soviet Union.[171] More than anything, confusion marked US policy towards China, as competing voices in the Washington bureaucracy struggled to respond to the fall-out from the impending Communist victory. The JCS had difficulty seeing the Chinese Communists as anything other than an adjunct of Soviet power, making them favour assistance to Chiang and denial of Taiwan to Mao and his followers, who might use the island to threaten sea lines of communication in the Western Pacific and the components of the offshore island chain. While in their planning the military tended to look to US requirements in the event of the outbreak of global war, State Department analysts were animated more by the possibilities of sowing dissension between Soviet and Chinese Communists (where US ties to Chiang would prove a hindrance), and in preserving Western prestige in a contest seen more in psychological and

[170] Gordon H. Chang, *Friends and Enemies: The United States, China, and the Soviet Union, 1948–1972* (Stanford, 1990), 26–35; and Steven M. Goldstein, 'Chinese Communist Policy toward the United States: Opportunities and Constraints, 1944–1950', in Borg and Heinrichs (eds.), *Uncertain Years*, 235–78.
[171] On Truman, see Arnold A. Offner, *Another Such Victory: President Truman and the Cold War, 1945–1953* (Stanford, 2002), 335.

political terms.[172] In issuing the China White Paper in August 1949, however, Acheson intended to signal that the United States possessed only limited means and ability to exercise influence on the Asian mainland; its effect, however, was merely to intensify the domestic political pressure on the administration, making early recognition of a new Communist government an unlikely prospect.[173] The same month saw the Soviet Union break the American nuclear monopoly, in a development which was far quicker than American analysts had predicted, and which heightened fears in Washington that more aggressive moves from the Soviet Union were possible while its own diplomatic initiatives would be constrained by the dangers of sparking a crisis which could result in war.[174]

Amid this debris, the authorities in Washington strove to agree a coherent policy towards the region as a whole, not least as Communist success in China might connect with the revolutionary situation encountered across South East Asia, an area which had hitherto been largely regarded as a European preserve, but whose raw materials and markets now seemed newly vulnerable. At the end of December 1949, the Truman administration approved NSC 48/2, a document which attempted to encapsulate American aims and objectives in Asia, and the policies that might accomplish them. Although the JCS continued to claim the importance of denying Taiwan to any hostile power, in the discussions preceding endorsement of NSC 48/2 they could find no ready response to Acheson's insistence that further military support for Chiang would be a futile waste, and serve only to alienate other Asian states who would see the Americans as the backers of reactionary regimes.[175] Accordingly NSC 48/2 merely noted that the United States should seek to deny Taiwan to the Chinese Communists by 'diplomatic and economic means', and that as this might well prove ineffective, and in a barely veiled reference to the likelihood of an early takeover of the island, then the American position in the Philippines, Ryukyus and Japan should be strengthened. The final form of NSC 48/2 had derived from an NSC staff study initiated in the summer of 1949 that had sought to address the concerns of the Secretary of Defense that American actions had not yet been formulated into any overall plan as to how to contain Communism in the Far East. In their subsequent work, the NSC staff had paid much greater attention to

---

[172] See the discussion in Borg and Heinrichs (eds.), *Uncertain Years*, 119–28; and Dingman, 'Strategic Planning and the Policy Process', 17. On Pentagon thinking being limited to the contingency of general war, see Bruce Cumings, *The Origins of the Korean War*, Vol. II: *The Roaring of the Cataract, 1947–1950* (Princeton, 1990), 386–7.

[173] Beisner, *Acheson*, 185–9.   [174] Leffler, *Preponderance of Power*, 326–7.

[175] Beisner, *Acheson*, 198–9.

the problems of South East Asia, now pictured in outlandish terms as 'the target of a coordinated offensive directed by the Kremlin', and where rising nationalism and local clashes with the colonial powers were seen as providing excellent opportunities for the spread of Soviet influence. Positing the disastrous worldwide repercussions if South East Asia were 'swept by communism', the staff study continued with a classic statement of the contradictory nature of American attitudes by averring that the United States should 'use its influence looking toward resolving the colonial-nationalist conflict in such a way as to satisfy the fundamental demands of the nationalist movement, lay the basis for political stability and resistance to communism, and avoid weakening the colonial powers who are our western allies'. However, the suspicions of Western influence that were prevalent throughout the area meant that the problem had to be approached 'from the Asiatic point of view in so far as possible', with Asian peoples providing leadership and initiative. 'In the conflict between the U.S. and the USSR,' the staff study concluded, 'the advantage in the long run in Asia is likely to rest with the side which succeeds in identifying its own cause with that of the Asian peoples and which succeeds in working in harmony with the dominant motivating forces in Asia today and in influencing these forces rather than attempting by direct or impatient methods to control them.'[176]

Two weeks after the official adoption of NSC 48/2, on 12 January 1950, Acheson delivered a major speech on US policy in Asia to the National Press Club in Washington, DC. The address became most famous for the Secretary of State's public delineation of the American defence perimeter in the Western Pacific, and the fact that though there was mention of US responsibilities towards South Korea, and the reliance that should be placed on collective obligations under the UN Charter, its omission from the list of territories that would be offered direct American protection might have served to invite later Communist aggression. In offering this strategic analysis, Acheson clearly thought he was on safe ground as he was merely recapitulating JCS policy and, for example, the views offered by MacArthur in March 1949 that the Pacific, with the end of the war, had 'become an Anglo-Saxon lake and our line of defense runs through the chain of islands fringing the coast of Asia. It starts from the Philippines and continues through the Ryukyu Archipelago, which

---

[176] See NSC 48/2, 'The Position of the United States with Respect to Asia', 30 December 1949, and NSC 48/1, 23 December 1949, in Thomas H. Etzold and John L. Gaddis (eds.), *Containment: Documents on American Policy and Strategy, 1945–1950* (New York, 1978), 252–76. The best coverage of the compilation of NSC 48/2 is provided by Robert M. Blum, *Drawing the Line: The Origin of American Containment Policy in East Asia* (New York, 1982), but see also Rearden, *Formative Years*, 234–8.

includes its main bastion, Okinawa. Then it bends back through Japan and the Aleutian Island chain to Alaska.'[177] However, adopting some of the themes that had informed the staff work behind NSC 48/2, Acheson had hoped that 'military considerations' should not dominate the thoughts of his audience, and indeed much of the speech was given over to recognition of the strength of Asian nationalism and the need for the United States to adjust to the new circumstances that the retreat of European colonialism and the aftermath of the Chinese revolution was producing. These new nationalist feelings were centred on a revolt against poverty, and against foreign domination, both issues with which Americans could identify. 'Throughout our history,' Acheson noted in grandiose (and inexact) fashion, 'the attitude of Americans toward the peoples of Asia had been an interest in them not as pawns in the strategy of power or as subjects for economic exploitation, but simply as people ... The outstanding factor in the interest of the American people in Asia ... was that over the years it had been parallel and not contrary to the interest of the peoples of Asia.'

American aid, Acheson had maintained, should go only where it was effective, a comment widely interpreted to mean that all support for the Nationalists now remaining on Taiwan would soon be terminated, while American intervention over the fate of the island would simply draw Asian criticism and incur the wrath of the Chinese people. Although there was no attempt to put an 'aggressive' tag on Chinese Communist actions, the Secretary of State attempted to scold Mao and other CCP leaders for being ready to subordinate China's national interests to those of their new friends in Moscow (at this time, of course, Mao was in the Soviet capital negotiating with mixed results the terms of the Sino-Soviet treaty of alliance). By emphasizing the imperialist ambitions of the Soviet Union in the Far East, and particularly Stalin's designs on Manchuria and Mongolia, Acheson hoped to promote the latent sources of tension in the Sino-Soviet relationship.[178] Clearer distance between Beijing and Moscow, Acheson was also privately anticipating, would help ease the path towards an eventual recognition of the PRC. Acheson closed his speech by reflecting on the changes that had swept over Asia in the previous decade:

the old relationships between east and west are gone, relationships which at their worst were exploitation, and which at their best were paternalism. That

[177] Dean Acheson, *Present at the Creation: My Years in the State Department* (New York, 1969), 356–7.
[178] Chang, *Friends and Enemies*, 65–6; Mayers, *Monolith*, 71–2; Stueck, *Road to Confrontation*, 139–43.

relationship is over, and the relationship of east and west must now be in the Far East one of mutual respect and mutual helpfulness. We are their friends. Others are their friends. We and those others are willing to help, but we can help only where we are wanted and only where the conditions of help are really sensible and possible. So what we can see is that this new day in Asia, this new day which is dawning, may go on to a glorious noon or it may darken and it may drizzle out. But that decision lies within the countries of Asia and within the power of the Asian people. It is not a decision which a friend or even an enemy from outside can decide for them.[179]

This was a positive vision of an Asia now free from colonial oppression and external domination ready to face the future in self-reliant fashion. It was also redolent of an American self-image where the United States stood ready to lend a hand in a spirit of friendship and partnership to those who were now enjoying the first moments of freedom but perhaps wary of the rocky shoals that lay ahead. But American actions were hardly in accord with this kind of sentiment, and ambiguous positions over colonialism, strong ties to the European powers and a tendency to subordinate all other concerns to its vehement opposition to Communism were doing much to diminish the respect the United States had earned through victory over Japan among many sections of Asian opinion.

A key part of Acheson's message was also to portray the Soviet Union as an imperialist power in the Far East (in many ways pursuing the same kind of policies as those of tsarist Russia at the end of the nineteenth century), intent on dominating Manchuria and northern China, and on working through its new surrogates in Beijing to curtail the independence that had just been won elsewhere in Asia. However, imperialism and the mentalities that lay behind it were firmly associated in Asia with racial discrimination, and, as long as Moscow projected its own ideology as upholding equality between peoples of whatever racial origin and of unremitting opposition to colonial oppression, it was difficult to make this particular charge stick. Furthermore, and as Acheson had acknowledged when writing to the FEPC in 1946, the treatment of African Americans within the United States, and the perception of American racism built up during and since the war, was another factor which militated against the aspirations towards genuine partnership contained in the National Press Club speech being realized, as Asian commentary seized on any evidence that Americans regarded Asians as of inferior status. Following Moscow's recognition of the DRV at the end of January 1950, C. L. Sulzberger, writing in the *New York Times*, proclaimed the opening of a 'Second

---

[179] Quoted in Thomas G. Paterson and Dennis Merrill (eds.), *Major Problems in American Foreign Relations*, Vol. II: *Since 1914*, 4th edn (Lexington, MA, 1995), 370–1.

Front' in the Cold War by the Soviet Union and the need for the Western powers to co-ordinate their policies in order to construct a new line of containment running from Turkey to the vulnerable states of South East Asia. However, the key to this approach was held by India which would have to eschew its previous neutral stand and support any defensive bloc. In this context, 'an issue which has a direct impact upon the Asiatic crisis is the fate of President Truman's civil rights program ... Only when the Orient is convinced that this Occidental democracy is what it says it is will Washington's diplomats have sound grounds for argument. Day after day the propaganda apparatus of communism is preaching the contrary.'[180] The coming to power of a Communist government in Beijing in October 1949 further complicated the task of winning adherents to the Western cause in Asia, as the most immediate adversary of the United States in the Far East became once again, as in 1941–5, a non-white power. Not only did the CCP demonstrate firm alignment with the Soviet Union, at least at this stage of Chinese development, but there would also be future opportunities, so some American officials believed, for the Communists to make appeals for pan-Asian solidarity in an anti-Western direction, feeding off past memories of shared colonial exploitation.

In this climate, as the Cold War in Asia became militarized during the course of 1950, and with the presence of the atomic bomb in the array of weaponry available to the United States becoming ever more conspicuous, it was possible to raise again the notion that the Western powers were prepared to sanction the use of nuclear weapons against their new Far Eastern enemies in China, Korea and Vietnam, not just because of an antipathy based around ideological rancour but also through an underlying racial prejudice that viewed Asian lives as of less intrinsic value than those of whites. Another component in the complex pattern of American–Asian relations that was emerging in the aftermath of the Communist triumph in China, this accusation, carried by the legacies of Hiroshima, was to become newly prominent as the United States went to war in wholly unanticipated fashion on the Asian mainland.

---

[180] 'Kremlin Opens Cold War Second Front in Asia', *NYT*, 5 February 1950.

2   The Korean War, the atomic bomb and Asian–American estrangement

Over the course of several days at the end of June 1950, the Truman administration took a series of momentous decisions that by committing American ground, air and naval forces to the fighting that had broken out on the Korean peninsula reversed the basic principle maintained by the JCS during and since the Second World War that American troops would not be committed to large-scale operations on the Asian mainland. The rollercoaster nature of the ensuing war, from the rapid retreat to the Pusan perimeter, to the heady days of the Inchon landings and advance to the Yalu river, followed by the deep depression when Chinese intervention seemed to spell disaster for the US and South Korean forces and the UN Command as a whole, was matched by the mood of popular opinion at home as American foreign policy in Asia became even more of an emotional and divisive issue in domestic politics. By the time the front in Korea had stabilized in the late spring of 1951, many Americans were left with the frustrating spectacle of debilitating involvement in a limited war with an implacable foe where few direct interests seemed to be engaged. Moreover, for senior figures in the Truman administration, even with the programme of wholesale rearmament launched in the summer of 1950, there was a pervasive sense that the Korean War was a draining distraction from the primary goal of bolstering the defence of Western Europe against any potential attack from a now nuclear-armed Soviet Union.[1] Though few doubted the wisdom of the original intervention of June 1950, seeing it as essential to oppose so blatant an attempt to expand Communist power in East Asia (with Truman picturing Korea as the 'Greece of the Far East'), Chinese participation in the war threw up a menacing new enemy. Having come to accept the thesis that Beijing was in close cohorts with Moscow, and that Chinese Communism, at least in the short term,

---

[1] As Acheson chose to put it, 'the great trouble is that we are fighting the wrong nation [in Korea]. We are fighting the second team, whereas the real enemy is the Soviet Union.' See memorandum of meeting at the Pentagon by Philip C. Jessup, 3 December 1950, *FRUS, 1950, VII: Korea* (Washington, DC, 1976), 1326.

was not about to follow the Titoist model, the war served to undermine any notion of accommodation with the PRC and to consolidate American support for the Nationalist regime on Taiwan.[2]

In this way, probably the most important consequence of the Korean War for the overall course of US policy towards Asia was the transformation in attitudes towards Communist China, both official and on the part of the wider public, that it helped to instil and then entrench. The feelings experienced during the late 1940s of intense disappointment, mixed with pique and annoyance, at how the Chinese had turned away from their American patron to embrace the alien creed of Communism and move towards alignment with the Soviet Union were supplanted by overt hostility as the forces of the PRC clashed directly with the Americans on the Korean peninsula from October 1950 onwards. China's sudden entry into the war, and the early successes achieved by the People's Volunteers, stunned Washington and reinforced notions of Beijing's perfidy in the American imagination. The sharp repulse that was given to the forces of the UN Command, under the flamboyant leadership of General MacArthur, was a shock to those who had become accustomed to American firepower and technological prowess guaranteeing victory on the battlefield. For many American officials there were few lower points in the Cold War than the winter of 1950–1, when US troops, alongside their South Korean and other UN allies, were sent streaming south in retreat back towards the 38th parallel, and the chances of a far wider war, encompassing a direct clash with the Soviet Union, became very high. The frustration of the situation on the ground, where quick and decisive victory over North Korea had been denied, only to be replaced by the ambiguities of limited war, led several commentators and even senior figures to call for direct military action against China. Only five years after the end of the Pacific fighting with Japan, Americans were once again engaged in direct combat with Asian adversaries, and in the search to redress the imbalance of conventional forces by using Western technological superiority to inflict crushing damage on the enemy, some were prepared to give consideration to the use of nuclear weapons. Yet there were always powerful reasons for not resorting to this drastic step, especially when the military situation, though serious, was by no means irretrievable. Lack of suitable targets for attack, the need to conserve the nuclear stockpile for use against the Soviet Union and strong objections from key Western European allies were all compelling arguments for not using the bomb. Furthermore, although not ultimately of central

---

[2] Mayers, *Monolith*, 80–4.

importance, negative evaluations of Asian reactions were beginning to form a consistent part of American appraisals of the outcome of nuclear use, where political factors would also need to be weighed alongside more purely military requirements, and it is to these that the following chapter aims to draw attention.

The fact that the Truman administration's decisions of June 1950 to actively intervene in the Korean peninsula were taken ostensibly to uphold the principles of the UN Charter and that the North Korean attack seemed such a clear-cut case of Communist aggression were important in generating public support, at least initially, for this new commitment on the Asian mainland.[3] In early August 1950, the British Ambassador in Washington, Sir Oliver Franks, was recording his impressions of the mood in the United States with the thought that 'there are too many Puritan avenging angels about, who feel that at last a straight moral issue of real principle has been raised and there is a clear Call to get on with punishing the guilty. To people in such a mood the longer processes of history, and the unfailing regularity with which all diplomatic chickens one day come home to roost, appear tiresome irrelevancies in the light of the Divine Call.'[4] After Beijing's intervention, images of a 'faceless' Chinese mass, exemplified in the 'human wave' attacks and the apparent indifference to casualties evinced by the Chinese armies in Korea, soon became embedded in popular stereotypes. These American ideas of their new enemy were reinforced by stories of Communist handling of prisoners of war (ranging from plain maltreatment, to the practice of 'brainwashing') and the resistance of Communist negotiators, once armistice talks got under way in July 1951, to the notion of voluntary repatriation of the prisoners held by the UN Command.[5]

Another crucially important by-product of American intervention in Korea was the decision by the Truman administration in June 1950 to interpose the US Seventh Fleet between Taiwan and the Chinese mainland, a move which, though presented as 'neutralization' of the strait, in effect protected the remains of Chiang Kai-shek's Nationalist regime from attack by Chinese Communist forces. Active protection of Taiwan marked another departure from the outlines of US policy towards East Asia that the Truman administration had begun to map only six months before, and signalled Washington's increasing hostility towards the new

---

[3] See the groundbreaking study by Steven Casey, *Selling the Korean War: Propaganda, Politics, and Public Opinion in the United States, 1950–1953* (New York, 2008), 30–6.
[4] Extract from Franks letter, 5 August 1950, F1022/24, FO 371/83014, TNA.
[5] The racial stereotypes prevalent on the American side during the war are discussed in Cumings, *Origins of the Korean War, II*, 690–6.

Communist Government in Beijing. In December 1949, and with the endorsement of NSC 48/2, Acheson had rejected renewed JCS recommendations to extend military aid to the Nationalists, finding it impossible to support such a corrupt and unreliable partner as Chiang, and hoping that tensions might soon develop between Beijing and Moscow on the assumption that the Russians would try to dominate the Sino-Soviet relationship. On 5 January 1950, Truman had reinforced the impression that the United States was distancing itself from the struggle by publicly declaring that the United States would not involve itself in the continuing Chinese civil conflict, sought no special bases or position on Taiwan and that, though economic aid would continue, military aid would not be forthcoming. A week later when Acheson outlined his concept of an American defensive perimeter in the Western Pacific before the National Press Club in Washington, Taiwan was conspicuous by its absence.[6] There seemed every indication that the United States was prepared to stand aside if later in the year Chinese Communist forces were used in an invasion to destroy the Nationalist remnants on the island, so making more likely eventual US recognition of the PRC.

Both domestic and international events, however, conspired to thwart Acheson's hopes. Two days after the Washington speech, and in a reminder of the Angus Ward affair, American consular offices in Beijing and Shanghai were seized by the new Chinese authorities (triggering the withdrawal, by the spring, of all US diplomatic personnel from the mainland), marking a sharp increase in tensions. Soon after, in February 1950, the fruits of Mao's six-week visit to Moscow and the arduous negotiations he had conducted there became evident when the terms of the Sino-Soviet Treaty of Alliance, Friendship and Mutual Assistance were made public. Though Acheson and his China hands in the State Department were still prepared to keep open the option of recognition, the PRC's alignment with the Soviet Union was now confirmed in their eyes. With 'forward' containment on the periphery of this new Chinese menace through the offshore island perimeter now of paramount concern, attaching Taiwan to the defensive chain began to appear more attractive to many – and as we have seen, the JCS had always argued it should be US policy to deny Taiwan to the Soviet Union in the event of general war but had previously been unwilling to earmark scarce resources for the task. Psychological factors also began to play a role, with many American policy-makers coming to believe that further territorial gains for Communism in Asia, however irrelevant to the overall strategic balance, held great significance

---

[6] See Acheson, *Present at the Creation*, 351, 357.

for how onlooking peoples and governments (not least those in Western Europe) perceived the willingness of Washington to respond to the Soviet challenge. This was the same kind of analysis reflected in the language of NSC 68, which argued in April 1950 that any extension of the area under Soviet control posed a threat to the American position in the Cold War and so placed a premium on the notion of an all-encompassing perimeter defence in the containment of Communist power.[7]

In the domestic context, Acheson's room for manoeuvre over China policy in the first few months of 1950 was further restricted by the enormous weakening of his political position that resulted from his stand over the Hiss case, and the vicious personal attacks that soon followed from Senator Joseph R. McCarthy. For those committed to unwavering support for Chiang Kai-shek, with sections of strong support within the Republican Party, it was another opportunity to undermine a Secretary of State whom they identified with 'appeasement' of Communism in the Far East. How much such domestic political considerations entered Acheson's policy calculations in early 1950 is open to question – it is easy, for example, to overestimate the coherence and effectiveness of the 'China lobby' – but these such constraints formed an essential part of the backdrop. With many of his colleagues, such as Dean Rusk, who became Assistant Secretary for the Far East in March, now urging a stronger stance in Asia, not least in the form of clear backing for Chiang's precarious position on Taiwan, Acheson's chances of keeping his China options open, by, for example, maintaining an ambiguous position on the efforts by the PRC to enter the UN, narrowed during the spring.[8] As for the President, there seems little doubt that Truman was worried by the domestic political implications of appearing weak over China policy (indeed, Truman had been instrumental in ensuring that all American assistance to the Nationalists was not ended in January 1950), and he was innately sceptical over the chance of fostering divisions between the Chinese and Russian brands of Communism. By May 1950, both the State and Defense Departments were re-evaluating their policy towards Taiwan, with a greater readiness to consider requests for military assistance and a more positive appraisal of Chiang's chances for survival.[9] At this stage recognition of Beijing was no longer under consideration within the State Department, and when the North Korean attack came in

---

[7] See John L. Gaddis, *Strategies of Containment: A Critical Appraisal of American National Security Policy during the Cold War* (New York, 2005), 89–90; and see Gaddis, 'Drawing Lines', 80–2.

[8] See Gaddis, 'Drawing Lines', 84–7; Beisner, *Acheson*, 273–80, 305–6.

[9] See Chang, *Friends and Enemies*, 72–5; Stueck, *Road to Confrontation*, 146–51.

June 1950, it appeared entirely natural to leading figures in the administration that elements of the Seventh Fleet should be moved into the Taiwan Strait both to prevent any provocation by Chiang, but also to forestall any Communist attempt to remove what was increasingly seen as a valuable anti-Communist outpost, whose existence would be an irritant to Beijing and might prove a stimulant to nascent forces of resistance on the mainland. This action, of course, was interpreted by Beijing, and by much of the watching world, as direct intervention in a civil war that still had one more act to play before final resolution. The fact that MacArthur then took the opportunity in July 1950 to visit the island and pledge American support for the defence of Taiwan, even though this was in defiance of the administration's wishes, served to identify the United States with the cause of the Nationalists even further.[10]

One reason why there had been increased interest in Washington for support for Chiang in the spring of 1950 was that it might draw Beijing's attention away from South East Asia, where in Indochina the Viet Minh were engaged in their bitter fight to oust French colonialism. Diplomatic recognition and military assistance for the Vietnamese Communists had been provided by Mao since the beginning of 1950, and there seemed every chance the anti-colonial insurgency would grow in intensity with this fresh outside support.[11] Indeed, to American policy-makers, it was in Indochina, during the period leading up to the outbreak of the Korean War, where the prime Communist threat in Asia was now assumed to lie and where US interests were most clearly at stake, and this was one of the messages conveyed in NSC 48/2. The prospect of a Viet Minh victory was greeted with outright alarm in Washington, where it was seen as merely a prelude to the almost inevitable fall of the rest of South East Asia to Communism as the domino theory – originally propounded by the British in 1949 – began to appear from now on in mantra-like form in American policy documents.[12] Nine years before, in 1941–2, it had been the Japanese who had swept with astonishing ease through South East Asia, either co-opting governments, as in Thailand, or employing force to overturn Western, imperial domination. Now, it was possible to imagine a similar process at work, where rapidly reformed colonial structures, as in Indochina and Malaya, would once again be pushed aside by local Communists in cohorts with the Chinese. Having earlier encouraged the French to go beyond the limited Vietnamese autonomy offered by the

---

[10] Offner, *Another Such Victory*, 384.
[11] Qiang Zhai, *China and the Vietnam Wars, 1950–1975* (Chapel Hill, 2000), 13–20.
[12] William Conrad Gibbons, *The U.S. Government and the Vietnam War: Executive and Legislative Roles and Relationships*, Part 1: *1945–1960* (Princeton, 1986), 64–8.

Elysée Accords, the Americans now recognized the need to moderate their anti-colonial strictures and to offer more substantive support to the French war effort. In February 1950 Washington duly embraced the so-called Bao Dai solution by recognizing the French puppet ruler of Vietnam, and in April Truman approved the supply of military and economic aid, so beginning a chain commitment that was to last for over two decades. By supplying aid directly to the Bao Dai Government, alongside the French authorities, the United States could maintain the fiction that it was sponsoring a reformed colonial administration which was steering the Vietnamese to eventual independence, but few were convinced by this device.[13] With the conflict in Indochina taking on such wider, international dimensions in 1950, Syngman Rhee's autocratic South Korean Government propped up only with US assistance, and the decisive move towards lending active assistance to Chiang on Taiwan, American approaches towards Asia were becoming ever-more firmly locked into support for anti-Communist regimes, whatever dubious credentials they might hold to be representative of popular wishes. Walter Lippmann had welcomed Acheson's National Press Club speech at the start of the year with its recognition of the new forces of Asian nationalism, but its depressing aftermath led him to criticize the fact that the administration had become 'hopelessly committed to … discredited or puppet regimes'.[14]

These developments in American policy helped to generate a feeling of estrangement and disillusionment among many non-aligned Asian leaders. Western diplomats acknowledged that India, through the moral weight it carried from its long and successful struggle against British imperialism, occupied a special place in influencing opinion throughout the region, and here the signs did not look encouraging.[15] Nehru's criticisms of American policy in Asia had become more vociferous in early 1950, focussing on Washington's support for the French in Indochina, obsession with communism and hostility to China; he was also nervous about American 'neutrality' over the Kashmir issue, and the growing warmth of ties between the United States and Pakistan. Matters

---

[13] For the most recent and comprehensive analysis of this shift in American policy, see Lawrence, *Assuming the Burden*, especially 255–61; see also Gary R. Hess, 'The First American Commitment to Indochina: The Acceptance of the "Bao Dai Solution", 1950', *Diplomatic History*, 2, 1978, 331–50.

[14] Quoted in Steel, *Walter Lippmann*, 467.

[15] Nehru was never one to downplay the significance of his own role and was certainly keen to emphasize how his country was regarded, telling one Congress party meeting, 'The world looks upon us as representing the centre of Asian feelings.' Quoted in Gopal, *Nehru*, 104.

were not helped by Loy Henderson, the US Ambassador in New Delhi, who was prone to lecturing his Indian audiences on their inability to appreciate the altruistic motives that lay behind American desires to offer technical and financial aid. In April, Henderson complained to Acheson how Indian 'unfriendliness' towards the United States had been 'steadily strengthening' over the previous eight months, with commentators dwelling on 'our treatment of American negroes, our tendency to support colonialism and to strive for the continued supremacy of white peoples, our economic imperialism, the superficiality of our culture, our lack of emotional balance as evidenced by our present hysteria in combatting Communism and our cynical use of "witch-hunting methods" in promoting domestic political ends'.[16] In May 1950, just before he left for his assignment as Indian ambassador in Beijing, Kavalam M. Panikkar wrote to one British correspondent that the emergence of what he called a 'new Asia' (which he defined as including 'not only India, Pakistan and Burma, but also South East Asia, *China and Japan*') was still strange to many in the West: 'They cannot easily reconcile themselves to the thought that these countries over which Europe had ruled or exercised sway only ten years ago are now factors to be counted with.' Britain alone, Panikkar averred, had understood this change, inferring that the Americans had still to adjust to the new realities.[17] To C. L. Sulzberger of the *New York Times*, Panikkar explained (so the former reported) that he was 'very distressed by American policy in Asia and by the manner in which it is presented, which offends Asiatic peoples. He said: "No country in Asia will accept to be bossed by America and any hint of such a desire by the United States causes immediate suspicion and hostility."'[18]

Despite the fact that in late June India backed the UN Security Council resolutions condemning North Korean aggression and calling for assistance to South Korea, Nehru took this action with some reluctance, and he detected no wider scheme of Soviet aggression behind events on the peninsula. Indeed, Indian diplomats, making clear their continuing commitment to a non-aligned foreign policy, strove throughout the summer to bring about negotiations which might end the fighting, efforts which

---

[16] See Singh, *Limits of British Influence*, 62–3, 72–3; H. W. Brands, *Inside the Cold War: Loy Henderson and the Rise of the American Empire, 1918–1961* (New York, 1991), 208–10; Henderson to Acheson, 12 April 1950, *FRUS, 1950, V: Near East; South Asia; Africa* (Washington, DC, 1978), 1461–3.

[17] Panikkar to Sir Ralph Stevenson, 5 May 1950, F1051/1, FO 371/83021, TNA. Panikkar himself was deeply distrusted by US officials for his 'innate sympathy for the Chinese Communists', with Livingston Merchant, for example, finding also that he was 'unconcealedly [*sic*] contemptuous of the white races'; see Brands, *Henderson*, 221.

[18] Entry for 25 April 1950, C. L. Sulzberger, *A Long Row of Candles: Memoirs and Diaries, 1934–1954* (London, 1969), 475.

Acheson tended to dismiss as naive, distracting and even damaging.[19] Underlying the Korean conflict, and notwithstanding the fact that American and United Nations support was being offered to the South Korean authorities, was also a sense that it represented some kind of potential or actual rupture between 'the West' and 'Asia'. This was due primarily to the phenomenon of Western forces being engaged once again with an Asian enemy, but also because of the ambivalent attitude of India towards the war, and the widespread feeling across the region that the American refusal to recognize and engage with Communist China amounted to an irrational failure to accept the new Asia that was emerging from the pre-war era of imperialist domination by the West. The US Consul General in Calcutta between 1950 and 1953 later recollected that it had come 'somewhat as a surprise to me to find that many of my Indian friends regarded [the Korean War] as a conflict between whites and non-whites'.[20] This was one of the reasons that Acheson took some pains to elicit troop contributions from as many friendly Asian states as possible (barring Nationalist China), as this would emphasize wide support for the UN action and, as the Secretary of State argued, counteract 'communist propaganda that this is whites fighting Asiatics'.[21]

It is in this context of the Korean War being projected in some quarters as a clash between Asia and the white West that the concerns over implications of any use of nuclear weapons in the fighting needs to be placed. At the time of the war's outbreak, the United States still enjoyed an overwhelming atomic superiority over the Soviet Union, with almost 300 bombs in the American stockpile, and over 260 Strategic Air Command (SAC) bombers converted to take nuclear payloads. The estimated ten to twenty weapons in the Soviet arsenal could only be delivered to targets in the United States on 'one-way' bomber missions, though Western Europe would be within relatively easy reach. Nevertheless, the United States was not completely invulnerable to Soviet attack and, even more to the point, its closest allies in Western Europe were likely to receive the brunt of any Soviet use of nuclear weapons in conditions of general war. The Atomic Energy Commission still retained custody over the entire US nuclear stockpile, and the Pentagon would have to follow carefully proscribed procedures involving presidential authorization before they could be

---

[19] See Merrill, *Bread and the Ballot*, 52; McMahon, *Cold War on the Periphery*, 82–4; Brands, *Henderson*, 212–14; William Stueck, *The Korean War: An International History* (Princeton, 1995), 51, 80–1.

[20] Evan M. Wilson Oral History, p. 77, Harry S. Truman Library (HSTL).

[21] In the event, token Asian contributions came only from the Philippines and Thailand, with India sending a field ambulance unit; see Stueck, *Korean War*, 72–3. The quotation is from Beisner, *Acheson*, 353.

passed to complete military control. There were as yet no nuclear weapons deployed overseas, and no agreements had been sought or reached with foreign governments for this to occur, let alone understandings made over consultation with host countries if they were to be used as a base for nuclear operations by the US Air Force.[22]

Such practical problems of availability and deployment did not prevent there being some Cabinet-level discussion within the Truman administration in early July about the idea of securing UN sanction for the possible use of the atomic bomb in Korea, largely in an effort to encourage the Russians to restrain the North Koreans. Soon after, and in line with his recommendations that the United States should improve its global readiness for war, Truman gave his approval to the temporary movement of nuclear-capable B-29 bombers to airbases in Britain, though the nuclear cores of their weapons remained at home. Within military circles, moreover, the topic of possible nuclear use against military targets in Korea was raised within the Operations Division of the Army General Staff as the poorly trained and equipped US ground troops who had been rushed from occupation duty in Japan and thrown into the early stages of the fighting struggled to check the southward advance of North Korean forces.[23] Public speculation on the same issue also began in mid-July, when in the *New York Times* Hanson Baldwin, despite comparing the North Korean advance with the barbarian invasions of Ghenghis Khan, returned to the theme he had first raised in 1945 over Hiroshima by arguing that the United States would risk its moral standing if it used the bomb under current circumstances. Atomic use would also carry the danger of expanding the war onto a global stage, and, 'Psychologically, the use of the atomic bomb would be almost certain to consolidate North Korea and most of Asia, even those few peoples of Asia who are still our friends, against us.' Pointing out that Communist propaganda was already branding the United States as a war-mongering aggressor for the emphasis it put on possession of the bomb, Baldwin delivered the warning that, 'If we want to lose what friends and what influence we have left in Asia, a good way to do it is to drop the atomic bomb on North Korea.' On a practical, military level, also, Baldwin judged that its use would be ineffective, considering the dearth of suitable targets for the few atomic bombs that the United States might be able to spare from its overall arsenal.[24]

---

[22] See Roger Dingman, 'Atomic Diplomacy and the Korean War', *International Security*, 13, 3, Winter 1988/9, 52–3; Robert D. Little, *Building an Atomic Air Force, 1949–1953* (Washington, DC, Office of Air Force History, n.d.), 115.

[23] See Dingman, 'Atomic Diplomacy', 56–60.

[24] See 'Atomic Bomb Is Not the Weapon', *NYT*, 17 July 1950.

The issue of nuclear use in Korea also began to attract the attention of the State Department at this time. Citing the opinion poll data that had been collected in the autumn of 1945 on the use of the atomic bomb against Japanese cities, Carlton Savage of the Policy Planning Staff felt that its use in Korea, as on the earlier occasion, would find approval among the US public if it would re-establish peace and save American lives. In prestige terms, however, the United States might lose credibility if it had to resort to such a measure while Chinese and Soviet involvement in the conflict remained limited. Moreover, if the bomb were used, but US forces were still driven off the Korean peninsula, the political results would be disastrous. Its use without UN concurrence would undermine the moral position of the United States, but obtaining such agreement might restrict American freedom of action in future situations. Savage therefore felt that atomic weapons should be used in Korea only if Soviet or Chinese forces had intervened, was necessary to restore a perilous military situation and could do so in decisive fashion, and if 'excessive destruction of non-combatants' could be avoided.[25] Savage's memorandum was received by Paul M. Nitze, who had taken over from Kennan as head of the PPS at the start of the year, and in the middle of July, aware that the subject was starting to generate public interest, he asked General Kenneth D. Nichols, the head of the Armed Forces Special Weapons Project, to come to the State Department to discuss the technical and planning issues surrounding the employment of nuclear weapons in the Korean fighting. Nichols largely concurred with the analysis offered by Savage but put forward the Pentagon's opinion that even in the absence of overt Soviet or Chinese involvement, the atomic bomb should be used if US forces were about to be driven off the Korean peninsula. UN agreement would be 'helpful', but public discussion might be of military advantage to the enemy. The Defense Department, Nichols advised, was still searching for a unified view on the issue.[26]

Meanwhile, by the end of July, the badly bruised US and South Korean forces had been driven back to the Pusan perimeter in the south-east corner of the peninsula, and pressure rose again for more drastic measures to be employed to reverse fortunes on the battlefield. One course pursued by the JCS was to sanction the heavier use of conventional bombing against urban-industrial targets in North Korea, and at the end of the month it was decided that two extra B-29 medium bomb groups from

[25] Carlton Savage memorandum, 'The Question of U.S. Use of Atomic Bombs in Korea', 15 July 1950, 'Atomic Energy – Armaments, 1950', box 7, Subject Files, records of the Policy Planning Staff (PPS), 1947–53, RG 59, NARA.
[26] See Nitze to Acheson, 17 July 1950, *ibid.*

SAC would be transferred to the Far East with this object in mind.[27] During a visit to MacArthur in Tokyo from the Air Force Chief of Staff, General Hoyt S. Vandenberg, and the Chief of Staff of the US Army, General J. Lawton Collins, the idea was raised by the Far East Commander that the atomic bomb could be used to isolate Chinese Communist forces if they entered the Korean fighting with attacks on their lines of communication. With the two SAC medium bomb groups soon scheduled to depart for the Pacific, back in Washington Vandenberg and the Secretary of Defense, Louis Johnson, pressed for the additional deployment of ten nuclear-capable B-29s with ten atomic weapons, though again without their fissile cores, to the island of Guam. Truman authorized the movement of the aircraft and non-nuclear components on 30 July, with the deployment to be completed by 12 August (shipment of the nuclear cores of the weapons to Guam would require another seventy-two hours following presidential authorization).[28]

In all probability Truman and Acheson viewed the movement as designed to signal American resolve to both Moscow and Beijing at a time when US forces had suffered a succession of setbacks, though no public announcements accompanied the B-29 movements; they also offered an in-theatre nuclear capability if the disaster of a Dunkirk-style evacuation had to be attempted from Korea and the President felt com-pelled to authorize nuclear use in order to cover the withdrawal.[29] The fact that the administration was becoming aware of the nuclear options that might be presented was also indicated when, in August, Truman moved to revive the NSC Special Committee on Atomic Energy, consist-ing of the Secretaries of State and Defense and the Chairman of the AEC. The Special Committee had originally been formed in early 1949 to advise the President on the momentous decision which was eventually made to develop the hydrogen bomb, but now it was in a position to become the key conduit for all major policy decisions in the nuclear field, including overseas deployment and even if presidential authorization for use of nuclear weapons was needed.[30] The Special Committee's fresh remit of considering together the military and political factors involved with

---

[27] See JCS 87522 to CINCFE, 31 July 1950, reproduced at www.trumanlibrary.org/whistlestop/study_collections/korea/sec3/kw132_1.htm

[28] See JCS 87570 to CINCFE, 31 July 1950, reproduced at www.trumanlibrary.org/whistlestop/study_collections/korea/sec3/kw133_1.htm

[29] See the speculation in Dingman, 'Atomic Diplomacy', 63–5, where the deployment is also seen as a possible response to Republican attacks on the alleged failings of the Truman administration's policies in Korea.

[30] See Doris M. Condit, *History of the Office of the Secretary of Defense*, Vol. II: *The Test of War, 1950–1953* (Washington, DC, 1988), 29–30.

nuclear use marked a step away from Truman's original and basic attitude to the bomb, underlined in 1948, that this was a 'retaliation' weapon of the very last resort, and towards the idea that its first use might have to be sanctioned in circumstances short of general war.

In any event, perhaps hoping to quell further public speculation about the issue, at his weekly news conference on 27 July, Truman gave a firm 'no' when he was asked if he was considering the use of the atomic bomb against North Korean forces.[31] On the same day as Truman's comment was made, a member of the Air Staff in Washington composed a memorandum which rejected nuclear attacks on industrial or civilian targets in North Korea as unlikely to be effective but argued that the use of between ten and twenty atomic bombs on troop concentrations could have decisive results. However, in the absence of such concentrations, and in view of the fact that the bomb would have to be used over South Korean territory, its employment could well be seen as a sign of US 'impotence, accentuated by cruelty'. Inconclusive use of the bomb was likely to have very grave repercussions, as it would open up the United States to criticism on human-itarian grounds, both at home and abroad, for killing large numbers of civilians for no apparent military gain. The outcry this might generate was likely to make it harder to use the bomb on later occasions. Moreover, 'if a pattern were set to use atomic bombs in peripheral areas, a widening of the conflict to other satellite fronts might lead to a waste of bombs, and thus play into Soviet hands'. West European confidence in the protection afforded by the US nuclear arsenal would also be dissipated if atomic bombs were seen to have less than decisive results on the Korean battlefield.[32]

For all these reasons, in early August the head of the US Air Force's Psychological Warfare Division was led to the conclusion that the use of the atomic bomb in Korea was 'undefendable [*sic*]'. The inevitable South Korean casualties if the bomb were used in the fighting, which was then confined to the southern half of the peninsula, would place the United States in an 'untenable propaganda position' while 'any utilization of atomic weapons in any of the areas [of Korea] could, in all probability, have the effect of consolidating Asiatic opinion against us'.[33] Studies by the Army's G-2 intelligence staff in the middle of July had reached a similar finding:

Use of atom bombs at this stage of the conflict would probably be interpreted as an indication of the ruthlessness of U.S. policy and a disregard for the lives of the

[31] See 'Truman Bars Atomic Bomb Now', *NYT*, 28 July 1950.
[32] Memorandum by Stefan T. Posony for Col. Walter B. Putnam, 'The Use of Atomic Weapons in Korea', 27 July 1950, 385.2 Korea (28 July 1950), box 906, Air Force Plans, RG 341, NARA.
[33] Memorandum by Col. O. L. Grover, 'Psychological Aspects of Atomic Weapons Consideration' (*sic*), 7 August 1950, *ibid*.

Asiatic peoples, or as a 'desperation measure' which would signify U.S. weaknesses and consequent inability to really help Asia, except by means of mass destruction and slaughter. In this respect, the resulting decrease of support by our Asiatic allies might well off-set the military advantage of such use.[34]

These appraisals mirrored those being compiled in London, where the British Chiefs of Staff (COS) had also considered the issue and arrived at the understated position that from a military perspective the 'dropping of an Atom Bomb in North Korea would be unsound. The effects of such action would be world wide and might be very damaging. Moreover it would probably provoke a global war.'[35] Despite the regrets of some in the American armed forces – General Nathan F. Twining (at the time the Vice Chief of the Air Force) later recalled that had an atomic bomb been dropped on a 'tactical target' during this early stage of the fighting, the later Chinese intervention would have been avoided – there were clearly strong military and political restraints operating against nuclear use during the summer of 1950.[36] Irrespective of all the military reservations over the shortage of both suitable targets in Korea and numbers of weapons in the overall US stockpile, having assembled a large coalition of partners and received the support of the UN for its military role in Korea, the Truman administration had no desire to prejudice this level of backing by resort to so drastic and controversial a measure. Within the United States, too, there were moral qualms over any resort to the atomic bomb, the Republican leader in the Senate, Robert A. Taft, for example, avowing to one correspondent in mid-July that he 'would not be willing to authorize the use of that weapon against people, most of whom are innocent, and all of whom are ignorant. The North Koreans are merely tools of the Soviet [sic], and I could not justify the destruction of millions of these people because the Russian Communists are unscrupulous.'[37] Moreover, analysts in the State Department and armed forces staff shared the belief that opinion across Asia would be completely alienated from the US cause if nuclear weapons were again on an Asian enemy.

---

[34] 'Intelligence Estimate of World-Wide and Soviet Reaction to the Use of Atomic Bombardment in the Korean Conflict', Assistant Chief of Staff, G-2, 13 July 1950, RG 319; quoted in Lloyd C. Gardner, *Approaching Vietnam: From World War Two through Dienbienphu, 1941–1954* (New York, 1988), 106.

[35] Confidential Annex to COS(50)97th meeting, 28 June 1950, DEFE 4/32 and in CAB 21/1988, TNA.

[36] See Nathan F. Twining, *Neither Liberty Nor Safety: A Hard Look at U.S. Military Policy and Strategy* (New York, 1966), 117; Twining lamented how 'political constraint on weaponry served to broaden and prolong the Korean War'.

[37] Taft to Julian Bishop, 19 July 1950, box 914, Robert A. Taft papers, Library of Congress (LC).

Indeed, concerns over the consequences of using the atomic bomb have also to be set against the background of the way the Korean War was perceived to be affecting overall relations between the West and Asia. One of the results of the war, officials from the Foreign Office's South East Asia Department noted in August 1950, was that, 'The Russians have had great success in arrogating to themselves the leadership of the anti-Colonial movement and of the feeling which, paradoxically enough, responded to the victory in 1904/5 by the Asiatic Japanese over the European White-faced Russians. These feelings have become much more intense in Asia today and can be played upon to further Communism.'[38] At the very same time, Nehru was speaking out more firmly about the Western powers taking 'decisions affecting vast areas in Asia without understanding the real needs and mind of the people' and that 'new types of colonialism and controlism' were being introduced. The *New York Times*, having welcomed India's previous backing for the UN action in Korea, interpreted these pronouncements as meaning that Nehru saw 'Asia and the Asians as part of a different world than the West, and that he was dividing the world in two on a racial as well as a geographical basis'.[39] The Truman administration's decision to interpose the US Seventh Fleet between the Nationalist Chinese remnant on Taiwan and the new Communist authorities on the Chinese mainland, coupled with the President's announcement that occupation of Taiwan by Communist forces would be 'a direct threat to the security of the Pacific area and to the United States forces performing their lawful and necessary functions in that area', was perhaps most instrumental in generating anxiety throughout Asia about the overall direction of US policy. Any settlement of the Korean fighting, this inferred, would not lead to a resolution of the Taiwan issue as Washington had now determined its retention in non-Communist hands was an essential component of their future vision for the region.[40] In one paper presented to the Cabinet in August 1950, Ernest Bevin, the British Foreign Secretary, maintained that

nothing in United States' Far Eastern policy since the war has inspired Asian countries with confidence, and the declaration on Formosa has caused both alarm and despondency because of the possibility which it has created of a conflict between the United States and China, with all the repercussions upon Asia which would be likely to follow. The doubts and fears to which the American action over Formosa have given rise have been given most expression in India, who [*sic*] has always been suspicious of American 'imperialism' and is especially worried now lest

---

[38] Russia Committee paper RC/122/50, Annex B, 'The Effect of the Situation in Korea on South East Asia', 10 August 1950, FZ10381/8G, FO 371/84529, TNA.
[39] 'India and the West', *NYT*, 5 August 1950.   [40] See Stueck, *Road to Confrontation*, 198.

American action should jeopardise the friendly relations which India herself is bent on establishing with China. But the feeling is probably more widespread that the United States is intervening in Asia and seeking to determine its future in a way unpleasing to the peoples of Asia and likely to be to their detriment. Though countries like Siam and the Philippines pay lip service to the United States they are not themselves held in high repute. India, on the other hand, has an undoubted influence upon Asian opinion. There is therefore a distinct possibility that, unless United States policy towards China, Japan and Korea takes more account of Asian opinion and Asian susceptibilities, we shall find that Asia is gradually alienated from the West, which could only be of benefit to the Soviet Union.[41]

A further adverse effect on perceptions of the West's behaviour in the region was the large-scale loss of human life and general destruction caused as the Korean conflict raged up and down the peninsula. As UN air power began to range behind Communist forces in attacks on lines of communication, a mounting toll of Korean civilian casualties was inflicted; mass bombing attacks against urban areas in North Korea, which as noted above were initiated by the US Air Force in late July 1950, contributed to the sense in which Western material and technological superiority was being directed against helpless Asian peoples and carried uncomfortable echoes of 1945. Within India, the growing ferocity of the war and its impact on Asians was one factor helping to fuel feelings of anti-Americanism: some Indians began to see Korea as being used by the United States as an unwitting stage for its more general conflict with the Soviet Union, and there was special resentment that it was Asians who were once more the victims of advances in the methods of war. In mid-August, the British Embassy in Washington was alerted by the Foreign Office to the possible effect on Asian opinion of US bombing policy if directed at North Korean targets in an indiscriminate fashion.[42] Communist propaganda was quick to point to the connections between the increasing loss of civilian lives from air attacks and the issue of race, with Radio Moscow alleging in August that 'the beastly bombing of peaceful citizens in Korea, racial discrimination, and the oppression of the colored people in the U.S.' were all 'links in the same chain'.[43] The *New York Times* reported in August 1950 that anti-US feeling in India had never been so prevalent, fuelled by news of the destruction of Korean towns by American air power and the conviction that the United States sought domination over Asia and should remove its bases from Japan, Korea and Taiwan. Support for the French in Indochina, along with

[41] CP(50)200, 'Review of the International Situation in Asia in the Light of the Korean Conflict', 30 August 1950, PREM 8/1171, TNA.
[42] See FO to Washington (for Franks), No. 3713, 17 August 1950, FO 115/4487, TNA.
[43] Quoted in Stueck, *Korean War*, 80.

development of the atomic bomb, had damaged US standing in India, and newspapers in New Delhi repeated the contention that the United States dropped atomic bombs only on Asian peoples.[44] In a column for the *Washington Post*, Marquis Childs reported that a 'dangerous hostility' had emerged between India and the United States, Acheson's rejection of Nehru's proposals to seat Communist China in the UN Security Council being seen, for example, as indicative of American disinterest in peaceful negotiations to end the fighting in Korea. Indian reaction against US bombing of Korean urban areas had to be understood, Childs explained, as representative of a 'deep and instinctive feeling that we in the West will ignore at our peril, that we are a small island of whites in a world of color. It is a feeling centering on the fact that the Americans and Europeans, who have been traditionally the powers exerting colonial superiority, are now with superior weapons killing Asians. It is a feeling that, in the Western attitude, Asians are considered expendable.' To Childs this highlighted the 'monstrous folly of any contemplated or proposed use of the atomic bomb in the Korean war ... Asians will never forget Hiroshima and Nagasaki where the bomb was used for the first and only time against civilians in two Asian cities.'[45]

The sceptical response of what was described as 'articulate Asian opinion' towards American actions in Korea was, Acheson signalled Henderson in New Delhi, 'seriously disturbing and foreshadows possibility [of] little Asian support shld [*sic*] further Commie aggression require deeper U.S. involvement in such trouble spots as Indochina and Formosa. It is apparent that important segments [of] Asian peoples are not yet convinced of our devotion to peace, lack of imperialist ambition and interest in Asian freedom and progress.' The State Department was hence considering the idea of suggesting a pattern of closer consultation with initially India and Pakistan on the problems of the area. Henderson, however, poured cold water on the proposal, which he felt would simply exacerbate tensions and disagreements, so far apart were New Delhi and Washington on basic issues relating to China policy, with Indian leaders likely to see the suggestion as a way to undermine their stance of non-alignment.[46] Acheson's message had been the result of a paper on a 'New U.S. Policy toward Asia' drafted by George McGhee, the Assistant Secretary for Near Eastern, South Asian and African Affairs, and which had been circulating around the State Department for much of August. In

[44] See 'Anti-U.S. Feeling Is On Rise in India', *NYT*, 13 August 1950.
[45] 'Friendship of Asia', *Washington Post* (hereafter *WP*), 16 August 1950.
[46] Acheson to Henderson, 15 August 1950; Henderson to Acheson, 23 August 1950, *FRUS, 1950, V*, 1468–70.

this, McGhee gave frank expression to his anxiety that should the present 'estrangement between Asia and the U.S. grow rather than diminish, the whole of Asia, except those areas where we or our non-Asian allies can maintain direct military control, can fall to Communism'. As well as putting forward the idea for more regular consultation with Asian governments, McGhee also wanted to see an increase in psychological warfare activities spreading the notion that the United States had an active interest in the welfare and freedom of the peoples of Asia.[47]

Such considerations, however, could, it was reckoned, be safely postponed while the United States seemed on the path to a quick victory over the Communist forces in Korea, a victory which it was thought would be the most effective way of stifling voices of dissent in the region. This seemed increasingly likely with the sudden reversal in fortunes for the UN Command's forces following MacArthur's Inchon landings of mid-September and the break-out from the Pusan perimeter. Although the UN Security Council resolution which legitimized the use of UN forces in combat operations in Korea had talked only of repelling the North's attack on the South and restoring peace and security, the Truman administration sensed an opportunity to inflict an even greater setback for the Communist cause in the Cold War by aiming for the complete destruction of the North Korean Army and the reunification of the Korean peninsula. MacArthur's own belief was that such an outright victory would help to reshape Asia's future, while there were strong moral arguments advanced throughout the government that North Korean aggression should be properly punished. In terms of domestic politics, there were many voices urging a move north, and with mid-term elections due in November, Truman did not want to open his administration up to Republican attacks for holding back MacArthur's exploitation of battlefield success. Even before Inchon, Truman had approved NSC 81/1, which anticipated authority for UN ground operations north of the 38th parallel provided there had been no entry into Korea of Soviet or Chinese forces, or threat that they would do so, and by the end of September, with Seoul recaptured and MacArthur now advancing rapidly, final permission was given to him to move north, again so long as there were no signs of direct Soviet or Chinese participation in the war.[48] On 7 October, US forces finally crossed the 38th parallel, setting the United States and the PRC on a direct collision course. American analysts predicted that, in view of their relative weakness, the

---

[47] 'A New Approach in Asia', Policy Paper by the Assistant Secretary for Near Eastern, South Asian, and African Affairs, 30 August 1950, *FRUS, 1950, VI: East Asia and the Pacific* (Washington, DC, 1976), 137–9.
[48] See Stueck, *Road to Confrontation*, 203–5, 219–20.

Communist leadership in Beijing would eschew intervention. They therefore wrote off the Chinese warnings delivered via Panikkar as a bluff
designed to deter Washington from further advances (using Panikkar as
an intermediary was also seen as an odd decision considering how unreliable he was regarded by the State Department). It was, however, Beijing's
sense of its own strategic vulnerability, particularly the threat to the key
region of Manchuria, that triggered the movement south across the Yalu of
the first contingents of Chinese 'volunteers' on 19 October.

What seems most remarkable in retrospect is that when the UN
Command began to detect the presence of Chinese forces there was no
new strategic appreciation attempted in Washington. Instead, following
on from the unsatisfactory Wake Island Conference, where MacArthur's
over-weening vanity was on full display as he deliberated (for all of ninety
minutes) with his notional Commander-in-Chief, the authorities in
Washington allowed their general in the field to take the war all the way
up to the Yalu river. Though some new restrictions were placed on hot
pursuit of enemy aircraft over the Chinese border and the bombing of the
northern side of the Yalu crossings, the JCS seemed oblivious to the fact
that its earlier admonition to MacArthur (conveyed in a loosely worded
directive of 27 September) to keep 'non-Korean' forces away from the
border areas 'as a matter of policy' and, in the event of PRC intervention,
to continue offensive operations if a successful outcome was judged
possible was now wholly unsuited to the changed circumstances.[49]

Asian perceptions of American intentions were also inevitably influenced by the move north of the 38th parallel, which was seen as going far
beyond the original UN mandate for international intervention. Even
before the move north, the CIA had delivered an intelligence estimate
which predicted that if the UN tried to destroy the North Korean regime,
it would result in divisions in the coalition and lead Asians to believe that
'the U.S. is, after all, an aggressive nation pursuing a policy of self-interest
in Asia'.[50] The Indian Government, in particular, was decidedly unimpressed that the Truman administration failed to take seriously the warnings it had transmitted in early October of Beijing's likely reactions if UN
forces approached the Yalu river.[51]

A further indication of the troubled state of relations between the West
and Asia was given by delegates to the annual conference of the Institute of

---

[49] See Offner, *Another Such Victory*, 388–93.
[50] CIA memorandum, 18 August 1950, *FRUS, 1950, VII*, 601.
[51] See Allen S. Whiting, *China Crosses the Yalu: The Decision to Enter the Korean War* (Stanford, 1960), 107–11; Rosemary Foot, *The Wrong War: American Policy and the Dimensions of the Korean Conflict, 1950–1953* (Ithaca, 1985), 79–83; Merill, *Bread and the Ballot*, 55–6.

Pacific Relations (IPR), held at Lucknow in India.[52] Nehru opened the conference with a speech which acknowledged the differences of Asian cultures and traditions and the vastness of Asia as a continent, but affirmed that, in spite of this, 'I think it is still true to say that there is such a thing as Asian sentiment.'[53] Those attending the gathering included representatives from India, Pakistan, Japan and the Philippines, and in discussion with their Western counterparts, they noted many sources of friction which were apparent between Asia and the West, including continued attitudes of racial superiority, the West's desire to subordinate Asia to its aims, the threat of military and economic domination which amounted to a new form of imperialism, and alignment of the Western nations with 'conservative groups'. Several delegates observed that the United States had replaced Britain as the prime target for Asian hostility, and that this was ascribed to the way US bases were being extended into the region, that the United States 'intends to fight Russia on Asian soil' (as in Korea), that it was 'willing to use the atom bomb in Asia but not in Europe', and 'regards the peoples of Asia as expendable and is indifferent to loss of Asian life in war'. Despite the fact, for example, that Western delegates at the conference pointed out that the bomb was ready for use only after the German surrender, this had little impact on general perceptions in the region. Whatever counter-arguments might be levelled to the list of complaints, 'it was agreed that right or wrong, Asians held deep-seated fears concerning the motives of the West'.[54] During the autumn of 1950, as one historian of the US–Indian relationship has put it, 'Indian intellectuals, journalists, politicians, and government officials excoriated the United States as a militaristic and imperialistic nation that represented a greater threat to international peace than the Soviet Union.'[55] American officials only expected that their expanding nuclear weapons programme

---

[52] 'Asian Parley Sees a Basis for Amity', *NYT*, 15 October 1950. An educational organization formed to spread greater knowledge of Asian problems and perspectives, build bridges between East and West, and influence official thinking, by this time the IPR was subject to much faction-fighting, while charges of pro-Communist leanings were soon to result in its final financial collapse; for its role in the Second World War, see Thorne, *Allies*, 81, 212–14, 540–2.

[53] 'Ferment in Asia', Nehru speech at Institute of Pacific Relations Conference, Lucknow, 3 October 1950, *Jawaharlal Nehru's Speeches*, Vol. II: *August 1949–February 1953* (Delhi, 1967), 240.

[54] 'Asiatics Impugn U.S. Aid Motives', *NYT*, 11 October 1950; Conference Document No. 4, Rapporteur's Reports, Second Series, Round Table D – Political Problems, 9–12 October 1950, Minutes and Documents of the Eleventh IPR Conference, pp. 117–19, box 472, Institute of Pacific Relations office files, Butler Library, Columbia University.

[55] McMahon, *Cold War on the Periphery*, 88; see also 'India's Neutrality', *WP*, 18 October 1950, where the continued influence of Gandhian principles of non-violence is seen as partly explaining Indian revulsion over the killing in Korea, as well as the 'suspicion that

would exacerbate this situation. At the end of October, the CIA produced a report on probable worldwide reactions to the first series of American nuclear tests to be conducted in the continental United States, which were scheduled to be held in Nevada during the spring of 1951. Soviet diplomacy and propaganda, it was predicted, would portray the tests as further evidence of aggressive US intentions. Though it was felt this was likely to have little tangible impact in overall terms, Indian attitudes would be strongly disapproving, with the tests seen as an attempt to 'intimidate' the Soviet Union. The government and the articulate public in India, it was noted, 'deplore the existence of the atom bomb and condemn its use [... moreover] they resent the fact that the bomb was used against an Oriental rather than a European or white people'.[56]

All this formed the backdrop to developments in the Korean War itself, where MacArthur continued to push his tired and stretched units northwards towards the Chinese border, carrying out a largely superfluous amphibious landing at Wonsan on the east of the peninsula that merely served to divide his command. At the same time, the numbing realization began to dawn in Washington that Beijing might have decided on a major introduction of Chinese troops to forestall the presence of US forces close to one of China's most strategically sensitive regions.[57] On 4 November, in a re-run of July's deliberations, Brigadier General Herbert B. Loper from the Armed Forces Special Weapons Project came to the State Department to discuss the possible use of the atomic bomb to counter Chinese Communist military action in Korea, seeing Nitze and Carlton Savage together. Here it was concluded that tactical employment of the bomb in Korea against such targets as troop concentrations or artillery support positions might certainly be effective, but it was felt there would not be many opportunities of this kind presented during the current course of fighting, meaning that decisive results for the pattern of the war as a whole were unlikely. Use of the bomb for 'strategic' purposes against Manchurian cities such as Mukden, Fushun, Anshan, Harbin and Dairen would lead to large-scale civilian casualties and probably bring the Soviet Union into the war. Savage advised that if the bomb were used against Chinese cities, 'it might be wise to issue a warning ahead of time in order to enable civilians to leave', a comment that recalls the criticism of

the West considers Asiatics expendable and that the desire of Europe and perhaps America is to fight the war against communism in Asia where weapons of mass destruction, such as the atomic bomb, can be used'.
[56] CIA intelligence memorandum No. 336, 'An Estimate of Soviet and Non-Soviet Reactions to U.S. Nuclear Energy Tests and Probable Consequent Actions and Results', 31 October 1950, CIA Freedom of Information Act Reading Room, www.foia.cia.gov/search.asp, accessed 20 March 2007.
[57] See, e.g., Beisner, *Acheson*, 406–9.

some of the scientists involved in the Manhattan Project that specific warnings had not been given prior to the atomic attacks on Japan. In any event, it was recognized that any use of the bomb 'would help arouse the peoples of Asia against us'.[58]

A few days later, John K. Emmerson, the Planning Adviser in the Far East Bureau of the State Department, compiled a memorandum for Dean Rusk on the use of the atomic bomb in China. Although he was ready to defer to JCS opinion, Emmerson assumed that China would offer few suitable targets because of its size, low levels of industrialization and dispersed cities, but if the latter were hit in a 'repetition of Hiroshima and Nagasaki', he predicted damaging political reactions: 'regardless of the fact that military results achieved by atomic bombardment may be identical to those attained by conventional weapons, the effect on world opinion will be vastly different. The A-bomb has the status of a peculiar monster conceived by American cunning and its use by us, in whatever situation, would be exploited to our serious detriment.' Without international sanction from the UN, the moral position of the United States would be 'seriously damaged' in view of the 'special place occupied by the atomic bomb as a weapon of mass destruction', the unity of the UN action in Korea would in all likelihood be shattered, and the Soviet Union might feel emboldened to enter a conflict where world opinion was more condemnatory of US behaviour. In the eyes of the world, Emmerson emphasized, the 'moral, political, and psychological position' of China was distinct from that of the Soviet Union, making using the bomb against the former a very different proposition. Moreover,

Should the next atomic bomb be dropped on an Asiatic population, it is easy to foresee the revulsion of feeling which would spread throughout Asia. Fears that we reserve atomic weapons for Japanese and Chinese would be confirmed, our efforts to win the Asiatics to our side would be cancelled and our influence in non-Communist nations of Asia would deteriorate to an almost non-existent quantity.

If decisive results against China were to be achieved, Emmerson pointedly noted, 'we should undoubtedly have to engage in atomic warfare on a wide scale', drawing the United States ever further into Asia, to the detriment of commitments in Europe. But failure to subdue the PRC would be disastrous for the US world position by undermining confidence that American possession of the atomic bomb was the best guarantee against

---

[58] See Savage memorandum, 'The Question of U.S. Use of Atomic Bombs to Counter Chinese Communist Military Action in Korea', 3 November 1950, and Nitze memorandum, 4 November 1950, 'Atomic Energy – Armaments, 1950', box 6, Subject Files, records of the PPS, 1947–53, RG 59, NARA. Some commentators were urging that a warning to the Chinese of possible nuclear use in Korea should be issued if large-scale intervention south of the Yalu occurred; see 'Neglect No Means', *WP*, 7 November 1950.

Soviet attack.[59] Similarly, for Gordon Dean, who had taken over the key position of chairman of the AEC in July 1950, two of the crucial questions that would have to be considered if the President ever had to decide on the use of nuclear weapons would be the effect on public opinion at home and abroad, and whether UN agreement had been secured beforehand.[60]

These discussions over possible nuclear use in Korea, echoing the earlier speculation in July, became steadily more pertinent as increasing numbers of Chinese troops began to probe the long front straddled by the UN forces. With the appearance of this new enemy, and possessing little knowledge of Chinese intentions and strength, MacArthur's mood oscillated between alarm and optimism, expressing frustration that he could not attack the 'privileged sanctuary' of the Manchurian bases over the border from which Chinese aircraft were beginning to operate, and always with an eye to transfer the blame for any setback to Washington. Nevertheless, a lull in battlefield contacts with Chinese forces in mid-November seems to have given him encouragement, and even though his own troops were tired, dangerously over-stretched and deficient in knowledge of the enemy, MacArthur did not want to let military realities intrude on what would be a fitting climax to his glittering career, and he proceeded to launch his command forward in an 'end the war' offensive. Almost as soon as it had begun, however, the anticipated final push began to meet determined resistance, and on 25 November a massive Chinese counter-attack began to drive back US and South Korean troops all along the line.[61]

Meanwhile, MacArthur's military superiors in Washington had already been considering how nuclear weapons might play a role in future operations, or even have to be used if the level of Chinese commitment to the war was stepped up. On 20 November, General Collins, the Army's Chief of Staff, warned that Chinese intervention raised again the possible use of the atomic bomb, which if employed against 'troop and material concentrations' could be decisive in allowing a defensive position to be held, or the Manchurian border to be reached. He was therefore anxious that the JCS planning machinery should begin to study the conditions under which the atomic bomb should be used, and against what kinds of targets.[62]

---

[59] Emmerson memorandum for Rusk, 8 November 1950, 711.5611/11–850, box 3173, Central Decimal File (CDF) RG 59, NARA; also reproduced in *FRUS, 1950, VII*, 1098–100.

[60] See entry for 10 November 1950, Roger M. Anders (ed.), *Forging the Atomic Shield: Excerpts from the Office Diary of Gordon E. Dean* (Chapel Hill, 1987), 89.

[61] Michael Schaller, *Douglas MacArthur: The Far Eastern General* (New York, 1989), 207–12.

[62] See memorandum by the Chief of Staff, US Army, on 'Possible Employment of Atomic Bombs in Korea', JCS 2173, 20 November 1950, 385.2 Korea (28 July 1950), box 906, Air Force Plans, RG 341, NARA.

Accordingly, the Joint Strategic Survey Committee (JSSC) began to consider the problem, but by the time they had completed their work at the end of November the general Chinese offensive was under way, and UN forces were beginning their traumatic retreat back towards the 38th parallel where the war had originally broken out in June. The sombre conclusion of the JSSC was that the bomb should be used 'in the face of imminent disaster that cannot be averted by other means', with the JCS to decide when such a situation had been reached (forced evacuation of UN forces from the Korean peninsula was one such obvious scenario).[63] Although SAC was placed on worldwide alert and two B-29 medium bomb groups were put on stand-by for transfer to the Far East, the immediate reaction of Air Force planners in Washington to the Army's recent interest in nuclear use was that there were many drawbacks to such a course of action, including, *inter alia*, the technical intelligence it was likely to offer the Russians, that prediction of weapons effects was still an inaccurate science, and that use of the atomic bomb 'could amount to a piece-meal commitment of advanced air weapons in an indecisive theater'; one senior planner was moved to conclude that 'in the light of the extraordinary reserve man power of the enemy, the Air Force might well warn that too much should not be expected of A-bomb use in Korea, unless reconnaissance shows targets of proper magnitude'.[64]

The large-scale involvement of Chinese forces marked, of course, a total change in the nature of the Korean War. For one, the predominantly American forces on the peninsula faced a battle-hardened and determined enemy enjoying a local numerical superiority, though often being deficient in heavy equipment, supporting firepower and logistical back-up. Another dimension to the direct clash between the United States and the PRC on the peninsula was the danger that it might also draw in Soviet participation, especially if the United States chose to expand the scope of the war by attacking military targets in China itself. Throughout the war, in fact, American commanders and many officials chafed at the restrictions placed on US air and naval operations, which meant that Chinese forces in Korea could be replenished from across the border in Manchuria, and that Chinese aircraft could return to their airfields in China with no fear of either hot pursuit or attack on the ground. On a more popular and emotional level, the Korean War helped to transpose wartime images of fanatical Japanese warriors into North Korean and

---

[63] See James F. Schnabel and Robert J. Watson, *The History of the Joint Chiefs of Staff*, Vol. III: *The Korean War*, Part 1 (Washington, DC, 1979), 372–3.

[64] 'Air-Ground Support with the Atomic Bomb', memorandum by Major General R. C. Wilson (Assistant Deputy Chief of Staff, Operations for Atomic Energy) for Lieutenant General Edwards, 1 December 1950, 385.2 Korea (28 July 1950), box 906, Air Force Plans, RG 341, NARA.

Chinese Communist 'hordes' who engaged in human wave attacks which seemed to epitomize the low value placed upon individual life perceived as rooted in 'Oriental' societies and systems of government.[65] Antipathy between the United States and the PRC, already pronounced following the disputes over treatment of American diplomats in China, Chinese ties with the Soviet Union, non-recognition and the status of Taiwan, now became almost total, as Chinese forces inflicted a series of humiliating and costly reverses on American troops.[66]

In the confused days that followed the start of the Chinese winter offensive, debates among senior policy-makers in Washington turned on both the wisdom and practicality of holding onto the position in Korea, especially when the main US adversary, the Soviet Union, remained aloof from the conflict. Some foresaw the possibility of evacuation from the Korean peninsula, but this was rejected as representing an unacceptable loss of face, which would leave the South Koreans to their fate and dishearten allies. Therefore, MacArthur would have to try to repel the Chinese advance as best he could with the forces at hand, for there were precious few reinforcements that could reach the front before the spring. However, even worse than a controlled evacuation would be if the UN forces were driven off the peninsula, in which case, as the JSSC had previously advised, nuclear weapons might have to be used to cover the withdrawal. The chance that carrying the war into China could trigger a Soviet response, which would lead to a more general war, also had to be considered, and this tended to induce caution over exercising nuclear options, Collins feeling, for example, that intervention by the Soviet air force would require the threat of use of atomic bombs to retrieve the position and so hence, 'We should ... hold back from bombing in China even if this means that our ground forces must take some punishment from the air.'[67] In these taut conversations, Acheson was at pains to remind the JCS that to attract international support, any military measures taken directly against the Chinese would have to be related to the safeguarding of US troops in Korea if they had to be evacuated, and not constitute 'mere retaliation' for the PRC's initial intervention, warning

---

[65] See, e.g., Sherry, *In the Shadow of War*, 186; Chang, *Friends and Enemies*, 170–1. Of the early Chinese successes in Korea, one historian has remarked that 'although American reports described the attackers as "hordes" coming in "human waves", the numerical balance of forces in December [1950] was not wholly out of line. The problem lay more in faulty leadership, training, morale, and tactics [among the American forces].' See Schaller, *MacArthur*, 213.

[66] The sense of American shame and humiliation over their military reverses at the end of 1950 is well captured by Max Hastings in *The Korean War* (London, 1987), 194–211.

[67] See memorandum of conversation by Philip C. Jessup, 1 December 1950, *FRUS, 1950, VII*, 1276–81.

that, 'If we get into general war with China and there are grave chances of general war with the Soviet Union soon then we would fight without allies on our side.'[68]

Indeed, the main concern of both Truman and Acheson was to avoid all-out war with China, which it was felt would only satisfy the Russians by diverting US strength to the Far East and so undermine the defence of Western Europe. Yet they were only too aware that any decisions regarding expansion of the fighting was not something over which they could exercise full control. Large-scale involvement in Korea by the Chinese Communist air force could put UN forces in even more jeopardy and prejudice the air superiority over the battlefield that most observers held as the crucial factor in holding up the Communist advance and preventing a complete rout. In this scenario there would be immense pressure on Washington to authorize air attacks on the Manchurian airfields, which might then bring in Soviet air involvement. All the time, moreover, domestic opinion in the United States was becoming increasingly inflamed at what was widely seen as Chinese 'aggression' in Korea and the unwillingness of the Truman administration to hit back against Beijing with stronger measures, while Republican gains at the recently held midterm elections (with McCarthy claiming credit for the loss of several key Democratic seats) made the political atmosphere even more uncomfortable for the President and his Secretary of State.[69] 'For weeks I've been fuming about these bitterly partisan bastards in the Republican camp who have been pushing our sons into a ten-year war with China,' Lilienthal, now freed from his responsibilities at the AEC, remarked in his diary. 'It makes me sick clear down to my lowest gut. It is a sad wretched ugly picture, this bunch of isolationists now suddenly weeping for the China they have despised (in the form of the Chinese people).'[70]

With American and UN forces in Korea continuing to retreat in disarray, on the morning of 30 November Truman entered the Indian Treaty Room in the Executive Office Building near the White House for his first press conference since the beginning of the Chinese offensive. The President was ready to convey a reassuring message from the administration to his news-hungry audience. Instead, his remarks were to spark renewed speculation over the role that nuclear weapons might play in Korea and also helped to confirm the State Department's fears over likely

[68] *Ibid.*, 3 December 1950, 1325; see also Stueck, *Korean War*, 133–4, for an excellent summary of these discussions.
[69] See Casey, *Selling the Korean War*, 109–11, 118–21.
[70] Entry for 28 November 1950, David E. Lilienthal, *The Journals of David E. Lilienthal*, Vol. III: *Venturesome Years, 1950–1955* (New York, 1966), 39.

Asian feelings if the United States were tempted to use the ultimate weapon in its arsenal in a Far Eastern setting. Truman began by asserting that the UN had no intention of abandoning its mission in Korea, but then, as Dean Acheson later recalled, 'the questions began, illustrating vividly the dangers that lurk in the American press conference, with its stress on candid answers to questions that seem to be without guile'.[71] Having avowed US determination to carry on the fight in Korea and to take 'whatever steps are necessary to meet the military situation, just as we always have', Truman was asked if these might include use of the atomic bomb. The President affirmed that there had 'always been active consideration of its use. I don't want to see it used. It is a terrible weapon, and it should not be used on innocent men, women, and children who have nothing whatever to do with the military aggression. That happens when it is used.' Continuing to be quizzed, Truman began to stumble, averring that 'the military people' would have to decide against which objectives it would be used, and, when pressed whether UN authorization would be required before its use, replied, 'The military commander in the field will have charge of the use of the weapons, as he always has.' The White House scrambled to release a clarifying statement within the hour, making plain that the President did not mean that any authorization had been given to commanders in Korea to use nuclear weapons, and that there was no change to the existing situation, but Truman's comments raised in a very public manner the distinct possibility that nuclear weapons might once again be used in Asia.[72]

The resulting international reactions were important for understanding later American fears over the political consequences that might follow from nuclear use. Among Asian representatives at the UN, there was widespread unease about the local impact of Truman's apparent admission. The Philippine diplomat Carlos Romulo offered the view that the 'moral effect' of the American use of the bomb in Korea was 'too fearful' to contemplate, with some Asian delegates warning that the 'hatred of 1,200 million Asian people' would be aroused against the United States.[73] One Saudi official told Eleanor Roosevelt, who was in the US delegation, that representatives from the Near East and Asia were 'profoundly distressed' by Truman's announcement that he was considering the 'possibility' of using the bomb, and that when the news reached Asia the word

[71] Acheson, *Present at the Creation*, 478.
[72] See 'The President's News Conference of November 30, 1950', *The Public Papers of the Presidents: Harry S. Truman, 1950* (Washington, DC, 1965), 724–8; James Chace, *Acheson: The Secretary of State Who Created the American World* (Cambridge, 1998), 305; Casey, *Selling the Korean War*, 152; Stueck, *The Korean War*, 131–2.
[73] Romulo is quoted in the *Hindustan Times*, 2 December 1950.

'possibility' would vanish. 'The people of the whole Asiatic continent would never understand why the American people had decided to use the atomic bomb against them. They would regard it as an action of the white race against the colored races. They would never forget that the atomic bomb was used first against the Japanese and later against the Chinese, but never against any white peoples. This fact would have a disastrous effect upon the relations of the United States with the rest of the world for years to come.'[74] The Indian and Pakistani delegates also 'agreed [that the] threat to use [the] bomb would reinforce [the] idea [that the] U.S. [was] willing to use mass destruction methods on Asians but not Europeans'.[75] Nehru made clear his own anxieties, via the Indian Ambassador to the UN, over the situation in Korea and the need for a cease-fire and the establishment of a demilitarized zone; it was a matter of 'absolute necessity' that use of the atomic bomb be avoided, noting the 'wide-spread feeling in Asia that the atomic bomb is a weapon used only against Asiatics'.[76]

In India, leading newspapers saw Truman's statement as a sign of warlike American intent and a callous attitude to the lives of Asians, with many editorials highlighting the fact it would be the third time weapons of mass destruction had been used in Asia. *The Hindu*, published in Madras, noted that, 'Asiatic opinion, which already strongly disapproved of the use of this terror weapon on Japan, will be horrified if Chinese or Korean cities are devastated in the same manner.' 'The dropping of an atomic bomb on Korea or Manchuria would destroy much more than the lives and habitations of Koreans and Chinese,' *The Times of India* intoned. 'It would cause as fierce a revulsion of feeling in Asia as to endanger calm thinking at a time when a sense of values was never more vital.' Atomic raids would 'alienate Asian opinion as nothing else will'. The *Indian News Chronicle* warned of the 'immense risk of earning the passionate hatred of Asian peoples'. One editorial writer posed the pointed question of why Truman was not considering dropping an atomic bomb on Moscow, if the Soviet Union was the main source of aggression

---

[74] Memorandum of conversation by Mrs Franklin D. Roosevelt, 1 December 1950, *FRUS, 1950, I: National Security Affairs; Foreign Economic Policy* (Washington, DC, 1977), 116. Eleanor Roosevelt replied that while the atomic bomb was indeed a terrible weapon, it was 'war itself that was the terrible thing', and that any decisions about use of the bomb in Korea would depend on the military situation at the time.

[75] New York to State Department, No. 931, 1 December 1950, 'Reactions to President Truman's statement re possible use of atom bomb', box 8, Korean War File, Staff Member and Office Files (SMOF), Harry S. Truman papers, HSTL; also reproduced in *FRUS, 1950, VII*, 1300.

[76] Memorandum of a telephone conversation by the Assistant Secretary of State for United Nations Affairs, 3 December 1950, *FRUS, 1950, VII*, 1334.

and instability in the world, leaving the inference that it was Asian peoples who were once again being targeted because of the colour of their skins.[77] The largest circulation newspaper in northern and central India, the *Hindustan Times*, carried reports that Senator Colin Johnston (Democrat, South Carolina) was calling for MacArthur to be given the go-ahead to drop atomic bombs in Korea and Manchuria. While Asian delegates at the UN had been supportive of the principle of collective security since the outbreak of the war in June, the paper reported, they had also been fearful that weaknesses in UN manpower would lead the United States to use nuclear weapons as it had 'once before used atom bombs in Asia in order to shorten the course of war'.[78]

Hostile press comment was not confined to India. The *Ceylon Daily News* noted that 'in Asia methods used to end the Second World War have not been forgotten or forgiven and [the] idea of using [the] same methods once again on Asian soil will alienate all responsible opinion throughout the East'. It would be seen not so much as a 'decisive blow to Communism but rather as [an] act of war by [the] Western world on Asia, where opinion [is] already shocked by [the] method [of] mass warfare found necessary in Korea. It is already remarked that Western powers are much readier to give "active consideration" to [the] use of atomic warfare on Asian soil than they ever were when war in [the] West was at its darkest and most desperate.'[79] In Indonesia, the US Embassy reported that the *Sin Po* newspaper was arguing that the Chinese offensive was a shock to American leaders because they could not believe that an 'army [of the] colored race can inflict such blows. White supremacy must be maintained so these leaders think of [the] atom bomb. White supremacy [was] more important than humanity.'[80] Intemperate comments from leading US political figures also contributed to Asian anxieties, with the perennial Republican presidential-hopeful Harold Stassen, for example, proclaiming while on a trip to Tokyo that the Chinese mainland should be attacked by air and sea and with nuclear weapons if necessary, if the Chinese did not agree to an immediate cease-fire and mediation talks.[81] The following February, American and British officials were still referring to Truman's

---

[77] See 'A-Bomb Threat Evokes Wrath of India Press', *Chicago Daily Tribune*, 4 December 1950, and Indian press summary contained in New Delhi to Secretary of State, No. 1383, 3 December 1950, 711.5611/12–350, CDF, RG 59, NARA.

[78] See *Hindustan Times*, 2 December 1950.

[79] Colombo to Secretary of State, 5 December 1950, No. 243, 711.5611/12–550, CDF, RG 59, NARA.

[80] Djakarta to Secretary of State, No. 730, 4 December 1950, 711.5611/12–450, CDF, RG 59, NARA.

[81] '"Cease Fire" Order from U.N. Urged by Stassen for Korea', *Chicago Daily Tribune*, 6 December 1950.

statement as 'having swept through Asia like wildfire' and as showing the ease with which 'anti-westernism' could be generated.[82]

Asian reactions to the possible use of the atomic bomb in the Korean War have to be seen in the context of the perceptions of the fighting that had been building up over the summer, and that were noted above. UN bombing of urban areas in the north and the numerous incidents where columns of refugees had been attacked from the air helped to create the impression that it was Asians who were suffering at the hands of the white powers (even if they operated under the guise of a UN Command). The press comments of December 1950 indicate that the atomic bombings of 1945 had a wider regional resonance which was only gradually coming to be appreciated, but which might have adverse consequences for overall American efforts to generate support for their policies in the Far East as a whole. They also served to confirm feelings common to some Western observers that racial divisions along occidental/oriental lines might come to play a more salient role in Asian views of the underlying nature of the Korean War; however, this might contradict professed American policy and attitudes, which were predicated on 'saving' Asians from Communist domination and takeover. Hanson Baldwin, writing in the *New York Times* and in an echo of the views he had expressed in July, warned that the atomic bomb should not be used in the current crisis, for it 'would range the whole Asian world against the Allies, both psychologically and polit-ically. Its use could be justified militarily – given such drawbacks – only if it were effective and there is little chance that it could be militarily effective in either Korea or Manchuria.'[83]

Truman's press conference statements also disturbed America's closest allies. In Britain, faced with a barrage of enquiries and questions in the House of Commons, Clement Attlee announced that he would fly to Washington for talks with Truman on the situation in the Far East. Among British observers there were concerns that the emotional mood of American opinion in the face of Chinese entrance into the war, and the known propensity of MacArthur to take matters into his own hands, might trigger a sudden resort to nuclear use. This would then, it was feared, lead almost inexorably to the direct involvement of the Soviet Union in hostil-ities, with probable military moves in Europe. American airbases in the United Kingdom, which had received the nuclear-configured B-29 deployment in July, would then become a prime target for Soviet atomic attack. Having committed its own troops to the Korean fighting in July

---

[82] Memorandum of informal US–UK discussions, 6 February 1951, *FRUS, 1951, VI: Asia and the Pacific*, Part 2 (Washington, DC, 1977), 1655–6.
[83] 'Crossroads in Korea', *NYT*, 6 December 1950.

1950, London expected that its voice should be heard over the critical situation in the Far East.[84] The British were therefore keen to press the argument that negotiations for a cease-fire with the Chinese should be pursued. Moreover, convinced that it was strategic folly to dissipate strength in the Far East, the British also wanted to secure American agreement to the principle that priorities should remain focussed on building up the defence of Western Europe against a possible Soviet offensive. As during the summer, the British Chiefs of Staff were dismissive over the idea of using the atomic bomb in the setting of the Korean War. On 1 December, the COS considered a paper composed by the Chief of the Air Staff, Air Chief Marshal Sir John Slessor, which examined the issue and came to the conclusion that its use could not be justified on military grounds. No suitable tactical targets were in evidence in Korea, while the destruction of Korean urban areas was felt to present no great psychological blow against the enemy, as 'life is cheap in Asia and the morale effect of casualties is not so great as with Western nations'. Moreover, Slessor was ready to introduce a moral argument by continuing that, apart from the lack of decisive results, when it came to attacks on urban areas 'we could not be a party to destroying cities and killing civilians in this way'. The essential British position was that the atomic bomb's prime value was as an insurance against the outbreak of a general war; its use in Korea would indicate to the Russians that the West regarded the stakes at play as so high that they were prepared to resort to extreme measures, and this was only likely to invite direct Soviet intervention.[85]

Warnings and concerns about the impact of a repeat use of the bomb on Asian opinion were common in Western capitals during this period. The Canadian Government was sufficiently disturbed to instruct their ambassador in Washington to deliver a memorandum to the State Department which outlined their fears and their feeling that, before any decision were made over its use, there should be consultation with allied governments. 'The military authorities may argue that the atomic bomb is just another weapon,' the paper ran, 'but, in the minds of ordinary people everywhere in the world, it is far more than that and has acquired an immensely greater intrinsic significance.' Use of the bomb against Chinese cities would risk destroying the 'cohesion and unity of the Atlantic community', while 'its use, for a second time, against an Asian people would

---

[84] See Pierson Dixon minute, 'Possible British Land Forces Contribution for Korea', 1 July 1950, FK1022/208G, FO 371/84091, TNA.

[85] Slessor's views received the endorsement of the COS and served as a brief for the subject of the British delegation during Attlee's visit to Washington; see Confidential Annex to COS(50)191st meeting, 1 December 1950, and Appendix I, 'Use of the A-Bomb in Korea', DEFE 4/38, TNA.

dangerously weaken the ties that remain between the Western world and the peoples of the East'.[86]

On 2 December, before leaving for Washington, Attlee and Bevin met the French Prime Minister and Minister for External Affairs to talk over the general situation in the Far East. Here Attlee expressed the view that 'it was necessary to bear in mind that the British and French were more alive to Asiatic sentiment than the Americans. For example, the suggestion that the atomic bomb might be used in Korea showed a lack of understanding for the Asiatic mentality, in that it suggested that Europeans and Americans had a low regard for the value of Asiatic lives ... [It was] essential to keep the Asiatic nations in step with the rest of the world in the stand against aggression, and for this reason any action proposed by the United Nations must be thought of in relation to its effect on Asian opinion.' When the French mentioned the fact that there would be much public disquiet in France if the bomb were used in Korea, Attlee responded by emphasizing the British position, in a reflection of popular feeling, that atomic bombs

could not be regarded on a level with other weapons. Their use would bring about a new era in warfare with consequences which no-one could appreciate. This question (like the question of bombing Manchuria) was one which could not be decided on purely military grounds. Short-sighted decisions designed to meet an immediate situation might be fatal, and the matter must be decided on the highest political level and not by one Power alone. It was the European countries who would get the retaliation, and though he did not say that atomic weapons must *never* be used in warfare, he took the same line as the French Government over their use in Korea.

As for Bevin, he 'very much regretted' the statements made by Truman at his recent press conference for they had caused a 'revulsion in Allied feeling' that had then required a retraction and which had helped to weaken the deterrent effect of the possession of nuclear weapons; the atomic bomb should 'be held in the background as an ultimate reserve. Any loose talk about its use, especially at a high level, was most danger-ous.' The French agreed that the statements had had a 'boomerang effect'.[87] The day after this meeting, the Prime Minister received a mes-sage of almost imploring tone from Nehru: 'I should like to impress upon

---

[86] See Canadian memorandum, 'Korea and the Atomic Bomb', 3 December 1950, and amended version given to Gordon Arneson, 7 December 1950, in Greg Donaghy (ed.), *Documents on Canadian External Relations, Volume 16, 1950* (Ottawa, 1996), 254–5, 256–7.

[87] Record of a meeting between Attlee, Bevin, Pleven and Schuman, 2 December 1950, F1027/6G, FO 371/83019, TNA; also in H. J. Yasamee and K. A. Hamilton (eds.), *Documents on British Policy Overseas (DBPO)*, Series II, Vol. IV: *Korea, June 1950–April 1951* (London, 1991), 229–36.

you the absolute necessity of avoiding use of the atom bomb. This will make world war inevitable. You can judge yourself the consequences of this in Western Europe. In Asia there has been a strong feeling that [the] atom bomb is used against Asians. Whoever first employs this weapon of tremendous destruction will I am sure forfeit the sympathies of people in this part of the world.'[88] As well as the dangerous results that would flow from an expansion of the war to China, Attlee therefore wanted to impress on the Truman administration the damage that the current evidence of US belligerence was doing to the entire UN cause in Korea, and the Western position as a whole in Asia. Most importantly he hoped to put the case for negotiations with Beijing that would include the future of Taiwan as well as a compromise settlement in Korea in one package deal, and urge the Americans to consider admitting the PRC to the UN.

The Americans were well aware of British anxieties before the talks with Attlee opened. In the briefing papers prepared for Truman, the State Department underlined the 'genuine fear shared by virtually all within the British community that we are drifting towards a third world war'. Furthermore, the British were seen as being worried that even if full-scale war with the Soviet Union were avoided, an exhausting war with China was a real possibility. Such a direct clash also raised the danger, in British minds, that this 'would turn all Asian opinion against the West'. Among the actions that could aggravate the situation was the 'fear of the effect on the Asiatic people of the use of the atom bomb, or even the open consideration of its use. There is a deep-seated belief that this would turn all the Asian people against the Western powers.'[89] Despite the soothing communiqué that was produced at the conclusion of the four days of talks in Washington, many British officials remained unsettled by the American attitudes on display. Truman had been ready to reassure Attlee that he would consult with the United Kingdom (and Canada also) over any decision to use the bomb, but Acheson and his senior officials were then quick to step the President back from this private

[88] Nehru to Attlee, 3 December 1950, Ind/50/25, FO 800/470, TNA.
[89] 'Overall Statement of Problem Involved', State Department briefing book, n.d. [but c. 3 December 1950], and 'Tab I: Use of Atomic Bomb', n.d. [but c. 3 December 1950], 'Truman–Attlee talks, Dec. 1950 – briefing book', box 141, Subject Files, Conferences File, President's Secretary's Files, Truman papers, HSTL. Truman apparently discussed this briefing material beforehand with Acheson; see Arneson memorandum for the record, 16 January 1953 [actually 1951], 711.5611/1–1653, CDF, RG 59, NARA. Further material on this issue can be found in drafts 1 and 2 of 'Use of the Atomic Bomb: Memorandum for Prime Minister Atlee [sic]', 2 December 1950, and Savage covering note, 4 December 1950, 'Atomic Energy – Armaments, 1950', Subject Files, box 6, records of the PPS, 1947–53, RG 59, NARA.

undertaking when they discovered it had been made, and went on to insist that all mention of consultation should be removed from the agreed records of the meetings.[90] Moreover, though admitting that war with China should be avoided and that attempts should be made to arrange a cease-fire to halt the current fighting, the Americans were unwilling to make the concessions that the British thought were essential in order to bring a negotiated settlement about. Above all concerned that what they regarded as Chinese aggression should not be seen to be rewarded (partly because it would destroy morale in Japan and the Philippines), Acheson and his officials admitted that it was not 'politically possible' for the administration to give any ground on the Taiwan issue at that particular moment, and that for the short term the American position was to hold on in Korea, and put as much pressure on China as possible through diplomatic measures at the UN. If driven off the peninsula, the Americans favoured the tightening of economic sanctions against the regime in Beijing, and promotion of subversive activity on the mainland (also mentioned was the fact that air action against targets on the mainland was then under study).[91] As far as the British were concerned, these steps (which they branded as 'limited war' against China) would very likely result in the wider war that all agreed should be avoided, while at the same time driving Beijing even closer towards Moscow. With the Americans stressing their strategic appreciation that denial of Taiwan to the enemy was now considered important, Truman told the Prime Minister that though he was 'anxious for [a] possible settlement' he was 'not in any mood for unconditional surrender. He thought time would bring the Chinese to realise that their friends were not in Siberia but in London and Washington.' Attlee's succinct reply was 'they would not realise it if limited warfare was waged against them'.[92]

Although Attlee projected the outcome of his visit to Washington in very positive terms, there was obviously still a big divide between the allies over the whole issue of negotiations with Beijing and what steps to take in the immediate future in the Far East. Considering the inflamed political temperature in the United States, and MacArthur directing operations in imperious fashion, there were some British officials who believed that the Americans would welcome a complete withdrawal from Korea as it would free them to pursue other military options against the PRC in what had

---

[90] See record of the fifth meeting between Truman and Attlee at the White House, 7 December 1950, ZP3/3, FO 371/124949; Washington to FO, No. 3315, 7 December 1950, FO 115/4521, TNA. See also Alex Danchev, *Oliver Franks: Founding Father* (Oxford, 1993), 130–1.

[91] See Franks to Bevin, No. 3282, 4 December 1950, in *DBPO*, series II, Vol. IV, 239–40.

[92] Extract from UK record of fifth Truman–Attlee meeting, 7 December 1950, *ibid.*, 245–6.

become, they felt, virtually a vendetta against the Chinese Communists. This was one way, it seemed, to account for the ineffectiveness with which MacArthur was greeting the Chinese offensive on the ground (and here it might be recalled that when MacArthur mounted a direct challenge to new instructions he received from the JCS at the end of December, it was on the basis of the incompatibility of both holding the line in Korea while also providing for the most adequate defence of Japan). The main achievement of the Attlee visit was to bring home to the Americans all the adverse military and diplomatic consequences that might flow from expanded actions against China.[93]

Such considerations were uppermost in Acheson's own mind, and he was still acutely aware that the United States faced isolation if it appeared to embrace the chance of all-out war with China with the attendant risk that the Soviet Union would be drawn into the conflict under the terms of the Sino-Soviet Treaty. He was also determined that the American military strength that came through the rearmament justified by NSC 68 and was expected to be fully apparent only over the next eighteen months should not be dissipated in the Far East but devoted to the crucial Western European setting (the so-called 'Great Debate' in Congress over the administration's plans for sending US divisions across the Atlantic to support NATO was just then building up steam). Nevertheless, like the President he served so loyally, he tended to see the PRC as being more and more subject to Soviet direction and control, while his approach to the Chinese Communist leadership was unyielding.[94] Called in to offer his respected counsel at this critical moment, even Kennan reinforced the hardline approach in evidence, telling Acheson and other senior officials on 5 December that the Chinese had 'committed an affront of the greatest magnitude to the United States ... what they have done is something that we can not forget for years and the Chinese will have the worry of righting themselves with us not us with them ... we owe China nothing but a lesson'.[95]

Meanwhile, despite demands from within Congress and among elements of public opinion for the use of atomic weapons, Pentagon thinking seems to have turned more firmly against any such action in the Korean

---

[93] See Stueck, *Korean War*, 137.

[94] There was, for example, little retrospective analysis of why China had entered the war beyond the simple notion that it was due to Soviet pressure, and it was assumed also that Beijing had been given assurances of Moscow's support if American attacks on China itself should then occur; see Foot, *Wrong War*, 123.

[95] Memorandum of conversation in the Secretary's Office, 5 December 1950, 'Truman–Attlee discussions, December 1950', box 8, Korean War File, SMOF, Truman papers, HSTL.

fighting during this period.[96] This was partly due to growing doubts about the tactical utility of the bomb against the kind of scattered and lightly equipped Chinese Communist forces that had swept south from the Yalu, and also the realization that if a wider war should occur involving the Soviet Union, the main theatres for nuclear operations should properly lie elsewhere. Even the ever-combative head of SAC, General Curtis E. LeMay, had signalled to Vandenberg on 2 December that 'analysis of available targets together with obvious considerations of possible adverse psychological reaction have led us to conclude that the employment of atomic weapons in the Far East would probably not be advisable at this time unless this action is undertaken as part of an overall atomic campaign against Red China'.[97] Only the disaster of an emergency evacuation from the peninsula under heavy enemy pressure would warrant the use of nuclear weapons, and as December wore on the JCS were beginning to see beyond the more alarmist reports from MacArthur's Command and to understand that, though serious, the situation on the ground was not yet critical and that the UN forces were starting to stabilize the position; on 6 December, General Collins, asked by newsmen following a tour of the frontlines whether the atomic bomb would be used tactically against the Chinese, was able to reply confidently in the negative. When Collins returned to Washington he reported to the President, Attlee (who was on the final day of this visit) and General Omar N. Bradley, the Chairman of the JCS, his belief that the Chinese would not be able to push UN forces out of Korea, even if their existing resources were not increased.[98]

Nonetheless, the outcome of the Attlee–Truman talks did little to allay the anxieties of the British military leadership that the Americans might be in the mood to bring on a general war as a way to settle current tensions. Having accompanied the Prime Minister to Washington, in mid-December Field Marshal Sir William Slim, the Chief of the Imperial General Staff, reported to the COS that the Americans 'were convinced that war was inevitable, and that it was almost certain to take place within the next eighteen months ... This attitude of the United States was dangerous because there was the possibility that they might think that since war was inevitable, the sooner we got it over the better, and we might as a result be dragged unnecessarily into World War III.' If forced to evacuate Korea, the Americans favoured sea blockade, bombing and

---

[96] See Dingman, 'Atomic Diplomacy', 67.
[97] LeMay to Vandenberg, 2 December 1950, B-8552, box B-196, Curtis E. LeMay papers, LC.
[98] See J. Lawton Collins, *War in Peacetime: The History and Lessons of Korea* (Boston, 1969), 230–3.

support for guerrilla elements in China, but the British considered this kind of 'limited war' would soon expand its scope. There had been signs in Washington, Slim felt, that the Americans recognized this point, but they were still averse to any policy that smacked of 'appeasement', while the effect on public opinion at home seemed to be the paramount consideration in the administration's debates over policy.[99]

With so many signs that the Americans would soon be drawn into direct action against China, the Joint Intelligence Committee (JIC) in London had also set about analysing Chinese vulnerability to Western bombing and blockade, and the measures that could be taken to ensure her defeat. In their resulting report, the JIC highlighted that even extensive air attacks on China's centres of industry and transportation would not achieve decisive results, while the Chinese army's disregard for casualties would allow it to maintain a strong defence.[100] Believing that a full-scale war with China would be 'militarily unsound and politically disastrous', the COS wanted a copy of this JIC paper to be given to the JCS in Washington, along with a note (drafted by Slessor, who was by most judgement the commanding intellect on the COS during this period) which laid out the consequences in stark terms of an Occident versus Orient clash along racial lines:

There could be no more dangerous outcome of the Korean affair than that it should develop into an issue between the white Western peoples on the one hand and the coloured Eastern people plus Russia on the other. That may at present look unlikely, but in our view it is by no means inconceivable and, if it happened, it would be militarily no less than politically catastrophic.[101]

In their subsequent formal advice to ministers on the same issue, the COS were led to the sobering conclusion that the Chinese were 'virtually

---

[99] See Confidential Annex to COS(50)206th meeting, 14 December 1950, DEFE 4/38, TNA.

[100] JIC(50)105(Final), 'Vulnerability of China', 7 December 1950, CAB 158/11; when passed to the COS this paper became COS(50)523, 14 December 1950. See FC1091/1G, FO 371/92254, TNA.

[101] See British Joint Staff Mission to Ministry of Defence (Tedder for COS), AWT 85, 21 December 1950; Slessor note, 22 December 1950; Ministry of Defence to British Joint Staff Mission (COS to Tedder), COS(W) 927, 29 December 1950 (incorporating Slessor note), FC1091/2G, FO 371/92254, TNA. The JIC study was duly passed to the Americans, though the US JIC response indicated sharp disagreement with their British counterparts on how bombing, blockade and support for anti-Communist guerrilla groups in combination could 'imperil' the Communist regime; see Note by the Secretaries to the JCS on 'Vulnerability of China', JCS 2118/18, 8 March 1951, enclosing JIC memorandum, OPD 381 China (29 Nov. 1950), sec. 2, box 732, Air Force Plans, RG 341, NARA.

invulnerable to Western attack' and that even the widespread use of nuclear weapons would not produce a successful outcome:

No doubt in course of time many or most of the large Chinese cities could be destroyed if the United States were prepared to devote their resources to that end. But that would not win the war. The vast proportion of China's 475 million do not live in or depend greatly upon their great cities, and human life in China is held very cheap. A historic tradition of flood and famine have rendered the Chinese people impervious to large scale disaster of the extent that could be imposed by atomic attack. Militarily, it is impossible to claim that this would make any appreciable difference to Chinese capacity to hold out.[102]

Similarly, for Asian leaders such as Nehru, belligerent American talk of expanding the war to China itself made no logical sense. Lilienthal, touring India in February 1951, was told by the Indian Prime Minister that 'China is like India. They too have suffered many, many disasters. So you could defeat China, but could not win her over; quite the contrary. Four hundred million people cannot be subdued by winning a war against them, or by visiting military punishment on them. They will never be won that way, no matter how great the military victory.'[103]

Such appraisals of the chances of success in a full-scale war with China (and of how such 'success' might be defined) were notably lacking in the US bureaucracy as it struggled to cope with the crisis, with officials tending to focus on either the short-term measures needed to stabilize the military situation, or on steps that could be taken to punish China for the effrontery of its intervention. During the remainder of December, confusing accounts of the battlefield situation in Korea continued to be received in Washington, as MacArthur painted a picture of desperate defence and imminent defeat, even to the extent that at the end of the month he submitted a list of 'retardation' targets in North Korea and China to Washington which he felt would require the use of up to thirty-four atomic bombs to check the Communist offensive, though it appears he did not go so far as to recommend their actual use.[104] However, more steady assessments were offered by the new commander of the Eighth Army, Lieutenant General Matthew B. Ridgway, who maintained that, though badly battered, the UN forces were capable of active and effective resistance and, as Chinese lines of communication lengthened and the full effects of UN air power began to be felt, there was every prospect of halting the Communist advance. More gloom enveloped senior US

---

[102] COS memorandum, 'War with China', Appendix to PMM(51)13, 6 January 1951, PREM 8/1408, and in F1102/1G, FO 371/92077, TNA.
[103] Entry for 23 February 1951, Lilienthal, *Venturesome Years*, 104.
[104] See Foot, *Wrong War*, 114–15, and Gaddis, 'Origins of Self-Deterrence', 116.

policy-makers in early January, when the Chinese mounted a second offensive that drove UN forces back below the 38th parallel, but on this occasion there was no sense of overriding panic, and Ridgway's unflustered approach to the business of command, combined with innate confidence in his troops, made a striking contrast to his military superior in Tokyo.

Still in overall command in the Far East, MacArthur was told by the JCS on 9 January that the blockade of the China coast that he had been urging must await either stabilization of the position in Korea or evacuation from the peninsula, and that naval and air attacks on targets in Communist China 'probably' could only be authorized if US forces outside Korea were themselves attacked.[105] Despite delivering this rebuff, the JCS were by now veering towards tougher measures, and in mid-January endorsed a memorandum composed by the Chief of Naval Operations (CNO), Admiral Forrest P. Sherman, presenting a series of options which in many respects reflected some of the steps MacArthur had himself been advocating, including a naval blockade, greater use of Chinese Nationalist troops, support for guerrilla groups in China, increased aerial reconnaissance of coastal areas and Manchuria, and, if Chinese Communist forces were to launch attacks on US forces outside Korea, naval and air strikes on mainland targets. Although this document was not ultimately endorsed by the National Security Council, neither was it disowned entirely, and ideas about inflicting some kind of retribution against the PRC for the pain it was inflicting on the UN Command in Korea, and for the damage it had done to American pride, were prevalent throughout the administration. In the meantime, however, Collins and Vandenberg had undertaken another tour of the Korean front, and their favourable report on UN prospects delivered on 19 January finally helped to convince the sceptics that the position could be held and evacuation from Korea, with its corollary of an expansion of hostilities to China proper, was an eventuality that need no longer be contemplated.[106]

In all these discussions, Acheson's strong reservations over expanding the war had helped to defer any irrevocable decisions, and the fact that an unreliable MacArthur would probably have had to oversee any such operations was a further factor making for immediate caution. In the background, pressure and lobbying from the British for restraint throughout January 1951 also made clear there would be little allied support for expanded actions against China. With all the talk of the previous

---

[105] JCS to MacArthur, 9 January 1951, *FRUS, 1951, VII: Korea and China*, Part 1 (Washington, DC, 1983), 41–3.
[106] See Foot, *Wrong War*, 118–22, 128–30; Stueck, *Korean War*, 149–51.

September of reunifying Korea under a new democratic government now appearing hopelessly unrealistic, in February 1951 Ridgway's rejuvenated forces inched back up towards the 38th parallel (Seoul was to be re-captured in mid-March), and the administration's position now coalesced around aiming for a cease-fire along this line, and an acceptance, at least in the short term, of a settlement which involved the political division of the peninsula. By the end of March, Bradley was telling his fellow Joint Chiefs that he thought it was 'unrealistic to shoot for a unified, independent, and democratic Korea. The 38th Parallel is a better line than the Yalu for us. We should be thinking in terms of the reestablishment of the *status quo ante* of June 25, and of withdrawing our forces from Korea. We should give up any idea of establishing a free and unified Korea.'[107] The objectives of 'limited war' in Korea, to hold territory already in friendly hands and inflict casualties on the enemy in the hope of first convincing him that battlefield success was unobtainable, and then inducing concessions in negotiations, appeared to have been finally established.[108]

American involvement in the Korean War and the events that culminated in the major Chinese intervention at the end of 1950 not only spurred the militarization of the Cold War in the Far East but also put paid to any notion that there could be any early reconciliation of the United States to the existence of a Communist regime in Beijing. Instead of the dust thrown up by the Chinese Civil War being allowed to settle (to paraphrase Dean Acheson), a veritable storm had arisen where Americans discerned the rise of a new and ominous adversary in Asia, whose potential power and resources, apparently harnessed to the will of the Soviet leadership in the Kremlin, represented an even more potent threat than that posed by the Japanese challenge of the early 1940s. In August 1950, as he cleared his desk in readiness for departure from the State Department (where he had held the position of Counselor since relinquishing the duties of head of the PPS to Nitze), George Kennan provided a valedictory on US policy in the Far East. 'The course upon which we are today moving,' Kennan warned Acheson, 'is one ... so little promising and so fraught with danger that I could not honestly urge you to continue to take responsibility for it.' Although he had agreed with the initial commitment to defend South Korea in June, Kennan felt that the administration had not set 'clear and realistic' objectives in relation to that country, while the 'emotional, moralistic' attitudes of public opinion and the 'establishment'

---

[107] Meeting of 28 March 1951, box 50, Meeting Summaries Project Files, Records of State-JCS Meetings, 1951–9, RG 59, NARA.

[108] The laconic comment of one British officer was that Ridgway's strategy was now 'homicidal not geographical'; see Stueck, *Korean War*, 167–9.

could easily lead to direct conflict with the Soviet Union. Current China policy, Kennan argued, was likely to result in 'serious conflict' with other Asian countries, as well as Britain and the Commonwealth, while American aid to the French in Indochina was enlisting support for a war which was unwinnable. Basing his position on considerations of 'pure national interest' rather than domestic politics, Kennan wanted to see the United States quickly terminate its involvement on the Asian mainland 'on the best terms possible', make clear to the French that the only course the United States was prepared to back in Indochina was withdrawal, even at the cost of spreading Viet Minh authority over the whole territory, and also recognize that it was beyond US capabilities to keep Korea permanently free of Soviet influence. In the long run, Kennan recommended agreement with the Russians over a demilitarized and neutralized Japan in return for an end to the Korean War, and UN control over the peninsula to be underpinned with forces drawn only from Asia itself. A proper American diplomatic relationship with Japan, a country described by Kennan as 'the most important single factor in Asia', could not be secured unless the large US military presence was removed and the Japanese encouraged to provide for their own defence.[109] For Acheson, burdened by the continuous assaults of Republican critics for his 'appeasement' of Communism in Asia, Kennan's memorandum 'mingled flashes of prophetic insight and suggestions … of total impracticality'. In the environment of policy-making in which he was operating, where public opinion and political pressures were ever present, Acheson later wrote, 'ideas such as these could only be kept in mind as warnings not to be drawn into quicksands'.[110]

By the end of the year, Kennan's warnings had evidently been insufficient to deter the authorities in Washington from the attempt to 'rollback' Communist power north of the 38th parallel, with the unwelcome final result that the prestige of the PRC had risen enormously as it forced into retreat forces from a technologically more advanced society. The irrationality of the refusal to even recognize the PRC was perhaps the most perplexing aspect of American policy for Asian observers to understand. Writing to a British correspondent in late November, Panikkar, now ensconced as Indian ambassador in Beijing, asserted:

China is not prepared to wait to be recognised as a great power in the Far East: nor does she feel in the lest [sic] frightened by American air power, [the] atom bomb or

---

[109] Kennan memorandum for Acheson, 21 August 1950, 'Chronological, 1950 (6)', box 34, records of the PPS, 1947–53, RG 59, NARA.
[110] Acheson, *Present at the Creation*, 445–6; see also Wilson D. Miscamble, *George F. Kennan and the Making of American Foreign Policy, 1947–1950* (Princeton, 1992), 325.

even the bluster of the Voice of America. She demands her place knowing that no one with the experience of Japan before them will attempt an invasion of China. Also her rear is guarded by a great power. So there is no use shirking the fact that America, whether she likes it or not, will have to realise that there has arisen a new power of the first magnitude, a power which does not suffer from the inherent weaknesses of Nippon's expansion. It is truly continental.

We are not passing out of the Korean crisis, but into it, and the preparations for a prolonged conflict are going ahead here. The issue has to be squarely faced. Is China to be a party in the settlement of the problems of the Far East (Japanese Treaty, Korea, Vietnam)? If so well and good – no war. If not, you have to fight and convince China, that being heathen Asiatics they are not allowed to have a voice in matters closest to them. Of course, from the point of view of the Americans they are only 'gooks', as I suppose we are 'wogs'. But the gooks and the wogs won't be persuaded so easily by the Yankee accents of the voice of America. So the West has to face the issue: whether in your fight against Communism, you want to raise the racial issue also against you. I know Britain realises this.[111]

It was, however, the 'racial issue' that was continually raised by the wide publicity given in Asia to the prevalence of segregation and discrimination in American life, while Truman's public airing of the possible use of nuclear weapons had also served to stoke up resentment and added to the lengthening list of grievances which some Asian observers held against the United States while its role in the region expanded.

The outpouring of concern from Asian and allied sources as the possibility arose of a repeat use of the bomb by the United States in the Far East helped to reinforce the caution that was shown by senior policy-makers in the administration when the prime US adversary was still the Soviet Union and American rearmament had yet to hit full stride. Anxiety over the reactions of that amorphous concept 'Asian opinion' was certainly present in the heated atmosphere of late 1950 but cannot be considered decisive in the outcome of debate. In one conversation held with his officials during the Attlee visit, Acheson noted the British felt that current US policy over Taiwan would alienate 'the Asians', who would probably 'neutralise themselves into a third force'. The Secretary of State 'countered [this] by saying that the Asians would probably do that anyway and he did not think we should pay a price for Asian opinion'.[112] In a similar vein, during the talks themselves, Acheson had responded to Attlee's point that nothing was 'more important than retaining the good opinion

[111] Panikkar to Guy Wint, 26 November 1950, FC1026/3, FO 371/92230.
[112] Memorandum of conversation in the Secretary's Office, 5 December 1950, 'Truman–Attlee discussions, December 1950', box 8, Korean War File, SMOF, Truman papers, HSTL.

of Asia' by remarking 'acidly' that 'the security of the United States was more important'.[113]

Though Acheson's dismissive response to concerns over how American policies might be received in Asia was partly indicative of his disdain for non-European peoples, it was also a product of the fact that the threat from Communist China at this stage of the Korean War was seen very much in terms of overt aggression and use of force. In such circumstances, the winning of Asian goodwill could be construed as secondary to the requirements of mounting the most effective military response to Communist tests of Western resolve. The allies that counted most for Acheson were, of course, the West European partners in NATO, on which the whole balance of power against the Soviet Union would depend, and whose support would also be critical in any expansion of the fighting with China. It would not, however, be possible to maintain this kind of position indefinitely, particularly as decolonization and the retreat of formal Western colonialism meant that more Asian states became significant actors in the region, and, even more pointedly, as the danger from Communism became increasingly seen in subversive terms, where influence was spread through more indirect means and the prospect of revolutionary and insurgent outbreaks became greater. In this environment, the political damage that might result from identification with racism, or showing indifference to the loss of Asian lives, was a consideration to be continually weighed. What is striking about the comments of so many US officials and commentators (and their British counterparts) is how entrenched by late 1950 had become the belief that nuclear use in Asia would have such adverse political effects: the view of many Western officials was clearly that, in the five years since 1945, Asian perceptions of nuclear use against Japan had become thoroughly informed with the belief that this was an act with a racist dimension. Moreover, discussion and planning for nuclear use was considered characteristic of the attitudes of Western dominance that had been exhibited in the region over the preceding decades. The 'new Asia' that was emerging with the demise of formal colonialism would, it was widely felt, instinctively criticize any Western resort to the methods of mass destruction warfare, and it was this 'new Asia' which was beginning to position itself away from the militarized and entrenched mentalities that the Korean War had done so much to foster.

[113] Quoted in Beisner, *Acheson*, 419.

3 Securing the East Asian frontier: stalemate in Korea and the Japanese peace treaty

The idea of the atomic bomb as a weapon of last resort, to be used only when national survival was considered at stake and all other means to prevent defeat or achieve victory in general war were deemed inadequate, was undermined, though not subverted completely, by the intervention of Chinese forces in the Korean War. Planning for all-out war with the Soviet Union increasingly relied on the use of nuclear weapons in Europe to offset Soviet conventional strength; in the standard picture of the time, the advance of dozens of Red Army divisions would be met with a series of shattering atomic blows at the centres of Russian power. By 1950, Strategic Air Command (SAC) was also beginning to redirect its targeting priorities to Soviet nuclear facilities and the airfields that might be used to launch Moscow's small stockpile of atomic bombs. In this overall context then, the strategic value of Korea in any general war with the Soviet Union had always been considered dubious by the JCS, and limited hostilities on the East Asian mainland served to tie down valuable resources that could be better deployed to more decisive areas. At the same time, the psychological and emotional shock that had been registered by the entry of China into the war, and the powerful images that were conveyed of mass 'oriental' armies overwhelming vastly outnumbered Western forces, generated strong impulses for the crude use of nuclear supremacy to redress the military balance in the Far East, even though, according to many evaluations, vital national interests were not imperilled. One opinion poll conducted in early December 1950, and so before the startling setbacks to MacArthur's forces had been fully absorbed, showed 52 per cent of respondents favouring the use of the atomic bomb against China in the event of war (though with 7 per cent of these 'as a last resort'), as opposed to 38 per cent against.[1] Bernard Brodie, who had just begun his brief period as an adviser to the Air Staff on targeting concepts, and whose influence on strategic thought was becoming significant, complained in

---

[1] 'The Quarter's Polls', *Public Opinion Quarterly*, 15, 1, Spring 1951, 168. See also Foot, *Wrong War*, 25, and *passim*.

December 1950 that, 'We have thus far given the Chinese every possible assurance that they could intervene with impunity … [We] should begin publicizing right now the fact that strategic bombing does not necessarily mean mass slaughter. All the gasping of horror which occurs every time the use of the atomic bomb is mentioned is extremely harmful to us politically and diplomatically.'[2] The clamour to hit back at China with the most powerful weapon in the American armoury raised the immediate issue of how the bomb might be used in the circumstances that were faced on the Korean peninsula.

Yet for Truman, ever mindful of the atomic attacks against cities he had sanctioned in 1945, the bomb was instinctively felt to be a weapon of 'mass destruction', whose very existence represented an underlying threat to civilization.[3] His press conference remarks of November 1950, where he had talked about its effects on 'innocent men, women, and children who have nothing whatever to do with the military aggression', was indicative of the President's basic attitude, while his handling of the issue in his talks with Attlee showed that he did not regard the current situation in Korea as sufficiently grave to warrant consideration of possible use.[4] The realization that the taboo that seemed to surround nuclear weapons, and the greater sense of vulnerability felt by allied nations who were physically closer to the Soviet Union, represented serious inhibitors on American freedom of action was actually becoming more widespread in some quarters. In late January 1951, Stuart Symington, the Chairman of the National Security Resources Board, had tried to argue in the NSC that possession of the atomic bomb was a 'political ace', but Acheson replied that it was, by contrast, a 'political liability', whose threatened use would 'frighten our allies to death'.[5] For military planners also, as well as members of the State Department, as we have seen, attacks against Chinese urban targets had been rejected as wasteful of the US atomic stockpile, likely to result in worldwide condemnation, and could trigger a strong Soviet response, with subsequent escalation to general war then a serious possibility. The nature of the fighting and terrain in Korea meant that appropriate military targets were difficult to identify, and there was a complete absence of tactical doctrine which might accompany the use of the bomb as a 'battlefield' weapon, with strategic air power theorists of Second World War pedigree having monopolized thinking about its

[2] Quoted in Kaplan, *Wizards*, 47–8.
[3] See Broscious, 'Longing for International Control', 17–20, 34–5.
[4] See, for example, Rusk's recollections about Truman's reactions to JCS talk of using nuclear weapons in Korea if the Chinese entered the war, in Dean Rusk, *As I Saw It* (New York, 1990), 126.
[5] Quoted in Dingman, 'Atomic Diplomacy', 69.

employment against the industrial and military heartland of the anticipated Soviet enemy; the results of its use in Korea, therefore, might be
inconclusive, undermining the role of the atomic bomb as an 'ultimate'
deterrent against Communist aggression elsewhere.

Even as these evaluations were being made, however, technological
developments began to suggest that smaller-scale use of tactical nuclear
weapons might be an increasingly realistic proposition. Improvements in
weapon design meant that lighter bombs with yields equivalent to or lower
than the 12–18 kiloton weapons used against Japan in 1945 could now be
carried by specially adapted fighter-bomber aircraft and delivered against
targets which could be defined as more strictly military, such as airfields,
troop concentrations and ports, while the US Army began to show
heightened interest in the use of smaller yield nuclear weapons for battlefield purposes.[6] Speculation about the new range of weaponry became rife
after an interview given by General Collins to *US News and World Report* in
February 1951 when he revealed that the army would soon have available
atomic artillery shells. The following month, MacArthur had received a
report entitled 'Tactical Employment of Atomic Weapons' from a special
Johns Hopkins University study group, which had looked at the way
atomic weapons might be used in Korea in support of ground operations.
In this it was asserted, in a cultural stereotype common for the period,
that, 'Given the general disregard of death among Asiatics compared with
Americans, [nuclear attack] might come to be accepted as a normal
hazard of war.'[7] There were some who were beginning to feel that the
self-imposed limitations on nuclear use that had featured in much public
comment about the bomb in the late 1940s were becoming ill suited to
current conditions in the Far East; in mid-1951, the JCS authorized
feasibility studies and exercises involving tactical atomic support for
ground operations in Korea, leading to simulated atomic bombing runs
in the autumn that went by the innocuous sounding name *Hudson
Harbor*.[8] Often expressed was the belief that American technological
superiority in the shape of possession of the atomic bomb would have to
be employed on Asian battlefields to redress the balance as Western
armies faced Communist weight of numbers on the ground. The support

[6] For background see David C. Elliot, 'Project Vista and Nuclear Weapons in Europe',
International Security, 11, 1, 1986, 163–83, which also shows SAC's hostility to any
proposals that challenged its tight hold over the nuclear role.
[7] Peter Hayes, Lyuba Zarsky and Walden Bello, *American Lake: Nuclear Peril in the Pacific*
(Ringwood, Victoria, 1986), 50, 61.
[8] See James F. Schnabel and Robert J. Watson, *History of the Joint Chiefs of Staff: The Joint
Chiefs of Staff and National Policy*, Vol. III: 2, *The Korean War*, Part 2 (Washington, DC,
1979), 613–14.

generated for MacArthur around the time of his dismissal from command of the UN forces in Korea in April 1951 – itself primarily the product of his restless insubordination and refusal to accept the limits of his role – seemed to demonstrate how widespread was the desire to break free of the various constraints that had been drawn around the fighting on the Korean peninsula by the administration in Washington. Indeed, early polls after MacArthur's recall showed 56 per cent in favour of attacks against Chinese supply bases above the Yalu.[9]

Following the successful *Ranger* test series of smaller warheads at the new Nevada proving grounds in early 1951, Gordon Dean at the AEC became particularly enamoured of the possibilities presented by designs featuring lower yields and lighter weights. Having witnessed the furore generated by Truman's press conference remarks of November 1950, Dean was evidently sensitive to the need to assuage and reassure a wide body of opinion, international as well as domestic, that the new classes of weapons being worked on by the research laboratories were of a different order from those produced before. The need to find some new terminology to describe smaller yield weapons was a particular preoccupation, and Dean only finally fell back to the clinical word 'tactical' once the somewhat ridiculous alternatives (such as 'small bang weapons') had been rejected; this labelling, as he made clear, was 'for the purpose of securing the support after the attack of people in the Middle East, Western Europe, Asiatics generally and for that matter the people of this country'.[10] At the level of formal national security policy, the Joint Strategic Survey Committee and State Department officials agreed in August 1951 that the United States had to retain the freedom to use atomic weapons in localized conflicts if the military situation demanded.[11] One aide to the Joint Congressional Committee on Atomic Energy enthused that tactical atomic weapons were the 'natural armaments of numerically inferior but technologically superior nations. They are the natural answer to the armed hordes of the Soviet Union and its satellites … they will decisively help to shift the balance of military power toward the free world and against the slave world.' Though recognizing their massive potential in

---

[9] See Casey, *Selling the Korean War*, 240, and Mueller, *War, Presidents and Public Opinion*, 229–30; though Michael Schaller cautions that the mass crowds that greeted the general upon his return to the United States, and opinion polls registering strong disapproval of Truman's action in removing him, should not necessarily be seen as an indication of widespread support for his Asian strategy. See Schaller, *MacArthur*, 241–4.

[10] Entry for 12 July 1951, Anders (ed.), *Dean Diary*, 158–60.

[11] See paper prepared by the Joint Strategic Survey Committee and representatives of the Department of State, 3 August 1951, *FRUS, 1951, I: National Security Affairs; Foreign Economic Policy* (Washington, DC, 1979), 871.

this regard, the author, however, lamented the fact that so little progress had been made in devising a doctrine for their deployment and use by the armed services.[12]

Use of nuclear weapons against targets such as airfields in Manchuria had actually been seen as a possibility earlier in the year at the very time when MacArthur was finally dismissed. In early April 1951, the UN Command in Korea had faced a fresh crisis as the Chinese prepared to launch their long-heralded spring offensive, and some US intelligence sources asserted that Communist air strength was being assembled north of the Yalu ready for an overwhelming assault. Fearing a surprise strike on UN ground forces and airfields in Korea, the JCS asked that MacArthur be given authorization to retaliate against the Manchurian airbases if his forces were subjected to a 'major attack' by air. As it transpired, MacArthur's incendiary and insubordinate letter to the Republican House Minority Leader, Joseph Martin, had just been leaked to the press, and on 6 April Truman and his advisers discussed what action to take against the recalcitrant Far East commander. Immediately after this meeting, the President also ordered the transfer of nine complete atomic weapons from AEC civilian control to military custody – the first time this step had been taken – so that a contingent of B-29 bombers could once more be sent to Guam. It is difficult to reconstruct Truman's thinking through the April crisis: he may have felt that the despatch of nuclear weapons to the Far East was a measure that could now be taken precisely because MacArthur's imminent removal meant that Washington would be able to exercise a surer grip on its theatre commander, or he may have wanted some insurance if MacArthur's relief was followed by a military disaster for which the UN Command was unprepared and where the administration would be assailed by its domestic critics. As Roger Dingman has argued, Truman could also have been signalling that despite the removal of MacArthur, he shared the thinking of the JCS regarding the measures that would have to be taken to ensure the security of US forces; MacArthur's removal may actually have been necessary to generate allied support for an expansion of the war to Manchuria, and to restore confidence in the chain of command from Washington if drastic action against China had to be taken.[13] On 22 April the Chinese launched their expected spring ground offensive, but air activity remained limited and although their forces advanced southward, they did so at a horrendous cost in casualties as the UN Command, now under Ridgway's steady overall control after MacArthur's dismissal on 11 April, absorbed and

---

[12] Memorandum by Mansfield for Brien McMahon, 15 August 1951, *ibid.*, 158–60.
[13] Dingman, 'Atomic Diplomacy', 74.

checked the attack. Nevertheless, Truman felt sufficiently concerned to order the despatch of a second group of B-29s to Guam at the end of the month, and a small SAC team was sent to Tokyo to plan possible nuclear strikes. Ridgway was also given some latitude in being able to launch air attacks against targets outside the Korean peninsula if his own forces were subject to a major air attack. The nuclear-armed B-29s finally returned home from Guam in June, the Chinese having broken off their offensive towards the end of the previous month, while the UN forces consolidated new defensive positions and settled down for a long and drawn-out attritional struggle.[14]

The April 1951 deployment raised once again important questions about the relationship between the political and military authorities, and the particular perspectives that they embraced, when it came to decisions over nuclear policy-making. When he learnt that the military might soon make a request over the transfer from the AEC of complete nuclear weapons, Dean was especially anxious, feeling that this was a step that should be handled with great care, warranting a debate in the full National Security Council once it had been considered by the select group on the NSC's Special Committee on Atomic Energy. Among the questions of concern to Dean was the subject of, 'What would be the effect upon the enemy of its use and the effect upon Western Europe and upon Asiatics generally who have felt that the "white man" picks only "yellow men" upon whom to drop bombs – this particular line having been exploited heavily by the Communists.'[15] This comment from Dean reflected what Samuel Cohen, an expert on tactical nuclear weapons who worked for the RAND Corporation, called a 'Hiroshima syndrome', something that was beginning to take hold among elements in the national security bureaucracy and involved a strong conviction that a repeat use of nuclear weapons in the Asian context would have disastrous political consequences.[16] Dean himself was adamant that AEC acquiescence in the transfer of complete nuclear weapons in no way signified advance approval for use and was determined that the Special Committee play a central role in assuring that several voices were heard in any decisions over the fate of the US nuclear stockpile, allowing proper discussion of State Department and AEC perspectives as well as more purely military judgements before a final presidential authorization to use could be given. In the event, Truman ordered Dean to carry out the transfer to military control without any discussion in

[14] Stueck, *Korean War*, 178–82, 185–9.
[15] Entry for 27 March 1951, Anders (ed.), *Dean Diary*, 129.
[16] Samuel Cohen, *The Truth About the Neutron Bomb* (New York, 1983), 33, and Tannenwald, *Nuclear Taboo*, 138–9.

the Special Committee, though assuring the AEC Chairman that it would be allowed a chance to explore the issues involved fully if a decision over use were to be made.[17] Some members of the bureaucracy were also inclined to question whether nuclear use would be appropriate to a crisis situation in the Far East. In one exercise undertaken in the middle of April by Carlton Savage of the PPS, and which also involved Nitze, it was argued that, 'While the atomic weapon is in some respects just another weapon in our national arsenal, its psychological impact is so great that use of it would doubtless precipitate general war, if war were not already under way. We are unlikely to use it, therefore, unless the vital security interests of the United States compel us to enter into general war with the Soviet Union.' If a major Communist air attack were launched against US forces in Korea, or there were Chinese attacks against US forces elsewhere in the region, Savage expected that the response would include air strikes and possibly some naval action against China proper. However, he did not anticipate that atomic weapons would be used as there were no suitable targets, except for 'three or four in Manchuria', and using them would 'help unite' the Chinese people against the United States.[18]

Towards the end of June 1951, the Soviet Union voiced its interest in seeing an armistice secured in Korea, and a flurry of diplomatic activity ensued as arrangements were finally made for talks to be convened between the major protagonists in the conflict. The resulting meetings between Communist and American negotiators which began the following month at Kaesong, before finally moving to Panmunjom, soon became stalemated over the vexed issue of repatriation of Communist prisoners of war. Fighting meanwhile continued, and with no prospect of any early resolution to the attritional nature of the struggle, further speculation was prompted that the new classes of tactical nuclear weapons could have special utility for the conflict. At one extreme were the visceral views of many Americans, such as the Republican Senator from Maine, Margaret Chase Smith (otherwise hailed for her 'declaration of conscience' against McCarthy), who maintained that if the armistice talks yielded no concrete results, the United States should 'drop the atomic bomb on these barbarians'.[19] In the more sober counsels of the AEC, the technological advances made by the weapons laboratories seemed to

---

[17] Entry for 6 April 1951, Anders (ed.), *Dean Diary*, 137; for a full exposition see Roger M. Anders, 'The Atomic Bomb and the Korean War: Gordon Dean and the Issue of Civilian Control', *Military Affairs*, 52, 1, 1988, 1–6.

[18] 'Circumstances under which the United States Would Be at War with the Soviet Union: Use of Nuclear Weapons', paper prepared by Savage, 12 April 1951, *FRUS, 1951, I*, 815, 819.

[19] Quoted in Stephen J. Whitfield, *The Culture of the Cold War*, 2nd edn (Baltimore, 1996), 6.

suggest that the shadow of Hiroshima could be lifted. This was the import of some of Gordon Dean's pronouncements from this period, to the extent that his previous firm adherence to the principle of civilian control, in the tradition of his predecessor Lilienthal, could be relaxed. Although aware of the dangers of a wider war, and that there would be State Department objections over such issues as the effect on '400,000 [*sic* – million?] people in the Middle East, ranging from Pakistan and India to Iran, with Nehru the most important', Dean believed that the American people would welcome effective nuclear use as the only way to break the Korean stalemate, noting how 'one of the real hurdles is that the A-bomb is associated in the minds of the people, and even in the minds of officials such as the President, with strategic targets, meaning specifically cities (Nagasaki and Hiroshima being the outstanding examples) in which civilians rather than military personnel would be the victims'.[20]

In a widely publicized speech, delivered at the University of Southern California in Los Angeles in October 1951, Dean announced that 'we are entering an era where our power to wage warfare with atomic devices is so great, even in comparison with the recent past, that our fundamental concepts of what atomic warfare is and what it might mean to us must undergo revolutionary change'. The types and variety of nuclear weapons now at American disposal, Dean confirmed, meant that they could be effectively used against the enemy's troops on the battlefield: 'with each passing day, our design and production progress is steadily adding to the number of situations in which atomic weapons can be tactically employed against military targets ... we are now at a place where we should give serious consideration to the use of an atomic weapon, provided it can be used effectively from a military standpoint'. This new way of thinking, Dean claimed, would hold the prospect of stopping 'these endless nibbling aggressions' without bringing on wholesale atomic devastation.[21] Few doubted that Dean was suggesting that tactical nuclear weapons could prove a way to break the Korean impasse. As if on cue, Senators Harry P. Cain (Republican, Washington), Edwin C. Johnson (Democrat, Colorado) and Bourke B. Hickenlooper (Republican, Iowa), the latter two members of the Joint Congressional Committee on Atomic Energy, pressed for American military commanders to be given the authority to use nuclear weapons against Communist forces in Korea whenever they deemed it militarily necessary to do so. Dean also felt that the new technological developments changed the moral position over the use of

---

[20] Entry for 12 July 1951, Anders (ed.), *Dean Diary*, 158–60.
[21] 'Dean Sees New Era in Atom Weapons', *NYT*, 6 October 1951; and see also Anders (ed.), *Dean Diary*, 276–85, and Tannenwald, *Nuclear Taboo*, 137–8.

nuclear weapons, so that 'we can with complete justification treat the tactical atom – divested of the awesome cloak of destruction which surrounds it in its strategic role – in the same manner as other weapons are treated'.[22] Removal of the moral stigma attached to weapons of mass destruction would be welcomed by some: one official in the State Department's Office of International Information found Dean's speech was the most important since that announcing the Marshall Plan, as it promised a time when the targets for atomic weapons would be confined to military formations rather than civilian populations, which 'takes us off the Hiroshima–Nagasaki moral guilt hook for good', and hoped that a publicity campaign emphasizing this point could be launched.[23]

In fact, publicity issues surrounding nuclear weapons began to receive much greater attention from the Truman administration as the size of the nuclear stockpile began an enormous expansion under the programmes set in motion by the acceptance of NSC 68's prescriptions. In October 1951, spurred again by uncomfortable memories of the President's press conference performance the previous November, the newly formed Psychological Strategy Board (PSB) commissioned a staff study on the procedures surrounding the release of public statements and information on the topic of what were euphemistically described as 'novel weapons'. 'Indiscriminate' statements about atomic weapons, the resulting report warned, served to weaken confidence in the free world, and 'encourage neutralism and stimulate the urge to stay out of the East–West conflict. They identify the U.S. with war and destruction and help Communist propagandists to fasten the "war-monger" label on us.' The general guidance it was recommended should be issued included, *inter alia*, the line that such weapons were deployed for defensive purposes, and that the United States stood for control of armaments and against 'city-bombing' in principle, and was in favour of greater target selectivity. Advice for handling these subjects when dealing with the 'Asiatic nations' was to reduce 'the effects of the moral guilt Asiatics habitually fix upon us' through simply avoiding the subject, and if it came up emphasizing the applicability of atomic weapons to any fighting in Europe but the 'lack of strategic targets in Asia'.[24]

---

[22] 'Senators Urge Use in Korea', and 'Dean Idea to Wage Atom War in Field Held Significant', *NYT*, 6, 7 October 1951.

[23] Memorandum from Llewellyn White for Charles P. Arnot, 8 October 1951, box 37, Psychological Strategy Board (PSB) Files, SMOF, Truman papers, HSTL.

[24] See memorandum for the Executive Secretary of the NSC, 'PSB Action on Publicity with Respect to Certain American Weapons', 27 February 1952, and PSB D-17, 'Staff Study on Publicity with Respect to Novel Weapons', 14 November 1951, box 37, PSB Files, SMOF, Truman papers, HSTL.

Elsewhere, securing the support of the 'Asiatic nations' for American Far Eastern policy was becoming a preoccupation of the Truman administration, now that the immediate crisis of the Chinese intervention in Korea had passed and the fighting front stabilized. Indeed, the lineaments of American policy, which had been in a state of flux since Acheson's National Press Club speech of January 1950 and thrown into further confusion by the onset of the Korean War, were finally becoming somewhat clearer. On 17 May 1951, Truman endorsed NSC 48/5, a comprehensive statement on 'United States Objectives, Policies and Courses of Action in Asia', which superseded NSC 48/2 of December 1949. In boiler-plate language, NSC 48/5 proclaimed that Soviet policy appeared to be directed towards 'bringing the mainland of Eastern Asia and eventually Japan and the other principal off-shore islands in the Western Pacific under Soviet control, primarily through the exploitation of the resources of Communist China'. This, the United States would strive to prevent by opposing Communist aggression where encountered, reducing the power and influence of the Soviet Union in Asia, undermining the Chinese Communist regime, and supporting and promoting 'stable and self-sustaining' non-Communist governments. These aims would be partly fulfilled by weakening Communist strength on the battlefront in Korea, encouraging the remaining forces of resistance within China, and denying occupation of Taiwan by Communist forces. It was also considered imperative to prevent a Communist victory in Vietnam, through fear that the effects would ripple across to Burma and down to Thailand. The over-stretch of American resources though, not least through the demands of the Korean War itself, meant that Washington should not commit its own forces to the defence of South East Asia. At the same time, the United States had to avoid steps which might expand the fighting in Korea into general war with the Soviet Union, or broaden hostilities with China into other parts of the region, particularly if this threatened to occur without allied support.[25] These were important restraints on American behaviour. They indicated the degree to which the risks of a general war involving atomic weapons with the Soviet Union, the need for support from European allies when NATO was still in its infancy and perceptions of the current limits of American capabilities if faced with an expansion of hostilities operated as determining influences on the administration's policies in the Far East.

[25] NSC 48/5 and attached NSC Staff Study, 'United States Objectives, Policies and Courses of Action in Asia', 17 May 1951, *FRUS, 1951, VI: Asia and the Pacific*, Part 1 (Washington, DC, 1977), 31–63.

Nonetheless, NSC 48/5 has rightly attracted additional attention for the recommendations it contained to continue to prepare plans for direct action against the PRC, including a naval blockade and attacks on Chinese Communist targets outside Korea, along with utilization of Chinese Nationalist forces, if Beijing launched another aggression elsewhere in Asia (the most probable areas being seen as Indochina and the Taiwan Strait), in what some have seen as a qualified departure from the limited war approach adopted in Korea.[26] This line was endorsed, of course, at the very moment when the administration was fending off hostile Republican critics of its policies in the Far East at the MacArthur hearings before the Senate Armed Services and Foreign Relations Committees. Here, the Chairman of the JCS, General Bradley, argued against any enlargement of the war, intoning the famous lines, 'Red China is not the powerful nation seeking to dominate the world. Frankly, in the opinion of the Joint Chiefs of Staff, this strategy would involve us in the wrong war, at the wrong time, and with the wrong enemy.'[27] Bradley, along with senior administration officials, had offered their testimony partly to underline and discredit MacArthur's parochial viewpoint that if left unchecked would have committed American resources to the mammoth task of defeating China in an all-out war. Yet despite these cool evaluations of strategic priorities, as we have seen, there were several occasions during the winter of 1950–1 when the JCS and leading figures in the administration were ready to contemplate an intensification of pressures against Beijing that might have led to this very outcome, making their belligerent and frustrated stance not entirely dissimilar from that displayed by their maverick commander in the Far East. Even in his careful testimony at the MacArthur hearings, Bradley had cautioned that while 'every effort should be made to settle the present conflict without extending it outside Korea', if such a settlement was not forthcoming, 'other measures may have to be taken'.[28] The hearings had nevertheless given the administration a crucial public opportunity to make a comprehensive case for limited war, for virtually the first time since the Chinese intervention, while opinion polls tended to show that the general public remained wary of all-out war against China when the Soviet threat appeared far more potent.[29]

---

[26] For comments about action against China, see, e.g., Foot, *Wrong War*, 147–8; Gaddis, *Strategies*, 122.

[27] Bradley testimony, 15 May 1951, quoted in Allen Guttmann (ed.), *Korea and the Theory of Limited War* (Boston, 1967), 37.

[28] *Ibid.*, 38.   [29] Casey, *Selling the Korean War*, 260–3.

Also of significance in NSC 48/5, however, was mention of some of the more general difficulties faced by American policy-makers in Asia. The NSC staff study which had yielded the analysis contained in the main document had been even more explicit about the threat from the PRC which, with the help of the Soviet Union, sought to extend its 'hegemony over Asia' by 'eliminating Western power and influence from the whole [of the] Far East'. In confronting the problem of China, there was some solace to be found from what were pictured as traditional Asian suspicions of Chinese intentions (particularly pronounced in Indonesia and the Philippines), but the recent successes of Chinese arms presented profound psychological problems for mobilizing support behind American policies: 'The effect upon the Chinese themselves and upon Asians generally of the prestige won by the Chinese Communists through their successful conquest of China must not be overlooked. Efforts by India and other Asian nations to rationalize the Communist revolution in China as basically a nationalist movement, and to establish friendly relations with the Peiping regime, probably stems in some degree from a basic admiration for the achievement of power by a regime which is Asian, revolutionary, and antagonistic to the West.'[30] In other words, the United States, because of its assumed role as the new standard-bearer for the West, would have much work to do to rally regional opinion behind an approach that was unremittingly hostile to Beijing when the Chinese Communist leadership seemed to represent the new Asia that was casting off domination by the imperialist powers. 'The United States,' warned NSC 48/5, 'faces a formidable political and propaganda task in establishing relations with Asia on a basis of mutual confidence and common interest, and in influencing the intense national-ism to take a direction harmonious with the interests of the free world.'[31]

As we have seen, compounding this problem was the fact that Washington's commitment to the Chiang Kai-shek Government on Taiwan, as well as assistance to the French military campaign in Indochina (to the tune of $316.5 million in the fiscal year 1951), was doing much to add to the sense that, despite their protestations of sym-pathy for Asian nationalism, Americans found it difficult to adapt to the new realities that had transformed the region since the end of the war against Japan. Having recently conferred with other British representa-tives, in December 1950 Sir John Sterndale Bennett, now filling the role of Deputy Commissioner General for South East Asia, was lamenting that

if the high purpose and material strength of the United States are our hope, it must regretfully be said that the methods of the United States are often our despair. It is

---

[30] Annex 1 to NSC 48/5, 17 May 1951, *FRUS, 1951, VI*, part 1, 43.   [31] *Ibid.*, 44.

their failure to appreciate the limits of intervention which are likely to be endured by any nation in its internal affairs that constitutes today one of the most difficult problems in Far Eastern, and indeed in world, policy. For over half a century America by her 'Open Door' policy and her encouragement of philanthropic enterprise had gradually acquired the position of China's friend and champion. The fact that after her assistance to China in the war against Japan, she is pilloried today as China's greatest enemy is due to her failure to appreciate the feelings which she aroused by her continued and uncritical support for Chiang Kai-shek in China's internal struggle even after he had obviously ceased to be the effective ruler of the country. This and her equally uncritical support of such discredited national figureheads as Syngman Rhee handicap American policy in the East, and particularly in India, and do much to weaken its approach.[32]

The successful American attempt to label and condemn the PRC as an aggressor in Korea through passage of a divisive resolution at the UN in January 1951, as well as heralding the imposition of wider economic sanctions, was seen by many observers as an initiative which could obstruct the path to early negotiations for a cease-fire. Compounding this was Dean Rusk's strident denunciation, in a speech delivered to the China Institute in New York in May 1951, of the 'Peiping regime' as a 'colonial Russian government – a Slavic Manchukuo on a larger scale. It is not the Government of China. It will not pass the first test. It is not Chinese.' By denying the agency of the Chinese leadership and denigrating them as the puppets of the Kremlin, Rusk not only signalled Washington's unremitting hostility to the PRC and a hardening of support for Chiang but also indicated that the United States rejected the outcome of the Communist Chinese revolution, one of the key developments taken by many as marking the arrival of a new Asia. In private, Rusk had a more nuanced view of the Sino-Soviet relationship, and the speech was primarily designed for domestic political consumption as the MacArthur hearings progressed and Acheson remained under intense fire from Republican critics, but such utterances left a lasting impression of an intransigent and backward-looking American policy.[33]

In terms of the anti-colonial credentials of the United States, moreover, the positive impression created by the granting of independence to the Philippines had been quickly overtaken by the perception that the weak and corrupt governments in power since then had been beholden to American business interests. The presidential election held in November 1949, which resulted in a victory for the incumbent Elpidio

[32] Singapore (Sterndale Bennett) to FO, No. 82, 29 December 1950, F10345/1G, FO 371/92067, TNA.
[33] See Stueck, *Korean War*, 151–7, 193; Warren I. Cohen, *Dean Rusk* (Totowa, NJ, 1980), 62–7; Rusk, *As I Saw It*, 172–4; Casey, *Selling the Korean War*, 255.

Quirino and his Liberal Party, was notable chiefly for the blatant fraud and vote-rigging on display. Though Washington despaired of Quirino – described by Acheson as a man who 'would prefer to see his country ruined rather than compromise with his own insatiable ego' – American policy-makers felt they had little option but to save his government from financial collapse in late 1950 as it struggled, amid much bureaucratic ineptitude, to overcome the Huk rebellion on Luzon. Not the least of American concerns, alongside the protection of commercial interests, was for the security of their air and naval bases in the archipelago, which since the 'loss' of China had assumed a new importance for the projection of American power into South East Asia and the defence of the offshore island chain.[34]

Adding to the picture of American alignment with the forces of reaction was Washington's attachment to the flimsy claims of the American-recognized Bao Dai Government of the Associated State of Vietnam to embody the Vietnamese people's aspirations for self-determination and genuine national independence. The senior US diplomatic representative in Indochina, Donald R. Heath, was admitting to his superiors in early 1951, in a rare moment of candour, that the only Vietnamese figure to enjoy any amount of national prestige was Ho Chi Minh. Even though privately many US officials had come to the conclusion that the Bao Dai Government would have to make way for one with a more broadly based appeal, Washington still had to work through the French colonial authorities in pressing their point of view, while the need for French co-operation regarding the defence of Western Europe militated against adopting an over-critical stance in Indochina.[35] Charlton Ogburn, the Regional Planning Adviser in the Far East Bureau of the State Department, was highlighting the problems of a growing gulf between the United States and the peoples and states of the region in January 1951, explaining:

The cause of the free world in Asia has become not an Asian cause (which it certainly should be, since it is the Asians and not we who are directly menaced) but an American cause in which we are pleading for adherents and turning ourselves inside out to keep afloat those we have. Those we have lined up with us in Asia have none of the sense of being the advance guard of a great and noble cause of which we are the base and Fatherland. Those Asians who give evidence that they *do* feel they are making history and have undergone sacrifices for great objectives and who evidently feel that they *are* moved by impelling ideals are the very ones we have

[34] See Karnow, *In Our Image*, 330–6, 344–6. Despite the prevalence of American influence in the Philippines, local political elites, not least Quirino himself, still had substantial latitude to manipulate the American presence for their own ends; for this key point, see Cullather, *Illusions of Influence*, 72–97.
[35] Gibbons, *U.S. Government and the Vietnam War*, Part 1, 88–93.

helped least and who are most wary of enlisting in a cause which they conceive of as an American snare. It is ironical but none the less true that Asians fighting on the Communist side with Mao and Ho, whom we feel the Asians should regard as the exponents of tyranny, have the inspiring sense of fighting for national freedom, while in the camps of Chiang, Quirino, and Bao Dai there is a strong feeling that we must see them through because they are serving *our* cause.

Ogburn's fundamental point was that the basic emphasis of American policy on anti-Communism and containment made it seem that Asian leaders extolling similar ideas were simply following Washington's own self-interest, rather than the interests of their own peoples, where issues of economic justice or continuing colonial influence might be of more immediate concern.[36]

The fighting in Korea, where Western, white soldiers, harnessing the superior firepower offered by their industrialized societies, inflicted a grievous toll of casualties on an Asian enemy and innocent civilian bystanders, was also a constant source of tension in relations with concerned Asian spectators. One Japanese commentator, who had spent three weeks in India during March 1951 and spoken with many Indian politicians, students, lawyers and journalists, came away with the impression that anti-American feeling, already aroused during the summer of 1950, remained strong and widely held. This came from many different sources, including resentment at the US occupation of a fellow Asian country (Japan), its pro-Pakistan stance over Kashmir, capitalist system, interventions in other countries, and that 'Americans have racial hatred. They used [the] atom bomb against Japanese and not against [the] Germans when they had one completed before Germany surrendered. Americans are dropping bombs mercilessly in Korea because they are Asians.'[37] The idea that modern 'mass destruction' methods were reserved for Asians was reinforced by the widespread use of napalm by the Americans. In February 1951, the American Consul in Bombay reported that one weekly news magazine, the *Forum*, published an editorial which described napalm as a weapon 'as horrible as the atomic bomb' producing thousands of non-combatant casualties in Korea and where Mustang pilots regarded its use as a 'favourite sport': 'When it comes to warring with an Asiatic nation, we know by now that the European nations [*sic*] are viciously ruthless in their methods of destruction and killing. When it comes to the testing of the atomic bomb, it was not the European civilians of Nazi Germany that became the victims of this

---

[36] Ogburn memorandum for Rusk, 15 January 1951, *FRUS, 1951, VI*, Part 1, 7–8.
[37] Takizo Matsumoto, 'Observations in India', enclosed in Tokyo to Department of State, No. 1482, 24 April 1951, 691.94/4–2451, CDF, RG 59, NARA.

most atrocious reign of death, but the innocent civilians of Nagasaki and Hiroshima. And they talk of Belsens and Dachaus!' With the United States having also provided napalm to the French for use in their campaign against the Viet Minh in Indochina, the purpose of the Americans was seen as being employment of Asian battlegrounds as 'the laboratories for their new-fangled war-weapons, with millions of Asians as guinea pigs'.[38] Contemporary appraisals of the insurgencies in Indochina and Malaya were not unnoticing of the racial elements they could carry and of the consequent need to use locally raised troops against the Communist enemy; an American survey of the military assistance requirements of the region, compiled at the end of 1950, carried the blunt observation that, 'Much of the stigma of colonialism can be removed if, where necessary, yellow men will be killed by yellow men rather than by white men alone.'[39] In a similar fashion, British Foreign Office officials had concluded that the 'use of white troops in operations against Asiatic guerrillas will tend to arouse a felling [sic] of solidarity with the guerrillas among Asiatics in the area'.[40] This consideration was one reason why American military assistance in Indochina put such a strong onus on building up a Vietnamese National Army, which might give greater credence to the role of the Bao Dai Government in prosecuting the war, although here US officials faced obstacles from the French insistence that they control the supply, administration and training of Vietnamese units.[41]

Among the most significant recommendations made by NSC 48/5 in May 1951 was that the United States should seek 'urgently' to conclude a peace settlement with Japan in order to end the occupation and restore sovereignty to the Japanese Government. Indeed, for many American officials, Japan represented the crucial arena for demonstrating American benevolence, and for counteracting the suspicions that were commonly held towards US intentions. Possessing great potential industrial and military strength, Japan was of fundamental importance to the geopolitical features of American containment strategy in the Far East, but whose progress towards a democratic, prosperous and stable society

---

[38] 'Behind the Headlines', *Forum*, 25 February 1951, enclosed in American Consulate General, Bombay, to State Department, No. 742, 27 February 1951, 711.5611/2–2751, CDF, RG 59, NARA. French aircraft first began to use American-supplied napalm bombs against the Viet Minh attackers of Vinh Yen in January 1951; see Ronald H. Spector, *Advice and Support: The Early Years of the U.S. Army in Vietnam, 1941–1960* (Washington, DC, 1983), 136–7.

[39] Final Report of the Joint Mutual Development and Assistance Program (MDAP) Survey Mission, 6 December 1950, *FRUS, 1950, VI*, 164–73.

[40] Russia Committee paper RC/122/50, 'The Effect of the Situation in Korea on South East Asia', Annex B, 10 August 1950, FZ10381/8G, FO 371/84529, TNA.

[41] Spector, *Advice and Support*, 131–4, 153–5.

after the upheavals of the first half of the century was also symbolic of the benefits that aid from and partnership with the United States could bring. Various drafts of a Japanese Peace Treaty had been attempted by the State Department on a desultory basis since the autumn of 1949 but had run into the firm opposition of the JCS to any agreement which might inhibit the freedom of action enjoyed by American forces operating from US bases, as well as the reluctance of several of the wartime belligerents, both Asian and Western, to hasten any normalization of relations with a Japan which was still reviled for its recent behaviour in the Pacific and not yet felt to be purged of militarism.[42] Nevertheless, despite constant stalling from the JCS, some progress had been made in treaty-drafting over the first few months of 1950 before the outbreak of the Korean War interrupted work; ultimately it was to be the latter event that acted as a catalyst and motor for ending the occupation regime in Japan.

One highly significant individual soon deeply involved in this process was John Foster Dulles, who had been enlisted by the Truman administration in April 1950 as a Special Consultant in the State Department in order to cloak Far Eastern policy with the aura of bipartisanship. With his immense experience and reputation in international negotiations, by the late 1940s Dulles had achieved notoriety as one of the Republican Party's leading spokesmen on foreign policy, and though his intense ambition to become Secretary of State had been thwarted by Republican defeat in the 1948 presidential election, he now seized the chance to further enhance his credentials. Though Acheson had already developed a healthy contempt for Dulles that was to infuse their relationship throughout the 1950s, he had been advised by Senator Arthur Vandenberg, as well as by Rusk, to appoint Dulles in order to mark a sharp shift in the State Department's approach to Asian affairs after Philip Jessup had been hounded out of his advisory post by the China lobby. The Secretary of State could see that Dulles might prove useful in shielding the administration from similar attacks from the Republican right, and this uncomfortable but realistic political calculation was also shared by Truman.[43] Dulles brought to his early views on the Far East the conviction that 'the 450,000,000 people in China have fallen under leadership that is violently anti-American, and that takes its inspiration and guidance from Moscow',

[42] See Beisner, *Acheson*, 208–9.

[43] Dulles himself also planted the suggestion of his appointment with Acheson through State Department intermediaries; for the background, see H. Alexander Smith Oral History, p. 193, Butler Library, Columbia University; Ronald Pruessen, *John Foster Dulles: The Road to Power* (New York, 1982), 435–6; Beisner, *Acheson*, 210; Ronald McGlothlen, *Controlling the Waves: Dean Acheson and U.S. Foreign Policy in Asia* (New York, 1993), 43–5.

and that the 'black plague' of Soviet Communism was intent on fuelling anti-colonial revolutionary nationalism which it would harness to its own ends of eventual world domination. His sermons on the need for spiritual regeneration in the West spilled over into a belief that Christianity might hold a key role in the peaceful transition from imperial rule to freedom in the colonized world, where he alleged that the missionary influence had in the past 'curbed and offset' the tendency for white Europeans and Americans to adopt attitudes of racial superiority and engage in exploitation.[44]

Soon after his appointment, Dulles was given the formidable assignment of crafting a Japanese peace treaty, a task which he turned to with alacrity, not least as he saw the consequences of failure as so serious.[45] Indeed, Dulles had quickly formed the opinion that the Communist attack in Korea, naturally instigated by the Soviet Union, was in part directed at American efforts to move forward the rehabilitation of Japan, making renewed efforts to this end all the more essential, telling Acheson 'if matters drift because of total preoccupation with the Korean war we may lose in Japan more than we can gain in Korea'.[46] In September 1950, Truman announced that the United States was ready to proceed with formal negotiations with the Japanese Government and allied nations, with a view to ending the occupation, though conclusion of the final peace settlement would have to wait until a favourable resolution to the fighting in Korea. By the end of 1950, however, with no early end to the war in sight, and with the Chinese now actively participating, there was an underlying concern that divisions between Asia from the West were widening, with China exercising a magnetic pull through its anti-imperialist fervour. The Pentagon wanted to delay any final treaty while priority was given to Japanese rearmament, but State Department officials and American diplomats began to argue that one way to show Asia that the United States could treat the peoples of the region on the basis of respect and equality was to end the occupation and restore a full measure of sovereignty to the Japanese authorities. Furthermore, this would, it was reasoned, be the best means to ensure a friendly and co-operative Japan as a secure rear base for the American military effort being waged on the Korean peninsula. Breaking the Japanese Government's desire to extend

[44] See Pruessen, *Dulles*, 441, 447–8.
[45] For the treaty-making process, see Takeshi Igarashi, 'Dean Acheson and the Japanese Peace Treaty', in Douglas Brinkley (ed.), *Dean Acheson and the Making of U.S. Foreign Policy* (New York, 1993), 133–58; Seigen Miyasato, 'John Foster Dulles and the Peace Settlement with Japan', in Richard H. Immerman (ed.), *John Foster Dulles and the Diplomacy of the Cold War* (Princeton, 1990), 189–212.
[46] Quoted in Pruessen, *Dulles*, 457.

its trading ties with the Chinese mainland now also became necessary, and new outlets secured for Japanese industry and commerce found in the rich maritime crescent of South East Asia.[47]

Dulles was particularly insistent that further progress on the treaty was vital, and, aware of the potential for the conflict with Communist China to divide Asia from the West, that the United States had to demonstrate it was capable of creating partnerships and friendships with Asian nations.[48] As early as 1947, it had been established in the State Department that any final settlement should be of a non-punitive nature if future anti-American sentiment were to be avoided, and early treaty drafts had included full restoration of sovereignty to the Japanese Government. This was all in accord with Dulles's belief that German treatment under the Treaty of Versailles had generated the aggressive and revisionist drives that had led to the Second World War in Europe, and that second-class status would similarly never be accepted by the Japanese. He was aware of the importance, as he told the British Ambassador in Washington, of 'not treating [the Japanese] as an inferior people'.[49] In early January 1951, Dulles tried to put new momentum into the process, warning that, 'The Japanese people and their leaders are coming increasingly to feel the danger of throwing in their lot with us in view of the fact that Communist power seems to be closing in upon them, and also upon their normal sources of food supply from French Indo-China, Siam and Burma.' Delays in pushing the peace settlement had not worked to American advantage, and it would now be necessary to negotiate the contents of the treaty rather than to simply lay down a series of vital conditions which could not be compromised.[50] The result was the despatch of Dulles on a preliminary mission to Japan as the President's Special Representative to discuss the terms of a treaty with MacArthur and leading Japanese figures; his principal goal, as set out in the letter of instructions he received from Truman, was to 'secure adherence of the Japanese nation to the free nations of the world and to assure that it will play its full part in resisting the further expansion of communist imperialism'.[51] Despite the fact that he had received Marshall's acquiescence to the conclusion of a peace treaty,

---

[47] Michael Schaller, 'Securing the Great Crescent: Occupied Japan and the Origins of Containment in Southeast Asia', *Journal of American History*, 69, 2, 1982, 392–414; Walter LaFeber, *The Clash: U.S.–Japanese Relations throughout History* (New York, 1997), 294–5.

[48] Roger Buckley, *US–Japan Alliance Diplomacy, 1945–1990* (Cambridge, 1992), 38.

[49] See memorandum of a conversation between Dulles and Franks, 12 January 1951, *FRUS, 1951, VI*, part 1, 793–4. See also John Swenson-Wright, *Unequal Allies? United States Security and Alliance Policy toward Japan, 1945–1960* (Stanford, 2005), 58–9.

[50] See Dulles to Acheson, 4 January 1951, *FRUS, 1951, VI*, Part 1, 781–3.

[51] Draft letter, Truman to Dulles, 10 January 1951, *ibid.*, 789.

with an accompanying security treaty before the end of fighting in Korea, Acheson remained pessimistic and could not see post-occupation relations with Japan developing in a smooth and friendly fashion.[52] In May 1951, the Secretary of State was expressing the bleak view that he could see 'nothing but disaster for us in Japan when the occupation is over'.[53] Among the threats detected to Japanese co-operation with the United States by U. Alexis Johnson, the head of the State Department's Office of Northeast Asian Affairs, were the 'racial and cultural affinities of Japan for the presently Communist-dominated areas of Asia' nearby, and 'the revival of the inherent Japanese spirit of nationalism and hypersensitivity to real or imagined discrimination which will again constitute a fundamental source of difficulty in relations, in particular between the "white" nations and Japan'. The Communists, Johnson predicted, could be expected to attempt to 'drive a wedge' between the United States and Japan by exploiting such issues.[54]

It thus became doubly essential, in the minds of many State Department officials, to restore a full measure of sovereignty to Japan when negotiating the peace treaty, and that the Japanese authorities were readily accepting of its final provisions. '[The] United States position in Japan becomes ... untenable, and a liability rather than an asset,' Dulles warned later in the year, 'if the Japanese people preponderantly resent it and want it to end, and if it can only be preserved by a show of force as against the Japanese.'[55] The final horse-trading over the treaty terms between Dulles and the Japanese Prime Minister, Yoshida Shigeru, saw an outcome reached involving a modest agreement over reparations linked to Japan's export trade, and the renunciation of Japan's territorial claims overseas; otherwise, however, there were no formal restrictions or limitations placed on the behaviour of the Japanese Government. The peace treaty also gave the United States administrative control in the Ryukyu and Bonin islands, though Japan would still hold 'residual sovereignty' over them (Okinawa in the Ryukyus was already forming a significant part in American planning for global war). The bilateral security treaty allowed the United States to retain bases on the Japanese home islands but gave no explicit guarantee that the United States would come to Japan's defence if it was attacked. The actual terms under which the American military presence in Japan would operate had also yet to be fully

[52] Beisner, *Acheson*, 474.   [53] Lilienthal, *Venturesome Years*, entry for 4 May 1951, 157.
[54] Johnson memorandum, 29 August 1951, *FRUS, 1951, VI*, Part 1, 1307–9. On the cultural and racial dimension to US–Japanese relations during this period, see Koshiro, *Trans-Pacific Racisms*, 78–88.
[55] Dulles memorandum for Rusk, 22 October 1951, *FRUS, 1951, VI*, Part 1, 1380–1.

determined, as an administrative agreement detailing such contentious subjects as consultation with the Japanese Government over use of American bases for overseas military action and the jurisdictional status of American personnel remained to be negotiated. The peace treaty was signed by Japan and forty-eight other states on 8 September 1951 at a carefully staged ceremony in San Francisco, but Senate ratification still had to be secured before its terms could be put into effect. This was placed in doubt when, later the same month, fifty-six senators sent a letter to Truman advising him that the establishment of relations between the PRC and Japan would be considered detrimental to US interests. Now charged with managing the ratification process, in December 1951 Dulles elicited from Yoshida his agreement to open ties with Chiang's Nationalist regime, and to eschew any initiatives to promote relations with the Communist regime on the mainland, so satisfying Senate opinion that Japan was not to be cast completely adrift, with the ability to undercut Washington's controversial China policy at will. Yet though it was Dulles who concocted the notorious Yoshida letter containing this pledge, there are several indications that the Japanese premier never intended to recognize Beijing at this stage and was happy that American wishes conformed with his own preferences; though he knew that agreement to the terms of the letter was essential if the peace treaty was to be approved, this did not amount to coercive diplomacy from the Americans, and Yoshida himself understood that Japanese national interests might be best served in the short term by an opening to Taiwan rather than the PRC, for all the attractions of future trade with the mainland.[56]

Outside the Communist powers, the chief source of criticism of American treatment of Japan in the build-up to the conclusion of the peace treaty during the summer of 1951 came from the Indian Government. Relations between India and the United States had continued on their downward and deteriorating path during the first half of 1951, as Indian representatives at the UN continued to urge a negotiated settlement in Korea which involved concessions to Beijing's position, and, with famine conditions threatening, resentment had been generated by congressional attempts to tie the provision of American food aid to indications from New Delhi that it would switch to a more pro-Western stance in the Cold War. American criticisms of non-alignment only served to make Indian leaders, bridling at American 'highhandedness', more determined to maintain their chosen course, while on the other side of the equation, as Dennis Merrill has commented, 'United States officials

---

[56] See Swenson-Wright, *Unequal Allies*, 87–91; also John W. Dower, 'Yoshida in the Scales of History', in *Japan in War and Peace*, 234.

compared Indian policymakers to "spoiled children", viewed non-alignment – in some measure – as a reflection of psychosis, and often ran roughshod over Indian sensitivities.'[57] Indian objections to the Japanese treaty were based on the continuing presence of American bases in Japan, and the failure to return the Ryukyu and Bonin islands to Japanese control, as well as the omission in the text of any mention of the need to revert the former Japanese colony of Taiwan to Chinese jurisdiction, as stipulated under the Cairo Declaration of 1943 (the latter problem, of course, rooted in diametrically opposed views held by Washington and New Delhi on what represented a legitimate Chinese authority). Having just approved the much-delayed legislation that would allow food aid to be shipped to India, the Truman administration, and many sectors of American public opinion, were outraged when New Delhi made clear during August that it would not sign the treaty and publicly attacked its provisions. As could be anticipated, this move earned the warm welcome of the PRC, and to some Americans it seemed, as one of Nehru's biographers has put it, all part of a 'general scheme to bring India, China and Japan into one orbit'.[58] Loy Henderson, the US Ambassador in New Delhi, and his staff were of the opinion that this was in accord with Nehru's policy of 'eventual exclusion from [the] mainland and waters [of] Asia [of] all Western milit[ary] power and what he w[ou]ld consider as Western polit[ical] and econ[omic] pressures'. By linking Indian rejection to the presence of US bases in Japan, Nehru was aiming to 'stimulate and gain influence over nationalistic and anti-white elements in Jap[an]', believing that with guidance and encouragement such elements could gain power in Japan, break the alliance with the United States and evict all American bases. Nehru, it was claimed, desired to foster an 'Asia for the Asians' movement under the banner of Asian nationalism. Thus far he had not had much success with drawing the PRC closer to this project and away from Russia, but he now had fixed his attention on moving Japan apart from the United States. The Chinese were unlikely to act strongly against Indian interests in Asia, it was predicted, 'because [of the] potential value of Nehru in helping stimulate hatred in Asia against peoples of Eur[opean] stock, particularly of U.S. . . .'[59]

From the Indian point of view, in fact, a prime cause of resentment over the treaty was the fact that Dulles had not visited or consulted New Delhi over its terms, alongside the general impression that the Americans simply

---

[57] See Merrill, *Bread and the Ballot*, 67–74.
[58] See Gopal, *Nehru*, II, 137–8, 177; also McMahon, *Cold War on the Periphery*, 101–8.
[59] New Delhi to the Secretary of State, No. 868, 6 September 1951, 611.91/9–651, CDF, RG 59, NARA; and see also Brands, *Henderson*, 229–30.

expected the Indians to follow Washington's lead; Sir Girja Bajpai, Secretary General of the Ministry of External Affairs, asserted that though having lived in the United States for five years and holding friendly feelings towards its people, 'in the past four years [he had] noticed a growing peculiar sort of power madness'.[60] British opinion was certainly perplexed by the hardening of American attitudes toward Nehru. 'It seems to me that the Americans are too inclined to assume that because Nehru is not actively co-operating with the West he is working against it,' one official opined in September 1951. 'They seem to believe that he is ready to ignore the menace of communism in order to preserve his "neutralism" between the communists and the West.' Advocacy of neutralism here was seen as coming from a 'desire to see "Asia for the Asians" – and not … as a result of any policy of balance and counterbalance in his attitude to East and West'.[61] In the midst of the controversy over Indian attitudes to the Japanese peace treaty, Nehru was asked by one reporter what he meant by 'Asia for the Asians', only for the Prime Minister to deny he had ever used such a term, and that he was 'not for pan-Asianism. Asia is far too big and varied for that [and] has an enormous variety of peoples.' Instead, what Nehru professed he wanted was a 'free Asia', where political and economic domination by the West was finished, while 'ultimately … it is the minds of the peoples of Asia that will make the difference'.[62]

It was in the context of external criticism of the treaty that Dulles and other State Department officials tried to impress upon the Department of Defense and the JCS the absolute imperative of cultivating friendship with Japan in the post-occupation phase, with Dulles clearly attuned to the racial implications that would be carried by treatment which was not based on the principle of equality. During the summer of 1951, and much to the annoyance of the State Department, the JCS began to repeat their insistence that, in contrast with the position in NATO, after the occupation legal jurisdiction over US military personnel and their dependants in Japan should reside with the American authorities. Dulles strongly disagreed, finding objectionable that there was a 'disposition on the part of the Armed Services to continue to treat the Japanese as defeated enemies and as orientals having qualities inferior to those of occidentals'. Changing the military's attitudes would be 'a major task of education', which would have to be begun immediately.[63]

---

[60] New Delhi to Department of State, Despatch No. 779, 4 October 1951, 611.911/10–451, CDF, RG 59, NARA.
[61] Foreign Office minute, 4 September 1951, FL10345/8, FO 371/92884, TNA.
[62] Robert Trumbull, 'Nehru Answers Some Basic Questions', *NYT*, 11 November 1951.
[63] Dulles to Webb, 10 September 1951, *FRUS, 1951, VI*, Part 1, 1344–7.

During October 1951, after the signing of the peace and security treaties, Dulles continued to express very real concerns that in their post-occupation presence and behaviour in Japan, the American military would insist on elaborate extraterritorial privileges under the still-to-be negotiated administrative agreement.[64] During the war, Dulles reminded Rusk, in views he also conveyed to Truman and Acheson, American soldiers had 'gotten into the habit of treating the Japanese as inferiors' and to alter such attitudes would be 'immensely difficult'. Nevertheless, the US military authorities in Japan would need to make the effort, or else squander the opportunity they had gained through victory in the Pacific War. Dulles then proceeded to expound at length on the wider importance of treating Japan as an equal:

The matter involves not merely our position in Japan but has broad implications as regards all of Asia. The Chinese Communists, using the old Japanese war slogan of 'Asia for the Asiatics', are attempting to rally all of Asia to rise up to eject violently all Western influence. India shows a tendency to move in that direction and in substance India's refusal to sign the Treaty of Peace was based on its Government's belief that it will prove impracticable for the United States to develop under the Security Treaty, the kind of 'friendly association' with a defeated nation of alien race, which is pledged by the Peace Treaty. If this Indian belief is verified, and if it is demonstrated to all Asia, which is intently watching, that Westerners as represented by the United States find it impossible to deal with Orientals on a basis of respect and equality, that will have grave repercussions throughout all of Asia. It will make it likely that all of the Asiatics will unite, under communist leadership, against the West. Then the situation would be more dangerous to us than when Japan attempted this same result under the same slogan.[65]

This, then, represented the main underlying concern nurtured by Dulles: that the new regime in Beijing would be able to mobilize a pan-Asian movement to expel Western and white presence from the region, while Indian policy was already showing signs that it was sympathetic to this general idea. However, if the Americans could work successfully in partnership with Japan, this would help to undermine the credibility of the Chinese message: treating the Japanese not as racial inferiors but as equals in the struggle against Communist imperialism would become the most effective riposte to those who would try to castigate US foreign policy as infused with the racism that was still endemic to American society.

---

[64] On the negotiation of the administrative agreement, see Swenson-Wright, *Unequal Allies*, 96–105.

[65] Dulles memorandum for Rusk, 22 October 1951, *FRUS, 1951, VI*, Part 1, 1381–2. Rusk also noted the need to 'guard against giving the Japanese any basis for belief that our policies are motivated by considerations of racial inequalities', *ibid.*, 1383.

Parenthetically, Dulles's mention of Japan's wartime cry of 'Asia for the Asiatics' helps to remind us of the intense ironies that abounded across a decade of war and upheaval in Asia and the Pacific: whereas between 1941 and 1945 the friendship and alliance with China had been essential to contradict the Japanese contention that their war effort was upholding the cause of a New Order in Asia against the imperialism of the white West, it was now seen as necessary to enlist Japan's assistance to undermine any attempt by Beijing to trumpet a similar message under the shadow of the Korean fighting.

The Indian Government's refusal to sign the Japanese peace treaty remained a source of deep anger to Dulles, colouring his attitudes to Nehru for many years to come, and fostering the sense of India's basic unreliability in the effort to contain Communism in Asia. In a revealing speech delivered on 2 December 1951 to the National Council of Christians and Jews in Cleveland on the theme of 'The Free East and the Free West', Dulles gave full vent to his feelings. The future Secretary of State outlined the 'fear' of Asian peoples and leaders that 'there cannot be cooperation with the West on the basis of equality, but that cooperation would subject the oriental to an offensive attitude on the part of the Westerners, many of whom in the past assumed racial, cultural and material superiority, and contempt for the rich and ancient cultures and civilizations of Asia'. Instead, 'what they hear mostly is Communist propaganda lauding the so-called racial tolerance that is practiced in Russia and contrasting it with the alleged racial intolerance practiced in the United States'. In an uplifting vision of the possibilities of cross-cultural communication, Dulles continued that, 'We Americans must realize that the free East and the free West are not going to join hands to preserve our common freedom unless our hand is a hand of fellowship which clasps the hand of the oriental as that of an equal.' The peace treaty that Dulles had spent so long negotiating was regarded by him as a test of this fellowship, built as it was on a spirit of reconciliation between West and East. In this respect, with India's rejection of the treaty, it had 'seemed to align itself with the Chinese Communists' line, which is that there cannot be "Asia for the Asians" unless all Westerners are rooted out of Asia'. This would only lead, Dulles warned, to an 'Asia for the Russians'. These alarming eventualities were likely to happen if Westerners did not work with Asians on a 'basis of equality'; the National Council had dedicated itself to eradicating racial and religious intolerance, Dulles reminded the gathering, and he was not underrating the problems of achieving this in Asia 'where there is a long background of Western arrogance and oriental sensitiveness and where Communism is using all of its propagandist skills to influence the people against the West and to magnify every unhappy incident'. Yet Dulles remained optimistic as he believed that Western values were based on the 'equal rights and equal dignity of all men', and 'that faith had its beginnings in Judea, where East and West met, and it held that all men, without regard to race and color, were the creation and concern of a universal God'.[66] This ecumenical vision was undoubtedly appealing to his audience, but the notion that there was somehow a shared connection between the spiritual values of Asia and the West, derived from some kind of common heritage and contact point in the Holy Land, was surely stretching the grounds of credulity.

The Cleveland speech reflected Dulles's acute sense of frustration with Nehru's obstinacy in not signing the treaty, but also his anxieties about the potential for Asian grievances over Western attitudes of racial superiority to spill over into a drive to evict the Western presence entirely from the region. Not unexpectedly, critical reactions came from India to Dulles's speech, and concentrated on the accusation that refusal to sign the treaty was tantamount to alignment with Beijing: the United States Information Service at the US Embassy in New Delhi reported that '"Surprising", "regrettable", "unfortunate" and "undiplomatic"' were some of the epithets employed by Indian editors in their comments, while a Ministry of External Affairs spokesman expressed his own astonishment that Dulles would want to disrupt a relationship that had shown signs of recent improvement, reflected in the appointment of the popular Democrat figure, Chester Bowles, as American ambassador in November 1951.[67] Bowles himself soon offered a different perspective on the underlying problems of US–Asian relations from his new vantage point, informing one American official soon after his arrival that

the greatest single triumph of Soviet propaganda is its success in convincing not only Indians but Asians generally that we Americans are incapable of treating the colored races of the world as equals. The terrible thing about it is that I am not wholly convinced in my own mind that as *a nation* we are actually able to meet this test. It would be hard for anyone who has not lived here for a while to believe the extent to which decent, honest and friendly Indians have become convinced that America as a nation is guilty of brutal practices toward her negro citizens.

. . . the people of India believe that lynching is a daily occurrence in America, that the Ku Klux Klan is a dominant factor in our political life and that we are unwilling to do anything about it. If we are unable to tackle the problem in an

[66] Dulles's address to the National Council of Christians and Jews, 2 December 1951, folder 243, box 94, Chester Bowles papers, Sterling Memorial Library, Yale University. See also the truncated report, 'Asians Are Testing U.S., Dulles Warns', *NYT*, 3 December 1951.

[67] 'Survey of Indian Press Comments for the Period December 4 through December 11, 1951', Press Analysis Section, USIS, American Embassy, New Delhi, folder 508, box 113, Bowles papers; 'Dulles' Criticism Hurts India Anew', *NYT*, 4 December 1951.

all-out manner, I can only say that we cannot expect to hold or to win the friendship of the one billion human beings who live in Asia.[68]

Bowles's views cast the spotlight back on America's own performance when it came to upholding the principles of freedom and equality at home. By contrast, Dulles, though he was certainly ready to acknowledge the harm that domestic American racism was doing to US policy abroad, was a believer in an incremental approach to change, and there is no evidence to show he favoured any acceleration in federal measures to bring about civil rights reform. Instead, Dulles hoped that the example of American treatment of its Asian allies, and particularly its former Japanese enemies, would help to convince others that there was substance to American claims that they stood for equality of treatment between peoples irrespective of race. In a subsequent article that appeared in *Foreign Affairs* in January 1952, Dulles continued to pursue the theme of forging partnerships across the divides between East and West when summing up his experiences in negotiating the peace and security treaties. Using the opportunity to drive home the message that the future relationship between the United States and Japan would be crucial in showing that 'friendly association' was possible across racial and cultural barriers, he opined that, 'Many Orientals fear that Westerners are incapable of cooperating with them on a basis of political, economic and social equality, and this fear divides the East and West. It has a long background of growth, and Communist propaganda in Asia concentrates on keeping it alive and whipping it up.' Stalin's goals had remained consistent since the mid-1920s, he argued, and involved the 'amalgamation of the Asian peoples into the political orbit of the Soviet Union', harnessing the human and natural resources of the area as a prerequisite before an open assault on the West.[69]

It was therefore of some importance to the State Department that the administrative agreement that would underpin the American military presence in Japan should conform to that used in the European context, so there was no leverage given to those Japanese who wanted to charge, as Acheson put it in early 1952, that 'we are trying to treat them as (1) not sovereign, (2) a defeated enemy, or (3) racially inferior. It will be difficult enough to maintain friendly relations between our forces in Japan and the Japanese people; it will be impossible if U.S. forces are looked upon as a symbol of western discrimination and arrogance toward Asiatics.' Extending his argument to Asia as whole, Acheson continued:

[68] Bowles to H. Sargeant Howland (Deputy Assistant Secretary of State for Public Affairs), 24 December 1951, folder 280, box 96, Bowles papers.
[69] John Foster Dulles, 'Security in the Pacific', *Foreign Affairs*, 30, 2, January 1952, 185, 187.

The entire non-white world will be watching closely the nature of our relations with Japan to determine whether we are willing to work with a non-white country on the basis of equality and partnership. *The one great issue which will be decisive in setting the basis of our future relations with Asia will be questions of equal treatment* [emphasis added]. Our discriminations at home are a great burden upon our relations with Asia: an attempt to practice similar discriminations officially in our relations with the Governments of Asia would be considered by them to be intolerable.[70]

For all his own disregard for the aspirations of African Americans, Acheson's comments about the damage that was being done to American goals in the Far East by domestic racial conditions at home helps to explain the support his department was prepared to offer the civil rights cases that were moving through the Supreme Court system at this time, and were to culminate in the *Brown* ruling of 1954.

When it came to the administrative agreement, nevertheless, the Pentagon and JCS mounted strong and sustained resistance to any concessions to the Japanese over criminal jurisdiction, and the final terms reached in late February 1952 were phrased as the US military had desired, though the Americans agreed to consider sympathetically requests for waivers in cases of particular importance. There was, however, in a reflection of State Department concerns, an additional understanding that once the status of forces agreements covering deployments in the NATO countries of Western Europe was put into effect (which Rusk privately hinted to the Japanese would be within a year), the Japanese Government could elect to be covered under the same principles, so that jurisdiction over American service personnel committing crimes against Japanese could be exercised by the local courts. With much speculation swirling around the final stage of negotiations, and accusations from its political rivals that Yoshida's Government was attempting to conceal the real nature of the bargains made with the Americans, Japanese press reaction to the administrative agreement was that it did not reflect the aspirations of sovereign equality between the parties that had been previously voiced.[71] In this way, the occupation period was to end on a sour note, as the United States relinquished its formal authority in Japan but continued to retain the capacity to influence Japanese internal political developments. American military administration of the Ryukyus and Bonins was also a source of lasting tension, as was the ubiquitous presence

---

[70] Acheson and Lovett memorandum for Truman, 18 January 1952, *FRUS, 1952–1954, XIV: China and Japan*, Part 2 (Washington, DC, 1985), 1098.
[71] See Sebald to State Department, 'Weekly Political Notes from Japan', 29 February 1952, *ibid.*, 1207–8.

of US service personnel and their dependants at American bases, which served as a constant reminder of the security treaty.

During the course of 1951, as the fighting in Korea settled into a gruesome stalemate, and the United States came increasingly to underwrite the French campaign in Indochina as well as stepping up its military assistance to Taiwan, American policy-makers became more aware than ever that the ideological challenge presented by the arrival of a strong and vigorous Chinese Communist government was every bit as daunting as the military threat it seemed to pose to Western interests. The PRC's emergence as a leading example of Asian nationalist assertiveness gave Beijing impeccable anti-imperialist credentials and its defiance of the Western powers was alluring to those who sought a similar sense of liberation from past patterns of oppression. Chinese Communist opposition to Western influence also had, it was widely acknowledged at the time, a racial dimension in its appeal to the shared Asian experience of subjugation by the occidental powers. To US officials this drive to expel Western influence from Asia had many of the characteristics that had been noted of the Japanese thrusts of the early 1940s, where the pan-Asianist banner was raised to rally the peoples of the region behind a message of anti-colonialism. 'We are witnessing right now the end of the white man in Asia as a dominant force,' MacArthur told one visitor to Japan in early 1951. 'The white man is through in Asia in the British sense, and will never come back again.'[72] In such an environment, it would appear essential that the United States dissociate itself from the practices and policies of the European colonial powers, and emphasize its sympathies for the needs and hopes of Asians who were still recovering from the physical and psychological traumas of the Second World War, and who were determined to find their own voice and to direct their own affairs. The unyielding anti-Communist stance of American political culture obviously made this a highly problematic task, when Communism itself held an innate appeal for its promise of economic justice and militant rejection of Western imperialism. In Indochina, this paradox was given its most graphic illustration. For many Americans, moreover, the demands of revolutionary nationalists, sometimes accompanied by the resort to violence, were simply seen as too threatening to regional stability. Despite much talk of working in partnership with Asians, there was still a pervasive element of paternalistic racism in the way Americans regarded many of the peoples of the region as not yet ready to cope with the problems of modernity, and of managing large and complex societies, as

[72] Lilienthal, *Venturesome Years*, entry for 9 March 1951, 121.

'immature' and almost childlike in their emotional bouts of disorder, and where the image of the Asian 'strong-man' as being a necessary way-station on the eventual road to democracy exercised an attractive pull. There was indeed, at this time, much wringing of hands in Washington as Asian nationalist leaders rejected Western economic systems, conceptions of social hierarchy and international norms of behaviour.[73]

The Korean War had also served to remilitarize the American presence in East Asia, as American power was projected onto the Asian mainland, and the offshore island chain bolstered by the construction of new bases and the injection of American military personnel. For many Americans, the only way to deal with the new situation they now confronted was to isolate and contain Communist China, oppose its probes for Western weakness with force and take steps to erode its power, while hoping that Beijing might one day detach itself from Moscow's orbit. But the militarization of the American presence, and the flaunting of its superior firepower in Korea, also served to alarm some Asians, who had no wish to see the domination of the West that had so recently been swept away by Japanese victories in the war years replaced by an overbearing and alien American influence. The fact that American rhetoric during the Korean War seemed to welcome the prospect of war with China, a country and a people who had so recently been an American ally, was perplexing for many observers, not least as such a catastrophic conflict would surely have served to undercut overall Western interests. In private, Dulles might avow to Lilienthal in May 1951, for example, that 'Bombing Chinese cities will solidify the people behind the regime more than any other thing we could do', but Asian audiences tended to pick up on the more extreme pronouncements of American spokesmen.[74]

The basic nature of one of the dilemmas faced by the United States as it tried to confront Communist power in Asia was that the military's requirements for an extensive base network and the rights that went with it, combined with the strategic imperative to plan for the use of nuclear weapons as these increased in both number and efficiency, created local unease, resentment and opposition, and were a boon to Communist propaganda keen to remind an Asian audience of the callous indifference of the Americans to the lives of non-white people. The State Department, for its part, was becoming increasingly concerned about the inability of the

---

[73] See Michael H. Hunt, 'The Decolonization Puzzle in U.S. Policy: Promise versus Performance', in David Ryan and Victor Pungong (eds.), *The United States and Decolonization: Power and Freedom* (London, 2000), 207–29; Donald F. McHenry, 'Confronting a Revolutionary Legacy', in Sanford J. Ungar (ed.), *Estrangement: America and the World* (New York, 1985), 90.

[74] Lilienthal, *Venturesome Years*, entry for 2 May 1951, 156.

United States to project a positive and progressive image in Asia, and the tendency for American policies to be seen as simply another variant on the old pattern of Western and white attempts to superimpose their own preferences and interests on others, as Asian territories were turned into the battlegrounds of the Cold War and colonial forms of control persisted. In this context, the identification of the United States with policies of racial discrimination and the practices of segregation did much to harm the pursuit of amicable relations and added force to the argument that there was a racial aspect to the way Americans seemed ready to use nuclear weapons in their efforts to contain Chinese Communist power, during an era when Beijing had no similar means of retaliation. The impression gained by Chester Bowles in December 1951 as he began to take up his duties as ambassador to India was of the 'success of Russian propaganda throughout the East on the race question' when a pro-American local revealed to him that 'many Indians were still deeply disturbed by the fact that we were willing to drop the atomic bomb on the Asian Japanese but unwilling to drop it on the white Germans'.[75] One Indian professor told Bowles that belief in innate American racism lay beneath the willingness of Indians to give some credence to Communist allegations that the Americans had used biological warfare in Korea: 'If only you had not dropped the atomic bomb on Asians! After that millions of Asians are willing to believe that, at least where Asian lives are concerned, you would not hesitate at even this new technique of mass killing of noncombatants.'[76] By June 1952, as the Soviet Union launched accusations in the United Nations that the United States was practising germ warfare in Korea, the *New York Times* warned its readers that this was part of 'newer charges, made by the Communists on all fronts now, that the United States is engaged in a systematic war against Asians and other "colored" races'.[77] The nuclear issue, however, was set only to provide more sustenance to such contentions, as over the next year American policy-makers turned their attentions to the wider problems of the defence of the Far East, and a new administration took office in Washington readier than previously to place nuclear weapons at the heart of its national security policies.

---

[75] Bowles to Donald Kennedy (Director of the Office of South Asian Affairs), 28 December 1951, folder 265, box 95, Bowles papers.
[76] Chester Bowles, *Ambassador's Report* (London, 1954), 224.
[77] 'Experts Discount Amity from Soviet', *NYT*, 19 June 1952.

4   A greater sanction: the defence of South
     East Asia, the advent of the Eisenhower
     administration and the end of the
     Korean War

By early 1952 it had become a central tenet of the Truman administration's Far Eastern policies that China was an aggressive and expansionist
power, whose ambitions for regional dominance, encouraged by a Soviet
Union content to see American manpower and resources consumed by
the inconclusive fighting in Korea, posed a dangerous threat to key
American interests. These interests had become enlarged to embrace
the rehabilitation and strengthening of Japan, a formal ally once the
security treaty came into operation in April 1952, and which through its
military-industrial potential was perceived as the principal prize in East
Asia. In January 1952, Acheson had avowed to British officials that 'the
heart of the matter in the Far East was to build up sufficient strength so as
to hold Japan on the side of the West', and pointed out the 'great shift in
the world power situation if Japan with its military virtues and industrial
capacity went over to the Communist side. While the chances of keeping
Japan on the side of the West were not overwhelming, everything had to
be done toward this end.'[1] This primary goal entailed also assuring
the security and stability of South East Asia, whose valuable markets
and raw materials were important in their own terms to keep out of
Communist hands, but also because access to them was seen as crucial to
Japanese economic growth and prosperity. If the Japanese Government
could not find an outlet for its gathering economic energies in South East
Asia, it was believed by American policy-makers, they would turn to traditional markets on the Chinese mainland and so come towards some kind of
accommodation with Beijing, and thereby prejudice American hopes for an
exclusively pro-Western orientation for post-occupation Japan.[2] Preventing

[1] US minutes of the third formal Truman–Churchill meeting, 8 January 1952, *FRUS*,
1952–1954, VI: Western Europe and Canada, Part 1 (Washington, DC, 1983), 783.
[2] See Andrew J. Rotter, *The Path to Vietnam: The Origins of the American Commitment to
Southeast Asia* (Ithaca, 1987), 214.

131

further Communist inroads in South East Asia necessitated support for the French war effort in Indochina, but the auguries here looked far from promising, with the infusion of American aid since 1950 having done little to check the Viet Minh's steadily growing hold over the Vietnamese countryside, particularly in Tonkin. Though there had been a brief French rally in the spring of 1951, lack of political progress towards genuine independence for the Associated States of Vietnam, Laos and Cambodia was glaringly obvious as the 'Bao Dai solution' proved devoid of any real substance, and American officials chafed at the obliviousness of their French partners to the anachronism of colonial mentalities when faced with their perilous position. Too much pressure on the French for reform, however, could erode their already fragile willingness to continue the costly struggle and leave Washington with the unenviable choice of either directly taking on the burden in Indochina or abandoning the territory altogether to Viet Minh control. There was also a crucial European dimension to American policy over the Indochina war, as French co-operation was vital to assure the creation of the European Defence Community, perceived as the necessary vehicle to permit the contentious rearmament of West Germany.[3] Acheson summed up prevailing administration opinion in testimony before the Senate Foreign Relations Committee in February 1952, offering the US objective as 'to keep [the French] doing what they are doing, which is taking the primary responsibility for the fight in Indochina and not letting them in any way transfer it to us'.[4]

Acheson's anxiety to avoid further calls on US military resources were, of course, partly conditioned by the fact that substantial American forces remained tied up on the Korean peninsula in a war the rationale for which had long been forgotten by many Americans. One of the most immediate goals of the administration when it came to Far East policy was to bring about a successful outcome to the armistice talks at Panmunjom, but this was also far from straightforward considering the bureaucratic conflicts within Washington over acceptable terms, the pressures of public opinion at home, the need to co-ordinate positions with the UN Command and the military negotiators on the spot, and the opinions of allies, let alone considerations of Communist tactics. Even though a number of outstanding practical matters had been settled by the end of 1951, the intractable issue of prisoner-of-war repatriation stood as a major hurdle to the early resolution of the talks. Moreover, the controversial decision reached in

---

[3] For the problems of the European Defence Community, see William I. Hitchcock, *France Restored: Cold War Diplomacy and the Quest for Leadership in Europe, 1944–1954* (Chapel Hill, 1998), 133–86.
[4] Quoted in Gibbons, *U.S. Government and the Vietnam War*, Part 1, 107.

February 1952 by the senior members of the administration, with Truman at the forefront, to stand firm on the position of voluntary repatriation in the expectation of Communist concessions, helped to produce deadlock in the negotiations.[5] Uncertain progress with the armistice talks made all the more relevant the background discussions that were being held on the course of action to pursue if these broke down entirely, or alternatively if they were to reach a successful conclusion, what reaction would follow if the Chinese should revive an attack in Korea, or engage in overt aggression in South East Asia. How to ensure the maintenance of an armistice, should one be agreed, was a topic that began to exercise the Truman administration by the end of 1951, and, still in the middle of the debilitating experience of bloody stalemate on the Korean peninsula, if fighting were to recur senior officials were determined that new military options of the variety already raised earlier in NSC 48/5 should be entertained.

The preferred expedient was that immediately after the conclusion of any armistice agreement a joint announcement should be issued by the sixteen states who had committed forces to Korea, containing a warning of the consequences that would follow if the armistice was violated by aggressive Communist action. Following protracted consultations among the interested parties to arrive at an agreed text, the so-called 'greater sanctions' statement took final form in February 1952 and concluded with the phrase that if there was a breach of the armistice, the consequences would be 'so grave that, in all probability, it would not be possible to confine hostilities within the frontiers of Korea'.[6] This raised the issue, however, of how the UN Command would go about such an expansion of the area of the fighting. Wanting no repetition of the frustrations of limited war, the JCS were clear that nuclear weapons would have to be used in reply to a fresh Communist onslaught, their Chairman, General Bradley, for example, telling Truman on 10 December 1951 that 'the biggest thing we could do to prevent a violation of an armistice would be to say that if the armistice is violated we will go all out against China', while Vandenberg 'would not attack Manchuria, but China proper, hitting at their ports, mining their rivers, etc.'[7] The JCS informed General Ridgway, the UN Commander in Korea, in categorical terms that 'the major deterrent to renewal of aggression must in last analysis be dependent upon realization by the Communists that a renewed aggression in

[5] See Rosemary Foot, *A Substitute for Victory: The Politics of Peacemaking at the Korean Armistice Talks* (Ithaca, 1990), 87–107; Stueck, *Korean War*, 259–65.
[6] See Foot, *Substitute for Victory*, 80.
[7] Memorandum for the President of a meeting held in the Cabinet Room, 10 December 1951, *FRUS, 1951, VII*, Part 1, 1292–3.

Korea would result in a new war which would bring upon China the full retribution which [the] United States and her Allies deem militarily desirable'.[8] Ridgway, mindful of this JCS injunction, was concerned that the implicit threat in the statement should not be a hollow one, and quickly reached the conclusion that 'the retributive potentiality of UN military power against Red China would be noneffective unless the full results of precipitating World War 3 were to be accepted, and the use of atomic weapons auth[orized]'.[9]

The administration, however, was not prepared to go quite this far. Indeed, when on 19 December 1951 the NSC had reviewed the formal US position on what a warning statement should convey, it had been decided to remove the original words 'or in the methods of warfare employed' after the stipulation that Communist aggression would 'result in a military reaction that would not necessarily be limited in geographic scope'.[10] This was a significant revision and reflected the administration's continuing sensitivity over expressly backing the use of nuclear weapons in the Far East even if the scope of the Korean fighting were to be expanded. Allied opinion was a crucial factor here: the British had already been wary over the import of the greater sanctions statement, fearing it might commit them in advance to a course of action which would make general war with the Soviet Union more probable. The ever-sceptical Air Marshal Slessor was surprised that the Americans seemed only to be contemplating a blockade and the bombing of airbases in Manchuria, and had no doubts that if aggression were revived there would be 'a clamour in America to use the atom bomb'.[11] In December 1951, the JIC in London produced a report on the consequences of extending the war beyond Korea which underlined the fact that conventional methods of bombing and blockade would probably be ineffective, and only atomic attack offered any hope of decisive results. As key communication hubs and supply points were usually located in or near towns such attacks were bound to be indiscriminate in nature, and there could not be complete confidence of the outcome, while 'all out atomic attack on China's major cities might force her to capitulate, though even this is open to doubt'. Most UN members, it was predicted, would prove reluctant to approve of

[8] See JCS to Ridgway, 19 December 1951, *FRUS, 1951, VII*, Part 1, 1378.
[9] See Ridgway to JCS, 7 January 1952, *FRUS, 1952–1954, XV: Korea*, Part 1 (Washington, DC, 1984), 11.
[10] See Acheson memorandum on NSC meeting, 19 December 1951, *FRUS, 1951, VII*, Part 1, 1375; and compare to original text of NSC 118/1, 'U.S. Objectives and Courses of Action in Korea', 7 December 1951, *ibid.*, 1261; see also Foot, *Substitute*, 80.
[11] Slessor minute on 'Action in the Event of a Major Break of an Armistice by the Communists in Korea', 3 December 1951, AIR 75/108, TNA.

the use of atomic weapons, despite the fact that UN forces would be under heavy pressure in Korea itself, and if used they would 'evoke vigorous protest and horror among the Asiatic nations and cause many heartsearchings in the West, particularly among the West European nations'. The Commonwealth Relations Office added their own view that the governments of India, Pakistan and Ceylon would offer the most determined opposition to any initiation of atomic warfare by the UN Command.[12] British suspicions were also aroused when in January 1952, during Churchill's first visit to Washington after his election victory the previous October, American ideas on how to respond to a violation of the armistice in Korea were explained, Bradley noting that it was not the American intention to use nuclear weapons, 'since up to the present time no suitable targets were presented', but added, more ominously, 'If the situation changed in any way, so that suitable targets were presented, a new situation would arise. So far this was entirely theoretical.'[13]

Theoretical or not, this new wave of American official thinking was greeted with disapproval by the British, who still balked at the prospect of full-scale war with China. 'In considering action against China,' the COS had affirmed in January 1952, 'it must ... be borne in mind that it is our first interest to avoid war with China since it is likely to lead to global war, and it would entail deployment of forces to the Far East where they would be misplaced.'[14] The overriding British fear was that expanding the war beyond Korea would trigger a Soviet reaction. The most immediate threat here was that bombing of Manchurian airfields would lead to the introduction of Soviet air force units into the fighting over Chinese airspace.[15] The discussions that ensued between the JCS and COS in February 1952 over the action to be taken if there was a breach of a future Korean armistice revealed that, as Slessor put it, the two sides were 'dangerously far apart'.[16] Current trends in American policy, which reflected the frustrations of the Korean stalemate, were the cause of continuing concern in London. In March 1952, the COS and senior Foreign Office officials

[12] 'The Possible Consequences of an Expansion by the UN Forces of the Korean War', JIC (51)115(Final), 13 December 1951, and Appendix B, 'Note by the Commonwealth Relations Office', 14 December 1951, CAB 158/13, TNA.
[13] Memorandum by Acheson of a dinner meeting at the British Embassy, 6 January 1952, *FRUS, 1952–1954, VI*, Part 1, 744–5; see also Gaddis, 'The Origins of Self-Deterrence', 116. The JIC paper referred to above was among the briefing materials that went with the Prime Minister to Washington.
[14] COS brief for ad hoc talks on the defence of South East Asia, COS(52)64, 26 January 1952, DEFE 5/36, TNA.
[15] See Northern Department paper for Russia Committee, 'Soviet Reactions to Western Pressure on "Sore Spots"', 1 February 1952, N51052/6G, FO 371/100840, TNA.
[16] Slessor to Bradley, 13 February 1952, AIR 75/108, TNA.

came together for talks on overall strategy in the Cold War. One of the most sensitive conclusions of these sessions was that 'the two most likely causes of world war in the next few years might well be: (i) Insistence by the Americans on a "show-down" when they found that they could no longer afford to maintain the weapon they had forged. Any appreciable scaling down in our own contribution might well encourage the Americans to stage a "show-down". (ii) Insistence by the Americans on a "show-down" with China, in the fond hope that Russia would not intervene.'[17]

Divergences were also in evidence when the first ad hoc staff talks between the United States, Britain and France on South East Asian defence were convened in January 1952. Alongside the greater sanctions statement, at the end of 1951 the JCS had been looking at US responses to possible Chinese intervention in French Indochina, where the Viet Minh-led insurgency was gaining ground day by day. The French High Commissioner and Commander-in-Chief in Indochina, General Jean de Lattre de Tassigny, had visited Washington in September 1951 to emphasize his need for more US equipment and supplies, and his concerns that with the convening of the Korean armistice talks (and if these talks should prove successful), the Chinese might transfer forces southward ready for a thrust into Indochina. During the course of these discussions, he presented an apocalyptic vision of the fate of the West if Indochina should succumb to Communism, saying that 'every day he asks those whom he meets in the United States if Indochina and Korea are not one war. The answer is always "Yes". ... General Collins had agreed with him that "if you lose Korea, Asia is not lost; but if I lose Indochina, Asia is lost". Tonkin is the key to Southeast Asia, if Southeast Asia is lost, India "will burn like a match" and there will be no barrier to the advance of Communism before Suez and Africa. If the Moslem world were thus engulfed, the Moslems in North Africa would soon fall in line and Europe itself would be outflanked.'[18] Intelligence reports in December 1951 that Chinese forces were gathering near the Indochina border spurred the Pentagon to consider what it could do to assist a French defence. Though the JCS were adamantly opposed to any commitment or involvement of US forces in South East Asia itself, regarding this as primarily a French and British preserve, Bradley thought it would be possible to transfer the 'greater sanction' principle from Korea to the Indochina setting, envisaging undertaking direct air and naval action against the Chinese mainland if Beijing should decide to stage an overt

---

[17] Minutes of meeting held 31 March 1952, DEFE 32/2, TNA.
[18] Record of a meeting at the Pentagon, 20 September 1951, *FRUS, 1951, VI*, Part 1, 517.

intervention.[19] When he explained this US thinking at the January 1952 staff talks with the British, Bradley also mentioned the issue of whether to use the atomic bomb as a threat, avowing that this should not be proposed unless there was every intention of carrying out the threat if it were ignored, while any ultimatum would need to make clear that the bomb would be used against military targets only, not civilian populations. However, Field Marshal Slim, the Chief of the Imperial General Staff, did not favour any use of the atomic bomb in this context and therefore preferred to keep mention of the type of retaliation that would be employed as vague as possible in order to add to Chinese uncertainty, an argument that Bradley was prepared to accept.[20] In fact, there had as yet been no consensus within the Truman administration over the course to take if the Chinese moved into Indochina; the JCS wanted to be told how much importance was accorded to holding Indochina, so they could determine the effort that should be devoted to its defence (when there were so many other pressing calls on US resources), while the State Department wanted to receive a military appraisal of options before offering a firm statement indicating the value of the territory compared to other US interests. At one meeting with the JCS, Paul Nitze explained how though there was a clear desire to issue a warning, it was also wished that this could be done 'without incurring the risk of general war and without using the atomic weapons'.[21]

The explicit line laid down in the first draft of NSC 124, the major document defining US objectives and courses of action in the event of Communist aggression in South East Asia, and issued by the NSC staff in February 1952, was that prior agreement with both Britain and France would have to be reached on what action to take if a warning was ignored before such a warning was given.[22] The problem here was that the French had reservations about launching any more general campaigns against China which might distract resources from the struggle in Indochina, and, as we have seen, the British wanted no part in an attack on the Chinese mainland designed to bring about the collapse of the regime and which might spark a global war with the Soviet Union, and they also had

---

[19] See memorandum of State Department–JCS meeting, 21 December 1951, *FRUS, 1951, VI*, Part 1, 570; JCS memorandum for Lovett, 28 December 1951, and Lovett to Acheson, 2 January 1952, *FRUS, 1952–1954, XII: East Asia and the Pacific*, Part 1 (Washington, DC, 1984), 4–7.

[20] Notes of tripartite military conversations, 11 January 1952, *FRUS, 1952–1954, XII*, Part 1, 9–10.

[21] Memorandum of State Department–JCS meeting, 23 January 1952, *ibid.*, 35.

[22] See NSC 124, 'U.S. Objectives and Courses of Action with Respect to Communist Aggression in Southeast Asia', 13 February 1952, *ibid.*, 48.

immediate concerns that Hong Kong would be the first Chinese target in the event of allied action against the mainland. Meanwhile, in Washington the Joint Strategic Plans Committee (JSPC) had been examining the military requirements that would flow from any decision to take direct action against China, and in a report produced in early April came forward with the conclusion that atomic weapons would have to be used. Their employment, it was estimated, would destroy the power of the Chinese Communist air force within ten days, while the logistics capacity of China to support aggressive military action could be reduced by 75 per cent in thirty days of bombardment; if conventional means alone were used, these times would stretch out to six weeks and nine months respectively.[23]

By June 1952, when the final draft of what became NSC 124/2 had been endorsed by the whole NSC, the emphasis of US policy had shifted to countering the far more immediate and pressing subversive Communist threat in the region, and the concomitant need to stiffen French resolve in Indochina, though how this was to be done remained the subject of contention.[24] Allied agreement for a joint warning of the consequences that would flow from overt Chinese aggression was to be sought, but (as in the February draft) before it could be issued Britain and France would also have to agree on the military steps to take if the warning was ignored, with a naval blockade the minimum level of response required.[25] Though during the summer the British seemed a little more forthcoming, their basic position was that while ready to see naval and air support offered to the immediate battlefront and bombing of Chinese lines of communication adjacent to any area of aggression, they were not prepared to subscribe to a more widespread campaign of bombing against mainland ports and communications, the mining of rivers, or a naval blockade of the Chinese coast.

British views were clouded by Churchill's personal interventions, where he tended to discount Chinese military capabilities and did not want Far East issues to come between London and Washington (especially when he had set about his second spell as prime minister determined to repair Anglo-American relations from what he felt had been the strains induced by the Korean War in 1950–1). In August 1952, in a display of his

---

[23] JCS 1992/146, 'U.S. Objectives and Courses of Action with Respect to Communist Aggression in Southeast Asia', and Enclosure A, 'Draft Memorandum for the Secretary of Defense', 1 April 1952, OPD 381 Asia (13 Feb. 1952), sec. 2, box 707, Air Force Plans, RG 341, TNA.

[24] See Gibbons, *U.S. Government and the Vietnam War*, Part 1, 116–17.

[25] NSC 124/2, 'United States Objectives and Courses of Action with Respect to Southeast Asia', 25 June 1952, *FRUS, 1952–1954, XII*, Part 1, 128–9.

unapologetic belief in 'Anglo-Saxon' superiority, he had minuted, 'I do not regard China as a formidable adversary . . . you may take it that for the next four or five years 400 million Chinese will be living just where they are now. They cannot swim, they are not much good at flying and the trans-Siberian railway is already overloaded . . . as long as we do not send American or United Nations troops into China or transport Chiang Kai-shek's people there, nothing very serious can happen in China. Do not let us be too hard on the Americans in this part of the world.' Churchill favoured limited air action against Chinese lines of communication, believing it would be enough to frustrate any advance into South East Asia: 'in the last war I never believed in the power of China. I doubt whether Communist China is going to be the monster that some people imagine.'[26] It was for this reason that the Prime Minister could see no sense in confronting China in the aggressive way that appeared to be favoured in some US circles; as he told the Cabinet's Defence Committee in March 1952, 'it would be silly to waste bombs on the vague inchoate mass of China and wrong to kill thousands of people for no purpose'.[27] With the Prime Minister ultimately prepared to conform with the wishes of his Cabinet colleagues, where the arguments for a more reserved and cautious position, as espoused by Foreign Secretary Anthony Eden, held sway, the British line was to press for further staff talks on the immediate needs of South East Asian defence rather than to make public any fresh statements on the retribution that would follow a Chinese attack (staff talks which the American military continued to regard with suspicion as a way to suck them into a commitment of forces for the defence of colonial territories or a regular system and machinery of staff consultation). In July, State Department representatives met with the JCS and discussed whether it would be possible to push the British any further, but Nitze, the head of the PPS, was not optimistic, particularly as now he could not see 'how we can accomplish much without using atomic weapons', and this was sure to lead to political difficulties. Bradley concurred that he and his colleagues believed the United States could not enter into what he called 'large-scale action against China' while keeping its nuclear weapons in storage, reasoning that 'we have been spending billions on them after all, and it seems to be a very effective weapon. I doubt if we can handle the problem without using them. One of the arguments against the [naval] blockade has been that it wouldn't be

---

[26] Churchill minute for Minister of State at the Foreign Office (Selwyn Lloyd), M.459/52, 26 August 1952, FO 800/782, TNA.
[27] D(52)2nd meeting, 19 March 1952, CAB 21/3280, TNA.

effective. I think that we could seriously interfere with the use of their main centers of communication if we used nuclear weapons.'[28]

Thus, by the summer of 1952, the Truman administration appears to have come round to the view that conventional air attack and naval blockade would not, of its own accord, provide a suitable or effective response to any further instance of Chinese Communist aggression in Asia, and that use of nuclear weapons had to be added to the range of responses that the military should have available. There were still political qualms over the likely attitudes of allies and Asian reactions, and NSC 124/2 mentioned the contingency that if there was overt Chinese intervention in Indochina, the United States would have to consider acting alone if allied agreement was not forthcoming.[29] It had also become a cardinal position, nevertheless, that British and French backing, at least at a political level, would be needed in the event of all-out war with China; as Charles Bohlen, Counselor of the State Department, put it in one meeting of early 1952, 'we have to get French and British support if we are going to war with Communist China, for without their support we might lose the whole NATO structure'.[30]

Nitze was certainly right to be concerned about British reactions if the use of nuclear weapons was brought into staff talks, and, just as at the time of the Attlee visit to Washington in 1950, British officials were conscious of the wider implications of any use of nuclear weapons in Asia, particularly with the shadow of the atomic bombings of Japanese cities still hanging heavily over the region, and key non-aligned states such as India harshly critical of the nuclear stance of the Western powers. Indeed, in their major Global Strategy Paper of July 1952, the COS had argued that, 'Conditions in East Asia are such that atom bombing of China – anyway on the scale we could afford to spare from the deterrent against Russia – is not only unlikely to be effectual but would operate to the disadvantage of the Allies by producing a strongly anti-Western reaction throughout Asia, a reaction of which Russia would make full use.'[31] At the end of that same month, Slessor travelled to Washington for high-level talks with the JCS and State Department representatives on the recent British strategic review. The conclusions of the COS, derived from Slessor's subsequent report, were that the American people would never accept another limited war such as Korea with troops engaged in an area like Indochina. Instead, more direct measures against the Chinese mainland would be undertaken, using US superiority in naval

---

[28] Memorandum of State Department–JCS meeting, 16 July 1952, *FRUS, 1952–1954, XII*, Part 1, 154.
[29] See NSC 124/2, *ibid.*, 132.
[30] Memorandum of State Department–JCS meeting, 5 March 1952, *ibid.*, 60.
[31] 'Defence Policy and Global Strategy', 9 July 1952, PREM 11/49; this paper can also be found at D(52)26, 17 June 1952, CAB 131/12, TNA.

and air power. In this response, the COS felt that American attitudes towards the potential bombing of China were 'governed more by emotion than by reason' and it was 'doubtful whether they have thought out their policy to its ultimate conclusion'. The American approach seemed to be that 'we must do something' if there was further Chinese aggression, but 'what the effect of that "something" would be they did not explain, but it is difficult to avoid the impression that their object – or at least that of the United States Navy – is to overthrow the Communist Chinese regime'. Even though the US and British intelligence communities had recently agreed on an assessment that a blockade of Chinese ports would have only slight impact due to the low volumes of seaborne traffic coming into them, US Navy leaders were still determined to pursue a naval blockade and the bombing of communications, leading the COS to conclude that they were 'a law unto themselves', while 'the influence of Admiral [Arthur W.] Radford [the US Commander-in-Chief, Pacific (CINCPAC)] ... is believed to be very powerful in favour of their "all-out" policy against China'.[32] Revisiting the same topic in September, the JIC found that disruption of Chinese aggression through attacks on the apparatus of centralized Communist control would require targeting thirty-five major centres of administration, and decisive results against these large towns and cities could be achieved only with atomic bombs; any use of atomic weapons would, however, elicit 'strong and determined opposition in East and West', particularly from Asian members of the Commonwealth.[33] The COS and their Joint Planning Staff felt that as well as increasing the risk of global war, widespread conventional bombardment of lines of communication in China would be 'unacceptable'. Such bombing would be unlikely to prevent the seizure of Tonkin and Hong Kong, and would increase the risks of global war. Moreover, it 'might be misinterpreted throughout Asia as an imperialist war of aggression' and 'alienate those eastern races now friendly to us'. Use of the atomic bomb was rejected in any campaign against China, 'as this would fatally estrange world opinion'.[34] Meeting in Washington in October, American, British and French staffs considered once again the kinds of retaliatory actions that might be taken against

[32] COS(52)443, 'Discussions in Washington on Global Strategy with the United States Joint Chiefs of Staff and the State Department', 18 August 1952, DEFE 5/41, TNA; the talks were actually held 29–30 July 1952.
[33] 'Military Courses of Action and their Implications in the Event of Further Chinese Aggression', JIC(52)57(Final), 4 September 1952, CAB 21/3274, TNA.
[34] See JP(52)113(Final), 'Possible Deterrents to Further Communist Aggression in South East Asia', 16 September 1952, CAB 21/3274, TNA; and 'Action in the Event of Further Chinese Aggression', COS(52)521, 19 September 1952, DEFE 5/41, TNA; these same conclusions were presented to a NATO meeting in Paris three months later; see 'Annex III: The Defence of South East Asia', COS(52)663, 5 December 1952, DEFE 5/43, TNA.

Chinese aggression. No mention was made of what difference nuclear weapons might make to the evaluations offered. The October discussions merely resulted in further exasperation on the part of the US military regarding the timidity of their Western allies, though in early 1953 it was decided to establish new loose arrangements for periodic staff consultations, involving Australia and New Zealand as well, to co-ordinate military planning among the five Western powers which might contribute forces for the defence of South East Asia.[35]

Despite the reservations of some American officials that this five-power staff agency, with an exclusively Western membership, could be seen as a 'white man's club', its first meetings went ahead in the spring of 1953, resulting in joint intelligence appreciations of the Chinese threat to the area and estimates of the force requirements that would be needed to oppose an overt aggression in South East Asia. Nevertheless, the Americans remained very uneasy about the existence of the staff agency, their doubts driven by a desire not to be pinned down by the other Western powers over their possible responses to a Chinese attack, and their sensitivities over the appearance of racial bias when dealing with the defence needs of an Asian area.[36] The British, for their part, remained alert to the possible damage to the Western cause that could be inflicted by underlying American attitudes. In December 1952, at the annual gathering of Britain's chief colonial, diplomatic and military officials in South East Asia, held at Bukit Serene in Malaya, the conferees 'recognised the fundamental generosity and idealism of United States policy but noted with regret that much of the good in American policy and action is often vitiated by the clumsiness of their methods and the deep-seated fear amongst Asians that the American attitude to China may lead either to an extension of the Korean War beyond Korea's boundaries or to a general war. These things provide exceptional opportunities for Communist propaganda.'[37]

Meanwhile, the rearmament effort launched by the Truman administration in late 1950 was beginning to bear fruit, as new US military equipment began to pour off the production lines, adding to general confidence in American strength and capacity to undertake an expanded war in

---

[35] For a summary see W. David McIntyre, *Background to the Anzus Pact: Policy-Making, Strategy and Diplomacy, 1945–55* (Christchurch, 1995), 370–3.

[36] For these reservations, see Charlton Ogburn memorandum for U. Alexis Johnson, 'U.S. Alliance with "White" Powers in Asia', 13 February 1953, 'Far East General' folder, box 5, records of the Bureau of Far East Affairs Subject Files, 1953, RG 59, TNA; see also Henry W. Brands Jr, 'From ANZUS to SEATO: United States Strategic Policy towards Australia and New Zealand, 1952–1954', *International History Review*, 9, 2, 1987, 261–3. For an Asian critique of 'white' planning in the area, see J. S. Singh, 'How to Win Friends in Asia', *NYT*, 28 September 1952.

[37] See MacDonald to FO, No. 100, 8 December 1952, DEFE 11/87, TNA.

Korea.[38] In April 1952, the Joint Strategic Survey Committee presented to their parent body, the JCS, a comprehensive list of military measures that should be considered in order to intensify pressure on the Communist side if a successful conclusion to the armistice talks was not reached before a predetermined deadline; now included was mention of the possible use of tactical nuclear weapons against enemy forces (the same month, incidentally, when the JSSC had first advocated the use of nuclear weapons against the Chinese mainland in response to overt aggression in South East Asia).[39] One major reason for the military's enhanced interest in nuclear options was that the US stockpile of weapons was now of vastly greater size than had been apparent only eighteen months before, making it no longer so risky to expend a proportion of the arsenal in the Far East as there would be adequate numbers still to face the Soviet Union if a general war were to result from action against China. In May 1952, in fact, senior figures in the Truman administration had approved a further expansion of the atomic energy programme that, as well as strengthening the production capacities of the United States for strategic nuclear weapons, placed a new emphasis on a rapid expansion of the stockpile of tactical atomic weapons, with concrete results expected by 1956. The military requirements which underpinned the whole programme, the Secretary of Defense noted, arose 'primarily from the necessity of meeting Communist aggression by more extensive use of our superior industrial and scientific resources rather than trying to match our potential enemy man-for-man'.[40]

Alongside this sense of burgeoning American power has to be put the intense frustration felt by wide currents of opinion over the losses entailed by a continuation of the Korean War in its current form, and a desire to punish the Communist perpetrators of the initial aggression. Restrictions over the means that could be used by the UN forces in Korea to break the stalemate at the front became a renewed topic of discussion among the JCS as the Truman administration, tiring of the deadlocked negotiations over armistice terms at Panmunjom, presented their final package of proposals over the central issue of prisoner-of-war repatriation in September 1952, which if rejected would result in the indefinite recession of the talks. When concessions were not forthcoming, senior US officials considered again how military pressure might be used to produce a change of attitude on the Communist side. A JCS staff study had already

[38] Stueck, *Korean War*, 283–4.   [39] Foot, *Wrong War*, 176–7.
[40] See memorandum by the Secretary of Defense for the Executive Secretary of the NSC, 16 May 1952, *FRUS, 1952–1954, II: National Security Affairs*, Part 2 (Washington, DC, 1984), 935; for American nuclear supremacy by 1952 and its temptations, see Marc Trachtenberg, 'A "Wasting Asset": American Strategy and the Shifting Nuclear Balance, 1949–1954', in *History and Strategy* (Princeton, 1991), especially 128–32.

concluded that if there was a breakdown in talks, a military victory in Korea would require eleven extra US divisions, much greater air and sea power, and use of atomic weapons.[41] When asked his opinion, the response from General Mark W. Clark, the American head of the UN Command, who had replaced Ridgway in May, was clear: a major augmentation of his forces was needed for a successful ground offensive in Korea, while casualties could be kept to acceptable levels only if the restrictions on the geographical scope of the fighting and the means at his disposal were lifted.[42] In a later submission, Clark was more explicit, advocating the use of atomic weapons against airbases in Manchuria and north China alongside his plans for a renewed effort on the ground.[43] With a presidential election due in November, it was obvious that no major decisions on future action would be taken until a new administration assumed office, and in the meantime the JCS continued to believe that an intensified campaign of conventional bombing of North Korea (a new round having been initiated in August 1952) offered the best immediate chance of weakening Communist resolve.[44]

The most effective message employed by the Republicans in their successful 1952 presidential election campaign was undoubtedly that their candidate would offer the American people respite from the casualties and taxes associated with the Korean War. Although not so bold as to mimic the Republican right's call for outright victory in Korea, Dwight D. Eisenhower nevertheless came to share in the attack on the Truman administration's conduct of the inconclusive armistice negotiations, and his leadership of a campaign which talked about the 'rollback' of Communist power suggested he would pursue a more aggressive policy. Having captured the Party's nomination in July from what he considered the dangerously isolationist hands of Senator Taft, he offered voters the ambiguous promise that he would bring what seemed an interminable war to an honourable and successful end.[45] Eisenhower would be joined in the

---

[41] Schnabel and Watson, *History of the JCS, III*, Part 2, 928–30.
[42] See Clark to JCS, 29 September 1952, *FRUS, 1952–1954, XV*, Part 1, 548–50.
[43] See Condit, *Test of War*, 166–7; also on Clark's thinking about use of nuclear weapons in Korea by late 1952, see Conrad C. Crane, 'To Avert Impending Disaster: American Military Plans to Use Atomic Weapons during the Korean War', *Journal of Strategic Studies*, 23, 2, June 2000, 82–3.
[44] These points are most effectively conveyed in Foot, *Substitute for Victory*, 143–52.
[45] For the campaign see Charles C. Alexander, *Holding the Line: The Eisenhower Era, 1952–1961* (Bloomington, 1975), 1–23. During June 1952, and before his nomination, Eisenhower had been very circumspect with reporters about the chances for success in Korea, and whether extension of the war offered any chance of its settlement; see Ronald J. Caridi, *The Korean War and American Politics: The Republican Party as a Case Study* (Philadelphia, 1968), 214–16. Eisenhower's essential moderation over using Korea to assail the Democrats is also emphasized in Casey, *Selling the Korean War*, 325–36.

stewardship of American foreign policy by John Foster Dulles, who had finally arrived at the culminating point of his long career as a lawyer and consultant specializing in international affairs. Easy to malign for his apparent slowness of thought and stiff demeanour, Dulles was a more complex character than first impressions would suggest. It is difficult to match the description offered by Marquis Childs, who observed the Secretary of State for many years as Washington bureau chief of the *Saint Louis Post-Dispatch*: 'A mixture of sophistication and evangelism, of great knowledge and a weakness for glib slogans, of shrewdness and windy idealism, of harsh realism, and the most naive wishful thinking, Dulles began [his time in office] with a self-centred confidence that he could quickly remedy the mistakes of the past.'[46] Having left his State Department assignment in March 1952 after Senate ratification of the Japanese peace treaty, Dulles began to forge a critique of what, in his famous *Life* magazine article in May, he alleged were the Truman administration's 'negative' and 'treadmill policies', which were sapping the economic vitality of the nation by their heavy expenditures for no apparent gain. Dulles staked out instead a grandly titled 'policy of boldness', which rejected any retreat into 'fortress America', or the initiation of a preventive war, in favour of developing 'the will and organiz[ing] the means to retaliate instantly against open aggression by Red armies, so that, if it occurred anywhere, we could and would strike back where it hurts, by means of our own choosing'. The 'means' referred to was 'atomic energy, coupled with strategic air and sea power', which would provide the 'community power to stop aggression before it starts ... In the hands of the statesman, [atomic weapons] could serve as effective political weapons in defense of the peace.'[47]

Dulles's conception that advance warning should be given of American readiness to 'hit an aggressor where it hurts' was clearly derived from the lesson of Korea that if the Communists had known beforehand the US response, they would never have dared to launch their attack of June 1950 in the first place and amounted to direct criticism of the ambiguous posture taken up by Acheson in his defence perimeter speech.[48] Though

[46] Marquis Childs, *Eisenhower: Captive Hero* (London, 1959), 174.
[47] See Gaddis, *Strategies*, 118–19; Townsend Hoopes, *The Devil and John Foster Dulles* (Boston, 1973), 127–8; and Michael A. Guhin, *John Foster Dulles: A Statesman and His Times* (New York, 1972), 225. For the early genesis of Dulles's ideas, see Samuel F. Wells, 'The Origins of Massive Retaliation', *Political Science Quarterly*, 96, 1, Spring 1981, 41–3.
[48] In one typical campaign speech, Dulles had declared, 'The only effective way to stop a potential aggressor is to convince them in advance that if they commit aggression, they will be subjected to retaliatory blows so costly that their aggression will not be a profitable operation'; see 'Mr Dulles' Program', *NYT*, 17 May 1952.

often identified with support for the Korean intervention, Dulles was well aware of the pitfalls of ground troop commitments on the Asian mainland, confessing in July 1950 to Walter Lippmann, for example, his 'doubts as to the wisdom of engaging our land forces on the continent of Asia as against an enemy that could be nourished from the vast resources of the USSR'.[49] In an address in Paris in early May 1952, Dulles argued that the best defence of Indochina and other vulnerable areas of Asia to Communist attack would be to threaten direct retaliation against the PRC or Soviet Union, asking, 'Is it not time that the Chinese Communists knew that if, for example, they sent their Red armies openly into Vietnam we will not be content merely to try to meet their armed forces at the point they select for their aggression but by retaliatory action of our own fashioning?' Large areas of China and the Soviet Union, including Siberia and Manchuria, Dulles highlighted, were 'vulnerable from the standpoint of transport and communication'.[50] The iteration of such an apparently dynamic new strategy was designed by Dulles, of course, as a contrast with the restraint exhibited by the incumbent Democratic administration. As we have also seen, however, the idea of retaliatory strikes against targets on the Chinese mainland in response to a direct move by Beijing into French Indochina was already a key part of US strategy in the Far East during 1952, and in October was to be the central topic of discussion with US allies in the newly formed five power staff agency concerned with the defence of South East Asia.

Where Dulles departed from existing administration policy, it becomes apparent, was in his willingness to be far more explicit in public about the response to aggression that was anticipated, primarily as he saw in nuclear weapons a means of deterrence, making the delivery of firm warnings to any potential aggressor essential. 'Upon entering office', as one of his biographers has remarked, Dulles 'believed that the strategy of and power for deterrence had to be more openly organized and clearly defined'.[51] Such an approach also presented opportunities to reduce the overall burden of defence spending by allowing for cut-backs to expensive overseas deployments of US ground forces, as well as the removal from

---

[49] Quoted in Steel, *Walter Lippmann*, 472, and see also Pruessen, *Dulles*, 455–6.
[50] See Robert E. Osgood, *Limited War: The Challenge to American Security* (Chicago, 1957), 201–4.
[51] Guhin, *Dulles*, 227. In June 1952, for example, Dulles had written: 'Our deterrent power does not, today, have anywhere near the reassuring power of which it is capable because no one knows whether, when or where it would be used. Complete precision on all these matters is of course neither practical nor wise. There is reason for calculated uncertainty and some flexibility, but there is never reason for the degree of political chaos which now involves this subject.' Quoted in Gaddis, *Strategies*, 149.

foreign territory of US troops which could easily become an irritant in relations with local peoples and governments. This last point was directly related to Dulles's experiences with the occupation regime in Japan and what he had learned of the attitudes of the military authorities. 'My personal feeling,' Dulles wrote in one letter of March 1952 to Chester Bowles, 'is that Japan would be stronger and more dependable ally [*sic*] if we relied upon the deterrent of striking power through our air and naval forces in the area and did not go into the business of trying to maintain large land forces on Japan. The continuing presence of large bodies of U.S. troops and their dependents is going to create vast ill-will (see our Declaration of Independence) ... '[52] Dulles's recognition that the presence of US bases and obtrusive military personnel could become the cause of anti-American feeling was an ever-present feature of his views, and increased the attractiveness of an American strategy that relied more explicitly on offshore naval and air power, bolstered with nuclear weapons.

Reductions in overall federal expenditures, as the route to lower taxation and a sounder economy, were also an essential part of Eisenhower's campaign, and his whole approach to government. The experience of the Korean War was again fundamental in shaping the new President's conviction that the health of the economy was inextricably linked to overall questions of national security policy. In Eisenhower's view, the Cold War was set to be a protracted struggle which, if American resources were not effectively marshalled, could place intolerable strains on the US economy and society as a whole. The ballooning defence budgets that had appeared since the eruption of the Korean crisis and the Truman administration's embrace of large-scale rearmament in September 1950 could become an inflationary recipe for disaster, with the federal government eventually having to impose illiberal controls on individual economic behaviour, and so sacrificing the very values that the United States was supposedly defending against the Communist challenge. A sound domestic economy was considered vital both for ensuring the United States could muster the resources necessary for the long haul of the Cold War, and as the bedrock on which the freedoms underpinning American society were built.[53] The arch-exponent and practitioner of this philosophy in the administration that took office in January 1953, apart from the President himself, was the powerful Secretary of the Treasury, George M. Humphrey, the

---

[52] Dulles to Bowles, 25 March 1952, folder 243, box 94, Bowles papers.
[53] See Alexander, *Holding the Line*, 29–30; Casey, *Selling the Korean War*, 331; Robert R. Bowie and Richard H. Immerman, *Waging Peace: How Eisenhower Shaped an Enduring Cold War Strategy* (New York, 1998), 44–5.

embodiment of conservative business ethos. At the Pentagon, as Secretary of Defense, Eisenhower installed Charles E. Wilson, the former head of General Motors, and it was Wilson the President came to reply on to steer through the budget cuts that made up what by the end of 1953 had come to be known as the 'New Look' in defence policy.

During the 1952 campaign, one of Eisenhower's overall messages was that he was the best candidate to ensure peace for the American people, and he had been far more reserved about echoing Dulles's ideas about the need for the United States to rely on nuclear retaliation as a deterrent to Communist expansionism, even insisting that all reference to 'retaliatory striking power' should be removed from the official Republican platform (the foreign policy sections of which had been composed by Dulles).[54] Once in office, however, Eisenhower showed no such squeamishness and, in marked contrast to Truman, felt as he entered the White House that, as Samuel F. Wells has put it, 'nuclear weapons presented real and usable military options' that he would be ready to employ 'in any situation where they would be militarily appropriate'.[55] Probably mindful of the first test explosion of a hydrogen bomb the previous November, when Truman had delivered his farewell broadcast to the nation in January 1953, he expressed his deep conviction that 'starting an atomic war is totally unthinkable for rational men'.[56] Aversion to giving detailed consideration to the circumstances in which nuclear use might be initiated was typical for Truman.[57] It was this reluctance to engage and think through such issues, however, that attracted criticism from Eisenhower and Dulles, among others. The new President was ready to examine these basic problems, and from an early stage of his administration wanted to explore the possibilities for tactical use of atomic weapons in Korea. Moreover, along with Dulles, Eisenhower was keen to remove the distinctions that had built up between nuclear and conventional munitions in popular perceptions. At an NSC meeting on 11 February 1953, when General Clark's complaint that the area around Keasong, where the armistice talks

[54] See entries for 6 and 9 July 1952, in Sulzberger, *Long Row of Candles*, 660–1, 662. Eisenhower also saw such statements as evoking the Taft wing of the Party's preference for a form of American 'neo-isolationism'; see Bowie and Immerman, *Waging Peace*, 73–4.
[55] Wells, 'The Origins of Massive Retaliation', 38.
[56] Farewell Address to the American People, 15 January 1953, *The Public Papers of the Presidents: Harry S. Truman, 1952–53* (Washington, DC, 1965), 1201.
[57] See, for example, mention of the 'lack of clarity' over American atomic intentions in the Far East and the fact the issue 'had been very incompletely examined by the American government' in the report of the high-level Panel of Consultants on Disarmament established by Truman in April 1952, 'Armaments and American Policy', January 1953, *FRUS, 1952–1954, II*, Part 2, 1070.

had first been held, was now being used as a sanctuary for the build-up of Communist forces was discussed, Eisenhower mentioned that it would make a good target for tactical atomic weapons and their use should be considered, while Dulles noted the moral problem faced with use of the atomic bomb and how the 'false distinction' set up between nuclear and conventional weaponry should be broken down.[58]

A further sign of new attitudes was given at the end of the same month during a meeting of the NSC's Special Committee on Atomic Energy, where in the middle of a discussion about whether the next US continental series of nuclear tests should be given wide publicity, Dulles interjected to offer his support and argue 'with some vigor' that the United States was

> doing itself a very great disservice by surrounding atomic weapons with a cloak of silence and mystery. This ... only adds to the tendency to place these weapons in a category apart from all other weapons and to reinforce the idea that their use was immoral. We tie our hands with this taboo. In the past, higher civilizations have always maintained their place against lower civilizations by devising more effective weapons. We must not, therefore, continue to play the Russian game ... it was inexplicable to him why it was moral to kill ten thousand people with ten weapons but immoral to do so with one.[59]

By the middle of March, Eisenhower was requesting that the Pentagon study the requirements of a major new ground campaign in Korea designed to inflict heavy losses on Chinese forces and secure a more defensible line at the narrow waist of the peninsula. He instructed that employment of nuclear weapons would be dependent on 'military judgment as to their use on military targets'.[60] At the end of the month, Eisenhower was remarking that the effect on the allies of any recourse to nuclear weapons in Korea would be very serious since 'they feel that they will be the battleground in an atomic war between the United States and the Soviet Union'. Despite this, both he and Dulles agreed that 'somehow or other the tabu [sic] which surrounds the use of atomic weapons would have to be destroyed'. Dulles, in fact, went even further by adding that 'in the present state of world opinion we could not use an A-bomb', and every effort should be taken to counteract this feeling.[61] In early May, Eisenhower had even speculated whether four Communist airfields in

---

[58] Memorandum of discussion at the 131st Meeting of the National Security Council, 11 February 1953, *FRUS, 1952–1954, XV*, Part 1, 769–70.

[59] Memorandum of a meeting of the NSC Special Committee on Atomic Energy, 24 February 1953, Declassified Documents Reference System (online version), document number CK3100129165. Henceforth cited in the form DDRS/CK3100129165.

[60] Memorandum by Cutler for Wilson, 21 March 1953, *FRUS, 1952–1954, XV*, Part 1, 815.

[61] Memorandum of discussion at a Special Meeting of the National Security Council, 31 March 1953, *ibid.*, 827.

North Korea which the Air Force had recently pinpointed for attack might prove a useful target to 'test the effectiveness of an atomic bomb'. This was accompanied by the thought that 'we have got to consider the atomic bomb as simply another weapon in the arsenal'.[62]

One of the clearest markers that the Eisenhower administration intended to remove any special status from nuclear weapons came in the way it was far more ready to accede to JCS requests that control of the US atomic stockpile should be transferred from civilian hands at the Atomic Energy Commission to the Department of Defense. When in April 1953 the NSC's Special Committee on Atomic Energy agreed to recommend to the President the transfer of all completed atomic weapons from the AEC to the Pentagon, it did so with the explicit backing of the State Department. In its supporting statement, the State Department noted its belief that custody for atomic weapons, like other weapons, should be in the hands of the user agency, adding to the sense that it was a 'normal' part of the military arsenal:

To the extent that such a transfer would help to reduce the uniqueness associated with these weapons at home and abroad, it will tend toward increased United States freedom of action in relation to this element of our military power. For the United States to continue to treat the custody of these weapons in a way different from other weapons would be inconsistent with efforts to convince the public at home or abroad that atomic weapons are to be considered an integral element of our arsenal and to reduce the moral stigma which has been associated with these weapons.

A note of caution did, however, enter into the State Department's position, holding that the timing and public announcement of any such transfer should be influenced by 'the state of world tensions and world developments in general', while major allies, particularly Britain and Canada, should be given advance notice.[63] This last proviso, as well as the comments of Dulles given above, were to become a constant feature of the administration's approach to nuclear issues throughout the rest of the 1950s, in that however much it might desire a transformation in attitudes, publics around the world were simply not prepared to accept that nuclear weapons were indistinguishable from conventional. This had a crucial

---

[62] Memorandum of discussion at the 143rd meeting of the NSC, 6 May 1953, *ibid.*, 975.

[63] See memorandum for Eisenhower by James Lay, 4 May 1953, and Appendix C, 'Statement by the Department of State', 22 April 1953, 'Atomic Energy – The President (May 1953–March 1956) (1)', box 1, subject subseries, NSC Records, Office of the Special Assistant for National Security Affairs, White House Office, Dwight D. Eisenhower Library (DDEL). It should be noted, however, that Truman had already reached a decision in principle to transfer a portion of the stockpile to military control in September 1952; see Condit, *Test of War*, 466.

bearing on the opinions and policies of US allies, many of whom would have to provide the bases for nuclear operations in any general war with the Soviet Union, and which were more vulnerable to Soviet nuclear retaliation, at least until the latter half of the decade, than the homeland of the United States.

As they began to disseminate new ideas on how nuclear weapons should be regarded, the administration searched for ways out of its Korean conundrum. During the presidential election campaign, Eisenhower and Dulles had offered few specifics about what new approaches they would try. The one concrete suggestion they did put forward was that more South Korean troops should be trained and equipped so that US forces on the peninsula could be reduced in number, an initiative which was presented in the context of the war having become a struggle with racial connotations. In early October, Eisenhower had declared: 'There is no sense in the United Nations, with America bearing the brunt of the thing, being constantly compelled to man those front lines. That is a job for the Koreans. We do not want Asia to feel that the white man of the West is his enemy. If there must be a war there, let it be Asians against Asians, with our support on the side of freedom.'[64] In an echo of these themes, Dulles delivered another speech a few days later advocating the replacement of US troops with South Koreans, presenting the strategic arguments for such a step in that it would release American strength from being tied up on the peninsula by Soviet pressure tactics. However, he also noted how the presence of US troops in Korea gave the Communists a 'colossal propaganda success' by being able to dub the conflict a 'race war'. If the South Koreans fought their own war this would 'automatically end one of the Communists' main talking lines. Then they can no longer misrepresent the war as a race war, with white men killing yellow men by methods white people would not use against each other.'[65] Though conceived as an appealing rebuff to Communist charges that the Korean fighting resembled in some ways the racial clash represented by the Pacific War of 1941–5, the idea that the United States was prepared to stand aside and let Asians kill Asians for the attainment of Washington's geopolitical goals quickly rebounded against the presidential candidate (the reception in India of such remarks was particularly poor). Indeed, when Eisenhower delivered his inaugural address in January 1953, there was an echo of the controversy in his declaration that 'we hold all continents and peoples in equal regard and honor. We reject any insinuation that one race or

---

[64] 'Eisenhower Wants Koreans to Bear Brunt of Fighting', *NYT*, 3 October 1952.
[65] 'Dulles Korea Plan Echoes Eisenhower', *NYT*, 5 October 1952. These speeches are also mentioned in Caridi, *Korean War and American Politics*, 230.

another, one people or another, is in any sense inferior or expendable.'[66] The use of the final word 'expendable' may have been an oblique reference to this earlier issue, but whatever the case, the sentiment expressed of support for racial equality is again indicative of how American presidents in the Cold War era were having to pay rhetorical attention to this principle in a global setting, even though the domestic race scene was so lamentable: by the early 1950s, the NAACP's demands for equality had been stifled through fear of being branded unpatriotic in its criticisms of American society, and southern segregationists lost no time in identifying advocates of racial change as dangerous communist subversives.[67]

As it transpired, the Korean War played its most notable role in the election campaign in late October 1952 when, only ten days before the presidential poll, Eisenhower dramatically announced that if elected he would 'go to Korea'. With this symbolic gesture, few doubted that Eisenhower's Democrat rival, Adlai Stevenson, faced clear defeat. Amid the euphoria of Republican victory, and the prospect of the party's first occupant of the White House for over twenty years, radical suggestions for ending the war were still in circulation. Eisenhower had been careful to keep MacArthur (a man he loathed) at a distance during the campaign, even though the controversial and now-retired general retained an adulatory following in some Republican circles. Nevertheless, in early December, while the President-elect was fulfilling his pledge to tour the front in Korea, MacArthur had seen fit to deliver a speech which asserted he had a solution to the war, but that it could be revealed only to Eisenhower himself. After some nervous discussion among his advisers, Eisenhower felt it appropriate to stage a meeting with MacArthur in New York, where the latter explained his idea to issue an ultimatum to Stalin containing the terms for a political settlement which if not accepted would lead to atomic attacks on troop concentrations in North Korea, the sowing of a radioactive belt to prevent the movement of supplies across the Yalu, and a major bombing campaign against China proper. According to an interview that Eisenhower gave to his biographer, Stephen Ambrose, he was appalled, being concerned not least that to use nuclear weapons again in Asia so soon after Hiroshima would, as Ambrose paraphrased it, 'make all Asians enemies of the United States'.[68]

---

[66] Inaugural address, 20 January 1953, *Public Papers of the Presidents: Dwight D. Eisenhower, 1953* (Washington, DC, 1955), 1.

[67] See George Lewis, *The White South and the Red Menace: Segregationists, Anticommunism, and Massive Resistance, 1945–1965* (Gainesville, FL, 2004).

[68] See Stephen Ambrose, *Eisenhower: The President* (London, 1984), 31–2, 35.

These intimations of concern for 'Asian opinion' are perhaps more revealing of Eisenhower's later reasoning for why nuclear weapons were not used as a way to break the stalemate in Korea as the war dragged on into 1953 (the armistice talks having gone into indefinite recess in October 1952). The President was certainly aware of the possibility of alienating Asian and allied opinion through resorting to the bomb, but as we have already seen he was keen for the military to study using tactical nuclear weapons against particular targets in North Korea in the first few months after the inauguration.[69] There was, nevertheless, some reluctance in Army circles to advocate the immediate use of tactical nuclear weapons, Bradley and Collins, the Army Chief of Staff, for example, being concerned once more that suitable targets did not present themselves, and the nature of the Korean terrain and the strength of the enemy's fortifications would reduce the effects of a nuclear attack. With demands for more forceful action to break the deadlock becoming more urgent, on the return leg of his trip to the Far East, Eisenhower had publicly affirmed his intention to depart from the approach of the previous administration, warning that the enemy would be moved only by deeds, and these would be 'executed under circumstances of our own choosing' (mirroring, of course, some of the rhetoric employed by Dulles in the recent campaign).[70] The flavour of the period was captured by Sir Roger Makins, the British Ambassador in Washington, who wrote to Eden in February 1953: 'Korea dominates [the] consciousness of the United States [...] The mood of the country, and the Middle West is the area which is most aroused, is one of impatience with allies, collective efforts, and consultation. Unilateral action by the United States would be very popular. There is no disposition to listen to the arguments for the maintenance of the *status quo.*'[71]

That changes in the American approach towards the war, and Far Eastern policy in general, were potentially in the offing was in fact suggested by the whole tenor of the Republican campaign of 1952, which had made much of the Democrats' comparative neglect of Asia in favour of a preoccupation with Europe, alleging this had resulted in damaging reverses for US interests. Moreover, 'Asia-first' Republicans were bolstered by the majorities that were secured in both the Senate and the House of Representatives in the November elections, with one of their

---

[69] Described as the most extensive high-level deliberation of specific nuclear use in the post-war era; see Richard K. Betts, *Nuclear Blackmail and Nuclear Balance* (Washington, DC, 1987), 38.

[70] Ambrose, *Eisenhower*, 34.

[71] Makins to Eden, 21 February 1953, F1023/7, FO 371/105180, TNA.

most prominent figures, Senator William F. Knowland (Republican, California), becoming the Senate Majority leader after Taft's sudden death in July 1953. Dealing with the China lobby became something of a preoccupation for Dulles, who had witnessed at close quarters the headaches it had caused for Acheson while serving in the State Department, and he moved to placate them with his early appointment of Walter S. Robertson as Assistant Secretary for Far Eastern Affairs, a stern Virginian known as an ardent partisan for the cause of Chiang Kai-shek and Nationalist China.[72] They were also delighted with the administration's announcement, proclaimed by Eisenhower in his first State of the Union address in early February, that it would withdraw the Seventh Fleet from the Taiwan Strait, so 'unleashing' Chiang, and implying this would give him greater freedom to conduct military operations against the mainland. In private, however, the administration (though ready to provide assistance for minor raids on the Chinese coast) had no intention of supporting any return to the mainland by Chiang, and kept a close watch on Nationalist intentions. Regarding many aspects of China policy, in fact, Dulles pursued a far more pragmatic course, within the limits of domestic political constraints, than his contemporary and public demeanour suggested, though there was still a strong basic attitude of hostility to Beijing and vigorous opposition to its attempts to spread Communist influence. In all this, therefore, there were more elements of continuity from the Truman period than points of difference.[73]

Nevertheless, Republican rhetoric mattered immensely in how American policies were perceived in parts of Asia, and some observers were alarmed by the new tone they detected in Washington. American statements over the Far East, Nehru proclaimed during a speech in February, had caused 'grave concern', and 'from the point of view of world psychology ... have had a disastrous effect'.[74] From his post as ambassador in New Delhi, Chester Bowles felt that Dulles's first pronouncements as Secretary of State had 'aroused widespread antagonism and a sense of fear' in India, and it was remarked how his positions 'lacked an appealing moral basis and seemed to reflect only a list of narrow short-term American military objectives'. American moves to support the

---

[72] See Nancy B. Tucker (ed.), *China Confidential: American Diplomats and Sino-American Relations, 1945–1996* (New York, 2001), 90–2.

[73] See Nancy B. Tucker, 'A House Divided: The United States, the Department of State, and China', in Warren I. Cohen and Akira Iriye (eds.), *The Great Powers in East Asia, 1953–1960* (New York, 1990), 35–62. In 1950, it is worth recalling, Dulles had even advocated admitting Communist China to the UN provided this faced no 'serious domestic resistance'; see Hoopes, *John Foster Dulles*, 262.

[74] In Lok Sabha, 18 February 1953, *Nehru's Speeches*, Vol. II, 346–7.

Chinese Nationalist position on Taiwan, or to use the remnants of their forces in northern Burma to put pressure on Beijing, raised concerns that the Chinese Communists might then respond with a move into Burma or Indochina. 'The question is gravely asked,' Bowles reported, 'what would America do then? She is apparently unwilling to use troops to invade China; cutting off sea traffic could not have a decisive effect and will only increase Chinese dependence on Russia; the bombing of Chinese cities with all their massed humanity would send a wave of horror through Asia which would have grave repercussions.'[75] In early February 1953, Bowles wrote to Dulles (in his usual verbose style) amplifying his anxieties over the overall situation in Asia in the light of the new administration's apparent aim to increase the pressure on Communist China in a bid to induce concessions that could bring about an end to the fighting in Korea. Bowles advised that encouraging guerrilla activity within China, or the arming of Nationalist irregular forces in Burma, would be largely ineffective, while a blockade of the coast would simply make Beijing more dependent on Soviet support. The extreme action of bombing of the mainland would also yield only negative results: 'the mass bombing of crowded Chinese cities would earn for us the bitter hatred of hundreds of millions of people throughout the world' and the Chinese Government 'would take the damage and the slaughter in their stride, with the knowledge that our action would tend to tip the scales of world opinion strongly in their favor'. Rather than possibly provoking the Chinese into an aggressive move into South East Asia through a programme of external pressures, Bowles hoped the new administration would instead concentrate its criticisms on the Soviet Union as the main impediment to a peaceful settlement in Korea as 'a policy of force that concentrates primarily and broadly on Communist China will increase the Asian tendency to sympathize with China, and lessen whatever chance may exist of a rift between China and the Soviet Union'. Within the Far East Bureau, U. Alexis Johnson, the Deputy Assistant Secretary, was dismissive of Bowles's concerns, principally as they were based on a false assumption that the administration was about to launch a broad range of military pressures against China, while the current Chinese leadership was unlikely to embark on aggressive action elsewhere in Asia because of the likelihood of US retaliation and the possibility it would lead to general war.[76] Already suspect to the incoming administration as a prominent New Deal/Fair Deal Democrat, Bowles lobbied to retain his posting but was removed in

[75] Bowles to Paul Hoffman, 2 February 1953, folder 92, box 86, Bowles papers.
[76] Bowles to Dulles, 5 February 1953, 611.91/2–553, and Johnson memorandum for Dulles, 20 February 1953, CDF, RG 59, TNA.

March, his final and forlorn protest over decisions to substantially reduce foreign aid to India from the budget allocations made under Truman standing as a suitable epitaph.[77]

The emphasis of the Eisenhower administration in its early period was on the provision of military assistance to friends and allies around the strategic periphery of the Sino-Soviet bloc. Economic aid to neutrals, though not neglected entirely, was a lesser consideration. Having formed a poor opinion of Nehru in the late 1940s and been angered by his refusal to sign the Japanese peace treaty, Dulles continued to find the Indian leader an irritating and condescending foil for the Cold War policies of the United States, particularly as Washington began to reach out to Pakistan (a country which the Secretary of State visited in May 1953, finding a government eager to co-operate with Washington and to form a part of the northern tier of anti-Communist states stretching across the Near East).[78] Another source of contention in Indo-American relations were the efforts of Nehru to act as an impartial mediator in the struggle to break the impasse over the Korean armistice talks. Despite having put forward, in November 1952, the UN resolution which suggested a four-nation 'neutral' commission which would decide on prisoner-of-war repatriation case by case, and which later formed the basis of the way this issue was resolved in the final armistice agreement, US officials tended to regard Indian initiatives with great suspicion as too vague and imprecise (not least as they were advanced in the UN by Krishna Menon, whose contempt for all things American was plain and who was felt to have a 'poisonous' influence over Nehru).[79] Asked by a presidential aide in March 1953 whether the United States should be glad or sorry if the Communist side accepted the latest Indian compromise proposal, Dulles shot back: 'We'd be sorry. I don't think we can get much out of a Korean settlement until we have shown – before all of Asia – our clear superiority by giving the Chinese one hell of a licking.'[80] This kind of reaction may well have reflected the Secretary of State's immediate sense of exasperation at what was seen as prolonged Communist intransigence, rather than his more reasoned views, but it also illustrated how sensitive the administration was to

---

[77] Merrill, *Bread and the Ballot*, 99. Eisenhower also felt that retaining Bowles would be unacceptable to the Republican leadership in the Senate; see George V. Allen Oral History, pp. 9–10, Butler Library, Columbia University.

[78] See McMahon, *Cold War on the Periphery*, 154–64.

[79] See Singh, *Limits of British Influence*, 98–106. Later in 1953, American officials also worked hard to exclude India from the Political Conference on Korea's future that it had been agreed would be convened after the conclusion of any armistice.

[80] Emmet John Hughes, *The Ordeal of Power: A Political Memoir of the Eisenhower Years* (London, 1963), 104–5.

matters of prestige and face, having failed to defeat Chinese forces on the battlefield.

The possibility of inflicting serious reverses against their Communist enemies in Korea preoccupied American policy-makers during the spring of 1953, even with the reconvening of armistice negotiations in April. Having considered the available military options if the current round of talks at Panmunjom failed, on 20 May 1953 the NSC, which Eisenhower had already elevated to become the administration's principal formal decision-making body when it came to national security and foreign policy, finally agreed that if the UN forces had to launch a major offensive in Korea, then it should be accompanied by use of nuclear weapons, though this renewed ground effort could not be mounted until the following spring.[81] That the President was serious about employing the nuclear option, even though he knew he would have a very difficult time selling it to his main Western allies, was indicated by the fact that soon after a series of messages, some more veiled than others, were delivered to the Communist side intending to warn that this step was now being planned in Washington if the final American offer over armistice terms, presented by General Clark on 25 May, was not accepted. Eisenhower's views were also conveyed to a meeting of senior officials on 30 May, when, the Communists having just mounted a new offensive, he asked Collins if atomic weapons could be used against the enemy, and then mentioned that if the armistice talks broke down 'it will be imperative immediately to discuss with our allies the necessity of using every available military resource, including atomic weapons, to bring a conclusion to hostilities … [he] emphasized that the weapons would be used tactically and that he saw no reason why our allies should disagree on the employment against enemy troops'.[82] In early June, the Communist negotiators moved close enough to the UN position on repatriation for an agreement to be reached, which even Syngman Rhee's provocative release of prisoners failed to derail, leading to the signing of the armistice at Panmunjom on 27 July (where the negotiators looked, James Reston of the *New York Times* noted, as if they were 'signing a declaration of war instead of a truce').[83]

---

[81] See memorandum of discussion at the 144th meeting of the NSC, 13 May 1953, *FRUS, 1952–1954, XV*, Part 1, 1012–17; memorandum of discussion at the 145th meeting of the NSC, 20 May 1953, *ibid.*, 1064–8. Some in the military had their eyes on the large-scale use of nuclear weapons on both strategic and tactical targets, in Manchuria as well as North Korea.

[82] Quoted in Richard M. Leighton, *History of the Office of the Secretary of Defense*, Vol. III: *Strategy, Money, and the New Look, 1953–1956* (Washington, DC, 2001), 4.

[83] Quoted in Stueck, *Korean War*, 342.

Both Eisenhower and Dulles later trumpeted that the signals that had been delivered to Beijing in late May – that the United States would expand the fighting in geographical scope and weaponry employed if the final terms were not accepted – were instrumental in bringing about a final agreement. As many scholars have noted, there were, however, grounds for doubting how effective the nuclear threats issued at this time actually were in forcing the hand of the Chinese Communist leadership, not least as Nehru, one of the administration's principal chosen message-carriers, later asserted that he had passed no hint of the American warnings to Beijing. More flexibility in the Communist position was already evident in late March, in fact, and it is reasonable to suppose that Stalin's death at the beginning of that month and the intensive UN conventional bombing campaign which pummelled North Korea in the spring of 1953 were all factors which conspired to produce the armistice agreement.[84] There can be no certainty over whether Eisenhower would have eventually sanctioned the use of tactical nuclear weapons in Korea if the war had continued. Many things could have occurred before the spring of 1954, when a new UN offensive may have been launched, while allied governments, given later British objections, were unlikely to have been supportive, and approval of contingency plans did not involve commitment to carry them out. But the balance of evidence points to Eisenhower being ready to order their use if considered militarily necessary in Korea, especially as warnings of such an escalation would have been issued and ignored, so placing American credibility at stake.[85] One more indication of the President's inclinations was given during an NSC meeting held just four days before the signing of the armistice, where US officials were nervous that the recent large-scale Communist ground offensive and build-up of troops meant that the apparent resolution of the truce talks was simply an enemy hoax to cover their real intentions. Alongside all the other reinforcements that Eisenhower wanted to despatch rapidly to Japan and Korea if this should be the case, he remarked that he would 'station extra [air] wings in the Far East, and in particular would see to it that atomic capabilities were available on Okinawa for possible emergency use'.[86]

[84] Most persuasive here is Rosemary Foot, 'Nuclear Coercion and the Ending of the Korean Conflict', *International Security*, 13, 3, Winter 1988/9, 92–112; and see also Foot, *Substitute for Victory*, 161–4, 177–8; Dingman, 'Atomic Diplomacy', 85–9; and Stueck, *Korean War*, 329.
[85] See Edward C. Keefer, 'President Dwight D. Eisenhower and the End of the Korean War', *Diplomatic History*, 10, 3, Summer 1986, 288; Betts, *Nuclear Blackmail*, 46–7.
[86] Memorandum of discussion at the 156th meeting of the NSC, 23 July 1953, DDRS/ 3100088439.

The route to closure of the Korean War was a powerful message to the Eisenhower administration that nuclear threats worked. For the President and Dulles, when faced with other crises involving China, there were always tempting analogies to draw about how Beijing would behave under similar coercive pressures. In early August, the sixteen nations contributing military forces to the UN effort in Korea issued their long-prepared greater sanctions statement, which warned that Communist renewal of the war would lead to consequences 'so grave that, in all probability, it would not be possible to confine hostilities within the frontiers of Korea'.[87] Although the other signatories of the statement would not have subscribed to the immediate use of nuclear weapons if the armistice was violated, for many US commentators there was also an inference that resumption of fighting would see previous restrictions on their use lifted; General Clark made the sentiment explicit when at a press conference held to mark his departure as head of the UN Command he was asked if he would favour using the atomic bomb in Korea if the conflict were renewed, and replied that he was in favour of using 'any and every weapon at the disposal of our country if we had to start hostilities again'.[88]

The end of the war left a bitter aftertaste, with American animosity towards their new Communist adversary very pronounced. Particular attention was given to the experiences of American prisoners of war who had suffered in Communist hands and were now returning with their stories of maltreatment. Detecting a different atmosphere from the previous times he had visited the country, in 1949 and 1952, Selwyn Lloyd, the Minister of State in the Foreign Office, remarked in August of how there was 'now in the United States an emotional feeling against Communist China and to a lesser extent about Russia which borders on hysteria'.[89] There would be no chance of diplomatic relations or even a dialogue developing between Beijing and Washington, and American attempts to isolate and weaken the mainland regime economically would continue. The threat from Chinese Communism was held to be the source of the entire region's problems, and to be particularly menacing in Indochina, where French fortunes against the Viet Minh remained at a low ebb. Indeed, in August 1953, the French Commander-in-Chief in Indochina, General Henri Navarre, predicted that the end of the Korean War, by releasing Chinese strength, might give Beijing greater latitude for direct intervention in Vietnam, and linked this with an appeal for American forces to enter the fighting if

[87] '16 Nations in U.N. Command Pledge to Resist New Attack', *NYT*, 8 August 1953.
[88] 'Clark Warns Foe on Truce Breach', *NYT*, 7 August 1953.
[89] Lloyd note, 23 August 1953, AU 1052/23G, FO 371/103518, TNA.

this should occur.[90] Only two days after the Korean armistice was signed, it was announced that another $400 million for the French war effort in Indochina would be included in the administration's foreign aid programme, and at the end of September a further $385 million was assigned to help finance the 'Navarre Plan', which with its major expansion of the Vietnamese National Army was envisaged by Washington as the path to victory (funding the plan was also intended to dissuade the war-weary French from being tempted to seek a negotiated end to the war in the wake of the Korean example).[91] On 2 September 1953, moreover, Dulles delivered a thinly veiled warning in a speech to the American Legion in St Louis, setting out that 'there is the risk that, as in Korea, Red China might send its own army into Indochina. The Chinese Communist regime should realize that such a second aggression could not occur without grave consequences which might not be confined to Indochina.'[92] This was an obvious echo of the greater sanctions statement issued the previous month over Korea, and indicated in clear terms that the administration was more than ready to employ the nuclear threats that had been levelled in the run-up to the Korean armistice agreement.

Eisenhower always rated ending the Korean War as probably the leading achievement of his administration. Yet, though clearly coming as a relief to the American people, the armistice agreement was not perceived in Washington as having raised American standing in Asian eyes. With the phenomenon of McCarthyism doing much to tarnish the American image abroad during this period, in the summer of 1953 the NSC was to ask for studies to be undertaken on why America's international reputation seemed so low. In the developing world, links with the older European colonial powers were still seen as a major problem, and suspicion of American imperialism was considered 'the single most adverse influence on American prestige'. In its analysis of the Far East, the Operations Coordinating Board (OCB) reported the prevalence of 'Racial sensitivity and antipathy to [the] Western powers', as well as the '[p]ersistent belief, despite U.S. professions to [the] contrary, that [the] U.S. regards Asiatic people as inferior, that [the] U.S. tends to patronize Asia, and that U.S. peoples and practices do not accord Asiatic governments genuinely equal status with [the] Western powers'.[93] In a tone of subdued irritation, one United

---

[90] 'Navarre Warns That Red China Is Free to Intervene in Indo-China', *NYT*, 7 August 1953.
[91] See Leslie H. Gelb with Richard K. Betts, *The Irony of Vietnam: The System Worked* (Washington, DC, 1979), 51; Spector, *Advice and Support*, 173–7.
[92] 'Text of the Dulles Address to the American Legion Convention', *NYT*, 3 September 1953.
[93] Study prepared by the OCB, 'Reported Decline in U.S. Prestige Abroad', 23 September 1953; see *FRUS, 1952–1954, I: General: Economic and Political Matters*, Part 1 (Washington, DC, 1983), 1466–7, 1489–90, 1531. The OCB was formed at the

States Information Agency (USIA) note highlighted that, 'We suffer among Asians and Africans and Latin Americans for every rememberance [*sic*] of insult or arrogance by a white "exploiter", whether or not the individual himself was American.'[94] The greater propensity of the Eisenhower administration to be prepared to use nuclear weapons, connected in an Asian context with the issue of race, and its willingness to make this posture public, was one more source of tension between the United States and its potential Far Eastern friends and allies. Nevertheless, the US atomic supremacy that was now in evidence, coupled with the conclusion to the Korean fighting, meant that the administration felt able to move ahead with some of the new directions in national security policy that had been sketched out in the 1952 presidential election campaign, and to underline in starker terms how nuclear weapons were to play an even more central role in the containment of Communist power in both Europe and East Asia across the decade ahead.

beginning of September 1953 and was assigned the task of co-ordinating and reviewing the implementation of NSC decisions and policies, and also took on the responsibilities of the old Psychological Strategy Board which was dissolved; in addition, the OCB would sometimes assume the role of planning how certain NSC directives would be carried out by the various departments and agencies of government; see Bowie and Immerman, *Waging Peace*, 93–5, and Kenneth Osgood, *Total Cold War: Eisenhower's Secret Propaganda Battle at Home and Abroad* (Lawrence, KS, 2006), 85–8.

[94] Infoguide, 'Supreme Court Decision on School Desegregation', USIA CA 564, 12 March 1954, AU 1828/3, FO 371/109162, TNA.

5   'Atomic Madness': massive retaliation and the *Bravo* test

The overriding conviction held by Eisenhower throughout his two terms as president was that the Cold War would be a long-drawn-out contest, where the United States would require a strong and healthy economy to prevail. The continual strain of heavy defence spending, Eisenhower feared, would eventually necessitate the imposition of economic controls by the state which would undermine the core American values of individual freedom that were presumed to differentiate the United States from its principal Soviet adversary. Surveying the landscape of national security policy on arrival in office, the new President, along with his Secretary of the Treasury, George Humphrey, believed that the rearmament efforts of NSC 68 and the demands of the Korean War had transformed the size and shape of the US military establishment in ways which were financially unsustainable and foreshadowed a 'garrison state' which would eventually undermine the Republic. Rejecting the notion of preventive war against the Soviet Union, Eisenhower would spend the first months of his presidency trying to inculcate the federal bureaucracy with his parsimonious philosophy and to find a new basis on which to contain the global Communist threat which most Americans discerned.[1]

Just before the Korean armistice, almost 1 million out of America's total military force of 3,555,000 were deployed overseas, compared with June 1950 figures of 281,000 overseas out of 1,460,000 service personnel. Germany, Japan and Korea, the key battlegrounds of the Cold War, were home to the bulk of overseas deployments. The defence budgets of 1953 and 1954 absorbed about two-thirds of entire federal spending, and would continue to consume over 50 per cent of the total for the rest of the 1950s.[2] During the first few months of 1953, the Department of Defense had struggled to produce new budget proposals and eventually settled on stretching out existing programmes and 'levelling off' rearmament.[3]

---

[1] See Bowie and Immerman, *Waging Peace*, 44–5, 47–8, 97–8; Gaddis, *Strategies*, 132–4; Hogan, *Cross of Iron*, 368–72, 384–410.
[2] Condit, *Test of War*, 535.   [3] Leighton, *Strategy, Money, and the New Look*, 73–82.

These modest outcomes were clearly unsatisfactory to the President, and by the summer of 1953, increased overall federal deficits were anticipated for the coming years. As a result, in early August, Eisenhower wrote to Wilson at the Pentagon in forceful terms: 'It is absolutely essential that you begin immediately to take every possible step progressively to reduce the expenditures of your department during the fiscal year 1954 [and] you will be expected to make substantial reductions in your requests for new appropriations and in the level of your expenditures for the fiscal year 1955, beyond those already indicated for the fiscal year 1954.'[4] The prime area where savings could be found was to reduce manpower levels, but without a new strategic concept to sustain the array of US global commitments, and with the incumbent service chiefs resistant to cuts, the economy measures demanded by the President appeared unobtainable. Cutting through this impasse would preoccupy much of the administration's time throughout the remainder of the year, until the public unveiling by Dulles of a new American strategy in his famous speech to the Council on Foreign Relations in New York on 12 January 1954.

Although a great deal of scholarly attention has been directed at the Solarium Exercise that Eisenhower initiated in May 1953, with its various task force reports on different options in the Cold War, of comparable importance to the eventual emergence of the New Look in national security policy was the President's appointment of a new set of figures to the Joint Chiefs of Staff, with Admiral Radford becoming Chairman of the JCS in August 1953.[5] Even before the formal assumption of their responsibilities, the President had handed the prospective new Chiefs an injunction that they prepare a fresh and succinct survey of US military capabilities in view of global commitments and the 'urgent need for a really austere basis in military preparations and operations'. 'What I am seeking,' Eisenhower continued in a familiar refrain, 'is interim guidance to aid the [National Security] Council in developing policies for the most effective employment of available national resources to insure the defense of our country for the long pull which may lie ahead.'[6] In his previous post as CINCPAC, Radford had already met Eisenhower and Wilson in December 1952 and convinced them both that he agreed with the need

[4] Quoted in *ibid.*, 145.
[5] On the Solarium Exercise, see Gaddis, *Strategies*, 143–4. For the JCS selections see Leighton, *Strategy, Money, and the New Look*, 8–9, 36–7; Robert J. Watson, *History of the Joint Chiefs of Staff*, Vol. V: *The Joint Chiefs of Staff and National Policy, 1953–1954* (Washington, DC, 1986), 15.
[6] See Watson, *The JCS and National Policy, 1953–1954*, 16–17; Leighton, *Strategy, Money, and the New Look*, 146–7; and *FRUS, 1952–1954, II: National Security Affairs*, Part 1 (Washington, DC, 1954), editorial note, 394.

for economy in defence spending and would be able to shed his previous service loyalties if made chairman. Until the end of his term on the JCS in August 1957, Radford was to prove the most effective military spokesman for the New Look and a powerful advocate of the wholesale integration of nuclear weapons into the US armoury, while he was also the champion of Republican proponents of an Asia-first policy and as CINCPAC had recommended the 'unleashing' of Chiang Kai-shek's forces on Taiwan.[7] Complementing Radford, the new Chief of Staff of the Air Force, General Nathan F. Twining, was also quick to point out to his colleagues that a greater emphasis on nuclear weapons might be one way to respond to the President's request for forces that could be 'maintained and operated for an indefinite period without forcing such a financial burden on the country as to endanger a strong, sound U.S. economy'. Nuclear weapons, Twining argued, should be accepted as 'accomplished facts' and employed more fully by the United States.[8]

Retreating to the Navy yacht the USS *Sequoia* at the beginning of August, the JCS produced a report which underlined the over-extension of US forces worldwide, leaving little left at home from which to build a strategic reserve, while continental air defence was dangerously lacking in the face of the Soviet Union's developing capacity for direct attack on the United States with atomic weapons. The basic idea behind the JCS approach was to rely more on indigenous forces in Europe and Asia to provide for local and forward defence against any initial Communist attack, allowing the United States to maintain a strong mobile reserve (much of it based in the United States itself) ready for quick deployment where needed, all backed by a 'capability for delivering swift and powerful retaliatory blows'. One of the main recommendations of the report was that the administration needed to devise and then announce 'a clear, positive policy with respect to the use of atomic weapons'.[9]

---

[7] See Ambrose, *Eisenhower*, 30, 33; Childs, *Eisenhower*, 181. Just before his appointment, Radford was telling one State Department official of his 'great admiration for Chiang Kai-shek and Syngman Rhee and in this conviction emphasized his doubts about the readiness of the peoples of Asia for democracy in a Western sense'; see 'Conversation with Admiral Radford about Far Eastern Problems', 19 May 1953, 'Far East General' folder, Miscellaneous Subject Files for 1953, box 5, records of the Bureau of Far East Affairs, RG 59, NARA.

[8] Memorandum from Twining for Radford, Ridgway and Carney, 20 July 1953, quoted in Watson, *The JCS and National Policy, 1953–1954*, 17.

[9] See Leighton, *Strategy, Money, and the New Look*, 151–3; Marc Trachtenberg, *A Constructed Peace: The Making of the European Settlement, 1945–1963* (Princeton, 1999), 151–5, and note 19; Bowie and Immerman, *Waging Peace*, 184–6. It is evident that despite signing the report, Ridgway, who had replaced Collins as US Army Chief of Staff in August, was very unhappy with much of its contents, and that Radford was the driving force behind its conclusions.

When the report was discussed by the NSC at the end of August, Humphrey described it, with some hyperbole, as 'terrific' and the 'most important thing that had happened in this country since January 20'. Dulles made the pointed observation that its heaviest impact would be in the area of reductions in troops in Central Europe, Japan and Korea, and he presumed this would involve greater dependence on the deterrent force of air power and nuclear weapons. Though he could appreciate the need for savings in defence spending, the Secretary of State was worried that a hasty withdrawal of US military personnel from overseas bases would send a wrong signal to US allies that Washington thought the Soviet threat had diminished. The Vice-President, Richard M. Nixon, wanted to know whether the JCS report meant that they were advocating both the strategic and the tactical use of nuclear weapons in the event of a major conflict. Radford answered in the affirmative and thought this should be reinforced by some public announcement: 'we have been spending vast sums on the manufacture of these weapons and at the same time we were holding back on their use because of our concern for public opinion. It was high time that we clarified our position on the use of such weapons if indeed we proposed to use them.' Although he was not present at this NSC meeting, Eisenhower himself was impressed with the JCS report and felt it was a good summation of the national security objectives of the administration.[10]

In a series of meetings held throughout October 1953, the NSC arrived at a new statement of basic national security policy, NSC 162/2, that embodied much of the thinking constituting the New Look. The place of nuclear weapons in this policy featured in many of the discussions, with much attention given to the critical paragraph 39b of the document, which contained the formulation that, 'In the event of hostilities, the United States will consider nuclear weapons to be available for use as other munitions.' This apparently clear injunction was, however, followed by the statement that, 'Where the consent of an ally is required for the use of these weapons from U.S. bases on the territory of such ally, the United States should promptly obtain the advance consent of such ally for such use. The United States should also seek, when feasible, the understanding and approval of this policy by free nations.' In other words, while the military sections of the New Look were clearly the provenance of the

---

[10] See memorandum of discussion at the 160th meeting of the NSC, 27 August 1953, *FRUS, 1952–1954, II*, Part 1, 443–55. For Eisenhower's emphatic approval, see also memorandum by the Special Assistant to the President for National Security Affairs to the Secretary of State, 3 September 1953, *ibid.*, 455–7, and Bowie and Immerman, *Waging Peace*, 186.

Department of Defense, the State Department, and other agencies of the national security bureaucracy, would have to conduct concurrent efforts to convince sceptical allied governments and their publics to accept that the new weapons were crucial to deter further Communist encroachments, and that talk of their possible use should not be the occasion for alarm.[11] It was Eisenhower himself who suggested that 'securing [the] understanding and approval of our allies should precede the use of these special weapons', and that 'nothing would so upset the whole world as an announcement at this time by the United States of a decision to use these weapons'. Concerned by the restrictions on nuclear use that were still implied by the President's comments to the NSC, Radford asked whether nuclear weapons could be used from bases where the permission of no foreign government was required. Even to this, Eisenhower 'reiterated his belief that we should issue no statements on this point until we have given our Government officials a chance to convince our friends as to the desirability of using these weapons'. The JCS could count on using nuclear weapons in their plans for general war, but 'should not … plan to make use of these weapons in minor affairs'. At this point, Dulles also chimed in with a repeat of his view that the taboo over nuclear use must 'somehow or other' be removed.[12]

A few days later, Radford raised the highly pertinent issue of whether the new policy would mean the JCS could plan on using atomic weapons in Korea if the armistice were broken. Dulles affirmed that they could 'if military considerations dictated their use', though he would like to have time to prepare the other UN members with forces on the peninsula for this step. At this point, Eisenhower asked whether this would lead to 'a dangerous breach in allied solidarity', and, though he believed 'we should use the bomb in Korea if the aggression is renewed', would like to check if this infringed any prior agreements with the allies.[13] This was not yet, therefore, a ringing endorsement of the view that nuclear weapons would automatically be employed when the United States was engaged in hostilities, but a more qualified instruction that the military should make plans for their use (so making possible reductions in conventional strength and overseas deployment), but with final decisions remaining dependent on the circumstances prevailing at the time, including the reactions of allies.

[11] See statement of policy by the NSC, NSC 162/2, 30 October 1953, *FRUS, 1952–1954, II*, Part 1, 593; and Bowie and Immerman, *Waging Peace*, 209–10.

[12] Memorandum of discussion at the 165th meeting of the NSC, 7 October 1953, *FRUS, 1952–1954, II*, Part 1, 533.

[13] See memorandum of discussion at the 166th meeting of the NSC, 13 October 1953, *ibid.*, 546.

As the administration moved to adopt NSC 162/2, it simultaneously planned to reduce the size of the combat forces it still had deployed in Korea, and it was in East Asia where the concepts of the New Look would find their initial application. The day before the NSC agreed the final text of NSC 162/2, it was discussed how to respond to a resumption of fighting in Korea, with the JCS and State Department being asked to review the courses of action that should be adopted if the armistice was broken by an overt act of Communist aggression.[14] In a further statement of intent, at a meeting dealing with reducing the future defence budget held on 11 November with the President, the Secretary of the Treasury and the Secretary of Defense, Dulles expressed his belief that US troops should begin to be withdrawn from Korea in the context of a basic policy of avoiding ground force commitments in Asia, overall cutbacks to Army strength and the dependence being placed on 'new weapons', a view which received general support.[15] A few days later, the JCS were given instructions from the Secretary of Defense to draw up their strategy and force requirements on the basis of the new assumptions contained in NSC 162/2, including that nuclear weapons 'will be used in military operations ... whenever it is of military advantage to do so'.[16] The resulting recommendations from the JCS, finally delivered on 9 December 1953, affirmed that 'our superiority in atomic weapons must be exploited to the maximum', with a strategic posture emphasizing 'offensive retaliatory strength and defensive strength – this to be based upon a massive retaliatory capability, including the necessary secure bases, an adequate continental defense system, and by combat forces of the United States and its allies suitably deployed to deter or counter aggression and to discharge required initial tasks in the event of a general war'. As greater reliance would be placed on allies for the indigenous forces required for local defence, American atomic capabilities would have to be stressed as the major contribution to collective security. The JCS assumed that US ground forces would be withdrawn from Korea, and eventually from Japan. Over the next few years, the US Army would face a cut of around one-third of its existing strength, while only six divisions were envisaged for eventual deployment overseas in the effort to build up the continental reserve that the Korean War had so denuded.[17]

---

[14] See NSC Action No. 949 (d), 29 October 1953, *FRUS, 1952–1954, XV*, Part 2 (Washington, DC, 1984), 1576; Watson, *The JCS and National Policy 1953–1954*, 228.
[15] See memorandum for the record by the President, 11 November 1953, *FRUS, 1952–1954, II*, Part 1, 595–6; Leighton, *Strategy, Money, and the New Look*, 170–1.
[16] Bowie and Immerman, *Waging Peace*, 195–6.
[17] JCS memorandum for Wilson, 'Military Strategy and Posture', 9 December 1953, 'NSC 162/2 (2)', box 11, Disaster File, NSC staff papers, White House Office, DDEL.

Military planning for the use of nuclear weapons in East Asia also moved forward, with the JCS in November 1953 proposing large-scale use of nuclear weapons against China if Korean hostilities were to resume.[18] In addition, as part of putting into effect the provisions of NSC 162/2, for the first time the JCS began to prepare for the long-term overseas storage of nuclear weapons, asking the Secretary of Defense for permission to deploy and store weapons in Britain, West Germany, French Morocco and Japan (the latter requirement being clearly related to the possible revival of hostilities in Korea).[19] When the NSC came to discuss the JCS proposals over action to take in Korea in early December, the President made plain his own opinion that 'if the Communists attacked us again we should certainly respond by hitting them hard and wherever it would hurt them most, including Peiping itself. This ... would mean all-out war against Communist China.' Radford agreed with the President's contention that any resumption of fighting would effectively mean war with China, and though operations would initially probably be 'limited' to Korea, Manchuria and North China, this would still mean 'we would have to strike against the Communist Chinese in the air from Shanghai all the way north'. Nevertheless, the State Department held strong reservations over the wider political consequences and the effect on allied opinion of such a general atomic targeting of China, not least as it could precipitate a general war with the Soviet Union by activating the terms of the Sino-Soviet alliance. Having mentioned British objections to anything other than attacks against Communist forces which were close to the area of the fighting in Korea, Dulles also told the NSC that the Japanese Government might restrict the use of US bases if they felt they might be subject to Soviet counteraction. Dulles felt it would be more appropriate to restrict US nuclear operations to the Korean peninsula itself, and to take such steps as a blockade of the China coast and the seizure of Hainan island. Responding to this more cautious advice, Eisenhower appears to have moderated his own language, acknowledging 'the necessity of distinguishing between airfields adjacent to the Yalu River as opposed to targets in the south of China. There was certainly a big difference.'[20]

---

[18] JSPC 853/179 and Appendix A, 'U.S. Courses of Action in Korea', 10 November 1953, OPD 381 Korea (9 May 47), sec. 28, box 899, Air Force Plans, RG 341, NARA.

[19] The JCS memorandum containing this important request for overseas storage (dated 25 November 1953) has yet to be declassified, but is directly referred to in a later telegram to General John E. Hull, the US Commander-in-Chief Far East (CINCFE), in Tokyo; see Chief of Staff, US Army (CSUSA) to CINCFE, DA 970996, 15 November 1954, 'Yoshida Visit', box 9, Subject Files, 1954, records of the Bureau of Far East Affairs, RG 59, NARA.

[20] See memorandum of discussion at the 173rd meeting of the NSC, 3 December 1953, *FRUS, 1952–1954, XV*, Part 2, 1636–42.

The administration's nuclear belligerence was moderated further when at the Bermuda summit with Britain and France which immediately followed, the British made clear to the American delegation led by Eisenhower and Dulles their firm opposition to a wider bombing campaign against China or the use of the atomic bomb, and would certainly expect to be consulted over any decision to employ the latter.[21] Having returned to Washington, on 10 December Dulles explained to the NSC that at Bermuda the British and French had 'exhibited very stubborn resistance to any idea of the automatic use of atomic weapons, even in the case of a Communist renewal of hostilities in Korea'. Although Churchill had been told that nuclear weapons would initially only be used in and adjacent to Korea, he had expressed his opposition, feeling that the UN allies would have to have agreed to such action in advance. The Prime Minister had emphasized the 'worldwide revulsion' that would follow any American use of nuclear weapons, prompting Dulles to comment that 'our thinking on the atomic weapon was several years in advance of the rest of the free world'.[22] These discussions over the difficulties of maintaining allied solidarity revealed one of the fundamental dilemmas of the New Look. Reductions in American forces deployed overseas necessarily entailed relying to a greater extent on the contributions of local allies to form the first line of defence to Communist incursions, and those same allies would have to provide the advance base during war for any nuclear offensive launched against the Soviet Union (or China in a Far Eastern context). Dulles would repeatedly remind the NSC throughout his time as Secretary of State that the United States did not have the resources to prosecute the Cold War in isolation but needed to work towards the idea of a common pooling of 'community power' if it was to face the threat posed by its totalitarian enemies. However, the administration's greater willingness to use nuclear threats and pressures, both public and private, and increased global concerns over the consequences of escalation of any confrontation with the Communist powers, placed alliance relationships under intense strain.[23]

[21] See, for example, Eden minute for Churchill, PM/53/337, 4 December 1953, FK1078/8G; Confidential Annex to BC(P)(53)4th meeting, 10.30 am, 7 December 1953, FK1078/9G, FO 371/105540, TNA; British dinner, 5 December 1953, Bermuda – Presidential notes 12/53 (1), box 3, International series, Ann Whitman File, DDEL. See also, in general, Kevin Ruane, '"Containing America": Aspects of British Foreign Policy and the Cold War in East Asia, 1951–54', *Diplomacy and Statecraft*, 7, 1, March 1996, 141–74.
[22] Memorandum of discussion at the 174th meeting of the NSC, 10 December 1953, *FRUS, 1952–1954, XV*, Part 2, 1654. See also the President's recollections of Churchill's objections and fears in Dwight D. Eisenhower, *The White House Years: Mandate for Change, 1953–1956* (New York, 1963), 248.
[23] For this point see, in particular, Trachtenberg, 'A "Wasting Asset"', 137–9.

These political realities were reflected in the final language incorporated in the text of a new memorandum on action to take in the event of a resumption of fighting in Korea and approved by the NSC on 8 January 1954, in which the State Department was also able to insert caveats to the effect that US military objectives should remain limited if full-scale Soviet intervention was to be avoided. Moreover, 'massive U.S. air attacks on numerous targets in China Proper, large scale landings on the China mainland, or possibly the seizure of Hainan, would stimulate Communist belief that ... the U.S. in fact intended to bring about the complete overthrow of the Peiping regime'. Similarly, allied and UN support would be prejudiced by such large-scale actions as they were likely to trigger active Soviet participation or even aggression in Europe. By limiting the American nuclear response to Chinese military targets directly supporting Communist aggression in Korea, it was hoped that in the immediate crisis period that would follow a resumption of hostilities in Korea some of the political objections to widening the scope of the war and the weapons employed might be surmounted.[24] Anxious that steps be taken to generate the savings in defence spending anticipated by the New Look, at the end of December Eisenhower announced the beginning of a progressive reduction of US ground forces in the Korean peninsula (initially involving the return to the United States of two divisions from the eight then deployed). The President was careful to repeat the warning issued by the UN members with forces in Korea that if the armistice was breached it would not be possible to confine hostilities to the peninsula, and emphasized that the US forces remaining in the Far East were sufficient to uphold commitments in the region and would have the capacity to oppose aggression with even greater effect than before.[25]

The intense discussions taking place in late 1953 over the new place of nuclear weapons in national security policy, relationships with allies and responses to a revival of fighting in Korea also helped to prompt a highly significant debate within the administration over the political factors that would have to be weighed in any resort to nuclear use. This fundamental issue arose because the JCS were inclined to believe that the vague wording of paragraph 39b of NSC 162/2, that, 'In the event of hostilities, the United States will consider nuclear weapons to be as available for use as other munitions', carried the assumption that they would be used on an

---

[24] See memorandum by the JCS to the Secretary of Defense, 18 December 1953; memorandum by the JCS and the Department of State to the Executive Secretary of the NSC, 7 January 1954; memorandum of discussion at the 179th meeting of the NSC, 8 January 1954, *FRUS, 1952–1954, XV*, Part 2, 1674, 1700–3, 1704–6.

[25] 'Statement on Troops in Korea', *NYT*, 27 December 1953; and see Leighton, *Strategy, Money, and the New Look*, 178–9, for the two division withdrawal decision.

automatic basis wherever military necessity dictated, including during conditions of limited war, and that this assumption should now be reflected in military planning. Meeting on 30 November 1953, in order to provide more precise guidance regarding the treatment of nuclear weapons in the US arsenal under the new policy, the NSC's Special Committee on Atomic Energy failed to agree on an interpretation of paragraph 39b, with the Pentagon holding to its position that nuclear weapons should be used for both strategic and tactical purposes wherever the military judged necessary. The State Department was conscious of the fact that this could be interpreted as advance authorization for nuclear use, and hence was an infringement of the principle established by Truman that any such decision must ultimately lie with the president. 'The Department of State had understood that the purpose of paragraph 39b was primarily to permit the military to make plans on the basis of the availability of nuclear weapons,' Walter Bedell Smith, the Under-Secretary of State, wrote to Eisenhower on 3 December:

It is also agreed that, as a corollary, custody of atomic weapons should in large part be transferred from the AEC to the Department of Defense. The Department of State, however, does not construe paragraph 39b to be a present decision that atomic weapons will, in fact, be used in the event of *any* hostilities. In its opinion, the decision to use atomic weapons will necessarily involve the gravest political and foreign policy aspects. For example, in cases of limited hostilities, it will be essential to consider whether the use of atomic weapons will widen the hostilities, lose the support of allies, or increase the danger of strategic use of atomic weapons by the enemy.

This was exactly the kind of perspective on nuclear use that was about to feature in British reactions at Bermuda to the suggestion that there should be employment of nuclear weapons against Chinese targets if limited hostilities broke out once again in Korea (Smith's memorandum, it should be noted, was sent at the same time that the State Department was pressing the political objections to JCS proposals to mount large-scale nuclear attacks against China).[26]

The State Department view was that the President should decide on nuclear use 'from case to case in the light of the circumstances', that paragraph 39b had not resolved such questions and that suitable procedures should be devised 'which will take account of the political issues' involved in such decisions.[27] The AEC supported the State Department position, with its Chairman, Lewis Strauss (who had taken over from

[26] See Leighton, *Strategy, Money, and the New Look*, 202–3.
[27] Smith memorandum for Eisenhower, 3 December 1953, 'Atomic Energy – The President (May 1953–March 1956) (2)', box 1, Subject subseries, NSC Records, Office of the Special Assistant for National Security Affairs, White House Office, DDEL.

Gordon Dean in July), maintaining that when the NSC had considered the new policy regarding nuclear weapons in October, 'There was no thought expressed that they would be so generally available that their use could be arbitrarily decided upon by a local commander.'[28] The problem for the Pentagon and JCS was that to make the savings in force levels demanded by the New Look they would have to integrate nuclear weapons into their planning assumptions and force structures for all varieties of combat. The JCS Chairman, Radford, as he explained to the NSC in October, thought it 'essential to settle this issue of the use of nuclear weapons. Only their use on a broad scale could really change the program of the Defense Department and cut the costs of the military budget.' What Radford was looking for was permission to use nuclear weapons 'in a blanket way'.[29] Nevertheless, Eisenhower was reluctant to agree to anything more precise than the formulation already offered in paragraph 39b and incorporated in NSC 162/2. With considerable confusion still obtaining over the issue several weeks later, a further meeting of the Special Committee on Atomic Energy was scheduled for 22 December in order to settle matters, this time with the President in attendance.[30] Just prior to his departure for the Bermuda meeting in early December, Robert Cutler, the President's Special Assistant for National Security Affairs, and James Lay, the Executive Secretary of the NSC, had discussed the whole dispute with Eisenhower. They both gleaned that Eisenhower's position was rather closer to that of the Pentagon than that held by the State Department. The President felt that paragraph 39b was phrased so that the military could 'make plans on the basis of full availability of the use of nuclear weapons', and that a 'distinction should be made between tactical and strategic use, difficult as it is in many cases to make. He was concerned with the level of decision in the military between strategic and tactical use. *The decision on tactical use might be left up to the commander in the field, but the decision on strategic use, particularly retaliatory, should be made here in Washington*' (emphasis added).[31] This directly cut across the advice (about to arrive) from both

---

[28] Strauss to Cutler, 3 December 1953, *ibid.*

[29] See memorandum of discussion at the 166th meeting of the NSC, 13 October 1953, *FRUS, 1952–1954, II*, Part 1, 546–7; and Leighton, *Strategy, Money, and the New Look*, 162–3, 196–7.

[30] See Lay memorandum for Eisenhower, 16 December 1953, 'Atomic Energy – The President (May 1953–March 1956) (2)'; and Bowie and Immerman, *Waging Peace*, 197–8.

[31] Cutler memorandum for the record, 2 December 1953, 'Atomic Weapons, Correspondence and Background for Presidential Approval and Instructions for Use (1953–1960) (1)', box 1, Subject subseries, NSC Records, Office of the Special Assistant for National Security Affairs, White House Office, DDEL.

Smith and Strauss, and had been exactly the kind of opinion concerning pre-delegation of authorization to use nuclear weapons to a local commander that had caused such troubles for Truman after his ill-judged press conference of 30 November 1950.

Despite this, following his meeting with the Special Committee on 22 December, Eisenhower approved a new interpretation of paragraph 39b which followed very closely the language of Smith's earlier State Department memorandum. This stipulated that while the paragraph should allow military planning to go ahead based on the availability of nuclear weapons and permit their transfer from the custody of the AEC to the Defense Department, this was not to be understood as a decision in advance that they would be used in any hostilities. The 'political questions' involved in the case of limited hostilities which it would be essential to consider included, in an echo of Smith's paper, 'whether immediate use of atomic weapons by the United States would increase the danger of their strategic use by the enemy, lose the support of allies, expose them to devastation, or widen the hostilities'. Inherent in the President's role as commander-in-chief was his power to make the final decision on nuclear use 'in the light of the circumstances existing at the time', while such decisions were 'so intimately bound up with the political and other factors that they cannot be governed by hard and fast rules adopted in the abstract'. The wording of this interpretation was finally approved by Eisenhower on 2 January 1954 and passed to the State Department, Pentagon and AEC. In view of this, the Special Committee of the NSC on Atomic Energy, originally created by Truman to advise him on nuclear issues, was formally abolished, but no institutional procedure to inform a presidential decision to use nuclear weapons was devised to take its place, as Smith had earlier recommended. The abolition of the committee was another clear sign of Eisenhower's innate confidence in his powers of judgement in this critical area, and that he did not want to be encumbered with a formal advisory mechanism involving other Cabinet members which might produce a different view from his own.[32] Six days later, when the NSC gave final approval for the course of action to adopt if hostilities were resumed in Korea, Eisenhower again made clear that any decision on nuclear use, even of a tactical kind, would be made by him in Washington, not by a local commander in the field.[33]

---

[32] See memorandum for Eisenhower by Lay, 31 December 1953, with handwritten note 'Approved by the President 1/2/54', 'Atomic Energy – The President (May 1953–March 1956) (2)'; 'Policy Regarding Use of Nuclear Weapons', memorandum from Lay for Dulles, Wilson and Strauss, 4 January 1954, 'Atomic Weapons, Correspondence and Background for Presidential Approval and Instructions for Use (1953–1960) (1)'.

[33] See memorandum of discussion at the 179th meeting of the NSC, 8 January 1954, *FRUS, 1952–1954, XV*, Part 2, 1705–7.

What had happened between the first and second meetings of the Special Committee to convince the President to accept almost verbatim the State Department's more restrained and guarded interpretation of the key section of NSC 162/2 dealing with the role of nuclear weapons in the administration's future strategy? It is difficult not to conclude that exposure to British fears and concerns at Bermuda played a key role in reinforcing State Department arguments that the attitudes of close allies had to enter into any discussion over nuclear use, and that political questions could not be ignored when such a momentous decision was taken. One notably emotive phrase that distinguished the text of the final interpretation emerging out of the second Special Committee meeting of 22 December from that previously offered by Smith in his memorandum of 3 December was the need to consider whether US nuclear use in limited war would 'expose [allies] to devastation'. It was just such a picture of nuclear destruction that Churchill had painted for the Americans two weeks earlier at Bermuda, when he had mentioned to Eisenhower the devastation that London would suffer if subjected to atomic attack.

The implications of the debate within the Eisenhower administration over the interpretation of paragraph 39b were wide-ranging and had significant repercussions for the relationship between the State Department and the Pentagon over nuclear policy in subsequent years. The President's final endorsement of the State Department's argument that political issues had to be taken into account in decisions over nuclear use gave space within the administration for consideration of the consequences that might follow in Asia, on allies such as Japan, and also on states whose allegiance in the Cold War was uncertain. Within just a few months the Pentagon's preferred approach to the integration of nuclear weapons into military planning – that they would be available for use according to military need – had been qualified by the need for explicit presidential authorization, where other factors might come to enter the decision-making process. Already, Dulles could see the difficulties that would lie ahead for the State Department in trying to foster a greater acceptance of nuclear weapons as having passed to 'conventional' status. He warned the NSC that while 'we regarded atomic weapons as one of the great new sources of defensive strength, many of our allies regard the atomic capability as the gateway to annihilation'. Nevertheless, as the President put it, 'preparing our friends behind the scenes for accepting our new strategic concept' was a task that would have to be fulfilled by US diplomats.[34]

---

[34] Memorandum of discussion at the 174th meeting of the NSC, 10 December 1953, *FRUS, 1952–1954, V: Western European Security*, Part 1 (Washington, DC, 1983), 452.

Inculcating a greater readiness to accept the implications of the existence of nuclear weapons was precisely the intention behind Eisenhower's own 'Atoms for Peace' speech, which he had delivered on his return from Bermuda and in front of the UN General Assembly on 8 December. The speech, and the policy initiative that it launched, had been the culmination of a prolonged debate within the administration over how to spread greater public understanding and awareness concerning nuclear weapons and present US nuclear policies in a more positive light, and in general terms reflected the new preoccupation of Eisenhower's administration with public relations and Cold War propaganda.[35] One of the main recommendations of the report of the high-level Panel of Consultants on Disarmament appointed by the Truman administration in 1952 was that greater openness should be exhibited by the American Government in explaining the issues raised by the existence of nuclear weapons and their role in national policy to the American people and to allied publics. By these means it was hoped to impart a sober realism in place of possible panic as the dangers of the arms race developed. The basic report that outlined the case for a greater disclosure of the tremendous power of nuclear weapons, NSC 151, was considered by the NSC in late May 1953. The ad hoc committee that drafted this report had stressed that the ethical distinctions made between nuclear and conventional weaponry had to be removed in the way nuclear issues were presented by the administration: 'Atomic weapons must be considered a part of our total weapons system, so that the question of morality will relate only to the way in which this or any other weapon is used. This will give us greater freedom of action with respect to all elements of our military strength ... The atomic weapon differs only in degree from other weapons ... Moral objections to the use of atomic weapons should be on the same basis as for other weapons capable of destroying life and inflicting damage.'[36] Although he had his doubts as to how far he should explain the problems raised by the report (saying he had no desire to go before the American people 'with some kind of horror story'), Eisenhower agreed in principle with the idea and over the next few months what became known as Project Candor gathered momentum, with various drafts of presidential speeches being composed.[37]

---

[35] For a comprehensive treatment, see Ira Chernus, *Eisenhower's Atoms for Peace* (College Station, TX, 2002); see also McGeorge Bundy, *Danger and Survival: Choices about the Bomb in the First Fifty Years* (New York, 1988), 287–94.

[36] Report to the NSC by the NSC Planning Board, NSC 151, 8 May 1953, *FRUS, 1952–1954, II*, Part 2, 1153, 1160.

[37] Memorandum of discussion at the 146th meeting of the NSC, 27 May 1953, *ibid.*, 1173.

The counterpoint to the adoption of NSC 162/2 in October 1953 was the realization that, while building up its atomic arsenal, the United States had to allay international anxieties and improve its own image by appearing to be animated by fundamentally pacific intentions when it came to nuclear power, especially in an environment when the Soviet leadership had managed to forge a consistent and attractive rhetorical commitment to disarmament.[38] In a reflection of the basic premise of the New Look, the final Atoms for Peace speech emphasized the huge explosive power of the rapidly expanding US armoury of nuclear weapons, which with their size and variety had 'virtually achieved conventional status' within America's military forces. Eisenhower went on, however, to propose the creation of a common pool of fissile material, made up of donations from the existing nuclear powers, which would be placed under UN supervision at a new International Atomic Energy Authority and used for peaceful purposes, such as for civilian energy needs or medical research.[39] Subsequent negotiations with the Soviet Union on the proposals yielded little except a counter-proposal from Moscow which involved a pledge that neither power would be the first to use nuclear weapons. Nevertheless, the administration wanted to press ahead with ideas for a new international body and planned to spread knowledge and technical expertise on the civilian uses of atomic energy to many nations in Europe, Latin America, Asia and Africa through travelling exhibits and educational exchanges.[40]

The reverse side of Atoms for Peace made its public appearance on 12 January 1954, four days after final NSC agreement on the military course of action to adopt in the event of a renewal by the Communist side of hostilities in Korea, when Dulles gave expression to the administration's strategic thinking in a now-famous speech to the Council on Foreign Relations. Elaborating on the new departures in national security policy recently adopted, he announced that it was not 'sound military strategy permanently to commit United States land forces to Asia to a degree that gives us no strategic reserve', and that 'there is no local defense which alone will contain the mighty land power of the Communist world', hence

---

[38] See Lawrence S. Wittner, *Resisting the Bomb: A History of the World Nuclear Disarmament Movement, 1954–1970* (Stanford, 1997), 155.

[39] See Bowie and Immerman, *Waging Peace*, 225–35; and also Shawn J. Parry-Giles, *The Rhetorical Presidency, Propaganda, and the Cold War, 1945–1955* (Westport, CT, 2002), 164–6.

[40] In his study of the psychological warfare programmes of the Eisenhower administration, Kenneth Osgood finds that the initiative was 'part of a broader effort to mould public perceptions in the thermonuclear age. Targeting U.S. allies, neutral nations, and domestic audiences, Atoms for Peace sought to manage fears of nuclear annihilation by cultivating the image of the "friendly" atom.' See Osgood, *Total Cold War*, 155, 170, 174.

such defence 'must be reinforced by the further deterrent of massive retaliatory power'. The basic policy decision of the administration 'to depend primarily upon a great capacity to retaliate instantly by means and at places of our choosing' (a phrase actually concocted by Eisenhower himself) was directly applicable in the first instance to the Far East. The new policy gave added strength to the previous warnings of what would happen in the event of Communist aggression in Korea where any fighting might spread 'beyond the limits and the methods [the enemy] had selected'. Dulles immediately followed this, if the message was already not clear enough, with mention that the United States intended to maintain its position in Okinawa 'to ensure adequate striking power to implement our new collective security concept'.[41] As one leading scholar of nuclear history has commented, this whole conception was 'more retrospective than prospective. It explained how the Korean War ought to have been fought [and] how a new war might be fought during the remaining period of grace of patent nuclear superiority.'[42]

The press was happy to dub the new approach a strategy of 'massive retaliation', and within a short while military commentators and domestic political opponents of the administration began to question its wisdom and prudence. Many critics argued that massive retaliation promised to reduce American options when faced with Communist probes or a minor aggression to unleashing nuclear attacks against the Soviet Union itself, so sparking all-out general war. Decrying the lack of flexibility inherent in the strategy, Hanson Baldwin cautioned that 'the A-bomb and air power provide neither a military nor a political answer to such forms of Soviet aggression or military danger as the recent guerrilla conflict in Greece and the current war in Indo-China'.[43] Adlai Stevenson, the defeated Democratic candidate in the 1952 election, accused the Republicans of breaking bipartisan accords on foreign policy and of threatening the unity of the anti-Communist alliance through belligerent talk of nuclear war.[44] Dean Acheson could barely contain his scorn for a policy that carried such huge potential costs, pronouncing in late March: 'If it is said ... that we cannot afford another war like Korea, the answer is that such a war is the only kind that we or anyone else can afford.' Massive retaliation, Acheson

---

[41] 'Text of Dulles' Statement on Foreign Policy of Eisenhower Administration', *NYT*, 13 January 1954; and see Bowie and Immerman, *Waging Peace*, 199.
[42] Lawrence Freedman, *The Evolution of Nuclear Strategy*, 2nd edn (London, 1988), 90.
[43] 'New Budget Emphasizes "New Look" in Defense', *NYT*, 24 January 1954.
[44] 'Democrats Criticize Defense Plan', *NYT*, 23 January 1954; and see Robert A. Divine, *Eisenhower and the Cold War* (New York, 1981), 38; Leighton, *Strategy, Money, and the New Look*, 217–25; and Gary W. Reichard, 'Divisions and Dissent: Democrats and Foreign Policy, 1952–1956', *Political Science Quarterly*, 93, 1, Spring 1978, 55–7.

warned, would invite Communist pressure and minor incursions precisely because Communist leaders would not believe that Washington was prepared to initiate a third world war for peripheral interests. It would also cause alarm and divide allies by exposing them to the risk of Soviet nuclear counteraction in a general war, while 'other nations not associated with either coalition but anxious to maintain their independence would be alienated from us by what they would undoubtedly regard as an immoral and reckless program calculated to plunge them into general turmoil and misery'.[45]

The administration's critics were also given extra ammunition by the developing crisis in French Indochina. Discussion of Indochina had figured little at the Bermuda Conference, where the French remained upbeat in their assessments of the situation. They were, nonetheless, keen to emphasize that domestic opinion now favoured a negotiated end to the war, and that military moves were designed to enhance the French bargaining position for when the inevitable talks finally began, a prospect which moved closer when, after the Berlin foreign ministers' meeting in February 1954, it was agreed that a conference would be held at Geneva to discuss outstanding Far Eastern tensions, including Indochina as well as Korea. To US officials, however, a negotiated solution remained anathema, involving as it would some concessions to the Communist side in the insurgency, as well as the possibility of Chinese participation in the forthcoming Geneva Conference, with all the de facto recognition this conferred on Beijing's enhanced status in Asia.[46] Many American commentators were led to ask how the new strategy of massive retaliation could be applied to such a Communist-backed insurgency, and pointed out how discouraged allies such as France would become if they could expect only limited assistance for local defence in these kinds of increasingly common 'brushfire' wars.[47]

Moreover, alongside the arguments advanced by those concerned with the credibility of deterrence or the strength of US alliances also stood considerations of morality and, in an Asian context, the impression of indifference on the part of a 'white' power over the loss of 'non-white' lives if massive retaliation were to be directed at China. This view was first articulated for an American audience by Senator Paul Douglas (Democrat, Illinois) who as well as putting forward the typical argument

---

[45] '"Instant Retaliation": The Debate Continues', *NYT Magazine*, 28 March 1954; see also Brinkley, *Acheson*, 19–22.

[46] See James Cable, *The Geneva Conference of 1954 on Indochina* (London, 1986), 36–9; George McT. Kahin, *Intervention: How America Became Involved in Vietnam* (New York, 1986), 40–1.

[47] See 'Indo-China Events Stir Test of "New Strategy" in Senate', *NYT*, 15 February 1954.

that the atomic bomb should properly be kept in reserve as an 'absolute' weapon also pointed to the fact that, 'Use of the atomic bomb on Asiatic cities and the killing of immense numbers of civilians would be exploited by the Russians as the waging of war by white men against colored peoples', with the result that, 'We would lose the support of all Asiatic and colored peoples.'[48] Already having highlighted how evidence of US racial discrimination at home served to disrupt relations between the United States and the peoples of Asia, Chester Bowles seized on Dulles's pronouncement as another potential source of estrangement. 'I deeply share your concern for our present "new look" foreign approach,' Bowles wrote to Joseph Alsop a week after Dulles's speech, 'not only on the grounds that it is inadequate as a military policy (particularly in Asia, where an atomic bomb can destroy very little except people) but also because it seems to ignore the danger of an imposed isolation as we drift further and further from the rest of the free world and its struggles and objectives.'[49] Bowles could see immense practical difficulties in coercing China, with its dispersed industrial base and highly mobile guerrilla-trained armies, through nuclear attack. China's cities might be left devastated by atomic attack, but its vast manpower would in all probability be left to overrun the rest of continental Asia. Most importantly, however, the United States would sacrifice its moral position if it had recourse to such a policy in reply to a Communist action. In a piece published by the *New York Times Magazine* at the end of February, Bowles maintained that 'if we threaten to bomb China's cities, we would seem to be proposing to wipe out millions of Chinese men, women and children, huddled in metropolises which, unlike those of the Soviet Union, are almost devoid of legitimate military or industrial targets. Are we prepared to exact this frightful toll of helpless people in order to punish the rulers who control them?' In an echo of the theme he had raised many times during his recent service as ambassador to India, Bowles continued:

Communist propaganda has already convinced hundreds of millions of Asians that we dropped the atomic bomb on Japan and not Germany because we considered Asians inferior people. Would not the atomic destruction of defenseless Chinese cities – while Russian cities remained untouched – turn all Asia into our bitter and unrelenting enemies?[50]

---

[48] 'A-Defense Dangerous: Douglas', *NYT*, 22 January 1954.
[49] Bowles to Alsop, 19 January 1954, folder 13, box 118, Bowles papers.
[50] 'A Plea for Another Great Debate', *NYT Magazine*, 28 February 1954. In an earlier version of these thoughts, Bowles had ruminated that 'we are now, almost casually, proposing to immolate millions of non-combatant men, women and children, in retaliation for an aggression launched by rulers over whom they have admittedly little control'.

The intelligence community was also aware that the new approach was likely to alienate important sections of world opinion if executed in an indiscriminate manner. In early March 1954, a Special National Intelligence Estimate (SNIE) was produced which attempted to forecast international reactions to various actions the United States might take if the Communist side were to attack in Korea. One of its conclusions was that atomic strikes against targets which were close to urban concentrations in North Korea or China would not be supported by the United States' European allies or the non-Communist world generally: 'They almost certainly would not consider that the issues of the Korean war justified such an act, even in the event of renewed Communist aggression.'[51] The administration found itself having to respond to the charge that it was planning to inflict large-scale nuclear attacks on Chinese urban areas if a limited war were to erupt again in Korea, or the fighting in Indochina were to expand. At his presidential news conference on 17 March, Eisenhower was asked by inquisitive reporters if the new policy meant bombing Moscow or Beijing and had to reply defensively that retaliation on this kind of scale for a small attack 'on the fringe or periphery of our interests ... I wouldn't hold with for a moment'.[52]

With the voices of disapproval mounting around him, Dulles published an article in the April 1954 issue of *Foreign Affairs* clarifying the meaning of the concepts he had publicly outlined in January. Playing down the more provocative aspects of his previous remarks, the Secretary of State was keen to underline that there were a wide range of nuclear weapons now available for US air and naval forces 'suitable not only for strategic bombing but also for extensive tactical use', and though certain types of Communist aggression might lead quickly to general war, 'the free world must have the means for responding effectively on a selective basis when it chooses'. Threatening the military assets of an aggressor with attack did not necessarily involve attacks on the industrial centres of China or the Soviet Union or 'indulging in atomic warfare throughout Asia'.[53] Nevertheless, many commentators continued to express concern. Thomas K. Finletter, Secretary for the Air Force during the Truman

See 'Some Observations on Foreign Policy Prompted by Secretary Dulles's Speech of January 12, 1954', pp. 14–15, 19–20, 12 February 1954, folder 750, box 166, Bowles papers.

[51] See SNIE 100–2–54, 'Probable Reactions of Communist China, the USSR, and the Free World to Certain U.S. Courses of Action in Korea', 5 March 1954, *FRUS, 1952–1954*, XV, Part 2, 1762.

[52] 'Transcript of Presidential Press Conference with Comment on Retaliation to Aggression', *NYT*, 18 March 1954.

[53] John Foster Dulles, 'Policy for Security and Peace', *Foreign Affairs*, 32, 3, April 1954, 358–60; on the background to the article, see Hamilton Fish Armstrong to Dulles, 5

administration, for example, warned in a major contemporary study of US foreign policy that on political grounds the use of the atomic bomb to block local aggression in Asia would be 'a blunder of the first order' as the first bomb dropped tactically would lead to more and more bombs being used and 'to deeper and deeper attacks into the Chinese homeland and to the destruction of what remains of Western prestige in the East. If our Far Eastern policy ends up in our burning and blasting Chinese cities to the ground with atom bombs it will have been a total failure.'[54] Though in his Atoms for Peace speech in December 1953 the President had tried to project the image of an enlightened and benevolent United States, ready to use its scientific and technological prowess for civilian purposes, the enunciation of massive retaliation by a pugnacious Dulles had served to foster entirely the opposite impression, of a country ready to threaten the first use of nuclear weapons when provoked, even when vital interests might not necessarily be in immediate danger.

These public debates over massive retaliation were also conducted in the context of a growing realization that the advent of the hydrogen bomb was likely to transform the strategic picture once again, and make the United States and its allies more immediately vulnerable to devastating attack. On 17 February 1954, in a speech delivered in Chicago by W. Sterling Cole, the Republican Chairman of the Joint Congressional Committee on Atomic Energy, the first official account was given of the dramatic results of the test explosion carried out by the US authorities of a thermonuclear device at Eniwetok Atoll in November 1952. Immediately after the *Mike* shot, in fact, there had been only partially successful attempts by the US authorities to shroud its outcome in secrecy, and Cole served to confirm what some of the eye-witness accounts that filtered back from the Pacific in 1952 had suggested: the huge blast had 'completely obliterated' Elugelab, the island chosen as a test site. As Cole explained, the area of total destruction was about six miles in diameter, with further damage extending for several miles beyond. The diameter of the explosion's crater, Cole told his audience, would in other words encompass all of downtown Chicago; equipped with one hydrogen bomb, a modern aircraft could carry the destructive force of all the conventional explosives dropped on Germany, Italy and Japan during the Second World War. The *New York Times* offered its readers a map showing the radius of destruction that might be expected if such a device were

February 1954, John Foster Dulles folder, box 25, Hamilton Fish Armstrong papers, Seeley G. Mudd Library, Princeton University. See also Bowie and Immerman, *Waging Peace*, 199–201; and Freedman, *Evolution of Nuclear Strategy*, 81–8.
[54] Thomas K. Finletter, *Power and Policy: U.S. Foreign Policy and Military Power in the Hydrogen Age* (New York, 1954), 151–2.

dropped in the middle of Manhattan.[55] Only the previous month, the AEC had announced a new test series in the Pacific, and as thousands of US service personnel, technicians and scientists, along with the ships and aircraft of Joint Task Force 7, headed once more for the scattered islands and anchorages of Bikini Atoll, where the first post-war atomic tests had been held in 1946, speculation grew that the major goal of the upcoming *Castle* series was the test of a deliverable hydrogen bomb, as opposed to the unwieldy 65-ton device that had featured in the *Mike* shot.[56]

The very high yields expected for the *Castle* tests had persuaded the AEC that Eniwetok, where the main US facilities and installations of the Pacific Proving Grounds were located, would be unsuitable, and so instead the larger and uninhabited Bikini Atoll, 180 miles to the east, was selected for the six test shots of various designs of thermonuclear weapon. A 50,000 square mile restricted zone was announced around Bikini, and all shipping warned to stay clear. As local fallout from *Mike* had been much lower than predicted in 1952, some US officials came to question the need for the kind of expensive precautions taken at Eniwetok; only pressure from the scientists with the task force saw the military retain an emergency evacuation capability to cover the small communities on the atolls of Rongelap and Ailinginae, forming a part of the Marshall Island chain, and which lay just over 100 miles east of Bikini. Nevertheless, in order to avoid the complications and expense of evacuation before the first test shot, the Department of the Interior (who administered the Marshalls as a US Trust Territory) recommended that the eastern border of the exclusion zone around Bikini should fall short of the two atolls, making accurate weather forecasting crucial so that the test could be timed to ensure fallout debris was blown safely away to the north.[57]

The first shot in the *Castle* series, dubbed *Bravo*, was fired on 1 March 1954 and was destined to be the most important event in forming public perceptions of the dangers associated with nuclear fallout and the wider consequences of the development of thermonuclear weapons. That the technical side of these processes were still in their infancy was given graphic expression by the test, which by producing an unprecedented

---

[55] 'Hydrogen Blast in '52 Dug Mile-Wide Crater in Sea and Wiped Out Island', *NYT*, 18 February 1954.

[56] See Robert A. Divine, *Blowing on the Wind: The Nuclear Test Ban Debate, 1954–1960* (New York, 1978), 5–6. On the *Mike* test, see Gerard DeGroot, *The Bomb: A History of Hell on Earth* (London, 2004), 177–9.

[57] For the *Castle* series, see Richard G. Hewlett and Jack M. Holl, *Atoms for Peace and War, 1953–1961: Eisenhower and the Atomic Energy Commission* (Berkeley, 1989), 164–6, 168–9, 171. See also Martha Smith-Norris, '"Only as Dust in the Face of the Wind": An Analysis of the BRAVO Nuclear Incident in the Pacific, 1954', *Journal of American–East Asian Relations*, 6, 1, Spring 1997, 1–34.

yield of fifteen megatons, against an estimate that had been in the five to seven megaton range, was to make it the largest ever US test explosion (*Mike* had registered just over ten megatons). Only a few minutes after *Bravo* was detonated, it was apparent to the nearest observers that the shot was producing greater radiation levels than had been predicted, while within an hour ships in the *Castle* task force began to see grey ash falling from the sky. The size of the explosion was also compounded by an unexpected shift in upper atmosphere winds which carried fallout debris much further than had been predicted. Twenty-eight US servicemen at Rongerik Atoll, there to make radiological and meteorological observations, were quickly evacuated as their readings began rising to dangerous levels. Despite heavy deposits of radioactive ash, 236 islanders on Rongelap, Ailinginae and Utirik atolls had to wait between two and three days after the shot before also being moved away from the area to a US military installation where they could receive treatment for their burns. Although the AEC tried to minimize the injuries that had been sustained by the islanders, they suffered from the health effects associated with acute exposure to radiation (receiving twenty-five times what was later considered to be a life-time dose).[58] Indeed, the AEC seems to have made a strong effort to clamp down on any information coming out from the Pacific Proving Grounds, with its Chairman, Lewis Strauss, personally demanding that 'no public release will be made in regard to fallout', combining his stringent regard for security and concern over the ramifications of general disclosure of what was effectively a nuclear accident.[59] Nevertheless, and inevitably given the number of American personnel attached to Joint Task Force 7, news began to arrive back in the United States of these disturbing events, prompting a bland report from the AEC on 12 March that a 'routine' test had led to precautionary evacuations of the Americans and Marshall islanders, all of whom were in good health.

Also in the path of the cloud of fallout produced by *Bravo*, eighty-five miles north east of Bikini Atoll and outside the established danger zone, however, was a 100-ton wooden Japanese tuna trawler, the *Fukuryu Maru*, or *Lucky Dragon*, which had left its home port of Yaizu on 22 January. Some members of its twenty-three crew saw the intense light of what they thought might be an American nuclear test in the early morning of 1 March, and all of them heard the crash of an explosion several minutes

[58] A. Costandina Titus, *Bombs in the Backyard: Atomic Testing and American Politics* (Reno, NA, 1986), 47–8; Stewart Firth, *Nuclear Playground* (Sydney, 1987), 15–17; Allen M. Winkler, *Life under a Cloud: American Anxiety about the Atom* (New York, 1993), 93–4.
[59] Strauss is quoted in Smith-Norris, 'The BRAVO Nuclear Incident', 7.

later. About two hours after the flash, white ash began to fall from the sky, coating the vessel and crew who had appeared on deck to witness the strange phenomenon. Worried by his low fuel and a poor catch, and fearful that the Americans might detain them if they lingered, the *Lucky Dragon*'s captain turned the trawler back towards Japan, where it arrived on 14 March, by which time almost all the crew had succumbed to headaches, nausea and diarrhoea.[60] Shortly after the return of the *Lucky Dragon* to Yaizu, the Japanese authorities were able to offer a firm diagnosis that the crew were suffering from radiation sickness.

With two of the worst affected crew members having been transferred to Tokyo University Hospital, on 18 March Dr John S. Morton, the director of the Hiroshima-based Atomic Bomb Casualty Commission, was asked by the AEC to examine their condition. The fact that Morton and his small team of doctors merely seemed to be taking the opportunity to study the radiation effects of American nuclear weapons on more Japanese victims was the cause of umbrage to local officials. Morton's subsequent delivery of a reassuring report following his initial examination merely fuelled Japanese suspicions of an American attempt to minimize the incident, while US reluctance to divulge what they knew about likely fallout content was the cause of further resentment. When three days later, Dr Merril Eisenbud, the head of the AEC's Health and Safety Division, arrived in Japan, the story of the *Lucky Dragon* was receiving extensive coverage in the local press, and the atmosphere had deteriorated. Eisenbud found his opportunities to carry out further tests on the remaining crewmen were limited.[61] Dr Masao Tsuzuki, the Tokyo physician who had prime responsibility for the crew's treatment, and who had just been made head of the new Japanese Institute of Radiological Sciences, was particularly alert to any suggestion that their care should be taken over by the Americans; he did propose, however, that full access would be granted if he were allowed to see the Marshall Islanders exposed to *Bravo*'s radiation.[62] One British diplomat at the Tokyo Embassy commented that the Japanese felt their own doctors had better experience at treating radiation sickness and that the Americans were 'more interested in using the victims as guinea pigs than in curing them'.[63] At Yaizu,

---

[60] See Divine, *Blowing*, 4–5; Roger Dingman, 'Alliance in Crisis: The *Lucky Dragon* Incident and Japanese–American Relations', in Cohen and Iriye (eds.), *The Great Powers in East Asia*, 187–9; Ralph E. Lapp's *The Voyage of the Lucky Dragon* (London, 1958) provides the best account.

[61] See Hewlett and Holl, *Atoms for Peace and War*, 175–7; Lapp, *Voyage*, 107–8.

[62] Lindee, *Suffering*, 157–8.

[63] Aubrey S. Halford to Colin Crowe, 24 March 1954, GE18/10; see also Halford to Crowe, 7 April 1954, GE18/25, both in FO 371/110695, TNA.

Eisenbud managed to see the rest of the fishermen on 25 and 26 March, finding that they had skin burns where radioactive fallout had settled.[64] These crewmen were finally transferred to Tokyo on 28 March, and access to the patients was thereafter restricted to exclusively Japanese medical teams, even as the American scientists proved reluctant to breach the security regulations of US atomic energy legislation by revealing all they knew of the properties of *Bravo*'s fallout, which they feared might give some clues to the design features of the weapon.[65] At first, the Japanese also kept US officials away from the *Lucky Dragon* itself, and the Americans grew concerned that fallout residue, or the stricken crew members themselves, could also yield damaging information.[66] In the meantime, the *Lucky Dragon*'s tuna cargo had been dispersed to fourteen different prefectures, leading to the development of an 'atomic fish' scare that temporarily crippled the Japanese tuna fishing industry (there were also protests when the US authorities announced they were extending the danger zone around the Bikini test site to a radius of 450 miles, closing off many traditional Japanese fishing grounds near the Marshall Islands).[67] Other boats working near the Marshalls had also returned with their catches, some with slightly contaminated tackle and cargoes, and by 10 May it was reported that 56 million pounds of tuna from sixty-one boats had been found to contain traces of radioactivity, and of these 207,460 pounds were disposed of as dangerous.[68]

The involvement of ABCC staff with examining the *Lucky Dragon*'s crew was particularly insensitive. The 'no treatment' policy of the commission had begun to come under greater local press criticism after occupation controls and restrictions were removed in 1952, and a number of citizens' action groups had also been formed to press for adequate medical care of the survivors of Hiroshima and Nagasaki. The very existence of the ABCC also served as a direct reminder of the atomic bombings and the link with past American actions and the current US presence in Japan; as one later United States Information Service (USIS) report noted, the ABCC site was on a prominent hill overlooking Hiroshima, and 'citizens [of the city] have indicated that they need no other reminder of

[64] See Smith-Norris, 'The BRAVO Nuclear Incident', 16.
[65] See Dingman, 'Alliance in Crisis', 194.
[66] On 20 March, though, what was described as a 'Top Secret Air Force team' made a detailed examination of the vessel (partly with a brief to look for unusual instrumentation on board); see memorandum for the record, 'CIA Investigation of Circumstances of Exposure of Fuku Ryu Maru (Fortunate Dragon) to Hydrogen Bomb Test', 28 April 1954, DDRS/CK3100123295.
[67] The panic induced in Osaka where many of the contaminated fish were sold is well conveyed in Lapp, *Voyage*, 84–9.
[68] See R. T. D. Ledward to F. W. Martin, 12 May 1954, GE18/30, FO 371/110695, TNA.

the bombing since the daily sight of the "overlords" is sufficient to bring back old memories'.[69] In the autumn of 1953, a delegation from the American Federation of Labor, led by George Meany, had visited Japan and listened to the plight of survivors. Dulles met Meany when he returned to the United States, receiving a memorandum recommending that American private finance should be raised to build a 'Peace Hospital' in Hiroshima to care for atomic bomb victims. A copy was passed to the AEC, asking if the commission would be willing to send doctors to help in this area. The AEC staff, however, were firmly of the view that it would be 'completely inappropriate' for the commission or the US Government to provide any kind of official aid.[70] In February 1954, when the US Embassy in Tokyo learned of the discussions that had been taking place about medical aid to atomic bomb survivors in Japan, they also sent their strong objections over a subject which 'has long been a propaganda stand-by of the Japanese left-wing, which had attempted to make "Hiroshima" the focus of its anti-rearmament, and anti-American exertions'. The Charge d'Affaires at the Embassy, J. Graham Parsons (later to become Assistant Secretary for the Far East at the State Department), highlighted that any kind of official sponsorship or support for treatment would reverse a principle that had stood for many years, and could have several negative consequences: 'To some degree we would be contributing to the sentiment in Japan which regards the last war as the central political fact of 1954 [and] supporting a belief that a special character attaches to atomic bomb deaths or casualties and that atomic bomb victims stand in some peculiar relation to the last war not shared in by other victims of other weapons ... we would be adopting a posture which could, and which we think would in Japan, be interpreted as an "apology" for the atomic bombs. We think we should, if possible, avoid all of this.'[71] Despite the fact that Strauss, in contrast to his staff, was personally in favour of exploring further whether more American doctors could be sent to Japan to assist the victims, the State Department was inclined to follow the advice of its diplomats in Tokyo, while to officials in the Far East Bureau the *Lucky Dragon* incident, with the problems over medical

---

[69] See 'Atoms for Peace Exhibit Hiroshima', p. 19, despatch by A. F. Fotouhi (Principal Public Affairs Officer, Hiroshima), enclosed in 'USIS Atoms for Peace Exhibition in Hiroshima', USIS Tokyo to USIA Washington, Despatch No. 52, 25 October 1956, Exhibit Studies: Atoms for Peace, box 2, Multi Area (World) Project Files, 1953–63, Office of Research, RG 306, NARA.

[70] See Gordon Arneson memorandum for Robert J. G. McClurkin, 8 March 1954, 'Japan (April–September 1954)', box 3, Subject Files, 1954, records of the Bureau of Far East Affairs, RG 59, NARA.

[71] Parsons to McClurkin, 18 February 1954, *ibid*.

treatment and access it had raised, 'offer[s] additional evidence of the unpredictable reaction in Japan over anything connected with this emotional issue'.[72]

The involvement of ABCC personnel in the initial US response to the plight of the crewmen was hence always liable to be seized on by critics of its work in Japan since 1947, feeding the allegations that the Japanese were being studied for the information they could provide on the effects of fallout on humans. In his initial efforts to gain access to the crewmen, Morton had apparently even offered to give them treatment at the ABCC facilities at Hiroshima. This gesture, however, even backfired, as it led many Japanese to question once again the US insistence that the ABCC was not there to treat other atomic victims, and that it was only interested in the crew members for research purposes. Providing the services of the ABCC for the afflicted crew members was, with good reason, seen as fundamentally inconsistent, implying either that the original rationale of the ABCC was false, or that the patients were to be treated as special cases for study.[73] Co-operation from the atomic survivors of 1945 with the ABCC began to decline further following the *Lucky Dragon* controversy.[74]

With public fear and concern in Japan spreading, severe strains were placed on relations between Washington and Tokyo. As demands for compensation from Japan's fishing industry multiplied, anger turned against the Japanese Government at a time when the Prime Minister, Yoshida Shigeru, was already subject to conservative pressure over his leadership. Uncertainty in Tokyo official circles over how to respond also gave Japanese scientists, lower-level bureaucrats and the press a licence to turn their attention to branding American behaviour as callous and irresponsible. 'It was as though a safety valve had been suddenly shattered,' Ralph Lapp later wrote, 'allowing the pent-up steam of almost a decade to blow off. Feelings of resentment, self-pity, personal anxiety and distrust broke through the surface of Japanese reserve.'[75] Within Washington's national security bureaucracy, the assumption quickly gained hold that the Soviet Union would use the *Lucky Dragon* incident to discredit the whole US approach to nuclear weapons. 'It is reasonable to suppose,' ran

[72] Drumright memorandum for Dulles, 'United States Aid to Japanese Atomic Bomb Victims', 3 May 1954, *ibid.*
[73] See the quotation from *Suhukan Asahi* of 4 April 1954, in Herbert Passin, 'Japan and the H-Bomb', *Bulletin of the Atomic Scientists*, 11, 8, October 1955, 291.
[74] Lindee, *Suffering*, 122–5. There was also some feeling that Morton had not offered the crewmen any words of consolation when granted access; see memorandum of conversation by the Acting Director of the Office of Northeast Asian Affairs, 22 April 1954, *FRUS, 1952–1954*, XV, Part 2, 1639.
[75] Lapp, *Voyage*, 95.

one memorandum reaching the OCB from the Pentagon, 'that Communist propagandists will make the most of the excellent opportunity they now have to exploit and develop their "peaceful" intentions regarding the atom as compared with what is apparently going on in the current US tests. This is all the more sensitive a point when considered in the light of Communist obsession with Nagasaki and Hiroshima as key targets for their propaganda.' They now had a chance to 'sow the same seeds throughout Japan with much greater potential effect'.[76] The OCB itself considered the US position with respect to injury and damage from *Bravo* at its weekly board meeting on 24 March but remitted the subject to its working group on Japan, contributing to the delay of the authorities in reacting to Japanese demands for compensation. The OCB finally decided to transmit an official note of regret to the Japanese Government, without implying any legal responsibility, while advising that 'official actions should tend to minimize the incident and ... undercut Communist propaganda'.[77]

In a situation where speed was called for to counteract the negative publicity that was being generated in Japan, the administration in Washington had dragged its feet, anxious primarily about the possible breaches in security that could come with the incident, and that no premature admission of responsibility should be made towards the crew members. When the US Ambassador in Tokyo, John Allison, finally received authority to enter into compensation negotiations with the Japanese Government, they proved to be a protracted and difficult affair. Allison himself ascribed the crisis to the 'lurid' stories being circulated by the sensationalist press, and the actions of a small group of publicity-hungry Japanese scientists and doctors, many of whom he caricatured as 'fuzzy minded leftists, pacifists, [and] neutralists'. Agitation had been mounted by left-wing activists with the aims of forming a breach in US–Japanese relations, gaining atomic intelligence, posing as the 'champions of Asian racialism [sic]', and to force the delay or suspension of the remainder of the nuclear test series. The Japanese Government was vilified by the Ambassador for its inability to control the situation, or even its own bureaucracy, with the Ministries of Welfare and Education

[76] 'Japan and Atomic Tests', memorandum for Elmer B. Staats (Executive Officer, OCB), from General Graves B. Erskine, Assistant to the Secretary of Defense (Special Operations), 22 March 1954, OCB 091 Japan (2), box 46, OCB Central Files series, NSC staff papers, White House Office, DDEL.

[77] Memorandum to the OCB from Staats, 30 March 1954, 'Atomic and Nuclear Energy, 1954', box 35, Lot 62 D430, records relating to State Department participation in the OCB and the NSC, 1947–63, RG 59, NARA.

blocking Cabinet attempts to comply with the embassy's requests to turn the *Lucky Dragon* over to the US Navy for sale of decontamination.[78]

From the point of view of many Japanese, however, the *Lucky Dragon* incident was a chance to express their anger at the perpetuation of American occupation-era attitudes, where legitimate Japanese grievances were overlooked. For the first time, Japanese could express their opposition to Washington's policies in a trend increasingly common throughout the rest of the decade, the alliance established by the Security Treaty of 1952 becoming the contested terrain of internal political debate. In many ways too, *Bravo* reinforced an emerging Japanese sense of victimhood, and by connecting so powerfully with Hiroshima and Nagasaki helped to put those two terrible events in a different and new narrative scheme, where the Japanese were marked out as the innocent atomic sufferers at the hands of Americans. This had the entirely negative effect, it might be added, of decoupling any Japanese feelings of responsibility for the war which had preceded the attacks of 1945, while they could now be figured as the first steps of a US attempt to establish a hegemonic position in the region, rather than the climax of a ferocious conflict which had its origins in Japan's own search for a New Order in East Asia.

Within the State Department there was growing anxiety over the possible impact of *Bravo*. An alarmed Dulles had called Robertson, the Assistant Secretary for Far Eastern Affairs, on the morning of 29 March to ask 'if we are watching the Pacific explosions in relation to public opinion in Japan'. Both men were unsure if a second test was planned, Robertson saying that the only information the State Department had was what appeared in the press, an obviously unsatisfactory state of affairs. With Robertson noting 'it was a tremendous situation in Japan', Dulles resolved he would call Strauss. When they spoke immediately after, Strauss was initially dismissive, maintaining that 'it was grossly exaggerated by those who wish we did not have such a weapon and don't care if Russia has it. Nothing was out of control. Nothing devastated.' Dulles replied that this was 'not correct from our [i.e. the State Department's] point of view. Japan and England are upset.' Strauss continued to argue (inaccurately) that the *Lucky Dragon* was within the designated danger

---

[78] See Allison to Department of State, 20 May 1954, *FRUS, 1952–1954, XIV: China and Japan*, Part 2 (Washington, DC, 1985), 1644–5. One 'dramatic gesture' suggested by the Ambassador was to issue a public invitation for the Japanese doctors tending the *Lucky Dragon* crew to observe the US treatment of their own service personnel at Honolulu who had been exposed to the fallout from *Bravo*. Bringing out that Japan did not have a monopoly of radiation patients might, Allison thought, have a 'beneficial effect on the Japanese doctors as well as the morbidly race conscious public'; see OCB Daily Intelligence Abstract No. 129, 3 May 1954, DDRS/CK3100092345.

zone, and that he was suspicious of the proximity of the vessel to the test site, while confirming that a second test explosion had already taken place on 26 March. Dulles pressed on, saying that 'international law is involved – can we have an operation that destroys all living things in an 800-mile radius?' The Secretary of State told Strauss that what should be kept in mind was 'the tremendous repercussions these things have. It should be kept under control. The general impression around the world is that we are appropriating a vast area of the ocean for our use and depriving other people of its use. There is panic re the fish being contaminated, etc. Some feel the British Isles could be wiped out, and so they better make a deal on the best terms possible with the Russians.' With Strauss finally conceding that the time had probably come for him to offer 'a careful explanation' in public, Dulles emphasized that 'it would be a good thing if something could be said to moderate [the] wave of hysteria [which was] driving our Allies away from us. They think we are getting ready for a war of this kind. We could survive but some of them would be obliterated in a few minutes. It could lead to a policy of neutrality or appeasement.' Dulles wanted Strauss to say something that would 'bring this back to the realm of reason'.[79]

One element complicating the American response to the fate of the *Lucky Dragon* was the belief held by some that espionage of one form or another was involved. Some senior State Department officials had been made suspicious by the seemingly unco-operative attitude of the Japanese, believing that this could 'stem from other than psychological grounds and that they have something to hide'.[80] Sterling Cole announced that until it was clear that the Japanese boat was not engaged in spying, the United States would make no commitments regarding compensation payments to the seamen. An increasingly under-pressure Strauss pushed the view that the whole affair had been manufactured by Communist elements in Japan either to generate adverse publicity for the testing programme, or even to acquire information on its results. Strauss could not reconcile himself to the idea that *Bravo* might be a genuine accident, or that the *Lucky Dragon* was an innocent victim of the test. On 2 April, he was voicing his suspicions that the vessel was a 'Red spy out-fit'.[81] If he were a Russian, Strauss reflected in a rare moment of whimsy, he would 'fill the

---

[79] Memoranda of Dulles–Robertson (10.12 am) and Dulles–Strauss (10.30 am) telephone conversations, 29 March 1954, box 2, Telephone Calls series, John Foster Dulles papers, DDEL; Strauss conversation also reproduced in *FRUS, 1952–1954, II*, Part 2, 1379–80.
[80] Dulles to Allison, 8 April 1954, *FRUS, 1952–1954, XIV*, Part 2, 1632.
[81] Entry for 2 April 1954, in Robert H. Ferrell (ed.), *The Diary of James C. Hagerty: Eisenhower in Mid-Course, 1954–1955* (Bloomington, 1983), 40.

oceans all over the world with radioactive fish. It would be so easy to do.'[82]
In fact, Strauss even asked the CIA to conduct an investigation into
whether the *Lucky Dragon* had deliberately exposed itself to the radiation
by sailing into the danger zone to collect fallout samples and to provide a
vehicle for anti-American propaganda. As part of this process, the
Japanese Ministry of Foreign Affairs was given a long list of questions by
a US Embassy official in Tokyo, asking about the political backgrounds
and possible Communist connections of the *Lucky Dragon*'s crew.[83]
The CIA also undertook enquiries over the matter of whether Dr
Tsuzuki was 'politically suspect'. The eventual conclusion of the CIA
probe, communicated in a letter to Strauss in late April from Frank
Wisner, the head of the agency's covert action arm, was that there was
no evidence to support the wilder theories then circulating (though
Wisner was not prepared to 'rule out the possibility of a certain amount
of irregularity').[84]

Although containment of the after-effects of *Bravo* was by now impossible, the administration's public presentation of the unfortunate results of
the test left much to be desired. At his regular press conference on 24
March, when Strauss was still away at the Pacific Proving Grounds,
Eisenhower admitted that, 'It is quite clear that this time something
must have happened that we have never experienced before, and must
have surprised and astonished the scientists. Very properly, the United
States has to take precautions that never occurred to them before.'[85] This
hardly represented the kind of statement that would halt the clamour for
more information about what exactly had happened at Bikini. Meanwhile,
informal Japanese requests that testing in the Pacific should be suspended
(particularly to minimize further disruption to the Japanese fishing industry) were summarily turned aside; US officials were simply not prepared
to compromise on continuing with the *Castle* series, citing the overriding
requirements of national security. On 30 March, Eisenhower decided that
official silence over *Bravo* was no longer an option, and calling Strauss in,
told him he would have to explain the facts behind the test in a prepared
statement for the news media in an effort to allay mounting concerns.
Strauss was already the subject of hostile comment from some reporters

[82] Entry for 4 April 1954, *ibid.*, 42. See also the disingenuous account offered in Lewis
L. Strauss, *Men and Decisions* (New York, 1962), 410–12.
[83] See Smith-Norris, 'The BRAVO Nuclear Incident', 11.
[84] See Wisner to Strauss, 29 April 1954, enclosing memorandum for the record, 'CIA
Investigation of Circumstances of Exposure of Fuku Ryu Maru (Fortunate Dragon) to
Hydrogen Bomb Test', 28 April 1954, DDRS/CK3100123295.
[85] President's news conference, 24 March 1954, *The Public Papers of the Presidents: Dwight
D. Eisenhower, 1954* (Washington, DC, 1960), 346.

because of his inept handling of the Oppenheimer case, and he cannot have relished the prospect of conveying the unappetizing news.

The next presidential news conference held on 31 March began in low-key manner, but Strauss, with the President alongside, soon turned to a briefing on the current American testing programme. The head of the AEC tried to downplay the whole incident, by claiming that there had been no wholesale contamination of tuna stocks, while the evacuated Marshall islanders were all in good health. Strauss also alleged that the injuries suffered by the Japanese fisherman were not caused by fallout, but by the heat from the explosion reacting with the coral reef. All these statements later proved to be inconsistent with the information available to the AEC at the time. As the press conference wound down, Strauss was questioned by journalists about the possible size of a thermonuclear weapon and remarked that 'it can be made to be as large as you wish, as large as the military requirement demands, that is to say an H-bomb can be made as large enough to take out a city'. Greeted with a concerted cry of 'What?' from the assembled reporters, the AEC Chairman repeated, 'To take out a city.' In answer to the almost inevitable query of 'How big a city?' Strauss responded, 'Any city', and then when asked if this could include New York, confirmed, 'The metropolitan area, yes.'[86] As James Hagerty, Eisenhower's Press Secretary, then so aptly put it, 'All hell broke loose.'[87] More maps, reminiscent of those used in February, appeared in newspapers showing the likely spread of destruction that would be caused to major US urban centres by a bomb the size of *Bravo*. Any hopes that administration officials might have had that the political effects of *Bravo* could be mitigated were quickly shattered, and the nascent anti-nuclear movement was galvanized by this powerful demonstration of the human and environmental consequences of atmosphere nuclear testing and the eruption of Cold War tensions into all-out war.[88]

The impact of *Bravo* was all the greater as it was felt at the same time as a major international crisis in Asia took hold. There has been surprisingly little attention paid to the confluence between widespread fears surrounding nuclear testing and fallout during the spring of 1954, and the anxieties over nuclear escalation prompted by the prospect of the United States intervening to forestall a Communist victory over the French in Indochina.[89] Notwithstanding the domestic pressures on the French Government to end the fighting, during the early part of 1954 the

---

[86] 'Text of 31 March 1954 Press Conference', *NYT*, 1 April 1954.
[87] Entry for 31 March 1954, Ferrell (ed.), *Hagerty Diary*, 36.
[88] See, e.g., Wittner, *Resisting the Bomb*, 1–26, 125–9, 144–8.
[89] A rare exception is Gardner in his *Approaching Vietnam*, 182–6, 191.

French High Command in Indochina had confidently prepared for a major clash with the Viet Minh in the remote valley of Dien Bien Phu, the outcome of which was likely to have a major bearing on the Geneva Conference which was due to open at the end of April. The Viet Minh assault launched in the middle of March against the French garrison led to quick, if costly, successes and cast instant gloom and despondency over policy-makers in both Paris and Washington. With the Eisenhower administration groping for ways to retrieve the increasingly desperate French position, Admiral Radford began to develop plans for active US intervention with the French military authorities, and aerial reconnaissance of Chinese airfields within reach of northern Vietnam was sanctioned in anticipation of a decision by Beijing to enter the fighting in a more direct manner. Meanwhile, on 29 March Dulles tried to prepare the diplomatic ground for more forceful measures by making a speech to the Overseas Press Club in New York calling for 'United Action' between the Western powers and friendly Asian nations in order to stem further Communist advances in South East Asia. It was on the same day that he held his worried telephone conversation with Strauss over the effect on allies such as Britain and Japan of the nuclear fears generated by *Bravo*.[90] Explaining his initiative to Sir Roger Makins, the British Ambassador in Washington, Dulles confessed that when he had talked of United Action, 'he had not had any specific plan in mind. Many courses were open. Much depended on the views of the Allies and how far they were ready to go in joint action.' To Makins it seemed that the Secretary of State was suggesting that the Chinese could be coerced by military threats into curtailing their support for the Viet Minh.[91] At the very least, Dulles hoped to form a coalition of the United States, Britain, France, Australia, New Zealand, the Philippines and Thailand, as well as the French-created Associated States of Vietnam, Cambodia and Laos, which could agree on common action in the event of either overt Chinese intervention, or a complete French collapse in Indochina.[92]

Though notably ambiguous in its precise meaning, the call for United Action, combined with the struggle of the besieged French garrison at Dien Bien Phu, triggered widespread speculation that the United States was preparing to enter the conflict. A powerful air strike could be mounted with the B-29 bombers of the Far East Air Force, staging through Clark

---

[90] See Gibbons, *U.S. Government and the Vietnam War*, Part 1, 180–2.
[91] See Geoffrey Warner, 'Britain and the Crisis over Dien Bien Phu, April 1954: The Failure of United Action', in Lawrence S. Kaplan, Denise Artaud and Mark R. Rubin (eds.), *Dien Bien Phu and the Crisis of Franco-American Relations, 1954–1955* (Wilmington, DE, 1990), 64.
[92] See George C. Herring and Richard H. Immerman, 'Eisenhower, Dulles, and Dien Bien Phu: "The Day We Didn't Go to War" Revisited', *ibid.*, 86.

Field in the Philippines, though this would take some time to plan and prepare. In addition, two American aircraft carriers steaming off the Vietnamese coast gave Washington a further and more immediate option of an attack against Viet Minh positions around Dien Bien Phu, and this course was pushed forward by a pugnacious Radford, even though his fellow Joint Chiefs were not prepared to join him in such a firm recommendation.[93] Although sceptical over the efficacy of immediate military action around Dien Bien Phu, a cautious Eisenhower and Dulles wanted, however, to keep their options open and were above all concerned to deter active Chinese intervention and fortify French resolve as the opening of the Geneva Conference loomed over the horizon. The President, moreover, was adamant that if the United States did become involved militarily in Indochina, it should be as part of a multilateral effort, involving both Western and Asian nations, in order to both remove any stigma of colonialism from US participation and to share the burden required. Always wary of the unhappy precedent of the Korean War, Eisenhower was also clear that congressional approval would have to be forthcoming. The congressional leadership was equally (if not even more) hesitant, and when Dulles and Radford presented ideas for military intervention to a cross-party group of senior figures on 3 April, the latter attached several conditions before they would give any advance approval for military action, including the stipulation of allied support. Exhibiting no real surprise at congressional responses, the President and his Secretary of State proceeded with the attempt to secure backing from US allies with interests in the area before contemplating again what more forceful action should be undertaken in Indochina or South East Asia as a whole. They were also determined that the French grant full independence to the existing governments of Vietnam, Cambodia and Laos before they would seek further congressional authority for intervention.[94] Dulles, for his part, felt that the presentation of a united front by the Western powers in the region could obviate the need for any action at all and would strengthen the French negotiating position at Geneva, rather than undermine the chances of a diplomatic settlement.

The principal objection to the formation of any coalition in support of United Action, however, came from a British government acutely conscious that if they gave a green light to military intervention, a cycle of escalation might be initiated that could lead to Chinese involvement, US

---

[93] See Gibbons, *U.S. Government and the Vietnam War*, Part 1, 182–97. Background on military preparations and plans for intervention can be followed in John Prados, *Operation Vulture* (New York, 2002).

[94] Herring and Immerman, 'Eisenhower, Dulles, and Dien Bien Phu', 88–9.

attacks on the mainland of China and Soviet action to prevent the demise of their Far Eastern ally. For Eden, the premature formation of a coalition might also scupper any chances of a negotiated settlement to the Indochina war at the forthcoming Geneva Conference. As the Foreign Secretary informed his Cabinet colleagues, he could see little chance that China would react to a joint warning by desisting from the line of policy she was pursuing in Indochina, leaving any coalition with the options of ignominious withdrawal or carrying out 'warlike action against China' through blockade or bombing, neither of which the COS had considered would be militarily effective at the time of the Korean War. If attacked, however, Beijing would surely invoke the Sino-Soviet Treaty, thus opening up the possibility of a wider world war.[95] Just as at Bermuda in December 1953, British ministers and officials foresaw the possibility of general war where the first target for Soviet atomic attack would be the US airbases in East Anglia and the urban sprawl of London.

Furthermore, reactions in Britain to the *Bravo* test had also been strong, and helped to give impetus to a growing anti-nuclear movement that found its support among peace activists, trade unionists, religious leaders and figures in the Labour Party.[96] Eden's Private Secretary at the Foreign Office, Evelyn Shuckburgh, noted the discrepancy between the scientists' expectations and the actual size of the test explosion with the thought, 'In other words, it was out of control. Very great excitement everywhere about it, as if people began to see the end of the world.'[97] Churchill had to come to the House of Commons on 1 April, where he made a statement defending the need of the United States to continue atmosphere testing of nuclear weapons. However, the Prime Minister was put under severe pressure from Labour backbenchers who were angry at how little the Government knew about the whole *Castle* series.[98] That evening, around one hundred Labour MPs (equivalent to about a third of the parliamentary party) signed a demand to stop hydrogen bomb tests, outlaw nuclear weapons and to move immediately to five-nation disarmament talks.[99] In

[95] See Eden's paper for the Cabinet, 'Indo-China', C(54)134, 7 April 1954, CAB 129/67; and subsequent discussion, CC(54)26th Conclusions, item 4, 7 April 1954, CAB 128/27, TNA.

[96] See, in general, Wittner, *Resisting the Bomb*, 16.

[97] Entry for 26 March 1954, Evelyn Shuckburgh, *Descent to Suez: Diaries, 1951–1956* (London, 1986), 155–6.

[98] This was the occasion for one of Churchill's worst performances in the Commons; see, e.g., John W. Young, *Winston Churchill's Last Campaign: Britain and the Cold War, 1951–5* (Oxford, 1996), 255–9. Churchill had presented his defence of US testing to the Cabinet the previous day; see CC(54)23rd Conclusions, item 1, 31 March 1954, CAB 128/27, TNA.

[99] See Divine, *Blowing*, 21; entry for 6 April 1954, Shuckburgh, *Diaries*, 160.

response to these signs of domestic unease, Eden privately urged the Americans to at least reconvene the then moribund talks with the Soviet Union in the Disarmament Committee at the UN, and in official circles there was much disquiet at the recent trends in US policy, even though it had to be publicly defended. Churchill had already written to Eisenhower in the middle of March, expressing his horror at the power of the new hydrogen weapons being developed, and stressing his concerns over the vulnerability of the densely populated British Isles, and London in particular.[100]

Only three months before the *Bravo* shot, Eisenhower had delivered his Atoms for Peace speech at the UN hoping to cast the American image in a new light by associating nuclear power with a benevolent and peaceful programme carried forward under American leadership. However, the results of the test and the subsequent publicity surrounding the ill-fated voyage of the *Lucky Dragon* placed the foreign policy objectives of the Atoms for Peace scheme in jeopardy. Symptomatic of the tensions within the administration's approach to the public relations issues surrounding nuclear weapons was the decision reached in mid-March, and before the full implications of *Bravo* had been digested, to release the AEC's film of the *Mike* test of November 1952, along with colour photographs of the immense fireball and resultant mushroom cloud. The materials were published and aired in the days after Strauss's press conferences, leading to yet more alarmed comment in newspapers across the United States. Sensing the damage that was being done, the US authorities tried to prevent distribution overseas of the colour images of *Mike*, but to no avail.[101] On one level, US officials reasoned that better information to the public about the new weapons might help to educate them about the realities of the new age in international politics that had now arrived, and of America's peaceful intent combined with its determination to face the Soviet threat. The negative consequences of this line were, however, only too apparent, with greater knowledge only stoking up fears over a coming thermonuclear conflagration. Among the peoples and governments of allies in Europe and Asia, this could have the effect of increasing pressures for negotiations with the Soviet Union that would result in damaging concessions, or to a distancing of relations with the United States. In April 1954, a National Intelligence Estimate (NIE) on the impact of growing nuclear capabilities concluded, with direct relevance to the

---

[100] See Churchill to Eisenhower, 9 March 1954, in Peter Boyle (ed.), *The Churchill–Eisenhower Correspondence, 1953–1955* (Chapel Hill, 1990), 122–4.
[101] See Divine, *Blowing*, 21–2; see also Progress Report of the Working Group of the OCB, 30 April 1954, *FRUS, 1952–1954, II*, Part 2, 1408–9.

Indochina crisis, that fear of a wider war would result in US allies being 'more reluctant than at present to repel local Communist aggression and more anxious to limit the scope of any local conflict', while their reactions could not be predicted if general nuclear war were imminent.[102]

The administration's internal debates over whether and when to release the film of the 1952 thermonuclear test, along with the importance assigned to the Atoms for Peace initiative, led to the active involvement of the Operations Coordinating Board of the NSC in managing the release of official statements relating to atomic energy matters, with the OCB interest defined as to 'assure maximum foreign support of the U.S. international position with respect to national policies, programs and objectives'.[103] As it began to assume the dimensions of a public relations problem of the first order, *Bravo* helped further galvanize the administration's approach, and recommendations soon reached the OCB calling for a 'vigorous offensive on the non-war uses of atomic energy' as the best method of countering the anticipated negative effects of the *Castle* series, possibly involving building an atomic reactor in 'Japan and Berlin, or any other tangible implementation of the President's [Atoms for Peace] speech which might be considered practical and of strong publicity value'.[104] The various projects associated with Atoms for Peace would, OCB officials resolved, have to be pushed forward with even greater urgency.[105] Animated by these issues, at the end of April 1954, the OCB decided to establish a special working group on nuclear energy and information programmes. Chaired by Gerard C. Smith, the State Department official who served as Dulles's Special Assistant for Atomic Energy Matters, the working group was to maintain a watching brief on government actions and programmes which were capable of significantly influencing the overseas climate of opinion towards nuclear weapons, and

---

[102] 'Probable Effects of Increasing Nuclear Capabilities Upon the Policies of U.S. Allies', NIE 100–54, April 1954, summarized in draft circular instruction, USITO 269, 10 March 1955, 'Fallout: Reactions and Statements' folder, box 243, records relating to Atomic Energy Matters, 1944–62, records of the Special Assistant to the Secretary of State for Atomic Energy and Outer Space (SASAE), RG 59, NARA.

[103] See memorandum for the OCB by Elmer B. Staats (Executive Officer, OCB), 'Coordination of Information and the Timing of Projects Related to Nuclear Energy', 6 March 1954, 'OCB General' folder, box 60, Subject Files Relating to National Security Policy, 1950–7, RG 59, NARA.

[104] Memorandum for the Executive Officer, OCB, from General G. B. Erskine, Assistant to the Secretary of Defense (Special Operations), 'Japan and Atomic Tests', 22 March 1954.

[105] Memorandum to the OCB from Staats, 30 March 1954, 'Atomic and Nuclear Energy, 1954' folder, box 35, records relating to State Department participation in the OCB and the NSC, 1947–63, RG 59, NARA.

to advise government departments how to craft their public statements and approaches to events such as upcoming nuclear test series.[106]

Whatever the administration did after *Bravo*, though, could not counteract the wide-ranging impact it had on perceptions of nuclear danger and the consequences of the arms race. For the vulnerable states and societies of Western Europe, it was difficult to see how the outcome of conflicts in peripheral areas of Asia warranted the risk of nuclear devastation, especially when on some readings it was the United States, a putative ally, which was behaving in a bellicose and provocative fashion. American officials, for their part, were becoming deeply concerned that their NATO allies, influenced by the trends of domestic opinion, would turn away from close alignment with Washington's policies, with the unfolding Indochina crisis a representative example. But *Bravo* was to have far wider reverberations than its impact on relationships between the Western allies, for it had a direct effect on the Asian region itself at the very moment when Asian voices and perspectives, particularly on such matters as imperialism and race, were beginning to be heard with increasing frequency. The regional relevance of *Bravo* and *Lucky Dragon* combined served to connect the legacy of Hiroshima with an identification of the United States with policies of racial discrimination, as Asian leaders and opinion-formers vented their suspicions that Americans were dismissive of the lives and welfare of those whose skin colour differed from their own. Whereas before *Bravo* 'Asian opinion' was a largely discounted factor to American policy-makers when it came to nuclear issues, the repercussions of the test, and the Indochina crisis that followed, became a steadily more significant consideration.

---

[106] See OCB Meeting Minutes, 28 April 1954, OCB 337 Minutes; OCB Progress Report on Nuclear Energy Projects and Related Information Programs, 22 November 1954, 'Atomic and Nuclear Energy' folder, box 35, records relating to State Department participation in the OCB and the NSC, 1947–63, RG 59, NARA.

6   The aftermath of *Bravo*, the Indochina crisis and the emergence of SEATO

By 1953–4, American soldiers, officials, businessmen and ordinary citizens were coming into contact with an ever-widening number of Asian states and societies, as the aftermath of the Korean War and the retreat of European colonialism saw a vacuum open up which American policy-makers and commercial interests, fearful of both Communist encroachments and losing new business opportunities, were eager to fill. Expansion of American power and influence also brought increased exposure and interest in the racial mores of American society. 'No American returning from Asia can doubt that the status of the American Negro is a key to our country's relationship with the awakening nations of Asia and Africa,' Chester Bowles declared in an article published in the *New York Times Magazine* in early February 1954. 'The colored peoples who comprise two-thirds of the world's population simply cannot think about the United States without considering bitterly the limitations under which our 15,000,000 Americans with colored skins are living. Communist propagandists, of course, exaggerate the picture. They tell Asians that lynch law is the rule with us. They make the fantastic assertion that the atom bomb was dropped on Japan and not on Germany because the Japanese are colored while the Germans are white. But make no mistake about it, the resentment would still be with us if the Communists shut up shop tomorrow.'[1] Although he recognized that there had been some progress made in improving the position of black Americans since the war, Bowles underlined how much still had to be done for full equality and freedom to be enjoyed by all American citizens. Having been exposed to the subject during his time in India, Bowles carried the message to his domestic audience that knowledge of racial oppression and injustice within the United States' own borders was undermining US professions of friendship for Asia and the promotion of democratic values in the Cold War.[2]

---

[1] 'The Negro – Progress and Challenge', *NYT Magazine*, 7 February 1954.
[2] Dudziak, *Cold War Civil Rights*, 77–8.

In the battle of ideas with Communism in Asia, where in the view of Supreme Court Justice William O. Douglas 'race and color consciousness is a dominant and often overriding factor in basic policy issues', it was difficult to accept American arguments that they stood for freedom and democracy when fundamental rights were denied to a significant element of their own population.[3] Following her own trip to India in 1954, Eleanor Roosevelt reported that 'we have against us their feeling that we, because our skins are white, necessarily look down upon all peoples whose skins are yellow or black or brown. This thought is never out of their minds [and] they always asked me pointedly ... about our treatment of minorities in our country.'[4] In one USIA guidance note sent to overseas posts in March 1954, the point was made that, 'Use of the term "colored" as a synonym for the American Negro has been damaging to us in Asia because it has automatically made people of yellow or brown skin identify themselves amongst those discriminated against.'[5] The State Department estimated that one half of all anti-American Soviet propaganda had race as its key theme.[6] It was for precisely this reason that in December 1952, in the last days of the Truman presidency, the Justice Department filed an amicus curiae brief for the plaintiffs in the upcoming Supreme Court case of *Brown* v. *Board of Education*, which was to consider the constitutionality of segregation in the public school system, emphasizing how such practices were harming the United States by exposing it to the charge of hypocrisy through its espousal of democratic values in the Cold War. Arguing that a change in the law was necessary in the interests of US foreign policy and that making segregation unconstitutional would have great symbolic value, the brief cited Acheson's views:

During the past six years [since Acheson's first letter to the Chairman of the FEPC in 1946], the damage to our foreign relations attributable to [race discrimination] has become progressively greater. The United States is under constant attack in the foreign press, over the foreign radio, and in such international bodies as the United Nations because of various practices of discrimination against minority groups within this country. As might be expected, Soviet spokesmen regularly exploit this situation in propaganda against the United States, both within the United Nations and through radio broadcasts and the press, which reaches all corners of the world. Some of these attacks against us are based on falsehood or distortion; but the undeniable existence of racial discrimination gives unfriendly governments the most effective kind of ammunition for their propaganda warfare. The hostile

---

[3] William O. Douglas, *Beyond the High Himalayas* (New York, 1953), 317.
[4] Eleanor Roosevelt, *India and the Awakening East* (London, 1954), 91.
[5] Infoguide, 'Supreme Court Decision on School Desegregation', USIA CA 564, 12 March 1954, AU 1828/3, FO 371/109162, TNA.
[6] Klein, *Cold War Orientalism*, 40.

reaction among normally friendly people, many of whom are particularly sensitive in regard to the status of non-European races, is growing in alarming proportions. In such countries the view is expressed more and more vocally that the United States is hypocritical in claiming to be the champion of democracy while permitting practices of racial discrimination here in this country.[7]

Awareness in Asia of the segregationist practices common within the United States was paralleled in many cases by scrutiny of American foreign policy towards the region, to see if there were any indications that it too contained discriminatory elements. Discussion of massive retaliation had already provoked some disquiet that the Far East was to be the setting of the new attitudes towards nuclear weapons that was beginning to distinguish the Eisenhower administration from its predecessor. The *Bravo* test, however, took Asian feelings over American policies to a new level, with the prevalence of a perception that the carelessness of the precautions that had been taken with the testing of thermonuclear weapons was related to the fact that those likely to be affected by its consequences were not white. In this way opposition to nuclear testing became a key theme that pulled together several strands of Asian and non-aligned opinion, helped to arouse Western fears over pan-Asian solidarity, and contributed to the global anti-nuclear movement. Outlining the 'helpless acceptance' that had greeted testing since 1945, *The Times of India* published an editorial on 24 March 1954 entitled 'Atomic Madness', which expressed the hope that the *Bravo* test would 'liberate the people – the common citizens of all nations sharing the common threat of this atomic madness – from their self-destructive apathy'. Noting the startled reaction of US scientists to the size of the *Bravo* shot, the editorial dubbed it a 'nightmarish achievement', possessing a destructive power six hundred times that of the bombs dropped on Hiroshima and Nagasaki. 'There can be no excuse,' it asserted,

for the errors of mismanagement and miscalculation which resulted in injuries to Japanese fishermen, islanders and American observers. Equally there can be no justification of any failure – by peoples or governments – to press forward towards international control and the abolition of atomic weapons ... No Government can absolve itself from the responsibility of being actively concerned with a matter beside which current political differences are insignificant. The combined weight of the smaller neutral States supported by the conviction and will of the people will be a force too formidable for the major powers to ignore.[8]

_____

[7] Acheson letter to the US Attorney General (James P. McGranery), 2 December 1952, cited in brief for the United States as Amicus Curiae, p. 7, *Brown* v. *Board of Education*, 347 US 483 (1954), as quoted in Dudziak, *Cold War Civil Rights*, 100–1, and see *ibid.*, 90–1.

[8] 'Atomic Madness', *The Times of India*, 24 March 1954; see also Foreign Service despatch, R. Smith Simpson, American Consul, Bombay, to Washington, No. 809, 26 March 1954, 711.5611/3–2654, box 3174, CDF, RG 59, NARA.

After the news that the second shot in the *Castle* series had been detonated, the same paper was writing in its leader a few days later that, 'The indifference and impatience with which expressions of concern throughout the world, and not least in Japan, have been received, will – without the slightest shadow of doubt – cause ... irreparable political damage to the United States ... and expose itself to the charge of fiendish inhumanity.'[9]

Several Asian political leaders made their concerns known. Attending a meeting of the prime ministers of the Colombo powers (India, Pakistan, Ceylon, Burma and Indonesia) at the end of March, Nehru told journalists of his anxieties over the unknown properties of fallout: 'Do you imagine that because these experiments are taking place in the Pacific that we in Asia are safe? ... How can we be sure that our children may not go gradually blind or contract some internal disease?'[10] On 2 April, in a speech before the Lok Sabha in New Delhi, Nehru called for a 'standstill agreement' among the atomic powers to cover testing and more publicity to be given to weapons effects. Expressing sympathy for the Japanese fishermen of the *Lucky Dragon*, the Indian Prime Minister concluded, as the chamber 'appeared to stir uneasily', with the comment that it was of 'great concern to us that Asia and her peoples appear to be always nearer these occurrences and experiments, actual or potential'.[11] With Tokyo already having passed an official note to the US authorities asking for testing to be suspended during the tuna fishing season between November and March, in early April both houses of the Diet passed resolutions critical of the tests in the Pacific and urging international controls on the practice.[12] Mirroring the appeals issued by Nehru, the Japanese Government soon also emerged as a leading proponent of international agreement to end all nuclear testing. On the day after Nehru's Lok Sabha speech, Ali Sastromidjojo, the Indonesian Prime Minister, lent his voice to the growing chorus by deploring current testing in the Pacific and endorsing Nehru's suggestion that the relation of Asia to the tests be discussed at a further conference of South and South East Asian prime ministers. The British Ambassador in Jakarta, Oscar Morland, warned Eden that 'there can be little doubt that the unfortunate results of the recent tests have been noted in thinking circles here with growing anxiety

---

[9] *The Times of India*, 31 March 1954.
[10] 'Nehru to Press Asians on Peace', *NYT*, 1 April 1954. The designation 'Colombo powers' came from their involvement in the British Colombo Plan scheme of economic aid and technical advice, first put forward in 1949.
[11] 'Nehru Proposes Atom "Standstill" Pending UN Curb', *NYT*, 3 April 1954.
[12] See 'Japanese Bid U.S. Curb Atom Tests', *NYT*, 1 April 1954; 'Tokyo Diet Calls for Atom Control', *NYT*, 2 April 1954.

and mistrust, while the more rabid nationalists have seized upon the opportunity to give vent to their anti-Americanism'.[13]

From Calcutta, the American Consul reported that the recent hydrogen bomb tests had aroused considerable coverage and editorial comment in the local press (both English language and vernacular), with much of it inclined to overlook Russian testing activities, and instead placing the onus for nuclear dangers on the United States. 'A sub-theme which appears in many editorials,' the Consul warned, 'is that America is conducting her experiments in the Far East so that Asians rather than white people would be subject to any possible after effects.' One newspaper asked the question, 'Why again are [the tests] being held in the Pacific and not in the Atlantic so that white people too may have some taste of bomb radiation?'[14] By the end of April, the American Consul General in Bombay was noting that the injury suffered by the Japanese crewmen of the *Lucky Dragon* had been 'much emphasised in both press and private conversations and has added a noticeably Asian factor to Indian reaction'. The explosions had 'appeared to reinforce that feeling which the Consulate General noticed developing last November from the relations of Indian and American officers in Korea, that America these days had a desire to fight'. Moreover, the emotional reaction to the tests had intensified the belief that US military assistance was 'detrimental to Asian stability, peace and independence from the West', while their overall effect had been to 'reduce American stock to a further lower level' even than that of the previous year, when the announcement of military aid to Pakistan had aroused the ire of India's political classes. Such was the climate of anti-American opinion in India that past and present elements of US foreign policy such as the Marshall Plan and NATO were increasingly seen as vehicles for American domination. It was becoming difficult for Indian leaders to side with the United States in discussion of current international affairs, while the Russians had gained a clear propaganda advantage within the subcontinent.[15]

The British High Commission in New Delhi placed the *Bravo* test in the context of the on-going Indochina crisis to provide an overview of Indian views of US policy. Against the background of Dulles's well-publicized

---

[13] Jakarta to Foreign Secretary, No. 66, 8 April 1954, GE18/26, FO 371/110695, TNA; see also *NYT*, 5 April 1954.

[14] Foreign Service despatch, J. T. McAndrew, American Consul General, Calcutta, to Washington, No. 501, 9 April 1954, 711.5611/4–954, CDF, RG 59, NARA. The quotation was from an editorial, 'Ban the Bomb', in the 31 March 1954 edition of *Amrita Bazar Patrika*.

[15] Foreign Service despatch, William T. Turner, American Consul General, Bombay, to Washington, No. 877, 22 April 1954, 711.5611/2–254, CDF, RG 59, NARA.

pronouncements about massive retaliation and the need to oppose Communist advances in Indochina, the Pacific testing programme, it was reported, had 'aroused a storm of criticism in the Indian press. Beneath the genuine sentiments of horror, the complex prejudices of anti-Americanism and "Asianism" are being exercised to the full.' Little attention was paid to recent Soviet tests, but the Americans,

due to their responsibility for the 'diabolic events at Bikini', are said to be ... forfeiting the leadership of the free world, whose views they now so obstinately disregard. It is feared that the voice of an America equipped with bigger and better bombs will become more and more strident, adding progressively to the dangers implicit in Mr Dulles's statements about 'instant retaliation' and 'united action' to resist Communist expansion in South East Asia 'by whatever means'. Mr Dulles's policy, backed by the H-Bomb, is seen as the 'surest way of bringing about the third world war and the destruction of the world'.[16]

These responses to *Bravo* in South and South East Asia were being noted by OCB officials, ever watchful of the 'psychological' aspects of US nuclear policies. In one OCB memorandum of April 1954, entitled 'Potential U.S. Vulnerability in Southeast Asia', it was noted that, 'The sensitive issue of race has been injected into reactions following the recent H-bomb explosion in the Pacific. In both Thailand and Indonesia the use of "Asian" waters for the test has been challenged and a lack of US regard for Asian lives has been strongly implied.' Such questions as why the United States chose a site so close to Asia for its tests, 'along with the implication of racial callousness', were said to have been circulating among Thais, and have been the comment of leading Indonesian newspapers. The Communist Party in India was seen as particularly culpable in spreading this message, and the 'nature of the charge and the obvious vulnerability to it in this racially sensitive area would seem to make it a logical theme for further Communist exploitation'.[17] In April 1954, the Indian Ambassador in Washington, J. J. Mehta, was telling David Lilienthal that US foreign policy lacked a 'moral basis', and that this belief existed 'because the atom bomb was dropped on Asians, and the H-bomb tested in Asian waters, which made people in Asia feel we did not value colored people's lives as we did white people's'.[18]

Indeed, the testing issue was arousing such worldwide concern, and leading to such widespread criticism of the United States, that the

---

[16] UK High Commission, New Dehli, to CRO, No. 46, Savingram, 9 April 1954, DO 35/7057A, TNA.
[17] Memorandum from Clyde Slaton to Louis T. Olom, 22 April 1954, OCB 000.9 Atomic Energy (8), box 8, OCB Central File series, NSC staff papers, White House Office, DDEL.
[18] Entry for 7 April 1954, Lilienthal, *Venturesome Years*, 497.

administration in Washington contemplated whether the programme should be sustained, or an initiative taken to end the practice through international agreement, as so many were starting to urge. At an NSC meeting on 6 April, with the Indochina crisis entering full swing, Dulles had passed a note to Eisenhower expressing his view that Nehru's recent call for a halt to testing should be given serious consideration.[19] At a time when international tensions were rising, this was evidently an attempt to meet widespread public disquiet over the effects of weapons-testing, Dulles, for example, avowing to Henry Cabot Lodge, the US Ambassador to the UN (and someone who had also put forward ideas to limit tests to below one megaton): 'I think this is an area where we have a chance to get a big propaganda advantage and perhaps results.'[20] Having discussed the matter with the British, Dulles again conferred with the President over a possible moratorium in the middle of the month, and Eisenhower affirmed his feeling that the United States should make such a proposal, though he wanted technical studies over its feasibility to be completed first.[21] In early May, the NSC heard a presentation from Dulles on the moratorium proposal, where its merits were argued largely on propaganda grounds. The President tended to be in favour, raising 'the necessity we were under to gain some significant psychological advantage in the world. Everybody seemed to think that we're skunks, saber-rattlers and warmongers. We ought not to miss any chance to make clear our peaceful objectives.' Outlining his support for a moratorium, Dulles argued that 'every day' the United States was 'losing ground' in Britain and other allied nations 'because they are all insisting we are so militaristic'. It was not possible to 'sit here in Washington and develop bigger bombs without any regard for the impact of these developments on world opinion. In the long run it isn't only bombs that win wars, but having public opinion on your side.' Strong opposition to any moratorium proposal came, nevertheless, from Wilson, Strauss and Radford, who all cited the significant strides made in thermonuclear capability during the *Castle* series, and how unwise it would be if the United States was seen to be bowing to international pressure over testing. The NSC decided to refer the subject for further study to Dulles, Strauss and Wilson.[22] By the end of

---

[19] See Hewlett and Holl, *Atoms for Peace and War*, 275.
[20] See Dulles to Lodge, 20 April 1954, 'Atomic Weapons and Proposals, 1953, 1954, 1955 (2)', box 4, Subject series, John Foster Dulles papers, DDEL.
[21] Memorandum of conference with President Eisenhower, 19 April 1954, 'Meetings with the President 1954 (3)', box 1, White House Memoranda series, John Foster Dulles papers, DDEL.
[22] Memorandum of discussion at the 195th meeting of the NSC, 6 May 1954, *FRUS, 1952–1954, II*, Part 2, 1424–9.

May, Dulles had changed his mind, converted by the technical arguments of the AEC regarding the difficulties of policing any moratorium, and his anxiety that it might be the Russians who would derive more propaganda advantages during the negotiations over testing by suggesting further measures of nuclear disarmament. Recognizing also that agreement to a moratorium would indirectly acknowledge the idea that nuclear weapons were 'morally bad' and in a different and special category from conventional arms, Dulles grandiosely described the final decision of the NSC on 23 June to oppose a moratorium as illustrating 'the power of reason against the power of will'.[23]

Greater pressure for an end to atmospheric nuclear testing came at the very time when the Eisenhower administration was trying to gather coalition partners for military intervention in Indochina should this be decided upon. Without such support, as congressional leaders had made clear during their pivotal meeting with Eisenhower on 3 April, there would be no domestic consensus behind military action, the legislators avowing 'we want no more Koreas with the United States furnishing 90% of the manpower' (the President was in any event sceptical of how effective intervention could be in the pattern of fighting then prevalent in Indochina).[24] Yet for several figures in the administration, the stakes in Indochina were very high, and the opportunity for a decisive display of US power, while the overall Soviet nuclear arsenal remained markedly inferior to the American, was only too apparent. The Chairman of the JCS, for one, was convinced that the Chinese would not intervene in Indochina even if the United States made an all-out effort to destroy the Viet Minh forces surrounding Dien Bien Phu, and even if they did, Radford reasoned, this would provide a useful pretext for his own preference for direct attacks against the PRC itself as the best method of addressing American problems in the region. On 7 April 1954, one of Radford's special assistants, Captain George S. Anderson, went to see Douglas MacArthur II, the Counselor of the State Department, to explain that a special Pentagon study group had made an estimate that the use of three tactical atomic weapons around Dien Bien Phu would be, as Radford put it, 'the best means of smashing [the Viet Minh] and cleaning up Indochina'. The JCS Chairman was hoping that some advance agreement with the French might be negotiated to allow the Americans to exercise this nuclear option

---

[23] See memorandum of discussion at the 203rd meeting of the NSC, 23 June 1954, *ibid.*, 1467–73; and also Hewlett and Holl, *Atoms for Peace and War*, 275–6.

[24] Gibbons, *U.S. Government and the Vietnam War*, Part 1, 189–95, provides the best analysis of the 3 April meeting with congressional leaders; and see also Leighton, *Strategy, Money, and the New Look*, 536–8; Betts, *Nuclear Blackmail*, 50.

if it was decided that American air power was to be directly engaged in Indochina. MacArthur was instinctively wary, feeling any such proposal raised 'very serious questions affecting the whole position of U.S. leadership in the world'. Doubting that the French would agree to any such plan, it was, furthermore, very likely to leak, causing 'a great hue and cry throughout the parliaments of the free world', particularly in Britain. American allies would then probably insist on firmer assurances over consultation before nuclear use was agreed to (MacArthur, one should recall, had been a member of the US delegation at the Bermuda Conference), while 'in addition to the Soviet propaganda, many elements in the free world would portray our desire to use such weapons in Indochina as proof of the fact that we were testing out weapons on native peoples and were in fact prepared to act irresponsibly and drop weapons of mass destruction on the Soviet Union whenever we believed it was necessary to do so'.[25]

Already troubled by the problems that assembling Dulles's United Action coalition would present, senior State Department officials were only too well aware that loose talk of using nuclear weapons would scotch the whole prospect of achieving a meeting of minds with the nervous British and French. It would also, in the shadow of the controversy over *Bravo* and nuclear testing, incur the hostility of Asian nations concerned that their region was becoming the nuclear playground of the US military. Moreover, Radford's approach glossed over some of the significant differences that had emerged within the military planning machinery during late March over the feasibility and effectiveness of atomic strikes around Dien Bien Phu, where the terrain and dispersed nature of the Viet Minh forces made target selection difficult. In addition some military planners on the Army and Air Force staffs worried that employing nuclear weapons involved the risk of Russian or Chinese counteraction, and consequent dangers of general war. The Office of Psychological Warfare in the Army's Plans Division warned of the 'resentment and distrust' that would be caused among American allies, while Asian states such as India, Burma and Indonesia would be completely alienated from US behaviour which Communist propaganda would portray as 'unstable, barbaric, and impatient'. The head of the office felt that the damage to US reputation that the use of nuclear weapons in Asia would produce would outweigh any loss of Western prestige as a result of the fall of Dien Bien Phu. Such arguments, combined with the belief that once US air and naval power had been committed to Indochina the employment of ground troops would

---

[25] MacArthur memorandum for Dulles, 7 April 1954, *FRUS, 1952–1954, XIII: Indochina*, Part 1 (Washington, DC, 1982), 1270–2.

inevitably follow, helped to confirm General Ridgway, the US Army's Chief of Staff, in his determined and consistent opposition to intervention.[26]

Arguments over the wider political consequences of nuclear use in Asia were also appearing more in the public domain as the Eisenhower administration found itself under increased pressure to explain how massive retaliation was supposed to work in the conditions found in Indochina. This was, after all, the first real test of the military policies of the New Look, but, as we have seen, more questions than answers were being raised, with critics of the administration seizing on the inappropriateness of mustering a nuclear response to such a local conflict, when it could lead to a sharp escalation to general war and so alienate the allies who were so essential in the overall confrontation with the Soviet Union. In this sense, the nuclear ingredients of the New Look threatened to cut across the administration's diplomatic strategy during the crisis.[27] In the *New York Times*, Hanson Baldwin, for example, added his voice to the debate by pointing out that, 'Small atomic weapons for tactical use might well be employed usefully by the French defenders [of Dien Bien Phu] against the enemy's outer lines, but at great political and psychological cost in Asia and at the risk that such weapons, which the Russians almost certainly possess, might be used in retaliation against the French concentrations and airfields at Hanoi, Haiphong, Saigon and elsewhere.' Almost certainly aware that such military planning for tactical use was then in progress at the Pentagon, Baldwin conveyed the message that nuclear weapons were of little or no use in fighting limited wars, and, as he had done in July 1950 (and to some extent in 1945 over Hiroshima), Baldwin chose to give prominence to the political damage it would bring to the US cause in Asia if they were ever employed in such a context.[28] Senator Mike Mansfield (Democrat, Montana), in a debate staged by the *New York Times Magazine* and moderated by Arthur Krock in mid-May, criticized the 'tremendous deficiency' in the concept of retaliatory striking power as 'when you get right down to it, the foot soldier is going to be the guy who is going to win any war'. Mansfield questioned whether atomic bombs could have any kind of effectiveness in Indochina, while China itself offered few obvious military targets, except cities such as Harbin or Mukden in Manchuria. 'I think that many of these people [in Asia],' Mansfield warned, 'are looking

---

[26] These points are detailed in Spector, *Advice and Support*, 200–1.
[27] See, e.g., Leighton, *Strategy, Money, and the New Look*, 223; Freedman, *Evolution of Nuclear Strategy*, 93–6.
[28] See 'The Bomb and a Battle', *NYT*, 1 April 1954; see also Baldwin's piece, '"New Look" Re-Examined in Light of Indochina', *NYT*, 2 May 1954.

to China today as the champion of the colored races. And they are going to say, "Why, these white folks are taking it out on us. They don't drop atom bombs on white people but they drop them on the Japanese, the Chinese." And I think the revulsion against us would be great.'[29]

Issues surrounding race also permeated the American task of assembling the coalition of Western and Asian states who might underwrite a – still highly speculative – collective military effort in South East Asia, against the background of a steadily deteriorating French position at Dien Bien Phu. This process led to much tension in Anglo-American relations during April and May (particularly between Dulles and Eden), as the British, ever mindful of the influence in South East Asia that India was assumed to carry, as well as her leading position among the newly independent Asian countries, felt that Nehru's involvement, or at least acquiescence, had to be secured, along with as many of the other Colombo powers as possible.[30] Eden was telling the Cabinet in late May that 'it was most important that the Western powers should retain the goodwill of the leading countries of Asia. Precipitate action for the establishment of a system of collective defence for South-East Asia would certainly have alienated India; and without India's goodwill, few of the other countries of South-East Asia would have been willing to participate in it.'[31]

Although recognizing the important role played by India in Asia, the Eisenhower administration was never able to give relations with New Delhi the priority many assumed they should command, while the extension of military assistance to Pakistan in early 1954 was a lasting source of alienation.[32] Indeed, the attitude of US officials became marked, above all, by deep frustration and resentment at the readiness of Nehru to adopt a conciliatory attitude towards Communist China. This was exemplified on 23 April 1954, when Indian and Chinese officials met to resolve differences over Tibet and agreed a statement of five principles (or *pan-chsheel*) that would govern their relations: these were mutual respect for each other's territorial integrity; non-aggression; non-interference in each other's internal affairs; equality and mutual benefit in relations; and

[29] 'Our Policy in the Far East: A Debate', *NYT Magazine*, 16 May 1954.
[30] See, e.g., John G. Tahourdin minute, 22 March 1954, DL1051/3, FO 371/112213, TNA; record of discussion on South East Asia between Eden and Dulles, 13 April 1954, ZP3/2G, FO 371/125123, TNA; see also Warner, 'Britain and the Crisis over Dien Bien Phu', 68–70; Singh, *Limits of British Influence*, 166–7.
[31] CC(54)35th meeting Conclusions, 24 May 1954, CAB 128/27, TNA.
[32] See McMahon, *Cold War on the Periphery*, 171–7. Nehru had launched a scathing denunciation of US policy in Asia in his speech to the Lok Sabha when rejecting Eisenhower's offer of comparable military assistance; see 'Nehru Decries U.S. Policy on Asia and the "Cold War"', *NYT*, 2 March 1954.

peaceful coexistence.[33] A day later, in a speech delivered in the Lok Sabha, Nehru denounced 'American statements which come near to assuming protection, or declaring a kind of Monroe Doctrine, unilaterally over the countries of South East Asia'.[34] It was the *panchsheel* that, perhaps more than any other statement at this time, best represented the philosophical gulf between an 'Asian' perspective on resolving outstanding issues between newly independent states and the fears of a bipolar division of the region into rival military blocs. Nehru believed that the extension of an area of peace, non-intervention and non-alignment in South East Asia was the best assurance of security, whereas the encroachment of military alliances directed by outside powers merely served to increase tensions by preparing for armed conflict. The aphorism that the Indian Prime Minister offered the following year best summed up his approach: 'One does not seek peace through security, but security through peace.'[35]

The impression of an emerging Asian voice was reinforced when, at the very end of April, a South Asian prime ministers' conference (involving India, Pakistan, Ceylon, Burma and Indonesia) was held in Colombo, leading to a declaration that colonialism was a violation of fundamental human rights and a threat to world peace, and further calls for the suspension of nuclear testing. There was also a proposal from the Indonesian Prime Minister that he should explore the notion of holding a wider conference bringing together leaders from both Asia and Africa.[36] The visit of China's Prime Minister, Zhou Enlai, to New Delhi and Rangoon (where Burma signed up to the five principles) in June 1954 emphasized concurrence with the Indian position that Asian solutions should be found for Asian problems and seemed to augur a new era in the politics of the region. Hindsight allows one to see that the *panchsheel* phase of inter-Asian diplomacy was to prove relatively short-lived, but all these developments nurtured fears in Washington that closer Sino-Indian ties might be an ominous sign of an emerging 'Asia for the Asians' movement, posing a threat to continued Western influence in the region, and the kind of combination that Dulles had warned about in 1951.[37] For some American observers, winning the allegiance of Asian neutralists had to become a central aim of American foreign policy if it was to fulfil its goals

---

[33] See Sarvepalli Gopal, *Nehru, 1947–1956*, 180; D. R. SarDesai, *Indian Foreign Policy in Cambodia, Laos, and Vietnam, 1947–1964* (Berkeley, 1968), 47–9.

[34] 'Nehru Condemns U.S. Proposal', *NYT*, 25 April 1954.

[35] SarDesai, *Indian Foreign Policy*, 51, 58.   [36] Colbert, *Southeast Asia*, 312.

[37] For more on this perspective, see Matthew Jones, 'A "Segregated" Asia? Race, the Bandung Conference and Pan-Asianist Fears in American Thought and Policy, 1954–1955', *Diplomatic History*, 29, 5, November 2005, 841–68.

in the confrontation with Communist China; as Chester Bowles put it in a contemporary analysis for *Foreign Affairs*, 'a defense system in Asia not supported by the Colombo Powers is a limited military expedient carrying obvious political liabilities'. Bowles's fear was that antipathy to the United States might eventually lead the Colombo powers 'to associate with Red China in the kind of "Asia-for-the-Asians" coexistence advocated by Chou [Zhou Enlai]', and that this would exclude the West from the region as a whole, including Japan: 'If Asia were once properly sealed off from Western influence, China would be in a position to step up her demands on her weaker neighbors, firmly assert her political and military leadership throughout Asia, and ultimately establish complete control from the Arabian Sea to Alaska.'[38] Dulles also certainly wanted to counteract any notion that there could not be effective co-operation across 'racial' divides when it came to opposing Communist aggression. To emphasize this point, he delivered a television and radio address on 7 May on the situation in Indochina:

Great effort is being made by Communist propaganda to make it appear as though there would be something very evil if Asian nations and the nations of the Americas or Europe joined to help each other and to assure that the peoples of Asia will really be able to secure their liberty. The Communist nations have … adopted the slogan 'Asia for the Asians'. Well the Japanese war lords adopted a similar slogan when they sought to subject Asia to their despotic rule. […] it is of the utmost importance that the United States participation in creating collective security in Asia should be on a basis which recognizes fully the aspirations, and the cultures of the Asian people. We in the United States have a material and industrial strength which these nations of Asia lack … But they also have cultural and ethical and spiritual values of their own, which make them our equal by every moral standard.[39]

This declaration of 'equality', rooted in respect for cultural values, was typical of what Christina Klein has described as an 'imaginary of integration', where American policy-makers emphasized the bridges that could be built within the non-Communist world, transcending barriers of race or religion. It was also an ideological worldview which allowed non-alignment to be stigmatized as a self-centred and narrow-minded expression of nationalism, opposed to the construction of an all-embracing and virtuous 'free world' community.[40]

---

[38] Chester Bowles, 'A Fresh Look at Free Asia', *Foreign Affairs*, 33, 1, October 1954, 65–6. Bowles did acknowledge the anomalous position of Pakistan among the Colombo powers as being firmly aligned with the United States and a signatory to the SEATO Treaty at Manila.

[39] 'Text of Dulles' Report to the Nation on the Geneva Conference', *NYT*, 8 May 1954.

[40] Klein, *Cold War Orientalism*, 41–8.

Nevertheless, the Eisenhower administration's preferred Asian partners were those who shared its own evaluation of the Communist menace
to the area and agreed with Washington on the best means to oppose it,
and India simply did not figure in this scheme of things. Walter Bedell
Smith, the US Under-Secretary of State, though admitting that Indian
association with collective efforts in South East Asia was desirable,
summed up the basic American view that India was unreliable, telling
the Australian Foreign Minister, for example, 'that "our" (i.e. the United
States') Asian nations (Siam and Philippines) would *fight* – whereas he
doubted whether any others would'.[41] Eisenhower administration officials felt that the inclusion of Thailand and the Philippines in arrangements for collective regional defence would meet objections that the
Western powers were planning to form a 'white coalition' to handle the
affairs of the region; as the President explained to the NSC in early May,
though small, 'such nations as Thailand at least provided the semblance
of Asian participation'.[42] However, the position of Thailand and the
Philippines as already close American allies made the British very doubtful that their participation would be effective in deflecting Asian
criticisms of any Western-led defence scheme.[43] On their side, the
Americans were concerned that Indian attitudes now had a hold over
British policy, Dulles informing Eisenhower in April of his belief that it
was Nehru's pressure that had led to Eden rejecting proposals for early
discussions on a security pact.[44]

That Washington would place a premium on building a coalition that was
willing to take firm action, rather than an 'ideal' line-up of Asian members,
was hardly surprising when the French position in Indochina looked on the
verge of collapse. By the last week of April, in fact, the situation around Dien
Bien Phu had become so critical that the French Foreign Minister, Georges
Bidault, meeting Dulles in Paris, requested an immediate and massive
American air strike against the besieging Viet Minh forces. Bidault even
later claimed in unlikely terms that Dulles had offered the loan of two

[41] Richard Casey diary notes of Geneva Conference, 13 June 1954, ZP22/4G, FO 371/
125137, TNA.
[42] See memorandum of discussion at the 195th meeting of the NSC, 6 May 1954, and
subsequent discussion between Eisenhower, Dulles and Cutler, 7 May 1954, *FRUS,
1952–1954, XII*, Part 1, 456, 458.
[43] As Eden put it in one message, 'Nobody ... regards Siam and the Philippines as truly
representative of Asian opinion.' See Foreign Office (from Eden) to Washington
(Makins), No. 1696, 19 April 1954, FE/54/21, FO 800/785, TNA.
[44] See memorandum of conference with President Eisenhower, 19 April 1954, 'Meetings
with the President 1954 (3)'; see also record of the Secretary of State's briefing for
members of Congress, 5 May 1954, *FRUS, 1952–1954, XIII*, Part 2, 1474.

atomic bombs in response.[45] The overriding American worry at this critical stage was that if the Americans failed to intervene before Dien Bien Phu fell, then the French would not carry on the fight in the rest of Indochina. Defeat at Dien Bien Phu, Bidault explained, would be a huge blow to French morale, with the implication being that the French Government would be under irresistible pressure to grant major concessions to the Communist side at the Geneva Conference in order to end the war.[46] In a final and ultimately fruitless bid to revive United Action before the opening of the Geneva Conference, Dulles and Radford travelled on to London from Paris and again pressed the British to underwrite an air strike at Dien Bien Phu, even if their support was limited to the diplomatic realm. Believing that US intervention by air power alone would prove both ineffective and likely to trigger direct Chinese involvement, the British wanted to give France every support in trying to secure a negotiated settlement to the fighting, something they believed outside military action would surely prejudice.[47] 'The British people would not be easily influenced by what happened in the distant jungles of South East Asia,' Churchill told Radford, 'but they did know that there was a powerful American base in East Anglia and that war with China, who would invoke the Sino-Russian Pact, might mean an assault by Hydrogen bombs on these islands.'[48] The presence of Radford was particularly unfortunate, for the belligerent manner of his demeanour worried many of the British officials he encountered. Dulles was informed immediately after that the British were 'very much disturbed and angered by Radford's coming over to London and trying to pressure the Cabinet and the Chiefs of Staff to come into Indo-China with sea and air power ... The British had a suspicion that Radford wanted to use this as a means of launching what Eden said was "Radford's war against China".'[49]

[45] See Dillon to Dulles, 9 August 1954; Dulles to Dillon, 9 August 1954; Dillon to Dulles, 10 August 1954, *FRUS, 1952–1954, XIII*, Part 1, 927–8, 1933–4. Such a categorical offer is difficult to reconcile with the Secretary of State's cautious operating procedures and customary divorce from any discussion of detailed military matters and may, as Dulles suggested, have arisen from a misunderstanding (and, in its later appearance in Bidault's memoirs, from a desire to pin responsibility for failure at Dien Bien Phu on capricious American behaviour during the crisis); see also the considered treatment of this issue in Bundy, *Danger and Survival*, 268–9.

[46] See memorandum of conversation by Merchant, 26 April 1954, and Dulles to State Department, 24 April 1954, *FRUS, 1952–1954, XIII*, Part 2, 1386–91.

[47] See Warner, 'Britain and the Crisis over Dien Bien Phu', 70–4.

[48] Record of conversation, 26 April 1954, PREM 11/645, TNA.

[49] Carl W. McCardle memorandum for Dulles, 30 April 1954, 'Strictly Confidential', box 2, General Correspondence and Memoranda series, John Foster Dulles papers, DDEL. Dulles later went so far as to advise Eden not to regard Radford (who Dulles was 'inclined to criticise') as any kind of authoritative spokesman for the official U.S. position; see Geneva (Eden) to FO, No. 86, 30 April 1954, PREM 11/649, TNA.

On 29 April, three days after the Geneva Conference officially opened, and having received the pessimistic conclusion from Dulles (who was present for the opening sessions at Geneva) that American intervention was likely to be matched by the Chinese, Eisenhower and the NSC decided that with none of the conditions for intervention set at the start of the month having been established, any military action in Indochina would have to be placed in abeyance pending the outcome of the on-going negotiations. The President was particularly adamant that lack of support from allies, which would be essential in conditions of general war, made the risks of unilateral US action too great, saying that 'a collective policy with our allies was the only posture consistent with U.S. national security policy as a whole. To go in unilaterally in Indochina or other areas of the world which were endangered, amounted to an attempt to police the entire world.'[50] Though the Americans were disappointed with their British allies, they were also exasperated with the French at this time who remained (as they had been throughout the crisis) stubbornly unwilling to surrender their military authority in Indochina as the price for more active US assistance, elusive in guaranteeing their future level of effort in Indochina once US intervention was under-way, and not prepared to grant genuine independence to Vietnam, Laos and Cambodia.

That same day, the NSC Planning Board held a significant discussion on whether nuclear weapons should be used against Viet Minh troop concentrations around Dien Bien Phu if a decision over intervention were to be taken. Amid the uncertainties discussed was whether use of the atomic bomb would, in fact, be decisive, and if the United States might even loan a weapon to the French. Assuming nuclear use, one of the possible consequences that the board considered was whether France and Britain would then 'take alarm, with possible repercussions on U.S. air bases overseas? If they should seek to cancel our bases on such a ground, how valuable are our allies and these bases?' Having heard these views, along with other arguments, the following day Eisenhower declared that he did not see how the atomic bomb could be used unilaterally by the United States in such circumstances, and that no mention of American intentions regarding nuclear weapons should be made before any United Action coalition was agreed.[51] In a later interview, Eisenhower also maintained he had exclaimed at this time: 'You boys must be crazy. We can't

---

[50] Memorandum of discussion at the 194th meeting of the NSC, 29 April 1954, *FRUS, 1952–1954, XIII*, Part 2, 1440.

[51] See memorandum by Cutler for Smith, 30 April 1954, *FRUS, 1952–1954, XIII*, Part 2, 1447; and Richard M. Nixon, *RN: The Memoirs of Richard Nixon* (New York, 1978), 154.

use those awful things against Asians for the second time in less than ten years. My God.'[52]

This particular outburst would seem to add credence to the notion that Eisenhower was alert to and responsive over the political costs to the US position in Asia of any repeat use of nuclear weapons. Eisenhower's remark was also consistent with the assertion in the first volume of his memoirs (published in 1963) that he had raised his voice in firm opposition to the use of the atomic bomb against Hiroshima in 1945; on that occasion he again referred to the atomic bomb as 'that awful thing'.[53] Just as the latter claim has been subject to serious scholarly doubt, there is no contemporaneous evidence to support Eisenhower's comments from 1954.[54] On several other occasions, it is apparent, Eisenhower had shown interest in the feasibility of using nuclear weapons in Asia. In June 1950, when hearing of the outbreak of the Korean War, he recorded in his diary the thought that every option should be prepared 'even if it finally came to the use of an A-bomb (which God forbid)'.[55] During the initial discussions the administration had held in early 1953 over ways to resolve the Korean deadlock, Eisenhower had shown no hesitation in considering the tactical use of nuclear weapons against military targets in North Korea. On a much later occasion in May 1962, when out of office, Eisenhower told two emissaries from President Kennedy that he recommended responding to a sharp deterioration of the situation in Laos with the introduction of US ground troops and 'would follow them up with whatever support was necessary to achieve the objectives of their mission, including – if necessary – the use of tactical nuclear weapons'.[56] These comments hardly seem consistent with the sentiments expressed in the ex-President's soon-to-be-published memoir, or concerns that such terrible weapons might be used against Asians. Nevertheless, one also needs to acknowledge that Eisenhower felt the need to register such thoughts with the wider public and for the benefit of future biographers. In considering his alleged comments from 1954, it must be recalled that the President was, of course, fully conversant with the nuclear anxieties on display in Asia in the spring of that year, for along with Dulles he had followed closely the repercussions of the *Bravo* test across the region, not

---

[52] Ambrose, *Eisenhower*, 184.   [53] Eisenhower, *Mandate for Change*, 312–13.

[54] See Barton J. Bernstein, 'Ike and Hiroshima: Did He Oppose It?' *Journal of Strategic Studies*, 10, 1987, 377–89.

[55] See entry for 30 June 1950, Robert H. Ferrell (ed.), *The Eisenhower Diaries* (New York, 1981), 176.

[56] Addendum to memorandum of discussion between Eisenhower, John McCone and Michael Forrestal, 10 May 1962, F-1998–01245, www.foia.cia.gov, accessed 3 June 2007.

least in Japan. When, on 11 May, Dulles later discussed with the President the forms US intervention in Indochina might still take, he was armed with a memorandum which warned that the 'use of atomic weapons will raise very serious problems of Asian opinion and [with the] attitude of our allies'.[57]

Irrespective of these deliberations, the fall of Dien Bien Phu on 7 May seemed to have finally put paid to the prospects for immediate intervention, and the convening the next day of the first plenary session at the Geneva Conference dealing with Indochina indicated that diplomatic efforts to resolve the crisis would now take centre stage. Nevertheless, while the French war effort continued and the prospect of Chinese involvement remained in the background, US officials, with Dulles to the fore, proved unwilling to completely foreclose the option of military action. In particular, the Secretary of State continued to canvas interested parties in discussing measures for the collective defence of South East Asia, being anxious to keep talk of US intervention alive in order to preserve some uncertainty among the Communist powers represented at Geneva as to what could occur if they chose to push home the Viet Minh's immediate military advantage against the French. Meanwhile, the British had now agreed that military staff talks might take place in Washington between the five Western powers – the United States, Britain, France, Australia and New Zealand – on how to guarantee any settlement that might be reached at Geneva against future Communist aggression, a remit which was later expanded to include the general problems of the defence of the area.[58]

In the background, and while the debates over possible Western intervention in Indochina had been proceeding, SAC was busy planning the nuclear strikes against Chinese targets that it anticipated would be needed if full-scale war were to occur with the PRC. However, rather than the selective approach to targeting which the NSC had agreed in January 1954 in relation to Chinese aggression in South East Asia, as head of SAC, General Curtis LeMay presided over a process which identified numerous industrial-urban 'complexes' throughout the Chinese mainland for atomic attack, with the aim of destroying the PRC's overall military potential. In mid-April 1954, the JCS even felt it necessary to hold a conference where planning representatives from SAC, the Far East and Pacific Commands and the Chairman of the JSPC could be reminded that the NSC had determined that the basic principles to govern strategy if

---

[57]   See memorandum prepared in the State Department, 11 May 1954, *FRUS, 1952–1954, XIII*, Part 2, 1534.
[58]   See entry for 5 May 1954, *Shuckburgh Diaries*, 192.

the Korean War resumed or if the Chinese directly entered the Indochina conflict were that while nuclear weapons would be used against the Chinese Communists, this was to be on a 'selective' basis, with targets having some tangible connection with the immediate area of the fighting.[59] Nevertheless, in the event that Communist aggression continued, SAC was also instructed to plan for an 'enlarged but highly selective atomic offensive in addition to attacks employing other weapon systems', designed, as the JCS put it, to 'reduce' China's 'war-making capabilities ... while keeping loss of civilian lives as low as possible'.[60] How multiple nuclear strikes against Chinese industrial and military infrastructure, much of it located close to or within urban areas, were to minimize the huge civilian losses likely to be produced was not made clear, and the evidence from this period points to a basic rejection by SAC of the idea – common also when it came to the Soviet Union – of selectivity and economy in its targeting approach.[61] The detail of this kind of nuclear planning was never, of course, shared with American allies, or even for that matter available to the State Department. Nonetheless, the glimpses that were sometimes offered of what the Pentagon and its subordinate commands understood by an approach of massive retaliation were a source of anxiety to those whose task it was to assuage the anxieties of Western governments or dissipate Asian suspicions that the United States was preparing to unleash widespread nuclear devastation across the area.

The problem of belligerent American military views undermining alliance cohesion became apparent when on 21 May the JCS produced a memorandum on responses to further overt Communist aggression in the region, assuming the 'loss' of Indochina, which rejected a Korean War-style static defence of Burma, Thailand and Malaya, and called instead for 'an offensive to attack the source of Communist military power being

---

[59] Memorandum for the record, 'Briefing Given by the Joint Chiefs of Staff to CINCFE, CINCPAC and COMSAC Planning Representatives', 16 April 1954, OPD 381 Korea (9 May 47), sec. 31, box 900, Air Force Plans, RG 341, NARA.

[60] JCS Secretariat memorandum for JSPC, 'Outline Plan for Renewed Hostilities in Korea', Enclosure A, 'Outline Plans in Event of Chinese Communist Aggression in Asia', SPSM-11–54, 17 April 1954, OPD 381 Korea (9 May 47), sec. 31, box 900, Air Force Plans, RG 341, NARA.

[61] In the summer of 1954, in fact, Ridgway launched a wide-ranging critique of SAC's expansive target planning against China, claiming it was in conflict with JCS planning guidance regarding 'selectivity or injunction against mass nuclear bombing'. See memorandum for the Chief of Staff, US Air Force, 'Strategic Air Command Far East Outline Plan 8–54', 8 June 1954, and memorandum by the Chief of Staff, US Army, for the JCS, 'Strategic Air Command Far East Outline Plan No. 8–54', 19 July 1954, OPD 381 Korea (9 May 47), sec. 33, box 900, Air Force Plans, RG 341, NARA; and in general see David Alan Rosenberg, 'The Origins of Overkill: Nuclear Weapons and American Strategy, 1945–60', *International Security*, 7, 4, Spring 1983, 6–7, 18.

applied in Southeast Asia'.[62] Probably mindful of Radford's earlier foray into international diplomacy during April, and with the five-power staff talks coming up in Washington, Dulles made known his concerns that 'the JCS viewpoint should be presented in a way which would have undesirable political repercussions'. Any inference that US intervention against Communist Chinese aggression would lead to all-out war with China involving nuclear weapons was best avoided, Dulles maintained, and outspoken expressions of Radford's military opinions might lead to US isolation: 'it was not politically good judgment to take it for granted that any defensive coalition would be bound to become involved in a general war with China, and perhaps with Russia, and that this would be an atomic war'. With all this, Eisenhower 'wholly agreed', saying he was 'strongly opposed to any assumption that it was necessary to have a war with China ... the JCS should not act in any way which would interfere with the political purposes of the Government, and he would try to find an occasion to make this clear'.[63] A few days later, Eisenhower had a chance to make the point to the JCS that 'the course which the U.S. would take was a political course, not determined entirely by military considerations and that we must take care not to frighten our friends in negotiations by bellicose talk'. Dulles, reminding the military chiefs of the views expressed by the British at Bermuda, affirmed that 'retaliation against overt Chinese Communist aggression was acceptable as a policy on a limited basis, but not in the broad context [indicated by the JCS] ... The U.S. to hold its allies would have to limit its counter-measures to targets having a demonstrable connection with Chinese aggression. If our plan were initially designed to destroy the total power of China, our allies would think we were heading toward general war ... if we leapt to general war all at once, our allies wouldn't leap with us.' As for the forthcoming staff talks involving the British, French, Australians and New Zealanders, the President repeated that 'our friends thought we were belligerent, wanted to fight, and were immature; therefore, we must be careful not to alarm them'. Eisenhower was particularly keen that the US representatives at the talks not be the first to raise the subject of nuclear weapons.[64] Such discussions showed how clear was Eisenhower's basic conviction that the United States could not pursue a war with China without allied support. In

---

[62] See memorandum by the JCS for Wilson, 'Defense of Southeast Asia in the Event of Loss of Indochina to the Communists', 21 May 1954, *FRUS, 1952–1954, XII*, Part 1, 514–17.

[63] See memorandum of conversation with the President, 25 May 1954, Mr Merchant Top Secret (Indochina) (2), box 9, Subject series, John Foster Dulles papers, DDEL; also in *FRUS, 1952–1954, XII*, Part 1, 512–13.

[64] Memorandum of conversation, 28 May 1954, *FRUS, 1952–1954, XII*, Part 1, 521–4. See also Eisenhower, *Mandate for Change*, 361.

early June 1954, for example, the President was averring to the NSC that 'any thought of going into China alone ... was completely contrary to all our basic objectives ... he realized that the main burden of such a war would have to fall on the United States. Our allies could be expected to provide little more than token forces. Nevertheless ... he did not wish the United States to stand alone before the world as an arbitrary power supporting colonialism in Asia.'[65] For Eisenhower, allied backing was essential not only for domestic political purposes, but also to cloak American actions with the veneer of international legitimacy.

After a week of deliberation and exchange in Washington, the report of the five-power military staff conversations was produced on 11 June. It began with an examination of the problem of stabilizing the current French position in Indochina against further Viet Minh gains, where it was estimated that holding the critical Tonkin Delta area through the summer and autumn would require the introduction of three new divisions and 300 aircraft. If Chinese forces were to intervene in Indochina, or commit aggression elsewhere in South East Asia, it was concluded that the best response would be immediate air attack against mainland Chinese targets, 'in the selection of which, however, political considerations cannot be ignored', while 'to produce lasting and maximum effect such air attack should use nuclear as well as conventional weapons from the outset'.[66] This mention of nuclear use in Asia caught the immediate attention of the COS back in London who warned ministers that this would have 'a serious impact on Asian opinion generally'.[67] The State Department had also raised political objections to the assumption made by the JCS in May that if the United States did undertake an intervention in Indochina, it would plan for the use of nuclear weapons wherever it was seen as militarily advantageous. Among these was the fact that 'adverse political reactions should be expected from most of Asia' if nuclear weapons were used, a view also conveyed by Bowie, the head of the PPS, in a personal paper for Dulles.[68]

For many American policy-makers, the most troubling aspect to the Asian response to the likelihood of a war between the United States and

---

[65] Memorandum of discussion at the 200th meeting of the NSC, 3 June 1954, *FRUS, 1952–1954, XII*, Part 1, 533.

[66] For a full copy of the report, see 'Five-Power Military Conference of June 1954', 11 June 1954, in D1074/130G, FO 371/111866, TNA.

[67] See Confidential Annex to COS(54)72nd meeting, 15 June 1954, D1074/133G, FO 371/111867, and also subsequent paper for the Cabinet's Defence Committee, D(54)26, 17 June 1954, CAB 131/14, TNA.

[68] See memorandum by Drumright for MacArthur, 24 May 1954; memorandum by Bowie for Dulles, 27 May 1954, *FRUS, 1952–1954, XIII*, Part 2, 1606, 1625.

China where nuclear weapons might be used was in how it might affect their relationship with Japan. Throughout this period access to Japanese bases remained important to US military planning in the Far East, while the political orientation of the government in Tokyo was even more crucial for overall American strategy in the Cold War, and particularly when the *Lucky Dragon* incident had introduced new elements of strain into the relationship. By the end of April 1954, US officials handling Japanese affairs in the State Department's Office of Northeast Asian Affairs were, according to one British diplomat, saying that the 'upsurge of Japanese nationalism and anti-American feeling had come as a considerable shock to many people in the Administration ... [who] ... had put too much faith in the apparent change of heart which came about during the American occupation'. When the British put forward their own view that 'it was a mistake to be too soft in one's dealings with the Japanese, who only took concessions as a sign of weakness', the American reply was that the United States 'could hardly afford to take a tougher line because of the vital importance of keeping [Japan] in the Western camp'.[69] Further tensions had been induced between Tokyo and Washington over the aftermath of the *Bravo* test by the Japanese Government's decision to send their own research vessel, the *Shunkotsu Maru*, to the Marshall Islands in order to monitor radiation levels and their effects on marine life. The Americans, in turn, reviving Strauss's fears about espionage, made plain that the ship would not be welcome close to their Bikini test site. By May 1954, Allison had reached a number of conclusions he described as 'unpleasant, some even ominous' in a long telegram seen by both Dulles and Eisenhower. The Indochina crisis had 'created [the] specter of [a] new and larger war not unrelated to Pacific tests in Japanese minds. If it came, most Japanese could not see how they could escape involvement, probably atomic involvement, and [the] prospect horrified them.' Allison felt that when faced with the *Lucky Dragon* incident, along with the pressure of prevailing tensions in the Far East, and a mounting sense of crisis which surrounded the scandal-hit Yoshida Government, 'the government and people cracked'. Allison continued:

What must now be recognized is depth of Japanese fear of nuclear weapons, their conviction of doom in the event of war, and, as consequences, their readiness to panic and their intense gullibility in nuclear matters. Throughout [the] past eight weeks, no report of long-range air or sea contamination, no story of food or water pollution, no theory of genetic deterioration seemed too wild for acceptance. To [the] unlimited targets of opportunity in Japan, to [the] total lack of civilian defense organization must now be added this dangerous psychological

[69] Michael Joy to Colin Crowe, 30 April 1954, FJ10345/2, FO 371/110412, TNA.

vulnerability of [the] Japanese to weapons and devices of nuclear technology. If Communists understand this latter element ... the consequences for our military planning with respect to Japan could be extremely grave. In the event of war or an imminent threat, if [the] Communists actively manage and carefully prepare a psychological-military operation involving [the] threat of nuclear weapons against Japan, this might well ... produce [the] national stampede that would sweep over any Japanese Government that attempted to halt it. In this process our own bases could be isolated or even made untenable.

Indeed, with sections of the Japanese press calling for assurances that Japan would not be used as a site for US nuclear attacks against any adversary, Allison predicted that revision of the 1952 security treaty would soon be on the political agenda. 'Neutralism in Japan,' the Ambassador warned, 'will vary in direct proportion to [the] conclusion Japanese leaders reach as to whether [a] relationship with [the] U.S. can provide, more than any other course of Japanese action, defense and security in [a] period when both U.S. and USSR possess thermonuclear weapons.'[70]

Having digested this report, a rattled Eisenhower called for State Department recommendations on improving relations with Tokyo. This prompted the reply from Robert Murphy, the Deputy Under-Secretary for Political Affairs at the State Department (and Allison's predecessor as ambassador), that the Japanese people were 'pathologically sensitive about nuclear weapons. They feel they are the chosen victims of such weapons.' In order to salve some of the wounds between Washington and Tokyo, Murphy recommended prompt compensation payment over the *Lucky Dragon* incident, and that the AEC pass over more information on radioactivity to the Japanese authorities, as scientific interchange was the 'best remedy for Japanese emotion and ignorance', while further expressions of regret should be made. Aside from encouraging the Japanese to do more to provide for their own defence, it was essential that the United States 'treat Japan as a full, free-world partner' if she was to 'count upon the use of Japanese bases and other cooperation in any future conflict'.[71]

The sensitivity of US officials to the issue of American bases in Japan, and Japan's attitude to nuclear questions, has to be understood within the context of the planning for nuclear operations in the Far East, much of which had been conditioned by the discussions in late 1953 over how the United States would respond to a revival of hostilities in Korea. As we have seen, in November 1953, the JCS had made clear the requirement to store complete atomic bombs at US bases in Japan. Such storage sites

[70] See Allison to Department of State, 20 May 1954, *FRUS, 1952–1954, XIV*, Part 2, 1643–8.
[71] Murphy memorandum for Eisenhower, 29 May 1954, *ibid.*, 1648–50.

would both allow for a prompt implementation of war plans over Korea, and give SAC the chance to strike targets in the Soviet Far East in the event of general war. In April 1954, President Eisenhower had granted authority to deploy complete nuclear weapons to US bases in Britain and French Morocco (the first 'permanent' deployments of nuclear weapons to bases in foreign countries); Japan and West Germany were next in line as sites for overseas nuclear storage. Accordingly, during May 1954, the State Department was asked by the Pentagon to 'take the necessary diplomatic steps to clear the way for the storage in Japan of nuclear and non-nuclear components of atomic weapons and, if feasible, to negotiate an advance authorization by the Japanese Government for the use of such weapons from United States bases in Japan'.[72] With the storm over the *Lucky Dragon* incident intensifying by the day, there could hardly have been a worse moment to make such a request. The State Department therefore recommended that while deployment of non-nuclear components of atomic weapons could go ahead, there could be no movement of their nuclear cores into the country until the political climate had altered.[73]

With this political clearance issued, in June the JCS were instructed by the Secretary of Defense to begin the construction of nuclear storage sites in Japan (at the same time as they were to begin similar work in West Germany), and at the end of that month authorization was finally given for the deployment of the non-nuclear components to the Japanese sites, though they did not actually arrive until early the following year. The initial intention had been that Yoshida and Okazaki Katsuo, the Japanese Foreign Minister, would be informed of the movement so that if asked they could accurately state – in a technically correct manner – that there were no nuclear weapons stored in Japan. However, even this idea was vetoed (initially by Robert Murphy), so much had the State Department's confidence in the Japanese leadership declined by this point.[74] Officials in

---

[72] See 'Reply to the Secretary of Defense's Letter of January 28, 1955, Concerning the Deployment of Nuclear Weapons to Japan', 11 March 1955, 'NN-Japan 1955', box 2, Country and Subject Files, 1950–62, SASAE, RG 59, NARA. In early February 1954, Eisenhower had refused to comment when asked about Air Force plans discussed in the Senate Armed Services Committee to build a 'world-wide chain of atom bomb storage bases'; see presidential news conference, 3 February 1954, *The Public Papers of the Presidents: Eisenhower, 1954*, 227.

[73] Gerard Smith memorandum for the file, 'Introduction of Weapons into Germany and Japan', 18 June 1954, 'NN-Japan, 1953–4', box 1, Country and Subject Files, 1950–62, SASAE, RG 59, NARA.

[74] See *ibid.*, and draft memorandum for the JCS, 'Use of Atomic Weapons', 8 February 1955, 'NN-Japan 1955', box 2, Country and Subject Files, 1950–62, SASAE, RG 59, NARA.

Washington looked on with mounting anxiety as Socialists in the Diet managed to disrupt proceedings and thwart the Government's measures for limited rearmament. Meanwhile, Yoshida postponed his trip to the United States as he fended off his domestic critics and struggled to unite the rival conservative factions who were lining up candidates to succeed him. In an evident expression of his pessimism regarding the current performance of the Japanese Government, Eisenhower concurrently made little secret of his concerns that if Japan should 'go Communist' then the United States 'would be out of the Pacific and it would become a communist lake'.[75] Reviewing overall US national security policy, the Deputy Director of the State Department's Office of Northeast Asian Affairs maintained that 'the one really formidable problem in keeping Japan on our side is the problem posed by our reliance upon nuclear weapons. This may overstate the situation, but not by much.'[76]

One of the consequences of American perceptions of the fragility of the Japanese political scene was that Japan's future economic prosperity had to be assured through continued access to South East Asian markets. Communist successes in Indochina it was believed, however, could threaten to bring about the collapse of the entire non-Communist position in the area, including such resource-rich territories as Malaya and Indonesia. This was one of the main reasons why the Eisenhower administration had been so anxious to see the French continue the struggle for Indochina even after defeat at Dien Bien Phu, and disapproving of any political settlement at the Geneva Conference involving a division of Vietnam which would, it was felt in Washington, soon be followed by a French withdrawal and the gradual erosion of any non-Communist Vietnamese government they left behind in Saigon. At the same time, the rhetoric of the administration had to be tempered by the need to attract allied support for the confrontation with the PRC that might follow any breakdown of negotiations at Geneva. In a bid to cool the worries of the administration's critics, on 11 June Dulles gave a speech in Los Angeles where he tried to refute any notion that the United States desired a 'military showdown' with China: 'There are some, particularly abroad, who seem to assume or pretend that the attitude of the United States flows from a desire for a general war with Communist China. That is clearly false. If we wanted such a war, it could easily have been based on the

[75] Notes on Eisenhower's meeting with legislative leaders, 21 June 1954, *FRUS, 1952–1954, XIV*, Part 2, 1662; see also 'Remarks at the National Editorial Association Dinner', 22 June 1954, *Public Papers of the Presidents: Eisenhower, 1954*, 587.
[76] Robert J. G. McClurkin memorandum for Ogburn, 'NSC 5422', 17 June 1954, 'NSC (January–June 1954)' folder, box II, Subject Files, 1954, records of the Bureau of Far East Affairs, RG 59, NARA.

presence of the Chinese aggressor in Korea.' At the same time, he repeated the warning that an overt Chinese intervention in Indochina would elicit a forceful American response.[77] A day later, on 12 June, hopes that the French would hold out at Geneva for a settlement which did not involve substantial concessions to the Viet Minh position vanished when the Government led by Joseph Laniel fell after a close vote in the French National Assembly over Indochina policy. Following five more days of uncertainty, Pierre Mendes-France became Prime Minister, staking his political future on reaching a rapid agreement at Geneva which would serve to bring about an end to the fighting.[78] In any event, the road to a Geneva settlement was already clearing with direct military talks between the Viet Minh and French representatives being staged, which were to lead to the idea of a temporary partition of Vietnam. Zhou Enlai, meanwhile, conceded recognition of the French-created governments in Cambodia and Laos, and the withdrawal of all foreign forces, in exchange for guarantees of neutrality for those states. Final agreement was not achieved at Geneva until 21 July, but in the meantime the Eisenhower administration turned its attentions to bolstering the position of the Vietnamese Government in Saigon, where Ngo Dinh Diem had been appointed as Prime Minister on 18 June. Diem's chief attraction to his early American sponsors was his Catholicism, the fact that he offered a nationalist alternative to the incapable Bao Dai and was untainted by any close association with the French colonial authorities.[79]

As the DRV Government assumed control in Hanoi, and consolidated its hold over the North, looking forward to the national elections supposed to be held in 1956 and which it was believed would lead to reunification, Dulles now took his opportunity to turn to his long-delayed task of assembling an international alliance dedicated to the defence of the remainder of South East Asia. Before the signing of the Geneva agreement, in fact, an Anglo-American study group was already at work in Washington during July trying to agree the principles and purposes of the new collective security pact. Among the JCS, Radford was not keen, holding that with the anticipated French withdrawal from the rest of Indochina, the only indigenous sources of substantial military power remaining in Asia lay in Japan, South Korea and Taiwan. The United

---

[77] 'Dulles Denies U.S. Policy Seeks Armed Showdown with Peiping', *NYT*, 12 June 1954.
[78] See Cable, *Geneva Conference*, 95, 102–3; Gibbons, *U.S. Government and the Vietnam War*, Part 1, 240.
[79] See Kahin, *Intervention*, 78–80; Seth Jacobs, *America's Miracle Man in Vietnam: Ngo Dinh Diem, Religion, Race, and U.S. Intervention in Southeast Asia* (Durham, 2004), 53–6; Kathryn C. Statler, *Replacing France: The Origins of American Intervention in Vietnam* (Lexington, MA, 2007), 119–20.

States should not waste its strength in trying to build up what would inevitably be a weak local defence in the remaining countries of South East Asia; a defensive pact would be 'undesirable and unwise', and the only effective response to further aggression, as Radford would never tire of repeating, was to strike directly at China.[80] Dulles, nevertheless, did not want to appear to abandon the rest of South East Asia after the setback in Indochina, seeing the rationale for a treaty in primarily political terms as a signal of US intentions to resist further Communist aggression (and hence to help deter it), provide some hold over the other Western allies to act to meet such a contingency and give a legal basis to sanction presidential authorization of direct action against China if it became necessary.[81] On 12 August 1954, the NSC duly endorsed a new document outlining US policy towards East and South East Asia in the light of the outcome of the Geneva Conference. NSC 5429 underlined the fact that Communist prestige had been given an enormous boost by events in Indochina, as had 'their capacity for expanding Communist influence by exploiting political and economic weakness and instability in the countries of free Asia without resort to armed attack'. To counter this trend in South East Asia, the United States had to 'protect its position and restore its prestige' by new initiatives, including the negotiation of a security treaty. However, any treaty should 'not limit U.S. freedom to use nuclear weapons, or involve a commitment for local defense or for stationing U.S. forces in Southeast Asia'.[82]

The outcome of this reassessment of policy was to be the signature by the delegates of eight nations meeting at Manila on 8 September 1954 of a South East Asia Collective Defence Treaty. Under the treaty terms, the United States, Britain, France, Australia, New Zealand, Thailand, the Philippines and Pakistan recognized that 'aggression by means of armed attack' in the treaty area would endanger their 'peace and safety', and they would in that case 'act to meet the common danger' in accordance with their constitutional processes. The American addition of a protocol to the treaty, which threw its protective cover over Laos, Cambodia and the 'free territory under the jurisdiction of the State of Vietnam', circumvented the provisions in the Geneva agreement that outlined the neutral status of Indochina as a whole, and was indeed taken by both the Chinese and the

---

[80] See memorandum of discussion at State Department–JCS meeting, 23 July 1954, *FRUS, 1952–1954, XII*, Part 1, 653–7.
[81] See Roger Dingman, 'John Foster Dulles and the Creation of the South-East Asian Treaty Organization in 1954', *International History Review*, 11, 3, August 1989, 462; also Gary R. Hess, 'The American Search for Stability in Southeast Asia: The SEATO Structure of Containment', in Cohen and Iriye (eds.), *The Great Powers in East Asia*, 280.
[82] See Gibbons, *The U.S. Government and the Vietnam War*, Part 1, 267–8.

Indians as a direct violation of the accords.[83] As the treaty discussions at Manila were pursued, the American delegation, with Dulles at its head, was mindful of the limitations in the US position that had been established over the undesirability of committing ground troops for a static defence of a fixed position on the South East Asian mainland. The Secretary of State made clear that the United States had 'no intention of earmarking specific forces for SEATO [South East Asia Treaty Organization]. It believed in mobile reserve striking power.'[84]

Just as the Manila meeting got under way, however, another confrontational crisis involving the PRC developed in the Far East which raised again the question of the applicability of massive retaliation and the political repercussions that might flow from nuclear use. On 3 September 1954, the Chinese Communists began an artillery bombardment of the Nationalist-held offshore island group of Jinmen (Quemoy), which along with Mazu (Matsu) and the Dachens had been used as bases for raiding, harassment and intelligence gathering against the mainland over the previous few years. The offshore islands also represented a physical expression of Chiang's claims that his government was the legitimate embodiment of Chinese sovereignty, and that his reach was not simply confined to Taiwan, containing the promise that they could become the potential stepping stones for an eventual return to the mainland. For the Chinese Communists, the offshore islands were a constant irritant, not least to the free passage of coastal shipping (Jinmen, garrisoned with 50,000 Nationalist troops, actually lay within the harbour and only four miles from Xiamen (Amoy)), and a strong reminder of the unfinished business of the Civil War. It is now clear that Beijing had no clear plans for their early invasion, and the bombardment may have been designed simply to attract attention to the Taiwan question as a whole and to drive a wedge between Chiang Kai-shek and the Americans. It also seems likely that the Chinese Communist authorities saw the shelling not as a distinct new phase of 'crisis' but as the continuation of the low-level hostilities that had featured between Nationalist and Communist forces in the coastal regions of South East China since late 1949. Nevertheless, American policy-makers perceived a new level of confrontation building across the Taiwan Strait, particularly as Washington (or so it thought) had

---

[83] *Ibid.*, 271–3.
[84] Memorandum of conversation by MacArthur, 5 September 1954, *FRUS, 1952–1954, XII*, Part 1, 851. On the eve of the Manila Conference, Radford would remind State Department officials that the JCS wanted no military planning machinery to accompany the treaty, and of his own view that 'the U.S. wants to avoid a definite commitment in that part of the world'; see memo of discussion at State Department–JCS meeting, 3 September 1954, *ibid.*, 831.

signalled during the summer that a Communist attack on the offshore islands might elicit a forceful response, leading them to feel that Beijing was deliberately flouting warnings of retaliation.[85]

To the Eisenhower administration, Beijing's actions corresponded with those of an expansionist power ready to take risks to establish its hegemony in East Asia, and followed from the confidence given to the Communist cause by the recent Geneva settlement, along with the discord that had seemed to mark the Western powers' response to the Indochina crisis.[86] Finding maintenance of the Nationalist footholds on the offshore islands 'important' rather than 'essential' on military grounds to the ultimate security of Taiwan itself, a majority of the JCS (Radford, Twining and Admiral Robert B. Carney, the CNO) nevertheless stressed the psychological necessity of avoiding any more loss of territory to Communism in Asia and favoured the commitment of US air and naval forces to their defence, almost inevitably entailing in addition attack against selected military targets on the Chinese mainland. Ridgway, ever the malcontent among his JCS colleagues, could not agree with this recommendation as he did not regard the islands as of any overriding strategic importance. Confronted with the problem of how to react to the Chinese bombardment, which many anticipated as preparation for actual invasion, Dulles told the NSC on 12 September that the United States found itself with 'a horrible dilemma'. The Chinese Communists might be embarked upon an irreversible path of expansion, with the firm intention of following a successful capture of the offshore islands with a follow-up assault on Taiwan. If the United States showed weakness in facing this probe, then it might send the wrong message to Beijing and bring on a larger-scale war at a later date. A Nationalist setback on the offshore islands might also bring about a complete collapse of morale on Taiwan, and the loss of Taiwan would have major repercussions in Japan and South Korea. On the other hand, taking a direct part in the defence of the offshore islands would in all probability lead to all-out war with China and the use by the United States of nuclear weapons against the mainland. In this situation, the Secretary of State warned, 'outside Rhee and Chiang, the rest of the world would condemn us, as well as a substantial part of the U.S. people'. This was a perception shared by Eisenhower, who did not feel that world or US opinion was ready for a war with China, telling the NSC: 'Letters to him constantly say what do we care what happens to those yellow men over

---

[85] See He Di, 'The Evolution of the People's Republic of China's Policy toward the Offshore Islands', in Cohen and Iriye (eds.), *Great Powers in East Asia*, 224–6; Gordon H. Chang and He Di, 'The Absence of War in the US–China Confrontation over Quemoy and Matsu in 1954–1955: Contingency, Luck, Deterrence?', *American Historical Review*, 98, 5, December 1993, 1500–8.

[86] See Chang, *Friends and Enemies*, 118–21.

there?' Just as over Indochina, the Eisenhower administration felt the need for general support at home, and from its allies abroad, if it were to go to war with China. The Secretary of State's own concern for the public image of the United States, and the power of international opinion to convince even Beijing to desist from its actions, was shown by his initiative to involve the UN in sponsoring a resolution which would attempt to uphold the status quo in the Taiwan Strait, and so defuse the tension over the islands. This was to be coupled with the offer of a Mutual Defense Treaty with Chiang Kai-shek, which would also have the effect of preventing any reckless attempt by the Nationalists to return to the mainland by requiring any large-scale military operations directed against the PRC to be discussed and cleared with Washington before they were mounted. Attempting to both restrain and reassure Chiang, Dulles would bank on the gradual development of a 'two-Chinas solution', though he could not say so in public.[87]

Avoiding war with the PRC, despite the provocations of Communist pressure against the offshore islands and Chiang's own inflammatory actions, which Eisenhower and Dulles both feared could draw the United States into unwelcome conflict, became the overriding pattern of policy towards the dispute in the final months of 1954. At the same time, American prestige was inevitably bound up with the preservation of Chiang's position on Taiwan, and the loss of the offshore islands might, it was believed, be such a serious blow to Nationalist morale that it would put the entire existence of the regime in question. Hence statements of US resolve and the raised commitment to Chiang represented by the Mutual Security Treaty that was finally agreed in December 1954 would serve, it was hoped, to deter Beijing from embarking upon any reckless attempt to capture the islands by overt invasion. The trick would be to keep the Chinese Communists guessing over US intentions and retaining flexibility. In November, Dulles told the NSC that 'public opinion throughout the free world would be against the United States if we went to war with Communist China over these offshore islands. The effect in Japan would be extremely bad. In short, if one paid any attention to the repercussions outside the immediate area concerned, it was plain that the price we would have to pay to defend the islands was too high. The Chinese Communists would win the sympathy of all our allies, and there would be devastating repercussions both in Europe and in Japan.'[88]

[87] Dulles memorandum, 12 September 1954, *FRUS, 1952–1954, XIV: China and Japan*, Part 1 (Washington, DC, 1985), 611; memorandum of discussion at the 214th meeting of the NSC, 12 September 1954, *ibid.*, 619–22.
[88] Memorandum of discussion at the 221st meeting of the NSC, 2 November 1954, *FRUS, 1952–1954, XIV*, Part 1, 833.

Dulles's comments were a reminder that the reverberations in Japan from the *Lucky Dragon* affair had continued to be felt throughout the summer of 1954, with relations between Washington and Tokyo remaining difficult, both sides having yet to resolve their differences over compensation payments, and the treatment of the afflicted sailors still attracting publicity.[89] There had been little vocal popular opposition to nuclear testing or even nuclear weapons themselves in Japan before 1954 (though here one must remember the restrictions imposed in this area by the occupation regime up to 1952 previously noted), but the *Lucky Dragon* acted as the stimulant to the emergence of a powerful anti-nuclear movement. By July over a million signatures had been collected on a petition calling for a ban on nuclear weapons, and a month later unprecedented numbers gathered for the peace ceremonies marking the anniversary of Hiroshima, where the following year saw the opening of the memorial peace museum and peace park. In September 1955, a mass organization, the Japan Council against Atomic and Hydrogen Bombs, was formed, with a leadership rooted in the Japanese Socialist Party and its trade union affiliates, as well as important Communist Party support, a political base that gave its large-scale anti-nuclear activism an even more dangerous quality to official American eyes.[90] By August 1954, a National Intelligence Estimate was predicting that neutralist sentiment was likely to increase over the period up to 1957, and that the Japanese Government would attempt to pursue a more independent line in foreign policy.[91] That same month, Dulles had been at pains to inform the NSC that though American policy had hitherto been to encourage a build-up of Japanese military strength, this might not be wise if Japan's political orientation was in doubt: 'Japan was the heart and soul of the situation in the Far East. If Japan is not on our side our whole Far Eastern position will become untenable.'[92] From Tokyo, Allison reported that recent Japanese behaviour suggested that Japan 'does not consider itself an ally or partner of the United States but rather a nation which for the time being is forced by circumstances to cooperate with the United States but which intends while doing so, to wring out of this relationship every possible advantage at the minimum cost'.[93]

---

[89] See Dingman, 'Alliance in Crisis', 196–7.
[90] See Wittner, *Resisting the Bomb*, 8–9; Dower, 'The Bombed', 136–7.
[91] See NIE-41–54, 10 August 1954, *FRUS, 1952–1954, XIV*, Part 2, 1697.
[92] Memorandum of discussion at the 210th meeting of the NSC, 13 August 1954, DDRS/ CK3100216577.
[93] Allison to the Department of State, 25 August 1954, *FRUS, 1952–1954, XIV*, Part 2, 1714.

Awareness of the continued suffering of the *Lucky Dragon*'s crew was rekindled in late September 1954 with the news that Kuboyama Aikichi, the radio operator on the vessel, had died. Although the US authorities denied that Kuboyama's death was directly related to the radiation sickness he had suffered earlier in the year, his wife received compensation payments from the US Embassy. In that same month, *Ashes of Death* was produced by the Shin Riken company, a thirty-minute feature film based on the effects of *Bravo*, which also covered the research voyage of the *Shunkotsu Maru* to the waters near the Marshall Islands and the hazards of contamination to which Japan might still be exposed. As well as noting its 'excellent technique', a US Embassy report on the film dubbed it an 'illustration of atomic morbidities, emotionalism and pseudo-scientific propaganda which have strained U.S.–Japanese relations since the Bikini incident'. One State Department information report considered by OCB staff found that the film would help to stimulate public interest and increase the tensions in bilateral relations, with the Japanese press still tending 'to emphasize the most sensational aspects of developments as well as to print exaggerated and inaccurate accounts of the effects of atomic energy. In addition, the continued passage of resolutions and circulation of petitions by private organizations calling for the banning of atomic weapons and tests is indicative of the sustained public interest in the problem of atomic energy.' Dulles's Special Assistant for Atomic Energy Matters, Gerard Smith, was treated to a showing of *Ashes of Death* by USIA. The film wove together footage of the ruins of Hiroshima and its maimed residents, shots of the treatment of injured fishermen from the *Lucky Dragon* and the work of the *Shunkotsu Maru* testing for residual radioactivity in the Pacific. Smith noted that the film was 'replete' with shots of 'particles described as radioactive ash recovered from the Fukuryu Maru', the 'dissection of laboratory mice which had been fed radioactive food, and the "shadows" produced by the radioactivity in the vital organs when they were placed on photographic film, *Shunkotsu Maru* scientists wearing heavy protective clothing and gloves while testing radioactivity in tuna caught near Bikini', diagrams which showed sea and air currents flowing between the Marshall Islands and the Japanese home islands, the dumping of a tuna catch because of high radioactivity readings, and finally rain 'perhaps from the radioactive upper-air – falling on Japanese rice paddies and vegetable gardens'. Smith felt that the effect on an average person watching the film 'must first be fear, if not terror, concerning this ubiquitous danger, and second, a strong dislike, if not hatred, for those responsible for such things'. Concluding that this was indeed the express intention of the filmmakers, Smith asserted that the 'primary purpose of this film is to create fear and anxiety in the Japanese people concerning the threat of ubiquitous radio-activity and hatred of the U.S. as the agent responsible for all this'.[94]

By the autumn of 1954 there was an accumulation of signs that a swing in Japanese policy away from an automatic pro-Western position might be in the offing. Warning that the force of Japanese neutralism should not be underrated, Allison would even note that there was a 'deep racial sentiment that Japan should not fight against Asians on the side of Western powers'.[95] Faced with an energetic peace movement, Yoshida and his Cabinet showed themselves reluctant to fall in with American wishes that Japan should contribute a greater share of its national income to defence. In its evaluation of the current state of relations with Japan compiled in October 1954, the OCB noted the existence of a 'psychosis' in Japan over nuclear weapons and concluded that, 'The violence of Japanese reactions to any matter relating to nuclear weapons is an element in all our relations with Japan and raises particular problems in connection with any further U.S. tests in the Pacific as well as in relation to U.S. actions in the development of peaceful uses of atomic energy.' The OCB called for a full-scale re-evaluation of the psychological strategy programme in Japan that had been operating rather ineffectually since 1952.[96] Against this inauspicious background, in November 1954 the Secretary of Defense made a further attempt to persuade Dulles that the State Department might approach the Japanese Government over the introduction of the nuclear components of atomic weapons to American bases in Japan. Hardly surprisingly, Dulles's response was cautious, merely telling Wilson he would do so 'if an opening occurs', while noting it was 'hard for me to think that this is very urgent because I understand that so far not even the non-nuclear components have been moved to Japan', following the authorization that had been granted in June. The Pentagon would have to wait.[97]

Tiring of Yoshida's inability to control either domestic public opinion or his own bureaucracy, in October the administration in Washington

[94] 'New Atomic Film Promises to Stimulate Further Popular Interest', IR-5550, 23 July 1954, OCB 000.9 Atomic Energy (8), October 1953–August 1954, box 8, NSC staff files, White House Office, DDEL; memorandum for the files, 13 September 1954, 21.52 Country File: Japan, Fukuryu Maru, 1954 (2 of 2), box 422, Subject Files, SASAE, RG 59, NARA.
[95] Memorandum by Allison for Dulles, 9 September 1954, *FRUS, 1952–1954, XIV*, Part 2, 1717.
[96] 'OCB Progress Report on NSC 125/2 and NSC 125/6, U.S. Objectives and Courses of Action with Respect to Japan', 27 October 1954, *FRUS, 1952–1954, XIV*, Part 2, 1766–7; for the psychological programme see Swenson-Wright, *Unequal Allies*, 181.
[97] Dulles to Wilson, 8 November 1954, 'NN-Japan 1953–4', box 1, Country and Subject Files, 1950–62, SASAE, RG 59, NARA.

began to show less interest in the immediate conclusion of a compensation settlement for the claims and damages arising from the *Bravo* test, not wanting to give the Japanese premier any ammunition he could use against criticisms from the conservative political factions who were now conspiring against him. Though he was received with formal correctness during his November visit to Washington, Yoshida did not manage to extract any significant concessions from Eisenhower and Dulles which might have provided for large-scale economic aid to Asia or relaxation of the American stance over trade with Communist China. In December, engulfed by scandal and with political support in his Liberal Party having ebbed away, Yoshida finally stepped down as premier, but his successor, Hatoyama Ichiro, even though he showed more interest in Japanese rearmament than his predecessor, was to prove a let-down for the Americans. For one, as part of the bargaining that had led to his assuming office, Hatoyama had courted Socialist support in the Diet, involving promises of an early general election, which was eventually held in March 1955. Left-wing gains in the poll, it was feared in Washington, could jeopardize American aims to have Hatoyama amend the Constitution to allow greater measures of rearmament to take place. The new Prime Minister was also known as a keen advocate of promoting trade ties with both Communist China and the Soviet Union. Nevertheless, the end of December 1954 finally saw US and Japanese negotiators agree a deal which involved payment of $2 million to settle the *Bravo* claims, though with no American admission of liability. Both Washington and Tokyo now hoped that they could move on from the travails of the past year, and the Eisenhower administration was relieved that conservative political dominance in Japan, at least for the moment, had been maintained even with the end of the Yoshida era. That said, the after-effects of the *Lucky Dragon* incident were not so easily dissipated, helping to move Japan away from the mentalities that had predominated during the occupation period and towards a more independent role on the international stage.[98]

The events of 1954 had helped to ensure that the idea of Asia's importance to the outcome of the Cold War as a whole assumed greater recognition in the consciousness of many Americans. The Korean War and the conflict with the PRC had already raised the stakes at play in the region considerably, as had American investment in the future of post-war

[98] See memorandum by the Assistant Secretary for Far Eastern Affairs to the Under Secretary of State, 29 December 1954, *FRUS, 1952–1954, XIV*, Part 2, 1815–16; Michael Schaller, *Altered States: The United States and Japan since the Occupation* (New York, 1997), 73–6; Swenson-Wright, *Unequal Allies*, 178–9.

Japan. Communist China's new-found stature was found especially alarming, and with the Korean armistice there was every expectation that it would use the freedom of manoeuvre it now enjoyed to spread influence among the weak and vulnerable states of South East Asia. The steady withdrawal of European power gave new opportunities for Communist gains to be made, particularly in Indochina. Fears of the further 'loss' of territories to Communism were attenuated by strategic evaluations of the economic significance of the valuable resources of South East Asia, such as tin, rubber and oil, and their significance for the 'Free World' economy, and the prosperity and stability of Japan, a point made by Eisenhower himself when explaining the domino theory to a presidential press conference in April 1954.[99] At the end of the year, Churchill wrote to Eisenhower expressing his long-held conviction that the threat of China in the Far East was overrated. China, the Prime Minister argued, 'is not important enough to be a cause of major hazards. Many people here exaggerate the power and importance of China as a military factor, and talk about six hundred million Chinese who, we are told, have all become Communists ... When I was young I used to hear much talk about "the Yellow Peril".'[100] The President was unconvinced, however, feeling that China posed a very real threat to the countries in its immediate vicinity, particularly as 'she can pay any price in manpower, with complete indifference to the amount ... I think it dangerous to dismiss too complacently the risks that the bad faith, bad deportment and greed of Red China pose to our world.'[101]

Eisenhower and Dulles had certainly considered nuclear options when it came to forestalling the French defeat at Dien Bien Phu, but their instincts were inherently cautious (the President markedly so), especially as the depth of allied opposition to intervention was made plain during April and the military implications of involvement were so uncertain. The main role envisaged for nuclear weapons after the opening of the Geneva Conference was as insurance against the rather remote contingency of direct Chinese Communist intervention – as Dulles had warned in his September 1953 speech to the American Legion at St Louis – and even here the emphasis had been on selectivity of nuclear strikes in order to try to garner as wide a range of allied support as possible in the event of war with the PRC. The general signs of US belligerence during the crisis, and the stance that was adopted towards the final Geneva agreements, were seen by most British officials as likely to alienate non-aligned Asian

[99] Ambrose, *Eisenhower*, 179–80.
[100] Churchill to Eisenhower, 7 December 1954, PREM 11/898, TNA.
[101] Eisenhower to Churchill, 15 December 1954, *ibid*.

opinion, but for the Eisenhower administration it was only the threat of a military intervention that had yielded the necessary concessions from the Communist side that had made final agreement at Geneva possible at all.[102]

By spreading such renewed and widespread concern over the vast destructive potential of nuclear weapons and the fallout they could create, *Bravo*, perhaps more than any other event, served to undermine all the hopes held by the Eisenhower administration to convince publics both at home and abroad that they were just another category of armament, to be employed according to traditional military criteria. The New Look's embrace of nuclear weapons could now be seen as a battle for political influence and public opinion. Referring to the need to sell the Atoms for Peace programme more vigorously, Dulles told the NSC in mid-August 1954 that propaganda depicting the United States 'as warmongers on account of our atomic capabilities' was doing 'incalculable harm'.[103] Debates over the utility of nuclear weapons for use in less than all-out conflicts had at the same time been spawned by the administration's own espousal of massive retaliation, and then, soon after, by the call for United Action against the menace from Communist China. This all called into question the viability of the administration's new strategic concept given the likely pattern of the Cold War in the coming years, where minor conflicts were set only to proliferate. Whatever the public rhetoric of the administration, decisions over nuclear use could not be determined solely by military criteria but would require the very careful weighing of political factors and consequences. At the height of the Indochina crisis, one PPS memorandum noted in April 1954 that in any presidential decision to use nuclear weapons, 'considerations other than strictly military ones have a bearing. In making it, the President will doubtless have regard for its effects on the governments and peoples of our allies and indeed on public opinion throughout the non-Communist world. It is exceedingly doubtful that the President would decide to use atomic weapons unless the act of aggression to which he was responding had so alarmed and outraged the free world that world public opinion could be expected to support his action.'[104] This was a categorical admission that nuclear weapons might

---

[102]   Bedell Smith's belief, for example, was that 'the only thing that produced an agreement at Geneva was the fear of the Chinese, probably strengthened by that of the Indians, that we would intervene'; see minutes of a meeting on South East Asia, 24 July 1954, *FRUS, 1952–1954, XII*, Part 1, 668.

[103]   Memorandum of discussion at the 210th meeting of the NSC, 13 August 1954, DDRS/ CK3100216577.

[104]   Study prepared by the Policy Planning Staff, 23 April 1954, *FRUS, 1952–1954, II*, Part 2, 1390.

not be useable in limited war, and undercut much of the premise behind the New Look.

In terms of the overall relations between the United States and Asia, the repercussions of the *Bravo* test and the Indochina crisis were thereafter indelibly connected. Disregard for the safety and welfare for Asian peoples who might be affected by fallout was then compounded by the intensive discussions that ensued between the Western powers over intervention in Vietnam – widely seen as an effort to shore up a discredited French colonialism – which might then have triggered an uncontrollable cycle of escalation, with all its attendant nuclear dangers for those closest to the fighting in Asia. For Western policy-makers concerned over winning the favour and allegiance of an attentive Asian public, *Bravo* was a public relations disaster, heightening the impression that nuclear weapons and the deadly fallout they generated were reserved for areas inhabited by non-white peoples.

Bravo also came during a period when relations between the West and Asia were often mediated through the lens of race. In this context, as has been noted, examples of domestic US discrimination and racism were given wide coverage in the Asian press, particularly as the white backlash against some of the economic gains made by African Americans during the Second World War, and the demographic and residential changes that accompanied them, began in earnest. The capacity of civil rights organizations to uphold the position of black Americans and campaign for genuine equality was inhibited by the pressures for domestic and patriotic conformity as Cold War histrionics permeated virtually every aspect of American society in the early 1950s. The vulnerability of the NAACP to red-baiting undoubtedly muted its effectiveness, and the Soviet Union's identification with critics of American racial conditions made it problematic for those who expressed dissatisfaction with the status quo.[105] While the legal challenge to segregation in the South was slowly moving through the federal court system in this period, the arrival of Eisenhower in office in 1953 did not portend any acceleration in federal intervention when it came to the issue of domestic civil rights, the new President, in fact, being largely indifferent to the plight of African-American citizens.[106] For those wanting to see quicker strides made towards full equality, some hope was offered by the Supreme Court's overdue and landmark 11 May 1954 ruling in the *Brown* v. *Board of Education* case establishing that segregation

---

[105] See, e.g., Lewis, *Du Bois*, 525–40; Richard Polenberg, *One Nation Divisible: Class, Race, and Ethnicity in the United States since 1938* (New York, 1980), 110–15, 150–3; Borstelmann, *Cold War and the Color Line*, 65–7.
[106] Borstelmann, *Cold War and the Color Line*, 87–92.

in the public school system infringed the constitutional right to equal treatment under the law, so overthrowing the doctrine of 'separate but equal' that had underpinned legal segregation in the South since 1896. Indeed, USIA lost little time in disseminating the ruling to its overseas posts, and trumpeting how well the impression of progress had been received by commentators in Asia, Africa and Latin America.[107] Nevertheless, the practical steps that were taken after the *Brown* ruling towards desegregation in the South were slow and halting, while Eisenhower – who had carried several Southern states in the 1952 election – made no effort to put the authority of the federal government behind the Supreme Court's decision. Southern politicians anxious for their own re-election began to realize the potency of a message which depicted them as the defenders of the region's racial practices against outside intrusion.

For an Asian audience also, the impact of the *Brown* ruling was muted by the more immediate evidence of American foreign and defence policy on display, and it was no surprise to see some reactions to *Bravo* dwell on the unsavoury racial undertones that were felt to lie beneath the apparent disregard for the health and environmental impact of nuclear testing in the Pacific on the inhabitants of the region, and the immediate response of the American authorities to the plight of those affected by fallout. The Vice-President of the All-India Peace Council, addressing a peace conference in New Delhi soon after *Bravo*, noted that, 'Our concern at the manner in which the H-bomb is being used is accentuated by the knowledge that the United States has thus far thought it fit to use Asians as guinea pigs for its experiments. It was on Asians that the first A-bombs were dropped. And again, it is in the Pacific Ocean, carrying peril to Asian peoples, that the new H-bombs are being tested.'[108] Writing in June 1954, Professor Tetsuzo Tanikawa, Dean of the Faculty of Literature at Hosei University, denied any feelings of anti-Americanism when decrying as 'plain national egoism' the paramount concerns over security rather than the welfare of the afflicted crew of the *Lucky Dragon* evidenced by many US officials: 'We cannot but conclude that this comes from a subconscious contempt for colored people.'[109] In one review of Indian–US relations compiled by the State Department in July 1954, the effect of testing was seen to have counteracted the more favourable impressions of

---

[107] Walter L. Hixson, *Parting the Curtain: Propaganda, Culture, and the Cold War, 1945–1961* (London, 1997), 130; Dudziak, *Cold War Civil Rights*, 107–9; Osgood, *Total Cold War*, 280–1.

[108] *The Times of India*, 2 April 1954.

[109] The quotation comes from the publication *Sekai* in June 1954 and is used in Passin, 'Japan and the H-Bomb', 289.

the United States that had been generated by news of the *Brown* ruling. The tests had induced 'widespread feelings of revulsion and anxiety' and 'the common Asian notion that the United States reserved the A-Bomb for application to the colored Japanese during World War II' was echoed by Nehru's statement of concern that Asians always seemed to be nearer to such nuclear events than other peoples.[110] 'Over and over again while I was India,' Chester Bowles recalled for American readers once again in his book *The New Dimensions of Peace* of 1955, 'I was confronted with the startling question whether we atom-bombed the Japanese because they were yellow, while we refrained from atom-bombing the Germans because they were white. No explanations ever quite seemed to silence doubts on this question.'[111] In one appraisal of US programmes in India compiled by the OCB in September 1954, there was reiteration of the point that the

extreme sensitivity of all Indians to matters of racial discrimination and color prejudice is a factor unfavorable to the United States. Indians, in general, believe that racial discrimination in the United States is much greater and more serious than it is and that Americans are much more influenced by color prejudice than they are. Thus, for example, Indians believe it is significant that the A-bomb was not used against the 'white' Germans but was employed against the Japanese and that the United States has conducted its tests in oriental waters.[112]

All these signs of mistrust and alienation between the United States and segments of Asian opinion would, some Western commentators feared, rebound to the benefit of a Communist China whose standing in the area had increased, and where Zhou Enlai's pursuit of peaceful coexistence and acceptance of the *panchsheel* was winning plaudits. In June 1954, Charlton Ogburn had composed the Far East Bureau's response to the NSC's latest review of overall national security policy. Hardly surprisingly, he found it gave insufficient emphasis to the importance of his area of responsibility, arguing 'the future course of the contest between the free world and the Communist camp will depend to a very considerable extent upon which side Asia's potential strength will be enlisted'. Ogburn also went on, however, to offer an astute analysis of the danger he felt was posed by Communist China to the West's position. This did not lie, he contended, in the direct application of military force or penetration and subversion, but that

[110] Quarterly Review of United States–Indian Relations, CA-300, 13 July 1954, 611.91/7–1354, CDF, RG 59, NARA.
[111] Chester Bowles, *The New Dimensions of Peace* (New York, 1955), 239.
[112] 'Evaluation of U.S. Operating Programs Relating to India', p. 55, OCB working draft report, 23 September 1954, DDRS/CK310011649.

by affording the spectacle of a backward and demoralized Asian country that has achieved national unity, international prestige, and the power and self-confidence to stand up to the West, it will have a magnetic effect upon other Asian countries, attracting them to its ideology and drawing them within the influence of its national power. We must recognize that already Communist China has won a considerable measure of admiration even from its enemies among the Asians. Every Asian has shared vicariously in the successes of Communist China and has gained in pride and self-esteem because of them.

Japan in 1941 had a similar impact upon the Asians and for all their short-sightedness and ultimate defeat, the Japanese doomed European rule in Asia for good. Had the Japanese avoided the provocation of Pearl Harbor and not made the same mistake as most of the Europeans made by treating the Asians who came under their control as inferiors, the 'Greater East Asia Co-Prosperity Sphere' might have been impregnable and European influence have been totally excluded from the Asian world. We cannot assume the Chinese Communists will make these mistakes.

Ogburn's use of historical analogy in his reasoning was typical for US officials of the period, as was his idea that Beijing was promoting a revival of the Japanese call for an 'Asia for the Asians' movement. It was also precisely why the Chinese strategy of embracing the *panchsheel* and developing ties with India was considered so worrying by the United States. For Ogburn, since the Second World War, the United States had also squandered its reputation as the champion of equality, freedom and anti-imperialism, 'as the result chiefly of our giving far more material aid to Western Europe than to Asia, of our temporizing in the Dutch–Indonesian dispute until the very end, of our supporting the French and Bao Dai in Indochina, of our standing constantly on the side of the European colonialists in Africa, and of our betraying in countless ways that we attach a secondary importance to Asia as a strategic area and to the Asians as human beings'.[113] By refusing to directly associate itself with the final Geneva settlement and by seeming to promote military action above the path of diplomacy, Washington appeared to be losing the battle for public opinion. Malcolm MacDonald, the British Commissioner General for South East Asia, was scathing in his summary of the wider impact of the American approach, concluding in August 1954:

The conduct of American foreign policy towards Asia during recent months has left the United States with few friends, many enemies and almost universal critics amongst Asian Governments and peoples. It has done America's reputation shattering harm, appears sometimes to Asians to support the Communist

---

[113] Drumright memorandum for Schwartz (though drafted by Ogburn), 'NSC 5422', 23 June 1954, 'NSC (January–June 1954)' folder, box 11, Subject Files, 1954, records of the Bureau of Far East Affairs, RG 59, NARA.

contention that the United States are the real 'war-mongers' in the world, and has left the United States virtually isolated here except for the support of the least influential Asian nations, like Siam and Chinese Nationalist Formosa. It is appalling that American statements and actions have caused such gigantic misunderstandings, and that the vast influence which America could exert for good has been turned to grave disadvantage to us all.[114]

It is hardly surprising then to find that it was the core of the Colombo powers who should be instrumental in summoning together another international conference, this time held at Bandung, and almost exactly a year after Geneva, which would explicitly exclude a Western presence and voice, and raise concerns in Washington that once again the Japanese wartime cry of Asia for the Asians would find a receptive audience.

---

[114] 'Note on Relations with the United States, China and the Colombo Powers', 8 August 1954, D1015/5, FO 371/111852, TNA.

7 'Asia for the Asians': the first offshore islands crisis and the Bandung Conference

By early 1955, many American observers were concerned that the United States was on the way to losing the Cold War in Asia. Commentators pointed to the setback of the emergence of a Communist regime in North Vietnam as a result of the Geneva settlement in Indochina of 1954, and many worries were expressed over the apparent effectiveness of the efforts of the PRC to build new and better relationships with the newly independent states of Asia, and the vulnerability of many of those same states to domestic Communist subversion. Popular anxieties were focussed on the notion that the large and restless populations of the region were peculiarly susceptible to Communist entreaties, and that once these human resources were harnessed by a hostile ideology, there would be no place for Western influence. The image that was immediately invoked for many Americans by 'Asia', as Harold Isaacs highlighted at the time, was of 'an undifferentiated crush of humanity', 'a dread blur of mystery and fearfulness, associated with vast numbers, with barbarism, and with disease'. What was also clear, moreover, was that Asia was restive and in ferment, consumed by the drive for self-determination and independence, with 'dark peoples determined to assert themselves'.[1] With the struggle against Communist China now fully engaged, adherents to an almost 'apocalyptic' perspective were making the free association: 'Soviet imperialism plus Chinese imperialism, overwhelming combinations of Asian populations; Western civilization is outnumbered, white civilization is outnumbered, and could go under.'[2] In newspapers, magazines and journals there was also a recognition that Americans themselves were doing much to alienate Asian peoples, through misguided policies and attitudes. What might be called *The Ugly American* syndrome was already rearing its head, with cultural disjuncture as American service personnel, diplomats, technicians and aid experts began to enter the region in ever

---

[1] Harold R. Isaacs, *Scratches on Our Minds: American Views of China and India* (New York, 1980; originally published 1958), 54–5.
[2] *Ibid.*, 58.

240

greater numbers. That post-Geneva gleam in John Foster Dulles's eye, SEATO, had yet to acquire any real substance, and its limited Asian membership and obvious domination by the United States gave it little credibility across an area where assertive expressions of nationalism were everywhere to be seen and where anything resembling the old-style colonial relationship of East and West was anathema.

It was against this background that the climax of the first offshore islands crisis was reached in March–April 1955, during which the Eisenhower administration gave serious thought to the use of nuclear weapons against the Chinese mainland if Beijing should take the decision to launch a direct attack against the Nationalist-held islands of Jinmen and the Mazu group.[3] The outlines and detail of the crisis have been traced at length elsewhere by scholars, but it is too often treated in isolation from other parallel developments both in the general sphere of the Cold War, and in a wider Asian context. There was, for example, a growing awareness on the part of publics around the world, but also of government officials, of the ominous implications of the arrival of the thermonuclear age; popular fears about fallout were experienced on a global basis, and in the United States itself they seeped into and permeated cultural and social life through books, plays, films, songs and works of art.[4] As we have seen, *Bravo* had done much to raise consciousness about fallout, but it was in 1955 that fuller data about its dangers became available.[5] It was in this setting that there was debate over the distinctions that could or should be drawn between tactical and strategic nuclear weapons, as scientists worked at both ends of the nuclear extremes, designing weapons that generated massive yields and large amounts of radioactive fallout, or those where yields were minimized and lighter bombs 'optimised' for 'battlefield' use.[6] These often bewildering technical developments convinced some that the tactical use of nuclear weapons against purely military targets was a perfectly feasible proposition, but made many others

---

[3] See, e.g., Betts, *Nuclear Blackmail*, 55–61; Divine, *Eisenhower and the Cold War*, 58–66; Bundy, *Danger and Survival*, 273–9; Kalicki, *Sino-American Crises*, 141–55; Bennett C. Rushkoff, 'Eisenhower, Dulles and the Quemoy–Matsu Crisis, 1954–1955', *Political Science Quarterly*, 96, 3, 1981, 465–80; Gordon H. Chang, 'To the Nuclear Brink: Eisenhower, Dulles, and the Quemoy–Matsu Crisis', *International Security*, 12, 4, Spring 1988, 96–123; H. W. Brands, Jr, 'Testing Massive Retaliation: Credibility and Crisis Management in the Taiwan Strait', *International Security*, 12, 4, Spring 1988, 124–51; Ronald W. Pruessen, 'Over the Volcano: The United States and the Taiwan Strait Crisis, 1954–1955', in Robert S. Ross and Jiang Changbin (eds.), *Re-Examining the Cold War: US–China Diplomacy, 1954–1973* (Cambridge, MA, 2001), 77–105.

[4] See, e.g., Winkler, *Life under a Cloud*, 90–108.

[5] See, e.g., Divine, *Blowing*, 36–50; Wittner, *Resisting the Bomb*, 4–13, 18–19, 27–8.

[6] For an early statement of these issues, see Bernard Brodie, 'Nuclear Weapons: Strategic or Tactical?', *Foreign Affairs*, 32, 2, January 1954, 217–29.

more anxious that any breach of the nuclear taboo that seemed to be developing would be disastrous, with an all-out exchange of strategic nuclear weapons a higher risk than some military experts supposed. For those in the new class of defence intellectuals, the advent of the hydrogen bomb bypassed traditional notions of strategy in ways that its atomic forebear of a decade previously had not even managed to do.[7]

Within the Eisenhower administration there was deep anxiety that the spectre of thermonuclear war would promote the development of neutralist tendencies among some of its key NATO allies, who might become increasingly nervous at confronting the Sino-Soviet bloc when Moscow had the capacity to devastate Western Europe, and one indication of this concern were the regular national intelligence estimates devoted to this subject. Indeed, in many respects, and although US officials were privately on alert for signs of Sino-Soviet tension, by projecting in public pronouncements the image of a close Moscow–Beijing axis, the Americans helped to create a wider strategic problem. The implication here was that with Sino-Soviet relations so strong, the terms of the 1950 treaty of alliance would almost certainly be invoked if the PRC was involved in a major war with the United States, with the Russians perhaps taking direct action against Western interests in Europe, and so bringing the threat of general nuclear war that much closer. Having sat through a typical exposition from Radford on the ease with which US power could overawe China, Dulles had to remind the JCS Chairman that 'the big danger resulting from a war between the U.S. and Communist China was not to be found in the realm of military action ... [but] was the possibility that it would alienate the allies of the United States and might indeed block all our best-laid plans for Western Europe'.[8]

In Asia itself, the offshore islands crisis also needs to be viewed in the context of the new dynamics created by the PRC's post-Geneva strategy of building relations with the non-aligned states of the region, exemplified by the repeated enunciation of the five principles of peaceful coexistence and the strengthening of Sino-Indian ties. To some observers indeed, a new spirit of Asia was beginning to emerge, partly out of the shadow of the *Bravo* test and the Indochina crisis of the previous year, and which was to culminate in the Bandung Conference of April 1955, where twenty-nine Asian and African states met to exchange and underline their shared opposition to colonialism and racial discrimination. The offshore islands

---

[7] See Ken Booth, 'Bernard Brodie', in John Baylis and John Garnett (eds.), *Makers of Nuclear Strategy* (London, 1991), 28.
[8] Memorandum of discussion at the 234th meeting of the NSC, 27 January 1955, *FRUS, 1955–1957, II: China* (Washington, DC, 1986), 138.

crisis, then, was conducted in an environment where tensions between Asia and 'the West', fears surrounding nuclear weapons, and the issue of race were swirling together in a potent mix. The political costs associated with nuclear use in this Asian setting were already becoming a recurring preoccupation for US officials, in terms not only of opinion in the non-aligned states, but also in Japan. Here, the aftershocks from the *Lucky Dragon* incident were still being felt, and a new government, led by Hatoyama Ichiro, had assumed office in late 1954, more disposed to steer an independent line in foreign policy than its predecessor. Japanese expressions of national pride and strength were to some extent welcomed in Washington, as a greater contribution from Tokyo towards defence efforts in East Asia was to be encouraged in the New Look era. Less favourable were indications that Hatoyama's conservative faction hoped to break subservience to the Americans, and the automatic alignment that had been a feature of Yoshida's long premiership.[9] At least, however, Japan was still ostensibly a US ally, tied to Washington by a security treaty which legitimized the presence of US bases and where it remained possible for American influence and pressure to be exerted, if in an increasingly circumspect fashion. More worrying perhaps for US officials keen to pursue their containment of Communism in Asia and to perpetuate a Western presence was the emergence of a vocal and increasingly active clutch of states which had emerged from European domination to push a new agenda in regional politics.

The Bogor meeting of South Asian prime ministers in late December 1954 had made concrete previous ideas to convene a wider grouping of Asian and African countries with a shared antipathy to colonialism, by issuing invitations to attend a conference which would be staged at Bandung in Indonesia. The conference call from the five Asian states had included a note of their 'grave concern' at the destructive potential of nuclear testing for the future of the whole world, and the subject was likely to be an important topic of discussion.[10] The forthcoming meeting was looked on with some anxiety in Western capitals, Eden telling the Cabinet in London, for example, that 'this was an unfortunate initiative and seemed likely to result in resolutions deprecating Colonialism and urging the prohibition of all further development of thermo-nuclear weapons'.[11] With the PRC's Prime Minister, Zhou Enlai, also invited at the express wish of Nehru, fears had been intensified in Washington that

---

[9] See Schaller, *Altered States*, 63–4, 84–6.
[10] See Homer Jack, 'The Afro-Asian Conference', *Bulletin of the Atomic Scientists*, 11, 6, June 1955, 221.
[11] CC(55)3rd Conclusions, 13 January 1955, PREM 11/881, TNA.

Sino-Indian relations, already cemented by the latter's visit to Beijing the previous October, could become even closer. The fact that the two most populous Asian states might be able to find common ground over opposition to Western imperialism in the region also raised a racial dimension to the challenge that Bandung was beginning to represent. In December 1954, having heard of the Bogor proposals, Robertson, the Assistant Secretary for Far Eastern Affairs, telephoned Dulles to relay his worries over what he called the 'Afro-Asian business', noting that while the first meeting of the SEATO Council due to be held in February 1955 in Bangkok would be with 'mostly whites and a few Asian people', Bandung 'would be practically all colored'.[12] With the likelihood that it would promulgate 'anti-colonial propaganda', the chief fear of the British Foreign Office was that the conference would 'present opportunities to the Communists to stir up racial feeling against the West'.[13]

Contemporary American press commentary was notable for the racial dimension to the Bandung meeting it chose to emphasize, and how the conference contained echoes of Japan's wartime attempts to forge pan-Asianism around the stand against Western imperialism's iniquities in the region. In January 1955, the *New York Times*'s chief correspondent in South East Asia, Tillman Durdin, wrote that Bandung represented a new 'Asia for the Asians rally' which was an 'aspect of the Asian reaction to three centuries of domination of Asia by the West … among many of the newly free brown and yellow peoples of Asia memories of the injuries and disruptions caused by the Occident are still vivid'. Moreover, following Nehru's criticisms of the alliance, it was now SEATO which was pictured as the new vehicle for the erosion of Asian sovereignty as the United States flexed its military muscles in the region. The underlying fear was that Communist China was 'energetically attempting to intensify Asia-for-the-Asians sentiments and deepen differences and ill-feeling between Asian nations and anti-Communist Western countries'.[14]

Partly in a reflection of such concerns, the Eisenhower administration moved quickly to establish an inter-agency working group to co-ordinate responses to the upcoming conference and to counteract the negative

[12] Dulles–Robertson telephone conversation, 31 December 1954, box 3, Telephone Calls series, John Foster Dulles papers, DDEL.
[13] FO to HM representatives, Intel No. 30, 4 February 1955, DO 35/6097, TNA.
[14] See '"Asia for Asians" Drive Stirs a Vast Continent', *NYT*, 9 January 1955. Two months later Walter Lippmann can be found opining of Bandung in the Paris *Herald Tribune* that 'it is very evident that this is no mere attempt to make a neutral bloc or a third force in between the giant military powers. Red China is no neutral and no third force. What this is, to put it plainly, is the most formidable and ambitious move yet made in this generation to apply the principle of Asia for the Asians.' Lippmann is quoted in Richard Wright, *The Color Curtain: A Report on the Bandung Conference* (London, 1956), 74–6.

impressions of American policy it threatened to generate. Dulles conjectured that 'if the nations invited to Bandung acquired the habit of meeting from time to time without Western participation, India and China because of their vast populations will very certainly dominate the scene and that one by-product will be a very solid block of anti-Western votes in the United Nations'.[15] Another problem for Dulles, as Robertson had also highlighted, was the contrast that would be presented between Bandung and the forthcoming SEATO Council meeting, but he hoped this might be turned to some advantage. To the Senate Foreign Relations Committee, Dulles made the point that Bandung would be 'limited to the non-white, non-Western countries' and therefore the SEATO Council, where Western and Asian powers met and worked together for a common interest, would be an 'antidote' to the Communist message that the peoples of Asia and Africa 'can get along better without any association at all with the Western white powers'. In fact, the 'big psychological value throughout Asia' of SEATO, the Secretary of State argued, was one of the reasons that the Senate should quickly ratify the Manila Treaty signed the previous September.[16] Just before his departure for the SEATO Council meeting in Bangkok, Dulles delivered an address to the Foreign Policy Association in New York which echoed some of the thoughts he had expressed in his Cleveland speech of December 1951 and subsequent January 1952 *Foreign Affairs* article on relations with Japan. He hoped that the Bangkok meeting would 'show the advantages of cooperation between the East and the West based on principles and on the common human interests of peoples, not on such factors as race or color'. The Secretary of State averred that some Asians 'retain a fear, derived from past colonial relationships, that close ties with the Western powers will lead to their being dominated by the Western powers. It is essential that this fear should be dispelled.' Soviet Communism, Dulles continued, preached 'a new doctrine of segregation. The peoples of Asia, it is said, must be segregated from the peoples of the West. The new nations of Asia must be segregated from association with others.'[17] By invoking the

---

[15] See memorandum of conversation, 7 January 1955, box 3, Secretary's memoranda of conversations, January–February 1955, RG 59, NARA. This full account of the meeting can be usefully compared to the expurgated version offered in *FRUS, 1955–1957, XXI: East Asian Security; Cambodia; Laos* (Washington, DC, 1990), 1–5; minutes of State–JCS meeting, 14 January 1955, box 51, records of State–JCS meetings, RG 59, NARA.

[16] Dulles statement, 13 January 1955, *Executive Sessions of the Senate Foreign Relations Committee (Historical Series)*, Vol. VII: *84th Congress, 1st Session, 1955* (Washington, DC, 1978), 8.

[17] See 'Our Foreign Policies in Asia', Dulles address to the Foreign Policy Association, 16 February 1955, and Bowie, 'Outline for Secretary's February 16th Speech', 9 February 1955, 'SEATO Council Meeting, Bangkok, February–March 1955', box 98, John Foster Dulles papers, Mudd Library; for another contemporary view see 'SEATO Parley Facing Afro-Asian Challenge', *NYT*, 20 February 1955.

image of segregation, so often employed in Communist propaganda against the United States and its domestic record on race, Dulles was attempting to discredit the idea of any 'racial' alignment of states in the Far East which might be formed in the wake of Bandung, which would, in his eyes, be subject to Communist manipulation.

In Dulles's rhetoric over the role that SEATO could play in Asia can be discerned a conviction that differences between peoples could be bridged through the empathy, commitment and engagement of ordinary Americans with a world emerging from colonialism. The compelling need to avoid any appearance of racism, to discard any association with the language and attitudes of imperialism and to bring about the political and economic integration of non-Communist Asia was characteristic of American policy during this period. Yet, from the policies and actions of the United States in the Middle East, Asia and South Africa, it was easy to draw the lesson that the US Government, as at home, identified with the interests of whites over others. As has been noted already, anti-American feeling and expression had gained increasing currency in important parts of South and South East Asia from the early 1950s onwards. In February 1955, the US Chargé d'Affaires in New Delhi, Donald Kennedy, was telling the *New York Times* correspondent C. L. Sulzberger that anti-American feeling in India derived from:

1. *Racism* – the American white-domination attitude.
2. *Imperialism* – the white man was the imperialist in Asia. We supported the French in Indochina and Chiang as a dummy against Mao. We are the all-powerful representative of the white West.
3. *Brutal honesty* – Americans are far too forthright, frank and open when the Indian would prefer subtle indirection.
4. *Bossiness* – the Indians tend to resent our aid because they feel we try too much to tell them what to do.
5. *Sense of humour* – their sense of humour is more restrained and subtle.
6. *Nehru* – Nehru is an intellectual snob who dislikes most Americans as 'uncouth'. Our ways irritate him: private investment, advertising, pushiness. And those around him, like Krishna Menon, share this view and feed it.[18]

Returning from a major tour of Asia, Harold Stassen, the director of the Foreign Operations Administration (and so responsible for administering US overseas aid programmes), warned Eisenhower, Dulles and other senior Cabinet members in mid-March 1955 that success for US policies in the region hung in the balance, and that 'joint actions of Asians with

[18] Entry for 8 February 1955, C. L. Sulzberger, *The Last of the Giants* (New York, 1970), 132.

Americans, or with other white men, participating as equals are crucial. The alternative is an Asia for Asians wildfire with Communists included and white men excluded, regardless of resultant economic chaos or suffering.'[19]

The image projected by Dulles himself, with his strictures about the iniquities of Communism and the perils of straying away from the orbit of the 'free world', did nothing to enhance the prospects for US policy finding sympathetic supporters among the developing nations. According to the later recollections of Bowles, 'Dulles never had any understanding of human aspirations. He dealt with the anti-colonial movement as a fact – he couldn't deny it was a fact – but I'm sure if you asked him if it was a good idea or not, he would say no, it wasn't a good idea at all. How could all these ignorant colored people run their own lives? It's incredible that they don't realize all the nice things the British and French have done for them.' The general tone of Dulles's views was 'sort of a disdain for these people', something which also reminded Bowles of the attitudes exhibited by Acheson.[20] In one meeting at the US Embassy in Delhi, Dulles had apparently told the staff that 'if we let the Indians alone they'd be crawling to the Americans on their knees', comments which had apparently leaked to the Indians.[21] Bowles, of course, had several axes to grind with Dulles, but his impressions are specific and unflattering. Wider criticisms were also being voiced about Dulles's conduct of American diplomacy, including his propensity for grandstanding, and the popular perception that he wanted to reserve all the crucial business at the State Department to himself; as one knowledgeable Washington commentator put it, there was 'growing distress with Dulles's insistence on having nothing but second-rate people among his State Department cronies. The only thing he wants from them is loyalty – not brains.'[22]

The Bangkok SEATO Council meeting in February 1955 was the setting where Dulles could explain to the other members of the alliance how the United States proposed to come to the defence of the treaty area if it came under overt attack. The JCS had made consistently clear that in the event of overt aggression they were against the deployment of ground forces for South East Asia, preferring instead that US air and naval power be used to strike directly at China, with nuclear weapons when necessary. Adopting this strategy also appealed to the JCS as the military could plan

---

[19] See 'Report on Journey to Asia – February 21 to March 13, 1955', Stassen memorandum, 14 March 1955, DDRS/310024618.
[20] Chester Bowles Oral History, p. 616, Butler Library, Columbia University.
[21] *Ibid.*, p. 645.   [22] Entry for 18 April 1955, Sulzberger, *Last of the Giants*, 167.

for the integration of nuclear weapons into the forces deployed in the Far East and also continue with the scheduled reductions in ground strength in the theatre that would allow the economies in defence spending required by the financial stringencies of the New Look to be accomplished. Nevertheless, the Eisenhower administration's review of its basic national security policy, undertaken at the end of 1954, had appeared to recognize the problems inherent in any blanket advance approval for the use of nuclear weapons, and the need to take the political consequences of nuclear use into account. At the same time, with the Pentagon's eagerness to find overall sanction for the cuts in conventional forces that it was planning, the discussions reflected the pressures to formally extend reliance on nuclear weapons into limited war situations. Hence NSC 5501, which was approved by the National Security Council on 7 January 1955 as a new statement of basic national security policy to supersede NSC 162/2, included the carefully balanced injunction that the United States must never allow itself to

> get into the position where [it] must choose between (a) not responding to local aggression and (b) applying force in a way which our own people or our allies would entail undue risk of nuclear devastation. However, the United States cannot afford to preclude itself from using nuclear weapons even in a local situation, if such use will bring the aggression to a swift and positive cessation, and if, on a balance of political and military considerations, such use will best advance US security interests. In the last analysis, if confronted by the choice of (a) acquiescing in Communist aggression or (b) taking measures risking either general war or loss of allied support, the United States must be prepared to take these risks if necessary for its security.[23]

The provocative final sentence was almost certainly approved with the frustrations of the Indochina crisis of 1954 in mind, where both lack of allied support and concerns about sparking a wider war had helped to forestall American intervention. Nevertheless, acknowledgement that 'political considerations' would need to be set beside military ones was a victory for those in the State Department who were concerned over the possibility that decisions over the use of nuclear weapons in situations below the level of general war might be predicated simply on the military recommendations of the JCS. This qualification had an obvious applicability when it came to the possibility of limited conflict with China.

---

[23] See NSC 5501, 7 January 1955, *FRUS, 1955–1957, XIX: National Security Policy* (Washington, DC, 1990), 32. One scholar of these debates has argued that this document represented a decisive renunciation of NSC 162/2 and the whole strategy of massive retaliation; see Campbell Craig, *Destroying the Village: Eisenhower and Thermonuclear War* (New York, 1998), 51–2.

These dilemmas may also have been on Dulles's mind when he held a meeting with Radford on 14 February to discuss the defence of South East Asia, and the approach of the US delegation to the upcoming SEATO Council meeting. Since the signing of the Manila Treaty, there had been little signs of any progress with developing the organization, and American officials were becoming concerned that they had to show its Asian members that membership brought tangible benefits, above all in the security field. Yet the JCS were adamantly against any kind of specific commitment of US forces to SEATO; as one later observer put it, 'SEATO resembled NATO chiefly in its initials'.[24] Therefore, when he saw Dulles, Radford made clear once again JCS opposition to the prior commitment of any forces to the forward defence of Thailand, believing instead that the United States should strike at the source of any aggression, affirming 'our strategy must be based on the use of appropriate atomic weapons'. In an oblique reference to his on-going concerns about the general state of Asian opinion, Dulles was at pains to make clear that while he was not opposed to such a course of action, 'the political and psychological factors involved could outweigh the immediate and short-term military advantage if the use of such weapons was not properly handled'.[25]

The careful handling of nuclear issues was certainly an issue that was a preoccupation of the State Department during this period. There was particular concern within the administration over international reactions to the release by the AEC on 15 February 1955 of a much-delayed report on the fallout effects of high-yield nuclear explosions. Ever since the furore over *Bravo*, there had been growing calls for more official information on the radiation effects of thermonuclear weapons, and a steady stream of newspaper and journal articles began to appear on this subject and the related dangers to human health posed by continued weapons testing.[26] In October 1954, State Department representatives had been briefed by the AEC on the fallout effects deriving from the *Castle* test series in the Pacific, with the result that several had urged deferral of any public release of information, and some opposed any release at all because of the harm it would do to US foreign policy objectives by spreading neutralist sentiment. Having received Gerard Smith's advice that publication should be deferred, a small committee composed of AEC, Office of Defense Mobilization and Department of Defense officials then proposed that information might be included in Eisenhower's State of the

[24] Osgood, *Limited War*, 228.
[25] Memorandum for the record by MacArthur, 14 February 1955, *FRUS, 1955–1957, XXI*, 35.
[26] See Divine, *Blowing*, 32–5; Hewlett and Holl, *Atoms for Peace and War*, 279–85.

Union address. This was in turn strongly opposed by the Secretary of Defense, and in December the OCB unanimously recommended against publication as it was liable to seriously prejudice 'foreign policy in both Europe and the Far East'.[27] Nevertheless, by now the AEC and Strauss were in favour of an official statement in an effort to quell public disquiet and what was seen as ill-informed speculation. It was also felt necessary to 'present the facts' to the American people in order that support for the civil defence programme could be consolidated. On 3 February 1955, the NSC considered the whole issue of publication once more, and finally decided to release the AEC report (it having been scrutinized line by line by Eisenhower); one pressing reason for a decision was that the British Government was itself shortly to release a statement in Parliament on the effects of fallout, potentially undercutting the US position.[28]

Although in its assessments of worldwide media reactions the State Department noted with relief that the 15 February report had generated little sustained and damaging comment, in Japan there was renewed alarm in the press. Many stories also carried a map showing the possible damage from fallout if Tokyo were bombed, with *Asahi* displaying a headline with the banner: '18,000 kilometres contaminated'. Japanese experts were quoted as saying that the new report showed that the danger zone from the *Bravo* test had been far too circumscribed, and even that large-scale weather changes might result from further atmosphere tests.[29] The administration took some comfort from what it perceived as the generally muted worldwide reaction to the AEC report, but this did not mean it was under any illusions about widespread public acceptance that nuclear warfare was somehow less threatening or that the long-term health effects of continued atmosphere testing could be discounted.

Nevertheless, when it came to the United States' Asian allies, the administration considered that it had vigorously to spread the message that reliance on nuclear weapons was the best means of deterrence. Presiding over the first meeting of the SEATO Council in Bangkok on 23 February, Dulles felt ready to again inform the assembled ministers about how the strategic concept of the New Look would apply to the treaty

---

[27] See Smith memorandum for the Acting Secretary, 'A Short History of the Delay in Releasing the "Fall-Out" Statement', 18 March 1955, Fallout: NSC and OCB Consideration, 1955 file, box 243, Subject Files, SASAE, RG 59, NARA; also Divine, *Blowing*, 36–7.

[28] See memorandum of discussion at the 235th meeting of the NSC, 3 February 1955, *FRUS, 1955–1957, XX: Regulation of Armaments; Atomic Energy* (Washington, DC, 1990), 12; also Hewlett and Holl, *Atoms for Peace and War*, 285–6.

[29] Tokyo to USIA, TOUSI 239, 18 February 1955, Fallout: Reactions and Statements file, box 243, Subject Files, SASAE, RG 59, NARA.

area. The Secretary of State made plain that the United States was opposed to any specific commitment of its military forces to SEATO, which would involve the 'chopping up' and tying down of its strength in the Pacific, and preferred to rely on the mobility of its air and naval forces, pointing out that US power in the region 'with modern [i.e. nuclear] weapons' was now greater than at the height of the 1941–5 war. This did not go down well with all those present, some of whom, such as the Australians, would have preferred to hear talk of deploying US troops on the ground as a more concrete deterrent to Chinese aggression, while others baulked when Dulles linked the problems of South East Asian defence with those associated with Taiwan and South Korea, picturing a single battleline with three separate but interlinked fronts.[30] Nevertheless, Dulles felt happy he had been able to give firm assurances to his allies that there would be positive US action if the treaty area were threatened. His mood was less upbeat after continuing his Asian tour to include Rangoon, Vientiane, Phnom Penh, Saigon, Taipei and Manila where he was given stronger indications by local US officials of the subversive and political challenge represented by Beijing's growing confidence and prestige. He later told the Canadian Cabinet in Ottawa that this trip had 'filled him with a sense of foreboding ... There seemed to be a general feeling in the countries he visited that the Chinese Communist regime represented the future.'[31] According to Sulzberger, who had accompanied Dulles on the tour, Beijing's threat to the region was doubly potent because it combined the organizational skills derived from Soviet techniques in Europe with 'an additional propaganda advantage. Japan's tarnished slogan "Asia for the Asians" burns deeply among peoples still or recently colonial. Peiping makes the most of this sentiment.'[32]

Dulles returned from his Asian trip in early March 1955 to signs that Beijing's pressures against the offshore islands were building to a critical stage. That the UN manoeuvres and Mutual Defense Treaty of late 1954 had failed to defuse tension in the Taiwan Strait had become apparent in mid-January, when Chinese Communist aircraft attacked Nationalist

[30] See telegram from the delegation at the SEATO Council meeting to the Department of State, 23 February 1955, *FRUS, 1955–1957, XXI*, 40; 'Dulles Affirms Intent to Defend Southeast Asia', *NYT*, 24 February 1955.
[31] Cabinet Conclusions, 18 March 1955, Greg Donaghy (ed.), *Documents on Canadian External Relations, Volume 21, 1955* (Ottawa, 1999), 664.
[32] 'Techniques of Expansion in Southeast Asia', *NYT*, 5 March 1955. Sulzberger, in fact, was appalled by Dulles's complacent and myopic view that the Council meeting had been a 'complete success', and recorded him as saying 'we are operating on a basis where more and more we treat atomic weapons as conventional ... It doesn't make sense to use one hundred shots or bombs to do exactly the same job as one atomic weapon and it is much more expensive'; see entry for 25 February 1955, Sulzberger, *Last of the Giants*, 135.

shipping in the isolated Dachen group of islands, about 200 miles north of Taiwan, and then the tiny island of Yijiangshan (Ichiang), just beyond the Dachens, was seized by Chinese Communist forces. Recognizing that the rest of the isolated Dachens were indefensible, the Eisenhower administration resolved to evacuate the remainder of Chiang's forces from the islands with US naval assistance but had also to respond to the obvious charge that it was engaged in retreat and appeasement. The Secretary of State saw Communist actions in the Dachens as the beginning of a series of military operations which would culminate in an attempt to capture Taiwan itself and felt the only way to deter this would be for the United States to announce its intention to intervene to defend the remaining offshore islands. However, he faced scepticism from both Wilson and Humphrey on the NSC, who discounted their value and preferred to stand on a simple commitment to Taiwan only, a position also backed by Robert Cutler, the Special Assistant for National Security Affairs. It was the President himself who suggested that the language used to express US intentions could be worded so that a firm and long-term commitment to the offshores could be sidestepped.[33] This more cautious stance was reinforced soon after when British views of the situation were received in Washington: Churchill's Government could not support any policy which involved military action over the offshore islands, and could not continue to work on moves in the UN to settle the dispute peacefully if the United States issued any public guarantee to defend them.[34]

In the face of these reservations, the administration chose to sponsor a carefully worded congressional resolution which gave Eisenhower the necessary authority to commit US forces to the defence of Taiwan and the Penghus (Pescadores). This was also extended to cover what were called 'closely related localities' (meaning the offshore islands of Jinmen and Mazu), though this was to apply only if an attack on the offshores was viewed as a prelude to a later and larger assault on Taiwan, and not merely as an end in itself. Backtracking on his earlier position, Dulles concluded it would be better 'not to nail the flag to the mast' with a detailed presentation of US intentions.[35] There was, however, no reduction in

---

[33] See memorandum of discussion at the 232nd meeting of the NSC, 20 January 1955, *FRUS, 1955–1957, II*, 70–1, 79–81.

[34] See memorandum of conversation between Dulles and Makins, 20 January 1955, *ibid.*, 86–9; also Michael Dockrill, 'Britain and the First Chinese Offshore Islands Crisis, 1954–55', in Michael Dockrill and John W. Young (eds.), *British Foreign Policy, 1945–56* (London, 1989), 173–96. The British envisaged a package deal which would have returned the offshores to mainland control in exchange for Beijing's renunciation of the use of force over Taiwan.

[35] See memorandum of discussion at the 233rd meeting of the NSC, 21 January 1955, *FRUS, 1955–1957, II*, 91.

the way the administration pictured current events as heading towards a showdown, Dulles, for example, in testimony before the Senate Foreign Relations Committee, asserting: 'We have got to be prepared to take a risk of war with China, if we are going to stay in the Far East. If we are not going to take that risk, all right, let's make that decision and we get out and we make our defenses in California.'[36] The public ambiguity attached to the circumstances under which the islands would be defended could be construed, of course, as putting uncertainty in the minds of the PRC leadership, while allowing the US position to remain flexible, and the administration took heart when both houses of Congress passed the Formosa Resolution by large majorities at the end of January.[37] Nevertheless, the placement of such high symbolic value on retaining the islands was thought unwise by many observers, while others were concerned that if Beijing chose to call Washington's bluff and make a move for them, the United States might find itself in an untenable position of facing war with China without crucial allied support. In private, more-over, and in order to secure his co-operation over the evacuation of the Dachens (which was completed in early February), the President went so far as to reassure Chiang that, if the Communists made a direct attack on the offshore islands, the United States would intervene.[38]

From the Chinese sources that are now available, however, it is clear that American policy-makers misconstrued Communist intentions, as they had done over the earlier initiation of the bombardment of Jinmen in September 1954. There were no Chinese plans or preparations made to seize Jinmen or Mazu in early 1955, and Mao saw the Dachen campaign as distinct and entirely separate from any bid to recover the other offshore islands further to the south. There was certainly a more strident tone about Beijing's attacks on the Nationalists, and belligerent noises about liberating Taiwan, particularly in February, but the Chinese leadership was in no position to carry out its claims and did not wish for direct conflict with the United States.[39]

By early March, both Eisenhower and Dulles were privately frustrated that they had not acted earlier to try to persuade Chiang to pull back his forces from their exposed positions on Jinmen and Mazu. Yet they also believed that their loss in the face of Communist pressure would do

[36] Statement by Dulles on Formosa, 24 January 1955, *Executive Sessions of the Senate Foreign Relations Committee, 1955*, 130.
[37] See, e.g., entry for 22 January 1955, *Hagerty Diary*, 171–2.
[38] On this important point, see Chang, 'To the Nuclear Brink', 104.
[39] Chang and He Di, 'The Absence of War in the US–China Confrontation over Quemoy and Matsu', 1509–11, 1514–15, 1517–18; Shu Guang Zhang, *Deterrence and Strategic Culture: Chinese–American Confrontations 1949–1958* (Ithaca, 1992), 218–21.

irreparable damage to morale on Taiwan and throughout Asia cast doubt
on US intentions to oppose Beijing's ambitions; in grim and determined
mood, they believed that the United States had to assist the Nationalists in
defending them from any assault from the mainland. However, to intervene effectively, it was also realized, US forces might have to employ
atomic weapons against the Communist gun emplacements and airfields
which were being built up opposite the offshores, in line with the repeated
advice coming from Radford and the JCS.[40] In a speech delivered to a
radio and television audience on 8 March 1955, and which had received
close scrutiny from Eisenhower, Dulles outlined the results of his recent
Asian tour and tried to refute Beijing's propaganda charges that the
United States was a 'paper tiger' that would retreat under pressure.
Everywhere he had visited, the Secretary of State explained, he had
found 'ominous evidence of the Communist efforts to terrorize, to beguile
and to subvert'. But in the new web of collective and bilateral security
agreements that he had recently negotiated, Dulles was able to profess US
willingness to stand firm, eschew the self-restraint shown in the past and
meet hostile force with even greater force; American sea and air forces in
the Western Pacific, he proclaimed, were 'equipped with new and powerful weapons of precision, which can utterly destroy military targets without endangering civilian centers'.[41] Eisenhower had specifically endorsed
the latter reference to US nuclear capabilities, though reminding Dulles in
ambiguous fashion that this did not mean the United States would use
what he termed 'weapons of mass destruction'.[42]

Dulles's speech marked the beginning of a flurry of statements from
the administration about the possible use of nuclear weapons, which
had the obvious aim of deterring Beijing from any precipitate action
against the offshores. Yet at the same time, they also had to convey the
message to a domestic and international audience now only too aware of
the effects of fallout that the United States was not considering the
'strategic' use of high-yield thermonuclear weapons, or planning to target
areas which could cause mass civilian casualties. Both the President and
the Secretary of State hoped that they might use the opportunity of the

[40] See memorandum of conversation between Eisenhower and Dulles, 6 March 1955,
    FRUS, 1955–1957, II, 336–7.
[41] 'Text of a Broadcast by Dulles of His Report to the Nation on His Trip to Far East', *NYT*,
    9 March 1955.
[42] See memorandum of conversation between Eisenhower and Dulles, 6 March 1955,
    FRUS, 1955–1957, II, 336–7; though see also Eisenhower to Dulles, 7 March 1955, in
    'SEATO Council Meeting, Bangkok, February–March 1955', box 98, John Foster Dulles
    papers, Mudd Library, where the President seems more circumspect towards overt
    mention of atomic weapons in the speech.

crisis to bring home to the public that it was necessary to regard the use of tactical nuclear weapons against military targets as no different from other forms of 'conventional' warfare. However, if they believed this message would be readily accepted, they were to be seriously mistaken. Dulles's assertions about the possibility of using nuclear weapons in such a selective manner were almost immediately subject to searching and critical analysis, Hanson Baldwin in the *New York Times*, for one, pointing out that the rather crude missiles and rockets then in the US inventory would be of no use against the kind of mainland targets threatening the offshore islands, leaving the accuracy of atomic strikes down to the ability of US fighter-bomber aircraft to deliver them with a degree of precision that was at odds with past experience of aerial bombing. This made it all 'hard to see how Mr Dulles can promise immunity to urban residents if atomic weapons should be used'.[43]

That Dulles was engaged with the problems of 'selling' nuclear use to a watching world was shown in very clear terms throughout this period. On 10 March, for example, the State Department reminded its overseas posts that it was 'interested in keeping under constant review world-wide political and psychological reactions to thermonuclear developments, generally, as well as U.S. actions and statements affecting such developments'. The main areas of concern included how growing nuclear capabilities might change neutralist sentiments, willingness to resist Communist aggression or subversion, or willingness to support US policies, and beliefs that the atmosphere had already been contaminated by tests, or that small-yield weapons were capable of producing damaging levels of fallout. One recent State Department intelligence estimate found that the 'already considerable fear of atomic and hydrogen bombs in Western Europe and Japan has, if anything, increased during the last year'. This led, it was noted, to widespread demands for an end to nuclear testing, and interest in promoting the idea of peaceful coexistence between East and West. With regard to Japan, its dependence on US military and economic support, and the presence of US forces in the country, led most Japanese to believe that their involvement in a general war would be virtually certain, but that over a longer period they might look forward to a greater freedom of action, so as to possibly escape such involvement.[44]

---

[43] 'The Dulles Report', *NYT*, 10 March 1955.

[44] See reference to IE No. 72, 'Recent Effects of Increasing Nuclear Capabilities on U.S. Allies', 16 February 1955, in draft circular instruction, USITO 269, 10 March 1955, Fallout: Reactions and Statements file, box 243, Subject Files, SASAE, RG 59, NARA.

On the same day this circular was issued, Dulles outlined to the NSC the stark choices confronting the United States in the crisis. On his recent Asian tour, US military officers had repeated the contention that nuclear weapons were the only effective means that could be employed against Chinese Communist mainland airbases and lines of communication, but an urgent effort was still needed to create a better public climate for their employment. The administration

> would have to face up to the question whether its military program was or was not in fact designed to permit the use of atomic weapons. We might wake up one day to discover that we were inhibited in the use of these weapons by a negative public opinion ... it was of vital importance, therefore, that we urgently educate our own and world opinion as to the necessity for the tactical use of atomic weapons ... much more remained to be done if we were to be able to make use of tactical atomic weapons, perhaps within the next month or two. Public opinion in Asia was not at all attuned to such a possibility.

Nevertheless, Dulles felt that Beijing would never accept the US position over the offshore islands until they had seen a demonstration of American resolve, blustering that the United States might have to '"shoot off a gun" in the area' to show the position 'by deeds rather than by words'. Radford followed this up with a further reminder to the NSC that the whole military structure had been built around the assumption of the use of nuclear weapons, and that the situation in the Far East, particularly in view of Communist air strength, could not be handled without them.[45] This, for the majority of the military, was the most important local factor: a sudden air attack launched from newly reinforced forward airfields at the offshore islands would be the logical prelude to an amphibious assault. Rather than wait for the Communist side to make its preparations undisturbed, many military leaders such as Radford and Admiral Felix Stump, who had taken the former's place as CINCPAC in the summer of 1953, wanted to see the Nationalists given an opportunity to conduct air operations over the mainland, and even, if the United States was resolved on retaining the islands, for the United States itself to give the Communists a bloody nose by air strikes at the airfields and gun emplacements threatening the offshores (Radford even at one point warning of a possible Pearl Harbor-style inquiry if the islands were suddenly seized by combined air and amphibious assault).

Yet as discussions within the administration during the crisis revealed, military considerations were not, ultimately, the controlling factors during the stand-off with Beijing. Concerns over the reactions of Asian opinion to

---

[45] Memorandum of discussion at the 240th meeting of the NSC, 10 March 1955, *FRUS, 1955–1957, II*, 347–9.

the outbreak of fighting with China were complemented in very significant ways by the desire of Eisenhower and Dulles not to induce any rupture in relations with the crucial Western European allies, particularly when the agreements that had been reached in the autumn of 1954 over the creation of the Western European Union and the accession of West Germany to NATO were still going through the process of formal ratification. German rearmament was the centrepiece of the administration's European policies at this stage of the Cold War, and there was deep anxiety that nothing be allowed to jeopardize this long-sought goal (especially when American policies earlier had been thrown into doubt by the traumatic collapse in the summer of 1954 of the European Defence Community scheme). On 11 March, Eisenhower and Dulles met the JCS to discuss US policy towards the crisis; although there were no serious indications that a direct attack on Taiwan was being prepared, the Chinese build-up opposite the offshore islands and their belligerent stance on the issue framed the discussion. Both the President and the Secretary of State mentioned throughout their wish to avoid direct intervention if at all possible, and the President laid down that the United States should put its emphasis on assisting the Chinese Nationalist forces on the islands to defend themselves. If it became necessary to intervene, Eisenhower stressed, this should be done at first with conventional weapons; nuclear use 'should come only at the end, and we would have to advise our allies first', while precipitate involvement 'might critically damage us in Europe'.[46]

One other action that Eisenhower took at this time was indicative of his sensitivities over retaining firm control over the nuclear option. Just prior to the 11 March meeting with the JCS, Eisenhower chose to review the interpretation of paragraph 39b of NSC 162/2 that he had agreed at the start of January 1954 on the need for presidential authorization of nuclear use, as this would now have to comply with NSC 5501, the new statement of basic national security policy adopted in January 1955. With what many would consider as less than vital security interests at stake over the offshore islands, the President did not want any of his more militant subordinates pushing for nuclear use beyond the boundaries established by the White House. Accordingly, Eisenhower now reaffirmed the interpretation of January 1954 as overriding guidance, stipulating that NSC 5501's mention that the United States could not 'preclude itself from using nuclear weapons even in a local situation' did not mean there should be automatic presumption of nuclear use in the event of any hostilities, and that 'political questions of the gravest importance' would have to be

---

[46] Cutler memorandum for the record, 11 March 1955, *ibid.*, 358–9.

taken into consideration. Final decisions would always be taken by the President in his role as Commander-in-Chief and there could be no 'hard and fast rules adopted in the abstract'.[47]

Dulles continued the administration's attempts to make distinctions between types of nuclear weapons when on 15 March he held a news conference and expounded at slightly greater length on how he thought the introduction of more precise, tactical nuclear weapons made it possible to envisage victory on the battlefield without the targeting of civilian areas or the use of hydrogen bombs, while the new weapons, he alleged, also presented no problems of radioactive fallout.[48] This was a message reinforced a day later by the President when he asserted during his own press conference (in an often quoted passage) that he could not see why nuclear weapons should not be used against 'strictly military targets and for strictly military purposes. I see no reason why they shouldn't be used just exactly as you would use a bullet or anything else.' The President, however, continued with a repeat of the important qualification: 'I believe the great question about these things comes when you begin to get into those areas where you cannot make sure that you are operating merely against military targets.'[49] One of the basic problems for the administration was the general sense of incredulity that surrounded any notion that the United States would embark upon wholesale use of nuclear weapons in reply to a Communist attempt merely to seize the offshore islands. These strategically insignificant specks of land were surely not worth the risks that would follow to world peace from breaking the nuclear taboo. By introducing the notion of a 'less-than-massive retaliation' (as some commentators began to describe this new rhetorical stance) through the possible employment of tactical nuclear weapons, the administration hoped to make its threats more credible and so increase the uncertainties in Communist decision-making circles. The intent behind these statements was, as Dulles and the President privately admitted, to impress Beijing with the seriousness of US resolve and its willingness to employ whatever were the most effective weapons to hand.[50]

---

[47] Cutler memorandum for the record, 11 March 1955, DDRS/CK3100452026; and Lay memorandum for Dulles, Wilson and Strauss, 'Policy Regarding Nuclear Weapons', 14 March 1955, 'Atomic Weapons, Correspondence and Background for Presidential Approval and Instructions for Use (1953–1960) (1)', box 1, Subject Subseries, NSC Records, Office of the Special Assistant for National Security Affairs, White House Office, DDEL.

[48] 'Dulles Says U.S. Pins Retaliation on Small A-Bomb', *NYT*, 16 March 1955.

[49] 'Transcript of Presidential Press Conference on Foreign and Domestic Affairs', *NYT*, 17 March 1955; Divine, *Eisenhower and the Cold War*, 61–2.

[50] Entry for 16 March 1955, Ferrell (ed.), *Hagerty Diary*, 211.

Yet these fresh statements served more to prompt further widespread doubts and criticisms over the administration's position. Responding to Dulles's claims about precision weapons, Edward R. Murrow, in a powerful CBS radio broadcast, wondered if what the Secretary of State had in mind was that staging areas for an invasion of the offshore islands could be hit 'without, at the same time, nuclear bombs being dropped on Shanghai and Peiping. But if nuclear weapons are used to stop an invasion of Quemoy and the Matsus, the cities of Amoy and Fuchou would be hit and its civilians would be endangered pretty much as were those in Hiroshima and Nagasaki. It would be a wholesale slaughter of civilians no matter what Mr Dulles seemed to promise.'[51] For Hanson Baldwin, as we have seen, Dulles was engaging in 'wishful thinking' in his view of limited use of nuclear weapons: 'Military targets, particularly airfields, are usually near towns or cities. A weapon large enough to insure the destruction of such targets will almost inevitably take a toll of non-military areas.'[52]

These doubts were not confined to such 'outside' observers but also extended to administration officials. Immediately after his press conference remarks of 15 March, Gerard Smith had approached Dulles to point out that even small nuclear weapons being used, for example, against airfields would create fallout, and that despite the increasing efficiency of tactical nuclear weapons, US Air Force thinking was still wedded to use of large-scale strategic bombardment, where military targets (airfields among them) might be attacked with megaton-yield bombs. Smith followed this up the next day with a session which also involved Robert Bowie, where he reminded Dulles of the briefing they had received from LeMay during their January visit to SAC headquarters at Offutt Air Force base in Omaha, and the general impression that if SAC war planning were implemented 'most major Russian cities would be destroyed and Russian casualties would be in the tens of millions', implying that similar outcomes might be expected in a war with China. The Secretary of State retorted that 'although he wanted to get the facts', he was very conscious that maintaining high levels of both conventional and nuclear strength was unsustainable. Though not disagreeing, Smith still wanted to 'urge that we avoid the dangers of "over-compensation" leading to the belief that nuclear warfare could be conducted without tremendous

[51] CBS broadcast, 'Edward Murrow Excerpts', 10 March 1955, contained in Joseph Hanson (USIA) memorandum, 'Atomic Weapons vs Weapons of Mass Destruction', 15 March 1955, box 342, Subject Files, SASAE, RG 59, NARA. A transcript of Murrow's broadcast was also printed in *Bulletin of the Atomic Scientists*, 11, 5, May 1955, 192–3.
[52] 'An Atomic Strategy', *NYT*, 17 March 1955.

destruction of civilians'.[53] Bowie also collected data on weapons effects from the AEC and used CIA sources on the distribution of the Chinese population near the artillery emplacements and airfields to be targeted opposite Jinmen in order to make a further presentation to Dulles on likely civilian casualties, which were estimated to be in the order of 12–14 million.[54] For Smith, who would eventually take Bowie's place as head of the PPS, this was the first of many interventions over the coming years, as he endeavoured to keep a close watch on the expansive nature of US nuclear planning. Always loath to pry into the details of such planning, these briefings may well have been eye-openers for Dulles, and from this point onwards one can discern a more cautious note to his comments about possible nuclear use, while Bowie certainly believed that the presentations had helped to inject a more sober understanding of the consequences of even 'limited' nuclear strikes.

Weighing the political costs in Asia and elsewhere of a resort to nuclear weapons continued to be the subject of speculation as the crisis peaked. As well as believing that to 'apply the word "precise" to an atomic weapon [was] a contradiction', in his column Hanson Baldwin was quick to see the wider problems associated with the policy, venturing that 'in Asia an atomic strategy of any sort is a two-edged sword. It might be militarily effective now – and Asians like to jump on the winning bandwagon – but Asians do not forget that atomic bombs have been used in war only against Asians. Used against Asians, in defense of Formosa or Matsu or Quemoy, for instance, the psychological result could only be a further hardening of hatred against the United States.'[55] Murrow, in the broadcast referred to above, also mentioned that it had long been considered a 'truism that the United States could not use atomic bombs against Chinese cities without forfeiting any hope of gaining the friendship of the Asian peoples. That may be why such care is taken to imply that the tactical use of nuclear weapons would not be like the strategic bombing of Japan in the last war.'[56] John C. Bennett, Dean of the Faculty at Union Theological Seminary, wrote to the *New York Times* to express his belief that even a limited war with China would alienate the rest of Asia, while use of tactical

---

[53] 'Discussion with the Secretary', Smith memorandum for the file, 16 March 1955, www.gwu.edu/~nsarchiv/NSAEBB/NSAEBB108/fire-2.pdf, accessed 27 January 2010. Dulles's visit to SAC headquarters is mentioned in the entry for 14 January 1955, Ferrell (ed.), *Hagerty Diary*, 161.

[54] Hoopes, *John Foster Dulles*, 278; see also the comments by Bowie on the briefing in Tucker (ed.), *China Confidential*, 126–7.

[55] 'Limited Atomic War: A New U.S. Strategy', *NYT*, 20 March 1955.

[56] CBS broadcast, 'Edward Murrow Excerpts', 10 March 1955, contained in Joseph Hanson (USIA) memorandum, 15 March 1955.

nuclear weapons would cause a 'moral revulsion' against the United States, particularly from the Japanese people:

There is a common feeling in Asia that we reserve atomic bombs for use on Asian peoples. We even do our most dangerous experimenting near their shores. We might win a military victory with these weapons but communism would win a moral victory in most of the free nations in Asia. Our acts of destruction would seem to Asians to be greater atrocities than those which we ascribe to the Communists ... The revulsion against our use of nuclear weapons would be combined with the old revulsion against any white man who attacks Asian soil.[57]

This was also a perspective held by other Western policy-makers. The Canadian Department of External Affairs made clear that Canada's support would not be forthcoming if the United States intervened to defend the offshore islands and tended to feel that Eisenhower would not authorize use of nuclear weapons if hostilities with China were to occur, partly as he 'cannot be unmindful of the deplorable effect that the use of nuclear weapons against Communist China would have on Asian opinion'.[58] Reacting to the efforts of the administration to distinguish between tactical and strategic use of nuclear weapons, the Chairman of the Canadian Chiefs of Staff Committee felt this would be a difficult division to sustain: 'First of all, once a war was started, it would be quite impossible to stick only to using small bombs, particularly if the desired results were not realized and US aims were not achieved, and secondly, whether or not a 20-kiloton or a 5 or 6 megaton bomb were dropped, the whole of Asia would be completely alienated by such action.'[59] In London, the Churchill Government had already signalled that while it would support the United States in a straightforward defence of Taiwan, it could not back Washington if US forces were used to shore up the Nationalist position on the offshore islands. 'You know how hard Anthony [Eden] and I have tried to keep in step with you and how much we wish to continue to do so,' the Prime Minister had written to Eisenhower in the middle of February, 'but a war to keep the coastal islands for Chiang would not be defensible here.' Moreover, the British believed that the Americans were being drawn into untenable positions by taking far too literally the strident line coming from Beijing that the 'liberation' of Taiwan was imminent, Churchill noting that it was probable 'the absurd Chinese boastings about invading Formosa are inspired by the Soviet desire to cause division

---

[57] 'Our Position in Asia', *NYT*, 21 March 1955 (letter composed 9 March 1955).
[58] Draft memorandum, 17 February 1955, *Documents on Canadian External Relations, 1955*, 1528.
[59] General Charles Foulkes comments, extract from minutes of meeting, 21 April 1955, *ibid.*, 1558.

between the Allies in the far more important issues which confront us in Europe. It costs very little to say, as the Chinese are now reported to be doing, that "the possession of the Tachens will help the liberation of Formosa". It adds to the pretence of Communist China's might and is intended to provoke the United States into actions and declarations which would embarrass many of us, and add influence to Communist propaganda.'[60]

It was this latter consideration which had also registered in London: besides the obvious dangers of an escalation of the crisis and the onset of a disastrous all-out war with China, the offshore islands were by any measure strategically insignificant, and standing by a discredited Chiang Kai-shek in their defence would put the West in an untenable position with wider Asian opinion. The British Ambassador in Washington, Sir Roger Makins, put forward an eloquent summary of British views to Dulles on 16 March, where he ventured that the Chinese would not launch overt attacks either on Taiwan or in South East Asia. Makins reasoned:

It will surely suit them better to try to win over Asian opinion and lull Asian suspicions by appearing moderate and peace-loving while at the same time pursuing their objectives under cover. The Bandung Conference will give them an opportunity to mobilise Asian opinion on their side in favour of such aims as non-interference, respect for national sovereignty, etc. They must know that they cannot take on the United States of America in open war with nuclear weapons. Their objective seems more likely to be to isolate the United States of America and to consolidate opinion on their side.

Therefore instead of our being faced with a showdown, the prospect in the Far East seems to us more likely to be a long drawn-out struggle for the support of Asia accompanied by Communist subversion and the constant threat of war. There may always be an explosion, but it seems to us that that would be more likely to come at present from miscalculation than deliberate policy on the part of the Chinese.

In view of this analysis, the British considered it crucial to 'exercise moderation in our statements and attitudes lest we frighten the Asians into China's arms', and this was one reason why London favoured evacuation of the offshore islands.[61] There was much in this that Dulles could privately agree with, but the administration had already tied US prestige to resisting any attempt to take the islands by force (it is interesting that Eisenhower would often indulge in cultural stereotyping when he pictured 'orientals' as driven by the need to preserve face rather than by rational

---

[60] Churchill to Eisenhower, 15 February 1955, in Boyle (ed.), *Churchill–Eisenhower Correspondence*, 193.
[61] Memorandum from Makins for Dulles, 16 March 1955, *FRUS, 1955–1957, II*, 374–5.

considerations, when in this crisis it was the United States, perhaps above all, that was motivated by fear of being branded a 'paper tiger').[62]

The British also believed that if nuclear weapons were used against China, the implications for the United States' most vital regional alliances in Asia could be severe. In the wake of the President's news conference remarks on nuclear weapons, the British Ambassador in Tokyo, Sir Esler Dening, wrote to Denis Allen, the Assistant Under-Secretary heading the Far East Department at the Foreign Office, wondering

whether the Americans, who seem to contemplate with comparative equanimity the prospect of an armed clash with China over these Islands involving the discharge of atomic weapons over the Chinese mainland, have ever paused to consider the Japanese aspect of the situation. For if atomic bombs were ever to be dropped on China, it seems to me very likely that both Russia and China might threaten Japan with retaliation in kind on American bases there. The mere threat – even if it is never put into execution – would have a profound effect on Japanese opinion, and I think it would be no exaggeration to say that it might be the beginning of the end of American influence in Japan. Not only would Japanese opinion turn against the United States but the Japanese would become firmly entrenched in neutralism and do their best to get out of the obligations under the Mutual [*sic*] Security Treaty and to get American forces out of Japan. Even if therefore, a clash between the United States and China did not lead to a wider conflagration, the result of using atomic weapons might well be disastrous in Japan and probably irretrievable.

Copies of Dening's letter were passed to Makins in Washington, while both the Permanent Under-Secretary, Sir Ivone Kirkpatrick, and Eden himself, wanted these points passed on to the Americans.[63] The Foreign Secretary found Dening's analysis 'interesting and important'; Eden, it was noted, had spoken along these lines to Admiral Stump at the Bangkok SEATO meeting, and though the latter had at the time 'seemed neither interested nor impressed by the reaction of world opinion to the use of nuclear weapons', even Stump, it was felt, could 'hardly look with equanimity on an increase in neutralist sentiment in Japan'.[64] When he relayed these views to Noel Hemmendinger, the Assistant Secretary for Northeast Asian Affairs, and Richard Finn, his Japan desk officer, one British Embassy official in Washington was told that they too shared the belief

---

[62] This was also an observation made by George Ball several years later when he lamented the Johnson administration's decision to bomb North Vietnam as 'a form of political therapy' which was the final resort of those who could not countenance the supposed humiliation of retreat from Vietnam: 'We seemed more concerned about "loss of face" than did the Orientals'; see his *The Past Has Another Pattern: Memoirs* (New York, 1982), 383.

[63] Dening to Allen, 16 March 1955, and Allen minute, 22 March 1955, FC1041/688, FO 371/115045, TNA.

[64] Allen to Scott, 6 April 1955, *ibid*.

that the 'effects were potentially serious, and admitted there was support for the view that the use of nuclear weapons against China might drive Japan into complete neutrality'.[65]

There were indeed deep concerns in Washington over Japanese reactions to the crisis, with memories still fresh of the upheavals that relations with Tokyo had undergone in 1954, while the reception of the AEC's fallout report in February within Japan left no room for complacency. A National Intelligence Estimate produced on 16 March warned that if nuclear weapons were used against China, 'the predominant world reaction would be one of shock'. Particularly negative responses would follow if they were used to defend the offshore islands, or to destroy Communist military concentrations before an attack on the offshores. While some Asian and European allies might condone a use of nuclear weapons to defend Taiwan itself, 'The general reaction of non-Communist Asians would be emotional and would be extremely critical of the United States. In the case of Japan, the Government would probably attempt to steer a more neutral course.'[66] From Tokyo itself Allison was especially sceptical, reporting back to Washington that, in a war over the offshore islands, the Americans could expect no support from Japan, and if this developed into an atomic conflict, the United States would even 'meet with active hostility'. In the Ambassador's view the Japanese simply did not regard the PRC and the Soviet Union 'in the same light. China to them remains an oriental country and more Chinese than Communist.'[67]

Lying in the background here was also the vexed issue of the storage of nuclear weapons at US airbases in Japan. In mid-February 1955, the State Department and Allison were told by the Department of Defense that the movement of the non-nuclear components of atomic weapons to American bases was going ahead (though this process actually appears to have begun at the end of 1954). At the same time, the Japanese Foreign Minister, Shigemitsu Mamoru, was informed of the deployment by General John E. Hull, the US Commander-in-Chief Far East. The State Department also began to issue advice to the JCS concerning the authorization they could give to the US Far East Command in Tokyo over

---

[65] Michael G. L. Joy to Colin Crowe, 28 April 1955, FC1041/820, FO 371/115049, TNA.

[66] NIE 100–4–55, 'Communist Capabilities and Intentions with Respect to the Off-Shore Islands and Taiwan through 1955, and Communist and Non-Communist Reactions with Respect to the Defense of Taiwan', 16 March 1955, *FRUS, 1955–1957, II*, 379.

[67] Allison's views are conveyed in the diary entry for 23 March 1955, Sulzbeger, *Last of the Giants*, 156. See also Sulzberger's column where he predicted Japanese hostility if atomic weapons were used to defend Taiwan, a conflict which might also bring to power a Socialist government in Tokyo, 'Why Japan Is Reluctant to Rearm', *NYT*, 26 March 1955.

deployment and use of atomic weapons from Japan. The nuclear components of the weapons 'then stored in areas under United States control
adjacent to Japan' (referring, in all probability, to Okinawa or Guam)
could be deployed immediately to Japan itself in a war emergency
declared through constitutional processes, if US forces were judged to
be subject to imminent attack, or if hostilities had broken out in the Japan
area. The State Department would determine whether it was advisable to
inform appropriate Japanese officials of this movement, while the Far
East Commander was authorized to plan on the immediate use of his
weapons if an attack on Japan were under way. In the latter case, the
Japanese authorities would be consulted prior to their use, but only if
feasible, while there could be no question of negotiating an advance
authorization for use.[68]

With authorization for the deployment of the nuclear components of
atomic weapons to Japanese bases having been postponed in the midst
of the *Lucky Dragon* crisis the previous year, the JCS and the Department
of Defense remained keen that this extra step should now be sanctioned.
As Wilson, the Secretary of Defense, put it: 'the Chiefs urge that in view of
the vital security interests involved the political obstacles be surmounted
as soon as possible'. However, it was precisely those political obstacles
that the State Department still saw as daunting, and when approached for
his advice from Tokyo, Allison again recommended that there should be
no change in existing policy regarding the introduction of nuclear components, or any attempt to seek advance authorization regarding use from
the Japanese Government. Indeed, the situation was viewed as even more
unfavourable than that obtaining in June 1954 when the original request
had been made. In making his recommendation, the Ambassador had the
support of General Hull, though with the proviso that it remained highly
desirable that both nuclear and non-nuclear components be stored in
Japan: 'If we wait until hostilities become imminent,' Hull had noted, 'it
may be too late to avoid disaster.'[69] On 11 March, now in the midst of the
offshore islands crisis and having given vent to his anxiety over Asian
reaction to any US use of nuclear weapons in the Taiwan Strait, Dulles
wrote to Wilson informing him that, while recognizing the military case
for deployment of the nuclear components of atomic weapons to US bases
in Japan, the political situation there made it inexpedient to recommend a

---

[68] See draft memoranda from the Secretary of Defense to the JCS with State Department
amendments, 'Use of Atomic Weapons', 8 February and 3 March 1955, 'NN-Japan
1955', box 2, Country and Subject Files, 1950–62, SASAE, RG 59, NARA.
[69] See Smith memorandum for Dulles, 'Reply to Secretary of Defense's letter of January 28,
1955, Concerning the Deployment of Nuclear Weapons to Japan', 11 March 1955, *ibid.*

change in existing arrangements.[70] The volatility that troubled the State Department was made all too plain at exactly the same moment, when Hatoyama brought down much criticism on his government by telling a press conference that Japan might not oppose the stockpiling of nuclear weapons on its soil if it was justified in thinking that what he called a 'peace sustained by force' was possible. A barrage of questions from the Opposition in the Diet followed over the next few months, with suspicions aroused that a secret undertaking had been made with Washington over deployment. Eventually, with the Government on the defensive, Hatoyama had to retract his statement and make clear that the administrative agreement that accompanied the security treaty gave the Americans no authority to introduce nuclear weapons to Japan, that there were no such weapons then in Japan, and Japanese consent would be required if there was ever a proposal that they should be introduced in the future.[71]

Despite his deference to Allison's advice regarding deployment issues in Japan, Dulles had reservations as he contemplated another unravelling of the administration's professed position that nuclear weapons should not be seen as a special category of armament, and immediately asked that further study be devoted to the problem. As Gerard Smith noted in one letter to Allison, 'I believe his [Dulles's] thinking on this matter is that having fully integrated these weapons into our weapons systems [sic], special foreign political restrictions on their storage and use should be submitted to only if clearly unavoidable.' The Ambassador was told that the weapons for deployment to Japan were of the 'tactical' variety, for use against military targets, and that this could influence Japanese responses to their introduction. The Department of Defense judged it feasible that they could be deployed with secrecy to Japanese bases, and Allison was also asked about his views on the introduction of nuclear components if no notice were given to the Japanese Government, but this was a line of action which he categorically rejected.[72]

Meanwhile, the administration also faced the problem that US intervention over the offshore islands was unlikely to receive bipartisan support at home, despite earlier backing for the Formosa Resolution. Senate Majority Leader Lyndon B. Johnson (Democrat, Texas) cautioned against 'an irresponsible adventure for which we have not calculated the risks', Senator Herbert Lehman (Democrat, New York) tried to sponsor an amendment which would remove the offshore islands from the pledge to defend Taiwan, and Adlai Stevenson voiced the 'gravest misgivings about risking a third world war in defense of these little islands'.[73] By the time of the President's news conference on 23 March, there were signs that the administration was beginning to back-pedal on the more out-spoken stance it had taken over nuclear use from the week before. When asked the direct question by a reporter whether he would use tactical nuclear weapons in defence of the offshore islands, Eisenhower replied that he could not give an answer in advance, and continued with the kind of memorable obfuscation of which he was so privately proud: 'The only thing I know about war are two things: the most changeable factor in war is human nature in its day-by-day manifestation; but the only unchanging factor in war is human nature. And the next thing is that every war is going to astonish you in the way it occurred, and in the way it is carried out. So that for a man to predict, particularly if he has the responsibility for making the decision, to predict what he is going to use, how he is going to do it, would I think exhibit his ignorance of war; that is what I believe.'[74]

However, other voices were ready to provide more direct and dramatic responses. In private after-dinner comments on 24 March, Admiral Carney, the US Chief of Naval Operations (CNO), told several pressmen that Eisenhower was considering a plan to destroy China's military poten-tial, so ending the expansionist threat that it posed, and that war would probably break out by the middle of April. Carney did not disguise the fact, one of those present reported, that both he and Radford believed 'that this is a moment for a showdown with Communist China', in which there was little likelihood of Russian intervention.[75] For the President, the CNO's intervention was a reprehensible example of the military infringing on the civilian prerogative. Eisenhower, concerned that the United States was perceived as 'looking for war' and fully aware that intelligence reports as yet indicated no major amphibious military build-up opposite the

[73] See Divine, *Eisenhower and the Cold War*, 63.
[74] See 'President Shuns Stand on Quemoy', and 'Transcript of the Presidential Press Conference on Foreign and Domestic Affairs', *NYT*, 24 March 1955.
[75] The dinner was apparently arranged by the reporter Marquis Childs after being contacted by one of Carney's aides. According to Childs, Carney had informed the newsmen that he was speaking with the full concurrence of Radford, and that Carney was contemplating a major war in Asia was made obvious by mention of the problems of military government of China, the fact that the Chinese lacked tactical atomic weapons, and that it was thought unlikely the Russians would supply strategic weapons or that Moscow would intervene at all. Childs felt the main purpose of the briefing was to curtail Eisenhower's freedom of action if the offshore islands should be attacked; see the revealing report in Canadian Ambassador in Washington to the Secretary of State for External Affairs, 29 March 1955, *Documents on Canadian External Relations, 1955*, 1547–8.

offshore islands, did not want to be backed into a corner.[76] He was probably also aware that Carney's comments undermined the administration's most recent attempts to be seen as positively working towards peace and to defuse the tensions produced by a burgeoning arms race by creating a new Cabinet rank position of Special Assistant to the President for Disarmament, to be filled by Harold Stassen (Stassen's appointment was itself testimony to the inability of the AEC, State and Defense Departments to co-ordinate a position on disarmament proposals).[77] The simple fact was that Carney's picture of Chinese forces massing for an amphibious attack on the islands did not accord with the intelligence available at the time: Allen Dulles, the head of the CIA, was of the opinion that Beijing was not going to mount an assault before the opening of the Bandung Conference, while it was increasingly apparent that use of nuclear weapons would endanger the very offshore islands they were supposed to protect via fallout, not to mention the city of Amoy on the mainland which lay close to Jinmen.[78]

With leading newspapers soon carrying paraphrased versions of Carney's remarks, the supposition was that they indicated a hardening of the administration's attitudes. The result was a far more intensive discussion of the consequences of an all-out war with China, and much comment that such a conflict would divide the country and lose America its allies.[79] Press commentary also included mention of the political impact in Asia of nuclear use. On 29 March, the *Washington Post* featured an editorial which speculated that the deadline for a Chinese Communist assault was fast approaching, picking up on Carney's warning of mid-April as a likely date; this would then raise the question of 'whether the counterattack should consist of an effort to blot out Communist airfields with tactical atomic weapons or whether it should aim at China's industrial potential'. Although the *Washington Post* could see that the use of atomic bombs in a large war would be inevitable, over the offshore islands, where much of the world was critical of the American position, 'to initiate

---

[76] See Alexander, *Holding the Line*, 89; Ambrose, *Eisenhower*, 240–1; entry for 28 March 1955, Ferrell (ed.), *Hagerty Diary*, 218.

[77] See the report of a conference between Eisenhower and Stassen, 22 March 1955, *FRUS, 1955–1957, XX*, 60–1. The widespread initial perception that Stassen would perform the functions of a 'Secretary for Peace' did not help to ease his relations with Dulles, who could not but feel that some of his job was being usurped (it was a title, incidentally, that both Stassen and the President were happy to see used); for relations between Stassen and Dulles, see Ambrose, *Eisenhower*, 401.

[78] Entry for 29 March 1955, Ferrell (ed.), *Hagerty Diary*, 220.

[79] Anthony Leviero, 'Policy Restudied: Eisenhower May State Get-Tough Decision at Coming Talks', *NYT*, 26 March 1955; James Reston, 'Quemoy–Matsu Trend: A Summation of the Factors Involved in Rising Opposition to Defending Isles', *NYT*, 7 April 1955.

the use of atomic weapons would be to cross a vast psychological bridge. Even if such weapons could be restricted to purely military targets, Asians have not forgotten that the only atomic bombs ever used in war were employed against an Asian nation; and Chinese propaganda would be sure to stress the point.' In further oblique references to Carney's injudicious briefing, the paper hoped that the President would not be 'stampeded by zealots into a holy crusade against communism' and that the administration should 'put a muzzle on the tough talk'.[80] A furious Eisenhower was busy doing just that, and he ordered Wilson to crack down on unauthorized comments to the press from the Pentagon and gave Carney what Drew Pearson described as 'the bawling out of his life'. Pearson's widely syndicated column 'Washington Merry-Go-Round' also intriguingly attributed Eisenhower's skittishness over the offshore islands to a letter he had recently received from Hatoyama which had denied the United States use of Japanese bases in the event of war with China.[81] If this letter actually exists, it has yet to come to light in the declassified archival sources, but rumours of its existence indicate the degree to which developments in the crisis and the question of use of Japan for possible nuclear operations were intertwined. In any event, Eisenhower, along with his Secretary of State, were by now resolved to find a way to defuse the sense that war was imminent.

There is further evidence to suggest that Dulles may also have gone through a modest nuclear epiphany during this period. Already having been made aware by Bowie and Smith that the Air Force would probably not hold back if a decision was taken to use nuclear weapons against the mainland, on 24 March Dulles was present when at the end of a largely nondescript NSC meeting (which had included a briefing from Allen Dulles on worldwide reactions to the crisis), a presentation was given by Pentagon officials on the 'effective bombing of hostile airfields'. Eisenhower asked the officers what was the 'cheapest' way to knock out enemy airfields, and received the unhesitating response, with high-yield nuclear weapons. When the President probed further and questioned whether studies had actually been completed on the best types of nuclear weapon to use against airfields, General Twining, the Chief of Staff of the US Air Force, had confirmed that they had, and that the most economical means would indeed be with 'the largest nuclear bombs'.[82]

---

[80] 'Atomic War Over Matsu?', *WP*, 29 March 1955.
[81] 'Washington Merry-Go-Round', 4 April 1955, http://dspace.wrlc.org/doc/get/2041/25053/b13f02-0404zdisplay.pdf, accessed 26 June 2007.
[82] Memorandum of discussion at the 242nd meeting of the NSC, 24 March 1955, DDRS/CK3100132881.

This was obviously far removed from the kinds of attacks against Chinese Communist airfields with small, low-yield weapons that Dulles had been envisaging only a few days before, and may have given pause for thought. A few days later, at a meeting with his senior State Department colleagues, Dulles noted in ironic mode that though they had no knowledge of JCS war plans for China, 'atomic or thermonuclear [i.e. very high-yield] weapons' would undoubtedly feature in attacks on the mainland, and this might not be the best way for Chiang Kai-shek to gain the support of the Chinese people.[83] On 30 March, at a meeting with legislative leaders, he conjectured whether the Russians might be encouraging the Chinese to try to seize the offshore islands 'causing us to use atomic weapons with the resulting great propaganda value to the Communists ... the use of these weapons could well result in a "fall out" which in turn might kill thousands of Chinese'.[84] The following day, when Radford finally gave an outline of JCS planning for war with China to the NSC, it was Dulles who immediately 'expressed considerable concern about the political repercussions of the proposed use of atomic weapons against Chinese Communist military targets', and he is unlikely to have been reassured by Radford's relaxed reply that 'precision atomic weapons would be used, and that except in one or two instances no large cities or concentrations of civilian population were involved in the targets'. Having already complained about the excessive use of nuclear weapons in targeting plans which the Air Force had produced for China in 1954, General Ridgway used this occasion to suggest that an intelligence assessment be compiled of the probable numbers of civilian casualties that might be produced if Radford's plans were implemented.[85] These attempts to quantify a gruesome tally of fatalities built on the earlier efforts by Smith and Bowie in mid-March to produce similar figures for Dulles and emphasized again the concern that indiscriminate nuclear attacks would lose the administration crucial global sympathy during any clash with the mainland and would in fact generate a revulsion against the United States which would prejudice the pursuit of its more general goals in the region.

On the side of several members of the military establishment, however, was a considerable amount of frustration that the administration was not prepared to use the crisis to deliver a decisive check to Communist China's pretensions to regional hegemony. Both Radford and Stump pressed unsuccessfully at times for authority that would allow the

[83] Memorandum of a conversation, 28 March 1955, *FRUS, 1955–1957*, *II*, 410.
[84] Memorandum of bipartisan congressional luncheon meeting, 30 March 1955, *ibid.*, 426.
[85] Memorandum of discussion at the 243rd meeting of the NSC, 31 March 1955, *ibid.*, 432–3.

Chinese Nationalists to launch direct attacks against airfields on the mainland opposite Taiwan, anticipating a Communist response that might necessitate direct US involvement.[86] In military circles, the political and propaganda aspects of nuclear use in the Far East were also under review, but in ways that were at odds to that found in the State Department. In April 1955, officers on the Air Staff in Washington prepared an outline programme of propaganda activities to support atomic operations in defence of Taiwan. Here it was argued that use of atomic weapons would 'initiate propaganda reactions throughout the world, on the part of United States allies and neutrals as well as by the Soviet bloc'. However, the emphasis was on the positive benefits that might accrue to American prestige by stressing that the United States was prepared to take firm and decisive action to offset Communist numerical preponderance in the region and prevent Soviet domination of friendly Asian states and neutrals. Hence, the United States, in order to 'strengthen a desirable climate of world opinion' regarding nuclear weapons, should be 'prepared to initiate coordinated propaganda addressed to friendly, neutral and hostile audiences immediately upon use of atomic munitions'.[87] These upbeat assessments were, of course, by no means universal. Among the JCS, for example, it was Ridgway who tended to exercise a moderating voice throughout, Hanson Baldwin reporting that the Army Chief of Staff opposed the use of tactical nuclear weapons to defend the offshore islands 'because of their adverse psychological effect upon Asia'.[88]

Nevertheless, officials in the Foreign Office in London were concerned that the aggressively interventionist tendencies they had seen exhibited a year before at the time of the fall of Dien Bien Phu were once again manifest in the positions of Admirals Radford, Carney and Stump. One senior official in the Far East Department noted, 'It seems clear … that the Chief of the American Joint Chiefs of Staff and the Head of the Naval Staff are in favour of what would amount to a preventive war against China now with nuclear weapons. The Canadian comment that they found this information frightening seems fully justified.' What alarmed British observers, above all, was their conviction that the Soviet Union would intervene to protect China rather than see its main Communist partner

---

[86] See memorandum of conversation between the President and Secretary of State, 11 April 1955, *ibid.*, 475.

[87] See memorandum by Colonel John J. Hutchison, Directorate of Plans, US Air Staff, 'Propaganda Support of Atomic Operations in Defense of Formosa', 8 April 1955, and attached draft directive for Commander, Far East Air Forces, 11 April 1955, OPD 381 Formosa, sec. 12, box 787, Air Force Plans, RG 341, NARA.

[88] 'U.S. Joint Chiefs Split on A-Bomb', *NYT*, 21 April 1955.

devastated by American nuclear attack. While Sir Harold Caccia, an Assistant Under-Secretary at the Foreign Office, thought that an outright preventive war was unlikely, he took seriously the idea that the military would act in a deliberately provocative manner. At the time of Dien Bien Phu, Radford had made obvious, Caccia reminded his fellow officials, that he was 'in favour of a policy of coat-trailing. Then if the Communists trod on the coat, the aggression would plainly be Communist aggression and the United States would be able, politically, to authorise military reaction.' This was also an attitude that Caccia had observed in Stump at Bangkok, leading to the conclusion that 'the islands of Quemoy and the Matsus have an additional value for the Admirals to the official explanations given by the President and Mr Dulles'.[89]

Eisenhower, however, was determined to keep a firm grip over his more militant subordinates, and during April the imperative became to search for political means to defuse tensions in the Taiwan Strait, and attention increasingly turned to addressing the anomalous position of the offshore islands themselves. To this end, the President began to entertain a scheme where Chiang would be persuaded either to evacuate the offshore islands, or at least to reduce substantially their garrisons, in return for the specific commitment of more American forces which would be deployed to Taiwan. In pursuing this course, Eisenhower was very much aware of what weak ground the United States would stand on if it had to fight over the islands; on 4 April, he was telling his Press Secretary that if the Communists attacked the offshore islands 'we ... could slow them up with atomic weapons, but [he] did not think that it would be wise, unless we are forced to do it, to atomize the mainland opposite them. And even if we did, they could just wait for a while and start the attack over again.'[90] A day later he wrote to Dulles that if the United States had to use nuclear weapons to defend the islands, 'we have ample forewarning of the adverse character of world reaction that would follow any such action ... Public opinion in the United States would, to say the least, become further divided. If conflict in that region should spread to global proportions, we would be entering a life-and-death struggle under very great handicaps ... We would be isolated in world opinion.'[91] By 8 April, Eisenhower and Dulles had agreed a new statement of US policy that favoured viewing the offshore islands as outposts rather than citadels or bastions to be held at all costs, and which might be relinquished rather than fought over on disadvantageous terms. One of the most important

[89] Caccia minute, 6 April 1955, FC1041/718G, FO 371/115046, TNA.
[90] Entry for 4 April 1955, Ferrell (ed.), *Hagerty Diary*, 224.
[91] Eisenhower to Dulles, 5 April 1955, quoted in Ambrose, *Eisenhower*, 245.

negative points if the United States was to come to their defence was that Chinese Communist offensive capabilities against the islands could not be nullified without 'so considerable a use of atomic weapons that there would be risk of large civilian casualties through after-effects, and indeed the inhabitants of Quemoy and even Taiwan might not be immune under certain atmospheric and wind conditions'. The essential problem, then, was becoming how to persuade Chiang to withdraw from these vulnerable positions.[92] The subsequent choice of Radford and Walter Robertson, two of the most pro-Nationalist die-hards in the administration, to act as emissaries to Chiang has drawn rightful criticism from many analysts of the crisis. Moreover, the offer they presented to Chiang, a Nationalist commitment to withdraw from the offshores in return for American 'interdiction' (i.e. blockade) of the sea-lanes opposite Taiwan (to prevent the build-up of Chinese forces which might be aimed at an unlikely invasion), seems fundamentally misconceived as it would have resulted in only a further phase of extreme tension if Chiang had chosen to accept it.[93] As before the onset of the crisis, the administration's responses were frequently conditioned by what would be acceptable to the Chinese Nationalist regime, and by extension, their supporters in Congress.

Nevertheless, by the middle of April, the high tide of popular expectations of direct conflict with China appears to have receded. Makins wrote to the Foreign Secretary from Washington that what he called the 'war party' of 'Senators Knowland and [Styles] Bridges and the Admirals' had little popular backing for their belligerent stance, with Carney's controversial press briefing of late March deemed important in swinging opinion behind a peaceful solution. Dulles had begun to signal the administration's change of tack with his public announcement on 5 April that the United States had no formal treaty obligations beyond the defence of Taiwan and the Penghus. Despite these signs, and in an echo of Eisenhower's comments about the consequences of being seen to back down, the British Ambassador warned that the situation was still precarious: 'there is a large element of face involved on the American side, which combines with hatred of Communists, particularly Chinese Communists, dislike of further retreat in the face of Communist pressure and other emotional attitudes to induce in some people a kind of resignation and disposition to bow to the inevitable. Dulles himself is not immune from the infection of fatalism.'[94]

---

[92] Draft statement prepared in the State Department, 8 April 1955, *FRUS, 1955–1957, II*, 459.
[93] See Chang, *Friends and Enemies*, 135–7, 140.
[94] Makins to Macmillan, 14 April 1955, FC1041/771G, FO 371/115048, TNA.

All participants in the crisis realized that the upcoming Bandung Conference had the potential to play a major role in its outcome. Although some pessimists in the administration felt that Bandung, if it led to endorsement of Beijing's claims to the offshore islands, might embolden the Communists into being more aggressive, Dulles and State Department analysts felt it was more likely that the PRC would use the meeting to underline its approach of peaceful coexistence with its Asian neighbours and pacific intentions. Nevertheless, this prospect in itself was seen as unsettling by many American observers, where fears were sometimes voiced, as noted above, of China, in cohorts with India, posing as the champions of an 'Asia for the Asians' movement against the influence of a white West identified with colonialism and racial discrimination. One *Washington Post* columnist made explicit the linkages between the offshore islands crisis, Bandung, nuclear weapons and race in late March. Noting how the crisis had brought forward the argument that defence of the islands with atomic weapons would 'mobilize Asian hatred against us', Malvina Lindsay also reflected on the fact that at Bandung there was likely to be discussion of thermonuclear testing where 'centuries of pent-up feeling against the West for colonialism, industrial exploitation, racism, and for the more recent employment of atomic weapons against an Asian people, will likely find outlet in talk'. The Chinese delegation could be expected to capitalize on speculation over American nuclear use, with most of non-Communist Asia blaming the United States for the nuclear peril facing the region because

the Americans dropped the first atomic bomb on an Asian city [and] that so many boasts and threats about nuclear weapons have been made by American legislators and warriors. Still another is that hydrogen bomb tests have been held in the Pacific and resulted in the poisoning of some Japanese fishermen. In many Asians' minds nuclear weapons are tied up with racial discrimination. Communist propaganda pictures the United States as brandishing an H-bomb over the world and threatening to make Asian peoples a proving ground for the weapon. Nuclear developments and test explosions of the Soviet Union are conveniently ignored.

There was a pressing need, in Lindsay's opinion, to see a more positive US approach to Bandung in order to offset the image of American 'atomic militarism', and this could usefully start with a reconsideration of the nuclear rhetoric that accompanied discussions of defence of the offshore islands, a point also made in a speech delivered by Thomas Finletter, the former Secretary of the Air Force, before the Philadelphia World Affairs Council.[95]

---

[95] 'U.S. Talk Aids Reds' Bandung Strategy', *WP*, 31 March 1955.

Though reluctant to acknowledge the role its own statements and attitudes towards nuclear weapons might have played in the resentments felt by elements of Asian opinion, within the Eisenhower administration there was also present a sense of foreboding over the omission of any white representation at Bandung. At one meeting, Robert Cutler called the Afro-Asian conference 'segregation of the worst sort' and suggested that a friendly delegate might urge that the conference 'not exclude Occidental nations and that [it] not practice race discrimination the way some Occidental nations have in the past'. This delegate might then, Cutler ventured in bizarre fashion, invite Israel and South Africa to join the gathering.[96] Worries over how the participants at Bandung might exploit the issue of race and the relationship this had to the offshore islands crisis were treated seriously by Dulles and found expression in early April with his dire warnings of the emergence of a pan-Asian movement determined to evict Western influence. One of the prompts for this was an address that Nehru delivered to the Lok Sabha at the end of March, which denounced Western policies, including the construction of military alliances around the world, but had little criticism to level at the Communist powers. In a harbinger of the line Nehru was expected to pursue at Bandung, the Indian Prime Minister specifically attacked SEATO, the Baghdad Pact, American support of Chiang Kai-shek over the offshore islands, as well as the West's failure to put any pressure on Portugal to leave Goa and its silence over apartheid in South Africa. 'Perhaps when the history of this time is written two things will stand out,' Nehru had claimed. 'First is the coming of atomic energy and the other is the emergence of Asia.' Citing the continuing relevance of Gandhi's message, Nehru avowed that only Asian spiritual values could save mankind, with adherence to the *panchsheel* the key. The efforts of the Americans 'to carry the burden of Asia on their shoulders' simply stifled Asia's own voice: 'on the one side one sees Asia, Resurgent Asia, awake – and ... on the other all these attempts in the name of helping Asia, in the name of preserving peace in Asia, promotion of discord and conflict in Asia'.[97] On 7 April Dulles told Makins and Douglas MacArthur II, the Counselor of the State Department, that he was 'considerably depressed ... in thinking over the general situation in Asia', and thought that Nehru's recent speeches meant that 'Asian solidarity in an anti-Western sense might be hardening'.

---

[96] See memorandum from Max W. Bishop for Henry Villard, 31 March 1955, 'Conferences and Meetings: Afro-Asian (Bandung Conference)', box 18, Subject Files, SASAE, RG 59, NARA.

[97] See 'Nehru Condemns the West; Says Alliances Hurt Peace', *NYT*, 1 April 1955; and *The Times of India*, 1 April 1955.

In Asia, Dulles continued, 'we were up against a bigger and more long-term problem than the details or incidents which make daily headlines in the press. In effect, [Dulles] felt that there were Asian elements that were pushing for a pan-Asian movement which would be by its very nature and concept anti-Western.' Makins was asked if the British could use their influence with friendly Asian countries attending Bandung to ease the tensions stirred up by the situation in the Taiwan Strait and the climate of pan-Asianism.[98]

A draft policy statement produced a day later and amended by Dulles emphasized the desirability of Chinese Nationalist forces assuming the main burden of any fighting that might occur over the offshore islands as it was 'of the utmost importance that the issue should not take on the appearance of a struggle between races. A strong effort is being made by the Chinese Communists to create all-Asian sentiment against the white West.' Any fighting should be portrayed as being between Chinese 'and not a fight between the "white" Westerners and the "yellow" Chinese'.[99] This was followed by a longer exposition by Dulles of the dire possibilities that Bandung opened up:

there was a real danger that it might establish firmly in Asia a tendency to follow an anti-Western and 'anti-white' course, the consequences of which for the future could be incalculably dangerous. In this sense the whole concept of human brotherhood, of equality among men, the fundamental concepts of the United Nations, are in jeopardy. It was true, of course, that in the past the record of the Western powers in Asia had not been without regrettable faults. There was nothing to be gained, however, by the Asian and African powers falling into the same faults, particularly the fault of racialism in the opposite direction ... If at the conference only the bad things in the record of the West are emphasized it would be easy to give impetus to an 'Asia for the Asians' movement. The West, of course, has been dynamic and aggressive and frequently shown a sense of racial superiority; but it also has contributed to human welfare in the realm of technical and material progress, and it has carried with it the Christian outlook on the nature of man. The West had carried good things as well as bad to Asia. It would be tragic if the Asians should select only the bad things in the record of the West, such as racialism, to imitate.[100]

In this far-fetched and tangled train of thought, what Dulles overlooked was that the Western record was also reflected in the on-going prevalence of colonialism in its various guises, support for a South African

---

[98] Memorandum of conversation, 7 April 1955, *FRUS, 1955–1957, XXI*, 80–1.
[99] Draft policy statement prepared in the Department of State, 8 April 1955, *FRUS, 1955–1957, II*, 460–1.
[100] Memorandum of conversation between Dulles and Dr Charles Malik, 9 April 1955, *FRUS, 1955–1957, XXI*, 83.

government which built its rule on notions of racial supremacy, and in the United States itself, domestic patterns of segregation and discrimination, on which the Supreme Court's *Brown* decision of 1954 was yet to have any appreciable impact. Indeed, the Court's follow-up implementation ruling in May 1955, which stipulated that the Southern school system should move towards integration with 'all deliberate speed', was sufficiently ambiguous to allow white segregationists to launch a campaign of 'massive resistance' to any attempt at wholesale racial change. The response of the Eisenhower administration, exemplified in the detached stance of the President himself, who was not devoid of the casual 'country club' racism so typical of the time, was to eschew any moves to force the pace and to defer to the aggrieved feelings of the white South.[101]

As the opening of the Bandung Conference approached, other commentators had deep cause for concern at the harm they felt being done to the US image in the region by the policies of the Eisenhower administration. In an article for the *New York Times*, Chester Bowles, by now a familiar voice on the limitations of the Republican approach to Far Eastern issues, warned that unless American policies were modified 'the day may not be far distant when we shall find the balance of power in Asia, and eventually the world, shifting inexorably against us'. Quoting Lenin's old maxim that 'for world communism the road to Paris lies through Peking and Calcutta', Bowles noted how Communist China's prestige had reached a high point as a nation which had broken free from Western domination and was tackling common Asian problems of poverty, illiteracy and low levels of industrial development. 'Moreover,' Bowles continued, 'there is a steadily growing anti-white racial consciousness, particularly in South Asia, which finds a powerful rallying point in the Chinese slogan "Asia for the Asians"', and which the Chinese could be expected to fully exploit at Bandung. Many non-Communist Asians had come to regard the United States as a militaristic nation because of the pronouncements of prominent American leaders; however, 'as the French discovered in Indochina, the decisive power lies not in bombs, but in people'. The key states to the stability of the region, and which had to be won over to the American position, were, Bowles maintained, India and Japan, whose populations made up 75 per cent of non-Communist Asia and contained most of its industrial potential.[102] Despite coming from near opposite ends of the political spectrum, it is striking how closely the

---

[101] Eisenhower often professed his scepticism over integration and his personal opposition to the 1954 *Brown* decision; see Harvard Sitkoff, *The Struggle for Black Equality, 1954–1980* (New York, 1981), 23–7.

[102] Chester Bowles, 'Memo: On Our Policy in Asia', *NYT*, 10 April 1955.

anxieties of Dulles and Bowles mirrored each other, especially when it came to the idea of China being able to pose as the leader of a new 'Asia for the Asians' movement in the shadow of Bandung and Zhou Enlai's approach of peaceful coexistence. It is also clear that the political costs associated with the rhetoric and policy of massive retaliation were felt most keenly in India and Japan, the two states where opposition to nuclear weapons and testing were strongest, and also the two states identified by Bowles as the keys to non-Communist Asia.

When it finally opened on 18 April, the Bandung Conference was, as anticipated, widely recognized for the symbolic importance it held as a gathering of non-white states that had emerged from an era of colonial domination by the West. While the governments of the West and the Soviet Union were preoccupied with the Cold War tensions of ideological rivalry, the balance of power in Europe and the pursuit of the arms race, delegates at Bandung pushed a different agenda of anti-colonialism, opposition to racial discrimination, non-alignment and calls for peace. In his opening remarks at Bandung, President Sukarno claimed that, 'This is the first inter-continental conference of coloured peoples in the history of mankind.'[103] According to Richard Wright, those gathering at the conference felt a sense of 'color consciousness, and they found that ideology was not needed to define their relations'.[104] For Peggy Durdin of the *New York Times*, the conference 'dramatized ... the fact that [the] day of special privilege, position and power for white men in brown and yellow and black men's countries is finished'.[105] To Ba Maw, the wartime Prime Minister of Burma, who had secured that distinction in May 1943 by working with the Japanese occupiers of his country, Bandung reminded him of the 'new spirit stirring in Asia' he had experienced when attending the Great East Asia Conference in Tokyo in November 1943 (an event which had brought together the notionally autonomous governments of Burma, the Philippines, Thailand, Manchukuo, and Wang Ching-wei's Nanjing regime in occupied China). Ba Maw even saw close parallels between the Tokyo Conference's enunciation of the five basic principles of a new order in Asia, and the five principles of the *panchsheel* embraced at Bandung.[106] The racial pattern to world events that Western observers felt that the Far Eastern War of 1941–5 had helped to underline was also being perceived again in the mid-1950s, where pan-Asian unity, under the

---

[103] See Tinker, *Race, Conflict and the International Order*, 103; Odd Arne Westad, *The Global Cold War: Third World Interventions and the Making of Our Times* (Cambridge, 2005), 99–103.
[104] Wright, *Color Curtain*, 150.
[105] Peggy Durdin, 'On Trial – The White Man in Asia', *NYT*, 5 June 1955.
[106] See Ba Maw, *Breakthrough in Burma*, 337, 339.

spur of the transnational struggle against colonialism, might serve to undercut the Cold War shibboleths emanating from Washington and complicate the task of isolating the perceived menace of Communist China.

Alongside the potential for Bandung to polarize issues across a white/ non-white dichotomy, American officials anticipated that the conference would become a forum for the mobilization of anti-nuclear sentiment, including criticisms of US nuclear testing in the Pacific. At the end of March 1955, for example, the OCB considered the probable anti-nuclear resolutions that could surface. Theodore Streibert, the head of USIA, wanted simply to collect information from friendly representatives about how the issue was likely to be presented, but Stassen thought that a 'really good offensive campaign' would be more appropriate. Resolutions could be introduced attacking Communist policies throughout Asia, while Nelson Rockefeller (then acting as a special presidential adviser on Cold War strategy), with support from Stassen, suggested that a resolution dealing with the peaceful uses of the atom, and emphasizing Eisenhower's contribution to this programme, would be helpful. There was general agreement among members of the OCB that a more positive stand on the question of atomic energy was needed at the conference.[107]

Zhou Enlai was certainly prepared to emphasize nuclear issues and themes at Bandung. Referring to the continuation of imperialism in the Afro-Asian region, in his opening speech to the conference, Zhou noted that the people of Asia would never forget that atomic bombs had first been dropped in Asia, that the first man to be killed by a hydrogen bomb had been an Asian (in a reference to Kuboyama Aikichi's death the previous September), and that bases were still being established by outside powers in the area for the purpose of waging atomic war. Espousing the unity and shared resistance of the peoples of Asia and Africa in their struggle against colonialism, Zhou supplemented his initial remarks to the conference with invitations for all the delegates from participating countries to visit China, asserting, 'We have no bamboo curtain, but there are people who are spreading a smokescreen between us.'[108] So much did

---

[107] See memorandum from Max W. Bishop for Villard, 31 March 1955, 'Conferences and Meetings: Afro-Asian (Bandung Conference)', box 18, Subject Files, SASAE, RG 59, NARA. See also Marquis Childs, 'Asian Opinion Moves Against U.S.', *WP*, 12 April 1955, where it was warned that the Chinese Communist 'peace offensive' would stress American nuclear testing in the Pacific, an area where Dulles's rhetoric played into Communist hands.

[108] Speech by Zhou Enlai to the full conference, 19 April 1955, Royal Institute of International Affairs, *Documents on International Affairs, 1955* (Oxford, 1958), 408, n. 2, 412.

Zhou hold the limelight at Bandung, in fact, that many observed that Nehru could not help but feel upstaged. Given that the conference had set itself a rule of unanimity, it was always going to be relatively easy for pro-Western delegates to scupper attempts to pass resolutions which were directed exclusively at the Western powers. Hence, although India and Japan played important roles in the Disarmament Subcommittee, it was possible for Turkey, Lebanon and Iran to ensure that outright demands for the cessation of nuclear testing were turned into more general appeals for all powers to reach agreement to suspend tests in the section of the final communiqué dealing with 'Promotion of World Peace and Cooperation'. On Indian initiative, in one of two separately issued Basic Conference Papers, it was recommended that a study be made of the way radioactivity from nuclear testing was spread through the atmosphere and oceans (the other paper dealt with the conference's shared abhorrence for racial discrimination).[109] The final conference declaration maintained that 'disarmament and the prohibition of the production, experimentation, and use of nuclear and thermonuclear weapons of war are imperative to save mankind and civilization from ... wholesale destruction', and in the meantime called for an international agreement to suspend testing.[110]

The relatively anodyne reiteration of this mantra in the declaration was overshadowed by the role Bandung played in bringing the first offshore islands crisis to a close. On 23 April, as the conference neared its end, Zhou Enlai indicated China's willingness to discuss directly with the US Government ways to reduce tension in the Far East and Taiwan Strait, and professed that the Chinese people did not want war with the United States. After initially and instinctively rejecting this overture, the administration indicated it was ready to begin bilateral talks with Chinese Communist representatives about arranging a cease-fire, something which Beijing would not consider as it did not see itself as being at war with the United States and judged the dispute with Taiwan an internal matter. Nevertheless, some kind of turning point had clearly been reached by the end of April, and with tensions now having eased, Dulles briefed several leading senators on the situation, choosing to emphasize that it was prudent to accept the Chinese offer to negotiate, and that the President was 'reluctant to see a wholesale use of atomic weapons against the densely populated mainland where land bursts would be required which would have fallout which might involve heavy casualties. This might alienate Asian opinion and ruin Chiang Kai-shek's hopes of ultimate welcome back to the mainland.'[111] One senator present recorded the

[109] See *ibid.*, 435, 437–8.   [110] See Wittner, *Resisting the Bomb*, 99.
[111] Memorandum of conversation, 27 April 1955, *FRUS, 1955–1957, II*, 526–7.

Secretary of State as saying that in order to defend the offshore islands, the United States would need to use 'the big bombs to attack the bases on [the] mainland and it might kill a million people'.[112] Dulles had come a long way from his previous talk of using only tactical nuclear weapons of high precision, where both fallout and casualties would be minimized. During May Chinese shelling of the offshores diminished and then stopped altogether, and in July agreement was reached to hold ambassadorial-level Sino-American talks in Geneva. Even though these proceedings often came to involve interminable polemical exchanges, they at least served to underline the point that the likelihood of direct armed conflict had now been much reduced.

Dulles had pulled back from the confrontational line he had initially adopted in January and February, when he had believed that a firm check to Chinese ambitions had to be delivered, to a position by April where he was ready to engage in a diplomatic dialogue of sorts with representatives of the PRC in order to arrive at a peaceful resolution to the dispute.[113] There were several reasons for this change of emphasis, but considerations of the impact of nuclear use on allied opinion, and increasingly on a watching Asian audience, played a significant role in persuading the Secretary of State that the political costs of limited war would be prohibitive. This was especially so when Dulles was made to understand that attacks on mainland airfields (which might even involve high-yield, thermonuclear weapons) were not going to be the virtually civilian casualty-free panaceas that he had at one time hoped. Instead, any retaliation with nuclear weapons was almost by definition going to be 'massive', and there was always a danger that, once nuclear use was initiated, the military would soon expand their actions to a much more extensive series of strikes against a wider Chinese target system.

Alongside this, there was also the special sensitivity that it was believed an Asian audience felt towards nuclear use, the atomic bombings of Japan having occurred less than a decade before, and with the impact of *Bravo* still echoing around the region. In the summer of 1955, USIA looked back on the issues it had had to confront during the crisis, where a 'common element in the varying reactions was the conviction that in a war with Communist China the United States would resort to the use of atomic weapons. In the Far East, USIA was forced to deal with mixed emotions regarding the use of atomic weapons against Asiatic peoples, and to

---

[112] Diary entry, 28 April 1955, box 282, H. Alexander Smith papers, Mudd Library.
[113] On Dulles's 'tough' line in February, see the discussion in Rushkoff, 'Eisenhower, Dulles and the Quemoy–Matsu Crisis, 1954–1955', 474–5.

counter communist propaganda designed to stir up race hatred.'[114] In the context of the Bandung Conference, where the dimension of race had figured so prominently, and where American leaders had evinced their fears over dangerous pan-Asian and anti-white sentiment forming, finding non-military means to resolve the crisis became all the more pressing. Dulles, in particular, had recognized that race, public pronouncements about nuclear weapons and the possibility of war with China had provided powerful propaganda for attacks on American policy. Eisenhower, for his part, had frequently voiced his concern over the political consequences that would flow from any use of nuclear weapons to defend the offshore islands.

In the aftermath of the first offshore islands crisis, there was a general realization on the part of administration officials that the New Look's goal of winning widespread acceptance of reliance on nuclear weapons for security as a permanent and necessary feature of international relations was a long way from being fulfilled. One factor here was the way the image of the United States was suffering due to its inability to put together convincing proposals for general measures of disarmament after all the publicity given Harold Stassen's new role. Rather than launching any new initiatives, Stassen was soon having to compose a response to the proposals introduced by the Soviet Union into the UN-sponsored London Disarmament Conference in May 1955, which had been deadlocked since it first convened in February. These indicated a greater degree of Soviet flexibility, in that they included ideas for the complete abolition of nuclear weapons and the cessation of tests, but were still deficient in US eyes as they were devoid of inspection checks and safeguards. Whatever one made of the genuineness of Soviet intentions, there could be no doubting that Moscow had boosted its credibility in the eyes of the anti-nuclear movement and, for some observers at least, appeared keener than Washington to ease the tensions of the accelerating arms race. Stassen's own proposals for the reduction of armaments, presented to the NSC in late June 1955, were comprehensively rejected by the Pentagon and JCS, who doubted any agreement with the Soviet Union was really possible unless a basic change in Moscow's attitude became apparent. Recognizing that the United States would have to be more forthcoming with schemes for disarmament if it were not to lose the support of public opinion in allied states and possibly the use of overseas bases, Dulles composed a memorandum in June 1955 which noted that the 'frightful

---

[114] NSC 5525, 'Status of United States Programs for National Security as of June 30, 1955', 31 August 1955, *FRUS, 1955–1957, IX: Foreign Economic Policy; Foreign Information Program* (Washington, DC, 1987), 531.

destructiveness of modern weapons creates an instinctive abhorrence to them and a certain repulsion against the strategy of "massive retaliatory power"'.[115] American nuclear sabre-rattling had indeed helped to intensify worldwide concerns over the apparently cavalier attitudes on display in Washington. As well as acting to undermine the administration's goal of removing the stigma attached by international opinion to nuclear weapons in general, it had made it extremely difficult to 'sell' the distinctions between the selective use of tactical nuclear weapons against military targets, and the more wholesale use of larger-yield thermonuclear weapons against urban centres of population.

The repercussions of these trends were perhaps felt most acutely in Japan, where use of American bases for nuclear purposes in the event of general or limited war was a subject of much private soul-searching from US officials. In May 1955, Allison responded once again to Dulles's continuing queries over whether it was now feasible to introduce the nuclear components of atomic weapons to US bases in Japan by repeating his earlier opposition to any such move, and this time asking whether General Hull could reassess the military need for such a deployment in the light of the political risks this step would carry. Hence, in early June, Dulles wrote to Wilson informing him that 'under present conditions it would be most unwise to attempt to introduce atomic weapons into Japan unless there is a present urgent military necessity to do so which could be made clear to the Japanese Government'. This was coupled with a request that the re-examination mentioned by Allison should be conducted.[116] Opposition agitation in Japan on the nuclear issue had not abated since Hatoyama's press conference remarks in March, which had suggested he would be willing to see US nuclear weapons stockpiled in Japan, and the Government's hand was forced when, on 27 June, Shigemitsu came before the Diet and explained he had reached an 'understanding' with Allison at the end of the previous month that US forces in Japan did not then have atomic weapons, and that Washington would not introduce them without the Japanese Government's approval. He also maintained that the security treaty and administrative agreement that accompanied it did not give the Americans authority to base nuclear weapons in Japan. This seemed to quell domestic unrest, as least temporarily, but such an assurance went much further than anything the Americans had actually

---

[115] See memorandum by Dulles, 29 June 1955, *FRUS, 1955–1957, XX,* 141. Dulles reiterated the point that more positive moves towards disarmament would need to be made at the NSC meeting held on 30 June 1955; see *ibid.,* 150.

[116] See Smith memorandum for Dulles, 'Deployment of Atomic Weapons to Japan', 2 June 1955; Dulles to Wilson, 3 June 1955, 'NN-Japan 1955', box 2, Country and Subject Files, SASAE, RG 59, NARA.

offered the Japanese. The State Department, moreover, felt they had enough legal cover through the administrative agreement to allow for deployment of nuclear weapons, if this was considered necessary in the future. Shigemitsu now appeared to be asserting the right of the Japanese Government to interpret such cardinal elements to the relationship with the United States in accordance with its own preferences.

Faced with this display of unwelcome clarity from Tokyo over arrangements where studied ambiguity was in best American interests, the administration decided that it could not allow this new position to stand. In a subsequent letter of 7 July, Allison informed Shigemitsu that he had made no commitments over nuclear weapons in a conversation that they had held on 31 May, and that the US Government was under no obligation to follow any particular course of action in this regard. In reply, Shigemitsu backed down and affirmed that he understood that the Americans did not feel themselves bound by any alleged understanding.[117] Yet at the end of the same month, another atomic storm was raised, when reports from Washington sources reached Japan that the US Army was deploying nuclear-capable artillery and short-range Honest John surface-to-surface missiles to the Far East, and that some of the latter were going to Japan under a secret agreement with the Japanese Government. Confusion may have arisen from a briefing General Hull had given Shigemitsu in March, where he had explained that he planned to introduce Honest Johns to the forces in Japan, and that though they were capable of firing either conventional or nuclear warheads, he had no intention of moving the latter to Japan except in a war emergency.[118] Whatever the case, Hatoyama and Shigemitsu had to publicly deny the existence of any secret agreement, or a plan to deploy Honest Johns with nuclear warheads, with the leading Japanese newspapers again giving the story major prominence. One result of this was that the Japanese Government's plans to force the passage of two controversial bills through the Upper House of the Diet, one which would have created a Defence Council to plan rearmament, and the other to look at revising the 1946 constitution to confirm the legality of rearmament, were derailed by the Socialists who were able to stage a filibuster centred on the atomic rockets issue until the Chamber recessed for the

---

[117] The Allison–Shigemitsu correspondence and its background is alluded to in State Department Office of Intelligence Research, Report No. 7466, 'The Relationship of Japan to Nuclear Weapons and Warfare', 22 April 1957, '21.52 Country File: Japan Intelligence Reports 1957', box 424, Country Files, SASAE, RG 59, NARA; see also Swenson-Wright, *Unequal Allies*, 139.

[118] See Martin E. Weinstein, *Japan's Post War Defense Policy, 1947–1968* (New York, 1971), 81–2.

session.[119] The fact that this latest controversy came just a few days before the tenth anniversary of the Hiroshima bombing added to the strength of the Opposition's attacks.

The exchanges between the Defense and State Departments during 1955 over the introduction of the nuclear components of atomic weapons into Japan were revealing on several counts. In being the final determiner of how such a movement would impact on US–Japanese relations, the State Department was able to curb and check the obvious enthusiasm of the military establishment to store nuclear weapons so that they would be available for immediate use. While initially being concerned that the Japanese case was undermining the New Look's assumption that nuclear weapons should be treated in the same fashion as conventional arms, by the summer of 1955 Dulles appears to have come round to the view, expressed by both his Ambassador in Japan and by Gerard Smith, his Special Assistant for Atomic Energy, that the military should re-examine their own requirements regarding deployment of the new weapons, in order that the political sensitivities of the host country should be recognized. Dulles's June 1955 comments about the 'repulsion' of international opinion against the concept of 'massive retaliatory power' came in the same month he had to acknowledge the overriding nature of Japanese political objections to deployment.

At no point did the State Department entertain the notion, floated by the Pentagon, that the nuclear components of atomic weapons should be introduced to American bases in Japan without the knowledge of the Japanese Government. Given the climate of opinion in Japan, it was clearly advisable that nuclear weapons should be stored in areas that were not subject to such searching public scrutiny or that did not involve interpretation of existing treaty provisions governing the operation of bases and consultation with foreign governments. Hence, the US bases on Okinawa were perceived as especially attractive as a prime location for the storage of nuclear weapons, and movement of complete atomic bombs to that island first seems to have occurred in late 1954 (while periodic deployments to the remoter location of Guam were under way as early as June 1951). It is also significant that in November 1955, at exactly the same time that the State Department was turning aside a renewed request from the Pentagon to consider deployment of nuclear components to Japan, Dulles mounted no objection to the dispersal of a small number of nuclear weapons to the Bonin and Volcano Islands. On 6 February

---

[119] See Tokyo to Department of State, No. 266, 30 July 1955, 711.5611/7–3055, RG 59; 'Atomic Artillery Sent to the Far East', *NYT*, 29 July 1955; 'Atom Gun Idea Disturbs Japan', *NYT*, 30 July 1955; 'Tokyo Diet Close Kills 2 Key Bills', *NYT*, 31 July 1955.

1956, the first weapon, with its nuclear core, was moved to a store on Chichi Jima.[120] As long as they could rely on Okinawa, the Bonins and Guam, the JCS were ultimately prepared to accept the constraints they faced when dealing with the Japanese base issue. In the longer term the Air Force looked towards moving away from primary reliance on the fleet of B-47 medium-range bombers that had underpinned the expansion of SAC in the early 1950s, to the new heavier and longer-range B-52, where in-flight refuelling meant that it could operate effectively from bases in the continental United States. To some this held the prospect of overcoming the overseas base dilemma, where nuclear issues always raised complicated matters of negotiation and consultation with host governments holding their own sets of interests and answerable to volatile domestic public opinion. Nevertheless, and as we shall see, growing fears for the vulnerability of the US base structure to an incapacitating Soviet first strike from 1957 onwards meant that the value of overseas bases for SAC's nuclear planning could not be discounted, as they allowed for a more dispersed air offensive against the Soviet Union and provided for a wider distribution of SAC's mushrooming stockpile of nuclear weapons.

For many American critics of the Eisenhower administration's whole tenor and approach to Asia, the offshore islands crisis was illustrative of the absurdities and dangers of applying the military practices of containment, which had first been devised in the European setting, to the Far East, where the problems of the area were so very different. It was, after all, some argued, the policy of 'unleashing' Chiang in 1953 that had led to the Nationalist garrisons of the offshore islands being reinforced so heavily, and to the islands being used as a base for small-scale raids on Chinese coastal shipping and various intelligence gathering and sabotage operations against the mainland. Despite the peaceful end to the first offshore islands crisis, by harnessing American credibility and prestige to such dubious figures as Chiang and Syngman Rhee, it was considered inevitable that wider American influence would suffer. Harold Isaacs composed a memorandum in mid-March 1955, summing up liberal complaints about the Republican conduct of policy over the previous two years. It charged that, 'American relations with Asia and the whole non-Western world are at a low and dangerous ebb. They are so low that even if there is time for a change, retrieval has become an overwhelmingly formidable task. They are so dangerous that we might at almost any hour stumble into an unwanted war with Communist China that will make

---

[120] See memorandum for Radford, 'Dispersal of Atomic Weapons in the Bonin and Volcano Islands', 4 June 1957, file 476.1, box 44, Chairman's Files: Admiral Radford, RG 218, NARA.

retrieval infinitely more difficult.' Turning the situation around would require a 'massive renovation of our entire approach to our world policy problems', including 'an extension of our steadily improving domestic race relations to the international sphere'.[121] 'The problem remains, as it has been since 1952,' Isaacs wrote to Chester Bowles one month later, 'whether these unbelievably incompetent people will wreck irreparable damage and carry us beyond the possibility of retrieval before it is too late.'[122]

For Isaacs, gatherings such as Bandung were representative of the new sense of Asian identity with which American policy would have to come to terms. Within the Eisenhower administration, though, the conference had been seen in a very different light. Rather than spur any fundamental reappraisal of US policy towards the developing world, Bandung induced a sense of relief in the administration with its relatively moderate and even-handed tone, while anti-Western and anti-white sentiment had not predominated in the way some had feared. Dulles explained that the conference had actually been 'dominated by a group of friendly Asian nations who believed in association with the West'. The final communiqué was felt to be an unobjectionable document, most of which the United States could even subscribe to, with its references to colonialism 'in accord with what we feel in our hearts (though we are unable to say them publicly)'. Most pleasing of all was that Zhou Enlai's conciliatory line was attributed to China's knowledge that the use of force in the Taiwan Strait would have been unacceptable to the other Asian leaders present, and so the conference could be deemed to have had a deterrent effect on otherwise aggressive Chinese behaviour and as such had 'played a decisive role at a most critical period in world events'.[123] In general, the administration congratulated itself that the psychological operations it had carried out in the build-up to Bandung, and the diplomatic work behind the scenes with friendly delegations it had undertaken, had done a very effective job at protecting American interests in the region.[124]

---

[121] Harold Isaacs, 'Draft on Asian Policy', 14 March 1955, folder 337, box 140, Bowles papers.

[122] Isaacs to Bowles, 21 April 1955, *ibid.*

[123] See minutes of a Cabinet Meeting, 29 April 1955; and memorandum of conversation between Dulles and Counselor of the Turkish Embassy, 4 May 1955, *FRUS, 1955–1957, XXI*, 91–2, 94–5.

[124] See Jason C. Parker, 'Small Victory, Missed Chance: The Eisenhower Administration, the Bandung Conference, and the Cold War', in Kathryn C. Statler and Andrew L. Johns (eds.), *The Eisenhower Administration, the Third World, and the Globalization of the Cold War* (Lanham, MD, 2006), 165–70.

In one sense, however, the most important outcome of Bandung was beyond doubt, witnessing as it did the emergence of the PRC as a leading player in independent Asia, respected for her role in challenging Western dominance rather than for the Communist ideology she had adopted, or the alliance she maintained with the Soviet Union. For decision-makers in Beijing, the succession of nuclear threats that Washington had employed against China since the arrival in office of the Eisenhower administration served to convince them that the security guarantee represented by the Sino-Soviet alliance of 1950 had to be augmented by Chinese acquisition of its own nuclear capability. Despite the enormous costs involved, and the uncertainties of a successful outcome, as the offshore islands crisis began to escalate in intensity in January 1955, the Chinese politburo initiated a major nuclear programme. A degree of Soviet help was readily accepted in the first instance, but with the emergence of the Sino-Soviet split by the end of the decade, it would be largely through immense indigenous effort and ingenuity that the Chinese would progress along their own nine-year path to an atomic bomb. The Chinese atomic programme meant that the charge that the bomb was a 'white man's weapon' would ultimately have a limited lifespan, but this point remained some time in the future, and in the meantime Beijing continued to echo the ongoing Soviet peace campaign and to highlight the way the United States used its nuclear weapons to intimidate in Asia.[125] Indeed, it was in this so-called Bandung phase of Chinese diplomacy that Beijing sought to woo neutralist states with its attacks against Western imperialism, which, it alleged, was perpetuated by a network of military alliances, with SEATO crucial in this context. Explaining the dilemmas of American defence policy in Asia, an area where there was 'fierce underlying resentment of real or believed attitudes of racial superiority in the West', Walt Rostow, busy crafting his reputation as a policy advocate and intellectual at the Massachusetts Institute of Technology's Center for International Studies, noted that 'the Chinese Communists are seeking to work around our atomic weapon delivery capability by diplomacy, blackmail, subversion, and limited military operations that afford neither satisfactory atomic weapon targets nor a political setting in which we find it possible to launch a direct attack upon the centers of Communist strength'.[126] As we shall see, responding to Communist propaganda attacks against the deployment of American nuclear power in the Far East became increasingly difficult as nuclear strength was nevertheless used to underpin the Western contribution to the defence of South East Asia.

---

[125] See John W. Lewis and Xue Litai, *China Builds the Bomb* (Stanford, 1988), 38–42.
[126] Walt W. Rostow, *An American Policy in Asia* (New York, 1955), 9, 41.

8   A nuclear strategy for SEATO and the problem of limited war in the Far East

The sense of relief that the course of the Bandung Conference and its immediate aftermath induced in the Eisenhower administration was relatively short-lived. Bandung may have failed to add momentum to any nascent 'Asia for the Asians' movement, generated no overriding current of anti-Western sentiment, and helped to reveal some of the tensions between India and the PRC over who should hold the limelight, but at the same time it had served to underline that there was an attractive path of neutrality open to newly independent states. The conference 'above all marked the watershed between neutralism as a negative refusal to take sides and a positive policy'.[1] The non-aligned movement, as it could now be termed, threatened to disrupt the close embrace with the West and rejection of contacts with the Communist world favoured by Washington; it also helped to mobilize a wide current of opinion behind an agenda that included both the principle of racial equality and opposition to nuclear testing. What most disturbed the Americans was the concern that home-grown Asian drives for independence and national self-assertion might be exploited by forces originating from outside the area. Therefore, it was especially worrying when, at the end of 1955, the Soviet Union embarked on a major effort to cultivate influence in the developing countries of Asia. Before this period, Moscow had shown little interest in taking direct initiatives in this part of the world, but now it seemed ready to offer generous amounts of economic aid, alongside its own model of state-led development for emulation.[2] The East–West conflict, as one NIE put it in November 1955, was 'shifting from a phase marked by direct Bloc threats and pressures to one marked by increasing emphasis on less obvious forms of Communist political warfare'. The West's reaction to the new Communist policies had to be considered, the NIE noted, 'against the background of growing concern over the devastating consequences of

---

[1] Wilfrid Knapp, *A History of War and Peace, 1939–1965* (London, 1967), 260.
[2] On the Soviet leadership's attitude to the developing world in the period after Stalin's death, see Westad, *Cold War*, 66–8.

all-out nuclear war. The most important effect of growing nuclear capabilities is to diminish the willingness of most governments and peoples to
incur risks of war.' As a result, it was conjectured, the West faced an even
more serious threat than that posed by Stalin's aggressive early post-war
policies, and it was now confronted by 'a period of less obvious hostility,
harder to identify as such or to meet by such means as deterrent forces or
military alliances'. This new phase of competition with the Communist
bloc was liable to see the 'gradual erosion of Free World positions' rather
than any dramatic showdown. In the countries of the non-Communist
world the fear of nuclear confrontation would produce more tendencies
for accommodation with the Soviet Union and PRC, and pressure for the
general reduction of armaments. Enhanced Soviet nuclear capabilities
might also lead to more local wars, as Soviet leaders calculated that the
United States and its allies would be unwilling to begin a nuclear war
which might bring on their own destruction.[3]

The basic problem about how to deal with local conflicts when worldwide abhorrence felt towards nuclear weapons showed no signs of abating, and when US military doctrine was geared more than ever to their use
in many different settings, was by now a perennial issue for US policy-
makers. In December 1955, Dulles was venting to Eisenhower his belief
that, '[O]ur whole international security structure [is] in jeopardy. The
basic thesis [is] local defensive strength with the backing up of United
States atomic striking power. However, that striking power [is] apt to be
immobilized by moral repugnance.'[4] Earlier that same month, the
Secretary of State had made some effort to again clarify the administration's stance when he had delivered a speech which mentioned that the
American 'arsenal of retaliation should include all forms of counter-attack
with maximum flexibility ... Our *capacity* to retaliate must be, and is,
massive in order to deter all forms of aggression. But if we have to *use* that
capacity, such use would be selective and adapted to the occasion.'[5] While
to Dulles this might have seemed a reasonable and proportionate position,
with the offshore islands crisis only a few months in the past, critical
observers were still aware that he was ready to see the United States
initiate the use of nuclear weapons against local Communist aggression,
with all the consequent chances of escalation to a wider nuclear exchange

[3] See NIE 100–7–55, 'World Situation and Trends', 1 November 1955, *FRUS, 1955–1957,
XIX*, 131–45; also Robert J. McMahon, 'The Illusion of Vulnerability: American
Reassessments of the Soviet Threat, 1955–1956', *International History Review*, 18, 3,
August 1996, 591–616.
[4] Dulles memorandum of conversation with Eisenhower, 26 December 1955, quoted in
Gaddis, 'Origins of Self-Deterrence', 142.
[5] 'Text of Dulles Speech on Tactic Soviet Now Uses', *NYT*, 9 December 1955.

with the Soviet Union. This prospect had become all the more menacing in November 1955, when at the end of its latest series of tests, the Soviet Union managed to air-drop a large thermonuclear weapon.[6] The resulting spread of atmospheric fallout was registered in Japan and across Europe, adding to anxieties about the consequences of war and the environmental impact of continued testing. By late January 1956, the Secretary of State was warning that current trends were leading to a situation where 'our allies will not permit us to have recourse to nuclear weapons except to retaliate for their use by the Soviets'; the Soviet capacity to mount a devastating nuclear attack and the 'repugnance to the use of nuclear weapons could grow to a point which would depreciate our value as an ally, undermine confidence in our "collective defense" concepts, and make questionable the reliability of our allies and the availability to SAC of our foreign bases'.[7] At the same time, although their testing was protested by anti-nuclear groups in the West and Japan, the Russians escaped some criticism for their behaviour by following their series with renewed calls for a reciprocal test suspension with the United States, which because it contained no safeguards against infringement, such as measures of inspection, was rejected by Washington. The Eisenhower administration could also hardly attack the Soviet Union for irresponsible testing when its own record was so poor, and when, urged on by the JCS, the AEC and the nuclear laboratories, it had every intention of maintaining a strong testing programme.[8]

When it came to the overall picture in Asia, the development that really shook Washington during this period was the tour undertaken by Nikita Khrushchev and Nikolai Bulganin to India, Burma and Afghanistan in November–December 1955 and the offers of aid that came in its wake. The Soviet leaders finished their visit to India by joining with Nehru in issuing a communiqué calling for the 'unconditional prohibition of the production, use and experimentation of nuclear and thermonuclear weapons'.[9] Moreover, Communist spokesmen now took it upon themselves to praise the practice of neutralism as a way of preserving independence. To Eisenhower, the new Soviet tactics promised to undercut long-held US positions, and in early December he was telling Dulles of his feeling that the international situation was in the process of being transformed, while to the NSC he offered the view that the character of the struggle with the Soviet Union was changing and meeting the new

---

[6] For the significance of this Soviet test, see DeGroot, *The Bomb*, 194–5.
[7] Memorandum of discussion at the 274th meeting of the NSC, 26 January 1956, *FRUS, 1955–1957, XX*, 298; Dulles memorandum, 28 January 1956, DDRS/CK3100502478.
[8] See Divine, *Blowing*, 65–6.   [9] *Ibid.*, 66.

threat was 'a very difficult job – almost as hard as it had earlier been to meet the military challenge'.[10] Congress was duly asked for an extra $100 million for long-term foreign aid to deal with the new Soviet policy, and the following month Dulles warned that defeat in the contest of economic development would be 'as disastrous as defeat in an armaments race'.[11] In the ideological battle for influence, US officials also believed that the Soviet Union, due to its supposed part-Asian 'racial' characteristics, possessed clear advantages in appealing to a non-European audience. Following an NSC meeting where it was asked why Communist aid programmes in the developing world seemed to be received more positively than American offers of help, Sherman Kent, the CIA's head of the Office of National Estimates, responded that this was due to the legacy of colonialism and the racial dynamic at play:

These former colonial countries suffer from an inferiority complex in dealing with the West. This causes them to react in the classic way of self-assertion and opposition. Also unfortunately over many decades Westerners have too often acted in a tactless and overbearing manner. They don't forget the Kipling concept of 'lesser breeds'.

The Communists are very astute in their approach. They have created the impression that they do not look upon these people as 'backward' or 'under-developed', phrases we have too often used. The struggle between the Soviets and U.S. and Western Europe, together with the racial and geographic background of the Soviets, have made it possible for the Soviets to get themselves accepted as non-Europeans, as fellow Asians.[12]

With the Soviet Union perceived to be holding such significant advantages in appealing to the developing states of Asia, it was all the more important, administration officials were coming to realize, that American racial practices at home should be either obscured for an overseas audience, or at least projected by USIA in a narrative of progress, and that American policy show no sign of the racial bias that acted to drive many newly independent nationalist elites in Asia away from close association with the United States. This certainly seems to have lain behind Dulles's thinking during this period; in early 1956 he had, for example, asked Dean Rusk, then heading the Rockefeller Foundation, to carry out a study of ways to improve

[10] See Eisenhower to Dulles, 5 December 1955, *FRUS, 1955–1957, IX*, 10; memorandum of discussion at the 269th meeting of the NSC, 8 December 1955, *ibid.*, 44–64; see also Merrill, *Bread and the Ballot*, 123–8.
[11] See 'Dulles Confirms Plan to Increase Foreign Aid Fund', *NYT*, 21 December 1955; 'Dulles Spurs U.S. in Economic War with Soviet Union', *NYT*, 12 January 1956; see also Connelly, *Diplomatic Revolution*, 95–6.
[12] Sherman Kent memorandum for Allen Dulles, 'Reasons for the Impact of the Soviet Orbit's Military, Economic and Cultural Drive in the Middle East, South and Southeast Asia', 29 November 1955, folder 9, box 100, Allen Dulles papers, Mudd Library.

relations with the developing world, and expressed interest in staging a 'reverse Bandung' conference, with the intention of 'demonstrating a community of interest across racial lines and a slowing down of the racially conscious antipathy now developing in non-white areas'.[13]

It was also in this context that the Eisenhower administration began to evince greater interest in neutralism as an approach that might lead gullible leaders into unhealthy relationships with the Soviet Union. American officials recognized that they had to do more to at least *appear* to be working towards the dismantling of the colonial empires if they were to win plaudits among the new nationalist leaders of the developing world. Nevertheless, there were few signs that these aspirations would feed through into active policy, particularly as the 'Europeanists' at the State Department cautioned against any initiative which might disrupt established relationships with generally reliable NATO partners (a case in point here was Dulles's ham-fisted public description and acceptance of Goa as a Portuguese 'province' in December 1955, which soured relations with India even further). If anti-colonialism was not to find practical expression, then the administration needed to revamp its aid policies towards neutralist states in order to compete with Communist overtures. This meant that US allies would not necessarily receive preference when it came to deciding aid priorities, Eisenhower informing the NSC in December, for example, that 'it was clearly to the security advantage of the United States to have certain important countries like India strong enough to remain neutral or at least "neutral on our side"'.[14] Dulles, for his part, seemed to oscillate between dire warnings about the perils of neutralism and denunciations of the immorality of it as an approach to international relations, to a more realistic appreciation that aid policies towards neutral states had to be flexible. In January 1956 he told Selwyn Lloyd, the British Foreign Secretary, that they should be

more vigorous than we have been in combatting the idea of neutralism. He said that he is more than ever convinced that it will become difficult to prevent a Communist take-over of the neutral governments if they continue to adhere to their view that the world problem is merely a power struggle between two blocs which does not affect their countries. This kind of thinking fits right into the whole Communist conspiracy to take them over ... These neutral governments do not seem to realize that the Communist intentions are so diabolical and so hostile to their freedom and independence. [Dulles] was afraid that they would eventually succumb unless they could develop a crusading spirit against the evil forces of Communism.

[13] Quoted in Cohen, *Dean Rusk*, 82–3.
[14] Memorandum of discussion at the 269th meeting of the NSC, 8 December 1955, *FRUS, 1955–1957, X: Foreign Aid and Economic Defense Policy* (Washington, DC, 1989), 47.

In the same conversation, however, he stressed that it was 'important to provide help to the neutral countries in order to help keep them from going over to the Communist side ... the all-or-nothing approach would throw them into the Soviet arms unnecessarily while there is still some salvation possible'.[15] His famous attack on neutrality as an 'immoral' and 'shortsighted' principle, delivered at Iowa State College in June 1956, was actually aimed at a domestic audience, when the administration's increased budget for the Mutual Security Program, which included foreign economic aid, was running into serious congressional opposition.[16] The Iowa speech illustrated the American dilemma in stark fashion: while the administration had to show that the alliances it sponsored and led served US interests, it also had to demonstrate to an international audience that they did not make mere stooges of their other members.

The balancing act that had to be performed in Asia was no better illustrated than over SEATO, whose existence was an affront to neutralist sensibilities, but which had also been trumpeted by the Eisenhower administration as an essential pillar of collective security in the region. Some American policy-makers would argue that the attractions of neutralism made it very important to highlight the advantages that membership of Western-led alliances could bestow on those lucky enough to be afforded their protection. Indeed, by the autumn of 1955 there was serious concern in the State Department over indications that the Asian members of SEATO had become disillusioned with that organization. The Americans were being criticized in Bangkok and Manila because, as Douglas MacArthur II, the Counselor of the State Department, put it, there was a 'general impression ... that the Manila Pact organization has bogged down and nothing really constructive is being accomplished'.[17] There was specific dislike of the way abrasive American commanders such as Admiral Stump tended to disregard the views of Asian officers at the initial meetings of SEATO staff planners and military advisers held in April and July 1955, respectively (the meetings themselves were regarded as a 'waste of time and resulted in nothing except making plans for future conferences').[18] According to MacArthur, there was an urgent need to 'breathe life into the blue baby' of SEATO, and that 'unless the Council

---

[15] Minutes of United States–United Kingdom Foreign Ministers Meeting, 31 January 1956, *FRUS, 1955–1957, XXI*, 169–71.

[16] See the persuasive discussion in Guhin, *Dulles*, 256–62.

[17] See memorandum by MacArthur for Dulles, 1 October 1955, *FRUS, 1955–1957, XXI*, 145, n. 2; see also memorandum of conversation, Department of State, 6 October 1955, *ibid.*, 144–9.

[18] See Lieutenant General Charles P. Cabell (Deputy Director, CIA) to Dulles, 12 September 1955, *ibid.*, 126–7.

could show at their [next] meeting in March [1956] that SEATO was real, and not just words on a piece of paper, the scepticism and disappointment which the Asian members were already expressing would become so great that SEATO would have no hope of recovery'. One major difficulty, as MacArthur explained to British officials in Washington, was the 'inability of the Asian members to play their proper part in directing it because of their lack of knowledge and experience. Inevitably the Western members must play the major role – but at the same time the Asian members must be made to feel that it was their show'.[19]

As part of these efforts to reassure their allies that they took their defence needs in South East Asia seriously, in October 1955 Admiral Stump and his staff at Honolulu drew up a paper which asserted that only the bombing of selected targets on the Chinese mainland, using both nuclear and non-nuclear weapons, offered an effective counter to a major Chinese attack directed through Laos and South Vietnam toward Thailand. These ideas were presented to the second conference of SEATO staff planners (held during the first half of November at Pearl Harbor).[20] British officials were, however, anxious that all this sudden new discussion of military planning, particularly mention of nuclear weapons, would have the effect of rekindling Asian neutralist feeling against SEATO.[21] Their fears were seemingly confirmed when a Reuters report carrying the substance of the staff planners' conclusions was published in the *Singapore Free Press* on 11 November with the eye-catching headline 'A-Plan to Beat Reds in S. E. Asia', leading one official to comment that 'public threats of atom bombing are scarcely likely to be helpful at the present stage and, when associated with the name of SEATO, are likely to give excellent propaganda opportunities to the neutralists'.[22] Sir Robert Scott, the Commissioner General for South East Asia, hoped that in future publicity about SEATO nuclear planning could be avoided, though this was problematic given the rhetorical stance adopted by the American administration.[23]

Anxieties about how an Asian audience might react to Western nuclear policies in South East Asia continued during the first half of 1956. At their

---

[19] Washington (Makins) to Foreign Office, No. 2924, 1 December 1955, D1071/468; Sir H. Graves to Denis Allen, 2 December 1955, D1071/473, FO 371/116932, TNA.

[20] See 'Report on 2nd Conference of SEATO Military Staff Planners', Annex to COS(55) 349, 23 December 1955, DEFE 5/63, TNA.

[21] See Scott to Allen, 29 November 1955, D1071/472, FO 371/116932, TNA.

[22] A. A. Dudley to F. S. Tomlinson, 12 November 1955, D1071/451, FO 371/116931, TNA.

[23] See also Scott to Allen, 13 December 1955, and Allen to Scott, 2 January 1956, D1071/502G, FO 371/116933, TNA.

second meeting held in Melbourne in January 1956, the SEATO military advisers had agreed to endorse the conclusions of the previous staff planners' conference: that in the absence of a large-scale commitment of conventional forces to the region, the alliance should accept that early nuclear counteraction was the only way that an overt Chinese Communist attack on South East Asia could be contained. It was recognized that this would give heart to its Asian members, but unfavourable responses were anticipated in India, Burma and Indonesia if this were publicized.[24] There already had been evidenced a ripple of concern over the fact that the first major military exercises staged under SEATO auspices (dubbed *Firmlink*), held in Thailand in mid-February, had involved American forces flying into Bangkok airport equipped with Honest John atomic-capable rockets, the same weapon system that had caused a stir of unease when first introduced into Japan the previous summer, underlining the fact that it would be difficult to keep the nuclear dimension to the potential American contribution to the alliance entirely quiet.[25] With the SEATO Council due to meet in Karachi in March 1956, where member states would give official endorsement to the report of the military advisers, and so explicitly accept a new strategy for the alliance that involved use of nuclear weapons, the issue became one of joint Anglo-American concern (the supposition of many Western officials was that lax security around the Karachi meeting meant that the news was bound to leak, and the British, in particular, felt that the Pakistanis would want it widely known in order to impress the Indians).

In London, the subject of the new SEATO strategy was judged of sufficient importance to be discussed by the full Cabinet at the end of February. The Commonwealth Secretary, Lord Home, presented a paper which admitted that acceptance of nuclear use for planning purposes was necessary, not least to sustain the morale of SEATO's Asian members, but went on to warn:

Unless matters are handled with great care, any publicity is likely to have serious repercussions throughout Asia and in India in particular. Very deep emotions may be aroused: Asia had not forgotten that the only atom bombs dropped have been on Asians. There is a danger that the effect may be to drive India, China and Russia into each other's arms and to raise the question of white superiority. (Atomic weapons would not – for the time being at least – be put into the hands of Asian troops but would be retained to be used by the 'white' Powers.)

---

[24] See Annex to JP(56)44(A), 17 February 1956, DEFE 6/34, and COS(56)87, 25 February 1956, DEFE 5/65; Scott to FO, No. 9 Saving, 18 February 1956, D1071/147G, FO 371/ 123221, TNA.
[25] See 'U.S. Forces Plan Thai Arms Test', *NYT*, 8 February 1956.

Home cautioned that everything possible must be done to mitigate the possible impact of the decision.[26] In the Cabinet discussion that followed, Selwyn Lloyd reinforced this with his own concerns over the effect in countries such as Malaya, where the British hoped to retain bases for the support of SEATO operations after independence had been granted (scheduled for August 1957 by negotiations which had only just been concluded, but the defence aspects of which had yet to be finalized). Lloyd, who would lead the UK delegation at the SEATO Council, was instructed to ensure at least that no explicit reference to nuclear matters be made in the final communiqué, while he would consult with Dulles over how to handle the issue.[27] Makins, the British Ambassador in Washington, was also instructed to deliver a memorandum to the State Department that conveyed the view that though the Government accepted the need to take account of nuclear weapons in military planning,

we consider it most important to recognise that the question of the use of atomic weapons, even if only as a basis for defence planning, is bound to be a particularly sensitive one in Asia. Any knowledge that SEATO military planning is proceeding on this basis is liable to arouse very deep emotions: Asia has not forgotten that the only atom bombs dropped have been dropped on Asians. These emotions will be exploited by the Communists and the results in the uncommitted countries, especially India, might well be far-reaching. Moreover, we have to give special thought to the situation in Malaya and Singapore ... we are hoping, in the course of future rapid progress towards full self-government for these territories, to secure defence agreements which will provide us with the base facilities we must have in order to continue to play an effective part in SEATO. This issue of nuclear weapons is perhaps more likely than any other, if wrongly handled, to prejudice our chances of securing such agreements, particularly as the opponents of the defence treaties will not hesitate to point to the dangers of nuclear retaliation.[28]

At exactly the same time as the Cabinet discussions in London, the NSC in Washington was debating the fact that recourse to the use of nuclear

---

[26] 'SEATO: Nuclear Weapons', CP(56)57, 27 February 1956, CAB 129/80, TNA. Home had earlier alerted the Prime Minister to this problem in a similarly phrased minute which noted the possibility of 'violent repercussions' and repeated that it raised the whole issue of 'white superiority in its acutest form'; see Home minute for Eden, 27/56, 25 February 1956, DEFE 13/228, and in D1071/165G, FO 371/123221, TNA.

[27] CM(56)17th Conclusions, item 1, 28 February 1956, CAB 128/30, TNA. These previously withheld documents were declassified following the author's request to the Cabinet Office.

[28] FO to Washington, No. 1125, 29 February 1956, D1071/165G, FO 371/123221, TNA; and see also FO brief for Lloyd discussions with Dulles, n.d. (but c. late February 1956), D10345/4, FO 371/123208, TNA. An internal note from November 1980 in FO 371/123221 reveals that the editors of *Foreign Relations of the United States, 1955–1957*, XXI sought permission to publish the British memorandum (contained in Telegram No. 1125), but this was refused; the telegram along with its parent file has now been declassified following the author's request to the Foreign and Commonwealth Office.

weapons could not be an automatic decision of national policy when faced with war, and that political factors had to be taken into consideration. Having been subjected to the familiar view of Admiral Radford, the Chairman of the JCS, that an imaginary dividing line between nuclear and non-nuclear weapons was hampering military planning efforts, the President responded by raising the implications of nuclear use in small or peripheral wars, pointing out that this would present 'serious political problems' considering the 'current state of world opinion as to the use of such weapons'. Eisenhower went on to predict that it would be some time before the United States could ignore the political repercussions of a military course of action. Dulles echoed the views of the President and advised that any decision on the automatic use of nuclear weapons 'might actually prove disastrous to the United States', and added a 'warning of the terrible repercussions which we would experience if we had recourse to the use of nuclear weapons against the colored peoples of Asia'.[29] When Makins presented British concerns to Douglas MacArthur II (the official Dulles relied on most in preparing for international conferences), he was reassured that the State Department appreciated the 'psychological' factors involved at Karachi, while it is clear from the evidence of the NSC discussions that Dulles was certainly alive to the racial element surrounding nuclear issues in the region.[30]

At the Karachi meeting itself, at the final session, Lloyd 'made a strong plea for secrecy' over approval for nuclear planning, and Dulles himself suggested adopting the line that, in its final communiqué, the Council would mention that it had merely 'taken note' of the military advisers' report, without revealing its contents.[31] This was all some way from the position that Dulles had adopted at the first SEATO Council meeting in Bangkok the previous February, where despite his own private awareness of the sensitivities surrounding the subject, he had been ready to explain in more public terms the 'mobile striking power' of American air and naval units equipped with 'modern weapons' which could be brought to bear in the region. It was an indication of how awareness of these issues had developed that he was now more circumspect about what could be presented in public. There was, of course, little realistic prospect of any detailed nuclear planning being done under the auspices of SEATO,

---

[29] See memorandum of discussion at the 277th meeting of the NSC, 27 February 1956, *FRUS, 1955–1957, XIX*, 203–6.

[30] See memorandum of a conversation between MacArthur and Makins, 'SEATO Military Planning', 29 February 1956, *FRUS, 1955–1957, XXI*, 179–80.

[31] See Karachi (from Lloyd) to Foreign Office, No. 55 DORAN, 8 March 1956, D1071/198, FO 371/123222, TNA; telegram from the US delegation at the SEATO Council meeting to the Department of State, 9 March 1956, *FRUS, 1955–1957, XXI*, 200–2.

such was American secretiveness about their nuclear intentions, where even their closest Western allies such as the British had to struggle to get the barest glimpses of Pentagon thinking from their contacts and sources in Washington. All the same, the British did manage to glean from their informal discussions with American officers that they were thinking of nuclear attacks on about fifty targets in southern China and North Vietnam, an estimate which tallied with British target studies and threat evaluations compiled at this time.[32]

Publicity surrounding the nuclear policies of the West always tended to be a contentious issue, but early 1956 was a particularly delicate moment for the issue of nuclear planning in SEATO to arise. Much of this was of the Secretary of State's own making. Amid concerns that the Eisenhower administration's foreign policy was failing to cope with the uncertainties of the developing Cold War, in January 1956 Dulles chose to give an interview to *Life* magazine where he expounded at length on the merits of a tough approach to the expansionist tendencies of the Communist powers. In particular he pointed to the warnings delivered to the Chinese in 1953 that the impasse in the Korean armistice negotiations had to be broken, the movement of aircraft carriers to the South China Sea in April 1954 at the time of the Dien Bien Phu crisis, and the uncompromising stance adopted over the offshore islands in 1954–5, as instances where his actions had averted aggression and defended American 'vital' interests. He further continued, in a classic example of Dulles's vanity and gift for the tactless statement:

You have to take chances for peace, just as you must take chances in war. Some say we were brought to the verge of war. Of course we were brought to the verge of war. The ability to get to the verge without getting into war is the necessary art. If you cannot master it, you inevitably get into war. If you try to run away from it, if you are scared to go to the brink, you are lost ... We walked to the brink and we looked it in the face. We took strong action.[33]

---

[32] For American views, see Annex to JP(55)119(Final), 14 October 1955, DEFE 6/31, TNA; 'Report on 2nd Conference of SEATO Military Staff Planners'; Secretary JIC (Far East) to Secretary JIC, SEC 242, 4 February 1956, DO 35/6052, TNA. The basic British study envisaged attacks on fifty targets using up to seventy nuclear weapons, each with a yield of no more than fifty kilotons; see 'The Probable Effect of Allied Nuclear Counter-Action on the Potential Communist Chinese Military Threat to Malaya and Thailand Starting from South China (1955–1960)', JIC(55)63(Final)(Revise), 18 November 1955, contained in DC(55)54, 25 November 1955, CAB 131/16, TNA.

[33] 'How Dulles Averted War', *Life*, 16 January 1956. Such statements had a wide resonance: one senior Foreign Office official cautioned the British Ambassador in Bangkok over a recent public remark where he had referred to SEATO as 'packing a potential punch' in the context of the suicidal effects of nuclear war, with the advice, 'you know our doubts about the wisdom of over selling SEATO on the publicity side. Apart from this we are particularly anxious on general policy grounds to go *very* easy for the present on the atomic

The Secretary of State's critics in the Democratic Party and beyond had a field day. Not only did they find his claims dubious, but his attachment to nuclear 'brinkmanship' (as it was soon dubbed), over what most regarded as peripheral rather than truly vital interests, attracted much scorn. By extolling the idea that bringing the world to the brink of a nuclear war in order to extract diplomatic advantage was some kind of esoteric art form and a legitimate approach, Dulles attracted an avalanche of criticism, while highlighting that such 'nuclear diplomacy' might be central to the conduct of US foreign policy was also hardly a message that the administration was happy to see conveyed. Adlai Stevenson attacked the remarks in a press conference, several Democratic senators called for his resignation, and the Speaker of the House, Sam Rayburn, lambasted Dulles for a 'pitiful performance' that would put a strain on US alliances.[34] While forced to publicly defend his Secretary of State, Eisenhower acknowledged that 'unfortunate expressions' might have been used in the *Life* article and, in what observers took as an implied rebuke for Dulles, expressed his view that he thought it improper to discuss the past, present or future decisions of the NSC in public.[35]

Nevertheless, public discussion of the role of nuclear weapons in possible limited war was becoming more prevalent by this time, fuelled by the output from the small industry of defence intellectuals and academic practitioners of the new field of strategic studies who were taking the study of deterrence and nuclear war into ever-more complex and involved realms. An increasingly common theme of much of this commentary on massive retaliation was how bankrupt the strategy was in view of burgeoning Soviet nuclear capabilities, and how ineffective or disastrous it could prove to be when peripheral areas were subject to Communist threat. How to ensure the 'credibility' of deterrence became the *sine qua non* of defence policy in the nuclear age, and to many this meant it was incumbent on the authorities in Washington to show less regard for the need to hold down budget expenditures, and more for increasing the conventional capabilities of US forces so that they acquired the capacity for 'extended deterrence'. For a contemporary critic such as Robert Osgood, the lessons of the Korean experience were clear: 'If the nation as a whole is unwilling to expend its lives and resources upon limited military engagements that

deterrent, especially in Asia and at the present stage of SEATO military planning. (The recent *Life* article on Mr Dulles and his policies is a good example of how *not* to handle it.)' Allen to Gage, 20 January 1956, D1071/58, FO 371/123216, TNA.

[34] James Reston, 'The Strange Case of John Foster Dulles', *NYT*, 15 January 1956; 'Rayburn Assails Dulles Stand', *NYT*, 17 January 1956.

[35] See 'Transcript of First Full-Dress News Conference Held by President Since Aug 4', *NYT*, 20 January 1956; also Hoopes, *John Foster Dulles*, 308–11; Sherman Adams, *First Hand Report: The Story of the Eisenhower Administration* (New York, 1961), 117–20.

promise no clear-cut resolution of the struggle for power, then no military establishment will be adequate to sustain a successful strategy of containment.'[36] A corollary to this debate was more analysis of the impact of tactical nuclear weapons on strategic calculations, and on whether their use in limited war was feasible or would simply hasten the stage at which escalation to a more general nuclear exchange would occur. The most famous of these contributions was probably Henry Kissinger's *Nuclear Weapons and Foreign Policy*, which spent thirteen weeks on the bestseller lists in the autumn of 1957.[37] While much of this literature concerned a NATO–Warsaw Pact confrontation in Europe, or possible scenarios over a future Berlin crisis, there was an obvious applicability of some of this thinking to the Far East, where massive retaliation had experienced some of its sternest tests. The main point to make in the Asian context however was that the United States faced a Chinese adversary which was non-nuclear, at least for the foreseeable future, making the question of at what point the Soviet Union would intervene to help its Chinese ally if it was subject to US attack with nuclear weapons one of the most central pre-occupations of Western intelligence analysts in the 1950s. As if to emphasize the damage the issues surrounding massive retaliation could cause, at the same time that Eisenhower was defending Dulles over the attacks that had followed his *Life* article, the President was also fending off accusations from Ridgway that had appeared in a *Saturday Evening Post* piece that he had cut the Army's funding in the 1955 budget round on the basis of political and financial considerations, rather than on grounds of national security (ever since his retirement as Army Chief of Staff in June 1955, Ridgway had been seething that his name had been associated with initial JCS approval for the New Look, and his criticisms of the administration were now becoming ever more vocal).[38]

The subject of when and how nuclear weapons would be used in conditions short of general war with the Soviet Union was a feature of

[36] See Osgood, *Limited War*, 189; probably the most important contribution to the debate was William W. Kaufmann (ed.), *Military Policy and National Security* (Princeton, 1956). Kaufmann's carefully presented arguments, defence of the Korean intervention and view that for any deterrent to be credible the punishment should fit the crime found a very receptive audience among Army officers suffering under the cuts of the New Look; see Kaplan, *Wizards*, 190–6.

[37] See Henry Kissinger, *Nuclear Weapons and Foreign Policy* (New York, 1957), and on the essentially derivative and flawed nature of this analysis, see Lawrence Freedman, 'Kissinger', in Baylis and Garnett (eds.), *Makers of Nuclear Strategy*, 105–7.

[38] 'President Denies Ridgway Charges', *NYT*, 20 January 1956. Ridgway's article was part of an advance serialization of his memoirs, which contained a fuller critique of massive retaliation; see Matthew B. Ridgway, *Soldier: The Memoirs of Matthew B. Ridgway* (New York, 1956).

several discussions within the confines of the NSC in this period, and one where Eisenhower can be found expressing contradictory or ambivalent views. In the February 1956 NSC meeting where the President had voiced his belief that political factors would need to be considered in any use of nuclear weapons in limited war, he also recalled the frustrations brought about by the limitations placed on US military action during the Korean War. This was a conflict, the President told the Council, 'which we were obliged to fight with handcuffs on ... in the future these peripheral wars must not be permitted to drag out. We must now plan to fight peripheral wars on the same basis as we would fight a general war. After all, there was no good reason for drawing distinctions between peripheral and general wars. Had we not made up our minds that if the Communists renewed their aggression against Korea we would go "all out" to meet it?' When Dulles, defending the State Department's position that US capabilities should remain flexible, asked if this meant the United States might drop atomic bombs on Beijing if North Vietnam attacked the south, Eisenhower replied in the negative but asserted rather that the bases in China which were supporting such aggression would be attacked.[39] Nevertheless, NSC 5602/1, the final updated document outlining the administration's basic national security policy, which was issued by the Council on 15 March 1956, retained and amplified some of the flexibility regarding responses to limited war that could also be found in the wording of its predecessor, NSC 5501. Forces to meet local aggression, it was maintained, had to be able to use both conventional and nuclear weapons, and

> must not become so dependent on tactical nuclear capabilities that any decision to intervene against local aggression would probably be tantamount to a decision to use nuclear weapons ... The apprehensions of U.S. allies as to using nuclear weapons to counter local aggression can be lessened if the U.S. deterrent force is not solely dependent on such weapons, thus avoiding the question of their use unless and until the deterrent fails. In the event of actual Communist local aggression, the United States should, if necessary, make its own decision as to the use of nuclear weapons.[40]

The ambiguities over whether and under what circumstances nuclear weapons might be used in limited war made it especially problematic for

---

[39] Memorandum of discussion at the 277th meeting of the NSC, 27 February 1956, *FRUS, 1955–1957, XIX*, 210–11. The present author's interpretation of this meeting is at some variance with that offered in Craig, *Destroying the Village*, 57–8, who sees Eisenhower as unambiguous in his stance over limited war. See also Kenneth W. Condit, *History of the Joint Chiefs of Staff*, Vol. VI: *The Joint Chiefs of Staff and National Policy, 1955–1956* (Washington, DC, 1992), 19.

[40] NSC 5602/1, 15 March 1956, *FRUS, 1955–1957, XIX*, 247.

the Pentagon to budget its programmes over the next few years, some-thing which Radford found increasingly frustrating. On a fundamental level, ever since the adoption of NSC 162/2 in late 1953, the Chairman of the JCS had accepted that the use of nuclear weapons had to be built into virtually all military planning assumptions, and that these in turn would yield the force requirements of the services. In June 1956, Radford reminded a Department of Defense conference that 'as we approach the year 1960, the possibility of military action not involving the use of nuclear weapons is going to become increasingly remote … We are simply in a position where we have to base our planning on using atomic weapons when militarily advantageous. It is important that every individual with a role in military planning know and understand this national policy.'[41] Radford was, however, uneasy whenever the reservations of those at the highest levels of government were made apparent on this basic question and knew that the budgetary savings emphasized by the New Look would not be attainable if a capability for conventional-only military operations had to be maintained alongside forces adapted for operations in a nuclear environment. Another problem was continuing dissent from the Army leadership over the adoption of the New Look and the painful cuts in manpower that they were now being required to make. Most annoying here was the fact that Ridgway's successor as Army Chief of Staff, General Maxwell D. Taylor, was proving just as obstinate when it came to accept-ing the administration's strong emphasis on the strategic nuclear deterrent.[42] Taylor foresaw a strategic environment where mutual deterrence at a general level would create only more opportunities for local and limited aggression, hence the United States needed 'balanced strength … in various forms appropriate to deter or to fight small wars' so that it could 'put out brush fires promptly before they can spread into general war'.[43] Testifying to Congress in early 1956, in a fashion that could only damage the administration, Taylor argued that the defence budget should put more emphasis on flexible land forces with the non-nuclear capability to meet the threat of limited aggression.[44]

During the spring and summer of 1956, in response to injunctions from the President that more economies in defence spending would have to be found, Radford tried to force through the JCS a new Joint Strategic Objectives Plan (JSOP, the basic medium-term US war plan) which

[41] 'Important Factors in Military Planning for 1956–1960', Radford address to Quantico Conference of Defense leaders, 23 June 1956, B-55025, box B-206, LeMay papers, LC.
[42] See Maxwell D. Taylor, *Swords and Plowshares* (New York, 1972), 170–1.
[43] Taylor speech, 31 October 1955, quoted in Andrew J. Bacevich, *The Pentomic Era: The U.S. Army between Korea and Vietnam* (Washington, DC, 1986), 51.
[44] See Watson, *New Look*, 613–15.

would determine force planning and goals up to 1960, and which contained deep cuts in US service personnel.[45] The opposition he encountered from Taylor and the Marine Corps led him in May to appeal to Eisenhower and to speak in the NSC of his 'great concern that occasions might arise when aggressions occurred and the armed forces of the United States would not be permitted to use atomic weapons to meet such local aggression'. In the absence of a decision in advance, he felt the Defense Department would still have to plan to equip its forces with both adequate conventional arms and nuclear weapons, with all the implications this held for the defence budget: 'the right to use atomic weapons in instances of local aggression was still the key question, and the National Security Council could not continue to straddle it'. Nuclear weapons could be used effectively to defend against local aggression, and the United States 'must have the courage to make the decision to do so'. Despite his own strong wish to control military spending, the President was not at this stage prepared to fully endorse Radford's line. Instead, Eisenhower preferred to place these arguments in a wider context, observing that the subject of limited war was 'not nearly so simple' as was imagined, and that 'strong opposition' would have to be overcome from some allies over the use of bases on their territory for the launching of nuclear attacks: 'While ... he agreed with ... the general theory [regarding the use of nuclear weapons in defence against a local aggression] we could not overlook all the political problems which were involved in it. We must proceed so that we are sure of retaining the friendship of the free world.' Though clarifying the position for the JCS was obviously desirable, Eisenhower cautioned that the United States must move very slowly in this area and cited progress with NATO allies, who 'were now clamoring that we share atomic weapons with them; whereas only a couple of years ago they had recoiled in horror from all thought of employing nuclear weapons'.[46]

Only four days later, however, Eisenhower was telling Radford in a private meeting that he was 'inclined to feel that we would not get involved in a "small war" extending beyond a few Marine battalions or Army units. If it grew to anything like Korea proportions, the action would become one for atomic weapons.'[47] Radford had gone to the President in order to appeal for support over Taylor's resistance to the budget cuts involved in

---

[45] *Ibid.*, 654–62.
[46] See memorandum of discussion at the 284th meeting of the NSC, 10 May 1956, *FRUS, 1955–1957, XX*, 397–9.
[47] See memorandum of a conference with the President, 14 May 1956, *FRUS, 1955–1957, XIX*, 302.

the new JSOP, and on 24 May Eisenhower had upbraided the Army Chief of Staff, holding that in limited wars, 'the tactical use of atomic weapons against military targets would be no more likely to trigger off a big war than the use of twenty-ton "blockbusters" … the support forces we provide [for small wars] would use the most efficient weapons, and over the past several years tactical atomic weapons have come to be practically accepted as integral parts of modern armed forces'. Taylor left the meeting understanding that Radford's views had the full support of the White House.[48] This kind of categorical stance, however, was not always reflected in Eisenhower's other statements from this period. For example, on 17 May, when confronted during an NSC meeting with the argument that a greater reliance on nuclear capabilities would allow forces to be reduced in Korea and Taiwan, Eisenhower demurred, countering with the thought that 'this business of arguing that you are going to defend these countries through recourse to nuclear weapons isn't very convincing. In point of fact, these countries do not wish to be defended by nuclear weapons. They all regard these weapons as essentially offensive in character, and our allies are absolutely scared to death that we will use such weapons.' Using nuclear weapons in anything other than the defence of the United States, the President noted, would prove 'very difficult'.[49] This hardly makes Eisenhower seem a model of consistency, when Radford was hoping for the services to plan on the use of nuclear weapons in the event of almost any degree of fighting, but merely reflected the uncertainties that swirled around these crucial issues.

These tensions were further displayed in the forum of the NSC in June 1956, when the State Department was this time ready to argue that the use of nuclear weapons should only be a matter of last resort, rather than the first response of the US military. The occasion was when Radford presented outline plans to the NSC on how South Vietnam would be defended by the United States from a North Vietnamese attack, now that the French Expeditionary Corps had finally been withdrawn. The plan envisaged US-trained and equipped South Vietnamese forces forming the main line of defence, with enemy troops and lines of communication being attacked with nuclear weapons by US air and naval forces; only three American regimental combat teams at most would be involved on the ground. It was expected that the SEATO Treaty would be invoked and token contributions of forces made by other member states.[50] In

---

[48] Memorandum of a conference with the President, 24 May 1956, *ibid.*, 311–15.
[49] See memorandum of discussion at the 285th meeting of the National Security Council, 17 May 1956, *ibid.*, 307.
[50] See Condit, *JCS and National Policy, 1955–1956*, 232; Spector, *Advice and Support*, 272–3.

response, Dulles called upon the Assistant Secretary for the Far East, Walter Robertson, to put forward the State Department's view that, 'of course, all members of the NSC would agree that the use of atomic weapons in Asia would have the very gravest impact on public opinion throughout Asia, and that we would not resort to the use of atomic weapons in that area except in the gravest of situations'. These kinds of political reservations did not please the JCS Chairman, and he specifically excluded himself from association with Robertson's remarks; Diem, Radford asserted, was, in fact, relaxed about the use of nuclear weapons in the face of Communist aggression.[51]

The concern that the Pentagon's determination to follow through on the logical implications of incorporating nuclear weapons into force structures and planning for limited war, backed with the seal of presidential approval, might produce negative consequences for American diplomacy in Asia was also seen in several small but revealing examples in the aftermath of SEATO's adoption of nuclear planning assumptions at the Karachi Council meeting. In one minor spat, in April 1956 Defense Department officials had sought what they thought would be routine State Department concurrence for involvement by US forces with atomic capability in forthcoming SEATO military exercises, but Dulles had vetoed their participation because of the possibility of 'serious political repercussions in Asia'. Officials from the Pentagon's Office of International Security Affairs protested, pointing out that *Firmlink* had already been carried out near Bangkok in February with US atomic capability on display with no apparent consequences (in fact, they claimed, it had been met with enthusiasm by the Thais), but these were rebuffed. Urged on by a frustrated CINCPAC, further representations were made by the Pentagon during May. At the beginning of June, Stump made a concerted appeal to the State Department which expressed concern over the future effectiveness of SEATO if US forces having an atomic capability were banned from military exercises. The CNO, Admiral Arleigh Burke, made a similar plea to the JCS to suggest to the Secretary of Defense that he raise the matter with Dulles in order that the impasse be resolved.[52]

Publicity surrounding use of nuclear weapons in the SEATO area was also the subject of further Anglo-American exchanges during this period. One outcome of Karachi was a decision to raise the organization's profile

[51] Memo of discussion at the 287th meeting of the NSC, 7 June 1956, *FRUS, 1955–1957, I: Vietnam* (Washington, DC, 1985), 699.
[52] See memorandum from Burke to Radford, 25 June 1956, and the attached summary of actions regarding SEATO, 092.2 SEATO, box 19, Chairman's Files, RG 218, NARA.

in the region through the appointment of a Public Relations Officer based in Bangkok.[53] Fearful that this new post would be turned by the pugnacious Americans into merely a source of what British officials called 'extreme or provocative' anti-Communist propaganda, the Foreign Office stepped in quickly with a draft directive to guide public relations policy. This included the proviso that the new officer should 'avoid any statement hinting however indirectly at the possibility of the use of nuclear weapons'.[54] By May 1956, the Americans were experiencing great problems accepting this part of the British draft, MacArthur telling Makins in Washington that Dulles had taken a personal interest in the issue, and that the State Department did not want to subscribe to any document that could give any apparent support to the view that the use of nuclear weapons was 'inherently wicked'. At the same time, they wanted some purely oral understanding 'based on the inexpediency of public references to the use of nuclear weapons in view of the climate of opinion in Asia'.[55] Perhaps the chief problem for Dulles was that he did not trust SEATO security, and that any leak of text from a directive that even mentioned nuclear use, especially following the Karachi endorsement of nuclear planning assumptions, would be seized on and exploited by those hostile to Western policies. The publication of any such wording might even carry the implication, so Dulles conjectured, 'that our hands were tied in the matter of use of nuclear weapons if the Russians committed an act of aggression'.[56]

Not all US representatives in the region were as attuned as Dulles and his State Department colleagues to the nuclear issue. Sir Humphrey Gage, the British Ambassador in Bangkok, hoped that the Foreign Office and State Department could settle the problem of how to restrict mention of nuclear weapons without appearing to do so, not least as his American opposite number was prone to advertise their utility at every opportunity. Gage reported that Max Bishop, the US Ambassador to Thailand, was

in favour of maximum publicity for all forms of military power (especially American) which are available for the defence of SEATO countries, and that he includes in this weapons such as 'Honest John' and certain types of aircraft which he gleefully emphasized have 'atomic capabilities'. He told me categorically that he

---

[53] On the role of the Public Relations Officer, see George Modelski (ed.), *SEATO: Six Studies* (Melbourne, 1962), 33.

[54] See F. S. Tomlinson minute, 31 May 1956, D1071/321G, FO 371/123229, TNA.

[55] Washington (Makins) to FO, No. 1129, 8 May 1956, D1071/293G, FO 371/123227, TNA.

[56] Washington (Makins) to FO, No. 1207, 24 May 1956, D1071/321G, FO 371/123229, TNA. The Philippines Government was regarded as the least secure in SEATO; see Cable minute, 10 March 1956, D1071/198, FO 371/123222, TNA.

did not believe that there was any particular sensitivity about nuclear weapons in South East Asia and that in fact all the Governments in the area were in their hearts glad that these weapons were available to deter would be aggressors.

Such displays of 'immoderate emotionalism in his approach to Communism', which stood in complete contrast to the low-key British approach, Gage thought should be stifled.[57] As a result, in early June 1956, MacArthur was presented by Makins with an Aide Memoire which outlined the central difficulty that the American and British representatives to SEATO were facing over publicity, with the former unable to agree to anything which implied any distinction between conventional and nuclear weapons. The Foreign Office wanted to remind Dulles that they felt from the conversations which had been held at Karachi that the State Department also subscribed to the view that nuclear issues were of particular delicacy in Asia; nothing should be revealed which might allow it to be implied that SEATO was resolved to use nuclear weapons in all circumstances. In this instance MacArthur reassured Makins that the US Ambassador in Bangkok had been told that he should reach an oral understanding with the British that SEATO's publicity materials should contain 'no mention or inference regarding the use of nuclear weapons' (it is also worthy of note that the NSC discussions over the adverse consequences on Asian opinion of any nuclear use in Vietnam occurred only a few days after these Anglo-American exchanges).[58]

These problems were symptomatic of the real dilemmas that US defence policy were causing the State Department as US force posture and operational doctrine in Asia were beginning to be transformed by the New Look. The programme embraced by the Pentagon in late 1953 had envisaged major cuts in conventional ground force strength in the Far East, and while the Indochina crisis of 1954 had placed a brake on rapid redeployment back to the continental United States, by 1955 the programme of troop withdrawals was again well under way. With the deactivation of the 1st Cavalry Division in Japan during 1956, the only ground forces remaining in the Far East would be the two infantry divisions in South Korea (7th and 24th), an army regimental combat team in Japan, and the 3rd Marine Division along with one further army regimental combat team on Okinawa.[59] Moreover, in June 1956, the Pentagon

[57] Bangkok (Gage) to FO, No. 268, 28 May 1956, D1071/321G, FO 371/123229, TNA.
[58] See UK Aide Memoire, 1 June 1956, and Washington (Makins) to FO, No. 1271, 2 June 1956, D1071/346G, FO 371/123230, TNA.
[59] See Wilson memorandum for the Executive Secretary of the NSC, 'Deployment and Strength of U.S./UN Forces in the Far East', 1 June 1955, US Policy toward Far East (1954–9), White House Office, box 8, briefing notes, NSC Records, Office of the Special Assistant for National Security Affairs, White House Office, DDEL.

disseminated the results of a full-scale review of the structure of its global unified commands, as part of the drive for economy and rationalization of effort. The major conclusion reached was that the Far East Command in Tokyo, covering Japan, Korea and North East Asia generally, was to be wound up, with its responsibilities transferred to a vastly enhanced Pacific Command based in Honolulu; Admiral Stump, as CINCPAC, would take over his wide-ranging new remit in July 1957. At the same time, the UN Command which had overseen Korean operations from its headquarters in Tokyo under the old and now defunct US Commander-in-Chief Far East was to be relocated to Korea itself. As well as the savings in personnel and efficiency gains anticipated by this reorganization, Radford also hoped that the move of the UN Command to Korea would boost Korean morale, and the abolition of Far East Command speed up Japanese willingness to shoulder a greater burden of their own defence.[60]

Though accepting the military and budgetary reasoning that lay behind these command changes, the State Department was, however, anxious about their political implications for relations with the Asian states which would fall under CINCPAC's new areas of responsibility. The principal reason for this was that the location of the Far East Command in Tokyo had allowed the US Embassy in Japan to exercise some degree of oversight over the activities of the CINCFE (at least after General MacArthur's dismissal), and for liaison to be developed with the US Ambassador. With the removal of this link, Dulles and the State Department pressed hard for the appointment of a Political Adviser (POLAD) to CINCPAC at Honolulu.[61] Pentagon officials initially appeared relaxed about this proposal, but opposition began to emerge, particularly from Admiral Stump himself, with backing from Burke, the CNO.[62] It took until March 1957 for Burke to be persuaded, but there then followed more protracted discussions over the terms of reference for the POLAD, with the CNO and Stump trying to cut down the role and the latter given the power to remove his State Department adviser if he was deemed 'unsatisfactory'.[63] Even when these matters were resolved, the State Department wanted its

---

[60] Radford memorandum for Goodpaster, 'Unified Commands', 22 June 1956, JCS (3) folder, box 4, Subject Files, Department of Defense, Office of the Staff Secretary, White House Office, DDEL.

[61] See memorandum of a conversation at the State Department, 2 July 1956, *FRUS, 1955–1957, XXI*, 226–7; and see Dulles to Wilson, 27 June 1956, 'CINCPAC (Administrative)', box 1, Subject Files of the Regional Planning Adviser, 1955–63, records of the Bureau of Far East Affairs, RG 59, NARA.

[62] See Marshall Green memorandum for William J. Sebald, 23 October 1956, 'CINCPAC (Administrative)', box 1, Subject Files of the Regional Planning Adviser, 1955–63, records of the Bureau of Far East Affairs, RG 59, NARA.

[63] See Burke to Stump, No. 20115, 4 March 1957, *ibid.*

choice for this tricky assignment, John M. Steeves, to have ministerial rank in order to boost his authority; as Marshall Green, the Regional Planning Adviser in the Far East Bureau, explained to Robertson, 'CINCPAC is a big, free-wheeling organization with an area of responsibility covering half the globe and half the world's population. The State Department has experienced considerable difficulty in maintaining proper liaison with CINCPAC and in having political considerations given proper weight in CINCPAC decisions and actions.'[64]

Wider tensions were beginning to emerge between the Pentagon and the State Department over the foreign policy implications of the US military posture in the Far East. Ostentatious displays of US nuclear prowess or resolve were necessary, so American military chiefs claimed, in order to reassure US friends and allies, and counteract any previous impression of weakness. Discussing coming to British aid if Hong Kong were ever subject to Chinese attack, Admiral Stump explained to one senior British officer in September 1956 that

certain difficulties within SEATO arose from doubts by the lesser SEATO powers that the Western powers would ever, in fact, use atomic weapons. This doubt was inspired by the failure to use these weapons at Dien Bien Phu in the face of opposition by the 'NATO Powers'. He considered it a sensible and practical step, and unprovocative, to announce clearly that atomic weapons would be used in any Far East conflict in spite of objection by the 'NATO Powers'. This was not said by the Admiral in any bellicose manner, but rather on the lines of regret that the Western Powers, in playing a difficult hand, were not prepared to use the cards they held, and which everyone knew they held, to the best advantage.

Discussing likely targets, Stump 'referred several times to the "Canton Complex" and to a subsequent shift to other areas if necessary, Shangai [*sic*] being mentioned ... It seemed clear that his thoughts were concentrated mainly on strategic targets, and that he had not so far given much consideration to the tactical problem.'[65] This attitude to nuclear targeting illustrated one of the central and underlying problems of the massive retaliation era. Even though at the NSC level, where Dulles could inject a State Department view, the injunction was for nuclear weapons to be used selectively and against military targets in situations of limited war as might occur in the Far East, the military authorities had a far more expansive conception of the way they would use the atomic power now at their fingertips.

[64] See Green to Robertson, 28 June 1957, *ibid.*
[65] Notes by Commander of British Forces, Hong Kong (Lieutenant General W. H. Stratton) on meeting with Admiral Stump, 21 September 1956, Appendix II to DCC(FE)(56)9, DEFE 11/172, TNA.

One deeper reason behind the appointment of a POLAD to Stump was to check this tendency to ignore the political ramifications of planning for the use of nuclear weapons, but in the event this step proved to be of negligible impact. Within months of his arrival at Honolulu in the summer of 1957, Steeves was noting that 'it is quite obvious that an area where POLAD should be more effective is in assessing the political assumptions made in connection with war plans. I am never invited into this area of discussion nor do I see any of the papers.'[66] Steeves's deputy, Richard B. Peters, wrote in December that 'the one thing the military cannot do is think like diplomatists. This consideration alone would make a Political Adviser's office here essential. The potential influence of this headquarters is too great to let its essentially military analyses and proposals go uninterrupted by the moderating influence of persons with first-hand experience (rather than just "foreign" experience).' Unfortunately, CINCPAC and his staff were not keen to take advantage of the diplomatic services on offer, while 'in a few important instances, we have been aware that the military has intentionally avoided us. And thus far, in the important "war plans" area, we have been completely excluded.'[67] Peters found the most disturbing aspect of his current work with CINCPAC was how he and Steeves saw 'how terribly restive the military is about its understanding of the growth of Communist strength in Asia. One sometimes senses a feeling of desperation among the staff of this Headquarters. Indeed, unless the American public is satisfied that we are "doing something", there is real danger that military policy will rush in to fill vacuums left by the absence or weakness of non-military American programmes in Asia.'[68]

What that military policy might entail was revealed to Christian Herter, the Under-Secretary of State, when he made a visit to Pacific Command Headquarters in August 1957. In Stump's briefing for the party from Washington, he chose to emphasize the need to reassure the 'leaders of the free countries of the Far East' of American intent in the face of Communist aggression. In recent conversations with Diem, Stump explained, the South Vietnamese president had agreed with his view that the US military response to an attack across the 17th parallel should include the use of nuclear weapons. He had also asked Chiang Kai-shek about Asian reactions to possible use of nuclear weapons against the

[66] Steeves to Walter Robertson, 19 November 1957, 'POLAD/CINCPAC-Letters from (1957)', box 1, Subject Files of the Regional Planning Adviser, 1955–63, records of the Bureau of Far East Affairs, RG 59, NARA.
[67] Richard B. Peters to Marshall Green, 18 December 1957, 'POLAD/CINCPAC-Memoranda', *ibid.*
[68] Peters to Green, 11 December 1957, 'POLAD/CINCPAC-Letters from (1957)', *ibid.*

Chinese mainland, where the latter's reply was that 'if the general populace were warned in advance to stay away from military targets' the popular Asian response would actually be favourable. Stump's Chief of Staff, Vice Admiral George W. Anderson, continued the briefing with a pessimistic appraisal of the situation in South East Asia and warned that the outcome of the Korean War and Dien Bien Phu had weakened the Western position throughout the region. 'As a means of attacking the problem of creating respect for our strength and determination,' Anderson opined, 'he thought it might even be desirable for the West to provoke incidents which would lead the Chinese Communists to overstep the mark, in order that the U.S. could retaliate promptly with overwhelming force.' Anderson dubbed this enterprising ruse a 'mousetrap operation'. When Herter asked what action CINCPAC would take if there was Chinese aggression against Vietnam, Laos or Thailand, Stump replied that he would 'strike heavily' against the support lines of the Chinese attack near the border; if this proved insufficient he would 'use powerful air strikes against the "Canton complex" and, if necessary, even against the "Shanghai complex"'. Stump felt that 'World War III would begin only if the Communists wanted it to begin and would not be determined by the circumstances of a retaliatory attack such as he had outlined'.

Obviously disturbed by what he had heard, Herter sent a copy of the briefing to Howard P. Jones, the Deputy Assistant Secretary for Far Eastern Affairs, and to Frank Wisner at the CIA, who was still head of its covert action arm, noting that there had been 'overtones' from Stump and his staff which had been left out.[69] At the end of September, Herter held a meeting in Washington with over thirty leading State Department, CIA and USIA officials where he reported on his recent trip in which he again shared his concerns over the contents of Stump's briefing and Anderson's notions of setting up a 'mousetrap' for the Chinese Communists (though his remarks were apparently curtailed by a hastily passed note from Walter Robertson warning him that what he had heard in Honolulu was too confidential to divulge to such a large audience).[70] Some of what Herter had described as the 'overtones' of Stump's briefing were indicated by Steeves, who wrote afterwards that Stump and Anderson had 'expressed themselves rather forcibly with respect to what they considered the lack of readiness in Washington to make the rapid fateful decision to use nuclear weapons in limited military action'. For

[69] Herter to Jones, 26 August 1957, and attached memorandum of conversation, 24 August 1957, *ibid.*
[70] See Green to Steeves, 27 September 1957, 'POLAD/CINCPAC-Letters from (1958)', [misfile], *ibid.*

Steeves, the episode brought up the subject of 'whether or not we have ever taken into full consideration in policy planning the fact that we are more and more relying on the ultimate weapon without ever having actually made the decision to use it'.[71]

This was once again a reminder of the ambiguities of the New Look. American war planning would proceed on the assumption of nuclear use where militarily necessary, but as long as the final decision over the use of nuclear weapons continued to rest with the President (something which Eisenhower had explicitly confirmed in January 1954, and reaffirmed in March 1955), then there could be no absolute certainty that their use would be authorized in the event of a Communist attack, including the various limited war scenarios that were possible in the Far East. The Eisenhower administration was, to be sure, beginning to discuss the procedure for pre-delegation of the authority to use nuclear weapons to various subordinate commanders in 1956–7, but this was only in a number of very tightly defined instances (such as in the air defence of the continental United States), and final instructions were not actually issued until 1959. Anxious that American resolve to use nuclear weapons at a very early stage of any fighting in his area of command should be signalled to the Communist side, and to reassure friends and allies, CINCPACs frequently expressed their sense of frustration. Just after Herter's visit in August 1957, Stump had signalled to Burke that it was time 'to stop pussy footing about use of nuclear weapons ... In personal conversations with 2 Presidents, Diem and Chaing [*sic*], they have insisted that we must use our atomic weapons capability, but they both have expressed disturbing doubts about our willingness to do so ... Our weak-kneed approach to atomic play in SEATO exercises is a prime example.'[72] In February 1960, Admiral Harry D. Felt (who had taken over from Stump as CINCPAC in August 1958) can be found arguing 'with vehemence that we were under a constant barrage of propaganda on a global scale emanating from the Communist bloc aimed clearly at undermining our determination to use these weapons, and perhaps more important still at persuading our friends that we lack such determination. To counter this propaganda, we must not only plan to use nuclear weapons if necessary, particularly against China, but we must also give clear evidence of our intention by openly "playing atomics" in our exercises.'[73] To State Department

---

[71] Steeves to Green, 9 September 1957, 'POLAD/CINCPAC-Letters from (1957)', *ibid.*

[72] Stump to Burke, CINCPAC cable no. 9480, 28 August 1957, quoted in Betts, *Nuclear Blackmail*, 70.

[73] Report by Air Marshal the Earl of Bandon on talks with Admiral Felt, 8 February 1960, Annex to COS 252/26/2/60, DEFE 7/2190, TNA.

representatives, on the other hand, there was a tendency to believe that this kind of behaviour served only to alarm states and attentive publics, many of them non-aligned and subject to Communist blandishments, where anti-nuclear sentiment could be a strong force in domestic politics.

In overall terms, during this period the Eisenhower administration was belatedly beginning to co-ordinate the public release of information regarding nuclear weapons, which was often required in order to control the speculation that sometimes surrounded such issues and to ensure that inadvertent disclosure of sensitive news or material was not made by any unwitting official spokesman. The unfortunate experience of Lewis Strauss in March 1954 was illustrative of the kind of headline-grabbing 'revelations' that were best avoided. This issue of information management became all the more pressing not only as the US testing programme continued to be a subject of both domestic and international controversy, but also as nuclear weapons became integrated into the structure and operations of military units. One small example of this was the Army's 8″ howitzer, and the way that with its capability to fire nuclear artillery shells it was assuming an important role in the new 'pentomic' divisions that began to be formed during 1956, where battlefield nuclear weapons were integrated into divisional structures and operational procedures.[74] In both February and September 1956, the OCB and Chairman of the AEC had blocked attempts by the Army to make official announcements about the new atomic capability of the howitzers. The OCB hoped that this knowledge should be allowed to leak out through unofficial channels rather than be part of the Army's statements about their new divisional organization; any public announcement, it was anticipated, 'would almost certainly be [a] major news item here and abroad, thus lending strength to the "ban the bomb" argument [and] raising further fears with respect to radiation fall-out'.[75]

Continuing State Department nervousness about the publicity surrounding nuclear issues in the Far East was further illustrated during the second half of 1956 over the major discussion that arose over the introduction into Korea of nuclear-capable weapons for the US forces on the peninsula. During 1953, US ground strength in Korea had peaked at eight divisions, but driven by the conventional cutbacks of the New Look, over the subsequent three years the Pentagon had substantially reduced this force while at the same time boosting the size of the South Korean Army. As the US Army now began to reorganize its divisions along

---

[74] See, e.g., Bacevich, *Pentomic Era*, 64–6, 84, 103–6.
[75] William H. Jackson memorandum for Eisenhower, 'Public Announcement of the Atomic Capability of the 8″ Howitzer', 10 October 1956, DDRS/CK3100230971.

pentomic lines, the JCS began to call for this modernization process to be extended to the two divisions that remained in South Korea. In the summer of 1956, the Army presented its requirements for replacing obsolete equipment in Korea, including the proposal to upgrade the fire-power of its units with the deployment of two short-range and nuclear-capable systems, the Honest John rocket and 280 mm cannon. The State Department was anxious over the implications of any such move, Walter Robertson finding it a 'particularly serious problem', not least as it would be a blatant infringement of article 13(d) of the Korean armistice agree-ments of 1953, which prohibited the introduction of new or 'reinforcing' military equipment to the peninsula.[76] Speaking for the JCS, Radford had no time for such State Department reservations and wanted to see the modernization accomplished without delay, along with the suspension of the tiresome legal straitjacket of article 13(d); 'the entire question', he asserted, 'was a matter of reducing the cost of our military commitment in Korea, and that this could only be done by modernizing the forces there to include weapons of atomic capability'.[77]

Coinciding with the need to upgrade the US forces in Korea with nuclear weaponry was the Eisenhower administration's imperative, by the autumn of 1956, to reduce the enormous costs of sustaining the South Korean military establishment (twenty regular divisions in the army alone), which was twice as large as its northern counterpart. During one NSC meeting in February 1956 where it was estimated that South Korea was absorbing about $1 billion per annum of US military and economic assistance, Eisenhower complained that the country was 'get-ting to be "a pretty expensive plaything"'.[78] With levels of military assis-tance to South Korea running at such high amounts, and under the spur of the Treasury, the Defense Department was looking at ways in which overseas expenditures could be reduced to more manageable proportions. There were also concerns that maintenance of such a large military establishment was having a damaging impact on the development of the South Korean economy. Equipping US forces in Korea with nuclear-capable weapons would, it was believed, convince Syngman Rhee that it was safe to acquiesce in Washington's plans to reduce the size of his conventional army. Yet despite the strong pressures mounting for nuclear deployment to Korea, the State Department remained sceptical.

[76] See Robertson to Murphy, 22 August 1956, *FRUS, 1955–1957, XXIII*: Part 2, *Korea* (Washington, DC, 1993), 300; Condit, *JCS and National Policy, 1955–56*, 219–20.
[77] See memorandum of State–Defense meeting, 11 September 1956, *FRUS, 1955–1957, XXIII*, Part 2, 306.
[78] Memorandum of discussion at the 276th meeting of the NSC, 9 February 1956, *ibid.*, 217.

Concerns were focused on the wider message it would send around the Far East region if US conventional strength were reduced, which could be interpreted as a sign of lack of resolve to defend its Asian allies, as well as the political difficulties that would accompany so conspicuous a display of US atomic power (it was generally acknowledged that it would be impossible to conceal the deployment of Honest John and the 280 mm cannon, the latter an unwieldy behemoth requiring two large tractors to haul it around the countryside). One Bureau of Intelligence Research report of November 1956 had already highlighted the fact that the introduction of what the public regarded as atomic weapons, even without their warheads, would have serious repercussions in Japan and Australia and throughout the SEATO region.[79] Considering the fact that many American allies as well as neutral opinion would see this step as a violation of the armistice, and how it was believed that Communist forces in the north were clandestinely augmenting their conventional capabilities with new aircraft, armour and artillery, the Far East Bureau did not feel that either introducing the new weapons, or reducing the size of the South Korean army, would be a wise policy to pursue; as Robertson put it, any cut would 'be clearly repeating the mistakes of 1948–1950'.[80]

The dilemmas and tensions generated by the growing presence of US nuclear weapons and delivery systems in East and South East Asia in the mid-1950s underlined a sharp dichotomy in how the Pentagon and the State Department regarded the major problems of American foreign policy in Asia. To the US military establishment, the introduction of nuclear weapons into the region and the planning assumptions that went with them was a necessary reassurance to loyal US allies, such as Thailand, South Vietnam, Nationalist China and South Korea, who were faced with a local preponderance of Communist conventional military power. Without the knowledge that a Communist aggression would be met by nuclear counteraction at an early stage of any fighting, it was believed that morale and confidence in these states might gradually diminish. In October 1957, Stump explained to an Australia, New Zealand, US Security Treaty (ANZUS) Council meeting that all his plans to meet aggression in the SEATO area included provision for the use of nuclear weapons. Both Chiang Kai-shek and Diem had told Stump, the latter explained, of their 'hope that the United States would come to their aid as soon as possible with everything it has, including atomic weapons'. As for Stump himself, he averred that he

---

[79] IR-7367, 'Probable Local and International Repercussions of Various Possible Courses of U.S. Policy in Korea', 1 November 1956; see *ibid.*, 353, 357–8.
[80] Robertson memorandum for Dulles, 29 January 1957, *ibid.*, 390–1.

favored the immediate use of everything available … there is a great deal of doubt in Asia about whether we will act fast enough if anything happens … Communist infiltration and action cannot be effectively resisted with conventional weapons. In all his discussions with the leaders in Asia he has informed them of what Secretary Dulles has often stated, that we are now stronger in the Pacific than at the close of the last war. It is necessary, however, that we make up our minds now that we would act immediately if necessary and use all our weapons to win.[81]

To the State Department, the intelligence community and USIA, however, 'Asian opinion' was not reducible to the attitudes of Chiang, Diem and Rhee, but was a catch-all phrase which was generally meant to refer to states and peoples outside the confines of American-led alliances, and who embraced a non-aligned approach (and had sometimes expressed hostility to organizations such as SEATO). In the wake of the Bandung Conference, it was to these developing states that the focus of the Cold War in Asia was, in many important respects, beginning to turn. Excessive identification with the authoritarian leaders of the right, it was also clear to many observers, had gone a long way towards producing that sense of alienation or estrangement between the United States and the peoples of the region that had developed over the decade since the Hiroshima and Nagasaki bombings. That said, it was Japan which still represented the most important source of non-Communist strength in East Asia, and it was in that country where the most vociferous anti-nuclear sentiments were to be encountered. It is therefore to the US–Japanese relationship in this period of the Cold War we shall now turn.

---

[81] US minutes of the ANZUS Council meeting, Washington, 4 October 1957, *FRUS, 1955–1957, XXI*, 392.

9 Massive retaliation at bay: US–Japanese relations, nuclear deployment and the limited war debate

In the previous chapter we saw how tensions began to develop between the Pentagon, in its desire to implement at a planning and deployment level in the Far East the reliance on nuclear weapons that underpinned the New Look, and the State Department which was anxious over how this would be received by Asian non-aligned states. But for US policy-makers it was in Japan, in the aftermath of the *Lucky Dragon* incident of 1954, that the most worrying trends in popular opinion towards nuclear weapons were encountered, and where the American stake in the outcome was highest. Alongside concerns over the state of public opinion were several unwelcome developments in the domestic political scene. Though Washington was happy to see a merger take place in November 1955 between the two main conservative parties in Japan to form the Liberal Democratic Party (LDP), and so thus instigating a system that would dominate government in Tokyo for the next forty years, much to the discomfort of the State Department, Hatoyama's administration was still determined to improve relations with the Communist bloc. Despite being diverted from making firm overtures to Beijing by signs of strong American displeasure, Japanese initiatives finally bore fruit when Hatoyama visited Moscow in October 1956 to sign an agreement which normalized relations with the Soviet Union and cleared the way for Japan's admission to the UN, giving Tokyo's foreign policy an increasingly independent tenor.[1] When Hatoyama finally stepped down as premier in December 1956, the LDP selected Ishibashi Tanzan as his successor, but his aim of trade expansion with the PRC made him Washington's least favoured candidate among those on offer. Meanwhile, the two wings of the Japanese Socialist Party had also come together to form a viable alternative to the Government,

[1] See Schaller, *Altered States*, 84, 114–23; Tadashi Aruga, 'The Security Treaty Revision of 1960', in Iriye and Cohen (eds.), *The United States and Japan in the Postwar World*, 62–3. The Foreign Office's annual review of Japan for 1956 noted that, 'The concept of China as a menace is one which has not yet penetrated the Japanese mind any more than the concept of China as a competitor'; see Tokyo (Dening) to FO, No. 12, 30 January 1957, FO 371/127522, TNA.

318

and, in American eyes, a dangerous home for neutralist sentiment. Socialist gains at the 1955 elections had, moreover, given them enough seats in the Diet to frustrate efforts at rearmament and constitutional reform.

Tensions in US–Japanese relations featured across a range of issues, including contacts with the Communist world, pressures from Washington for Japan to expand its own self-defence forces and take a greater role in regional security arrangements, American domestic discrimination against Japanese textile exports, nuclear testing in the Pacific, the jurisdictional arrangements that covered US service personnel based in Japan, and the status of the Ryukyu and Bonin islands, where 'residual sovereignty' was said to lie with Tokyo under the 1951 peace treaty, but the American authorities showed no signs of relinquishing their physical control, with Okinawa a pivotal part of the offshore island defensive chain in the western Pacific. Lying at the centre of these frictions was the security treaty, which was seen by all shades of political opinion in Japan as one-sided, providing no right of consultation over the use of the American bases, or over the deployment of nuclear weapons. Japanese governments were determined to secure its eventual revision or replacement with a new agreement that had 'mutuality' as its basis. Ties with the United States in the economic and security fields remained of critical importance to Tokyo, but with the emergence in the post-Yoshida era of a nationalistically minded leadership in the LDP, relations were entering a new phase, and, in a more general sense, Japanese historians of this period have often noted the 'love–hate' feelings in evidence towards the United States, when 'Japanese identification with America as a model of democracy and assimilation went hand in hand with anti-Americanism on a political level'.[2]

Over nuclear issues there remained many signs that the rupture to US–Japanese relations caused by the *Lucky Dragon* incident would be difficult to repair completely. One revealing picture of Japanese opinion was conveyed by Herbert Passin in an article published by the *Bulletin of the Atomic Scientists* in October 1955. Passin, one-time Research Associate with the Department of Sociology and Anthropology at Ohio State University, had also worked in Japan for the US occupation authorities conducting social research, but was now engaged in a three-year stint as Far East representative for *Encounter* magazine.[3] 'There is a feeling among the Japanese

---

[2] See Nagayo Homma, 'America in the Mind of the Japanese', in Iriye and Cohen (eds.), *The United States and Japan in the Postwar World*, 211.

[3] At this time, *Encounter* was the recipient of covert CIA funding; see Francis Stoner Saunders, *Who Paid the Paper? The CIA and the Cultural Cold War* (London, 1999), 165–89.

these days bordering on paranoia that they are the fated victims of American atomic policy,' Passin claimed, with *Lucky Dragon* and Kuboyama having 'become household words that stir a deep sense of resentment'. When the United States made an offer to Japan of a quantity of enriched uranium for its embryonic civilian reactor programme in the summer of 1955, it served to spark a fresh debate in scientific, academic and media circles over the motivations behind American actions, revealing 'a real distrust of American atomic policy'. With the widespread belief in Asia that the United States dropped the first atomic bomb on Japan 'because the Japanese are "colored people" and the Germans are "whites"', Passin reminded his readers, some Asian observers had come to connect Communist charges of germ warfare in Korea with the Pacific nuclear tests of 1954.[4]

Despite these discouraging signs, the Pentagon remained determined that the nuclear components of atomic weapons should be deployed to US bases in Japan. Having carried out a further study of the problem, by the autumn of 1955 the JCS, while admitting that immediate action was probably not possible, were asserting that 'the requirement still is valid and should be accomplished at the earliest time consistent with the maintenance of a satisfactory state of United States–Japan relations'. It was this final consideration, of course, that gave the State Department and the embassy in Tokyo the leverage they needed to argue against any steps that would upset the already delicate state of play with the Japanese Government. The impatience of the Pentagon was underlined in November 1955, when Reuben B. Robertson, the Deputy Secretary of Defense, reminded the State Department that greater appreciation by the Japanese of the peaceful uses of atomic energy would be 'useful in reducing existing psychological barriers as well as fostering a greater appreciation of the realities of the military atomic program'. The State Department's reaction was to highlight the work that had already been done in this field: Japan was the first country to receive an atomic energy library, Japanese students were attending courses at the School of Nuclear Science and Engineering, an agreement on nuclear research reactor assistance and material had been signed, and Japanese participation in the International Atomic Energy Conference at Geneva had 'to some extent dispelled Japanese misapprehensions about atomic energy and has oriented Japanese thinking toward the benign uses of the atom'. Though ready to accept a Pentagon suggestion that a joint examination be conducted into the possibility of influencing the Japanese leadership into a

[4] Passin, 'Japan and the H-Bomb', 289–92.

more favourable view of US military atomic policy, State Department officials were adamant that much was already being done.[5]

The main vehicle for this effort was USIA's on-going attempts to soften Japanese attitudes to the bomb by propagating the Atoms for Peace programme. Roving exhibits showing films, displaying models of the atom and atomic reactors, alongside new scientific instruments, and illustrating various medical and industrial applications of atomic energy, were sent out around the world from 1954 onwards as the administration sought to spread the impression the United States was determined to harness the new source of power for peace, not war.[6] USIA was particularly pleased with the year-long tour of its Atoms for Peace exhibit through Japan, which opened in Tokyo in November 1955, the agency describing in hyperbolic terms the resulting change in mood towards atomic energy as 'spectacular ... Through an intensive USIS campaign, atom hysteria was almost eliminated and by the beginning of 1956, Japanese opinion was brought to popular acceptance of the peaceful uses of atomic energy ... Substantial progress has been made in improving Japanese opinion toward the U.S. and thereby taking some of the pressure off the Japanese Government on account of its pro-American policies.'[7]

The most sensitive site for the tour of the exhibit was naturally Hiroshima, with planning for the event beginning in May 1955. By early 1956, with the exhibit already making its way around Japan, some local resistance from atomic bomb survivors and representatives of the Council against Atomic and Hydrogen Bombs was being encountered, not least due to the fact that it was to be mounted in buildings in the Peace Memorial Park (one of which was the museum). Efforts were made to overcome this through public meetings where concerned survivors were reassured that the aim of the exhibit was not to erase the memory of the bombings themselves, while several Japanese officials in the municipal government were very supportive of the educational themes of the programme. USIS also showed many films with Atoms for Peace material in the Hiroshima area over the period, while numerous articles promoting the peaceful uses of atomic energy appeared in the press. A US Navy aircraft dropped 100,000 leaflets in Iwakuni, Hiroshima and Kure urging people to visit the exhibit. Television stations carried special features, and visits were made by USIS officers to neighbouring cities to hold meetings

[5] See Herbert Hoover Jr, letter to Reuben B. Robertson, 18 November 1955, 'NN-Japan 1955', box 2, Country and Subject Files, 1950–62, SASAE, RG 59, NARA.
[6] On the worldwide Atoms for Peace programme, see Osgood, *Total Cold War*, 174–80.
[7] See *ibid.*, 179, and also on USIA in Japan, Swenson-Wright, *Unequal Allies*, 181–3.

with municipal representatives, school boards, cultural and educational organizations, and the media. The prefectural board of education for Hiroshima ordered all public schools to send students to the exhibit, with attendance for senior high school students being obligatory. By the end of its three-week stay in Hiroshima, which began in May 1956, the exhibit had attracted over 120,000 visitors and, according to USIS officials, was regarded as a runaway success, with 'active support by community leaders' seen 'as an indication of the effectiveness of USIS operations in this area'. The 'positive' approach exemplified by the staging of the exhibit was felt to underline American 'sincerity and goodwill', while the 'rank and file of friendly groups in Hiroshima continues to grow. Leftist movements are overshadowed by the increasingly overt pro-American attitudes supported by groups, individuals and newspapers in this area.' The USIS office in Tokyo was also gratified to note that, after the exhibition, the local authorities decided to devote two-thirds of the space in the Hiroshima Peace Museum to Atoms for Peace material (when up to that point the museum had displayed only relics from the atomic bombings and pictures of the decimated city and injured survivors).[8]

Nevertheless, despite the laudatory commentary and self-congratulatory tone of USIA reporting of their work in Japan, there was also much evidence to show they still had a long way to go to persuade Japanese popular opinion of the beneficent qualities of American Cold War policies. In fact, US officials remained deeply concerned with the currents of Japanese opinion and the potential strength of the Socialist Party on the Japanese political scene. The idea that the Japanese public looked on the United States as somehow a 'natural' ally and counterweight to Communist China, and even the Soviet Union, was refuted in 1956 by USIA surveys conducted by officials attached to the US Embassy in Tokyo (actual interviewing was carried out by a Japanese polling organization, without evidence of US involvement). One poll taken in January 1956 asked respondents whether Japan should take sides if war came between the United States and the PRC. While 29 per cent felt that Japan should join with the United States, 48 per cent said they would prefer their country to adopt a neutral posture. Another question asked whether respondents thought US bases were a good or bad thing for Japan, with only 16 per cent answering affirmatively, while 51 per cent

[8] See 'Atoms for Peace Exhibit Hiroshima', despatch by A. F. Fotouhi (Principal Public Affairs Officer, Hiroshima), enclosed in 'USIS Atoms for Peace Exhibition in Hiroshima', USIS Tokyo to USIA Washington, Despatch No. 52, 25 October 1956, Exhibit Studies: Atoms for Peace, box 2, Multi Area (World) Project Files, 1953–63, Office of Research, RG 306, NARA.

felt negatively.[9] As the Tokyo Embassy reminded the State Department in April 1956: 'for many Japanese "complete independence" includes the concepts of "neutrality" and "disengagement" from the United States in a politico-military sense. These neutralistic tendencies are believed to derive in large part from fear that military alliance with the United States, particularly the presence of American atomic bases in Japan, may involve Japan in an American war and thus bring about Japan's destruction.'[10]

The data from the embassy surveys conducted in 1956 were interpreted in two joint State Department–USIA reports, both of which were seen by Dulles and passed on to the President. The first of these, produced in April 1956, highlighted Japanese sensitivity to atomic issues 'being the only people who to date have found themselves on the "business end" of atomic bombs – a memory vividly revived by the injury of the Japanese fishermen at the time of the Marshall Island tests. (Those so injured *would*, of course, have to be Japanese.)' An outright ban on nuclear weapons was favoured by 55 per cent of the general public, it was noted, even if this would leave the anti-Communist powers militarily weaker than their Communist opponents. This figure rose to 61 per cent for the upper socio-economic groups, and 73 per cent for those with a college or university education. Over half of those surveyed tended to blame both the United States and the Soviet Union equally for Cold War tensions.[11] The second report, compiled in September 1956, identified a clear trend towards neutralism, with over one half of college- and university-educated respondents feeling that Japan should take neither side in the Cold War. Perhaps most worrying was the weakness of the governing LDP, which because of 'paralyzing apprehension of immediate domestic political consequences and divisive bickering among its members' was unable to offer clear leadership to public opinion on the basic issues surrounding the Cold War and Japanese security. American prestige as a whole was on the decline, due to continued atmosphere testing of nuclear weapons, the status of the Ryukyus, the presence of US military bases, and the belief that the United States had little interest in general disarmament.[12]

[9] See FE-19, 'Japanese Trends in Neutralism, Judgements of U.S. vs Soviet Strength and Reactions to U.S. Troops', May 1959, box 1, Public Opinion Barometer Reports, 1955–62, Office of Research, RG 306, NARA.
[10] Tokyo to State Department, No. 942, 16 April 1956, 'Japan Correspondence 1956', box 13, Country Project Correspondence, Office of Research, RG 306, NARA.
[11] See 'Japanese Public Opinion on International Issues', 25 April 1956 (transmitted to Eisenhower by Dulles, 11 May 1956), 'Japan 1953–56 (2)', International Series, box 33, Ann Whitman File, DDEL.
[12] See 'Japanese Public Opinion: Mid-1956', 27 September 1956 (transmitted to Eisenhower by Dulles, 18 October 1956), 'Japan 1953–56 (1)', *ibid.*

The large-scale presence of American forces in Japan, who much to local resentment also retained significant areas of agricultural land for use in military exercises, was a constant reminder of the recent occupation period, as well as the 'unilateral' aspects of the security treaty that underpinned the American bases. The Tokyo Embassy bluntly advised the State Department in 1956: 'We must remember that Japan has been occupied only once – by us. No matter how "benevolently" it was carried out, the Occupation was an enormous shock to a proud and sensitive people, and it left a residue of bitterness toward the United States which still has by no means completely healed.'[13] One of the reasons given for the decision to dissolve the Far East Command in Tokyo and to run down US ground troop strength, as Wilson, the Secretary of Defense, told the NSC in July 1956, was that it formed part of an effort to 'scotch the idea so prevalent in Japan that that country was still occupied. If we could not succeed in destroying this idea, we stood to lose our entire position in the Japanese islands.'[14] Another key source of tension was the refusal of Washington to cede their control over the Ryukyu Islands, where Okinawa served as the hub of the American presence. Despite requests from Tokyo to consider reversion, Okinawa remained under anachronistic US military government and was home to a Marine Division, amphibious lift and crucial nuclear storage facilities for the US Air Force. With 40,000 US service personnel, and two 12,000 foot runways at Kadena Air Force base, the longest in the Far East, the island's reputation, as proudly proclaimed by the words on the US Army-issued licence plates of the American cars on Okinawa, was that of being America's 'keystone of the Pacific'.[15]

There were also tremors of anxiety through the US bureaucracy as planning for the summer 1956 Pacific test series, dubbed *Redwing*, got under way, for at the beginning of that year both Houses of the Diet had passed resolutions calling for suspension of the tests. AEC officials were eager to emphasize that their weather forecasting techniques had improved since the *Bravo* incident of 1954 and there would be no shots under 'marginal' conditions, while predictions of fallout patterns were also more advanced. Very careful patrolling of an enlarged danger area was to be conducted, and more radiation safety stations established on

---

[13] Tokyo to State Department, No. 942, 16 April 1956, 'Japan Correspondence 1956'.

[14] See memorandum of discussion at the 290th meeting of the NSC, 12 July 1956, *FRUS, 1955–1957, XXIII*, Part 1: *Japan* (Washington, DC, 1991), 188–9.

[15] See LaFeber, *The Clash*, 289–91; 'Base on Okinawa is U.S. Keystone', *NYT*, 14 April 1956. As of late June 1958, for example, SAC had Mk-6 and Mk-39 nuclear bombs stored at Kadena (its only overseas storage in the Far East); see History of the Strategic Air Command, 1 January 1958–30 June 1958, p. 90, Historical Study No. 73, Vol. I, www.nukestrat.com/us/afn/SAC01-0658.pdf, accessed 25 May 2007.

uninhabited atolls. One military officer commented that 'if a [monitoring] team had been stationed on Rongelap at the time of the first *Castle* test the natives could have been advised to bathe frequently and would not have suffered ill effects'. In any event, evacuation plans were drawn up for the inhabitants of Rongelap 'should there be an untoward incident'.[16] In early March 1956, nevertheless, State Department officials met Strauss and other senior AEC officials to discuss their concerns about the upcoming tests on Japan. Reporting the views of the US Embassy in Tokyo, it was noted that there was a 'considerable amount of steam behind the propaganda against the test series', that Japanese opinion continued to be averse to nuclear weapons, and that 'unless something can be worked out to ameliorate the situation with respect to the tests there is a possibility that the Government might fall'. Moreover, Japanese scientists were concerned that their aspirations to develop civilian sources of nuclear power were being jeopardized by general public prejudices against atomic energy. The most important steps the US authorities could take to mitigate some of this local impact, it was felt, were some concession to the Japanese view that their fishing interests should be compensated for the loss of access to grounds covered by the test areas in the Pacific (while it was even held possible that Communist agents might 'spike' tuna fish in Japan in order to trigger another radioactive fish scare). One proposal was that the Americans co-operate actively with Japanese oceanographers intending to survey the waters around the danger area for possible contamination to fish stocks, though with no prior commitment to compensate.[17] Testing continued to touch raw nerves in the summer of 1956. In one bizarre but indicative episode, the AEC wanted to procure several Japanese houses and ship them to the Nevada testing range for the upcoming domestic *Plumbob* series so that the radiation dosages received by Japanese civilians through a nuclear attack might be more accurately estimated. This was deemed important, it was argued, in order that the condition of the Japanese survivors from 1945 could be better understood by ABCC doctors, but the US Embassy in Tokyo mounted strong opposition to any such experiment, the detail of which could easily leak and be

---

[16] Memorandum for the files by George C. Spiegel, 'Weapons Testing: Redwing', 16 February 1956, Weapons Testing: Redwing folder, box 345, Subject Files, SASAE, RG 59, NARA.

[17] Memorandum for the files by George C. Spiegel, 'Discussion of Japanese Concern over Nuclear Tests', 2 March 1956; draft memorandum for the Acting Secretary, 'Alleviation of Japanese Fears and Countering Communist Propaganda in Japan Re Pacific Nuclear Tests', 8 March 1956, *ibid*. In the event, Japanese reactions to the 1956 series were not as strong or outspoken as many US officials had feared; see Swenson-Wright, *Unequal Allies*, 184.

interpreted as American preparations for a future war where Japan would be a principal target.[18]

During the summer of 1956, the Defense Department tentatively tried to explore with General Lyman L. Lemnitzer, the new head of the Far East Command in Tokyo, the steps that could be taken to reduce the political obstacles to deployment of the nuclear components of atomic weapons in Japan.[19] However, with the support of the State Department, Allison remained firmly opposed to any attempt by the US authorities to stage special programmes explaining the role of nuclear weapons in defence policy in order to influence public opinion or the Japanese leadership. Having weathered the storm of the *Lucky Dragon* incident two years before, the Ambassador now argued that 'the question of the use of atomic weapons should, for the present, be left strictly and deliberately alone by all American officials dealing with the Japanese and ... we should wait for relationships in other fields to develop further before proceeding'. Japanese leaders had first to accept the need to build up their own self-defence forces and take the military requirements of security more seriously before atomic issues were broached. 'The dangers in opening the subject prematurely,' Allison warned in late 1956, 'even in the more general "educational" terms without any specific reference to our desire to bring the nuclear components in, would be that we might well get carried along to the point where we would be forced to give assurances ... to the effect that we would not bring them in or use them without the Japanese Government's approval.'[20]

Indeed, several voices in the State Department were acutely aware that Japanese sensitivities were unlikely to dissipate, meaning that Washington would simply have to adapt to a more restrictive environment than the military felt necessary. In December 1956, the Far East Bureau's Regional Planning Adviser, Marshall Green, composed a memorandum on reconsidering the US military position in Japan, which began by arguing that the Japanese regarded the American presence as a 'carry-over of the occupation period, as a form of foreign control earmarking Japan for involvement in any major war which, moreover, is likely to be a war involving nuclear weapons with which the Japanese have a deep morbid preoccupation'.

---

[18] The AEC even suggested that the CIA be utilized to bring Japanese houses back clandestinely to the United States, but the Agency would have nothing to do with the scheme, and instead the houses were simply constructed on site with American materials. See State Department to Tokyo, 10 July 1956; Howard L. Parsons draft letter to Allison, 9 July 1956; State Department to Tokyo, 27 July 1956; Smith memorandum for Foster, 16 July 1956, all in 'Weapons Testing, U.S. Tests 1957', box 347, Subject Files, SASAE, RG 59, NARA.

[19] See Smith letter to Allison, 12 September 1956, 'NN-Japan 1956–57', box 2, Country and Subject Files, SASAE, RG 59, NARA.

[20] See Smith draft letter to Gordon Gray, 3 December 1956, *ibid.*

Green foresaw that without a change in policy, American bases were only tenable for the next two to four years, while even during this period US ability to use its bases for military operations outside the area of Japan or for deploying nuclear weapons 'may be seriously restricted'. As a people the Japanese had yet to recover from the shocks of defeat, occupation and a return to the international community, and they 'somehow still connect the appearance of their new-found liberties and ways of life with the disappearance of Japan's strong defense establishment'. 'We must avoid as far as possible,' Green cautioned, 'justifying our military presence in Japan on the need for advance bases from which to reduce Chinese and Russian cities to rubble ... we will have to take pains to meet Japan's understandable psychosis on the subject of involvement in any nuclear war.'[21]

The Pentagon, nevertheless, were not easily dissuaded and at a mid-January 1957 inter-agency meeting, Gordon Gray, the Assistant Secretary of Defense for International Security Affairs, impressed on State Department representatives his hope that more could be done to influence public opinion in Japan, in the same way that NATO allies had been persuaded to accept nuclear weapons. Another Pentagon official noted that the problem was 'basically a matter of getting the right to store nuclear warheads in Japan where they would be ready at hand' and wondered if a Japanese training programme in dual-purpose weapons such as the Nike surface-to-air missile system might be a step forward. Douglas MacArthur II, who had been selected to replace Allison as US ambassador in Tokyo, was, however, much more circumspect. Any proposal for training would have to come from the Japanese themselves, while the whole question was 'extremely delicate as the Japanese were the only people in the world to have had the bomb used against them'. Though they might come to accept civilian uses for atomic energy, it seemed doubtful the same could be said for its military application; the weakness of the current government and 'immaturity' of the Socialists made for a bad situation. With little agreement evident, on Gray's suggestion it was decided that the issue of 'indoctrinating' Japanese leaders as to the need for nuclear weapons would be referred to an informal ad hoc working group of Defense and State Department officials with additional representation from the CIA and USIA.[22] The potential for any mention of US nuclear plans to

---

[21] Marshall Green memorandum for Howard L. Parsons, 'Reconsideration of Our Military Position in Japan', 13 December 1956, 'Japan 1956–1957 (1)', box 3, Subject files of the Regional Planning Adviser, records of the Bureau of Far East Affairs, RG 59, NARA.

[22] See memorandum of conversation, 'Introduction of Nuclear Weapons to Japan', 14 January 1957, 711.5611/1–1457, CDF, RG 59, NARA; Smith memorandum for the file of meeting in Mr MacArthur's office, 14 January 1957, 'NN-Japan 1956–57', box 2, Country and Subject Files, SASAE, RG 59, NARA.

unsettle a domestic Japanese audience was underlined only a short time afterward when reports began to surface in the Japanese press (derived from stories circulating in Washington) about the withdrawal of the US 1st Cavalry Division from Japan and its replacement by an 'Atomic Task Force'. The State and Defense Departments had to issue a joint press release denying that any such decision had been taken, but this did not stop Socialist criticism of the Government. With the source of the leak being traced back to the Far East Command Headquarters in Tokyo, Dulles sent a stiff letter to Wilson complaining that such disclosures were undermining American objectives in Japan.[23]

The controversy came at a time when the Eisenhower administration was keeping a close watch on political developments in the volatile LDP. Washington had anticipated a difficult relationship with Japan under an Ishibashi premiership, with his professed desire for closer ties with Beijing, but after only two months in office, he was forced to step down through ill health. Though just as much a Japanese nationalist, the LDP's selection of Kishi Nosubuke as Ishibashi's successor in February 1957 was a far more acceptable choice as prime minister to the Americans, and he soon proved willing to work closely with Washington on the issues that divided the two states, establishing a particular rapport with MacArthur. Kishi's stress on the need for greater measures of Japanese rearmament was particularly welcome to American officials who had been urging progress in this area ever since the end of the occupation in 1952.[24] Even under this new leadership, however, the Americans could expect that agitation for change in the relationship would grow, as Japan's dramatic economic recovery continued apace and demands for equal treatment came from both sides of the political spectrum. Walter Robertson had already fired a warning shot in a memorandum for Dulles in January 1957 which underlined that 'the strategic value to the United States of Japan as a close friend and ally is tremendous, and our entire strategic position in the Western Pacific is anchored on Japan'. It was important for the United States not to underestimate the chances of neutralist sentiment taking hold, while the Japanese government was showing clear signs of wanting to assert its independence as it began to conduct a more active foreign policy, and might even be tempted to assume a leadership role in the 'Afro-Asian bloc' in the UN. Japanese leaders were increasingly restless with the

---

[23] See memorandum from Robertson to Dulles, n.d.; Dulles letter to Wilson, n.d. (but *c.* mid-February 1957), '21.52 Country File: Japan Weapons 1957–1961', box 425, Country Files, SASAE, RG 59, NARA.
[24] See Schaller, *Altered States*, 124–5, 130; Swenson-Wright, *Unequal Allies*, 224.

pattern of their relations with the United States, and Robertson saw a need by the Americans to 'recognize the ground swell' in Japan and make adjustments in policy, rather than be overtaken by events and have their hand forced. The major issues that would need addressing included Okinawa and the Ryukyus, what he pointedly termed 'the present unmutual "Security Treaty"', and the problem of American bases and installations in Japan.[25]

The Atomic Task Force controversy was most concerning to the State Department because it feared that continual airing of the issue of nuclear deployment and use would force the Japanese Government to give categorical assurances that it would be consulted by Washington before any introduction of such weapons into the country, and in general for the impetus it gave to Socialist criticisms of the security treaty. The potential damage that could be done was illustrated on 11 February 1957 when questions in the Diet led Kishi to refer to the 'Allison–Shigemitsu agreement' (of May 1955) as assuring Japanese neutrality when it came to atomic weapons, thus reopening the uncomfortable fact that Washington, at least in private exchanges with Tokyo, denied that any such agreement existed. Moreover, Kishi was soon forced to issue a much firmer declaration that he would never consent to nuclear weapons storage in Japan, asserting that Japan would be 'indefensible' in war with such armaments.[26]

The highly charged atmosphere generated by these issues conspired to make Dulles very averse to any renewed attempt to push the issue of deployment with the Japanese Government. In one further meeting with his officials in early February 1957, the Secretary of State expressed his desire that the present arrangements regarding nuclear deployment in Japan should continue. Referring to his belief that Western European governments had come to accept in NATO that nuclear weapons should be considered as conventional, he went on to note that the case of Japan was different, and that it might be necessary 'to take actions in conjunction with the Government of Japan which recognize the peculiarities of the Japanese picture'.[27] Dulles may have had in mind a concerted public information programme, but the inter-agency ad hoc group previously

---

[25] See Robertson memorandum for Dulles, 7 January 1957, *FRUS, 1955–1957, XXIII*, Part 1, 240–4.

[26] See State Department Office of Intelligence Research, Report No. 7466, 'The Relationship of Japan to Nuclear Weapons and Warfare', 22 April 1957, '21.52 Country File: Japan Intelligence Reports 1957', box 424, Country Files, SASAE, RG 59, NARA.

[27] Memorandum of conversation, 4 February 1957, '21.52 Country File: Japan Weapons 1957–1961', box 425, Country Files, SASAE, RG 59, NARA.

mooted never seems to have been formed.[28] The 'peculiarities' of the prevailing Japanese scene were emphasized even more in a comprehensive report issued in April 1957 by the State Department's Office of Intelligence Research on 'The Relationship of Japan to Nuclear Weapons and Warfare'. Since Hiroshima, it noted, the Japanese public had been 'horror-stricken' at the thought they might be involved in a future nuclear conflict, in a fixation that was judged probably 'unique in the world'. This was an attitude and concern shared by all political parties, social groups and intellectual levels. Successive Japanese governments had been 'intimidated' by popular opinion on the subject, and the issue of nuclear war played a prominent role in political debate, with memories of the attacks on Hiroshima and Nagasaki 'recalled with a religious fervor'. Wide publicity continued to be given to the illness and deaths of many of the survivors, and the *Lucky Dragon* incident had set off a further 'wave of hysteria', captured most recently by on-going protests about the current round of British atmospheric testing at Christmas Island in the Pacific. The development of so-called 'clean' nuclear weapons, with less fallout, had done little to dissipate the public's anxieties. Fearful of being subjected to another nuclear attack, the Japanese people believed that their best way of escaping such a fate lay in rejecting the storage or use of US nuclear weapons. There was little likelihood of this view changing in the immediate future, and even if there was some slight modification, the avoidance of nuclear war would still 'take priority over questions of justice, other national interests and obligations, or even calculation of the ultimate victory'. If general nuclear war were to become imminent, panic was expected to sweep the country, and the Government might even order Japanese forces to prevent the use of nuclear weapons from American bases, though it would be 'more likely to concentrate upon appeals to world opinion for the withdrawal of U.S. forces, and upon efforts to identify Japan with the neutral nations of Asia'. In any event, a general strike of Japanese labour and demonstrations against the American presence would be probable. In sobering tones, the report concluded that, in effect, 'Japan's commitments to the U.S. would be of doubtful dependability'.[29]

The American image in Japan was also suffering during this period from the repercussions of the Girard case. At the end of January 1957, William

---

[28] One memorandum from Gerard Smith's assistant, Philip Farley, makes clear that the Pentagon had still not found a satisfactory representative for the group in June 1957; see Farley memorandum for the file, 'Japan Weapons', 3 June 1957, 'NN-Japan 1956–57', box 2, Country and Subject Files, SASAE, RG 59, NARA.

[29] State Department Office of Intelligence Research, Report No. 7466, 'The Relationship of Japan to Nuclear Weapons and Warfare'.

S. Girard, an American soldier based at Camp Weir near Somagahara, shot dead a Japanese woman collecting spent cartridge cases for scrap at an army firing range. The Japanese press was suspicious that the death was not just an accident, and the Socialists organized demonstrations calling for a full investigation and for the Government to take jurisdiction in the case. Though wary of the precedent that might be set if Girard were tried in a Japanese court, the US military authorities knew that the Girard case was a potential powder keg (he had, it transpired, acted with intent, and the woman had been shot in the back while running away) and in May decided to relinquish their rights to jurisdiction. By way of compromise, the Japanese authorities also agreed to charge Girard with 'wounding resulting in death', rather than a more serious offence, and to influence the court to mitigate any sentence that might be imposed.[30] However, strong congressional pressure caused the Pentagon to try to unpick the decision, rescind its agreement with the Japanese and proceed with a military court martial. Suitably alarmed at the damage this could cause, Dulles and the State Department intervened to block any hasty action, and preferred to discuss American dilemmas and preferences with the Japanese at a high level through the diplomatic channel.[31]

Other indications that the American presence in Asia was a lightning rod for resentment were given in May 1957 when an angry crowd attacked the US Embassy in Taipei following the acquittal on a charge of voluntary manslaughter of Master Sergeant Robert G. Reynolds after he had killed a Chinese national; several members of the embassy staff had been injured and the local police were reported to have stood by while the building was gutted.[32] The implications of both cases prompted Dulles to warn the President that, 'The situation is serious. These developments in Taipei are going to have a chain reaction in Japan. The issues at stake are tremendous.' Eisenhower was only too aware of the possible ramifications, noting that 'we must have a very serious look at these Asiatic countries, and decide whether we can stay there. It does not seem wise, if they hate us so much.'[33] Dulles believed that if Girard was not turned over to the Japanese as had recently been agreed 'we might as well write Japan off', while the President told Dulles that it was his 'strong feeling

---

[30] See Schaller, *Altered States*, 127–8, 131–2; memorandum from Robertson to Dulles, 20 May 1957, *FRUS, 1955–1957, XXIII*, Part 1, 293–6.

[31] See draft memorandum for Eisenhower prepared in the State Department, 25 May 1957, *FRUS, 1955–1957, XXIII*, Part 1, 323–5.

[32] The Reynolds case had a decidedly murky background, some of which is conveyed in Tucker, *China Confidential*, 140–1.

[33] Memorandum of conversation between Eisenhower and Dulles, 24 May 1957, *FRUS, 1955–1957, III: China* (Washington, DC, 1986), 528.

that prompt and radical steps had to be taken to cut down the number of our armed forces in foreign territories … it was inevitable that they would sooner or later produce [a] strong anti-American feeling'.[34] Insistence by American congressional and public opinion on maintenance of extra-territorial rights for American service personnel meant, as Dulles told members of the press in a background briefing in late June, the United States would find itself having to withdraw from its overseas bases: 'Our world-wide system of security, and our present bases system, which gives us diversified retaliatory power against the Soviet Union, all that is apt to collapse.'[35]

The situation in Japan with regard to US bases and the attendant problems of nuclear deployment was, of course, wrapped up in the administration's continuing efforts to integrate nuclear weapons more fully into force structures and war planning. The ramifications of this were felt throughout the Far East. In Korea the Pentagon began to press more forcefully in early 1957 for the 'modernization' of the weapons available to US forces on the peninsula. The whole subject came before the NSC for discussion at the end of January 1957, the NSC Planning Board having prepared a paper laying out the various policy alternatives, none of which yet called for the storage of nuclear weapons in Korea.[36] The board predicted that if it was decided to deploy short-range Honest John rockets and 280 mm cannon to Korea to give US forces a 'battlefield' nuclear capability, as had been initially proposed the previous year, the United States was likely to face censure from several of its allies and Asian neutral states; moreover, the Communists could be expected to launch a new propaganda campaign charging the United States with violating the armistice agreements, increasing tensions in the Far East and 'planning again to use atomic bombs on Asians'.[37] Robert Bowie, the head of the Policy Planning Staff, felt particularly strongly about the issue, arguing that 'the State Department has consistently maintained that the

---

[34] Memorandum of a telephone conversation between Eisenhower and Dulles, 24 May 1957, *FRUS, 1955–1957, XXIII*, 316; and memorandum of conversation with Eisenhower, 24 May 1957, 'Meetings with the President 1957 (5)', box 6, White House Memoranda series, John Foster Dulles papers, DDEL.

[35] Background conference before the San Francisco Press and Union League Club, 28 June 1957, 'Japan and the Girard Case' folder, box 118, Selected Correspondence, John Foster Dulles papers, Mudd Library.

[36] See Byron R. Fairchild and Walter S. Poole, *History of the Joint Chiefs of Staff*, Vol. VII: *The Joint Chiefs of Staff and National Policy, 1957–1960* (Washington, DC, 2000), 199.

[37] See NSC 5702, 'Evaluation of Alternative Military Programs for Korea', 14 January 1957, *FRUS, 1955–1957, XXIII*, Part 2, 380; see also Robert J. Watson, *History of the Office of the Secretary of Defense*, Vol. IV: *Into the Missile Age, 1956–1960* (Washington, DC, 1997), 623–5.

introduction of such weapons would violate the armistice and have adverse consequences out of all proportion to the benefits in the absence of incontrovertible evidence of the introduction of nuclear weapons into Korea by the Communists'.[38] At the NSC meeting itself, Dulles rehearsed this line, stressing that increased Communist propaganda would result, while neutrals and some allied nations would not consider such a violation of the armistice agreement as justified; yet at the same time the Secretary of State was not about to renounce so easily the idea that nuclear weapons should play a role in enhancing the capabilities of US forces to fight in limited war. In the last resort, Dulles was prepared to acquiesce in the deployment if the Pentagon could supply publishable intelligence showing that the Communist side was also upgrading its own equipment with nuclear-capable weaponry.[39]

When the NSC Planning Board over the next month turned to the task of devising a new military programme for Korea based on modernization of US equipment and a reduction in Korean forces, more differences emerged, as the State Department opposed the JCS's proposals to allow for nuclear storage on the peninsula.[40] In early April, Dulles had still seen no intelligence indicating the presence of Communist nuclear-capable weaponry in Korea, and so he again brought to the NSC State Department objections over the introduction of the 280 mm cannon and Honest John rockets, citing the possible worldwide reaction, and the fact it was 'certain to stir up serious repercussions in Japan'. On this occasion, the President seemed to side with the State Department's reservations, and he was particularly keen to discuss the whole issue with the United States' NATO allies (he made no mention of possible Asian reactions).[41] Almost simultaneously, the OCB's ad hoc committee on publicity concerning the overseas deployment of nuclear-capable weapons was meeting to discuss the guidelines that should operate in this area. The immediate prompt for the formation of the group was the decision to deploy a squadron of nuclear-capable Matador surface-to-surface missiles to Taiwan and how this was to be announced, James Hagerty, the President's Press Secretary, fearing it would be 'headline news all over

---

[38] Bowie memorandum for Dulles, 29 January 1957, 'Korea', box 130, records of the PPS, 1957–61, RG 59, NARA.

[39] See Dulles's comments at the 311th meeting of the NSC, 31 January 1957, where Dulles appears to backtrack on his position; and Sebald memorandum for Bowie, 15 March 1957, where Dulles's agreement to the deployment is mentioned as conditional on production of the evidence, *FRUS, 1955–1957, XXIII*, Part 2, 395, 400, 408.

[40] See Fairchild and Poole, *JCS and National Policy*, VII, 199–200.

[41] Memorandum of discussion at the 318th meeting of the NSC, 4 April 1957, *FRUS, 1955–1957, XXIII*, Part 2, 422, 425–6.

the world'. Abbott Washburn, the Deputy Director of USIA, was concerned over the repercussions in Asia which would 'add fuel to the propaganda fire', while 'the peoples of the Far East could be expected to react in a highly emotional manner to Soviet charges that once again the US was proving that it had in mind the nuclear annihilation of the Asiatic peoples'. The committee proceeded to concoct a statement which highlighted the defensive role of the Matadors and also worked on new instructions on any oral or written statements made by government officials regarding nuclear weapons, which would all have to be cleared and co-ordinated by the OCB. The guidelines for statements on the overseas deployment of dual-capable weapons emphasized that they should be 'brief and factual', should stress the defensive purposes behind American actions and make mention of the joint agreements that underpinned the presence of US forces in host countries.[42] On 2 May, the NSC approved the OCB's final recommendations over publicity arrangements, Robert Cutler, the President's Special Assistant for National Security Affairs, explaining that their chief purpose was as a means to control 'the tendency to "play up" nuclear weapons in official statements'. Meeting the new guidance with approval, Wilson felt that the 'sooner our statements were able to carry the impression that the movements of nuclear-capable forces were routine, the better it would be'. Eisenhower could only agree, adding that he hoped that minimal publicity would in future be given to such movements.[43] These disputes and anxieties over nuclear deployment in Asia within the bureaucracy were, in fact, emblematic of some of the larger arguments then being pursued over the whole implementation of the New Look.

During the first half of 1957, the Eisenhower administration had engaged in a vigorous high-level debate, much of it conducted at NSC meetings, where the President supported the budget cuts to conventional Army forces mandated by the Pentagon's search for economies, and had to face criticism from a State Department that saw the wholehearted embrace of a national security policy based on nuclear weapons as detrimental to the wider goals of US foreign policy, especially in a context where worldwide anti-nuclear feelings showed no signs of abating. As in 1956, this debate over the role of nuclear weapons was conducted against a background where the problem of limited war was receiving extensive

---

[42] Memorandum of meeting of OCB ad hoc committee on publicity concerning overseas deployment of nuclear-capable weapons, 5 April 1957, OCB 000.9, box 11, OCB Central File series, NSC staff papers, White House Office, DDEL.
[43] Memorandum of discussion at the 321st meeting of the NSC, 2 May 1957, DDRS/CK3100501983.

discussion in scholarly circles from the likes of Robert Osgood and Henry Kissinger.

Although expanding Soviet nuclear capabilities were very important in undermining the credibility of massive retaliation in a European setting, feeding pressures for greater expenditures on US conventional forces, in its Far Eastern counterpart China, by contrast, had no capacity to retaliate in kind to a nuclear attack and during this period US intelligence appraisals tended to suggest that Moscow would not come to Beijing's direct assistance unless the destruction of the Communist regime itself was threatened. In other words, one of the key inhibitions about using nuclear weapons in a limited war setting – the danger that they might spark escalation to a more general nuclear exchange – was not as readily apparent in Asia. Instead, what one sees at regular intervals in the limited war debate during 1957 and after was mention of the disastrous political consequences it was believed would flow from a repeat use of nuclear weapons against an Asian and non-white adversary. This was also a factor that received attention, it should be noted, when ample evidence of the racism and discrimination still present in American society was projected to an international audience by the Little Rock school crisis in September 1957. Within the administration, the key source of doubt over the role of nuclear weapons in national security policy was the Policy Planning Staff of the State Department, first under Bowie's direction, but after September 1957 led by Gerard Smith (who had, of course, had extensive exposure to the arguments over massive retaliation as Dulles's Special Assistant for Atomic Energy since 1954).[44] Reinforcement for the PPS's position came from the State Department's Far East Bureau, whose officials were sensitive to the currents of Asian anti-nuclear opinion, and the links this had with race. These voices within the State Department were increasingly joined, it is ironic to note, by John Foster Dulles himself, who was beginning to recognize that massive retaliation, a phrase which he had done so much to fix in the public mind, was an approach that lacked credibility and represented a handicap to the pursuit of American diplomatic objectives.

The State Department's concern over the trajectory of US military planning had begun to be aroused in late 1956 when Smith became drawn to the possibility that if the United States became involved in future hostilities in the Middle East, the Defense Department would exert strong pressure to permit American forces to use low-yield nuclear weapons. Dulles was alerted by Smith to the fact that the Secretary of State would

---

[44] See Gerard C. Smith, *Disarming Diplomat: The Memoirs of Gerard C. Smith, Arms Control Negotiator* (Lanham, MD, 1996), 74–7.

then have to advise the President on the political ramifications for the US global position if nuclear weapons were used in the region, yet no one in the State Department was responsible for preparing any such estimate, or for any planning as to how the effects of use might be moderated in the international political field.[45] On this occasion Dulles did not approve the recommendation that officials investigate the problem further, but in March 1957 Smith returned to the subject by suggesting to Christian Herter, the Under-Secretary, that a study be made of the political effects of the possible use of nuclear weapons in limited warfare (Smith noting that Herter had himself raised the idea at an earlier NSC briefing). In turn, Herter asked that Bowie conduct such an exercise among a very restricted group of State Department officials in the PPS, with a view to eventually consulting the regional bureau. ('Naturally,' Herter warned, 'it will be important to be very circumspect in the work you do on this subject.')[46]

The NSC debates that took place in the spring of 1957 over proposed revisions to the annual draft paper covering basic national security policy served to expose important differences between the Pentagon and State Department in this whole area and helped to generate more intervention by the latter in the field of defence policy. By this time, Eisenhower himself seems to have wanted to tighten up the language of the papers when it came to the role of nuclear weapons.[47] In one NSC meeting of April 1957, Radford noted that the JCS and Pentagon were then engaged in pursuing a policy where nuclear weapons would be used if necessary in any action involving US forces, and called for a new NSC directive to avoid future confusion. This position was supported by the President, who wanted the Pentagon to provide an explicit statement of the military elements of national strategy and added that, 'What was important was to see to it that from now on our basic policy gets into line with the planning which had been going on in the Department of Defense for over two years.'[48] Certainly, American field commanders were already primed to believe that there would be few restraints on the use of the nuclear resources

---

[45] Smith memorandum for Dulles, 'Political Aspects of Possible Use of Nuclear Weapons in the Middle East', 3 December 1956, 'Atomic Energy – Armaments', box 125, records of the PPS, 1957–61, RG 59, NARA.

[46] See Smith memorandum for Herter, 'Political Effects of Limited Use of Nuclear Weapons', 14 March 1957, and Herter memorandum for Bowie, 19 March 1957, *ibid.* This author could find no trace of this exercise in the PPS papers, and it may well have been overtaken by the debates witnessed over basic national security policy in the spring of 1957.

[47] See Craig, *Destroying the Village*, 62–6; and Fairchild and Poole, *JCS and National Policy*, VII, 12–14.

[48] Memorandum of discussion at the 319th meeting of the NSC, 11 April 1957, *FRUS, 1955–1957, XIX*, 472.

under their control. The Pentagon was evidently determined to use the annual NSC discussion of basic national security policy in order to gain wider acceptance of the principle that nuclear weapons would be used as a matter of course in response to virtually any limited conflict. These discussions were also framed by NSC evaluations of the world situation in early 1957, which anticipated that the Soviet capacity to destroy the United States in an all-out nuclear exchange might encourage more aggressive Communist policies at a local level (calculating that Washington would feel inhibited from any nuclear response).[49]

The old language featured in the 1956 paper on basic national security, NSC 5602/1, had talked of the need to use 'force' selectively to counter local aggression; by contrast, the Defense Department's draft proposals for its replacement (contained in paragraph 15 of NSC 5707/7) narrowed this down by merely mentioning the need to use 'nuclear weapons' selectively. Bowie felt that NSC 5707/7 threatened to change existing policy in three crucial ways: by making the sole criterion for the application of force the achievement of 'military objectives'; by planning for only nuclear capabilities to be used in 'any type of engagement larger than a border skirmish'; and by proposing the transfer of nuclear warheads to 'selected allies'. Bowie reported that the State Department was unanimous in objecting to the Pentagon's draft paper. All the Assistant Secretaries in charge of the regional bureau, the Counselor and the Special Assistants for Atomic Energy, and for Intelligence, found that the limited war proposals would 'forfeit freedom of maneuver and choice, estrange and divide our allies, jeopardize our overseas arrangements, lower will to resist, unacceptably risk the broadening of hostilities, and prejudice our moral leadership'. Ultimately, Bowie maintained, the new proposals ignored the fact that military policy and strategy should serve political purposes, including the alliances and overseas military arrangements which were themselves vital to national security.[50]

Bowie's summary had reflected the objections contained within a succession of papers submitted throughout May 1957 from the regional bureaus. 'There are strong, rising emotional tides – especially in the Far East – against atomic bombs and atomic tests,' Walter Robertson argued in his contribution. 'It is all very well to state – as do the draft revisions – that our allies "must accept" nuclear weapons as an integral part of our arsenal

---

[49] See Watson, *Into the Missile Age*, 103–4; Craig, *Destroying the Village*, 64–5.

[50] Memorandum by Bowie for Dulles, 'Basic National Security Policy (NSC 5707/7)', 23 May 1957, 'NSC 5707/1 Basic National Security Policy' folder, box 60, Subject Files Relating to National Security Policy, 1950–7, records of the PPS, 1957–61, RG 59, NARA.

and that they must recognize that their prompt use will provide the best means of avoiding general war. But will they accept it?' The Assistant Secretary for the Far East went on to note Japanese fear of atomic attack and radioactivity, and that at present it was 'inconceivable that any Japanese Government could agree to the storage of nuclear weapon components in Japan or to the use of Japanese bases for nuclear attacks. Our Embassy at Tokyo has recently reported that "the time has not yet come when the storage and use of atomic weapons in Japan can be profitably discussed, even in the strictest privacy, with Japanese leaders".' The equipping of US forces in Japan with just a nuclear capability would, it was predicted, become intolerable for the Japanese Government, and this consideration could not be lightly dismissed when there were, Robertson noted, 'over 400 bases and other operating facilities in Japan and that Japan occupied a key position in the free world defense chain'. As for South East Asia, the countries here were 'uneducated in the atomic facts of life', but they might come to 'share the attitude of their fellow Asians, the Japanese ... Certainly the Communists will be hard at work, assisted by intellectual, labor and socialist groups, to whip up Southeast Asian opposition to any form of military cooperation with a big power solely reliant on nuclear weapons. If it should eventuate that we were solely reliant on nuclear weapons to fight even brushfire wars, and if our friends in Southeast Asia meanwhile became deeply opposed to any nuclear protection, would this not in itself be a factor spurring the Communists to aggress against them?' Moreover, providing US nuclear weapons with warheads to 'selected major allies', which it was presumed would be European, gave all the impression of discriminatory treatment as other 'non-European allies' would be merely encouraged to rely for support on US capabilities, raising the issue of race once again. The Americans would then have two kinds of military associates: '(1) the Europeans and caucasians, the technologically advanced, the ones whom we can trust with atomic weapons: therefore the real allies; (2) the Asians and non-whites, the backward peoples, the ones who cannot be trusted with atomic weapons but who must look for atomic support to the U.S.' Robertson would not argue for giving nuclear weapons to Far Eastern allies ('quite the contrary') but any 'distinction between white ally and yellow dependent would cause an ever-widening rift between us and our Asian allies'. Robertson's concern, it should be emphasized, was also that the United States might find itself 'frozen into inaction' in responding to various situations, including guerrilla insurgencies, if the only means at its disposal were nuclear ones.[51]

---

[51] Memorandum from Robertson for Bowie (though in all probability drafted by Marshall Green), 'Basic National Security Policy', 7 May 1957, *ibid.*

In addition to this Asian perspective, all the regional bureaus pointed out that early resort to nuclear weapons in limited war would remove any chance of using diplomatic means at the outbreak of any fighting in order to achieve a settlement before escalation took hold. Officials were also united in their belief that no firm evidence existed to support the conviction of the JCS that use of nuclear weapons in limited war was unlikely to broaden into general war, and in fact were inclined to reach the opposite conclusion as Soviet nuclear capabilities were built up and the logic of deterrence was reinforced. The Counselor of the State Department, G. Frederick Reinhardt, could only concur with the various bureaus, noting the particular sensitivities of Germany and Japan in regard to nuclear weapons, and that, 'Our actions must take account of political currents in these countries in order to avoid a situation in which a government which continued military collaboration with us could not remain in power.' The embassy in Japan, for example, reported that it would be 'political suicide' for any Japanese government to consent to introduce nuclear weapons into Japan. Reinhardt concluded: 'knowledge that the U.S. armed forces had no capability except to fight with nuclear weapons would tell our allies that the decision which they consider an exceedingly critical one and one which has major implications for their future national existence has in effect already been made by the U.S. In such a situation it seems quite likely that U.S. forces would no longer be welcome on the soil of many or most of our allies and the use of facilities on their territory would be increasingly denied.'[52] This analysis, it must also be recalled, came at the same time that Washington was trying to deal with the repercussions of the Girard case for relations with Japan, and Eisenhower himself was beginning to wonder how tenable was the overseas base structure when anti-American feelings, particularly in Asia, appeared to be on the rise.

Dulles signalled his objections to the Pentagon's proposals to alter the language in the existing document at an important NSC meeting on 27 May 1957, where he questioned the assumption that a limited war could be waged with tactical nuclear weapons at all, highlighting his belief that the smallest weapons in the US armoury were of the type that had 'produced such sensational results at Hiroshima'. Moreover, he argued that the United States 'could not disregard important elements of world opinion' and 'was convinced that world opinion was not yet ready to accept the general use of nuclear weapons in local conflicts. If we resort to such a use of nuclear weapons we will, in the eyes of the world, be cast as

---

[52] 'Comments on Draft Revisions of NSC 5602/1, April 30, 1957', memorandum from Reinhardt for Bowie, 6 May 1957, *ibid.*

a ruthless military power, as was Germany earlier.' To emphasize that this was a widely held perspective, Dulles pointed out that the assistant secretaries who headed the State Department's regional bureau had all recorded their unanimous and strong opposition to advance approval for nuclear use because of the 'disastrous effect on public opinion' in their various areas of responsibility. Though Dulles recognized that small-scale and selective use of nuclear weapons might be the 'wave of the future', now was not the time to alarm allies and alienate popular opinion.[53] Radford's reply to these kinds of objections was to assert in characteristically blunt fashion that the essentials of the Pentagon's preferred draft of NSC 5707/7 had actually been adopted back in 1953 when the administration had embraced the New Look, and so current military planning was, whatever the semantics involved, proceeding along the lines stipulated in the new and narrower language of its controversial paragraph 15.

In order to break the impasse, Eisenhower and Cutler came up with a compromise form of words holding that 'military planning for U.S. forces to oppose local aggression will be based on the development of a flexible and selective capability, including nuclear capability for use as authorized by the President'. In addition, Cutler proposed a further modification to paragraph 11 of NSC 5707/7, which, as Dulles explained, the State Department would like changed so that nuclear weapons would be used 'when required to achieve national objectives', replacing the Defense Department's draft of 'military objectives'.[54] There seems to have been no challenge made to this alteration, though as Bowie claimed at the time, the 'single most important change in the basic paper' was the insistence by Dulles that the phrase 'national objectives' replace 'military objectives' as the criterion on which to judge the use of nuclear weapons.[55] The final version of what became, after presidential approval, NSC 5707/8 read that, 'It is the policy of the United States to place main, but not sole, reliance on nuclear weapons; to integrate nuclear weapons with other weapons in the arsenal of the United States; to consider them as conventional weapons from a military point of view; and to use them when

---

[53] See memorandum of discussion at the 325th meeting of the National Security Council, 27 May 1957, *FRUS, 1955–1957, XIX*, 499–501. A summary of State Department views and objections to the Defense Department's draft of NSC 5707/7 can be found in Bowie memorandum for Dulles, 'Basic National Security Policy', 23 May 1957, 'S/P Chronological, 1957–59', box 205, records of the PPS, 1957–61, RG 59, NARA.

[54] Memorandum of discussion at the 325th meeting of the NSC, 27 May 1957, *FRUS, 1955–1957, XIX*, 502–3.

[55] See Bowie memorandum for Herter, 'Politico-Military Cooperation', 3 August 1957, 'Atomic Energy – Armaments', box 125, records of the PPS, 1957–61, RG 59, NARA.

required to achieve national objectives.' The document also dropped its predecessor's injunction that US forces 'must not become so dependent on tactical nuclear capabilities that any decision to intervene against local aggression would probably be tantamount to a decision to use nuclear weapons'.[56]

The seemingly arcane discussions over the text of NSC 5707/8 were indicative of the contrasting priorities of different members of the policy-making bureaucracy. The Department of Defense and JCS (excepting the Army and Marine Corps), with strong support from the US Treasury, wanted to plan their overall strategy, force goals and overseas deployment on the basis of a general conflict with the Soviet Union and its allies. Limited war forces were a diversionary luxury from this overriding aim, and 'local aggression' would have to be met by the forces of regional allies, backed up with American air and naval power, delivering nuclear strikes as required. If American ground troops had to be introduced, such had been the cut-backs to the Army, they could only be committed in small quantities, and they would operate with their own tactical nuclear capability to compensate for inferiority in numbers. By contrast, the State Department were acutely aware of the political sensitivities surrounding nuclear issues, particularly when it came to Asia (and where 'local aggression' was probably most likely), and preferred to maintain flexibility over the kind of force that would be employed in limited war, and, by extension, hoped that conventional options could be retained. The ability to counter a local attack with non-nuclear force could also increase the credibility of US alliance commitments when questions were increasingly being asked over whether the ultimate American nuclear guarantee would still operate as Soviet strategic nuclear capabilities expanded. To several State Department officials there was an additional and related concern, which echoed the objections expressed in late 1953 over the JCS interpretation of NSC 162/2: with nuclear weapons dominating all the military's planning assumptions for limited war, there was an implicit tendency to downgrade the importance of ultimate presidential authorization for nuclear use in this context, and when such a decision would necessarily be based on a variety of political considerations, and not just narrow military criteria, as the Pentagon favoured (hence Bowie's note of satisfaction about the insertion of the phrase 'national objectives' in the language related to nuclear use). Despite this concession, NSC 5707/8 was important, as the official historians of the JCS have noted, because it 'moved closer to a policy of using nuclear weapons against local

---

[56] See Watson, *Into the Missile Age*, 107–10, for an overall summary of the debates over the wording of NSC 5707/8 and its meaning.

aggression but without affirming categorically that they would be used',
while its approval 'marked the apogee of the New Look'.[57]

The whole set of problems over limited war, force structure and the
effect on relationships with allies suggested that a greater degree of State
Department input was necessary to the way national defence policies were
formulated before they reached the higher forum of the NSC (or were
even discussed by the interdepartmental Planning Board that supplied its
major policy papers). Yet the evidence suggests that at this stage, during
the deliberations over national security policy and military posture in
1957, Dulles was unwilling to force this key question with the JCS and
Pentagon. At the NSC meeting in late May 1957, where the draft of NSC
5707/7 was discussed, Dulles was noticeably conciliatory, frequently
affirming that his own views were not greatly different from those of
Radford and Wilson, the Secretary of Defense. He was ready to agree
that it was inevitable that in the future the use of nuclear military power
would be accepted as 'conventional', and his anxieties simply lay in the
fact that the rest of the world was not yet ready to accept this notion.[58]
Perhaps most revealingly, when Cutler turned to Dulles to ask him if he
agreed with the State Department suggestion, contained in the annex to
NSC 5707/7, that a study should be made by an 'informed and disinter-
ested group' on the problem of limited war, using a number of hypothetical scenarios, the Secretary of State demurred (it was a proposal also
opposed in emphatic style by both Eisenhower and Radford).[59]

Nevertheless, and despite the hesitancy of Dulles, the May 1957 discussions of limited war capability in the NSC seem to have acted as a
catalyst for the State Department to involve itself more directly in the
Pentagon's closely guarded remit of military planning. Again it was
Gerard Smith who played an important role, drafting a memorandum to
Dulles in early June arguing that 'civilian Government officials should
acquire a better grasp of military planning for the use of and defense
against nuclear weapons'. With the increasing destructiveness of nuclear
weapons, Smith noted, there was a greater case for more involvement by
civilian officials, yet, 'The reverse seems to be the case. There seems to be
a reluctance on their part to know much about planning for wartime
employment of nuclear weapons. Perhaps because of his great military
experience, there is a tendency to assume that the President alone can
bring to bear the necessary civilian judgment on such planning. But the

[57] Fairchild and Poole, *JCS and National Policy*, VII, 16–17.
[58] See Dulles's comments in memorandum of discussion at the 325th meeting of the NSC,
27 May 1957, *FRUS, 1955–1957, XIX*, 499.
[59] *Ibid.*, 504.

responsibility for any decision to use nuclear weapons is too heavy for one person to assume.' Highlighting that war planning had traditionally been regarded as an exclusive preserve of the Pentagon, Smith maintained that with the advent of nuclear weapons, it should no longer be considered a technical matter beyond the understanding or responsibility of civilian officials. Smith's initial idea was that Dulles might simply approach the Secretary of Defense to suggest some State Department involvement in military planning. Herter, though, held up this proposal, and instead wanted the PPS to work up something more specific, and to think more carefully about tactics in presenting such ideas.[60]

In July 1957, the NSC continued to examine defence budget assumptions and planning for the next few years, with the Pentagon outlining proposed redeployments and reductions of forces overseas. It was in this context that Dulles now called for greater State Department participation in such planning so that the political implications could be properly assessed at an early stage. Eisenhower subsequently approved an NSC Action which directed the Secretaries of State and Defense to jointly consider the foreign policy aspects of the US military programme for 1959 while in its planning stages.[61] Bowie considered this development a 'unique opportunity' to press for State Department involvement in military planning, especially as Wilson had himself just suggested that continuing arrangements to handle this problem were necessary. The head of the PPS now felt that the State Department 'should take full advantage of this suggestion to arrange a firm basis for continuing joint consultation on politico-military matters, including the use of nuclear weapons'. However, Bowie felt that any move to gain access to 'war planning' was unrealistic; instead the emphasis should be placed on carrying forward the directives of NSC 5707/8.[62] In September 1957, in accordance with the earlier instruction of the NSC, Dulles met Donald A. Quarles, the Deputy Secretary of Defense, where the latter outlined his department's thinking over levels of military spending and forces over the next few years. The Secretary of State used the occasion to remind Quarles of the need to consult with the State Department well in advance over the foreign policy implications of proposed reductions in overseas deployments. Responding to Dulles's call for better co-ordination in

---

[60] Smith memorandum for Dulles, 'The Need for Additional Non-Military Participation in Planning for the Employment of Nuclear Weapons', 3 June 1957, and Herter memorandum for Bowie, 12 June 1957, 'Atomic Energy – Armaments', box 125, records of the PPS, 1957–61, RG 59, NARA.

[61] See memorandum of discussion at the 332nd meeting of the NSC, 25 July 1957, *FRUS, 1955–1957, XIX*, 561, and NSC Action No. 1755 of 31 July 1957, *ibid.*, 564, n. 8.

[62] See Bowie memorandum for Herter, 'Politico-Military Cooperation', 3 August 1957.

military planning, Quarles suggested that senior figures from the two departments should meet on a regular basis. But Dulles was after something more, proposing (ultimately unproductively) that his officials 'have contact with the planning group within Defense before the plans had jelled and been presented to the JCS'.[63]

The outcome of the review of national security policy, Bowie felt, was that the Pentagon and JCS had been 'sharply reminded that the use of force cannot be isolated from controlling political considerations'. As regards nuclear weapons, the debates had also shown the need for 'early contingency planning to establish integrated political and military criteria for their use in local situations'. It was urgent that there should be 'joint State Department–Defense consideration of a concept to coordinate the selective and flexible application of nuclear force with the achievement of limited political objectives'. Civilian officials outside the Pentagon knew too little about the physical effects of nuclear weapons, while military officers needed to know more about the likely political effects of weapons usage and 'must understand that *nuclear weapons differ from all other weapons not only in the magnitude of destructiveness but in the fact that their effects cannot be measured solely in terms of numbers killed*' (emphasis added).[64] Nothing could be further from the rhetoric associated with massive retaliation, where the moral distinctiveness of nuclear weapons was to be ignored, or from the planning concepts favoured by Radford. Formulating a national doctrine for responding to local aggression was becoming a leading preoccupation of the PPS. It was, moreover, a subject that excited the interest of Cutler, who in August 1957 can be found pressing Eisenhower to lift discussion of limited war onto a new plane, perhaps by creating a special committee of the NSC which could study US capabilities to deal with local hostilities on a continuing basis 'starting in trouble spots (such as Korea, the Offshore Islands, Syria, Indonesia, Indo-China, Thailand, Israel, etc.)'.[65]

By this stage there were indications that Dulles was also coming round to the view that the political issues surrounding nuclear use would have to be given greater consideration by defence planners, and that this

[63] Howard P. Jones memorandum for Walter Robertson, 'Meeting State–Defense September 5, 1957', 9 September 1957, 'FE 2500–3100', box 1, TS Files of the Regional Planning Adviser, records of the Bureau of Far East Affairs, 1955–63, RG 59, NARA.
[64] Bowie memorandum for Herter, 'Politico-Military Cooperation'.
[65] Cutler memorandum for Eisenhower, 'Limited War in the Nuclear Age', 7 August 1957, 'Military Doctrine and Organization (1956–1960) (5)', Department of Defense subseries, Subject series, Office of the Staff Secretary, White House Office, DDEL, and see two attached memoranda, 'Increasing Emphasis on Firepower' and 'Increasing Reliance Upon Deterrent Capabilities', both 11 July 1957.

was also related to the vexed issue of deployment of nuclear weapons to overseas locations. We have already seen how the Secretary of State was reluctant to follow military advice when it came to the movement of nuclear-capable weaponry to Korea. With the embassy in Seoul supportive of modernization, however, and Dulles clearly divided on the issue, pressures on the State Department to adopt a more flexible approach mounted. In early June 1957, Walter Robertson came out in favour of pressing ahead with the programme, though without actual warheads to accompany the dual-capable weapons; Bowie was still opposed, some State Department officials even believing that the JCS talk of 'modernization' was merely a sham to conceal the fact that the policy was designed to 'dump' in Korea unwieldy and outmoded weapons systems whose range and mobility made them unsuitable for most projected military operations. Dulles himself could see no military rationale for the deployment, feeling that US fighter-bomber aircraft based on Okinawa and in Japan could provide any necessary nuclear firepower: the only reason that carried weight with Dulles was over using the arrival of the weapons as a lever to help to convince Syngman Rhee to reduce the large size of the South Korean standing army.[66]

On 13 June 1957, with the Pentagon and the State Department still divided, the NSC considered once more the whole issue of modernization of forces in Korea. Raising the general problem of overseas deployment of nuclear weapons, Dulles cautioned the Council that 'to advertise the existence of such huge weapons as these would be bound to cause very serious repercussions for the United States throughout Asia. Sending such weapons to Korea would be resented throughout Asia because [they] were identified with the West and with the hated doctrine of white supremacy, quite apart from the weapons effects themselves.'[67] The modest savings which the Defense Department anticipated would come from reductions in Korean military assistance were not enough, in the Secretary's eyes, to 'compensate for the political and propaganda liabilities which would be thrust upon us'. Radford defended the military case for deploying the weapons, but he also tried to respond to Dulles's points about the political ramifications by mentioning that in his past visits to 'friendly' Asian nations, most of the military men he encountered accepted the necessity of a nuclear defence to offset Chinese conventional strength, with Japan being the only exception. The President remained sceptical, however, and it appears that though he was prepared to see the

---

[66] *FRUS, 1955–1957, XXIII*, Part 2, 439–43.
[67] Memorandum of discussion at the 326th meeting of the NSC, 13 June 1957, *ibid.*, 445. The remarks immediately after Dulles's comments here have not been declassified.

nuclear-capable weapons deployed to Korea, he hoped that this could be expressly linked to a more wholesale reduction in South Korean forces (a trade-off which was in accord with Dulles's own wishes). A decision was thus deferred pending further approaches to Rhee. It seems surprising that Eisenhower believed this kind of rational logic would work with Rhee, and ever true to form, the South Korean President rejected any idea of a major cutback to his army, at least until his ultimate goal of unification had been achieved: in Rhee's mind, of course, military strength and the latter objective were explicitly linked. As diplomatic approaches to the South Koreans continued, pressure mounted from the JCS for a deployment decision, and news began to seep out that the transfer of nuclear-capable weapons to Korea was held up. Already, on 21 June, the UN Command had announced it was suspending adherence to article 13(b) of the armistice agreement, paving the way for modernization of conventional equipment for the American divisions to move forward. There were also concerns that Rhee would take reluctance to deploy the nuclear-capable weapons as a signal of weakening will on the part of Washington, and Eisenhower himself seems to have become increasingly impatient with the technicalities holding up the whole process and (perhaps mindful of the recent OCB guidelines on nuclear deployment announcements) felt there was no special reason why this category of weapon system should have any extra attention drawn to it.[68]

The matter was discussed at another NSC meeting on 8 August 1957. In the absence of the 'package deal' linking major reductions in South Korean forces with the introduction of the 280 mm cannon and Honest John rockets, Dulles remained opposed to their immediate deployment, feeling this was the only 'trump card' the United States held over Rhee (a man he described as an 'Oriental bargainer'). In the event, the NSC decided, in principle, to proceed with the move of the nuclear-capable weapons, but the timing of the deployment would be left to the President, after consulting the Secretaries of State and Defense.[69] Final presidential authorization for the movement of the nuclear-capable weapons seems to have been forthcoming in December 1957. Despite Dulles's belief that deployment should be dependent on South Korean acquiescence to US plans for conventional force reductions, Rhee's calculated procrastination appears to have been effective at decoupling the two issues, and South Korean readiness to study the whole issue once modernization was under

[68] See memorandum of conference between Eisenhower and Lemnitzer, 23 July 1957, *ibid.*, 471.
[69] See memorandum of discussion at the 334th meeting of the NSC, 8 August 1957, *ibid.*, 480–9, and NSC 5702/2, 9 August 1957, *ibid.*, 489–98.

way seems to have been enough to convince an anxious Pentagon that there were now no longer any grounds for delay of changes which they regarded as valid on their own terms for the US forces deployed in Korea. There was still some confusion over the storage of nuclear munitions in Korea: Radford had commented at the August NSC meeting that there were no official instructions to prepare for storing nuclear warheads in South Korea, something which surprised Eisenhower who had felt this had already been agreed in June. The official historians of the JCS comment that in mid-July the chiefs had asked for storage policy in Korea to be reconsidered, but that this was not approved by the administration. Cutler's recollection (concurred in by Dulles) was that 'at least by the Council meeting on August 8 it was understood by the President, by the Secretary of State, and by Defense that nuclear warheads might be stored in Korea as appropriate', though again further authorization would be required from Eisenhower for the specific timing of deployment. This authorization to change storage policy in Korea seems to have been eventually issued to the JCS by the Secretary of Defense on 17 January 1958, the same time that Honest John rockets and 280 mm artillery pieces were also finally deployed. The Air Force followed this up at the end of the year with a Tactical Missile Group equipped with the Matador surface-to-surface cruise missile, all under the watchful eye of a wary State Department.[70]

That Dulles had seen fit to raise the issue of race at the NSC meeting held on 13 June which discussed nuclear deployment in Korea also seems of significance when considering how he was framing the issues at stake. The following day, at the annual Secretaries of Defense conference at Quantico in Virginia, having discussed with one general over breakfast 'the hate the yellow man has for the white man', Dulles ruminated on the lasting legacy of Western colonialism and resultant racial discrimination

---

[70] See Leonhart memorandum for Smith, 'Nuclear Storage in Korea', 17 October 1957, and Cutler notes, 16 October 1957; Farley memorandum for Smith, 'Deployment of Nuclear Weapons to U.S. Forces in Korea', 1 November 1957, all in 'Korea', box 130, records of the PPS, 1957–61, RG 59, NARA; Fairchild and Poole, *JCS and National Policy*, VII, 201; Robertson to Sprague, 8 January 1958, and Sprague to Robertson, 21 January 1958, *FRUS, 1958–1960, XVIII: Japan; Korea* (Washington, DC, 1994), 424, 431; Watson, *Into the Missile Age*, 627. Some US Air Force officers felt that the Matadors might prove useful in a 'strategic' role; one assistant to the Chief of Staff of the US Air Force felt that 'the Matador in Korea could be a potential Korean Strategic Retaliatory Strike Force. Should Korea be threatened by Chicom [*sic*], the U.S. could turn over to ROK the Matadors with nuclear weapons, and thus enable ROK to announce that an atk [*sic*] on ROK would result in ROK attack upon industrial centers of China with nuclear wpns [*sic*]', note by Lt Col James C. Sherrill on Major General M. A. Preston memorandum for General Thomas White, 11 September 1957, 'Command Pacific', box 6, Thomas C. White papers, LC.

in parts of Africa and Asia. With a staggering degree of myopia, the Secretary of State continued that the United States had been 'relatively free from the practice of those discriminations abroad although by no means wholly so, but in any event we are just lumped with the western Europeans, the whites, in that respect'. This represented one of the 'grave liabilities' to which the United States was exposed, especially as Communist propaganda exploited 'our own racial problems here at home', using them to 'indicate this sense of white superiority'. This issue was a 'very grave problem' that 'affects our whole military-political strategy particularly in Asia'. Moreover, in what constituted the most revealing aspect of Dulles's remarks, he went on to mention that discussions with a senior political officer who had just returned from South East Asia led him to the conclusion:

While it is quite true that the top political people and top military people are, I think, increasingly open-minded to the use of atomic weapons, still there is in the feelings of the masses identification of the atomic weapon with this white supremacy and its having been used first by the United States against members of the so-called yellow race, and there is a greater measure of tolerance toward the development of atomic weapons, the testing of atomic weapons, by the Soviet Union than there is to that development and testing by the United States or Great Britain because a good many of the Asians take a certain degree of quiet satisfaction over the fact that a nation that is at least partly Asiatic, which has never been identified with the white Europeans in terms of colonialism, that that is now getting in a position to challenge the power which heretofore has been a monopoly of western whites.[71]

In the Secretary of State's comments one can see an obvious attempt to communicate to his military audience the political and diplomatic dangers attached to the identification of nuclear weapons with notions of white superiority. How this concern might influence overall strategy was outlined in the prepared speech that Dulles gave to the conference, where under the title 'The Political Importance of Flexible Military Strength' he emphasized the need to supplement retaliatory nuclear capacity with sufficient local strength to convince allies that smaller conflicts could be contained without recourse to all-out war.

What Dulles called 'our own racial problems here at home' were shown again all too clearly only three months later when in September 1957 the Little Rock school crisis exposed the continuing prevalence of segregation in the South to an international audience. As the governor of Arkansas

---

[71] See Dulles's speech and question and answer session at Department of Defense Secretaries Conference, Ellis Hall, Quantico, Virginia, 14 June 1957, 740.5/614–57, box 3143, CDF, RG 59, NARA.

moved to block the admittance of nine African-American students to
Little Rock's Central High School, and baying mobs shouted abuse as
they were finally escorted by federal troops to their classrooms, USIA's
hopes that the earlier *Brown* ruling would symbolize racial progress in the
United States was dealt a resounding blow. Harold Isaacs, in a contemporary analysis, noted that Little Rock was 'certainly the most heavily
reported U.S. story abroad in 1957', and began when the impact of events
in 1955–6, such as the Emmett Till trial and the Montgomery Bus
boycott, was just dying away.[72] With images of white racial intolerance
and bigotry being broadcast around the world, the administration worried
about reactions in Africa, Asia and the Middle East. 'At a time when we
face grave situations abroad because of the hatred that Communism bears
toward a system of government based on human rights,' Eisenhower told
the American people in a radio and television address (in comments that
were actually scripted by Dulles), 'it would be difficult to exaggerate the
harm that is being done to the prestige and influence, and indeed to the
safety, of our nation and the world.'[73] The situation at Little Rock, Dulles
complained to the Attorney-General, was 'ruining our foreign policy. The
effect of this in Asia and Africa will be worse for us than Hungary was for
the Russians.'[74] One prominent conservative Japanese citizen, a reporter
based in India, noted of these events: 'If Americans can regard Negroes as
inferior, how do they really regard Asians?' Incidents such as Little Rock
'serve to drive more and more Asians to the conclusion that there cannot
be, at least not in this sorry generation, any real meeting ground between
Occident and Orient'.[75] Eisenhower sanctioned federal intervention in
Little Rock because of the need he felt to uphold the constitutional order,
and because of the harm images of white violence were doing America's
reputation, not through any basic attachment to notions of equality. In an
attempt to repair some of the damage that had been done, the administration publicized the role of federal troops and the US Government in
defending the constitutional rights of the African-American students, but
dispelling original impressions was far from easy.

   A 'meeting ground between Occident and Orient' was certainly what
Dulles and the State Department were trying to achieve when it came to

---

[72] See Harold R. Isaacs, 'World Affairs and U.S. Race Relations: A Note on Little Rock',
Public Opinion Quarterly, 22, 3, Autumn 1958, 364.

[73] Radio and television address to the American people, 24 September 1957, *Public Papers of
the Presidents: Dwight D. Eisenhower, 1957* (Washington, DC, 1958), 694; and see
Dudziak, *Cold War Civil Rights*, 131–4, for the background.

[74] Memorandum of telephone conversation between Dulles and Herbert Brownell, 24
September 1957, *FRUS, 1955–1957, IX*, 613.

[75] Quoted in Dudziak, *Cold War Civil Rights*, 137.

US relations with Japan and the thorny issue of revision of the security treaty, against the unpromising background of the Girard case. In a series of talks between Kishi and MacArthur held in April 1957, the Japanese Prime Minister argued that most Japanese regarded the treaty as a sign of subordination to the United States through the way it granted the unilateral right to station American forces in Japan and to use them without regard for Japanese views. Stressing his primary desire to strengthen the US–Japanese relationship, Kishi wanted the treaty revised to make deployment and use of American forces the result of mutual agreement, and also a time limit set for its provisions after which the treaty might be terminated by either party. Convinced that revision was now essential, MacArthur informed his superiors in Washington that 'we have reached the turning point in our relations with Japan' and concessions to the Japanese position involving putting relationships in the security and economic fields on an equal basis would be required. The alternative, the Ambassador predicted, would be a Japan 'headed in the wrong direction. They might adopt neutralism, perhaps on the Swiss, but perhaps on the Indian, model. They might even turn to work with the Communists.'[76]

Nevertheless, Dulles was not yet ready to see full-scale revision or even replacement of the treaty (the latter would be politically challenging in any case, with Congress highly restive over the Girard case), and so though sympathetic with developing a more co-operative basis to relations, when Kishi visited Washington in June he was offered only a joint US–Japanese Committee which would allow for consultation over problems arising under the existing agreement. Seeing the continuing presence of almost 100,000 US military personnel in Japan as an important source of friction, and in concomitant moves, the administration also decided to implement another round of troop reductions, with an army division being moved to Korea, where it would replace one of the two divisions already deployed there (which in turn would then be disbanded), and the remaining Marine contingent transferring to Okinawa. By the end of 1957, it was planned to have removed virtually all ground combat units from Japan, air force personnel now making up the bulk of the 60,000 or so forces remaining in the country.[77]

Though Kishi's June visit had not produced any dramatic breakthrough, there was every sign that the Eisenhower administration realized that the Japanese Prime Minister was their 'best bet' (as Dulles termed it)

---

[76] See Tokyo to State Department, 17 April 1957, *FRUS, 1955–1957, XXIII*, Part 1, 277–9; and MacArthur's comments in memorandum of conference with the President, 18 June 1957, *ibid.*, 358.

[77] See Schaller, *Altered States*, 130–3.

if conservative control was to be assured over the long term against the Socialists and a close relationship with the United States maintained. One manifestation of this was the beginning of the covert supply of funds to LDP candidates by the CIA in the build-up to the May 1958 Diet elections, and the similar promotion of moderates within the structures of the Socialist Party.[78] During the summer of 1957, in addition, Dulles had already come to the view that the right of consultation with Tokyo over the disposition of US forces would have to be conceded, in line with the arrangements that obtained within NATO. As a consequence it seemed inevitable that treaty revision would eventually follow, and that the Pentagon's propensity to link revision to speedier progress with Japanese rearmament and willingness to play a wider military role in the region would be overridden. In an analysis of the overall trends in opinion towards the United States compiled in September 1957, it was concluded that the cumulative impact of such incidents as the Girard case, as well as the continuing controversy surrounding nuclear testing, was doing serious harm to the American image. With the prestige of the PRC deemed to be on the increase, 'if the present converging trends are not arrested the time must be anticipated when Communist China will begin to vie with the United States in Japanese esteem'.[79]

It was also at this time that Dulles attempted to offer a more palatable version of massive retaliation in 'Challenge and Response in United States Policy', an article that appeared in the October 1957 issue of *Foreign Affairs*. Allen Dulles had mentioned his brother's June Quantico speech to Hamilton Fish Armstrong, the editor of *Foreign Affairs*, who thought it might be a good follow-up to the piece that he had published in April 1954, where the Secretary of State had sought to clarify the meaning of massive retaliation. This idea had also occurred to John Foster Dulles himself, who in turn asked that Bowie, in one of his final acts as director of the PPS, prepare an article on the main lines of current US foreign policy which Armstrong could use to mark the 35th anniversary of the journal. Eager to catch the current debate over limited war, in August Armstrong had himself encouraged Dulles to outline the shape of his thoughts about current national security policy with the prompt: 'Isn't one of the needs of diplomacy to know that behind it there exists an American capacity to fight a limited war? ... Would you not feel better able to deal with a wide variety of contingencies in all parts of the world if you had the backing of a

---

[78] See *ibid.*, 136; LaFeber, *The Clash*, 318.

[79] FE-13, 'Trends in Japanese Attitudes toward the U.S. vs Communist Powers and Toward the Present State of Relations with the U.S.', 4 September 1957, box 1, Public Opinion Barometer Reports, 1955–62, Office of Research, RG 306, NARA.

more flexible power which could be used where the all-out deterrent is ineffective?'[80]

In the piece that was eventually published, Dulles argued that the United States had not been and was not content to base its strategy merely on 'a capacity to destroy vast segments of the human race', a concept which was 'acceptable only as a last alternative'. The development of low-yield and 'cleaner' tactical nuclear weapons offered a way out of the limited war conundrum (as Kissinger was then arguing) by reducing the extent of the devastation that nuclear use would produce; 'the resourcefulness of those who serve our nation in the field of science and engineering', the Secretary of State had averred, 'now shows that it is possible to alter the character of nuclear weapons. It seems now that their use need not involve vast destruction and widespread harm to humanity. Recent tests [most likely a reference to the 1956 *Redwing* series] point to the possibility of possessing nuclear weapons the destructiveness and radiation effects of which can be confined substantially to predetermined targets. In the future it may thus be feasible to place less reliance upon deterrence of vast retaliatory power' so that, for example, invasion routes could be covered by nuclear artillery (in what may have been intended as passing reference to the role of 280 mm atomic cannon in defending the paths from the Korean armistice line to Seoul).[81]

In many ways, this was a reaffirmation of the 'selective' targeting response to minor Communist aggression that the administration had laid out in the spring of 1954 in order to meet the original critics of massive retaliation. Now, Dulles was saying, technology allowed such a limited and controlled use of nuclear weapons to become a proportionate reply to minor Communist probes of Western resolve. These claims, however, simply lacked credibility in the eyes of wider public opinion, especially when strategic analysts considered low-yield atomic weapons still to be in the order of 15–20 kilotons, and so comparable to the Hiroshima and

[80] See Allen Dulles to John Foster Dulles, 7 July 1957; John Foster Dulles to Allen Dulles, 9 July 1957, 'Deterrent Strategy' folder, box 115; Armstrong to Dulles, 12 June 1957; Bowie memorandum for Dulles, 3 August 1957; Armstrong memorandum telephoned to Dulles, 8 August 1957, 'Armstrong' folder, box 113, Selected Correspondence series, John Foster Dulles papers, Mudd Library. That Dulles held Armstrong in high regard is shown by the fact that he offered him the job of head of the PPS when Bowie stepped down from that position.
[81] See John Foster Dulles, 'Challenge and Response in United States Policy', *Foreign Affairs*, 36, 1, October 1957, 25–43, especially 31; see also Rosendorf, *Cold War Statesmen*, 81–2. That Bowie's PPS played a large role in crafting the article is apparent from Bowie memorandum for Dulles, 3 August 1957, 'China, People's Republic' folder [misfile], box 113, Selected Correspondence series, John Foster Dulles papers, Mudd Library; it is also apparent from this material that Eisenhower himself read and checked through the text in mid-August 1957.

Nagasaki bombs in explosive power: the casualties from the use of only a few such bombs would still be horrendous for the European or Asian states over whose territory a limited war would be fought. Coupled with that, the risks of escalation to a strategic nuclear exchange, where vastly more powerful hydrogen weapons would be employed, were still enormous once the nuclear threshold had been crossed. This was the most significant point of all: whatever the rhetoric of the administration, popular opinion saw a sharp distinction between conventional and nuclear weapons, and the stubborn prevalence of this belief made heavy reliance on nuclear weapons as a means of deterrence an inherently problematic policy to sell to friends, allies and non-aligned states around the world.

Widespread unease about an apparently limitless nuclear arms race, which in the absence of superpower agreement might only be ended by mutual destruction, was common by the late 1950s, and was given graphic demonstration by the opposition to the continuation of nuclear testing. The Eisenhower administration had always implicitly recognized the presentational problem of the New Look's reliance on nuclear weapons by maintaining the stance that it was willing to discuss steps towards disarmament, or arms control, with the Soviet Union, though always with a carefully crafted set of conditions attached to the proposals that were put forward. In his 1957 *Foreign Affairs* article, Dulles had highlighted American interest in disarmament measures and had professed that the United States recognized 'armaments alone are no lasting guarantee of peace'. Nevertheless, over the previous two years, and since Stassen's appointment as a special assistant on disarmament to the President, the administration had struggled to formulate a coherent and attractive programme of proposals to reduce tensions and curb the arms race. Although Eisenhower could often be found in NSC meetings expressing his anguished view that something had to be done to halt the ascending spiral, little of substance came out of the White House, and it is hard to avoid the conclusion that key officials, Dulles included, simply did not feel agreement with Moscow on these kinds of issues was a practical proposition, while disarmament initiatives were designed largely for cosmetic purposes, with the knowledge they were almost certain to be rejected.[82]

Over atmosphere nuclear testing, the AEC and its Chairman, Lewis Strauss, with strong support from the Department of Defense, were able to frustrate Stassen's attempts to push forward a bolder position by initially dispensing with insistence that proper inspection and monitoring controls should accompany any moratorium. As for Stassen himself, his

---

[82] See Wittner, *Resisting the Bomb*, 175–80.

maverick performance in the 1956 election campaign (where he had opposed Nixon's nomination as Eisenhower's vice-presidential running mate) along with evident political ambition had contributed to his isolation in Republican circles, while his tendency to advance personal proposals without official sanction was a constant irritation to Dulles. In February 1958, Stassen finally resigned from the administration, his latest ideas for a two-year US test moratorium having been turned down by the NSC, and the President having finally wearied of his disarmament adviser. At the same time, public alarm over fallout from testing, both at home and abroad, remained strong. By mid-1957, for example, opinion polls were registering that 64 per cent of the American people favoured an international agreement to prohibit tests, and the President was also showing increasing signs of scepticism at the burgeoning number of test shots that each new programme produced by the weapons laboratories and the AEC seemed to incorporate as necessary.[83] Nevertheless, and despite mounting domestic and international pressures, as long as the Soviet Union carried out its own extensive programme of testing, and designed and built ever-more powerful thermonuclear weapons, it was difficult to counteract the arguments of the military establishment that, without continued American testing, the United States might fall dangerously behind in certain crucial areas of weapons technology.

Meanwhile, the idea that the United States' own strategic superiority in nuclear weapons would suffice to deter attack and, at a lower level, provide the shield that would allow limited nuclear use in the event of a local Communist aggression was in the process of being eroded by apparent Soviet breakthroughs. Knowledge that the Soviet Union had tested the first Intercontinental Ballistic Missile (ICBM) in August 1957 was compounded by the public shock experienced in early October when the Russians also launched the world's first artificial earth satellite, driving home an image of Soviet technological and scientific prowess. According to the British Prime Minister, Harold Macmillan, who visited Washington soon after, the mood induced by the *Sputnik* launch 'has been something equivalent to Pearl Harbour. The American cocksureness is shaken … the President is under severe attack for the first time … Foster [Dulles] is under still more severe attack. His policies are said to have failed everywhere.'[84] Inflated fears of a 'missile gap' opening up with the Soviet Union

---

[83] Eisenhower was clearly annoyed with the number and size of some of the shots initially proposed for the *Hardtack* series in the Pacific planned for 1958; see Hewlett and Holl, *Atoms for Peace and War*, 456–7.

[84] Macmillan diary entry, 23 October 1957, MSS Macmillan dep. d. 50, Bodleian Library; and in general Robert A. Divine, *The Sputnik Challenge: Eisenhower's Response to the Soviet Satellite* (New York, 1993).

became the political currency of the day, and the American homeland seemed exposed like never before to a crippling nuclear strike.[85] The administration's position was also made uncomfortable by the conclusions of the Gaither Committee which had been assembled by the President earlier in the year to investigate US civil defence, but which had chosen to expand its remit to look in an overall sense at American vulnerability to Soviet attack. Its provocative report, presented to Eisenhower in early November, and quickly leaked to the press and partisan opponents of the administration, portrayed SAC's bomber force as exposed to a surprise Soviet first strike, using its new ICBM potential, with a high-point of vulnerability being reached as early as 1959–60. The Gaither panel therefore called for a rapid hike in US defence spending, and an extensive series of measures to improve American preparedness and increase retaliatory capabilities.[86] Eisenhower's sober, almost dismissive, treatment of the Gaither Report appears entirely commendable in retrospect, and the President was correct in his scepticism over estimates of Soviet strength which later proved to be wildly inaccurate.[87] Nonetheless, the impression of approaching strategic nuclear parity, or even of Soviet superiority, served to undermine the credibility of massive retaliation yet further.

The Gaither Committee had, moreover, devoted attention to the limited war debate in its deliberations and received evidence from, among others, disgruntled senior Army officers, and members of the State Department's PPS.[88] Of particular importance here was the role of Paul Nitze, the former head of the PPS and principal drafter of NSC 68, who since 1954 had been an outspoken critic of massive retaliation and had pressed for an emphasis on graduated deterrence in articles and commentaries on current national security policy.[89] Nitze played a leading part in writing the Gaither Report, which included as a 'highest value measure' the recommendation to augment US and allied forces for limited military operations, and (as the PPS had also been urging) to undertake a national study 'to develop current doctrine on when and

---

[85] See Peter J. Roman, *Eisenhower and the Missile Gap* (Ithaca, 1995).

[86] See David L. Snead, *The Gaither Committee, Eisenhower, and the Cold War* (Columbus, OH, 1999).

[87] See Bundy, *Danger and Survival*, 334–42; though see also Snead, *Gaither Committee*, 154–8, who argues that Eisenhower was less dismissive of the report than other scholars have supposed.

[88] See Snead, *Gaither Committee*, 97–102.

[89] See, e.g., Paul H. Nitze, 'Atoms, Strategy, and Policy', *Foreign Affairs*, 34, 2, January 1956, 187–98; and Paul H. Nitze, *From Hiroshima to Glasnost: At the Centre of Decision: A Memoir* (London, 1989), 151–2, 164–9.

how nuclear weapons can contribute to limited operations'.[90] The cumulative impact of these developments was to cast doubt on the competence of the administration in the field of national defence, where the charge was frequently levelled that the shibboleths of fiscal prudence were putting at risk the security of the nation. As one study of these issues has contended, 'the autumn and winter of 1957–1958 witnessed the rise of a coalition of forces, each (for its own reasons and in its own interest) seeking to overturn the Eisenhower program of defense'.[91]

In response to the Gaither Report's recommendation over compiling a study of limited war capabilities, the Defense Department argued that it alone should carry out the exercise, but when the NSC came to discuss this recommendation in January 1958, Dulles argued strongly for State Department participation in any Pentagon work on limited war doctrine so that 'political and foreign policy considerations should be meshed into the study ... from the very beginning'.[92] By early March 1958, after some foot-dragging, the Pentagon finally came forward to the NSC with a formal proposal for a major inter-agency study of US and allied capabilities for limited war, involving representatives from the JCS, State and Defense Departments, and input from the CIA.[93] Already discernible at this early stage was the extreme reluctance of the Pentagon and JCS to review the issue of limited war capabilities on anything other than their own terms and their endeavours to marginalize the foreign policy aspects of the problem that State Department officials would certainly try to emphasize. We can also see a change in emphasis from the Secretary of State: in May 1957 he had sided with Radford and Wilson in rejecting the need for a study of limited war, but Dulles now gave his backing to those in the State Department, such as Gerard Smith, who had been pressing for such a survey.

Any such appraisal of limited war was likely to have to deal with the issue of American dependence on its overseas bases for the effective

[90] See 'Report to the President by the Security Resources Panel of the ODM Science Advisory Committee on Deterrence and Survival in the Nuclear Age', 7 November 1957, *FRUS, 1955–1957, XIX*, 643; and for Nitze, see Snead, *Gaither Committee*, 69–71, 115–16, 120.
[91] Richard A. Aliano, *American Defense Policy from Eisenhower to Kennedy: The Politics of Changing Military Requirements, 1957–1961* (Athens, GA, 1975), 54.
[92] See memorandum of discussion at the 352nd meeting of the NSC, 22 January 1958, *FRUS, 1958–1960, III: National Security Policy; Arms Control and Disarmament* (Washington, DC, 1996), 27.
[93] See Lay memorandum for the NSC, 'Capabilities of Forces for Limited Military Operations', 7 March 1958, with enclosed Quarles memorandum, *FRUS, 1958–1960, III: National Security Policy; Arms Control and Disarmament: Microfiche Supplement* (Washington, DC, 1998), fiche 23; Watson, *Into the Missile Age*, 301–2.

conduct of military operations, and here nuclear issues were bound to be of importance in influencing the attitudes of host governments to the American presence, particularly in the Far East. This was brought home to the President and his senior policy-making advisers in December 1957 with their receipt of the Nash Report, a major (and voluminous) study of the worldwide US overseas base structure. As we have seen, through the summer of 1956 Eisenhower and Dulles had had many indications that with the threat of overt Communist aggression apparently receding, fears of nuclear fallout increasing and local nationalism also on the rise, opposition was mounting in many countries to US military bases.[94] Eventually, in October 1956, Frank C. Nash, a former Assistant Secretary of Defense, was directed by the President to compile a large-scale study on the problem and all its juridical, political and military aspects. After over a year of work, involving the despatch of questionnaires to US military and diplomatic personnel, interviews with high-ranking officials and several field trips, Nash produced a comprehensive set of general recommendations on how the base network could best be preserved against local pressures, featuring twenty-nine specific country studies.[95]

There had already been indications that nuclear issues would be a major feature of Nash's study. The Far East Bureau of the State Department felt that given the continuing reliance on the manned bomber for deterrent striking power, general base requirements in the region were unlikely to change over the subsequent decade, yet irritations and grievances such as 'criminal jurisdiction and status of forces, antipathies generated by higher U.S. standards of living, occupation of agricultural land, U.S. automobiles and traffic accidents, economic impact, jet noise, [and] special local issues' were always to be expected. Marshall Green was alert to the fact that Nash's survey would pay particular attention to local sensitivity to the presence of US nuclear weapons and the connections to American posture for limited war, noting in August 1957:

With the increasing incorporation of atomic weapons into the U.S. arsenal, public opinion and governmental attitudes in allied countries on the subject of atomic weapons have ever greater bearing on the ability of the U.S. to secure and maintain operating facilities abroad. In several allied countries, there is a body of public opinion opposing atomic weapons, which is strong enough to restrain the governments of those countries from full cooperation with the U.S. This public opinion is based partly on moral considerations and partly on a conviction that the presence of U.S. atomic forces will automatically involve the host country in nuclear warfare should fighting break out. This concern may be heightened by a growing alarm

[94] See Dulles letter to Wilson, 28 June 1956, *FRUS, 1955–1957, XIX*, 333–7, and n. 2.
[95] See editorial note, *ibid.*, 709–10.

that the U.S. will use atomic weapons in all situations, however small and limited, and that this will lead automatically to the use of larger weapons and to general nuclear war. Unless we can resolve this question in reasonably satisfactory fashion, it will play hob with our base positions overseas and ... with our alliances. What renders the problem almost insoluble is the insistence of many host countries, in the course of negotiations on the introduction and storage of atomic weapons, on advance consultation before those weapons may be used.

For the moment, all the State Department could do to mitigate this problem was to engage in public information programmes to explain the roles of both conventional and nuclear weapons in deterrence, avoid statements which drew attention to US nuclear capabilities and deployments, involve selected allied militaries in training schemes for dual-capable weapons, and observe strict secrecy concerning the arrangements with allied countries over the introduction, storage and use of nuclear weapons.[96]

The final conclusions of the Nash Report, particularly when it came to its sections on the Far East, did not make for reassuring reading. In most countries where the United States had bases, it was pointed out, the Sino-Soviet threat was not seen as immediate and pressing, with the result that many Asians believed the bases were there for solely American purposes. As long as the Soviet Union or the PRC did not make overt moves of aggression, then the forces of neutralism and nationalism were likely only to increase, and pressures for the reduction or removal of US forces would gather pace. The present defence chain in the Western Pacific had 'serious weaknesses in every link'. Okinawa was not ideal as a base because its concentration of military facilities made it potentially vulnerable to air attack. Taiwan and the Philippines had unpredictable and sometimes unstable internal political environments, while the US forces in Korea were tied to a particular role and so lacked flexibility. The report noted that the bulk of US tactical air power in the region was still based in Japan, making it home to the 'most valuable U.S. base complex in the whole Pacific area. It is not only the great strategic prize in the area; it also affords port facilities, tool shops, skilled labor, and industrial back-up that could not be duplicated elsewhere in Asia. No comparable logistical base for supporting our current efforts in the cold war could be established west of Hawaii, and possibly not west of California or north of Australia. It is, therefore, essential to U.S. security that Japan become militarily secure and remain politically aligned with the United States.' However, Japanese

---

[96] Green memorandum for Robertson, 'Nash Survey', 12 August 1957, 'Hong Kong' [misfile], box 3, Subject Files of the Regional Planning Adviser, records of the Bureau of Far East Affairs, RG 59.

fears of 'a second atomic devastation' (amounting to an 'almost psychotic attitude') had led to a ban on the introduction of US nuclear weapons and severely limited the retaliatory potential of US forces located there: 'we have no assurance that we can count on the full use of our logistic complex or air bases to support hostilities in Korea or elsewhere, unless Japan should be directly involved'. Reductions in the number of US service personnel deployed in Japan were believed to offer some prospect that tensions over the American presence might be somewhat lessened, and over nuclear issues Nash (echoing Green) put his faith in educating Japanese political and military leaders in the new, dual-capable weapons, with, for example, joint training exercises. It was evident, nevertheless, that there were no easy answers, and the problem could even widen in scope. 'The opposition in Japan to the use of atomic weapons is explicit and vocal,' Nash warned. 'There is always the possibility ... that a general wave of emotional reaction against atomic weapons might arise in Asia, which, fanned by Soviet propaganda, might hinder the effective use of these weapons from any bases except those in territory controlled by the United States.' It was partly for this reason that Nash advocated dispersing US forces to areas directly under American control, such as the Bonin and Mariana Islands groups, the latter held as Pacific Trust Territories.[97]

The Nash survey was a powerful reminder to senior policy-makers in the Eisenhower administration of the connections that existed between the nuclear requirements of the New Look, the attitudes towards the United States of governments and peoples whose territories were home to American bases, and the overall objectives of US foreign policy in maintaining what was often grandly referred to as 'Free World cohesion'. The basic problem was that containment of Communist China had entailed building a ring of bases and alliances around the periphery of the mainland, while bolstering non-Communist Asian governments with military and economic aid in a bid to reinforce their capacity to deal with internal subversion, and to resist the electoral and popular appeal of left-wing forces.[98] For many Asian states, however, their foreign policy was not predicated upon American notions of how best to check the alleged expansionist ambitions of Chinese Communist power (especially when Beijing was engaged in the 'Bandung diplomacy' of the 1954–7 period)

[97] 'United States Overseas Bases', December 1957, pp. 26–7, 30–1, 51, box 27, Administrative series, Ann Whitman File, DDEL. I am grateful to David Haight of the Eisenhower Library for highlighting to me the importance of the Nash Report.
[98] For contemporary perspectives, see Hanson Baldwin, 'U.S. Forces in Orient', *NYT*, 29 May 1957, and Percy Wood, 'U.S. Prestige Wanes in Asia Despite Cash', *Chicago Daily Tribune*, 7 July 1957; also Klein, *Cold War Orientalism*, 19–22, for an excellent discussion of *Newsweek* magazine's June 1957 report on worldwide anti-American feelings.

but was animated by the need to assert an independent pattern of development as they moved away from conditions of colonial domination or
occupation. Viewed from this angle, the greater danger was seen to lie in
the belligerent policies of the Eisenhower administration, where its support for Chiang's anachronistic regime on Taiwan, as well as Rhee's
authoritarian Government in South Korea, was complemented by a sterile
effort to isolate Beijing.

Despite the criticism that this latter policy approach was beginning to
draw from some domestic American quarters, there was little sign of the
administration moderating its stance, even though Eisenhower himself
harboured the private view that the trade embargo with the PRC should
actually be relaxed. Indeed, in late June 1957, Dulles delivered one of his
most trenchant speeches in San Francisco where he defended the firm
approach of China policy, reiterated adamant American opposition to
recognition and admittance of the PRC to the UN, and talked of the
mainland government as a 'passing and not a perpetual phase'.[99] As
Rosemary Foot has argued, by pointing out Beijing's aggressive intent
and flouting of international norms of behaviour, the speech was designed
to undermine China's growing prestige and its claims to legitimacy, as
well as to reassure Chiang's still powerful backers in Congress that under
the current Republican administration there would be no major changes
in policy towards the mainland.[100] Nevertheless, to many observers it was
a patent absurdity to suggest that the PRC would soon disappear or that
Chiang had any hope of usurping the Communists' position on the mainland, and in fact Dulles was privately ready to acknowledge that a 'two
Chinas' solution to the recognition problem was probably inevitable.
Robert Bowie signalled his own objections to the Secretary of State in a
memorandum which argued that holding to the policy of isolating China
was unwise for it would anchor American prestige and resources to an
effort that would eventually fail, handing a clear political victory to
Beijing. The negative tenor of Dulles's address, Bowie added, was a
distraction from the more urgent task of 'developing strong counterweights to Communist China in Japan and India'.[101]

The concern of many critics of Dulles's inflexible public stand was that
it was doing immense harm to the American image in Asia, particularly in
those societies which feared being dragged into a Sino-American war

---

[99] See Hoopes, *John Foster Dulles*, 418–21; Chang, *Friends and Enemies*, 161; Foot, '"We the
People": U.S. Public Opinion and China Policy', in *Practice of Power*, 92–3.
[100] Foot, 'China as the "Wave of the Future": The Chinese Politico-Economic Model', *ibid.*,
206–7.
[101] Bowie memorandum for Dulles, 19 June 1957, *FRUS, 1955–1957, III*, 545–9.

which might engulf them in nuclear devastation. Bowie's mention of the importance of Japan and India as 'counterweights' to China was also a reminder that in these two countries anti-nuclear sentiments were probably the highest in the region. The military component of the containment of Chinese Communist power, encapsulated in the idea of massive retaliation and reliance on first use of nuclear weapons to repel any Communist attack, could also be seen as a counterpart to the rigidity of the diplomatic policy of non-recognition and isolation. The protracted debates over the deployment of dual-capable weapons systems to Korea, and their accompanying warheads, revealed for the State Department the fundamental dilemma of US defence policy. It was viewed as essential to stand firmly by Asian friends and allies, and to contribute to their defence against the local conventional military threat presented by China, but the pressures on the defence budget, and the belief that overseas garrisons attracted nationalist resentments and anti-American feelings, also meant that there was a growing imperative from the mid-1950s onwards to withdraw conventional military forces from their overseas bases, or in the Korean instance to reduce the high levels of military assistance provided at a direct cost to the US Treasury. The substitute for when these props were removed was the new power represented by US nuclear weapons, particularly the lower-yield tactical or battlefield varieties, which might give American allies the reassurance they needed. However, nuclear weapons themselves presented special political problems in the Asian setting for American officials and diplomats sensitive to the wider currents of Asian opinion, and though in some ways they were a quick fix to the overstretch felt by the Pentagon in the latter 1950s, their high visibility and special qualities raised issues, many of them connected to Western identification with 'white superiority', that could not be ignored. These dilemmas were already adding to a growing sense that reliance on nuclear weapons to deter conflict across all levels of intensity and scope was simply not a viable basis for overall national security policy, and as the next chapter will show, massive retaliation would come under even more sustained attack during the final years of the Eisenhower administration.

10 The second offshore islands crisis and the advent of flexible response

During the late 1950s, as Cold War tensions in Europe gathered fresh impetus in the form of confrontation over the status of Berlin, searching enquiries into the Eisenhower administration's national security policy were conducted in the public sphere of the academic writings of civilian defence intellectuals, as well as among informed commentators in the press and Congress. Some of this fresh impetus was attributable to the reception given to the Gaither Report and the concomitant *Sputnik* launch. The vision of burgeoning Soviet ICBM capabilities, and anxiety over the vulnerability of the continental United States and the SAC bomber force to a devastating attack, made many question the American stance over limited war. It no longer seemed credible, so the argument went, to threaten immediate escalation to large-scale use of nuclear weapons when faced with minor or local Soviet aggression, perhaps along the flanks of NATO, when the United States' own cities would be destroyed in the counter-blows that might then result. In this context, it was queried how much faith the NATO allies in Europe would continue to have in the US deterrent, leading to a loosening of the ties of the alliance and perhaps to a greater readiness to show accommodation to the Soviet Union.

One remedy proposed was to augment conventional capabilities in NATO, but the costs involved appeared prohibitive, and the Europeans themselves seemed very reluctant to devote a greater share of their resources to defence. Another idea, which received its most extensive airing in Henry Kissinger's writings at this time, was to employ low-yield battlefield nuclear weapons in reply to Soviet incursions and to work towards a formal doctrine of limited nuclear war (though this could hardly be considered attractive to the European populations who would be at the receiving end of such a nuclear exchange). A further controversial notion, and one that came to be favoured by Eisenhower himself, was that the West European allies should be given control over their own theatre-level nuclear forces in various mooted schemes of 'nuclear sharing'. This had the added attraction to the President of possibly allowing the United

States to withdraw some of the conventional forces it had deployed to the European continent in support of NATO and on a 'temporary' basis in 1951. Bernard Brodie, still one of the leading academic strategic thinkers of the period, and certainly the most lucid, published his own summation of contemporary arguments in 1959. *Strategy in the Missile Age* projected limited war where 'deliberate' and 'massive' restraint in the tools of warfare was the prime requirement of the strategist as inherently preferable to the mutual suicide of total war. Brodie also stressed that, in his view, there were no intrinsic differences between so-called 'tactical' and 'strategic' nuclear weapons, with high-yield weapons just as 'efficiently' usable against military targets as low-yield. In what seems a clear refutation of the ideas being propounded by Kissinger, and which had been echoed by Dulles in his October 1957 *Foreign Affairs* article, Brodie argued that 'between the use and non-use of atomic weapons there is a vast watershed of difference and distinction, one that ought not to be cavalierly thrown away, as we appear to be throwing it away, if we are serious about trying to limit war'.[1]

Within the confines of the Eisenhower administration, there were many officials who now nursed deep reservations over the whole approach to deterrence that was being adopted by the military establishment with the explicit endorsement of the President. The most important of these was now Dulles himself, and while in the summer of 1957 he had embraced the idea of ever-smaller and cleaner nuclear weapons as holding some promise as to how limited forms of Communist aggression might be countered, by the spring of 1958 he had also begun to favour increased US conventional capabilities as the best solution to the dilemmas produced by mutual deterrence. At a March 1958 meeting of the NSC, Dulles had mocked Robert Cutler for again raising the notion that in coming years the Soviet Union would be tempted to mount or promote small-scale aggression. However, only a few days later the Secretary of State was expressing his own private doubts to Eisenhower over the whole concept of massive retaliation.[2] As annual revision of basic national security policy came before the NSC once more in May 1958, Cutler now found he had a more resilient ally in his efforts to change the language contained in NSC 5707/8, so that greater flexibility would be introduced into how the United States responded to each case of limited war.

Nevertheless, and despite support coming from both General Taylor and Admiral Burke among the Joint Chiefs, the advocates of allocating

---

[1] See Bernard Brodie, *Strategy in the Missile Age* (Princeton, 1959), 309–10, 325–7.
[2] See, e.g., John L. Gaddis, 'The Unexpected John Foster Dulles', in his *The United States and the End of the Cold War*, 73.

greater resources to enhance limited war capabilities faced determined opposition from the Secretary of Defense, Neil H. McElroy (who had replaced Wilson in October 1957), and the new Chairman of the JCS, General Nathan F. Twining, Radford having completed his own term in this post in the summer of 1957. Both McElroy and Twining were determined that there should be no watering down of the reliance on nuclear means to resist limited aggression. Eisenhower was also loath to abandon the policy he had laid down only the previous year of putting the onus on forces for general war, rather than for limited engagements, seeing no scope for devoting greater resources to the defence budget without the introduction of economic controls and eventually leading to what he pictured as a garrison state. Moreover, thinking of the situation in central Europe faced by NATO, he simply could not see how the outbreak of a local aggression could be prevented from developing into a general war: better, then, to prepare for the latter contingency, and make the prospect of any war so awful that both sides would avoid direct conflict (this may have had a certain logic when applied to the US–Soviet stand-off in Europe but had less relevance to the Far East, where the principal adversary had no easy access to nuclear weapons). During the spring of 1958, it was finally decided that there would be no wholesale change to basic national security policy, now encapsulated in NSC 5810/1, but it was agreed that the military paragraphs of this new document should be subject to continuing scrutiny by the Pentagon and State Department. This arrangement, it was felt, might also then allow proper consideration to be given to the still-incomplete inter-agency Limited War Study begun earlier in the year.[3]

The contentious report of the Limited War Study finally emerged in late May 1958. To those who had hoped it would provide further ammunition in the assault on massive retaliation, such as Gerard Smith at the PPS, the report proved a disappointment. The study had been guided by the important assumptions that operations involving Soviet forces would be omitted (it being held that such a scenario would constitute the start of general war), enemy forces would not have access to nuclear weapons, and in the Far East setting that the United States could engage in 'effective action' against the Chinese mainland without the risk of provoking a

---

[3] Memorandum of discussion at the 359th meeting of the NSC, 20 March 1958, *FRUS, 1958–1960, III*, 54; memorandum of conversation by Dulles, 1 April 1958, *ibid.*, 57; memorandum of meeting in the Office of the Secretary of Defense, 7 April 1958, *ibid.*, 62–4; memorandum of discussion at the 364th meeting of the NSC, 1 May 1958, *ibid.*, 79–90. See also Craig, *Destroying the Village*, 76–8, which, however, omits all mention of the Limited War Study and has a prime focus on Europe, and the summary in Fairchild and Poole, *JCS and National Policy*, VII, 19–21.

general war. Smith found all of these prior assumptions contestable, and given this starting point he considered it hardly surprising that the conclusions offered by the study were drawn in reassuring terms. The final report noted that US capabilities for limited military operations were adequate, but only if the use of nuclear weapons to achieve military objectives was authorized. This was a crucial proviso: although scenarios situated in Europe and the Middle East had been examined, it was in its sections dealing with the Far East that some of the study's most arresting findings were found and where nuclear use was judged most necessary but also most problematic. Preponderant Communist conventional power in the hypothetical scenarios considered (Korea, the Taiwan Strait and Indochina) meant that nuclear strikes would have to be employed in all the situations envisaged in order to destroy enemy forces and 'neutralize' bases, airfields and war-making capabilities. 'In the case of aggression against Quemoy and Matsu, Taiwan or the ROK [Republic of Korea],' it was highlighted, 'this would require air strikes deep into Chinese Communist territory. Despite careful and selective use of nuclear weapons, heavy civilian casualties would result.'

The political ramifications which would arise from such nuclear use in an Asian setting, it seems apparent, were pushed forward by the State Department representatives on the study team. For example, Japanese bases and transit rights would be very important for US military, naval and air operations in the Far East limited war scenarios, yet as the report noted, it was 'very probable that Japan would deny us the use of its territory for launching nuclear strikes; moreover, in the circumstances of our use of nuclear weapons in defense of Quemoy and Matsu, Japan might deny us all access to its territory'.[4] In even more forthright fashion, in the final section of its summary, the study highlighted the disconcerting fact that the

clear requirement for the use of nuclear weapons had been established in that area of the world where such use will have maximum adverse political consequences for the U.S. The deep seated Asian aversion to the 'atomic bomb' does not rest solely on the weapon's horrifying lethal effects. It rests also on Asian racial and color sensitiveness, and the widespread Asian conviction that the 'atomic bomb' is the white man's weapon which he is cold-bloodedly willing, if not eager, to use against colored peoples. No rational explanation will serve to overcome these visceral convictions and should the need arise to use nuclear weapons in the Far East, we

---

[4] All the evidence would point to Marshall Green as being the author of these remarks; see the contribution he offered to the study in his memorandum, 'Situations Most Likely to Involve the U.S. in Limited Military Operations: Quemoy and Matsu', 27 March 1958, '18.3 Weapons: Limited War, 1958', box 341, Subject Files, SASAE, RG 59, NARA.

would have to accept the consequences of long-lasting damage to our relations with much of Asia.

As we have seen, this was exactly the point that Dulles himself had raised when meeting Pentagon officials in conference in June 1957, while in the meantime the domestic US racial scene, encapsulated by the Little Rock School crisis in particular, had since done nothing to reduce the international salience of such issues. In what undoubtedly represented a final concession to State Department opinion, the report included a significant recommendation that the Director of the CIA should compile a Special National Intelligence Estimate (SNIE) on the subject of 'Sino-Soviet and Free World Reactions to U.S. Use of Nuclear Weapons in Limited Wars in the Far East'.[5]

The resulting SNIE was disseminated by the CIA towards the end of July 1958. In its first area of interest, it was concluded that there was a 'grave risk' that if the United States used nuclear weapons to meet local aggression, then the Soviet Union would probably feel compelled to lend an equivalent form of assistance to their Communist allies in the Far East (perhaps through covert supply of weapons), thus invalidating one of the initial assumptions of the Limited War Study. On the second question concerning 'Free World Reactions', the SNIE concluded that though there might be some encouragement felt at a prompt and resolute American response to aggression, 'U.S. use of nuclear weapons would arouse widespread fear of general war and would tend to obscure Communist responsibility for initiating hostilities.' The United States would face condemnation by popular opinion, while this would be

particularly strong throughout most of Asia. Here such use would tend to be looked upon as callous white indifference to the lives of Asians. Indeed the inflicting of large-scale casualties on Asian civilians might have enduringly adverse consequences for the anti-Communist position in Asia. The reaction in Japan would be especially adverse, in view of deep Japanese emotional antagonism to the use of nuclear weapons, and Japan would probably not allow U.S. use of bases on its territory.

The only compensation that could be found in this picture was the belief that if American use of nuclear weapons led to a swift victory without high numbers of civilian casualties, then the 'attitude of repugnance' would

---

[5] For the full text of the Limited War Study's report, see 'U.S. and Allied Capabilities for Limited Military Operations to 1 July 1961', 22 May 1958, 'Elbert G. Matthews Chronological', box 204, records of the PPS, 1957–61, RG 59, NARA. For a short summary of assumptions and findings, see McElroy memorandum for the NSC, 17 June 1958, *FRUS, 1958–1960, III, Microfiche Supplement*, fiche 63/pp. 1–4. For further discussion, see Watson, *Into the Missile Age*, 301–2.

tend to diminish.[6] This last conclusion was one with which not all would agree: when Anglo-American intelligence staffs met for an exchange of views on the Far East in late October 1958, British officials were shown a copy of the SNIE but expressed their doubt that 'light civilian casualties would overcome the present continued revulsion of Asian countries to the use of nuclear weapons as such, and more especially by Europeans against Asians'.[7]

The Limited War Study itself was discussed at an NSC meeting in late June 1958, giving Dulles an opportunity to emphasize its finding that the United States lacked a non-nuclear capability for limited war in the Far East and that this was a 'weakness' as there would be 'very serious political implications in using nuclear weapons once again against the Asiatics' with important repercussions especially in Japan and India. Referring to the possible response to a North Vietnamese invasion of South Vietnam, Dulles averred that the United States was 'muscle bound' if it could only reply with nuclear weapons and went on to recall that in 1954 the use of nuclear weapons had been rejected as politically impossible, and the United States 'should avoid being placed in such a fix again'.[8] Having noted its contents, the NSC went on to refer the study to the Secretaries of State and Defense who were to use it in their efforts to keep under review the military aspects of national security policy so recently reaffirmed in NSC 5810/1. For Gerard Smith, the time had now come for what he called 'a real show-down within our government' on an issue he considered the most important he had handled since taking over the PPS from Bowie. However, with the NSC set for another debate on 24 July, Smith was unsure how far he could rely on his political master, as limited war doctrine was an area where in the past Dulles had been 'loath to define strong views, regarding it as a predominantly military problem'. Smith wanted it impressed on Dulles how 'deeply and unanimously' the State Department felt on the need for an adequate conventional capability so that he would make a strong case to the NSC, and where support would be found from among the services in the Army, Navy and Marines, as well as from the CIA.

Once again all the interested bureaus in the State Department forwarded memoranda on the limited war problem to Smith which could

[6] SNIE 100–7–58, 'Sino-Soviet and Free World Reactions to U.S. Use of Nuclear Weapons in Limited Wars in the Far East', 22 July 1958, *FRUS, 1958–1960, XIX: China, Microfiche Supplement* (Washington, DC, 1998), fiche 22/pp. 1–12.
[7] 'Report of the UK and U.S. Teams', 1 November 1958, contained in S6/MODA/2/A, 'Anglo/U.S. Talks on the Far East', 14 November 1958, DEFE 7/1722, TNA.
[8] 'NSC Meeting – June 26, 1958', 'Gerard C. Smith Files 1958 (3)', box 1, Gerard C. Smith series, John Foster Dulles papers, DDEL; memorandum of discussion at the 370th meeting of the NSC, 26 June 1958, *FRUS, 1958–1960, III*, 121.

then be distilled for Dulles.[9] From the Far East Bureau, for example, came a paper warning that, in Asia, Soviet and Chinese strategy, through a blend of political, economic and psychological measures, with local military and subversive action, appeared to be unfolding in most ominous fashion, and it was 'reasonable to forecast that Communist expansionism is likely to be prosecuted in ever subtler and more ambiguous guises'. In the future, the enemy challenge would be 'posed in ways where nuclear weapons would be either ineffective or politically disastrous'.[10] Reliance on simply a capability for massive retaliation, Smith told Dulles, was leading to a position where American freedom of action would be reduced to two choices: 'total nuclear war with unimaginable death and destruction' and 'cumulative retreat before Communist menace and subversion'. In the Far East the Limited War Study had shown that these stark alternatives might already obtain.[11] Yet there was no final showdown at the NSC level on this fundamental matter as Smith had desired. With McElroy unwilling to modify NSC 5810/1 to accommodate a more flexible approach to planning force levels, and Dulles concerned not to ventilate once again such a controversial subject in a large meeting, both men agreed that the existing document would be endorsed, but they would hold future joint discussions on the overall strategic concept.[12]

The outcome of the debate represented a short-term victory for the Pentagon. Over subsequent months, little seems to have happened, the sudden emergence of the second offshore islands crisis in August–September, and then the onset of fresh tensions over Berlin in November 1958, overtaking minds and bureaucratic energies. In that same month, Dulles and McElroy held a round of desultory talks on the strategic concept, but with budgetary pressures now even more paramount, any talk of expanding conventional limited war capabilities was overshadowed by general concern over where the Treasury's axe would fall. On this the Secretary of State's senior advisers had few doubts: 'If

---

[9] See Marshall Green memorandum for J. Graham Parsons, 'Basic National Security Policy on Limited War', 9 July 1958, 'Top Secrets OD-NSC', box 2, TS Files of the Regional Planning Adviser, records of the Bureau of Far East Affairs, 1955–63, RG 59, NARA.

[10] See J. Graham Parsons (drafted by Green) memorandum for Smith, 'Basic National Security Policy on Limited War', 11 July 1958, 'Limited War', *ibid.*

[11] Smith memorandum for Dulles, 15 July 1958, 'S/P Chronological, 1957–59', box 205, records of the PPS, 1957–61, RG 59, NARA. Dulles approved this memorandum.

[12] McElroy memorandum to the NSC, 18 July 1958, and memorandum of discussion at the 373rd meeting of the NSC, 24 July 1958, *FRUS, 1958–1960, III*, 125–31; Smith memorandum for Dulles, 19 July 1958, *FRUS, 1958–1960, III, Microfiche Supplement*, fiche 76; Bosner memorandum for record of Dulles–McElroy discussion, 22 July 1958, *ibid.*, fiche 80; Dulles to Eisenhower, 23 July 1958, *ibid.*, fiche 81; Fairchild and Poole, *JCS and National Policy*, VII, 22; Watson, *Into the Missile Age*, 303.

additional budget cuts are essential the foreign policy argument favors a placing of the burden of the reduction on the massive retaliation capability and not on the limited war capability.'[13]

The second offshore islands crisis had helped to reinforce the latter conviction and was the principal event in the late 1950s that brought home to many in the State Department the potential political costs associated with any US use of nuclear weapons in Asia. Based on JCS military planning for the contingency of a Chinese attempt to capture the islands, the 1958 Limited War Study had included the comment that 'very few people around the world would consider that they were of sufficient significance to justify nuclear strikes 500 miles into Communist China, some of which would endanger major population centers'.[14] This observation became especially pertinent in early August when Chinese Communist air power began to be built up on the mainland opposite the islands and frequent clashes arose with Nationalist aircraft, with many observers seeing this as presaging an attempt by Beijing to interdict the vulnerable seaborne supply routes to the bloated Nationalist garrisons, or even to begin preparations for a major assault.

The predominant view of senior administration officials was that Nationalist morale on Taiwan would crumble if the offshore islands were lost, for besides the troop strength deployed there, they also represented stepping stones for that fundamental *raison d'être* of Chiang Kai-shek's regime, an eventual return to the mainland. In mid-August, Smith alerted Christian Herter to the fact that current JCS plans for the defence of the offshore islands called for 'nuclear strikes deep into Communist China, including military targets in the Shanghai–Hangchow–Nanking and Canton complexes where population density is extremely high'. Referring Herter to the previous Limited War Study, Smith pointed out that though so-called low-yield weapons would be used, these would still be comparable to the twenty kiloton bombs dropped on Hiroshima and Nagasaki, and that before hostilities were over there would probably be 'millions of non-combatant casualties'. The implications of this outcome, coupled with the SNIE on Sino-Soviet reactions to US use of nuclear weapons in the Far East (which predicted a likely Soviet nuclear response), led Smith to conclude that the United States did not have a

[13] Murphy/Reinhardt/Smith memorandum for Dulles, 8 November 1958, *FRUS, 1958–1960, III, Microfiche Supplement*, fiche 108.

[14] 'U.S. and Allied Capabilities for Limited Military Operations to 1 July 1961', 22 May 1958, 'Elbert G. Matthews Chronological', box 204, records of the PPS, 1957–61, RG 59, NARA.

'politically feasible capability' to defend the offshore islands.[15] Soon after, and with Dulles absent in New York attending the UN General Assembly, the JCS briefed Herter, Smith, Walter Robertson and Robert Murphy, the Deputy Under-Secretary for Political Affairs, on their latest thinking about the growing tensions in the Taiwan Strait. From this meeting, it was apparent that some officers were not attracted to the exercise of restraint once any hostilities had begun to defend the offshore islands, and even greeted the prospect of escalation to a full-scale war with equanimity. When Herter asked General Twining about plans for US intervention if the islands were about to fall, the Chairman of the JCS replied that Chinese bases on the mainland would have to be hit and, rather airily, that 'political as well as military factors would be controlling in how we went about the operation. Probably we would not do the job all at once but start out by hitting a few [later defined as 6–8] of the airfields in the Amoy area ... it would be necessary to use low-yield atomic bombs in the 10–15 KT range.' If the fighting did not desist, Twining continued, then 'we would be left with no alternative but to conduct nuclear strikes deep into China and as far north as Shanghai involving likely Communist nuclear retaliation against our positions in Taiwan, and possibly on Okinawa and elsewhere', adding ominously, 'In other words, if it is our national policy to defend the Offshore Islands, then we must face the possible ultimate consequences of that policy.'[16] While Robertson was prepared to back this degree of force to hold the islands, others were far less convinced: in a further memorandum, this time addressed to Dulles, Smith warned that implementation of JCS plans in the event of a blockade or invasion of the offshore islands would lead to general war with Communist China, and therefore a serious risk of war with the Soviet Union. The President, Smith urged, should direct the Pentagon to prepare a local defence of the islands that did not involve nuclear strikes against the mainland, but if this were not feasible, he wanted to re-examine the whole US commitment to the offshores.[17]

On 23 August, Chinese Communist artillery batteries began an intensive bombardment of the islands, signalling to some that the crisis was entering a new and yet more dangerous phase (though not, one might note, an apparently imperturbable Dulles, who returned to Washington

[15] Smith memorandum for Herter, 'August 14 Discussion of Taiwan Straits', 13 August 1958, 'S/P Chronological 1957–1959', box 205, records of the PPS, 1957–61, RG 59, NARA.
[16] State Department–JCS meeting, 15 August 1958, box 51, records of State–JCS meetings, RG 59, NARA.
[17] Smith memorandum for Dulles, 15 August 1958, *FRUS, 1958–1960, XIX: China* (Washington, DC, 1996), 57–9.

briefly on that same day, only to depart again for a week-long vacation cruise on Lake Ontario). For his part, Eisenhower was extremely cautious about sanctioning any nuclear response to a Communist attack on the offshore islands, though if such an attack extended to Taiwan (which he considered improbable), this would become a much more serious matter. In mid-August he told one meeting of senior officials that in the former contingency 'we should be very careful ... that we do not take instantaneous action which would spread the hostilities', and that US responses should have 'fixed definite limits'.[18] Two days after the bombardment began, Eisenhower, though authorizing the military to prepare to use nuclear weapons if necessary, ordered that a conventional defence should be tried in the first instance if the Chinese should attempt invasion.[19] The President was certainly sensitive to the wider public relations side of US actions: at the end of August, he talked of the United States being the 'prime target in the cold war. If we moved in at once on this situation (and attacked the Mainland) we would lend credence to Communist propaganda charging us with aggression.'[20] Throughout the crisis it is evident that Eisenhower was determined to maintain tight control of the military actions undertaken by the United States, and while perfectly willing to have nuclear weapons available as a threat to deter China from an invasion, he was eager that he should not have to be confronted with any momentous decision over whether to actually use them.[21] Perhaps Eisenhower's overwhelming feeling was of annoyance and frustration that Chiang's progressive reinforcement of the islands had led to the current position, coupled with a determination that Chiang's provocations should not drive the United States into an unnecessary war.[22]

When Dulles returned to Washington at the start of September, he was briefed by the JCS on their belief that nuclear weapons would have to be used to defend the islands if the Chinese Communists mounted a large-scale and determined assault. In one telephone exchange with Twining before the briefing was held, Dulles confessed he 'did not know where we now stand on use of nuclear weapons. There was no use having a lot of stuff and never being able to use it.' The Chairman of the JCS confirmed

[18] Memorandum for the record, 14 August 1958, *ibid.*, 52–5, and for an unexpurgated version, see DDRS/CK3100568438.
[19] Memorandum of meeting, 25 August 1958; telegram from JCS to Felt, 25 August 1958, *FRUS, 1958–1960, XIX*, 73–6. A few days later, Eisenhower was commenting that 'we should probably hold back on nuclears' even in the event of an assault on the islands; see *ibid.*, 96–7.
[20] Memorandum of meeting, 29 August 1958, *FRUS, 1958–1960, XIX*, 98.
[21] See the persuasive analysis in Bundy, *Danger and Survival*, 283–6.
[22] See, e.g., memorandum of Eisenhower–Dulles telephone conversation, 1 September 1958, *FRUS, 1958–1960, XIX*, 113.

they were indeed usable, and that this 'was not the place to use conventional ones'.[23] At the briefing itself, Twining explained current military planning for the use of tactical nuclear weapons (of up to ten kilotons) against five coastal airfields, after which 'we would stop to observe the effect on Communist intentions'. Although raising the issue of possible Japanese objections to the use of US bases for operations in the Taiwan Strait, Dulles seemed to accept the JCS view of available options, noting that 'if we shrink from using nuclear weapons when military circumstances so require, then we will have to reconsider our whole defense posture', but also observing that the JCS arguments for the necessity of nuclear use 'had important implications affecting the government's whole foreign policy'.[24]

Dulles revealed his own perspective a day later, when he told a meeting of State Department and Pentagon officials that he considered current Chinese objectives to be 'internal development' and that the action over the offshores was 'essentially a probing operation' designed to test US intentions, perhaps under Khrushchev's prompting.[25] On 4 September, having conferred with Eisenhower at Newport, Rhode Island, Dulles issued a strong statement that the President had authority from the Formosa Resolution to use force to defend the offshore islands, warned this was becoming more likely, and that the Chinese, as in the Korean example, should not 'defy the basic principle upon which world order depends, namely, that armed force should not be used to achieve territorial ambition'.[26] He complemented this with background briefings for the press which emphasized US determination to defend the offshore islands, remarking that 'if I were on the Chinese Communist side, I would certainly think very hard before I went ahead in the face of this statement'.[27] Meanwhile, US naval and air units in the Taiwan area were substantially reinforced. These concerted actions appeared to bring dividends when, on 6 September, Zhou Enlai announced Chinese preference for a peaceful settlement and their willingness to renew the ambassadorial-level Sino-American talks that had previously been held in abeyance. The subsequent resumption of these talks in Warsaw, and the reduction of Chinese artillery fire on the offshore islands to harassing levels by the end of September, marked the end of the crisis, while the

---

[23] Dulles–Twining telephone conversation, 2 September 1958, Dulles papers, quoted in Bundy, *Danger and Survival*, 279.
[24] Memorandum of conversation, 2 September 1958, *FRUS, 1958–1960, XIX*, 118.
[25] Memorandum of conversation, 3 September 1958, *ibid.*, 126.
[26] 'Text of Dulles Statement on the Far East', *NYT*, 5 September 1958.
[27] 'U.S. Decides to Use Force if Reds Invade Quemoy; Dulles Sees Eisenhower', *NYT*, 5 September 1958.

Nationalist garrisons had been kept resupplied there in a very effective operation organized by the US Navy.

To Smith and other PPS members, the crisis underlined once again the interconnections between Asian (and world) sensitivity over nuclear use and the need for the State Department to play a larger role in the arena of military planning. The regular State Department–JCS meetings were a useful forum for the exchange of information but did not allow the former's officials access to deeper military thinking or any say when plans were in the formulation stage. As had been a feature of the first crisis in 1955, the concern of some State Department officials was that any clash between US and Communist Chinese forces in the Far East was likely to trigger not a measured and limited response from local commanders (such as the new CINCPAC in Honolulu, Admiral Felt), but be the pretext for the initiation of a strategic strike against mainland Chinese military and industrial targets identified in general war concepts as holding the PRC's prime war-making capacities.[28] When Smith saw Dulles on 2 September, in an exact repetition of the warnings he had delivered in March 1955, he expressed his concern that the Secretary of State was 'not getting the full flavor of the military planning for the possible use of nuclear weapons against mainland China'. Smith feared that, if they were used, they might not be limited to a few airfields near Jinmen and Mazu and that nuclear strikes far deeper into China would be needed, as the scenario in the Limited War Study had suggested. That same morning, Smith informed Dulles, Twining had been telling a staff meeting that if the United States intervened, 'we should "shoot our wad", and if by chance this lead [sic] to the destruction of Formosa we would just have to "go home"'.[29]

Anxiety over alienating international opinion through nuclear use also figured in the thinking of senior administration officials. Although very hawkish over the need to retain the islands and ready to employ force, Robertson reminded the JCS that 'precipitate use of large nuclear weapons would leave us with no friends in the world. We would be completely isolated. It [was] very much in our over-all interests that we put the Chicoms [sic] on warning through graduated steps, using conventional weapons as long as possible and using atomics only as a last resort and then only on particular military targets.' These were 'crucial political and public opinion factors that must be borne in mind'.[30] By contrast, Smith

[28] See Hayes, Zarsky and Bello, *American Lake*, 57.
[29] See memorandum of conversation between Smith and Dulles, 2 September 1958, 'Gerard C. Smith Files, 1958 (3)', box 1, Gerard C. Smith series, John Foster Dulles papers, DDEL.
[30] State Department–JCS meeting, 5 September 1958, box 51, records of State–JCS meetings, RG 59, NARA.

was opposed to any nuclear use to prevent the loss of the offshore islands, as he was conscious of the huge civilian casualties that were likely to come with the employment of tactical nuclear weapons which had similar yields to the Hiroshima bomb. Again, just as in March 1955, Smith later recalled, he arranged for a briefing to be given to Dulles over the casualties in nearby cities such as Amoy if low-yield nuclear weapons were used against the artillery emplacements shelling the offshore islands: 'I think this made a substantial impression on his mind, from the point of view not of religious scruple, but just of the political price the United States would have to pay around the world if it resorted to nuclear weapons in that sort of a limited type of hostility.'[31] If nuclear strikes were used, Dulles was told by Smith, 'we would be involved in the most unpopular war with the most unpopular weapons' and their limited use 'might sharply stimulate world drives' to ban them altogether.[32]

Following one staff meeting during the crisis, George Allen, the head of USIA, felt the need to alert Dulles to how disturbed he was by the military options on offer. Allen found it 'difficult to emphasize too strongly the adverse reaction which would result if the United States were to use atomic weapons again, particularly in the Far East. The only two atomic weapons have been used in that area, and most of the non-white people of the world feel that the United States is building its armaments to keep the non-white races in subjection [sic]. They frequently say that we wouldn't dare use atomic weapons against another white nation.'[33] In a USIA study of reactions to various possible US courses of action, it was predicted that intervention with nuclear weapons would be condemned and opposed by most governments around the world. Within Asia, approval would be forthcoming from only Nationalist China, South Korea, South Vietnam, Thailand and the Philippines, though among the populace of these countries there would be mixed feelings and fears of retaliation, while many opinion leaders in the Philippines were also likely to be critical.

Informed by such surveys, Abbott Washburn, the Deputy Director of USIA, wrote to Eisenhower on 9 September to warn him that if nuclear weapons were used to hold the islands, the United States 'could lose the respect of mankind, possibly for all time'. Moreover, Gallup polling was showing that American domestic opinion did not favour help to the Nationalists in holding the islands if this involved the use of atomic

---

[31] Gerard C. Smith Oral History, pp. 4–5, Mudd Library. This briefing is also alluded to in Betts, *Nuclear Blackmail*, 69, where the figure of 8 million possible casualties is mentioned.

[32] See memorandum of conversation between Smith and Dulles, 2 September 1958, 'Material from Gerard C. Smith Files, 1958 (3)'.

[33] George V. Allen Oral History, pp. 30–2, Mudd Library.

weapons and the attendant risk of all-out war. Washburn advised that a prudent evacuation of the offshore islands would garner widespread approval and not result in a 'chain reaction' with irreparable loss of morale on Taiwan. On the other hand, the bulk of world opinion would 'experience revulsion' if nuclear weapons were employed in the area, and this might serve to jeopardize use of overseas bases in such areas as Japan and Morocco. Pointing out that civilian populations totalling over one and a half million people lay close to the airbases located at Foochow, Amoy and Swatow, Washburn highlighted that, 'Another atom-burning by the U.S. of Asian civilians would do incalculable damage to the U.S. in the eyes of Asian and all colored peoples and governments for years to come.' There was also the possibility that covert Soviet nuclear help might be sent to China, where bases on Taiwan, Okinawa, Japan and the Philippines made inviting targets: 'As Jim Hagerty remarked the other day, "There is probably no such thing as a limited atomic war." ... In defending Quemoy and Matsu, therefore, we would be virtually going it alone – with Chiang and Syngman Rhee our only enthusiastic allies (each with his own reason for trying to draw the U.S. into a conflict with Communist China). Even our best friends are dropping away from us in the present situation.'[34]

This was hardly an enticing prospect, and standing at the centre of State Department concerns in early September, as ever, was the effect on Japan if hostilities escalated to nuclear level.[35] At his JCS briefing referred to above, Dulles informed the assembled chiefs that he had been advised that if the United States used nuclear weapons to defend the offshore islands, Japan might demand the withdrawal of all American bases, and continued that this 'posed a very basic question with respect to our defense posture in the Far East: namely if anticipated reactions against our use of nuclear weapons were to be so hostile that we would be inhibited from using them except in the NATO theater or in retaliation against a Soviet attack, was our reliance on their use correct and productive?'[36] Having read a paper prepared by Dulles on the stakes at play in the crisis, which reiterated the inflated fear that if Jinmen were taken by the Communists, then the whole Western position in East and South East Asia would unravel, Smith

[34] Washburn to Eisenhower, 9 September 1958, and attached 'Estimate of Free World Reaction, Country by Country to Three Possible Courses of Action by the U.S. in Quemoy-Matsu [sic]', 6 September 1958, box 29, Administration series, Ann Whitman File, DDEL.

[35] See, e.g., Robertson memorandum for Dulles, 19 August 1958, 'Taiwan Straits Background Paper', box 1, TS Files of the Regional Planning Adviser, records of the Bureau of Far East Affairs, 1955–63, RG 59, NARA; 'Japan Seeks Voice on U.S. Bases' Use', *NYT*, 2 September 1958.

[36] Memorandum of conversation, 2 September 1958, *FRUS, 1958–1960, XIX*, 120.

underlined the fact that US intervention might have exactly the same consequences, warning 'if we use nuclear weapons, our intervention may force Japan, the Philippines and other Asian nations further in the direction of neutralism and eventual accommodation with Peiping [sic]'.[37] When they conferred together at Newport, Dulles and Eisenhower produced a paper laying out the issues in the crisis which has rightly drawn criticism for the overblown estimates it contained of the consequences for the region if the offshore islands were taken by the PRC.[38] However, the memorandum also incorporated Smith's perspective by mentioning that if nuclear weapons were used in their defence, 'there would be a strong popular revulsion against the U.S. in most of the world', and this would be 'particularly intense in Asia and particularly harmful to us in Japan'. Nevertheless, it continued, in a reflection of the optimistic assessments coming from the JCS, these possible political repercussions could be minimized if 'small detonations were used with only air bursts, so that there would be no appreciable fallout or large civilian casualties' and if the conflict were over quickly. The conclusion of the paper, however, was far more guarded, noting that 'it is not certain, however, that the operation could be thus limited in scope or time, and the risk of a more extensive use of nuclear weapons, and even a risk of general war, would have to be accepted'.[39]

A critical point in the thinking of Dulles, at least, seems to have been reached in early September. From the one side he was exposed to the arguments of Twining and others that the use of low-yield tactical nuclear weapons against mainland airfields would be essential in any defence of the offshore islands against attack; these would also be used in air-bursts, so the military reassured him, designed to lessen the degree of fallout produced. This represented the practical implementation of the revised version of massive retaliation that the Secretary of State had outlined in his *Foreign Affairs* article in October 1957, where the notion was that the punishment should fit the crime of aggression in a local setting, and where 'clean' nuclear weapons might be employed to that end. But Dulles was also subjected to the more sceptical arguments of his chief policy planner, Gerard Smith, who was far less sanguine about the effects of tactical nuclear weapons, dubious about the claims of the JCS and ready to point out the severe political costs involved with any nuclear

---

[37] Smith memorandum for Dulles, 3 September 1958, *ibid.*, 123.
[38] See Bundy's comments in *Danger and Survival*, 274.
[39] Dulles memorandum, 4 September 1958, *FRUS, 1958–1960, XIX*, 133; see also Zhang, *Deterrence*, 248–9. It is noticeable, as ever, how closely Dulles and Eisenhower worked to co-ordinate their approaches at such important moments.

use, especially in an Asian context. The hawkish background briefing that Dulles delivered to reporters on 4 September (at the time, newspapers had described their source as a 'high official') reflected the military analysis of the JCS, and the Secretary of State, as we have seen, was wont to defer to 'military experts', as this was an area where he professed to have little knowledge. Smith later recalled that Dulles 'was very sensitive to stay out of the jurisdiction of other people ... in the case of Lewis Strauss and also in the military field, he was very sensitive to the fact that his writ did not extend beyond the State Department'.[40] However, once the foreign policy implications of nuclear use became clearer, particularly in relation to the impact on Japan, the private comments of Dulles, as well as Eisenhower, were much more cautious. By 11 September, the President was telling Dulles that his understanding was that the JCS were now saying the offshore islands were not essential to the defence of Taiwan, and 'said he is quite prepared to see the abandonment of Quemoy, but, of course, this cannot be said publicly at the present stage'.[41] A few days later Eisenhower attended the UN General Assembly in New York where he saw the British Foreign Secretary, Selwyn Lloyd, who reported the President as saying that it was 'out of the question to use nuclear weapons for a purely local tactical counterbattery task. If nuclear weapons were to be used that should be for "the big thing".' Eisenhower had added, in a fashion that stood in marked contrast to the public position adopted by the administration ever since 1953, 'When you use nuclear weapons you cross a completely different line.'[42] Another manifestation of this, it is worth noting, is that administration officials made no repeat of the very public declarations about how nuclear weapons were considered in the same category as conventional when it came to possible military responses, as had occurred during the height of the 1955 crisis.

Relations with Japan were also very much on Dulles's mind throughout the 1958 crisis as it occurred just when the issue of revision of the security treaty was coming to a head. Pressures for changes to the treaty regime had accumulated both before and immediately after the LDP's improved showing in the May 1958 Diet elections, which had served to strengthen Kishi's position within his party. In what appears in retrospect to mark a major change in attitude (and where the Nash Report mentioned in the

[40] Gerard C. Smith Oral History, pp. 3–4, Mudd Library.
[41] Dulles memorandum of conversation with Eisenhower, 11 September 1958, DDRS/ CK3100324073.
[42] New York to Foreign Office, No. 1071, 21 September 1958, FCN 1193/250G, FO 371/ 133532, TNA.

previous chapter may have played an important role), Dulles composed a memorandum for his senior officials on 19 January 1958 which held:

I do not think that we can safely continue our present posture in Japan and Okinawa. If we try merely to sit on our treaty rights, we shall end by being blown out by popular sentiment, spearheaded by a Japanese government of hostile and neutralist, if not pro-Communist, sentiments. We have in Kishi a more able and more friendly Prime Minister than any in the past and probably any we are very likely to see in the future. I believe we should move forward actively to readjust our position.[43]

Opinion polling conducted by USIA also showed that feeling against the American military presence continued to be sharply negative. A sample taken in March 1958 registered that 56 per cent felt that American bases were 'not a good thing', as opposed to 19 per cent having a positive response, and the same group showed 75 per cent opposing US forces in Japan being equipped with nuclear weapons, with only 6 per cent in favour.[44] One official at the British Embassy in Tokyo concluded that there was little Japanese appreciation of the importance of Taiwan for the containment of the PRC, and most influential Japanese would in fact 'welcome [the] collapse of the Formosa regime as affording the only solution for an otherwise permanent and corrosive problem'.[45] From the Tokyo embassy, MacArthur urged that the administration now tackle the security issue head on, or risk the build-up of more neutralist tendencies, and in June recommended that a new treaty should be negotiated, rather than amendments merely made to the existing 1951 agreement (the embassy had, in fact, already drawn up a new draft treaty in February).[46]

During the summer, the State Department and the Pentagon struggled to agree on a new treaty text which acceded to Japanese needs for 'mutuality' and included the right of consultation over the introduction of nuclear weapons to US bases in Japan, as well as tackling the use of the American bases for operations going beyond the immediate defence of Japan. From 10 to 12 September, the Japanese Foreign Minister, Fujiyama Aiichiro, visited Washington to discuss the negotiations over a new treaty with Dulles and raised these specific issues, citing the on-going offshore islands crisis as a clear example where there would be concern about

[43] Dulles memorandum, quoted in Dulles to MacArthur, 10 February 1958, Strictly Confidential – M (1), box 3, General Correspondence and Memoranda series, John Foster Dulles papers, DDEL.

[44] Japan Opinion Survey (March 1958), Part III, pp. 30, 34, box 62, Country Project Files, Office of Research, RG 306, NARA.

[45] Tokyo to Foreign Office, No. 257, 10 September 1958, FCN 1193/125G, FO 371/133528, TNA.

[46] See Schaller, *Altered States*, 137–8; Tokyo to State Department, 5 June 1958, *FRUS, 1958–1960, XVIII*, 34–6.

Japanese bases being used for action against the Chinese mainland.[47] While Dulles and the State Department were ready to be responsive to Japanese fears, the Pentagon were adamantly opposed to anything that gave the Japanese a right of veto over how US military power was deployed and used in the region. Even so, the JCS recognized that the strength of anti-nuclear feeling in Japan precluded any effort to modify the position that had been adopted on moving the fissile components of atomic weapons to US bases. In the formal paper encapsulating JCS views preceding the Fujiyama talks, the following assertion was made:

With regard to introduction of nuclear weapons in Japan, including visits of U.S. ships with nuclear armaments, there is virtually no prospect of a solution which will satisfy both sides. The 'atom bomb' in any context still remains in Japan a matter of the utmost emotional intensity. Until such time as this feeling moderates to manageable proportions, it would be altogether unrealistic to expect to obtain Japanese agreement for the introduction of nuclear components into Japan, although this remains a highly desirable military objective toward which to work. It therefore appears advisable now to seek to maintain the status quo with respect to weapons in Japan.

Moreover, while rejecting the idea of any Japanese veto power, the JCS were now prepared to concede the right of consultation before action was undertaken involving US forces operating from Japan.[48]

For the Far East Bureau of the State Department, the message of the offshore islands crisis was clear: the current US military posture was unsustainable in view of local pressures connected with the presence and possible use of nuclear weapons. The Deputy Assistant Secretary for the Far East, J. Graham Parsons, outlined the basic problem in December 1958 when speaking to the Marine Corps School at Quantico:

The increasing incorporation of atomic weapons into the U.S. arsenal is already raising serious problems regarding the use of our bases. Many Asians are concerned lest the presence of United States atomic forces will automatically involve the host country in nuclear warfare should fighting break out. This concern could be heightened by alarm that the United States would use atomic weapons in all situations, however small and limited, and that this would automatically lead to the use of larger weapons and general nuclear war. This issue could play hob with our base complex.[49]

[47] See Arthur J. de la Mare to Peter Dalton, 22 September 1958, FJ 10345/8, FO 371/133592, TNA; memorandum of conversation, 9 September 1958, and memorandum of conversation, 11 September 1958, *FRUS, 1958–1960, XVIII*, 64–9, 73–84.
[48] See JCS 2180/120, 'Security Treaty – Japan', 10 September 1958, *FRUS, 1958–1960, XVIII*, 71.
[49] 'United States Security Arrangements in the Far East', p. 16, speech delivered 15 December 1958, folder 3, box 12, Parsons papers, Georgetown University Library.

The conviction that nuclear use in the Taiwan Strait would do serious political damage to US interests throughout Asia helped cast doubt on how long the Nationalist position could or should be sustained in the offshore islands. Dulles complained that the 1958 crisis had 'strained our relations with Congress and foreign governments almost to breaking point'. Eisenhower was adamant that Chiang must be persuaded to defuse tensions with Beijing by pulling back some of his forces from the islands and to moderate his inflammatory talk of liberating the mainland through armed invasion. To this end, Dulles travelled to Taiwan in October 1958 where he managed to secure Chiang's agreement to a package deal. This would provide Chiang with more amphibious lift for his forces on Taiwan, in order that a return to the mainland could be contemplated in the event of mass unrest in China, but in return he would have to withdraw troops from the offshore islands and pledge to work through 'political' means (rather than the overt use of force) to effect change in the PRC.[50]

In April 1959, the Far East Bureau produced a paper which recommended a reconsideration of US policy towards the offshores, involving greater pressure on Taiwan to accelerate the evacuation of its vulnerable garrisons. In any repeat of the 1958 crisis, where nuclear weapons had to be used to repel a Chinese assault, 'aside from the appalling risks involved in a nuclear war', any such recourse might be 'politically disastrous in Asia. We must bear in mind that such is our dependence on nuclear weapons today that their employment would be required in many situations ... [and] a strong argument can be made that if we ever have to initiate the use of nuclear weapons it should certainly be in a situation, unlike the offshore islands, where we have maximum international understanding and support.' Moreover, and as well as the perennial problem of the availability of US bases in Japan, along with those in the Philippines, for nuclear operations, the use of such weapons 'against the mainland Chinese, killing untold numbers, would set the hearts of the Chinese people against the GRC [Government of the Republic of China] in a way which might well destroy any possibility of carrying out its long term objectives'.[51] In June 1960, a further memorandum on the Taiwan Strait problem, produced by the PPS, maintained that there were 'grave objections' to the use of nuclear weapons to defend the islands: 'the political costs throughout Asia, including Japan with its important U.S. bases, would be high if not well-nigh prohibitive'.[52]

---

[50] See Chang, *Friends and Enemies*, 198; Zhang, *Deterrence*, 263–4.
[51] Far East Bureau memorandum, 'Considerations Affecting a Reconsideration of Our Policies Toward the Offshore Islands', 1 April 1959, *FRUS, 1958–1960, XIX, Microfiche Supplement*, fiche 569/pp. 1, 7–8.
[52] 'Taiwan Straits and Offshore Islands Problem', S/P-6050, 28 June 1960, *ibid.*, fiche 757/p. 14.

In more general terms, the 1958 crisis also underlined for many senior officials the increasing redundancy of relying on nuclear weapons to cope with the kind of limited war scenario likely to be present in the Far East (and, for that matter, over maintaining access to West Berlin). In November 1958, Dulles delivered a speech to the National War College in Washington, where he mentioned that it was 'necessary to have more than the deterrent of a retaliatory striking power, primarily represented by SAC; it is necessary also to have limited warfare capabilities, because the reality is (and certainly it would be judged to be a reality) that we would not in fact use retaliatory striking power if there was what appeared to be a relatively minor incident'.[53] Only six months before his death, Dulles can thus once more be found repudiating the utility of a concept with which he had been so closely identified at the beginning of the administration. During the first half of 1959, as the annual NSC discussion of national security policy came to the fore, Smith pressed that the long-delayed meetings with the Defense Department on the basic strategic concept be held. As Smith explained to Dulles in January 1959, it was up to the State Department to take the initiative as his discussions with the Director of the Joint Staff and others at the Pentagon had convinced him that 'Defense and the Chiefs seem to be paralyzed by inter-service differences'. The PPS had accordingly drafted a paper on 'A Concept of U.S. Military Strategy for the 1960s' that called for a deterrent limited war force that was highly mobile, widely deployed with a flexible mix of air, sea and ground power, and able to fight effectively without using its nuclear capabilities.[54] However, with the Berlin crisis hanging over the administration and Dulles himself overtaken by his final struggle with cancer, little progress seems to have been made, and it was not until mid-April 1959 that Smith met John N. Irwin, the Assistant Secretary for International Security Affairs in the Defense Department, for preliminary discussions over the future direction of national strategy. Following this initial meeting, the State Department produced another paper stating that, 'We need from the point of view of foreign policy a capability and a doctrine that are flexible enough to enable us to deter and to defeat limited Communist

---

[53] Speech to National War College, 'Current U.S. National Strategy', 23 November 1958, box 136, John Foster Dulles papers, Mudd Library. On the 'conversion' of Dulles to flexible response, see also Gerard C. Smith Oral History, p. 20, Mudd Library.

[54] Smith memorandum for Dulles, 'Review of Strategic Concept', 20 January 1959, attached memorandum, 'A Concept of U.S. Military Strategy for the 1960s', 5 January 1959, and draft letter Dulles to McElroy, 24 January 1959, *FRUS, 1958–1960, III, Microfiche Supplement*, fiche 131. See also Watson, *Into the Missile Age*, 326–7.

aggression in ways that are acceptable to Free World public opinion and that minimize the danger of expanding local war into general war.'[55]

With a majority of the Joint Chiefs by now also finding sole reliance on massive retaliation an unacceptable way to plan force levels and strategic posture, when the NSC came to consider basic national security policy in the summer of 1959, the State Department's efforts to revise the controversial paragraphs of NSC 5810/1 appeared about to bear fruit.[56] However, McElroy, his deputy, Thomas Gates, and Radford (who had returned in a temporary capacity to the JCS while Twining had surgery) remained firmly wedded to the commitment to use nuclear weapons as military considerations demanded, and opposed what they called the 'dangerous policy implications' contained in the State Department's attempts to revise the language of the new draft statement of national security policy (NSC 5906); indeed, it was felt that the President should be encouraged to 'affirm in the NSC his willingness to use tactical nuclear weapons in limited war when necessary'. Radford maintained that there were 'practical restrictions' on the use of nuclear weapons, that there would be 'no casual use; use would be in accordance with careful prior planning', and that it would take five years to reconstruct the military establishment to allow it to fight limited wars without recourse to nuclear weapons. In the Asian context, the United States 'could not keep its present forces in the West Pacific unless they were armed with and could use nuclear weapons. If they found it necessary to put ground forces in Viet Nam [in response to a conventional Communist attack], they would have to have nuclear weapons [to prevent] from being overrun.'[57] Even though ill, Twining also added his own strong objections to any departure from the course that had been laid down in 1957. Smith found the Defense Department's views 'discouraging', believing, as he told Herter, who had assumed the duties of an ailing Dulles in April, that current strategic doctrine simply did not meet the requirements of US foreign policy with its suppositions over nuclear use in limited conflicts; Herter himself, Smith added, had raised the 'anomaly of our planning for

[55] See Herter to McElroy, 25 April 1959, and PPS paper, 'Summary Statement of Foreign Policy Requirements Bearing upon U.S. Strategy', 24 April 1959, *FRUS, 1958–1960, III*, *Microfiche Supplement*, fiche 153.

[56] The Chief of Staff, US Army, the Chief of Naval Operations and the Commandant of the Marine Corps all registered their opposition to the new draft statement of national security policy (NSC 5906) submitted by the NSC Planning Board; see JCS memorandum for the Secretary of Defense, JCSM-239–59, 20 June 1959, *FRUS, 1958–1960, III*, *Microfiche Supplement*, fiche 166.

[57] Memorandum for the record of State–Defense meeting on military paragraphs of NSC 5906, 30 June 1959, *ibid.*, fiche 168.

the use of nuclear weapons having a yield of over 1 megaton for tactical purposes'.[58]

Although he was obviously weary of the discussion, having confidence in his own ability to make the crucial judgements over nuclear use, Eisenhower himself could see his subordinates were still having problems implementing his wishes. For the President, the budgetary considerations that underpinned the original adoption of the New Look overruled the arguments placed before him by the State Department, while Herter did not command the authority of his predecessor as Secretary of State. In a meeting held to thrash out these issues on 2 July 1959, Eisenhower was prepared to recognize that 'the world is "scared to death" of atomic bombs, and that we could lose all our allies in one ill-advised act', but asserted that 'the crux of the matter was that we just could not deploy ground forces all over the world. Main reliance would have to be placed on nuclear weapons and mobile forces.' Eisenhower tried to explain how he was not advocating nuclear use in minor-scale actions, as might materialize in Central America or the Middle East, but only in the instance of a major attack in Central Europe or Korea, and he was also insistent that delegation of authority for nuclear use should be tightly controlled if the State Department's concern was that a local commander might take matters into his own hands and employ his local nuclear capability. In reacting to Communist probes, the United States must 'not use excessive means to meet our tasks. Just as a man cannot use a pistol against another who is simply trying to give him a bloody nose, there is need for judgment and care in selecting the weapons with which we would respond … Our military people should continue the incorporation of atomic weapons into our military structure, but at the same time should make sure that we can use the forces we have in a maximum conventional role and thus avoid unnecessarily causing all-out war to occur.'[59] A few days later, Eisenhower was evincing sympathy with the State Department's concerns about having the capacity to, what he called, 'stabilize small situations' without having to use nuclear weapons. However, in any repetition of fighting on the scale of the Korean War, or in a major clash with China, such as might arise if there were a direct attack on Taiwan, it was 'inconceivable' to the President how nuclear weapons would not be used.[60]

[58] Smith to Herter, 1 July 1959, *FRUS, 1958–1960, III, Microfiche Supplement*, fiche 169. See also Fairchild and Poole, *JCS and National Policy*, VII, 23–4.
[59] Memorandum of conversation (by Goodpaster), 2 July 1959, *FRUS, 1958–1960, III, Microfiche Supplement*, fiche 171; memorandum of conversation (by Smith), 2 July 1959, *FRUS, 1958–1960, III*, 228–35. See also Craig, *Destroying the Village*, 109–10.
[60] See memorandum of discussion at the 412th meeting of the NSC, 9 July 1959, *FRUS, 1958–1960, III*, 238–53.

After extended debates in the NSC, the wording of the crucial paragraph of NSC 5906/1 (which was crafted by Eisenhower himself) read that,

It is the policy of the United States to place main, but not sole, reliance on nuclear weapons; to integrate nuclear weapons with other weapons in the Armed Forces of the United States; and to use them when required to meet the nation's war objectives. Planning should contemplate situations short of general war where the use of nuclear weapons would manifestly not be militarily necessary nor appropriate to the accomplishment of national objectives, particularly in those areas where main Communist power will not be brought to bear.[61]

Much of the convoluted discussion over the language that was employed here was in any case academic. Gordon Gray, who had taken over from Cutler as Special Assistant to the President for National Security Affairs in July 1958 and was instrumental in managing the disputes between the State and Defense Departments over the document, maintained that whatever the new language now said, Eisenhower did not believe this 'represents any change in policy, and that it will not allow additional strength for the Army nor a "doubling or tripling" of the Defense budget for additions to the limited war capability. If the Secretary of State believes that a change in policy is involved, or that any increase in our limited war capability will result ... he is wrong.'[62]

The State Department was only too aware, however, that part of the political foundation on which nuclear use in limited war planning for the Far East was built was already shifting, most notably in the context of use of the Japanese base complex. Fujiyama's visit to Washington in September 1958 had seen some essential concessions made to the Japanese position over revision of the security treaty. There was every expectation that detailed negotiations could be completed quickly, but Kishi had to admit to US officials that factionalism in the LDP (with some elements not wanting to gift the Prime Minister what might be seen as a diplomatic coup) meant that Tokyo could not arrive at a settled negotiating position until the spring of 1959. When talks between MacArthur and Fujiyama finally got under way in April, the familiar sticking points revolved around whether Japanese forces might be used in other parts of the Far East for the purposes of collective defence as

[61] Paragraph 12, NSC 5906/1, 5 August 1959, *ibid.*, 295–6. In the opinion of the JCS historians, by raising the notion that limited war without use of nuclear weapons was a 'distinct possibility', the new document 'marked a discernible retreat from NSC 5707/8'; see Fairchild and Poole, *JCS and National Policy*, VII, 25, 29; Eisenhower's comments throughout would indicate, however, that this was not his basic intention.
[62] Letter from Howard Furnas of the PPS to Smith, 15 July 1959, *FRUS, 1958–1960, III*, 255–9.

defined by the new treaty, consultation over use of bases in Japan by US forces for operations not connected to the immediate defence of Japan (i.e. in Korea, the Taiwan Strait, or in attacks directed against the Chinese mainland), and the storage of nuclear weapons on Japanese territory. This final issue proved one of the most difficult, with the United States eventually undertaking by a secret exchange of notes with the Japanese Government not to 'introduce' nuclear weapons to Japan without prior consultation with Tokyo, though this was not interpreted to mean that US aircraft and ships equipped with nuclear weapons could not transit at will through Japanese bases or ports. This provision gave scope for the offshore storage of nuclear weapons on US ships and barges, which could, in an emergency, quickly transfer their cargoes to American airbases in Japan.[63]

A new mutual co-operation and security treaty was finally signed at a ceremony in Washington in January 1960, but this was merely a prelude to the eruption of discontent to come as the subsequent ratification process in Japan provoked a storm of protest. The Diet approved the treaty in June, but the opposition Socialist Party had boycotted the vote, and mass demonstrations led by labour and student organizations had already taken hold against the continuation of close security ties with the United States, as well as the increasingly autocratic leadership style of Kishi. With violence accompanying the anti-treaty protests, perceptions growing that Kishi could not guarantee public order and intense criticism in the media, the Prime Minister's LDP factional rivals lost little time in exploiting the situation to the full.[64] In late June, with final preparations well under way for a visit by Eisenhower to Japan to mark ratification of the new treaty, US and Japanese officials showed mounting nervousness over the physical safety of the President, and at the last minute Kishi was forced to withdraw the invitation, announcing also his intention to resign. Kishi's successor as LDP President and Prime Minister, Ikeda Hayato, proceeded to steer the party to further electoral success in November 1960, building his appeal around a concentration on the uncontroversial goal of furthering Japan's astonishing economic growth and respect for the niceties of parliamentary government, while avoiding the treacherous ground

---

[63] See Schaller, *Altered States*, 140–1. The notes remain classified and whether 'consultation' infers Japanese consent is a moot point; for an American interpretation, see Watson, *Into the Missile Age*, 637–8.

[64] See Schaller, *Altered States*, 143–62, and Tadashi Aruga, 'The Security Treaty Revision of 1960', in Iriye and Cohen (eds.), *United States and Japan in the Postwar World*, 61–79; Swenson-Wright, in *Unequal Allies*, 231–5, emphasizes the intra-LDP features of the treaty ratification struggle and highlights the resilience of LDP electoral strength in the rural areas of Japan throughout the period.

of rearmament and any constitutional revision which would allow the country to adopt a greater regional security role.[65]

For the United States, the smooth way in which Ikeda took over the LDP's reins in July 1960 was certainly reassuring, as was the abrupt end to the anti-treaty protests that followed Kishi's departure. Nevertheless, a real blow had been dealt to the US–Japanese relationship, and the cancellation of the President's visit was a graphic sign of how times had changed since the end of the occupation. Even though the new treaty provided the Americans with their minimum desiderata, by allowing the retention of bases in Japan and not offering Tokyo any formal veto on their use, the Japanese reaction to its signing was a stark illustration of the likely consequences if it was necessary to use the bases in a limited war context where the main target for US nuclear strikes would be the Chinese mainland. Not only could local disturbances and opposition present immediate security problems for the operation of the bases, but the political stability of Japan might be undermined, with the left standing ready to make gains at the expense of the LDP. In this scenario there was every likelihood that an LDP government would itself raise objections to use of the bases rather than face the subsequent political fallout, creating a further crisis in US–Japanese relations. Furthermore, rather than forming an essential pillar in the structure of containment built around China, Ikeda's new Government embarked upon a course in the early 1960s where its drive for economic expansion led it towards the traditional path of trade with the Chinese mainland.

Meanwhile, in the aftermath of the 1958 offshore islands crisis, many Americans grew ever-more concerned about their ability to intervene with conventional forces in a local Asian setting. This was an issue given new salience during the summer of 1959 by the deteriorating situation in Laos, where fighting between the Hanoi-backed Communist Pathet Lao and the fragile government in Vientiane had raised alarms that North Vietnamese influence might soon extend all the way down to the Thai border on the Mekong river. As the Pathet Lao pressed forward, the SEATO allies (spurred by a worried Thai Government) considered their options for armed intervention on the pretext that Hanoi's involvement constituted 'outside aggression'.[66] The British noted the signs that the US military were anxious about how they would deal with the ambiguities of conflicts such as Laos. In November 1959, informal Anglo-American staff talks

---

[65] See LaFeber, *The Clash*, 322.
[66] See Hugh Toye, *Laos: Buffer State or Battleground* (Oxford, 1968), 127–9; David Kaiser, *American Tragedy: Kennedy, Johnson, and the Origins of the Vietnam War* (Cambridge, MA, 2000), 24.

were held in Washington on global strategy. On his return, the British representative noted that Twining and Thomas Gates, the Secretary of Defense-designate, were 'greatly worried at their apparent incapacity to meet the threat of limited war; they remain convinced of the need for the deterrent, but were disturbed as [sic] being unable, despite their vast nuclear potential, to control a situation such as that in Laos, where they could not use it'.[67] In December 1959, Parsons, who had taken over as Assistant Secretary for the Far East after Walter Robertson's retirement in June, reminded the Pentagon that the State Department set great store on ensuring that conventional capabilities were kept up to strength in the region for what he called a 'time-phased reaction to a Communist probe'. 'As was demonstrated at Quemoy,' Parsons explained, 'tranquilization can be achieved by a graduated conventional response which may be stepped up until the degree of risk for the Communist aggressor becomes greater than that which he was prepared to accept. If we were to lack conventional strength, our choice of withdrawal in the face of Communist attack or resort to nuclear retaliation must be faced at once, without the advantage of time in which graduated military plus diplomatic and psychological measures could prove effective.'[68]

This was as good a definition of 'flexible response' as could be found anywhere at this time and indicates how far this kind of thinking had permeated the Far East Bureau. At the annual meeting of American Far Eastern Ambassadors, held at Baguio in March 1960, where Laos was high on the agenda of discussion, it was the unanimous view of those present that, 'The aversion in Asia to the use of any type of nuclear weapon is so strong that such use would without question be at great political cost.'[69] As talk of possible SEATO intervention in Laos continued, the Far East Bureau, echoing voices within the PPS and from American diplomats in the area, expressed its anxieties over the absence of suitable US conventional capabilities to wage the kind of limited campaign that might be required in South East Asia. 'Recent studies have tended to indicate,' Parsons noted in May, 'that with increased Chinese Communist military power we might well be unable to turn back a determined Communist thrust ... short of the use of nuclear weapons, which we believe would bring virtually prohibitive political costs. Furthermore, at least in Laos the use of nuclear weapons would appear to be unprofitable

---

[67] See Confidential Annex to COS(59)74th meeting, 1 December 1959, DEFE 32/6, TNA.
[68] Parsons to Irwin, 15 December 1959, *FRUS, 1958–1960, XVIII*, 597.
[69] See Parsons to Herter, 7 April 1960, 'Far East Chiefs of Mission Conference', box 3, Subject Files, Assistant Secretary for Far Eastern Affairs, 1960–3, records of the Bureau of Far East Affairs, RG 59, NARA.

in any event, and we could be faced with the necessity of striking elsewhere in order to relieve the pressure on Laos if it were persistent and great.'[70]

Parsons's mention of 'recent studies' was probably a reference to a further limited war study that was then being compiled in response to the reservations voiced over the inadequacies of the 1958 exercise. Gerard Smith had been particularly unhappy with the latter because its hypothetical limited war scenarios assumed that the United States would retain its monopoly over use of nuclear weapons, and indeed that this was essentially the reason that the 1958 study was able to conclude that US capabilities were sufficient. This assumption ran counter to the arguments contained in the SNIE of July 1958, which suggested that US nuclear strikes against mainland China could provoke a Soviet nuclear response against Taiwan (and when discussion of just such a possibility had occurred during the subsequent crisis in August 1958). As a result, during 1959 it was decided by the Secretaries of State and Defense that another limited war study would be undertaken where Communist nuclear capabilities and intentions would be taken into account.[71] The final State–Defense–JCS–CIA inter-agency study that emerged in July 1960 reduced the twelve geographic areas considered in the 1958 study to five: Korea, offshore islands/Taiwan, Iran, Berlin and Laos/Cambodia/Vietnam. In its Laos scenario, which covered a SEATO intervention after large-scale North Vietnamese support for an insurrection, the study commented on the restraints that would operate when considering possible use of nuclear, chemical and biological weapons in terms that echoed its predecessor when it came to race:

Insofar as use of nuclear weapons is concerned, it would be necessary to take into account not only a general world-wide reaction to the use of nuclear weapons anywhere, but also a special Asian sensitivity. We have thus far used atomic weapons only against Japan. Their use in Laos would give credence among Asians to the damaging charge that we regard them as the white man's weapon against Asians.[72]

For Smith, the new study still had not confronted the issue of two-way use of nuclear weapons in limited war ('because the JCS finds it an extremely

---

[70] Parsons to the Acting Secretary, 'Military Preparedness in the Far East', 19 May 1960, 'Far East, General, January–June 1960', box 1, Geographic Files, Assistant Secretary for Far Eastern Affairs, 1960–3, records of the Bureau of Far East Affairs, RG 59, NARA.

[71] See Smith to John N. Irwin, 28 September 1960, 'Limited War (1) (1957–61)', box 12, Briefing note subseries, NSC series, Office of the Special Assistant for National Security Affairs files, White House Office, DDEL.

[72] See 'United States and Allied Capabilities for Limited Military Operations to 1 July 1962', 14 July 1960, 'Limited Military Operations (1960) (1)', box 5, Subject subseries, NSC series, Office of the Special Assistant for National Security Affairs Files, White House Office, DDEL.

offensive subject in view of the present doctrine on the use of nuclear weapons'), but it at last brought out the fact, though in language that was 'carefully hedged', that the United States did not have an adequate limited war capability. The situation was most alarming in the Far East where any use of nuclear weapons 'would be at prohibitive cost to the U.S. in terms of world public opinion including the support of our allies'. The study suggested that there was an urgent need for the military to pursue dual planning, both nuclear and conventional, rather than the current 'planning for half-hearted conventional limited wars with the expectation that use of nuclear weapons will always get us out of any jams. While this philosophy may have been sound in 1950, it is no longer valid.'[73] Speaking for the Far East Bureau, Parsons warmly endorsed the study's ideas to develop greater capacity for limited military operations, arguing that the United States was 'dangerously deficient in capability to meet precisely the kind of military threat that is most likely to face us in the next few years in the Far East and elsewhere'. When it came to subtle nuances over how nuclear weapons might be targeted in limited war, Parsons was dismissive: 'the important fact for most of our allies and friends in Asia would be that nuclear weapons have again been used in Asia and again on U.S. initiative. This could have irreparable consequences.'[74] The political impact in the Far East of any American initiation of nuclear use was again raised in the full NSC when it came to consider the Limited War Study in October 1960.[75]

Although the JCS and the Department of Defense, thinking especially of Korea and the Taiwan Strait, continued to maintain that US willingness to use nuclear weapons was crucial as the best deterrent against limited war occurring in the first place, there were some fleeting signs that their old resistance to some State Department input on the planning side might be breaking down. The British Ambassador in Washington, Sir Harold Caccia, noted that the presence of a State Department representative (Foy Kohler) at the November 1959 Anglo-American staff talks was 'a new development here. Gates more than once during our discussion stressed the need to have the State Department alongside in defence planning, so that defence problems are not looked at in a political

[73] See Smith memorandum for Herter, 28 July 1960, *FRUS, 1958–1960, III*, 435; and Smith memorandum for the Acting Secretary, 'U.S. Limited War Capabilities', 5 October 1960, 'S/P Chronological, 1960–61', box 205, records of the PPS, 1957–61, RG 59, NARA.
[74] See Parsons memorandum for Herter, 'Inter-Agency Study on Hypothetical Limited War Situation', 12 September 1960, 'FE 4000–4999', box 1, TS Files of the Regional Planning Adviser, records of the Bureau of Far East Affairs, 1955–63, RG 59, NARA.
[75] See memorandum of discussion at the 462nd meeting of the NSC, 6 October 1960, *FRUS, 1958–1960, III*, 485.

vacuum.' Moreover, Robert Murphy was reported to have begun attending some meetings of the JCS, while Smith had made a private arrangement to hold regular weekly meetings with the Director of the Joint Staff
for an off-the-record discussion of current issues. Caccia welcomed this
change, which he felt mirrored more the integrated British approach, and
hoped it 'augurs well for what might happen in the Gates–Herter period
during the remainder of this Administration'.[76]

These were, however, largely straws in the wind, and without the
President being willing to re-examine nuclear policy in a fundamental
way there was no likelihood of expanding conventional capabilities for
limited war. Indeed, his determination to effect savings in defence spending between 1956 and the end of 1960 saw the overall size of the armed
forces drop by over 300,000 personnel, with the Army undergoing the
severest cuts from just over a million to just under 870,000 (representing
15 per cent of the total); Army active combat divisions went down from
eighteen to fourteen, with three of the latter engaged in training duties
rather than being ready for immediate deployment.[77] Eisenhower had
evinced his concern over the huge numbers of tactical nuclear weapons
that were in the US arsenal during 1960, and at how difficult it would be to
prevent a limited war from becoming general if the threshold of nuclear
use was so low, but he was not prepared to grapple with the problem with a
view to finding a solution.[78] For some scholars this has been a mark of
Eisenhower's basic adoption of a 'war avoidance' strategy: by making the
consequences of the outbreak of any limited or general war so devastating,
aggression would be prevented from occurring in the first place. This was
deterrence at its purest and simplest and was held to have operated well in
both the second offshore islands crisis and the Berlin crisis of 1958–9.
This, however, overlooks the question of war as a result of miscalculation,
or inadvertence, especially in the tension of a crisis situation where 'backing down' could be perceived by all sides as a major political defeat. It is
easy to see why Eisenhower was criticized by his contemporaries for
intellectual laziness towards the end of his presidency.[79] In this way, his
stance on limited war resembled that towards his attitude to the massive
expansion of the overall US stockpile of nuclear weapons in the latter half
of the 1950s, and the Single Integrated Operational Plan (SIOP), compiled during 1960, that would launch the great bulk of US nuclear weapons in one overwhelming strike against the Soviet bloc. Although he could

[76] See Caccia to Dean, 24 November 1959, CAB 21/5706, TNA.
[77] See Watson, *Into the Missile Age*, 776.   [78] See Bundy, *Danger and Survival*, 323.
[79] See, e.g., Bruce Kuklick, *Blind Oracles: Intellectuals and War from Kennan to Kissinger*
(Princeton, 2006), 67–9, 105–6.

see the tremendous amount of 'overkill' involved in these plans, the President held back from any intervention which might produce a more discriminating range of nuclear options. As President Kennedy's Special Assistant for National Security Affairs, McGeorge Bundy, later remarked, Eisenhower 'was aware of the profoundly excessive character of the strategic forces he had approved and aware also of the possibly catastrophic consequences of their use, but he did not act on his awareness'.[80]

While the opportunities for change in the American stance towards limited war were negligible under Eisenhower, there were many clear indications outside the confines of the administration that the debate over the futility of persevering with a primary reliance on nuclear weapons to deter local aggression had already been resolved in favour of 'flexible response'. Maxwell Taylor's dissent from official policy reached its zenith with the appearance of his tract *The Uncertain Trumpet*, which contained ideas he had been prevented from presenting in print while still serving as Army Chief of Staff.[81] Freed of this constraint by his retirement in July 1959, Taylor's work and views were sought out by Democratic politicians restive at what they regarded as the reckless defence policies of the Republicans. Included among these was Senator John F. Kennedy who had written to Taylor commending him for *The Uncertain Trumpet*, noting he had found it persuasive and helpful with his own thinking on strategic issues.[82] In one speech of October 1959, Kennedy had expounded on the problem that nuclear retaliatory power was insufficient to deter the full range of Communist aggression: 'It cannot protect uncommitted nations against a Communist takeover using local or guerrilla forces. It cannot be used in so-called "brush-fire" peripheral wars.' The real danger facing the West, the Senator explained, was continual Communist nibbling away at the fringe of the Western position, with each move not enough to justify massive retaliation. Yet under the Eisenhower administration, he charged that 'we have been preparing primarily to fight the one kind of war we least want to fight and are least likely to fight'.[83] In holding this kind of perspective, Kennedy was also very much in line with other leading Democratic Party

---

[80] Bundy, *Danger and Survival*, 325.
[81] Taylor had intended to publish a critique of massive retaliation as early as 1956 in *Foreign Affairs*, but this had been blocked by the Pentagon. 'Although I never regarded the article as world-shaking,' he later commented, 'their attitude was suggestive of the "thought control" established at the time over the opponents of Massive Retaliation'; Taylor to Armstrong, 12 June 1959, 'Maxwell D. Taylor' folder, box 61, Armstrong papers, Mudd Library.
[82] See Taylor, *Swords and Plowshares*, 175, 178, 180; also Lawrence Freedman, *Kennedy's Wars: Berlin, Cuba, Laos and Vietnam* (New York, 2000), 18–19.
[83] Kennedy speech, 16 October 1959, in Allan Nevins (ed.), *The Strategy of Peace* (New York, 1960), 184. In January 1954, Kennedy had criticized Dulles's massive retaliation

critics of the New Look.[84] With the Soviet Union now in a position to inflict devastating damage on the United States in any nuclear exchange, causing millions of civilian casualties, and any all-out nuclear war increasingly seen as a threat to life on the planet as a whole, the risks of threatening nuclear escalation during a local or minor crisis were seen by many as quite unacceptable. This was the prevailing logic behind advocating a policy of flexible response to the whole range of Communist threats and pressures, which would be met on their own terms. Furthermore, in situations where Western forces were unlikely to be able to inflict defeat on a Communist conventional aggression because of the greater numerical strength enjoyed by the latter, they could at least delay the point at which nuclear options might have to be exercised and enable political contact and messages to be sent between the opposing sides of the conflict.[85]

Even within the highest reaches of the incumbent administration there was an appreciation that change could not be deferred for much longer. On the same day as Kennedy's narrow election victory in November 1960, Christian Herter prepared his own notes on the major problems which would confront the incoming administration. Listed under those needing early attention was what Herter called 'the nuclear balance, and the inevitable abandonment by the U.S. of massive reliance on massive retaliation'. This would involve a review of basic national security policy and 'painful withdrawal symptoms as we move away from "massive retaliation" to dependence on more useable types of military power'.[86] The first NIE on the world situation that confronted the Kennedy administration in January 1961 highlighted some of the problematic issues surrounding any use of nuclear weapons in a limited war or tactical environment, which would, along with risking escalation to general war, 'alienate large and influential sectors of world opinion from the cause of the user, however just it may have been'.[87]

Soon after its arrival in office, then, the Kennedy administration communicated its belief that the non-nuclear means of deterrence had been neglected, and that it wanted to expand the range of options available when meeting various levels of Communist aggression.[88] At the end of

policy as completely inappropriate for opposing Communist advances in guerrilla war situations such as in Indochina; see Philip Nash, 'Bear *Any* Burden? John F. Kennedy and Nuclear Weapons', in Gaddis *et al.* (eds.), *Cold War Statesmen*, 122.

[84] See Aliano, *American Defense Policy from Eisenhower to Kennedy*, 231–4.

[85] See Gaddis, *Strategies*, 214.

[86] Herter notes, 'Memorandum for the Incoming Administration', 8 November 1960, DDRS/CK3100313268.

[87] See NIE 1–61, 'Estimate of the World Situation', 17 January 1961, *FRUS, 1961–1963, VIII: National Security Policy* (Washington, DC, 1996), 7.

[88] See Gaddis, *Strategies*, 202.

March 1961, Kennedy began to rectify the lack of conventional capabilities for limited war that he had earlier identified by requesting a supplemental appropriation for the 1962 defence budget. In the message to Congress that accompanied this request, he explained that, 'Non-nuclear wars, and sub-limited or guerrilla warfare, have since 1945 constituted the most active and constant threat to Free World security.' American forces overseas were best engaged, he maintained, in 'deterring or confining those conflicts which do not justify and must not lead to a general nuclear attack ... our objective now is to increase our ability to confine our response to non-nuclear weapons, and to lessen the incentive for any limited aggression by making clear what our response will accomplish'.[89] A powerful reminder of the urgency of the new president's request was being given at that very moment by the discussions over US military intervention in Laos that were then being pursued by the administration.

The Eisenhower administration's ill-fated backing for General Phoumi Nosovan in the hope of installing an anti-Communist right-wing government in Vientiane during the autumn of 1960 had appeared to reap dividends when his forces took the Laotian capital at the end of the year and drove out the moderate and neutralist figure of Prince Souvanna Phouma, whom the Americans took to be little more than a Communist stooge. However, Souvanna managed to rally neutralist forces and began to receive supplies from the Soviet Union as well as assistance from the Pathet Lao, who had no intention of seeing Laos turn into a pro-Western bastion. Phoumi's attempts to move north from Vientiane soon met firm resistance, and by early 1961 the Pathet Lao were preparing for a counteroffensive that might drive the rightist forces in the Royal Lao Army back towards the capital. Already North Vietnamese and Soviet involvement in the unfolding civil war had caused deep concern in Washington, and the Pentagon urged that consideration should be given to SEATO, or even unilateral US intervention if external support to the Pathet Lao should look like producing an outright Communist victory in Laos, the reverberations of which would be felt in Thailand, America's key ally on the mainland of South East Asia (and when the Thai leadership had close links with Phoumi). Eisenhower himself was adamant that Laos could not be allowed to succumb to Communism.[90] In the first few days of January 1961, as the Republicans prepared to leave office, Gerard Smith felt it necessary to despatch a reminder to Herter of some of the conclusions reached by the 1960 Limited War Study. These included the view that in

[89] Special Message to the Congress on the Defense Budget, 28 March 1961, *Public Papers of the Presidents: John F. Kennedy, 1961* (Washington, DC, 1962), 232.

[90] See Toye, *Laos*, 159–65; Kaiser, *American Tragedy*, 26–32.

the event of a SEATO intervention in Laos where North Vietnamese forces were present in any numbers, decisive results could only be achieved by a direct sea, land and air attack on North Vietnam itself, while 'selective and timely use of tactical nuclear weapons in Laos and Vietnam would be militarily effective against a DRV intervention in Laos'. However, such action could trigger a 'Soviet sponsored response in kind' while allied operations would need the use of US bases in Japan, Okinawa and the Philippines. Once more, the conundrum was raised of how use of nuclear weapons in limited war in Asia might cut the ground from underneath American feet by alienating Japanese opinion, making it impossible to operate from some of the key American bases in the Western Pacific.[91]

Laos duly became the first major foreign policy crisis to be faced by the new Kennedy administration. Kennedy was clearly unimpressed with the chances of securing military success on the ground and soon shifted to a position which sought a diplomatic solution involving a reconvened Geneva Conference where the great powers with an interest in the conflict could underwrite a settlement, and the neutralization of Laos under a national unity government led by Souvanna. Before this could occur, however, the new administration wanted to see a cease-fire in the fighting, and military options for intervention remained the topic of intensive discussion in Washington. One of the things Kennedy found disturbing about these was the JCS view that if North Vietnamese or Chinese forces were to enter Laos in large numbers to face American or SEATO troops, use of tactical nuclear weapons was the only way to avoid defeat. Once nuclear strikes began, Kennedy appreciated, they would probably extend to targets in southern China, making the possibility of direct Soviet involvement all the greater, and he was not ready to start a nuclear war over such an apparently insignificant territory.[92] Kennedy was also clearly disturbed about the paucity of US conventional capabilities for rapid deployment and resupply after the rundown of the Eisenhower years.[93] Diplomatic moves, and the onset of monsoon weather in late April, eventually brought about a cease-fire in Laos, and the Geneva Conference was convened in early May where prolonged negotiations

[91] Smith memorandum for Herter, 'Study of Limited War in Laos', 4 January 1961, 'Laos', box 130, records of the PPS, 1957–61, RG 59, NARA.
[92] See Arthur M. Schlesinger Jr, *A Thousand Days: John F. Kennedy in the White House* (New York, 1965), 332, 337–8; memorandum of conversation, 29 April 1961, *FRUS, 1961–1963, XXIV: Laos Crisis* (Washington, DC, 1994), 152; and Freedman, *Kennedy's Wars*, 302–3.
[93] See Schlesinger, *Thousand Days*, 315–16; and Lawrence S. Kaplan, Ronald D. Landa and Edward J. Drea, *History of the Office of the Secretary of Defense*, Vol. V: *The McNamara Ascendancy, 1961–1965* (Washington, DC, 2006), 233.

finally produced a settlement based around neutralization the following summer.

Studies of the Laos crisis of early 1961 have rightly drawn attention to the unappetizing nature of the military options on offer to Kennedy, and the fact that direct US or SEATO intervention was not favoured by Congressional opinion, while the British were also highly sceptical. 'We looked long and hard at the Laotian situation,' the new US Secretary of State, Dean Rusk, later recalled, 'and the more we looked, the more forbidding was the prospect of landing American troops.'[94] In the wake of the Bay of Pigs fiasco of mid-April, it was unlikely that Kennedy would embark on another uncertain military adventure, and one where the risks of triggering Chinese intervention were considered so high. Though never a central consideration, possible Asian reactions to any resort to nuclear weapons was a further background factor present in the administration's thinking. Behind this concern lay, once more, the position of the US bases in Japan as the Government in Tokyo emerged from the bruising battles of 1960 over the ratification of the new security treaty. Having been publicly critical of Eisenhower for his insensitivity towards the problems of the newly independent states of Asia, and of non-aligned opinion more generally, leading figures in the Kennedy administration were likely to be even more alert to the potential of nuclear use to alienate some of the key players in the region. In March 1961, Chester Bowles, now installed as the Under-Secretary of State, warned Rusk that, 'If powerful ground troops are thrown at us and our forces are overwhelmed, we face an impossible choice: either we retreat under fire, with the most humiliating implications to our prestige and influence, or we resort to nuclear weapons, which would be catastrophic in its effects on Asian and world opinion.'[95] A State Department Policy Planning Council (PPC) paper of May 1961 argued that fear of nuclear war was common for all neutralist states, who may have had no part to play in its inception but suffer all the terrible results, while 'the Asian and African nations see the nuclear bomb as a white man's weapon and there are racial overtones in their anti-nuclearism'.[96]

Attempting to profit from the Laotian experience, in July 1961, John Steeves, now the Deputy Assistant Secretary of State for Far Eastern Affairs, requested the production of an estimate by the intelligence community on world reaction to the use of nuclear weapons in response

[94] Rusk, *As I Saw It*, 428.
[95] See Chester Bowles, *Promises to Keep: My Years in Public Life, 1941–1969* (New York, 1971), 338.
[96] PPC 61–1, 'Neutralism: Suggested United States Policy Toward the Uncommitted Nations', 29 May 1961, 'Policy Planning: Neutralism', Subjects series, box 303, National Security File (NSF), John F. Kennedy Library (JFKL).

to Communist aggression in Asia. Because of the 'highly controversial nature of this subject', Steeves felt it best if this took the form of a SNIE mirroring the one completed in July 1958, and which examined the consequences of nuclear use in Korea, the offshore islands and Laos. As well as gauging likely Soviet and Chinese reactions, the SNIE should include 'Japanese reactions including those relating to United States ability further to use Japanese bases'. Just as the 1958 SNIE, in conjunction with the 1958 Limited War Study, had proved 'highly useful in policy discussions concerning the 1958 Offshore Islands crisis', Steeves hoped that a new SNIE might supplement the 1960 Limited War exercise, while it had obvious relevance for Laos.[97] As it transpires, no SNIE appears to have resulted, but in a fascinating parallel (showing, as in 1956 over SEATO's adoption of nuclear planning assumptions, the shared anxieties of the Western powers over the subject), the British intelligence community had undertaken a similar exercise. In early July 1961, the JIC in London considered the consequences if nuclear weapons were used following SEATO intervention in Laos triggering a commitment of Chinese ground forces. Their conclusions were decidedly pessimistic. The JIC felt that the terrain in Laos, difficulties of target selection and probable Chinese infiltration tactics meant that any Communist advance was unlikely to be blunted by limited nuclear use in the area of the ground battle; SEATO would inevitably be faced with the prospect of more extensive use (against targets in North Vietnam and southern China). Any advantage that nuclear strikes might gain in terms of showing Western resolve would be counteracted by the 'very adverse consequences in the psychological and propaganda fields which would be fully exploited by the Soviet Union'. African and Asian states would react in a 'bitter and emotional' way, with even moderate governments having to condemn SEATO action. The Commonwealth might break up under the strain, while there could be expected a 'particularly sharp emotional reaction from Japan. The position of Western bases in Afro-Asian countries would be jeopardised. Even Thailand and South Vietnam might have to reappraise their pro-Western policies.'[98] Given the frequent exchange of appraisals between British and American intelligence staffs, it is quite possible that these bleak prospects were conveyed to the JIC's counterparts in Washington.

---

[97] See Steeves memorandum for Hilsman, 'Request for Intelligence Estimate', 28 July 1961, 'FE 5000–5599', box 1, TS Files of the Regional Planning Adviser, records of the Bureau of Far East Affairs, 1955–63, RG 59, NARA.
[98] See JIC(61)48(Final), 'Use of Nuclear Weapons Following SEATO Intervention in Laos and the Likely Consequences', 7 July 1961, CAB 158/44, TNA.

By the early summer of 1961, having gone through both the Laos and Cuban crises, officials in the Kennedy administration were more aware than ever that an adequate US capacity for intervention in settings where limited war was a distinct possibility was an essential requirement of foreign policy for the coming decade. Robert Komer, one of the key assistants on McGeorge Bundy's NSC staff, composed a typically hard-hitting memorandum in May 1961 which called for big increases in the Pentagon's budgeting for limited war forces, particularly so that two regional crises could be handled simultaneously without affecting the overall US posture for general war. 'Moreover,' he continued, 'I am convinced that our limwar [sic] planning is still all too closely tied to the idea that if a fracas got above a very modest level we would use nuclear weapons.'

Looking at the world of the 60s one is struck by two facts. First we are going to be a lot more reluctant to use nuclear weapons locally as well as strategically; the other fellow appreciates this too, so this deterrent is simply a lot less credible. Second, if the first few months of '61 are any guide we are likely to be confronted with numerous crisis situations around the globe which will require a credible deterrent and, if this fails, an adequate capacity for intervening. Given Mr Khrushchev's current ebullient mood and Peiping's intransigence we may well have more than one crisis on our hands at any given time. Ergo, we need a far more flexible limwar capability, one not tied too exclusively to nucs [sic] and one which gives more than a single punch.[99]

This kind of message was beginning to be absorbed by the Pentagon under the new stewardship of Kennedy's energetic Secretary of Defense, Robert S. McNamara. Though no great difference was apparent in the absolute size of the US Army and Marine Corps through the subsequent Kennedy years, the number of active US divisions was raised to sixteen, and, even more importantly, the combat effectiveness of US forces was increased through better provision of more modern equipment, and greater air and sea-lift capacity.[100] More responsiveness from the JCS to the new ideas coming from the White House and McNamara's Pentagon staff was also assured when Kennedy moved to replace the existing Chairman, General Lyman Lemnitzer, with his favourite general, Maxwell Taylor, in the summer of 1962.[101]

---

[99] Komer memorandum for Bundy and Rostow, 'Grappling with the Conventional Force Syndrome', 9 May 1961, 'Staff Memoranda, Robert Komer', box 321, Meetings and Memoranda series, NSF, JFKL.

[100] Kaplan, Landa and Drea, *McNamara Ascendancy*, 57–8, 65–6.

[101] On Kennedy's reordering of the JCS in 1962, see H. R. McMaster, *Dereliction of Duty: Lyndon Johnson, Robert McNamara, the Joint Chiefs of Staff, and the Lies that Led to Vietnam* (New York, 1997), 22.

The dominant approach to thinking about US defence policy and the role of nuclear weapons in the later 1950s has tended to centre on changing evaluations of the strategic balance and the erosion of the credibility of massive retaliation when the Soviet Union gained the capacity to deliver a crippling nuclear attack on the continental United States. This kind of explanation can certainly provide a logical and persuasive explanation as to why doubts about excessive reliance on nuclear weapons to deter Communist threats began to arise, and how an alternative stance of flexible response gained adherents. However, this does not convey a complete picture of the contemporary debate, particularly when one examines the Asian scene, where there were much lower chances of a Communist response in kind to first use by the United States of nuclear weapons. While Taylor's dissent of 1959 has captured a great deal of attention, it is also important to note that within the Eisenhower administration the political and moral aspects to nuclear use, and the racial connotations nuclear weapons carried in Asia as a symbol of 'white superiority', were a frequent topic of comment and concern. Such was the degree of unease surrounding the possible repeat employment of weapons of mass destruction in a Far Eastern context that by the end of the 1950s the State Department had come to believe that *any* nuclear use, in however limited a fashion, would alienate large swathes of public opinion and could prove disastrous to US interests in Asia.

Since the Korean War, officials had worried almost constantly about the estrangement they saw as developing between the United States and the peoples and states of Asia: the brandishing of American nuclear capabilities, in a region where the memories of Hiroshima and the *Lucky Dragon* incident were still near, was one more aspect to that phenomenon. Although US military chiefs continued to anticipate that nuclear weapons would be used in response to a large-scale Communist aggression, during this period one sees the State Department mount a strong and concerted effort to make its voice heard, and to inject political factors into the Pentagon's jealously guarded realm of defence planning and force structures (in fact, one of the signs that times were changing under Kennedy was the creation, in 1961, of a new Bureau of Politico-Military Affairs in the State Department, mirroring in some ways the Pentagon's own Office of International Security Affairs).[102] For many of the critics of massive retaliation, who had entertained doubts about the approach since Dulles's initial formulation of the policy in 1954, the offshore islands crisis of 1958

---

[102] See Raymond L. Garthoff, *A Journey through the Cold War: A Memoir of Containment and Coexistence* (Washington, DC, 2001), 121–2.

was the final straw.[103] Writing in the *New York Times*, James Reston attacked the drift he saw present in the Eisenhower administration and asked, 'Is United States power in balance with its commitments – honestly in balance for non-atomic as well as atomic war – or would we have to use atomic weapons once more against Asians in order to prevent an all-out invasion of Quemoy?'[104] Within the official bureaucracy, by the time that Kennedy arrived in office the stage was already set for a new strategic doctrine more attuned to the issue of limited war, with all the political ramifications it raised.

The acceptance by the Kennedy administration of a strategy of flexible response signalled the basic conviction of many US officials, one concurred in by public opinion, that general nuclear war involving the Soviet Union would be a recipe for national suicide. The experience of the Berlin crisis of 1961 had only reinforced the belief that the range of military options available to the President had to be increased. In the European setting, the administration, as McNamara explained in his seminal Athens speech to the NATO Council in May 1962 (and made public during another speech at Ann Arbor the following month), wanted to boost the ability of allied conventional forces to withstand a Soviet attack, so as to delay the point where local commanders might have to appeal to political authority for permission to use tactical nuclear weapons on the battlefield. The extension of this phase of any land battle might allow for pauses in fighting and for negotiations. As a corollary to this, the administration also wanted to develop a greater range of nuclear options, and certainly to modify the all-or-nothing SIOP that SAC planners, who dominated the joint targeting staff at Omaha, had devised by the end of 1960.[105]

Notwithstanding these basic developments in strategic thought, however, there was also present among the civilian members of the Kennedy administration a growing conviction that once any nuclear use had been sanctioned, on whatever scale, escalation to all-out nuclear war would be virtually impossible to avoid. This appears to have been the case with McNamara, who later recollected that in the early 1960s he had privately told Kennedy that he should never, under any circumstances, authorize

---

[103] See, e.g., Brinkley, *Acheson*, 63.
[104] 'Drifting and Dreaming on the Potomac', *NYT*, 7 September 1958.
[105] See McNamara speech to NATO Council, Athens, 5 May 1962, in Philip Bobbitt, Lawrence Freedman and Gregory F. Treverton (eds.), *US Nuclear Strategy: A Reader* (London, 1989), 205–22; Freedman, *Evolution of Nuclear Strategy*, 233–5, 296–301; Robert S. McNamara, 'The Military Role of Nuclear Weapons: Perceptions and Misperceptions', *Foreign Affairs*, 62, 1, Fall 1983, 63–4. It is clearly significant that William Kaufmann, one of the leading critics of massive retaliation in the mid-1950s, played a central role in the drafting and content of the Athens speech; see Kuklick, *Oracles*, 108.

the first use of nuclear weapons, advice which was repeated to his successor, Lyndon Johnson.[106] Despite his enthusiasm for the application of flexible response to NATO strategy and the development of more options in the face of Communist conventional military power, Kennedy's essential view was that once nuclear weapons began to be used, in however controlled an initial fashion, it would be extremely difficult to avert rapid escalation to a larger and more catastrophic nuclear exchange.[107] In this scheme of things, nuclear weapons were only valuable as a deterrent to a Soviet nuclear attack, or as a weapon of very last resort when a Soviet conventional offensive might be in danger of overrunning Western Europe, but certainly not to be employed in a limited war setting.

How these doctrinal shifts in thinking about nuclear use in the Kennedy years affected strategy in the Far East is more difficult to determine. Here, of course, the principal American opponents would not be armed with nuclear weapons at all, at least until China attained a nuclear capability. One reason a non-nuclear capacity for fighting limited war was seen as important was that Soviet intervention could not be discounted if the Communist Chinese regime was threatened with destruction (and there was always the possibility that Moscow might supply nuclear weapons to Beijing in an emergency), but the idea of Soviet nuclear assistance looked increasingly unlikely as the Sino-Soviet split became evident from 1960 onwards. It took some time for Washington to appreciate the full significance of the fracture in Sino-Soviet relations, but by 1962 the gulf between the two Communist powers was unmistakable, even to State Department sceptics. With the danger of a nuclear response from the Soviet Union having receded, this made the political objections to nuclear use in Asia of even more relevance, and once again it was reactions in Japan and among the non-aligned states of the region that provided the cause for concern, with race appearing as a factor. Finally, and most significantly, as China moved ever closer to its first test explosion of a nuclear device, American strategy would have to adapt to the changing political environment that this important event would generate.

---

[106] McNamara, 'Military Role of Nuclear Weapons', 79; and also Daniel Ellsberg, *Secrets: A Memoir of Vietnam and the Pentagon Papers* (New York, 2002), 59–60.
[107] See Taylor, *Swords and Plowshares*, 206.

11 The Chinese bomb, American nuclear strategy in Asia and the escalation of the Vietnam War

For President Kennedy, the insurgencies in Vietnam and Laos, even though the latter was temporarily stifled by the neutralization agreement reached at Geneva in July 1962, were potent signs of the immediacy of the Communist threat facing the fragile states and societies of South East Asia, and tests of how the United States would meet the danger to regional stability they represented. Indeed, the ideological struggle of the Cold War showed every sign of intensifying across the decade to come, with Khrushchev's acceptance of peaceful coexistence, and recognition that a direct military clash between the United States and Soviet Union was a quick route to mutually assured destruction. In this context, the battle for 'hearts and minds' in the developing world held even greater significance, by moving areas notionally on the periphery to the centre of conflict. As far as the Kennedy administration was concerned, this had been the main import of Khrushchev's 'wars of national liberation' speech in January 1961, which signalled a transfer of the major battleground of the East–West competition to regions newly liberated from overt Western domination (though as we have already seen worries over Soviet inroads being made in the developing world had first emerged in Washington in the mid-1950s, and economic aid to key non-aligned states such as India had been enhanced as a result).[1] Addressing the NSC in January 1962, Kennedy identified Khrushchev's remarks as 'possibly one of the most important speeches of the decade', where the Soviet Premier had 'made clear the pattern of military and paramilitary infiltration and subversion which could be expected [and that] in response we must strengthen our conventional forces and our capability for military leadership in dealing with that kind of war'. In what encapsulated his own beliefs of where the priorities of defence policy should lie, Kennedy felt that 'all forces – Army, Marine, Air and Navy – must learn how to fight on the edges of the world. The record of the Romans made clear that their success was dependent on

---

[1] See, e.g., memorandum of discussion at the 295th meeting of the NSC, 30 August 1956, *FRUS, 1955–1957, XXI*, 243.

their will and ability to fight successfully at the edges of their empire.' This striking imperial metaphor was then followed, when looking ahead to the future, by the President's mention of 'special unsolved problems', including the effect on 'our dispositions in Southeast Asia' of China's acquisition of 'missiles and bombs and nuclear weapons'.[2] In linking Beijing's possession of a nuclear capability and American intervention on the Asian periphery, the President was beginning to signal what would become an abiding strategic issue for his successor as the war in Vietnam began to consume American attention.

Throughout the first part of Kennedy's presidency, American policymakers detected the Soviet Union's influence behind the outbreaks of unrest in the developing world that the United States had sought to contain, through the support and encouragement offered to surrogates in Hanoi and Havana, or by its direct role in fuelling the conflicts in the Congo and Laos.[3] However, during 1962 there were several indications that these trends were shifting, and that the Russians might be reacting to events rather than instigating them. Rational dialogue leading to agreement with Moscow began to seem eminently possible. One sign of this was given by the Geneva Agreement on the neutralization of Laos in July 1962, and the fact that a constructive exchange of sorts was becoming possible over Berlin and the potential for West Germany to develop nuclear weapons.[4] The decision to install missiles in Cuba, itself connected to the German problem and Berlin, was a Soviet miscalculation, but the fact that it was successfully resolved through Moscow's acceptance of American proposals for resolution of the crisis, which involved mutual concessions, gave encouragement to Washington. The basic rationality of Soviet policy had ultimately been demonstrated by Khrushchev's willingness to retreat from the nuclear brink. As the Americans came to see it, the Russians might be dangerous adversaries, but they were also essentially pragmatic realists who did not want competition with the West to turn into an all-out war which would bring disastrous consequences for everyone involved.

No such attributes were ascribed to the Chinese Communists, whose implacable hostility was reflected in an unremitting and militant barrage of propaganda and commentary, much of it playing down the destructiveness of nuclear war for a country possessing the vast size and population of

---

[2] Summary of President Kennedy's remarks to the 496th meeting of the NSC, 18 January 1962, *FRUS, 1961–1963, VIII*, 240.

[3] Westad, *Cold War*, 166–70.

[4] For the development of US–Soviet understanding over Berlin and the German problem in 1962–3, see Trachtenberg, *Constructed Peace*, 327–8, 341, 344–50, 379–90.

China, and espousing the coming global revolution in the Afro-Asian world that would overthrow capitalist imperialism. The Chinese were considered virtually unreachable, their diplomatic isolation, despite the American role in its instigation, increasingly conceived of as self-imposed, while the mass famine that consumed the Chinese countryside in the early 1960s, following the catastrophic experiment of the Great Leap Forward, only served to reinforce a picture of indifference to human suffering.[5] The development of the Sino-Soviet split underlined the unpredictable and volatile nature of Mao's leadership in Beijing, which now criticized the Russians for their apparent climb-down in the face of American nuclear superiority over Cuba, and their lack of commitment to the international class struggle. Within the United States, public attitudes towards China as an enemy were also changing as détente with the Soviet Union became more of a feature of great power relations after 1962. In early 1964 one report considered by McGeorge Bundy, the President's Special Assistant for National Security Affairs, detailed the results of interviews conducted with a wide geographical spread of Americans the previous autumn, and revealed that the PRC was now viewed as a bigger threat to world peace than Russia. Fear of war with the Soviet Union was declining, but respondents could see a nuclear-armed China as posing more of a danger in the future. The survey showed, moreover, that while in 1961 only about 5 per cent talked about a Chinese threat 'in terms of a racial struggle or as a conflict between western and Oriental civilizations', these aspects were now mentioned by almost 20 per cent of those interviewed; the image of a growing conflict between 'the West' and an Eastern world led by China, it was suggested, was related to greater public awareness of the Sino-Soviet split and identification of Russia with the values of Western civilization. Perhaps most remarkably, it was also concluded that somewhere between a quarter and a third of the electorate were 'moving mentally towards a possible eventual alliance of the U.S. with Russia against Red China'. Overall, the public was pictured as lacking confidence with how China's growing strength could be addressed, while 'deep in their minds lies the dread that Red China is moving inexorably towards a nuclear, racial war and that so far we do not know what to do to change this drift of events'.[6]

---

[5] George Kennan voiced a common feeling when he avowed that, 'We have much more difficult problems with the Chinese than with the Russians. The latter have more in common with Western civilization'; see record of Policy Planning Staff meeting, 8 February 1961, *FRUS, 1961–1963, V: Soviet Union* (Washington, DC, 1998), 63.

[6] 'Report on Changes in Public Attitudes toward Communist China by Samuel Lubell Associates', and covering note from Forrestal to Bundy, 18 February 1964, China Memos, Vol. I, Country File, box 237, NSF, LBJL.

Kennedy had begun his presidency prepared to re-examine elements in the China policy he had inherited from Eisenhower, but he was still very wary of the residual China lobby in Congress and its capacity to complicate his more important objectives elsewhere, while the narrow margin of his election victory in 1960 precluded potentially divisive changes.[7] In May 1961 he had apparently told Dean Rusk (according to the latter's recollection) of his desire that the State Department launch no new initiatives over China policy, citing Eisenhower's pre-inaugural warning that he would publicly speak out against any attempt to confer recognition or seat the PRC at the UN.[8] Whatever early interest Kennedy may have exhibited in the possibility of a 'two Chinas' solution to the dilemma of Chinese representation at the UN – with the idea of shifting the blame for PRC exclusion to Beijing's obstinacy rather than American capriciousness – it was tempered by his unwillingness to break the alliance with Chiang, while the overt hostility with which Beijing had greeted his arrival in the White House did not improve matters. By October 1961 flirtation with notions of modifying the American stance at the UN on the representation issue had been discarded and replaced by a secret pledge to use the American veto in the Security Council to protect Nationalist China's seat.[9] For the President and his senior advisers, in fact, there was an abiding belief that the PRC was an aggressive and expansionist power, intent on usurping American influence in Asia. China's active promotion of revolutionary causes in the developing world, and the conviction it was instrumental in fostering militancy throughout South East Asia (including the growing insurgency in South Vietnam), made its continued containment and isolation a firm plank of official policy, reinforced by the influence of an unrepentant Rusk at the State Department. With Rusk as Secretary of State, and given the powerful domestic political constraints that Kennedy perceived, there was very little likelihood of any dramatic shift in China policy, notwithstanding the occasional trial balloon floated by the likes of James C. Thomson of the NSC staff, or Roger Hilsman, the Director of the State Department's Bureau of Intelligence and Research.[10]

[7] See, in general, Noam Kochavi, *A Conflict Perpetuated: China Policy during the Kennedy Years* (Westport, CT, 2002); and also Rosemary Foot, 'Redefinitions: The Domestic Context of America's China Policy in the 1960s', in Ross and Changbin (eds.), *Re-Examining the Cold War*, 264–6.

[8] See Rusk, *As I Saw It*, 282–3; Kochavi, *Conflict Perpetuated*, 56.

[9] Bundy to Cline, 11 October 1961, *FRUS, 1961–1963, XXII: Northeast Asia* (Washington, DC, 1996), 154–5.

[10] See James Fetzer, 'Clinging to Containment: China Policy', in Thomas G. Paterson (ed.), *Kennedy's Quest for Victory: American Foreign Policy, 1961–1963* (New York, 1989), 178–97; Foot, 'Redefinitions', 281–4.

One approach to the likely increase of Chinese influence in Asia was to improve ties to India, and Kennedy had long considered that the fate of the region would probably depend on whether its peoples looked to the revolutionary tenets of the PRC, or to the example of democratic India, as an appropriate model of economic development.[11] The phenomenon of Sino-Indian tension and rivalry, latent in the aftermath of Bandung, had become an increasingly significant feature of the international politics of Asia during the late 1950s. Chinese suppression of the Tibetan rebellion in 1959, and the refuge that the Dalai Lama found at Dharamsala, was one source of discord, but the outbreak of the serious border dispute in that same year over the McMahon line in northern Assam and the disposition of the Aksai Chin in western Tibet sent relations into rapid decline. These problems between New Delhi and Beijing finally dissipated the fears of a Sino-Indian combination working together to expel Western influence from the region that had animated the worldview of some Americans in the mid-1950s. Less encouraging, however, was the evidence that Nehru also sought to improve his links with Moscow and the fact that the US alliance with Pakistan meant that the Indians could not see their way to a closer relationship with Washington. Furthermore, American attempts to broker a resolution to the Kashmir dispute simply engendered resentment and suspicion in New Delhi, and congressional criticism of the administration's aid policy to the subcontinent was a further and important source of friction.[12] Indeed, the attractiveness of Soviet models of centrally planned development to the Indians was still a concern to modernization theorists in the Kennedy administration, who hoped that capitalist-led economic growth might be to the tool that could lure newly independent countries away from Communism.[13] Increasing Sino-Soviet competition for influence was also a factor here, where the Great Leap Forward experiment in mass action revealed just how far Beijing had moved from Moscow's direction. With its dismal economic failures, the PRC had fallen a long way from being a leading representative of the optimistic 'new Asia' that emerged from the wreckage of Japanese imperialism and war after 1945. Nevertheless, China's continued defiance of US imperialism still won it plaudits in Asia, and from 1964 onwards Mao began to articulate 'three worlds theory', where the two main superpowers were grouped together in a First World enjoying a

---

[11] Schlesinger, *Thousand Days*, 522.   [12] McMahon, *Cold War on the Periphery*, 272–86.
[13] See David C. Engerman, 'West Meets East: The Center for International Studies and Indian Economic Development', in David C. Engerman, Nils Gilman, Mark H. Haefele and Michael E. Latham (eds.), *Staging Growth: Modernization, Development, and the Global Cold War* (Amherst, MA, 2003), 199–223; Merrill, *Bread and the Ballot*, 170–86.

hegemonic relationship with an industrialized Second World, while China led the poor (and non-white) countries of the Third World in revolution.[14]

The idea of a brewing transnational racial conflict which was suggested by some of the propaganda coming from Mao's China at this time coincided with a period of unprecedented racial change within the United States itself, as the civil rights movement advanced towards the accomplishment of its major legislative goals, mobilizing support through non-violent action and protest, and holding up to a global audience the response of the Federal Government to Southern white resistance. Black Americans and Africans saw close parallels between the American racial scene and the determination of white minority governments in Southern Africa to meet any challenge to their control with force. These transnational linkages between the struggles against white supremacy were not lost on US officials, particularly as the many African states that gained independence in the pivotal year of 1960 began to find a voice at the United Nations (and it was in Africa, too, where the PRC was to begin to carve out new diplomatic initiatives during 1964). Aware of the domestic political pitfalls, not least within his own Party, that awaited any open embrace of the cause of equal rights for African Americans, during the final year of his presidency Kennedy shifted only reluctantly towards an acceptance that decisive federal action was needed. The widespread international media attention that was given to the civil rights movement when it encountered a violent white response, most notably during the protests at Birmingham, Alabama, in April–May 1963, has been cited as one reason why the President felt that America's image in the Cold War was being tarnished by the denial of basic freedoms to so many of its citizens and that he should adopt a less equivocal position.[15] Rusk later recalled that 'race relations within the United States during the sixties had a profound impact on the world's view of the United States and, therefore, on our foreign relations ... I regularly testified before Congress that racial discrimination in the United States had great significance for our foreign policy and that our failure to live up to our proclaimed ideals at home was widely noted abroad.'[16]

After succeeding to the presidency Lyndon Johnson, a committed liberal on race issues, was determined to lead his country into a new era of domestic reform where racial discrimination and poverty might be

---

[14] See Westad, *Cold War*, 162; Tinker, *Race, Conflict and the International Order*, 117–18.

[15] On international perceptions of Birmingham and the Kennedy administration's response, see Dudziak, *Cold War Civil Rights*, 169–85, and Borstelmann, *Color Line*, 157–62.

[16] Rusk, *As I Saw It*, 586.

eradicated, and the United States prove a model for the rest of the world to emulate. The great irony of his huge achievements in managing the passage of the Civil Rights Act of 1964 and Voting Rights Act of 1965 through Congress were that they were accomplished when he was launching the United States on another war on the Asian mainland with the bombing of North Vietnam, and the despatch of combat troops to the South. It was as though every act of escalation in South East Asia warranted some counterpoised act of domestic racial atonement. Thus, for example, abolition of the national origins system through the October 1965 Immigration Act, where previously Asian immigration had been severely restricted by a racially defined quota, can be seen to hold a transnational significance.[17] As Thomas Borstelmann has commented, the new law represented a 'sharp break with the past: the United States would no longer legally seek to preserve an identity as a homogenous white society. There was little coincidence in this change being enacted in the wake of both the civil rights movement and the dispatch of American troops into war with an Asian enemy. The Johnson administration was determined to minimize racial conflict on all fronts.'[18]

The notion of China entering the ranks of the existing occidental nuclear powers with its first test explosion also contained a racial dimension, as did the related subject of American nuclear strategy in the Far East during the Kennedy era. The Chinese nuclear programme had, of course, been watched closely by the American intelligence community ever since its inception in the mid-1950s, but concrete knowledge of developments, as opposed to supposition and conjecture, was rare. Western analysts had noted a step change during 1960 in Chinese pronouncements about nuclear weapons, not least a withdrawal from all forms of anti-nuclear weapon propaganda in the Far East, which seemed to indicate that the path to acquisition of a nuclear capability was clearer for Beijing.[19] The dramatic withdrawal of Soviet advisers from China as Sino-Soviet relations continued to deteriorate in that same year was presumed to have delivered a major setback to the programme. However, the huge effort devoted by the Chinese Communist leadership to acquiring the bomb and the indigenous talents of China's own nuclear physicists and engineers were starting to bear fruit by 1961, and this was reflected in the more confident assertions of a number of Chinese military figures. As early as the spring of 1961, Kennedy was talking, so the *New York Times* columnist Arthur Krock later recalled, of the need to continue with the test-ban

---

[17] See Polenberg, *One Nation Divisible*, 202–6.   [18] Borstelmann, *Color Line*, 194–5.
[19] See Foreign Office minute (Atomic Energy and Disarmament Department), 'Chinese Interest in Nuclear Weapons', 17 June 1960, IAE 410/8G, FO 371/149546, TNA.

negotiations at Geneva because of an 'intense desire to do everything possible to assure that Communist China won't have a bomb'.[20] The President's belief in the dire political consequences of a Chinese bomb even led him to doubt that holding the line in Vietnam would be an effective counter to Beijing's ambitions. When Krock asked him in October 1961 if he believed in the domino theory, and that the fall of Vietnam and Laos would lead to the subjugation of the remainder of the region, Kennedy demurred, replying with his doubt 'that this theory has much point anymore because ... the Chinese Communists are bound to get nuclear weapons in time, and from that moment on they will dominate Southeast Asia'.[21]

The uncomfortable knowledge that it was now only a question of when rather than whether the PRC would stage its first test explosion spurred the State Department into considering the policy implications of the PRC's attainment of a nuclear capability. The PPC was inclined to emphasize the psychological importance of this development, rather than any of its military aspects, seeing it as adding to China's prestige and the impression of growing strength. This might then have the effect of creating political pressures on China's neighbours to align themselves with Beijing. George McGhee, the head of the PPC, even suggested to Rusk that India could be offered nuclear assistance, so that a non-Communist Asian state would be the first to mount a test explosion, but the Secretary of State was not in favour of measures which might lead to greater nuclear proliferation.[22] In late October 1961, the PPC produced a long paper on US policy towards Communist China which included a recommendation for a covert propaganda campaign in Asia aimed at the reduction of the impact of the anticipated first Chinese test explosion and to 'lessen its contribution to the belief that Communism provides a superior blueprint for national development'. Furthermore, in what was to be a constant theme, it recommended that non-nuclear US military capabilities in the western Pacific area should be enhanced, and studies made of what reassurances could be given to Asian allies that they would not be subject to nuclear blackmail from Beijing. One step tentatively suggested in the latter context was the stationing of more nuclear forces in friendly Asian countries (or in the case of Japan, offshore on ships), but this was almost immediately contradicted, in a sign of the nuclear

[20] Arthur Krock, *Memoirs: Sixty Years on the Firing Line* (New York, 1968), 370.
[21] *Ibid.*, 358.
[22] George McGhee to Rusk, 'Anticipatory Action Pending Chinese Demonstration of a Nuclear Capability', 13 September 1961, as quoted in William Burr and Jeffrey T. Richelson, 'Whether to "Strangle the Baby in the Cradle": The United States and the Chinese Nuclear Program, 1960–64', *International Security*, 25, 3, Winter 2000/1, 61–2.

anxieties that it was known still prevailed in Asia, by the idea that nuclear weapons might instead be moved away from bases near the Chinese mainland, where they could present inviting targets, to US-held territories further to the east.[23]

After Walt Rostow was made head of the Policy Planning Council by Kennedy in November 1961, he set about completing an ambitious revision of the numerous basic national security papers that had been an annual feature of policy-making during the Eisenhower presidency, with the aim of producing an agreed strategic concept that could help to guide the new administration. Following several long and exhaustive versions, which attracted the scorn of some senior US officials for their verbosity and unrealistic scope (this was, after all, an administration that liked to see the rather dry task of 'planning' as an intrinsic element of on-going operations, rather than as a separate and distinct function), Rostow's exercise had run into the bureaucratic sand by the summer of 1962.[24] However, among the essential planning tasks he had identified for further treatment was the issue of determining the implications of China's acquisition of nuclear status, a study which he now entrusted to one of his staff members, Robert H. Johnson. Having worked on Far East problems as part of McGeorge Bundy's NSC staff during the first year of the Kennedy administration, Johnson had been transferred to the PPC in the spring of 1962. Even as Johnson set about his task, officials also began to give concrete shape to some of the PPC's earlier recommendations, and in September 1962 Rusk approved a proposal for a co-ordinated propaganda campaign to counteract the possible political impact of a successful Chinese test. A joint State–Defense–CIA effort would have to be mounted, so it was claimed, in the context of the 'vast ignorance and strong emotionalism' that tended to feature in Asian views of nuclear weapons, and in the expectation that a Chinese test would have 'dramatic repercussions'. Beijing would undoubtedly seek to exploit its position as the first Afro-Asian country to join the nuclear club, and in the long term a Chinese nuclear programme could have a 'degrading effect on the U.S. political and military positions in Asia'. While an overt information programme run by the State Department would seek to increase awareness of US strength in the region and downplay the growing fear of Chinese power, the CIA would launch a covert programme to spread unattributable stories in the

[23] 'U.S. Policy Toward China', draft paper prepared in the Policy Planning Council, 26 October 1961, *FRUS, 1961–1963, XXII*, 165.
[24] The exercise was actually begun by McGhee, Rostow's predecessor as head of policy planning; see Gaddis, *Strategies*, 199. On the reception given to Rostow's drafts, see David Milne, *America's Rasputin: Walt Rostow and the Vietnam War* (New York, 2008), 110–17.

media that the explosion was long-anticipated, had been held up by economic problems and lack of Soviet support, that a Chinese nuclear capability was an expensive luxury, and that American nuclear power was far superior.[25] The State Department side of this work was handled by William J. Jorden, the head of the Interdepartmental Psychological-Political Working Group, which was itself positioned under the auspices of McGhee, now the Under-Secretary for Political Affairs.[26]

At the same time as the State Department began to analyse in a systematic fashion the consequences of Chinese acquisition of nuclear status for the region, the Kennedy administration was also initiating a little-noticed but highly significant review of its overall nuclear strategy in the Far East. Although the centrepiece of this reappraisal was the nature of the US commitment to the defence of South Korea, it was soon caught up in the repercussions of a future Chinese nuclear capability and the whole American stance towards limited war. The basic motivation for this exercise was – as in the initial phases of the New Look in 1953–4 – derived from efforts to reduce the financial burden incurred by the US global military presence. In the spring and summer of 1962, the very substantial Military Assistance Program (MAP) for South Korea had come under scrutiny, with some civilian officials at the Pentagon keen to pursue the cost-cutting measures suggested in a report compiled by Major General John B. Carey.

The Carey report, produced in April 1962, had seen reductions in South Korean forces with consequent savings in MAP support as militarily acceptable, as long as the sanction of US nuclear retaliation to any North Korean and Chinese attack lay in the background as a deterrent, though it had warned of possible adverse political repercussions. As General Maxwell Taylor, then serving as Kennedy's Military Representative, made clear to McGeorge Bundy, this basic political assurance over the authorization of nuclear use would need to be forthcoming before the responsible military authorities were likely to recommend cuts in Korea.[27] Attention also moved to redeploying one of the two US

---

[25] Rusk memorandum for McGhee, 'Program to Influence World Opinion with Respect to a Chinese Communist Nuclear Detonation', 20 September 1962; McGhee memorandum for Harriman, 24 September 1962, with attached paper, in 'Psychological Political Elements of Policy' folder, box 13, Subject Files of the Regional Planning Adviser, records of the Bureau of Far East Affairs, 1955–63, RG 59, NARA; and see also Jeffrey T. Richelson, *Spying on the Bomb: American Nuclear Intelligence from Nazi Germany to Iran and North Korea* (New York, 2006), 147.

[26] See Harriman letter to Roswell Gilpatric, 18 June 1963, 'Psychological Political Operations', box 496, W. Averell Harriman papers, LC.

[27] See editorial note, *FRUS, 1961–1963, XXII*, 550; McNamara to Hamilton, with attached Carey report, 27 April 1962, *ibid.*, 558–62; Taylor to Bundy, 18 June 1962, *ibid.*, 576–7.

divisions in South Korea to Okinawa, mainly in order to make balance of payments savings, with Rusk particularly keen that this should be examined for the extra flexibility this appeared to offer US capabilities in the region. The JCS, though, registered their opposition in August, fearing, *inter alia*, that this would lead to a dilution of the local deterrent to Communist aggression and to questioning by the South Koreans over the command arrangements in the area considering the obvious disparity in ground troops that would remain on the peninsula. While confident a North Korean attack alone could be repulsed by existing forces, the JCS felt that if they were joined by Communist China the outcome would be far less clear, making any reduction in the American presence unwise. Within the State Department, it was also reasoned that cuts in MAP levels for South Korea would be harder to sell if US troops were also in the process of being withdrawn.[28]

Nevertheless, fresh impetus to the debate over redeployment options and its impact on nuclear strategy was given by a three-week tour of the Far East that Maxwell Taylor conducted in September 1962. During the summer, Taylor had been nominated by Kennedy to take Lemnitzer's place as the new Chairman of the JCS, and the tour was conducted as preparation for his fresh assignment. Taylor returned impressed by the greatly increased threat that a modernizing and expanding Chinese Communist air force presented to the US position, and with a conviction that the conventional forces available in the region to meet a Chinese attack were so limited (and likely to remain so) that there was a pressing requirement for new guidelines enabling local commanders to plan for the use of tactical nuclear weapons. In Taylor's view, as he put it in his memoirs, 'we badly needed an integrated plan for the deterrence of China, one that would take into account all allied and U.S. assets to include our nuclear weapons'.[29] During his inspection tour, Taylor came to the conclusion that reductions in the Korean MAP and in US ground forces were possible, as long as the assumption was made that nuclear weapons would be used at the start of any combined North Korean/Chinese Communist offensive.[30] Taylor presented his views to President Kennedy and his senior advisers at a White House meeting on 25 September, where he explained that with Chinese conventional military power increasing, there was no prospect, for example, of making

[28] Gilpatric to Rusk, 28 August 1962, *FRUS, 1961–1963, XXII*, 596–7; Johnson to Rusk, 15 September 1962, *ibid.*, 599–600.
[29] Taylor, *Swords and Plowshares*, 256–7.
[30] 'Impressions of Korea', paper prepared by Taylor, 20 September 1962, *FRUS, 1961–1963, XXII*, 601–5.

reductions in US ground forces in Korea, particularly as current planning did not assume the use of nuclear weapons if there was an attack across the 38th parallel. Having already talked over the idea with McNamara, Taylor now wanted the President to approve a study on the use of nuclear weapons in the Far East, with a view to making a future redeployment of forces. Kennedy was receptive to these ideas and authorized the new work to go ahead.[31]

Taylor's enthusiasm in the autumn of 1962 for planning for the early use of nuclear weapons seems at odds with his earlier advocacy of flexible response in Europe, with its avowed reliance on an extended conventional defence and raising the threshold at which decisions about nuclear use would have to be taken. However, Taylor had always been eager to examine the possibilities for selective targeting and use opened up by lower-yield tactical nuclear weapons, and in the NATO setting had been more than happy for these to be added to the armoury of responses that was available to the theatre commander. To some officials, there seemed little difference between the strategic posture adopted in Europe and East Asia: as Robert Komer of the NSC staff put it, 'in either case we resist conventionally unless and until confronted with an overwhelming attack'. As was the case in Europe, US nuclear forces stood ready in the theatre to be used if the remote contingency of a major Chinese offensive move were to occur, while a Chinese build-up in North Korea would be very difficult to conceal, giving time to prepare a more adequate conventional defence. Any change in the assigned mission of US forces in Korea resulting from the new studies being undertaken would, in Komer's estimation, be essentially 'a bookkeeping transaction', with no change to the existing nuclear threshold, and would merely make more explicit what was then implicit.[32]

In the Far East, the attractions of tactical nuclear use seemed in many respects even greater by the early 1960s, as with the advent of the Sino-Soviet split it seemed increasingly unlikely that Moscow would come to Beijing's aid if a Chinese aggression in Korea or the Taiwan Strait were faced with limited use of nuclear weapons by the United States. This distinction was acknowledged by all concerned: when Kennedy pointed out that adopting a stance involving rapid escalation to tactical nuclear use in Korea represented in some senses a reversal of the emphasis in Europe,

---

[31] Taylor meeting recording, 25 September 1962, in Timothy Naftali and Philip Zelikow (eds.), *The Presidential Recordings: John F. Kennedy, The Great Crises*, Vol. II (New York, 2001), 157–60; and see Forrestal memorandum for the record, 26 September 1962, *FRUS, 1961–1963, XXII*, 605, n. 1.

[32] Komer memorandum for Carl Kaysen, 26 September 1962, *FRUS, 1961–1963, XXII*, 606–7.

McNamara agreed, averring, 'I think the conditions are reversed. In Europe the reason our strategy [is] as it is, [is] because we're faced with a nuclear force and a very strong one. In China we have no nuclear force opposing us. And it seems to me this is enough of a difference to warrant at least consideration of a different strategy.' McNamara had already been studying this kind of problem at the Pentagon in connection with the defence budget for 1964, and was certainly keen for a further examination.[33]

Following Taylor's report to Kennedy, McNamara duly initiated a study by the JCS on the effects of US and allied force requirements and levels of military assistance assuming the use of nuclear weapons at the start of Chinese Communist aggression in either South East Asia or against Taiwan. The JCS concluded in the summer of 1963, in unremarkable fashion, that since existing force requirements, dating back to studies from the 1950s, were themselves based on the assumption of early nuclear use, no reductions were warranted. As the President had earlier instructed, the Joint Staff also worked on a radical plan to withdraw both of the US divisions from Korea, substituting them with an expanded US army missile command (equipped with Sergeant and Pershing missile units). Under this scheme current troop strength could be cut from 54,400 to 17,250 by the end of 1965, leading to an annual gold flow saving of $44.9 million. The whole plan was again dependent, however, on prior presidential agreement that nuclear weapons would be used from the outset of a major aggression against South Korea; the missile command was intended to provide a visible and tangible indication of American intent to pursue a nuclear strategy.[34]

One crucially important issue overshadowing all of these discussions, and that would influence the kind of strategy adopted in the Far East, was the perennial problem of the use of Japanese bases for nuclear operations. This was something which Kennedy certainly recognized, and when discussing Taylor's ideas for planning nuclear responses to a Korean attack, he brought up the point that the bases would almost certainly be unavailable. Taylor's initial tendency was to downplay the role of US bases in Japan. During his Far East tour of 1962, he had reported back that he thought they were of 'uncertain' value; in conditions of limited war, the bases would probably be available for operations 'provided the US

---

[33] Taylor meeting of 25 September 1962, in Naftali and Zelikow (eds.), *Great Crises*, II, 161.
[34] Talking paper for the JCS Chairman, 'Effect on Force Requirements in Korea of U.S. Use of Nuclear Weapons at the Outset of Major Aggression', 16 April 1963, box 1, memos concerning proposed US and South Korean Troop Withdrawal and Reductions in South Korea, 1962–3, records of the Deputy Under-Secretary for Political Affairs, RG 59, NARA.

moves no nuclear weapons into or out of Japan. Since our primary enemy in the Far East is Red China and it would probably be necessary to use atomic weapons in an all-out war with that enemy, the foregoing is a serious limitation on the usefulness of Japanese bases.' In conditions of general war with the Soviet Union, the bases would be largely irrelevant to the implementation of the SIOP. Taylor's conclusion from this was that there was 'no justification' for the United States to pay any great price for US bases in Japan, while general Japanese apathy to the needs of their own defence made them 'a poor bet as a military ally' and as a result military considerations should not determine the future direction of US–Japanese relations.[35] When meeting Kennedy in September, Taylor had to acknowledge that two-thirds of US combat aircraft in the area were located at Japanese bases and that the Air Force and Navy considered them 'virtually indispensable' in peacetime, and it was possible they might be 'neutralized' in war. William Sullivan, a senior official in the Far East Bureau, chimed in with the comment that the 'principal handicap' to the adoption of a new strategy for Korea was the question of nuclear weapons in Japan, a subject on which the Japanese were 'fanatical ... for understandable reasons'.[36]

In the event, Taylor's challenge to the received wisdom regarding the value of the Japanese bases to the US position in the Far East was not sustained. Objections to downplaying their importance were levelled by the American Ambassador in Tokyo, Edwin Reischauer, and Admiral Felt, still holding the position of CINCPAC at Honolulu. Reischauer maintained that predominant military opinion still considered the Japanese bases essential to support the US position in Korea, while positions 'further south' would also be weakened if the bases were lost.[37] The Ambassador's intervention was reinforced by a memorandum from the Far East Bureau, which maintained it was 'not sufficient' to view Japan from the perspective of the 'military asset' that it represented to the United States, as Taylor had done. The negative 'military, economic and political results which would ensue were Japan to fall under Communist domination and control' also had to be brought into the equation. The alliance with Japan and the American bases had the effect of anchoring Japan in the 'free world', and without this connection Japan might decide to reach an accommodation with the Communist powers. Moreover, Japanese bases were still judged essential for defeating with non-nuclear

[35] Taylor's message was dated 20 September 1962; see editorial note, *FRUS, 1961–1963, XXII*, 741–2.
[36] Taylor meeting of 25 September 1962, in Naftali and Zelikow (eds.), *Great Crises*, II, 163–4.
[37] See Reischauer to Harriman, 22 October 1962, *FRUS, 1961–1963, XXII*, 744–5.

warfare a North Korean attack: 'It is true that our inability to store nuclear weapons in Japan would involve delay of perhaps four and a half hours in the time by which nuclear-armed air forces in Japan could take off. However, nuclear war is only one of the forms of aggression we need to be able to deter or defeat in the Far East.' In terms of overall doctrine, Taylor's apparent suggestion of lowering the threshold at which nuclear weapons would be employed seemed 'to run counter to our policy of fighting limited wars without use of nuclear weapons, and of endeavoring to prevent their escalation', the Bureau citing the conclusions of the March 1960 Baguio Conference that the most likely dangers in the Far East over the coming years was low-level insurgency and aggression and that 'aversion in Asia to the use of any type of nuclear weapon is so strong that such use would without question be at great political cost'. The Bureau felt it was not safe to assume that a one-way use of nuclear weapons against China was possible without Soviet involvement. Moreover, and in an argument which would gather in force over the coming months, it was avowed that, 'When the Chinese acquire a nuclear capability, a principal Asian reaction will be the fear of being drawn into a Chinese–US nuclear war. *If we cannot convince Asian countries that they can be defended without resort to nuclear weapons, they are likely to seek accommodation to Chinese political demands* [emphasis added]. We will be unable to convince them if our advertised means of dealing with local aggression is a nuclear counter-attack.'[38] Taylor's doubts over the value of the bases also prompted McNamara to ask the JCS for an evaluation of their role. In December 1962, the JCS replied with a memorandum (signed off by Taylor, who had by now assumed the role of Chairman) which described the bases as 'essential to the maintenance of the US deterrent posture in the Far East', and required for supporting American forces in Korea.[39] This reaffirmation of the importance of the Japanese bases made it more difficult to rely on the use of nuclear weapons in limited war on the Asian mainland, as it would be precisely this kind of action which was most likely to jeopardize their maintenance, if not the entire US–Japanese relationship.

The idea that such a limited war remained a possibility was suggested by the additional evidence of Chinese belligerence and confidence that the events of 1962 served to provide. In June, a third offshore islands crisis

[38] Edward E. Rice memorandum for Jeffrey C. Kitchen, 'General Taylor's Report', 15 November 1962. I am grateful to William Burr for providing me with a copy of this document.
[39] Memorandum from the JCS for McNamara, 7 December 1962, *FRUS, 1961–1963, XXII*, 761–3.

flared up in the Taiwan Strait, as Chinese Communist troops were built up, in what may also have been a defensive measure to foil any last-ditch effort by Chiang to return to the mainland. Although not as apparently serious as the previous crises of the 1950s, the 1962 affair led to renewed contingency planning in the event that Beijing decided to invade at short notice. The crisis quickly blew itself out, Kennedy having both made clear that the United States would not support any reckless attempt by the Nationalists to launch a large-scale attack against the mainland, and authorized a few low-key steps to raise military preparedness in the region, while McNamara was dismissive of the kind of amphibious threat represented by the PRC's forces, which the intelligence community had supposedly discerned massing opposite the offshore islands.[40]

American perceptions of the dangers to regional stability posed by Communist China were then given a new dimension by the outbreak of the Sino-Indian border war in late October 1962. With its successes achieved on the battlefield, followed by the announcement of a unilateral cease-fire and a withdrawal to a more defensible line, Beijing had demonstrated its capacity and willingness to act forcefully when it considered vital national interests were at stake. As Roger Hilsman later put it, the Chinese had shown 'skill and sophistication' in their handling of the conflict with India: 'Their attack had been a masterpiece of orchestrating military, political, and psychological instrumentalities as a single, limited, disciplined, and controlled operation directed toward and subordinated to a political end.'[41] It was also apparent that Beijing's line in the border dispute with India during 1962 was related to the continuing tensions in Sino-Soviet relations, with Moscow's ties with New Delhi seen as an attempt by the Soviet Union to win favour in wider parts of the developing world. The ideological struggle between Beijing and Moscow for control of the world Communist movement was beginning to enter a new phase, as the militancy of Chinese propaganda and rhetoric steadily increased, attacking both the revisionism of the Soviet system under Khrushchev and actively promoting the revolutionary class struggle against imperialism. In South East Asia some of these tendencies were manifest in Chinese efforts to build relations with Indonesia (sealed by the visit of Liu Shaoqi, the President of the PRC, to that country in April 1963), and the beginnings of arms supplies to North Vietnam following an initial request from Hanoi in the autumn of 1962.[42]

[40] Freedman, *Kennedy's Wars*, 254–5; Roger Hilsman, *To Move a Nation: The Politics of Foreign Policy in the Administration of John F. Kennedy* (New York, 1967), 317–19.
[41] *Ibid.*, 338.
[42] See R. B. Smith, *An International History of the Vietnam War*, Vol. II: *The Struggle for South-East Asia, 1961–65* (London, 1985), 80–9, 104–5.

Along with the belligerence of Chinese rhetoric at the time of the Cuban Missile Crisis, the Sino-Indian war seems to have acted as a catalyst for the President's own concerns over the extent of Chinese ambitions. Rather than seeing the Chinese acting with discretion and caution in their prosecution of the dispute with New Delhi, as had several contemporary observers, the spectre of Chinese armies flooding down towards the plains and cities of Bengal seems to have excited some geopolitical imaginations. The border war heightened the sense in the Kennedy administration that China was determined to expand its influence in Asia if given the chance, and added to the imperative need to prevent Beijing attaining a nuclear capability. In early December 1962, welcoming a Japanese trade delegation in Washington, Kennedy gave expression to his belief that 'our major problem' was now to deal with the 'rise of Communist power in China combined with an expansionist, Stalinist philosophy'. Containing Communist expansion in the Far East was necessary 'so that we do not find the Chinese moving out into a dominant position in all of Asia, with its hundreds and hundreds of millions of people in Asia, while Western Europe is building a more prosperous life for themselves [sic]'. The President saw the current phase as a period of 'great danger for Asia', where Japan and the United States should work as partners against a Communist movement 'which is in its essence today a believer in not only the class struggle, but also in the international class struggle of a third world war'.[43]

Although American intelligence on the Chinese bomb programme was still very sketchy throughout the period, impressions of steady progress were treated with mounting concern in Washington, with Kennedy growing ever more animated by the subject.[44] As McGeorge Bundy explained to John McCone, the head of the CIA, in early January 1963, Kennedy felt that the Chinese programme 'was probably the most serious problem facing the world today ... the President was of a mind that nuclear weapons in the hands of the Chinese Communists would so upset the world political scene it would be intolerable to the United States and the West', while Bundy himself 'intimated that we might consider a policy of indicating now that further effort by the Chinese Communists in the nuclear field would be unacceptable to us and that we should prepare to take some action unless they agreed to desist from further efforts in this

---

[43] 'Remarks at a Luncheon in Honor of a Japanese Trade Delegation', 3 December 1962, *The Public Papers of the Presidents: John F. Kennedy, 1962* (Washington, DC, 1963), 850–1; for Kennedy's concerns over China, see also Schlesinger, *Thousand Days*, 903–4, and Fetzer, 'Clinging to Containment', 180–3.

[44] See Richelson, *Spying on the Bomb*, 142–6, 150–2.

field'. Along with Cuba, McCone himself noted, the nuclear threat from Communist China was the 'foremost issue' in Kennedy's mind, and hence 'an intense intelligence effort' was being made to discover more about the state of the Chinese programme, though current information was meagre.[45] At one of Kennedy's rare meetings of the full NSC on 22 January, he reiterated his great concern over the emergence of a Chinese nuclear capability and the importance of the test-ban negotiations as a possible way to impede the Chinese programme; as for the Chinese Communists, they 'loom as our major antagonists of the late 60s and beyond'.[46] Appearing on the television programme *Meet the Press* a few days later, Rusk avowed that the 'psychological and political effect of the achievement of a nuclear weapon by Red China would be very severe. It would not for many, many years affect the general strategic balance in the world, but there is no question that this would have a serious and negative effect. This is one of the reasons why we are very much interested in such a thing as a nuclear test ban, for example, or agreement which might serve to limit the transfer of weapons from one nation to another.'[47]

Averell Harriman, the veteran diplomat who Kennedy had made Assistant Secretary for the Far East in November 1961, and then promoted to Under-Secretary for Political Affairs in April 1963, was pleased that the President had recognized the importance of trying to prevent Beijing from attaining nuclear status. Having heard Kennedy's remarks to the NSC in January 1963, he wrote to convey his belief that co-operation with the Soviet Union might be one way to arrest the Chinese programme. The bait offered to the Russians could be that the United States would exert all its influence to prevent West Germany from developing its own independent nuclear capability. Harriman even suggested that Moscow might agree to joint action to threaten China's nuclear facilities if Beijing would not agree to enter into a test-ban regime.[48] Kennedy's subsequent strong push for a nuclear test-ban treaty with the Soviet Union, conducted in the face of his own belief that it would be extremely difficult to secure Senate ratification and might have domestic political costs, was to a large extent driven by his conviction that this measure would help to frustrate Beijing's nuclear ambitions. The President was even prepared, as Harriman had suggested, to enlist Soviet help to this end. Hence, when Harriman travelled to Moscow to negotiate the Partial Test Ban Treaty in

---

[45] Memorandum for the record by McCone, 11 January 1963; see editorial note, *FRUS, 1961–1963, XXII*, 339.

[46] Notes of 508th meeting of the NSC, 22 January 1963, *FRUS, 1961–1963, VIII*, 462, n. 6.

[47] Text of Rusk interview of 27 January 1963, in Washington to Foreign Office, No. 50 Saving, 30 January 1963, IAD 1125/2, FO 371/171244, TNA.

[48] Harriman to Kennedy, 23 January 1963, *FRUS, 1961–1963, XXII*, 341.

July 1963, having been hand-picked for the task by the President, he did so with authority to draw out from Khrushchev his view of the 'means of limiting or preventing Chinese nuclear development and his willingness either to take Soviet action or to accept U.S. action aimed in this direction'.[49] As it transpired, Harriman did not have an opportunity in Moscow to present any proposal along such precise lines to Khrushchev, and his attempts to discuss the Chinese nuclear issue with the Soviet leader were rebuffed. Khrushchev, embroiled in the struggle with Beijing over leadership of the Communist movement, did not want, at this stage, to lose ideological credibility by being pulled into a US–Soviet condominium aimed at China. Despite this setback, Kennedy still believed there might exist a shared interest with the Soviet Union in preventing a Chinese bomb, and on 1 August he gave voice to his continuing fears when pronouncing at a presidential news conference that, in a decade's time, a China with 700 million people and a Stalinist regime which was 'determined on war as a means of bringing about its ultimate success' and equipped with nuclear weapons would present the United States with a situation 'more dangerous than at the end of the Second World War'.[50]

While the White House considered the steps it might take to retard the Chinese nuclear programme in the summer of 1963, the debate over American nuclear strategy in the Far East, prompted by the proposal to withdraw conventional forces from Korea, had taken several more turns. During April 1963, State Department representatives gave a critical reception to the JCS's latest ideas for securing advance presidential authorization for the very early use of nuclear weapons in Korea in the event of a resumption of Communist aggression which involved Chinese forces, a step which was considered essential if troop strength in the peninsula was to be drawn down. Apart from the fact that all present intelligence estimates rated the chance of a Communist attack in Korea as highly improbable, Robert Johnson, informed by his on-going work on the Chinese nuclear problem, found many other weaknesses in the overt acceptance of prime reliance on nuclear weapons in such a limited war context. As Johnson noted in a long memorandum, present contingency planning for a resumption of hostilities in Korea, dating back to the adoption of massive retaliation in 1953–4, involved early use of nuclear weapons, the JCS proposals would merely make 'clear and manifest' what

---

[49] See Kennedy to Harriman, 15 July 1963, *ibid.*, 370; and also Chang, *Friends and Enemies*, 243.
[50] Presidential news conference, 1 August 1963, *The Public Papers of the Presidents: John F. Kennedy, 1963* (Washington, DC, 1964), 616.

had already long been implicit (an argument also advanced by Komer the previous autumn). Any use of nuclear weapons in the Far East, furthermore, would 'breach the unmistakable barrier that [exists] in the continuum extending from limited conventional operations to general nuclear war'. This qualitative distinction over breaking the nuclear taboo was also allied to the uncomfortable view that 'once the process of nuclear escalation is begun there will be no militarily logical stopping point'. Despite the Sino-Soviet split (and even because of it), Johnson felt it would be unrealistic to expect the Soviet Union to stand aloof while another Communist power was subject to nuclear attack. When the PRC itself acquired a limited nuclear capability, there was the strong chance that it would retaliate against US bases in the Far East if American nuclear weapons were used against the mainland. Johnson concluded his paper with a political argument that had echoed throughout the previous decade and still carried resonance in the 1960s:

An important potential consequence of a clear public posture of primary reliance upon nuclear weapons in Korea when we are arguing for a different strategy in Europe [of an extended conventional defence] would be the apparent racialist character of our strategy. It would appear, despite any efforts we might make publicly to differentiate the strategic situation, that we valued the lives of white men more than the lives of Asians. The new increasingly strong effort by Peiping to appeal to Africans and Asians on a racialist basis would find useful ammunition in such a U.S. posture.

China's acquisition of a nuclear capability might also be employed 'to reenforce [sic] this racialist appeal', as this was likely to be justified on the grounds of the US nuclear threat in the Far East, while the Chinese would probably also combine their nuclear status with calls for nuclear-free zones and removing American nuclear weapons from the region.[51] Johnson's analysis was composed just as the domestic American racial crisis at Birmingham was building to a climax, with the focus of international media attention directed at the disjuncture between American professions of support for equality and freedom on the global stage and the treatment being given to African Americans demonstrating on the streets of the South.

In early May 1963, the NSC met ostensibly to discuss proposals to provide for the air defence of Indian cities in the event of another Chinese offensive. The discussion soon turned to the question of offering some

---

[51] Robert H. Johnson memorandum for Kitchen, 'JCS Proposals Relating to Korea', 29 April 1963, box 1, memos concerning proposed US and South Korean Troop Withdrawal and Reductions in South Korea, 1962–3, records of the Deputy Under-Secretary for Political Affairs, RG 59, NARA.

more general guarantees to the Indians in the event of overt Chinese aggression, which Kennedy felt had the merit of holding a deterrent value, referring to the analogy of Korea before the outbreak of war in 1950. Taylor wanted to open out the discussion from the possible defence of India to the more general problem of 'how we can cope with Communist China over the next decade', doubting it 'possible to deal with the Chinese on the ground in non-nuclear warfare'. Taking his cue from this, McNamara raised the point that the defence of India against large-scale Chinese attack would involve the use of nuclear weapons, and that a similar issue had just arisen over Korea, where the JCS were now ready to agree to reduce US forces as long as an overt commitment on nuclear use could be given as insurance against Communist aggression. For his part, the Secretary of Defense 'preferred the use of nuclear weapons to the use of US forces on the ground in Asia'.

This whole line of argument prompted George Ball, the Under-Secretary of State, to caution that if this shift in strategy back to a reliance on nuclear weapons was to be agreed, 'we should be aware of the reaction which might occur in Asia, i.e. we are prepared to use nuclear weapons against yellow people but are not prepared to use them against white people in Europe'. McNamara backtracked slightly by stating he was not recommending any change in strategy, but that extra commitments, such as towards the defence of India, would involve dealing with the nuclear issue. There seemed to be few qualms on this point, however, in Kennedy's own mind. He told the NSC meeting that if the United States 'were overrun in Korea, in Formosa, or in Western Europe, we would obviously use nuclear weapons. If we are prepared to defend Korea and Thailand, ... why should [we] not be prepared to commit ourselves to defend India.' The President wanted to know whether American guarantees to the Indians would serve as a deterrent to a Chinese Communist attack.[52] The aftermath of this NSC meeting was instructive for illustrating the confusion that still seemed to obtain over the Kennedy administration's nuclear stance in the Far East. Paul Nitze, the Assistant Secretary of Defense for International Security Affairs, interpreted McNamara's position to be that 'our present strategy calls for the use of nuclears against the ChiComs and, therefore, conventional capabilities in the Far East, beyond counterinsurgency, have a low priority; and that the President said just as in Europe we would use nuclears if there was no other way of avoiding defeat, so we would in the Pacific'. Nitze understood this to mean that Kennedy believed there was really no difference in strategy

---

[52] Summary record of the 514th meeting of the NSC, 9 May 1963, *FRUS, 1961–1963, XIX: South Asia* (Washington, DC, 1996), 583–8.

between Europe and the Far East, and that 'if a policy of giving the President maximum options in Europe makes sense, it would also seem to make sense in the Pacific'. When it came to Sino-Soviet relations, Nitze could see, however, that reliance on nuclear means to deter the Chinese had serious drawbacks, as 'the Soviets might have less reason to restrain the Chinese in aggressive action if our only possible response were a nuclear response *which the circumstances might make politically difficult for us and thus of dubious credibility* [emphasis added]'.[53] Once more, it was the political aspects to nuclear use in the Far East that drew the attention of senior officials, amounting to recognition that in some senses they represented a liability for the pursuit of American foreign policy goals.

The official and negative response of the State Department to the JCS proposals for adoption of an overtly nuclear strategy in Korea was conveyed in a letter sent by U. Alexis Johnson, the Deputy Under-Secretary for Political Affairs, to General Taylor at the end of May 1963. Johnson explained that the withdrawal of the two US divisions would not be politically feasible, involving as it did reliance on the early use of nuclear weapons to repel any attack. Such a new stance would be impossible to conceal, and to bolster South Korean morale President Kennedy would presumably have to offer some 'firm and binding advance commitment' to employ nuclear weapons, something which raised a multitude of legal and political obstacles. Re-equipment of US forces in Korea to make them solely nuclear-reliant would give an opportunity to the Communists of 'getting out their propaganda line on U.S. nuclear policy'. When it came to Japan, a nuclear commitment would present 'insurmountable political problems' of maintaining use of American bases for Korean operations, and any Japanese government would feel obliged to disassociate itself from such a US strategy, while some of the present more encouraging trends in Japanese attitudes towards defence co-operation with the United States could be reversed. Alexis Johnson continued, in an echo of the arguments made by both Robert Johnson and Ball:

In Japan, as in many places elsewhere in Asia, an announced exclusively nuclear strategy for the defense of Korea, particularly when set against our policy of

---

[53] Nitze memorandum for McNamara, 11 May 1963, *FRUS, 1961–1963, XXII*, 367–8. In a later conversation with an official from the State Department's Bureau of Politico-Military Affairs, Nitze expressed his concern that a Korean redeployment would entail the almost automatic reliance on the use of nuclear weapons against China, and that he was 'by no means certain that this represented a clearly, thought-through, well considered policy', and that he was also doubtful over alleged Communist Chinese air superiority over the West; see Seymour Weiss memorandum for Kitchen, 'Discussion with Paul Nitze', 11 June 1963, box 1, memos concerning proposed US and South Korean Troop Withdrawal and Reductions in South Korea, 1962–3, records of the Deputy Under-Secretary for Political Affairs, RG 59, NARA.

seeking to achieve a conventional option in Europe, would give much opportunity for unfriendly elements to exploit what could be termed a 'racist strategy'. That is, our policy would be interpreted as a greater willingness to use nuclear weapons against non-white races. This would give Peking much useful ammunition in its appeals to African nations on racial issues.

The adoption of flexible response when it came to NATO strategy, in other words, made it all the more difficult to 'sell' American reliance on nuclear weapons to an Asian audience attuned to detecting signs of racism in Washington's policy-making.

Taylor was also informed by Alexis Johnson that once the Chinese acquired a nuclear capability, friendly Asian governments would look towards a US conventional defence as providing the best immediate response to 'Chinese Communist nibbling acts' rather than an American nuclear riposte. In the long run, a greater tendency towards accommodation with Beijing might be induced if it was felt that acceptance of US military commitments would lead to an inevitable nuclear exchange with devastating local consequences. Johnson also doubted the premise that Soviet involvement could be discounted and that the United States would be free to 'fight a one-sided nuclear war in Korea'. It was unlikely, Johnson felt, that use of nuclear weapons would be confined to tactical targets on the Korean peninsula, and that attacks on targets on the Chinese mainland would be required. In these circumstances, Moscow would face many policy dilemmas and might even feel compelled to provide nuclear weapons to the Communist side, a contingency which could become more likely if hostilities had increased in intensity and Beijing had used its assumed small nuclear capability against American bases in the Far East. 'Which side would win a two-sided nuclear war over Korea seems to us a matter requiring further examination,' Johnson soberly noted, continuing, 'it would appear to depend in large measure upon the assumptions or estimates as to where the process of escalation would stop'.[54]

With the political situation in South Korea remaining uncertain following the imposition of military rule in 1961, there were also strong arguments that nothing should be done which might destabilize the local scene by such a change in policy. State Department officials felt, moreover, that the JCS staff study on defending South Korea through nuclear means, though it emphasized the varied American inventory of tactical nuclear weapons and number of available targets for possible interdiction, was built on weak ground. One member of the Bureau of Politico-Military Affairs advised Alexis Johnson:

[54] U. Alexis Johnson to Maxwell Taylor, 28 May 1963, DDRS/CK3100316244.

I think we need to take a hard look at the presumed military advantages of the proposed use of nuclear weapons against targets in North Korea and China in the event of resumption of hostilities ... considerations involving methods of logistic support employed by North Korean/Chinese forces, ability to move at night, limited intelligence, mountainous and otherwise difficult terrain, etc. all place serious limitations upon the effective use of nuclear weapons in an interdiction role ... it is clear that good target acquisition is an absolutely vital requirement for effective tactical nuclear employment. Accordingly, the added margin of military efficiency gained from use of nuclear weapons, as contrasted with conventional explosives, particularly in the interdiction role, may not be great or in any event decisive. However, once committed to the employment of nuclear weapons military logic will inevitably drive us toward employment where such weapons would do the most good, i.e, harm to the enemy. This, inevitably, means against the Chinese industrial complex located in China's large urban centers. The war then becomes one of city busting, with all of its political (as well as moral) implications.

The JCS would have to be pressed to explain exactly which targets would be attacked by nuclear weapons and what the estimated effects of such attacks would be for the State Department to be more convinced of the case.[55] In the face of these kinds of objections, the idea of withdrawing US troops from Korea was for the moment placed in abeyance, but members of the NSC staff continued to look for possible future savings in the $200 million of MAP aid that was budgeted for the bloated South Korean Army during the next financial year, aware that Congress had targeted the administration's foreign aid bill for cuts.[56] In fact, the administration's MAP request was finally reduced to $153 million, meaning that the issue would once again have to be confronted during 1964, but this time by a different administration.[57]

As the debates over Korea helped to illustrate, perhaps the central issue facing US strategic posture in the Far East was how it would be affected by the arrival of a Chinese nuclear capability. This was not, however, so much a question of devising an adequate war-fighting stance in the event of all-out Sino-American hostilities, as this kind of conflict was still considered improbable, and – as Kennedy had told the NSC – it was long established that nuclear weapons would be used in the event of a large-scale Chinese Communist assault that overwhelmed a local conventional defence. Moreover, as the State Department's Bureau of Intelligence and

[55] Seymour Weiss memorandum for U. Alexis Johnson, 2 July 1963, box 1, memos concerning proposed US and South Korean Troop Withdrawal and Reductions in South Korea, 1962–3, records of the Deputy Under-Secretary for Political Affairs, RG 59, NARA.
[56] Robert W. Komer memorandum for Kennedy, 31 May 1963, *FRUS, 1961–1963, XXII*, 647–8.
[57] For the administration's problems over the MAP budget, see Kaplan, Landa and Drea, *McNamara Ascendancy*, 435–7.

Research reiterated in May 1963, it was predicted that China's acquisition of a nuclear capability would not change its fundamentally cautious behaviour, and awareness of overwhelming US nuclear superiority made any offensive use of nuclear weapons highly unlikely. China's possession of the bomb, though, would serve to boost its international standing, encourage neutralist tendencies among its near neighbours, and enhance its image among revolutionary movements in the Afro-Asian world.[58] The chief problem hence became the public perception of what kind of defence in limited war in Asia would be mounted by the United States, and the political message that this was intended to convey. The July 1963 SNIE produced on the Chinese nuclear programme, as well as analysing the latest findings of aerial photographic missions over the PRC's nuclear facilities, also speculated that once Beijing had acquired a nuclear capability, China's Communist leaders might believe they were in a better position to deter US intervention on the Asian mainland. This, in turn, could make China more assertive in the areas closest to their own borders, with obvious implications for the situation in South East Asia.[59]

The point was underlined the following month when Rusk informed McNamara, in very significant fashion, that 'politically and psychologically it will become even more important after a Chinese Communist nuclear detonation to have adequate US conventional capability in the Pacific so that free Asian nations will believe that we can assist in defending them against at least limited Chinese Communist attack without necessarily involving them in nuclear war'.[60] In the build-up to the first Chinese test, Beijing's propaganda line, furthermore, had begun to re-focus on the nuclear dangers facing Asia: in August 1963, at the Warsaw Sino-American ambassadorial talks, the Chinese representative offered a denunciation of US nuclear deployment and 'blackmail' in the Pacific and, in a new initiative, put forward the idea of a joint proposal declaring a nuclear-free zone in the Asia–Pacific region, which would involve the withdrawal of all American bases from the territories surrounding the PRC.[61]

The conclusion that became established among senior policy-making circles in the year leading up to the first Chinese test was that American

[58] George C. Denney to Rusk, 6 May 1963, box 250, records of the PPC, 1963–4, RG 59, NARA.
[59] See SNIE 13–2–63, 'Communist China's Advanced Weapons Program', 24 July 1963, *FRUS, 1961–1963, VIII: National Security Policy, Microfiche Supplement.*
[60] Rusk to McNamara, 1 August 1963, *FRUS, 1961–1963, XXII*, 377.
[61] Thomas L. Hughes memorandum for the Acting Secretary of State (Ball), 'Peiping Focuses on Nuclear Question at Warsaw Talk', 10 August 1963, 'Nuclear Test Ban, General, 8/63', box 261A, Departments and Agencies series, NSF, JFKL.

conventional forces, designed for limited war on the Asian mainland, offered the best reassurance to the PRC's nervous neighbours. The corollary to this was that the United States should not appear to be intimidated from using them when Asian allies and friends called for help. This was also one of the findings made by Robert Johnson, who by the autumn of 1963 had completed his report on the implications of a Chinese nuclear test and acquisition of a nuclear capability, allowing his superior at the PPC, Walt Rostow, to begin disseminating the study throughout the bureaucracy.

Johnson's most important point was that in view of overwhelming US nuclear superiority and Chinese vulnerabilities, Beijing was highly unlikely to initiate the use of nuclear weapons, except if the mainland itself was under direct attack in a way that threatened the survival of the Communist regime. Cautious probing, rather than outright aggression, was the pattern of behaviour that could be expected from China, and here Beijing would be influenced not by any false reading of its military strength, but on its estimation of the 'psychological situation in Asia' and the reactions of the United States and its allies to such tests of Western resolve. There was no doubt, Johnson maintained, that the Chinese would try to exploit their nuclear status by putting fresh political pressures on the Western presence in Asia, and to spread fear of China's new power while emphasizing that it was still the United States which presented the greater nuclear danger in the area. Asian allies were likely to turn to the United States for reassurances, and an American ability to respond to Communist aggression without 'undue reliance' on nuclear weapons would be important in this regard. As hitherto 'military thinking and planning for the Far East has tended to prefer a relatively low nuclear threshold', Johnson felt that revisions in American strategy and force posture were required:

It is evident that effective strategy for Asia must find an appropriate blend between an implicit nuclear threat and an evident visible ability to deal conventionally with Communist aggression. When the ChiComs have a nuclear capability there will be increased fear in Asia of the possibility of a nuclear war on Asian soil. An evident (declared or undeclared) U.S. policy of major reliance upon nuclear weapons will in this circumstance make Asian states more reluctant, if not afraid, to seek U.S. assistance, more concerned that the U.S. would not respond adequately to lower levels of aggression that would not justify nuclear weapons use, and less likely to give the U.S. continued access to bases and facilities (particularly in Japan).

Beijing's calls for the creation of nuclear-free zones might also have more appeal in a situation where US dependence on nuclear weapons was pronounced. Johnson obviously favoured raising the US nuclear threshold in Asia by ensuring that conventional forces could at the very least enforce a pause in the event of a Chinese aggression, and he rejected such measures as creation of a tailored nuclear force with the specific task of offering a deterrent to China, or deploying Medium-Range Ballistic Missiles (MRBMs) in East Asia.[62] In a later paper opposing the idea of deploying MRBMs in the Far East, Johnson argued that existing carrier or land-based aircraft were perfectly capable of delivering the tactical nuclear weapons that were widely considered a suitable deterrent against what was likely to be a very limited future Chinese nuclear threat. Aircraft were also felt advisable, Johnson highlighted, because they were dual-capable, and 'we do not want to give the impression to Asians now, and even less after the Chinese develop a nuclear capability, that we intend to employ nuclear weapons at an early stage in future conflicts in Asia. A military posture which left this impression would make Asian states more reluctant to seek our help, more inclined to forestall our military involvement in other countries, and more likely to give in to Communist demands backed by an implicit nuclear threat.'[63]

As head of the PPC, Rostow had already had a chance to present Johnson's conclusions to some of the United States' allies, for the topic of China's acquisition of a nuclear capability was exercising not only Washington during this period. In 1962, on British initiative, the Atlantic Policy Advisory Group (APAG) had been formed within the structures of NATO as a forum where foreign policy planners from member states could gather in informal surroundings to exchange ideas on problems of common concern in the Cold War which usually went beyond the alliance's familiar terrain of the military and political confrontation in Europe. For the APAG's fourth meeting, held at Royaumont near Paris in October 1963, British officials prepared a paper which explored the implications of a Chinese nuclear test, which the JIC thought lay only a year or so away. China, the British paper argued, would 'command respect as the first underdeveloped country to achieve nuclear status. The benefit of Chinese prestige could to some extent be mitigated

[62] Planning Statement, 'A Chinese Communist Nuclear Detonation and Nuclear Capability: Major Conclusions and Key Issues', 15 October 1963, S/P Papers, box 275, records of the PPC, 1963–4, RG 59, NARA. See also the analysis in Burr and Richelson, 'Whether to "Strangle the Baby in the Cradle"', 76–8. For an earlier draft, where Johnson again stressed the lack of credibility of threatening to respond to a conventional aggression with nuclear weapons, and that what he called a 'nuclear dependent strategy' would also increase the pressure on Japanese bases, see Robert H. Johnson draft policy statement, 10 September 1963, 'China Nuclear', box 15, Subject Files of the Regional Planning Adviser, 1955–63, records of the Bureau of Far East Affairs, RG 59, NARA.
[63] Memorandum from Robert H. Johnson to Henry Owen, 'The Utility of MRBMs in the Far East', 26 November 1963, 'Defense Affairs, Def 18', box 16, Subject Files 1963, records of the Bureau of Far East Affairs, RG 59, NARA.

by the fact that nuclear weapons may still be associated for some Asians with Hiroshima and are looked upon as contrary to Asian ideals. But this feeling would be far outweighed by admiration for China's success in breaking the nuclear monopoly of the industrialized states of Europe and North America. China's claim to leadership in Asia will be greatly strengthened.' Echoing American appraisals, it speculated that insecurity among Western allies in Asia would probably increase during the period after a Chinese test, not least as it would be assumed that China's nuclear weapons, though its stockpile would be very small, would have a tendency to cancel out American nuclear capabilities in the Far East, making the balance of conventional forces in the area of prime importance. India, though it was likely to adhere to a policy of non-alignment, might seek greater military aid from the West and develop its own nuclear programme. Although elsewhere in the world there would be respect for China's achievement, this could be mitigated by disapproval from those elements of non-aligned opinion which viewed nuclear weapons as morally wrong, and prestige could suffer if Chinese tests were conducted at a time when a test-ban agreement was in force among the existing nuclear powers. Whatever the case, there would be increased pressures to admit the PRC to the United Nations and other international organizations from which it was then currently excluded.[64]

The State Department's Bureau of Intelligence and Research was generally in agreement with the British paper, though felt it would probably take China somewhat longer before it could stage its first test and doubted that Asian reactions to the event would amount to admiration, as opposed to fear. Johnson, whose draft views on the subject would form the basis of the American presentation to the APAG's meeting, thought similarly that sharp distinctions between admiration, respect and fear would be difficult to distinguish.[65] At the meeting itself, Rostow advanced the idea that

[64] Permanent Under-Secretary's Department Planning Section paper, 'The Implications of the Acquisition by China of a Nuclear Capability', SC(63)32, c. 6 September 1963, WUN 1075/28, FO 371/173383, TNA. 'We must face the fact that a Chinese test will have a considerable political and psychological impact on governmental and public opinion in Asia which the Chinese will exploit,' one later Foreign Office paper ran. 'The fear and awe of their neighbours may be mingled with pride (though not in India) that an Asian country has matched an achievement hitherto attained only by Europeans [sic].' 'Emergence of China as a Nuclear Power: Counter-Publicity Themes', FO Intel No. 19, 19 February 1964, DO 182/163, TNA.
[65] See Allen S. Whiting to Robert H. Johnson, 'Comments on British Paper on Communist Chinese Acquisition of Nuclear Weapons', 30 September 1963; Robert H. Johnson memorandum for Rostow, 'APAG Discussion of the Implications of a Chinese Communist Nuclear Capability', 2 October 1963, 'CSM-1 Nuclear Explosion', box 15, Subject Files of the Regional Planning Adviser, 1955–63, records of the Bureau of Far East Affairs, RG 59, NARA.

Chinese acquisition of the bomb would make her more cautious rather than adventurous, Beijing being afraid of inviting a pre-emptive strike if China engaged in provocative actions. With its new status, China was, nevertheless, felt likely to try to frighten its neighbours and to persuade them to disengage from alignment with the West.[66]

When a final version of Robert Johnson's report on the impact of China's gaining of nuclear status emerged in October 1963, it met with general approval from Rusk and his State Department colleagues. Its sober conclusion that a Chinese Communist nuclear capability did not present dramatic new problems for American policy chimed with the views of many American diplomatic representatives in East Asia, and its dismissal of the effect on the military balance was in accord with JCS studies. The potential political impact remained a worry, however, as did the idea that the Chinese might seek to intimidate their Asian neighbours through the perception of enhanced military strength. As Rusk put it in deadpan fashion at one staff meeting he presided over: 'the threat of one nuclear bomb on Calcutta could conceivably give Communist China considerable political leverage'. Set against this was Beijing's awareness that they could expect nuclear reprisal if they attacked any of their neighbours with nuclear weapons, thus 'US countermoves and the US military posture in the area will go far to determine the course which China's Asian neighbours will adopt once China has the bomb'. The United States, it was proposed, had to maintain a strong conventional capability, and the willingness to deploy it. Picking up on the racial implications of a Chinese bomb, there was also a feeling that 'the colored peoples of the world might rally to a nuclear-armed China', but this was balanced by the fact that there might also be fear of China and pressure on her to enter into international negotiations over disarmament.[67] Reporting the views of an interdepartmental group of high-level officials, Robert Komer felt that Johnson's conclusions meant there should be less pressure to 'strangle the baby in the cradle' through a pre-emptive strike at China's nuclear facilities, and the 'consensus was that the Chinese would remain basically cautious in the overt use of force even after they acquired a few nucs [sic]; first use by them would be highly unlikely – instead they would see their nucs as a deterrent to escalation by us'.[68]

---

[66] J. N. Henderson memorandum, 16 October 1963, and attached note on 4th meeting of the Atlantic Policy Advisory Group, held 7–10 October 1963, WUN 1075/41, FO 371/173383, TNA.

[67] Highlights from Rusk's Policy Planning Meeting, 15 October 1963, *FRUS, 1961–1963, XXII*, 399–402.

[68] Memorandum from Komer for Bundy, 5 November 1963, *ibid.*, 404–5.

Robert Johnson's report languished in the national security bureaucracy over the next few months. In the wake of Lyndon Johnson's arrival in the White House, Rostow passed summaries of the report to McNamara and McCone, and in January 1964 gave a version to Bundy in the hope he might pass another summary to the new President. Rostow's belief was that the report should be considered at length and further conclusions issued in the form of a National Security Action Memorandum, but both Bundy and Komer were opposed to the idea, seeing the paper as largely having served its 'educational' purpose.[69] A very short summary was finally sent to Lyndon Johnson by Rostow in April 1964, underlining the basic conclusion of the paper that despite its psychological effects in Asia, no major changes in American policy were required in response to the Chinese nuclear programme.[70] It was also agreed that Robert Johnson should draw up a further set of actions that might be taken by the United States in response to the occurrence of a Chinese test, and, incorporating the deliberations of an interdepartmental group (with officials drawn from the State Department, Pentagon, Arms Control and Disarmament Agency, Agency for International Development and the CIA), these were eventually presented by Rostow to Bundy in late September 1964. The implications of a Chinese nuclear capability conveyed here were familiar enough from Johnson's previous studies of the issue:

The basic military problems we will face are likely to be much like those we face now: military probing operations designed to test the level of the U.S. commitment and response; relatively low-level border wars; 'revolutionary' wars supported by the ChiComs [*sic*]; and pressure to keep U.S. nuclear weapons from the area. The ChiComs will value their nuclear capability as a deterrent to attack on the mainland, and for its psychological effects in weakening the will of countries resisting insurgency, in inhibiting their requests for U.S. assistance and in stimulating and exploiting divisions within Asia and between Asian countries and the West. It will be used to put political pressure on the U.S. military presence and to obtain support for Chinese claims to preeminence in Asia and to status as a world power.

When it came to the effect on other Asian states and the need for American reassurance, it was also noted that 'if there is evidence that the Free World effort is not succeeding in containing communism in Asia, a ChiCom detonation and capability will tend to cause some Asian

---

[69] See Rostow to Bundy, 24 January 1964; Komer to Bundy, 26 February 1964; Komer to Bundy, 24 March 1964, 'China (CPR), Nuclear Explosion Capability', Files of Robert Komer, box 14, NSF, LBJL.

[70] Rostow memorandum for the President, 'The Implications of a Chinese Communist Nuclear Capability', 30 April 1964, China Memos, Vol. I, Country File, box 237, NSF, LBJL.

nations to move increasingly toward accommodation with Communist China. Other Asian nations may instead seek reinsurance via Moscow.' Johnson's specific recommendation was for an American 'posture of calm and assurance', involving a flexible military stance and reassurances to American friends and allies that the United States had the capability and will to resist Chinese aggression or threats with non-nuclear means.[71]

The eventual adoption of a relatively relaxed attitude to Chinese acquisition of the bomb by the Lyndon Johnson administration was by no means inevitable. Direct military action against Chinese nuclear facilities had been under discussion within the Pentagon since the summer of 1963. Although the JCS were generally sceptical over such an operation, a covert attack, possibly using Nationalist Chinese commando teams, or unattributable air strikes, were felt worthy of serious study by McGeorge Bundy and, it would seem, President Kennedy himself.[72] Having spent so much time already on the Chinese nuclear problem, Robert Johnson was again asked by Rostow to examine possible preventive action that could be taken against Beijing's programme. Johnson produced his findings in April 1964, and perhaps not surprisingly given his relatively sanguine attitude to China's development of a nuclear capability, they were not encouraging; denying China nuclear status in the short term, Johnson concluded, would not 'justify the undertaking of actions which would involve great political costs or high military risks'. Not only was it virtually impossible to guarantee the success of such drastic steps as air strikes or sabotage operations in the face of the intelligence deficit that was apparent with regard to the Chinese nuclear programme, even if significant damage were done to Chinese facilities this would only retard development by about four or five years. Moreover, Beijing might take retaliatory action against Taiwan or American bases in East Asia and so increase the chance of much broader hostilities, Soviet reactions were unpredictable (Johnson discounting the possibility they would acquiesce in an American attack), and coercive action against China was likely to risk alienating widespread segments of allied and non-aligned opinion. Without the Chinese themselves engaging in provocative behaviour, it would be difficult to justify

---

[71] Rostow memorandum for Bundy, 25 September 1964, 'A Program of Action to Deal with Effects of a Chinese Communist Nuclear Detonation and Nuclear Capability', in 'Nuclear Testing, China', Subject File, box 31, NSF, LBJL; and also Komer memorandum for Bundy, 13 October 1964, which indicates that there was no great urgency taken in implementing Johnson's recommendations, in 'China (CPR), Nuclear Explosion Capability', Files of Robert Komer, box 14, NSF, LBJL.

[72] See Burr and Richelson, 'Whether to "Strangle the Baby in the Cradle"', 68–74; Richelson, *Spying on the Bomb*, 154–6; for Bundy's enthusiasm for military action, see Andrew Preston, *The War Council: McGeorge Bundy, the NSC, and Vietnam* (Cambridge, MA, 2006), 59–62.

preventive action, and, in a reflection of the racial dimension that still lay in the background of nuclear issues in Asia, an American attack would 'play into the hands of efforts by Peiping to picture U.S. hostility to Communist China as the source of tensions and the principal threat to peace in Asia. It is also likely to be viewed, with the help of Peiping's propaganda, as a racialist effort by the U.S. to keep non-white countries in a state of permanent military inferiority.'[73]

Determining how much influence was carried by Robert Johnson's negative conclusions is difficult to gauge, and there is no evidence to show that the President was even exposed to his lengthy arguments.[74] McGeorge Bundy remained interested in the possibilities of taking force- ful action in the first few months of 1964, though his deputy Komer was more sceptical. Some military voices expressed a readiness to adopt firm measures in order to retard Chinese nuclear development. The new CINCPAC at Honolulu, Admiral Ulysses S. Sharp, for example, felt increasingly concerned by the intelligence reports he was receiving that a Chinese test was expected in the near future. In July 1964, he signalled to the JCS that when this event occurred, 'it is estimated that the effect on Asia at large will be very great. The Asian rank and file will not discrim- inate between a bread-board test [sic] and a genuine bomb, and the Chinese will acquire overnight the status of a nuclear power in their minds. Such a development cannot help but hurt our cause, and every- thing possible should therefore be done to defer the day when the Chinese detonation takes place.' Sharp went on to enquire if covert action could be taken against the instruments or devices that formed part of the nuclear programme.[75] However, Rusk's customary caution was evident throughout the policy discussions of 1964, and there was no indication whatsoever that the Russians would be prepared to open discussions on joint action, Moscow taking for granted that the Chinese would soon acquire nuclear weapons and that this was essen- tially an extra strategic problem for the United States alone. As for President Johnson, it would be very difficult to conceal American involvement in any action taken against Chinese nuclear installations,

[73] Robert H. Johnson memorandum, 'An Exploration of the Possible Bases for Action Against the Chinese Communist Nuclear Facilities', 14 April 1964, and covering mem- orandum from Rostow to Bundy, 22 April 1964, China Memos, Vol. I, Country File, box 237, NSF, LBJL; see also the analysis in Burr and Richelson, 'Whether to "Strangle the Baby in the Cradle"', 80–2.

[74] Though Rostow did include brief mention of Johnson's position against preventive action in a memorandum for the President of 1 May 1964; see Burr and Richelson, 'Whether to "Strangle the Baby in the Cradle"', 82–3.

[75] CINCPAC to JCS, 13 July 1964, China Cables, Vol. I, Country File, box 237, NSF, LBJL.

and with an election due in November he had every incentive to avoid a dangerous confrontation with the PRC, especially with the image he was cultivating as the candidate of peace and moderation as against the belligerent Republican challenger, Senator Barry Goldwater. By the middle of September 1964, all the senior policy-makers in the administration, including Bundy, Rusk and McNamara, had come to the view that 'unprovoked unilateral U.S. military action' should not be taken against Chinese nuclear installations, although they still wanted to explore co-operative action with the Soviet Union to inhibit Chinese nuclear development if there was any interest from Moscow; this was a view with which the President concurred.[76]

It still remained to deal with the repercussions of the Chinese test. From the State Department, William Jorden's Psychological-Political Working Group had prepared a public statement that could be issued when it became evident that the test was soon to occur, so that it would be apparent that the United States had not been taken by surprise and was prepared for the new circumstances that a Chinese bomb would create. Such a statement would also carry domestic political advantages, of course, in that the Republicans could not accuse the administration of having been caught unawares. On 29 September 1964, Rusk duly announced that a Chinese test was expected soon, deplored China's disregard for efforts to ban atmosphere testing and tried to reassure Asian allies by making the point that a successful explosion would not mean that China now possessed a large stockpile of weapons or the means to deliver them, while the United States had taken full account of Beijing's nuclear potential in its own military planning and preparations.[77] The *New York Times*, while agreeing that the military equation was likely to remain unchanged for many years to come, predicted that the political and propaganda consequences were likely to be 'formidable. Peking can be expected to argue that it has broken the "white man's monopoly" of nuclear weapons and that this is one more reason why the underdeveloped nations of Asia, Africa and Latin America should look to the Chinese for leadership and support.' Moreover, Chinese possession of the bomb might spur non-nuclear states such as India and Japan to try to develop their own nuclear weapons programmes.[78]

When the test explosion finally occurred on 16 October, President Johnson reaffirmed the established line that a Chinese nuclear capability

---

[76] Bundy memorandum for the record, 15 September 1964, Intelligence File, box 9, NSF, LBJL.
[77] See Morton H. Halperin, *China and the Bomb* (London, 1965), 83–4.
[78] 'Those 700 Million Chinese ... and China's Bomb', *NYT*, 30 September 1964.

would have no effect on American readiness to fulfil its defence commitments in Asia, while the United States enjoyed overwhelming nuclear strength in the region. The test was a 'tragedy for the Chinese people', Johnson claimed, as Beijing's nuclear ambitions had consumed valuable resources that could otherwise have been used for peaceful economic development. Pledges of support for any state threatened with nuclear blackmail by China soon followed.[79] In the propaganda battle that ensued, the Chinese authorities tried to counteract the negative publicity that their test attracted and displayed their disdain for the test-ban treaty. 'The atom bomb is a paper tiger,' a statement issued from Beijing maintained. 'This famous saying by Chairman Mao Tse-Tung is known to all. This was our view in the past and this is still our view at present. China is developing nuclear weapons not because we believe in the omnipotence of nuclear weapons and that China plans to use nuclear weapons. The truth is exactly to the contrary. In developing nuclear weapons, China's aim is to break the nuclear monopoly of the nuclear powers and to eliminate nuclear weapons.' The Chinese went on to call for the prohibition of all nuclear weapons, and, in a repeat of their proposal from the year before, for a nuclear-free zone in the Pacific. To reinforce the message that it had developed a nuclear programme as a purely defensive measure and as a response to previous American nuclear threats, Beijing also pledged that it would never be the first to use nuclear weapons (a right which the United States was not, of course, prepared to renounce).[80]

Immediate reactions to the test from the PRC's Asian neighbours varied. Chiang Kai-shek made a strong but fruitless personal appeal to Johnson for further planning co-operation over action that could be taken to destroy Chinese nuclear facilities, but the dominant impact on Taiwan seems to have been resignation that a return to the mainland was now inconceivable. Feeling newly vulnerable and exposed, the Indian Government condemned the Chinese test but affirmed its commitment to a non-nuclear stance, a response which was echoed in Japan. Most Japanese press commentary discounted the military significance of the Chinese achievement but could see that the event would boost Beijing's prestige on the world stage; indeed, many editorials spoke of the need for the West to reach an accommodation with the PRC, and to at least bring it into dialogue over disarmament and joining the test-ban regime. As could be expected, laudatory comment came from North Vietnam, North Korea and Indonesia, with the test seen as delivering a blow against

---

[79] Halperin, *China and the Bomb*, 87–8; and Foot, *Practice of Power*, 183–4.
[80] Halperin, *China and the Bomb*, 90–3.

Western imperialism in Asia.[81] Many African states, as well as Pakistan, Indonesia and Cambodia, saw the achievement as enhancing the stature of the Afro-Asian world that had been inaugurated at Bandung. Pressures for greater international engagement with China were only likely to increase, and there was no easy discounting of the political significance of the PRC's acquisition of nuclear status, or the anomaly of her not being represented at the UN and of not holding the Chinese seat on the Security Council, when the other four permanent members were also nuclear powers.[82] By June 1965, CIA reports were indicating that many of the new African members of the UN would support the PRC's admission, and the 'overwhelming majority' of UN member states felt that China would have to be included in any meaningful discussions concerning disarmament. Most tellingly, a key factor in convincing many 'Afro-Asian' states to favour Chinese admission was its recent acquisition of nuclear status, while some African nations were 'proud that China has developed a "colored bomb"'.[83]

Some observers had already noted how China's Asian neighbours were resigned to the inevitability of Beijing's nuclear status and even conjectured that their worries over the consequences might be mixed with a certain degree of racial pride. 'The sophisticated in all Asian countries,' one *New York Times* columnist opined, 'have never forgotten that the first and only atomic bombs to be aimed at people – the Hiroshima and Nagasaki bombs of 1945 – were aimed at Asians', and now 'China's fellow Asians … may be experiencing a grim exhilaration. At least Asians do it, too!'[84] In the context of its growing rivalry with the Soviet Union, China's prestige in the 'underdeveloped' areas of the world was likely to be enhanced, a *New York Times* editorial highlighted, as 'like them, it is a nonwhite nation faced with the task of building a modern state out of a primitive peasant society'. Moreover, the newspaper could see previous calls for 'neutralization' within South East Asia, deriving from concerns

---

[81] Several reports on world reactions to the Chinese achievement reached Johnson's desk from USIA just after the explosion, affirming in self-congratulatory fashion that the preparatory work done by US agencies on the ground had reaped rewards through the generally calm responses that were recorded; see Carl Rowan memorandum for the President, 19 October 1964, and attached report 'Foreign Media Reaction to Communist China's Nuclear Device', USIA Research and Reference Service, R-158–64, 18 October 1964, 'Nuclear Testing, China', Subject File, box 31, NSF, LBJL. See also parallel reporting from the Foreign Office, 'World Reactions to the Explosion of the First Chinese Nuclear Device', B.718(R), 27 October 1964, IAM 1018/61, FO 371/176434, TNA.

[82] Foot, *Practice of Power*, 185–8.

[83] CIA Intelligence Information Cable, No. 95979, 22 June 1965, DDRS/CK3100099714.

[84] 'Asia Resigned to a Nuclear China', *NYT*, 18 October 1964. See also Halperin, *China and the Bomb*, 89.

over the effects of the war in Vietnam, being reinforced as perceptions of Chinese strength grew.[85]

China, therefore, had acquired new prestige and status following its first nuclear test, but the question exercising American policy-makers during 1964–5 was whether it would be able to capitalize on this by the further spread of revolutionary change in South East Asia, where the conflict in Vietnam was now assuming a place of central importance. There was a danger, some US officials believed, that the perception of Chinese Communist power moving into ascendancy across the region might soon gain hold. In South Vietnam itself, the removal of the Diem regime in November 1963 had done nothing to stem the rising scope and intensity of the Communist-led insurgency. Though the indigenous and southern roots of unrest were sometimes belatedly acknowledged in Washington, the inclination of the Johnson administration was to see Hanoi's hand as directing the moves of the National Liberation Front, with Beijing also working through the North Vietnamese to destabilize the whole of South East Asia.[86] Any weakening of American resolve in Vietnam, or even the withdrawal of American commitment, might be interpreted as a sign that China's new nuclear status was having a direct pay-off as US policy became more timid. In one White House meeting in September 1964 where Lyndon Johnson was given the view of Maxwell Taylor (now the US Ambassador in Saigon) that 'sooner or later we would have to act more forcefully against the North', the President asked those present if there were any doubts over whether American efforts should be expended holding South Vietnam. Taylor's response that Hanoi could not be allowed to win was reinforced by General Earle G. Wheeler, who had taken over as Chairman of the JCS in June, who claimed that 'if we should lose in South Vietnam, we would lose Southeast Asia. Country after country on the periphery would give way and look toward Communist China as the rising power of the area.' Rusk and McCone then also underlined their emphatic agreement with this appraisal.[87]

In its crucial report of November 1964, the NSC Working Group on Vietnam, chaired by William P. Bundy (and including, it might be noted, Robert Johnson), argued that the effects of the loss of South Vietnam on Asia generally would depend on the manner in which defeat was incurred, and 'whether the loss did in fact greatly weaken or lead to the early loss of

---

[85] 'China's Bomb', *NYT*, 18 October 1964.
[86] See Robert D. Schulzinger, 'The Johnson Administration, China, and the Vietnam War', in Ross and Changbin (eds.), *Re-Examining the Cold War*, 238–42; Robert S. McNamara, *In Retrospect: The Tragedy and Lessons of Vietnam* (New York, 1995), 116–17.
[87] Memorandum of a White House meeting, 9 September 1964, *FRUS, 1964–1968, I: Vietnam, 1964* (Washington, DC, 1992), 752–3.

other areas in Southeast Asia. Nationalist China (shaken already by the Chicom nuclear explosion and the UN membership crisis), South Korea, and the Philippines will need maximum reassurance. While Japan's faith in our military posture and determination might not be shaken, the growing feeling that Communist China must somehow be lived with might well be accentuated [...] the picture of a defense line clearly breached could have serious effects and could easily, over time, tend to unravel the whole Pacific and South Asian defense structures.'[88] The advice offered by one contemporary analyst, Morton Halperin (who was then a consultant for the RAND Corporation but in 1966 would join the Department of Defense), was that the smaller states of Asia must be assured by the United States 'that the existence of a Chinese nuclear capability has not seriously affected the military balance in the Far East. They must be convinced that a Chinese nuclear capability makes U.S. intervention more rather than less likely.'[89] Standing by American commitments and maintaining 'credibility' in the region appeared all the more vital, then, in a context where non-Communist Asian states might fear that the development of a Chinese nuclear umbrella in the coming years would increase Beijing's assertiveness and reduce the proclivity of the United States to employ military force in their defence.

The central point to make here is that the policy debates over escalation of American involvement in the Vietnam War witnessed in late 1964 and the first few months of 1965 were carried out in the shadow of the recent Chinese test.[90] Even though the re-evaluation of nuclear strategy in the Far East conducted under the Kennedy administration in 1962–3 was usually framed in terms of a conventional and overt instance of Communist aggression leading to limited war, rather than under conditions of insurgency, the political objections to any nuclear use which were again voiced within the US bureaucracy, as well as the implications of the arrival of a Chinese nuclear capability, in a number of ways had a bearing on the posture subsequently adopted in Vietnam. An obvious effect was in bolstering the strong aversion of the Johnson administration to taking military steps against North Vietnam which might provoke the introduction of Chinese ground forces and so instigate a dangerous cycle of escalation. During early 1964, as it became clear that the situation in South Vietnam was continuing to deteriorate, the JCS came forward with a series of proposals intended to curb the Communist insurgency

[88] Paper prepared by the NSC Working Group, 21 November 1964, *ibid.*, 918.
[89] Halperin, *China and the Bomb*, 115.
[90] One of the few scholarly works on the Americanization of the Vietnam War to make this fundamental point is Kaiser, *American Tragedy*, 353–4, 362.

by bringing military pressure to bear directly against Hanoi. If Chinese intervention was triggered as a result, then the JCS were convinced that nuclear weapons would have to be used to repel Communist forces and to assure American victory.[91] In offering such advice, the military were simply reflecting the nature of the planning that had developed over responses to Chinese intervention ever since the subject had first received detailed study by the Eisenhower administration in 1954. However, to the civilian members of the Johnson administration, attuned to the recent dangers of nuclear escalation during the Cuban Missile Crisis of 1962, such mention of nuclear strikes was deeply troubling, despite the fact that China as yet had no deliverable nuclear capability. The Cuban crisis had evidently given leading policy-makers such as McNamara a degree of confidence that they could control and manage a process of escalation, but had also imparted an even greater sense of the consequences of failure. Though the JCS might discount the possibility of Soviet involvement if limited war involving China expanded to encompass US nuclear attacks against Chinese targets, there was a widespread appreciation that the Russians might not simply stand by and see their erstwhile Communist ally devastated.[92]

While the authorities in Washington wrestled with the problem of how to sustain the revolving door of anti-Communist governments in Saigon during the course of 1964, the debate over nuclear posture elsewhere in East Asia was also continuing and again served to underline State Department estimates of how deep Asian opposition to nuclear use would be. During a visit to Taipei in April 1964, Rusk had told Chiang Kai-shek that the United States had to be careful about the way it went about opposing Communist advances in South East Asia, as it was 'not going to deal with large masses of men on the Asian mainland with conventional US forces'. The implication was that nuclear weapons might have to be used if the PRC was provoked into direct intervention in Indochina, and the Secretary of State warned that, 'It may be that Southeast Asia cannot be made secure unless the Chinese Communists are hurt and hurt badly, but this would build up a legacy of hate against the United States.' Chiang's reaction may have surprised Rusk, for the Nationalist President now avowed that he was opposed to the use of nuclear weapons 'in this part of the world', continuing that it would

---

[91] See, e.g., McNamara, *In Retrospect*, 111.
[92] This was one product of a major study undertaken by State and Defense Department representatives in the spring of 1965; see Llewellyn Thompson memorandum for Rusk, 'China Study', 15 July 1965, *FRUS, 1964–1968, XXX: China* (Washington, DC, 1998), 187.

'hurt the United States more than anything else and it was unnecessary'.[93] Returning from his trip to Taipei, Rusk told the NSC that the most interesting part of his talks with Chiang had been the latter's 'passionate statement that nuclear war in Asia would be wrong'.[94] This represented a major change from the apparently nonchalant attitude Chiang had adopted to the idea of using nuclear weapons against mainland targets in the late 1950s.

Chiang's opinion was also registered at the same time as a revitalized policy discussion was being conducted over force reductions in Korea, with Lyndon Johnson pressing for savings in overseas expenditures as he tried to trim the federal budget and accommodate domestic spending priorities.[95] By early June 1964, both the State and Defense Departments had come around to the shared view that it was not an opportune time to cut back on US force deployments in the Korean peninsula (especially when the South Korean Government was then dealing with large-scale student demonstrations and a wave of unpopularity which led to the imposition of martial law). One draft memorandum produced by Rusk argued that any American withdrawal would 'inevitably and undesirably focus attention throughout the Far East on the already heavy nuclear emphasis in our Korean posture'. In his recent talks with Chiang Kai-shek, Rusk pointed out, the former had 'sharply rejected any possibility of the use of nuclear weapons by the US in Asia as being completely contrary to US interests'. Hence, the 'entire military rationale' of the proposal gave Rusk cause for concern, while the reduction might excite memories of the complete pull-out of American forces in 1949 that had preceded the North Korean invasion, and so undermine confidence in US intentions at a difficult moment for the Government in Seoul. A concomitant staff study could see major political problems in any overtly nuclear strategy for Korea, as it was 'important for Asian countries not to suppose that any form of an attack would automatically lead to making nuclear battlefields of their countries. If it appeared in Japan, for example, that any military effort would mean a nuclear war, there would be danger of the Japanese Government's being forced to re-examine US rights under the US–Japanese Security Treaty of 1960 *and related arrangements to launch nuclear*

---

[93] Memorandum of conversation, 16 April 1964, *ibid.*, 47.
[94] Summary record of the 528th meeting of the NSC, 22 April 1964, *FRUS, 1964–1968, I*, 258. See also Rusk's (misplaced) allusion to this conversation in his memoir, *As I Saw It*, 288.
[95] Bundy to Alexis Johnson, 20 December 1963, *FRUS, 1961–1963, XXII*, 672; embassy in Korea to the Department of State, 21 January 1964, *FRUS, 1964–1968, XXIX*, Part 1, *Korea* (Washington, DC, 2000), 1–2; National Security Action Memorandum 298, 5 May 1964, *ibid.*, 21–2, and note 3.

strikes in defence of Korea from US bases in Japan' (emphasis added). Recent military appraisals, it was maintained, had suggested that a conventional defence of Korea was in any case feasible with existing forces, even against a combined North Korean/Chinese Communist attack, obviating any immediate need to exercise a nuclear option.[96]

The study's mention of a possible understanding with Tokyo over use of American bases for nuclear operations relating to Korea is intriguing and adds another element to explanations as to why both the US and Japanese governments have thus far refused to reveal the full records of the negotiations surrounding the security treaty. In addition, the State Department's doubts concerning the robustness of the understandings over the use of the bases is apparent from this and other contemporary evidence. As the Johnson administration moved in the autumn of 1964 to commit American power to war on the Asian mainland once more, it did not seem the time to undertake any radical revision of force posture in Korea which might give Hanoi or Beijing the wrong impression about Washington's intentions and resolve in South East Asia. The South Korean Government was meanwhile indicating its own strong support for the American stand, despatching a small group of 2,000 non-combat troops to aid the South Vietnamese Government in its struggle to contain the Communist insurgency, a gesture of solidarity from another Asian state warmly received by the US administration. By May 1965, when President Chung Hee Park visited Johnson in the White House, the South Koreans were approached with the request to contribute a full division of troops for Vietnam, and this was eventually fulfilled.[97] The *quid pro quo* for this deployment was Washington's agreement not to denude its forces in South Korea by substantial levels (though they were run down somewhat as the demands of the ground war in Vietnam increased during 1965–6), while the decline in MAP support would also be arrested.[98]

The issue of the entrenched perception of the atomic bomb as a 'white man's weapon', having already made an appearance when the State Department had considered nuclear policy and responses to Communist aggression in Korea during 1962–3, was also mentioned in

---

[96] See Rusk draft memorandum for the President, 'Study of Possible Redeployment of U.S. Division Now Stationed in Korea', and attached State-Defense-AID study, 8 June 1964, 'Korea', box 254, records of the PPC, 1963–4, RG 59, NARA.
[97] Memorandum of conversation, 17 May 1965, *FRUS, 1964–1968, XXIX*, 97–9. For South Korean deployments to South Vietnam, see also Kahin, *Intervention*, 333–4.
[98] See Kil J. Yi, 'The U.S.–Korean Alliance in the Vietnam War', in Lloyd C. Gardner and Ted Gittinger (eds.), *International Perspectives on Vietnam* (College Station, TX, 2000), 159–60.

the debate over possible nuclear use in Vietnam. On 24 May 1964, Barry Goldwater drew fresh attention to his hawkish views by suggesting in a television interview that low-yield atomic weapons could be used along South Vietnam's borders in order to clear the jungle and so expose Communist supply routes, though this would be done after 'consultation' with the Chinese and North Vietnamese and in a fashion that would not endanger life.[99] This unique answer to the problem of defoliation, and Goldwater's first major recommendation on Vietnam war strategy as he stood poised to secure the Republican nomination, was a gift to Democratic Party campaign managers who wanted to position Johnson as a responsible man of peace, and someone best placed to handle Vietnam in a way that both upheld US interests and commitments and avoided such extreme measures. Goldwater's remarks prompted the re-emergence of notions that any use of nuclear weapons in Asia would carry disastrous political consequences. U Thant, the Burmese Secretary-General of the UN, responded by telling reporters that anyone advocating use of atomic weapons in Vietnam was 'out of his mind'. Citing as reasons the radioactive fallout that would result, the elusiveness of the Viet Cong enemy and the 'widespread resentment and bitter criticism' that would come from many quarters previously unmoved by the war, U Thant reserved his final comment for what he called 'a very important element ... there is some racial factor in such a projected operation. In 1945 when atomic weapons were dropped over Hiroshima and Nagasaki in Japan, there was a widespread feeling in many parts of Asia that these deadly atomic bombs were dropped on Japanese cities because the Japanese were non-whites, and it was also argued at that time that the atomic bombs would never have been dropped over cities in Nazi Germany.'[100]

At the beginning of June, only a few days after the press flurry prompted by Goldwater's views on Vietnam, Rusk was in Saigon for meetings with General Nguyen Khanh, the South Vietnamese Prime Minister. The Secretary of State took the chance to inform Khanh that if the Chinese intervened in response to American escalation of the war, this would likely result in use of nuclear weapons as the United States 'would never again get involved in a land war in Asia limited to conventional forces'. Rusk noted that this was something which many leaders in the 'free world'

[99] 'Goldwater Urges Atom Use in Asia', *NYT*, 25 May 1964.
[100] Andrew W. Cordier and Max Harrelson (eds.), *Public Papers of the Secretaries General of the United Nations*, Vol. VI: *U Thant, 1961–1964* (New York, 1976), transcript of press conference, 26 May 1964, 591–2; 'Thant Deplores Talk of Using Atomic Weapons in Vietnamese War', *NYT*, 27 May 1964; 'Thant Opposes A-Bombing of Viet Cong Area', *Chicago Tribune*, 27 May 1964.

would be against, and that even Chiang Kai-shek had relayed his opposition to this course of action, continuing 'many Asians seemed to see an element of racial discrimination in use of nuclear arms; something we would do to Asians but not to Westerners'. Khanh, however, demurred, avowing he had no quarrel with American use of nuclear weapons, that using the bomb against Japan in 1945 had saved not just American but also Japanese lives, and the only answer to the mass forces fielded by the Chinese was 'superior firepower'.[101] Such remarks were an echo of those proffered by Diem to Admiral Stump in 1957 when the latter had outlined a similar process of nuclear escalation after a North Vietnamese attack across the 17th parallel, though presumably with more enthusiasm than the Secretary of State; Khanh's views also showed the inherently problematic task of arriving at a settled and uniform reading of 'Asian opinion' regarding nuclear weapons when a variety of perspectives were present in the region. From Saigon, Rusk had travelled on to Honolulu, where he attended a major conference of American diplomatic and military representatives which discussed US objectives in South East Asia and what measures could be taken to convince Hanoi of American resolve to defend South Vietnam. If US air action against the North produced Chinese intervention, this would, McNamara pointed out to the assembled group, lead to the question of having to use nuclear weapons. Admiral Felt asserted that 'there was no possible way to hold off the communists on the ground without the use of tactical nuclear weapons, and that it was essential that the commanders be given the freedom to use these as had been assumed under the various plans'.[102] This kind of approach was anathema to the Secretary of Defense: in his memoir of the war, McNamara professed that both he and Lyndon Johnson were 'shocked' by the 'cavalier' way the JCS entertained the risks of a possible use of nuclear weapons in South East Asia, something which his later approach to the controlled use of air power against North Vietnam was above all designed to avoid.[103]

McGeorge Bundy recalled later that fear of reprisal was not a major factor that weighed in the calculations of the Johnson administration over whether the use of nuclear weapons in Vietnam should be given serious thought. That the issue was dismissed had more to do with the fact that

---

[101] Rusk to State Department, 1 June 1964, *FRUS, 1964–1968, I*, 410.

[102] *The Pentagon Papers: The Defense Department History of United States Decision-Making on Vietnam*, Senator Gravel Edition, Vol. III (Boston, 1971), 175. See also Ellsberg, *Secrets*, 63–4.

[103] McNamara, *In Retrospect*, 160–1. See also Randall B. Woods, 'The Politics of Idealism: Lyndon Johnson, Civil Rights, and Vietnam', *Diplomatic History*, 31, 1, January 2007, 9–10.

political reactions in Vietnam to the widespread Vietnamese casualties that would result from their use would likely prejudice any future for the American presence in the country, the intense international revulsion that could be expected and the improbability that nuclear use in a setting of limited war would ever receive the overall support of domestic public opinion. In the 1964 election campaign, President Johnson, positioning himself against the irresponsibility of Goldwater, had declared that 'there is no such thing as a conventional nuclear weapon', proclaiming that any decision to use the bomb was a 'political decision of the highest order' that could never be delegated to the military. 'By 1964,' Bundy recorded, '[Johnson] was entirely clear in his own mind that he would have no interest whatsoever in ordering the use of even one bomb, ever, except in the context of some overwhelmingly dangerous and direct confrontation with open Soviet aggression.'[104] Morton Halperin, in one contemporary analysis, did not think that the United States could completely rule out Soviet assistance to the Chinese in the event of a US nuclear strike, leading him to the conclusion that 'on these grounds alone, it is doubtful whether American military commanders will ever be given the authority to launch tactical nuclear weapons against China'. Moreover, Halperin also pointed out that the use of such weapons carried serious political consequences in the Asian setting, where aversion to the atomic bomb was still much in evidence, reflected in support for the Partial Test Ban Treaty and UN motions calling for nuclear-free zones. 'It is unlikely,' Halperin concluded, 'that the United States will be in a situation in which the winning of a single battle seems to outweigh the political disadvantages that will always accompany the use of tactical nuclear weapons.' A large-scale Chinese invasion of, say, India would be a different matter, and in such cases strategic nuclear retaliation might be called for, but the United States should, Halperin advised, indicate that it could deal with lower levels of Chinese aggression with conventional forces.[105]

Both McNamara and Rusk, it seems, held deep moral reservations over any first use of nuclear weapons, except in response to the unlikely scenario of a massive Soviet attack in Western Europe, where NATO was facing overwhelming defeat.[106] In addition, Rusk, another Southern racial liberal like Johnson, was clearly sensitive to the damage that the United States' own domestic record on race was doing to its international

---

[104] See Bundy, *Danger and Survival*, 536, 538. As one scholar of this subject concludes, in Vietnam nuclear weapons 'were politically unusable, and for some officials, even morally unacceptable'; see Nina Tannenwald, 'Nuclear Weapons and the Vietnam War', *Journal of Strategic Studies*, 29, 4, August 2006, 677.

[105] Halperin, *China and the Bomb*, 103–5.

[106] See, e.g., McNamara, *In Retrospect*, 345; Rusk, *As I Saw It*, 248.

image, and was conscious of how the nuclear issue carried a particular resonance for an Asian audience. The historical analogy that was most suggestive to administration figures during this period (none more so than Rusk himself) was that of Korea in 1950, when American involvement had been followed by the Chinese intervention and the traumatic retreat back to the 38th parallel, prompting widespread speculation that only the use of nuclear weapons would reverse the dire situation at the battlefront.[107] This was an experience that had to be avoided at virtually all costs and was one reason, alongside doubts that military success was feasible in the South, why some officials and members of Congress, such as the Senate majority leader Mike Mansfield, were prepared to advocate reducing the American commitment in Vietnam.[108]

In October 1964, as his dissent from the Vietnam policies of the Johnson administration began its forlorn path, George Ball compiled a long memorandum which summarized why winning the war in the South was an unobtainable object and put forward a case for cutting American losses through a political solution which would allow for American withdrawal. Ball felt that if the United States were to make a prolonged and large-scale commitment of ground troops to Vietnam which also led to substantial casualties, and certainly if the Chinese should intervene, then domestic pressures would mount for the use of tactical nuclear weapons: 'the American people would not accept again the frustrations and anxieties that resulted from our abstention from nuclear combat in Korea'. There would be major political costs to any such course of action, and in his appraisal of these Ball made explicit the connections between race and nuclear use in Asia, and the relevance of the previous Korean example:

Our employment of the first tactical nuclear weapon would inevitably be met by a Communist accusation that we use nuclear weapons only against yellow men (or colored men). It is Communist dogma that this is the reason that we used atomic bombs against Japan but not against Germany in World War II. There would be profound shock around the world not merely in Japan but also among the non-white nations on every continent ... we should recall the reactions in December 1950 when President Truman even suggested the possibility of using atomic bombs in the Korean War – at a time when we still had the nuclear monopoly.[109]

---

[107] For a thorough analysis, see Yuen Foong Khong, *Analogies at War: Korea, Munich, Dien Bien Phu, and the Vietnam Decisions of 1965* (Princeton, 1992), 97–147.

[108] Though Mansfield and others were still very reluctant to voice their doubts publicly; see Fredrik Logevall, *Choosing War: The Lost Chance for Peace and the Escalation of War in Vietnam* (Berkeley, 1999), 137–9, 285.

[109] Ball memorandum, 'How Valid Are the Assumptions Underlying Our Viet-Nam Policies?', 5 October 1964, in George W. Ball, 'The Light That Failed', *Atlantic Monthly*, July 1972, 42. For the background, see Ball, *Past Has Another Pattern*, 380–3.

Even though Ball's full 'devil's advocate' paper on withdrawal did not immediately find its way to the President, Johnson was also fully aware of the risks attached to expanded action against the North.[110]

Yet the three leading foreign policy-making figures in the Johnson administration (aside from the President himself), Rusk, McNamara and McGeorge Bundy, realized that more needed to be done if the deterioration of governmental control in South Vietnam was to be reversed. Once the presidential election was out of the way, at the end of November 1964, the foreign policy 'principals' in the administration were freer to consider the alternative courses of action set out by William Bundy's NSC Working Group on Vietnam. During these discussions, McNamara explained to his colleagues, regarding the place of nuclear options, that 'he could not imagine a case where they would be considered'.[111] Ultimately, they all moved to embrace 'calibration', or the fine-tuning of actions to avoid the extremes of excessive and provocative escalation or passivity resulting in defeat and humiliation.[112] Following the Viet Cong attack on the American base at Pleiku in February 1965, the administration accepted McGeorge Bundy's programme of 'sustained reprisal' through bombing the North, though Ball was now accorded a more direct opportunity to warn Johnson of the possible consequences of Chinese intervention, along similar lines to his October memorandum. Use of tactical nuclear weapons in this instance, the Under-Secretary repeated, would 'obviously raise the most profound political problems', generating 'probably irresistible pressures for a major Soviet involvement' but also leaving the United States 'vulnerable to the charge that it was willing to use nuclear weapons against non-whites only'.[113] The limits of American action against North Vietnam subsequently established by the President and his main advisers were of course designed to avoid the wider conflict and possible use of nuclear weapons that Ball had warned about, but, as Ralph Smith once highlighted in his multidimensional history of the war, it also entailed risks of a different kind, which had featured in the earlier Korean intervention of 1950, that of 'large-scale ground war on the

---

[110] Logevall, *Choosing War*, 243–6.
[111] At this meeting of 24 November, McGeorge Bundy did raise the issue that there might be 'great pressure' for nuclear use from the military and 'certain political circles' under 'certain circumstances' (presumably Chinese intervention); see *Pentagon Papers*, III, 238. For an extensive analysis of the Working Group and the reception of its conclusions, see Logevall, *Choosing War*, 255–74.
[112] See the discussion of calibration as applied to Vietnam in Gaddis, *Strategies*, 241–50; also Lawrence Freedman, 'Vietnam and the Disillusioned Strategist', *International Affairs*, 72, 1, 1996, 133–51.
[113] Memorandum from Ball to Johnson, 13 February 1965, *FRUS, 1964–1968, II: Vietnam, January–June 1965* (Washington, DC, 1996), 255.

Asian mainland, which was a more daunting prospect for Washington than for Hanoi or Peking – or, since it would not be directly involved, for Moscow'.[114] Here lay the great irony of the American belief that calibrated pressure against Hanoi would yield dividends in the South, or at least preserve the edifice of a non-Communist government in Saigon, when all it would serve to do would be to enlarge the American stake in the conflict, draw in more resources and hand the strategic initiative to Washington's adversaries.

In overall terms, American strategy in the Far East between 1962 and 1965 was reconfigured as the problems associated with the emergence of China as a nuclear power were digested by American policy-makers. The pressures to reduce overseas defence spending had initially led the Pentagon to develop the idea of placing greater reliance on tactical nuclear weapons in order to deter and then meet overt Communist aggression, in a return to the thinking that had predominated at the outset of the Eisenhower administration in 1953–4. As in that former case, the setting for this reconsideration of strategy was Korea, where MAP expenditures and the deployment of two US divisions were a major financial burden. However, it was not so easy to discard the logic of flexible response just as it was being introduced by McNamara in the European theatre, and the attempt to do so quickly encountered strong objections. One of the several arguments advanced by the State Department was that 'turning back the clock' to the days of massive retaliation would appear as a 'racist strategy' to an Asian audience, where the atomic bomb was still viewed as the 'white man's weapon'. Another, as we have seen, was that China's anticipated first nuclear test would erode the credibility of an American nuclear response, for now China would have the means to strike back if she were subject to nuclear attack, and the likeliest targets for such a Chinese counterblow were American bases located on the territory of Washington's Asian friends and allies. This kind of reasoning made it apparent to the Kennedy administration by 1963 that conventional capabilities for limited war in the Far East had to be given even greater emphasis if a necessary sense of reassurance was to be spread around the region and as the date of a Chinese nuclear test approached. Once the techniques of counter-insurgency were seen to have failed in South Vietnam following the overthrow of the Diem Government, the Johnson administration would proceed to use enhanced American conventional capabilities for limited war while it deepened involvement in the fighting during 1965 and after.

---

[114] Smith, *International History of the Vietnam War*, II, 257.

From some American officials during this period, one can see concern over how the phenomenon of a Chinese bomb might raise Beijing's image and status in what was often termed the 'non-white' or 'colored' world. The symbolic significance that an occidental monopoly on nuclear weapons was in the process of being broken was widely recognized, and there was much discussion of the best tactics to adopt in response. A further consequence of Chinese acquisition of a nuclear capability discerned by the Johnson administration was that it would accelerate the process of nuclear proliferation. Although not yet an overwhelming preoccupation, the problem of nuclear diffusion would be regarded as one of the major sources of international instability during the latter half of the 1960s, and its ramifications were first brought home to the administration by the work of the Gilpatric Committee, which produced its comprehensive (and in retrospect seminal) report on proliferation and how it might be averted in January 1965.[115] In Asia, the Chinese test prompted concerns that pressures would build for India and Japan, the two states previously most associated with anti-nuclear sentiment, to create their own nuclear programmes, a development not seen to be in overall American interests. Reassurances that the United States would stand by any state which was subject to Chinese nuclear blackmail was one suggestion for how Washington might forestall this eventuality, but a concrete willingness to confront Communist power in South East Asia was another. In evidence he gave to the Gilpatric Committee in December 1964, Walt Rostow made this abundantly clear, explaining that one of the factors that would influence an Indian or Japanese decision over whether to produce their own nuclear weapons would be 'whether US military power proves relevant and credible in containing Communist China in Southeast Asia. If Southeast Asia should crumble, the judgment in India, and to a lesser extent in Japan, may be that whatever the scale and quantity of our [nuclear] hardware, it is not relevant to the defense of Asia against Communist China, and they had better look to their own devices.'[116] From this it was not difficult to extrapolate that the United States had to be willing to face with conventional military power the immediate Communist challenge in Vietnam, where Beijing's ambition to drive the United States out of Asia was in most immediate evidence.

[115] See Glenn T. Seaborg with Benjamin S. Loeb, *Stemming the Tide: Arms Control in the Johnson Years* (Lexington, MA, 1987), 137–49; Hal Brands, 'Rethinking Nonproliferation: LBJ, the Gilpatric Committee, and U.S. National Security Policy', *Journal of Cold War Studies*, 8, 2, Spring 2006, 83–113.
[116] 'Summary of Statement Made before Gilpatric Committee, December 13, 1964', 17 December 1964, 'Briefing: Rostow Statement', Committee File, box 4, NSF, LBJL.

Perceptions of the rising power and influence of China, underlined by its new nuclear status, lay behind much of the American involvement in Vietnam.[117] Justifying American participation in the war in his famous address at Johns Hopkins University in April 1965, Lyndon Johnson, having outlined the way North Vietnam was fuelling the conflict in the South, went on to warn that, 'Over this war – and all Asia – is another reality: the deepening shadow of Communist China. The rulers in Hanoi are urged on by Peking. This is a regime which has destroyed freedom in Tibet, which has attacked India, and has been condemned by the United Nations for aggression in Korea. It is a nation which is helping the forces of violence in almost every continent. The contest in Viet-Nam is part of a wider pattern of aggressive purposes.'[118] For Johnson and his advisers, according to Warren Cohen, 'Concern about a militant China armed with nuclear weapons was fundamental in their decision-making', and to someone like Dean Rusk, China's infringement of the norms of international society and 'civilized' behaviour during the 1960s was a direct challenge to the world order that the United States had sought to promote since 1945.[119] McNamara, for his part, seems to have been deeply impressed with the concept of 'people's war' as popularized by Lin Biao, China's Defence Minister, in an article published in September 1965 which talked of the rural areas of the world enveloping the cities of the industrialized countries (implying that the class struggle against US imperialism would receive support from the PRC wherever it occurred).[120] Two months later, McNamara was warning the President that

China – like Germany in 1917, like Germany in the West and Japan in the East in the late 30s, and like the USSR in 1947 – looms as a major power threatening to undercut our importance and effectiveness in the world and, more remotely but more menacingly, to organize all of Asia against us. The long-run U.S. policy is based upon an instinctive understanding in our country that the peoples and resources of Asia could be effectively mobilized against us by China or by a Chinese coalition and that the potential weight of such a coalition could throw us on the defensive and threaten our security.[121]

This kind of alarmist thinking had a lineage that can be traced back to the fears of pan-Asianism expressed by John Foster Dulles and Chester

---

[117] See Chang, *Friends and Enemies*, 253–4, 258–60.

[118] 'Peace without Conquest', address at Johns Hopkins University, 7 April 1965, *The Public Papers of the Presidents: Lyndon B. Johnson, 1965* (Washington, DC, 1966), 395.

[119] Cohen, *Dean Rusk*, 282–4.

[120] See McNamara, *In Retrospect*, 215; also Chang, *Friends and Enemies*, 269–70, and Foot, *Practice of Power*, 159–60.

[121] Draft memorandum by McNamara to President Johnson, 3 November 1965, *FRUS, 1964–1968, III: Vietnam, June–December 1965* (Washington, DC, 1996), 514.

Bowles in the mid-1950s, and to the images of Japan leading an 'Asia for the Asians' movement that had been at work during the Second World War.

Nevertheless, as many observed (and some American analysts had predicted), China's international behaviour after acquisition of nuclear status in 1964 became, if anything, even more cautious and pragmatic. A limited nuclear capability might give some feelings of insurance against arbitrary use of nuclear weapons by the United States against the mainland, but that same capability remained highly vulnerable to pre-emptive attack. With a major American ground force active in Vietnam on its southern flank, and American air and naval power on conspicuous display in the seas and skies around China during the middle and late 1960s as the convulsions of the Cultural Revolution began to gather momentum, Beijing did not seek military confrontation with Washington and set limits to the assistance it was prepared to give Hanoi.[122] Rather than noting the setbacks to Chinese diplomacy that were encountered during 1965, including the outcome of the Indo-Pakistan War and the October failed coup in Jakarta that led to the destruction of the Indonesian Communist Party at the hands of the army, Washington focussed on the inflammatory rhetoric coming from Beijing and worried about China's enhanced status in Asia being used to spread revolutionary violence, some of which – particularly with the Sino-Soviet split widening – contained the implicit message of racial confrontation between Occident and Orient. The United States, having some fifteen years before embarked upon a costly and protracted limited war in Asia, for all its presumed power and nobility of purpose, was now set upon a similar course where no clear path to victory lay ahead.

[122] Foot, *Practice of Power*, 177–8; Qiang Zhai, *China and the Vietnam Wars*, 138–45.

Conclusion: from massive retaliation to flexible response in Asia

The use of atomic bombs against Japan was emblematic of the technological and material supremacy of the United States in mid-century as its productive capacities and human resources were mobilized for total war. From one perspective, the atomic attacks could be seen as heralding a period of American ascendancy in Asia and the Pacific, as the United States, its global power and reach obvious to all, took the lead role in occupying Japan and then overseeing the restoration of the Japanese economy following the reverse course of 1947–8. Victory over Japan had coincided with high hopes that with US leadership it would prove possible to forge 'One World', where American values would be universally acclaimed and the international system refashioned in its own image. Instead, during the decade that followed, the Cold War preoccupations of policy-makers in Washington had often carried little resonance for indigenous Asian peoples and governments coping with a very different agenda, and where perceptions of the United States were not always positive. Moreover, one of the most significant and far-reaching consequences of the Second World War was to raise the saliency of the issue of race, which was now increasingly operating in a transnational fashion, breaking down the traditional distinctions maintained between domestic and international contexts. In its immediate setting, the dropping of the bomb in 1945 had done much to drown out Japan's wartime rallying call of 'Asia for the Asians' and its challenge to Western influence. Yet, in the opinion of many observers, the employment of weapons of mass destruction, and future threats to use them in Asia, held a continuing association with the racial animosities that had featured in the war of 1941–5 and so served as a further source of estrangement between the United States and an Asia rebuilding itself after the traumas suffered in those years.

American material prowess was not universally regarded as a benevolent force intrinsically associated with virtue, but sometimes as a menacing and unwelcome intrusion, while the process of decolonization and national self-assertion required some divorce from alignment with the West, or even rejection of Western values altogether. The United States, as a self-consciously 'white' power in an area where anti-colonial senti- ment had an underlying racial dimension, often saw itself classed in the same category as the Europeans, especially when, despite professions of anti-imperialism, administrations in Washington continued to lend sup- port and assistance to the colonial powers as they struggled to retain control over their remaining possessions in the Far East. As well as representing a great potential adjunct to Soviet strength in the Cold War, the establishment of the PRC in 1949 operated as a serious setback to American hopes for post-war order and stability in Asia, with concerns that Beijing would work to spread revolutionary and subversive tenden- cies among the fragile states and societies of South East Asia. The quick onset of hostility between the United States and Communist China, sealed by Chinese entry into the Korean War, pushed sublimated racial tensions and factors to the surface, as Americans faced again a non-white adversary, only a few years after their triumph over Japan. Moreover, far from being regarded as a dangerous development, some Asians saw the emergence of a Communist regime as one more sign of the 'new Asia' that was rising from the wreckage of the war years and the challenge to Western dominance. Despite China's own attitudes towards Tibet, this tended to be the Indian position and, combined with Nehru's enunciation of the principles of non-alignment, made for much tension in Washington's relations with New Delhi.

During the Second World War, American victory over Japan had been attained primarily by the dominance established in the Western Pacific by US naval and air power, which had made the 'island-hopping' campaigns of 1943–5 a possibility for the Army and Marine Corps. When Japanese armies on the Asian mainland had been confronted it had been done mainly by American allies, with heavy US material support. By the late 1940s, as the American position in China was undercut, and the last US troops were withdrawn from Korea, Washington faced a very different set of strategic circumstances, necessitating the adoption of the offshore island defensive perimeter concept as the on-going division of Europe absorbed American resources and attentions. Although there were strong signs that the Truman administration's policy towards the Nationalist position on Taiwan was changing in the spring of 1950, not least as domestic political pressures on American Far Eastern policy began to intensify, the outbreak of the Korean War signalled a dramatic shift in the previous situation, making the subsequent American military commit- ment seem, in retrospect, like such an aberration. To many Americans, however, the Korean intervention of 1950 was perceived as a clear-cut case of upholding the principles of the United Nations in the face of a flagrant aggression by the Communist powers, while for Washington policy-makers the North Korean attack was interpreted as a straightforward sign of Soviet expansionist intent, which if not checked would merely be the prelude for further tests of Western resolve in areas of more vital interest. American credibility and the whole fabric of order in East Asia that the United States had hoped to uphold now appeared to be on the line, while Acheson's long-term expectation of seeing Sino-Soviet tensions develop – as anticipated in his National Press Club speech – was completely subordinated to the current and apparently overwhelming evidence of a rapacious Moscow–Beijing axis. Moreover, with American troops soon engaged in bitter fighting on the Korean peninsula, in a conflict featuring large-scale civilian and battlefield casualties, the spectacle of the United States confronting another Asian adversary, to some at least, carried racial undertones of the recently finished war against Japan. The crossing of the 38th parallel in October 1950 created a fresh stir of unease for Asian observers, who now, along with other critical commentators, questioned whether the United States was merely acting as an instrument of the will of the international community, or taking advantage of the war to complete the destruction of the North Korean regime. American championing of the authoritarian leadership of Syngman Rhee also helped convince many that there was a glaring gap between the rhetoric attached to the UN's cause on the peninsula and the reality of political rights and freedoms that could be enjoyed by the Korean people. China's intervention, and Truman's careless comments at his November 1950 press conference about possible use of the atomic bomb in Korea, set off much excited reporting around the world and underscored the capacity of the fighting to become global in scope. As well as making clear how alarmed Washington's close allies were by the dangers of escalation, Asian reactions to Truman's remarks brought home to American officials how ingrained was the notion that there was a racial aspect to proposed nuclear use in the Far East, and that memories of Hiroshima and Nagasaki were still visceral in the region. In the immediate circumstances of the Korean fighting, nevertheless, there was little indication that the Truman administration considered this a major obstacle in whatever line of nuclear policy it chose to pursue.

The protracted and debilitating stalemate of the Korean War – in Senator Albert Gore Snr's words, 'a meat grinder of American manhood' – where outright victory seemed impossible without bringing on a third world war, and whose limited aims were unacceptable to a wide range of domestic critics, convinced many Americans, including 'Asia firsters' in the Republican Party, that the commitment of American blood and treasure to the Asian mainland had been a mistake.[1] Instead, reverting in some ways to the patterns of strategy adopted between 1942 and 1945, it was considered more prudent for the United States to bolster its anti-Communist Asian allies, who would provide the ground troops necessary for local defence, while American naval and air atomic supremacy would be employed to deter, and if necessary defeat, the Chinese Communist enemy through direct attacks on mainland targets. The JCS had begun during 1952 to incorporate these kinds of assumptions about the need to use nuclear weapons in their planning for further offensive operations in Korea, and in responses to a Chinese intervention in Indochina, but it was under the Eisenhower administration that the atomic bomb was readily assimilated into the range of options that policy-makers would employ if faced with evidence of further Communist aggression in the Far East. The utility of American nuclear threats and pressures had seemingly been demonstrated in the period that preceded the conclusion of the Korean armistice in July 1953, and the philosophy lying behind the New Look entailed breaking down the distinctions between conventional and nuclear weapons and so allowing for economies to be found in defence spending.[2]

Both Eisenhower and Dulles placed maximum value on the deterrent effect of American nuclear capabilities and their rhetorical willingness to use the atomic bomb in the event that hostilities were resumed in Korea, or Communist probes encountered elsewhere in Asia. In other words, limited wars would not be permitted to recur, because the United States would rather escalate them by inflicting decisive defeat on the enemy through the best means at its disposal. Such an approach, however, carried several significant drawbacks and risks, of which senior administration figures were only too well aware. The most obvious was that the emergence of a substantial Soviet nuclear capability during the period 1953–5, including the successful testing of a hydrogen bomb, meant that expansion of the fighting to general war carried much greater dangers of nuclear devastation for the United States and, even more so, its West European allies. Though the exact condition of the Sino-Soviet relationship was often a subject of conjecture, there was always the possibility that Moscow would come to the assistance of Beijing if the limitations that had

---

[1] Albert Gore Snr to Truman, 14 April 1951, folder 692A, box 1528, Official File, Truman papers, HSTL; and see Sherry, *In the Shadow of War*, 177, 181; for a contemporary view, see Finletter, *Power and Policy*, 144.

[2] See, e.g., Divine, *Eisenhower and the Cold War*, 33–4; and for Eisenhower's conviction that there should never be another war like Korea, see memorandum for the record by the President's Special Assistant for National Security Affairs, 23 January 1956, *FRUS, 1955–1957, XIX*, 191.

been imposed on the geographical scope of US combat activities during the Korean War were to be lifted, and the Chinese mainland itself was subject to direct American attack. The chances of Russian intervention were felt to be even higher if nuclear weapons were used and Moscow's principal Asian ally faced destruction.[3] As over Korea earlier, the dangers of escalation inherent in any use of nuclear weapons in the Far East would, American officials anticipated and feared, lead to deep reservations and even to growing neutralism on the part of their closest allies. All this placed in doubt the credibility of the administration's avowed intention to use nuclear weapons at the early stages of any outbreak of limited war.

One of the consequences of this was that over the Far East the administration had tried to present the specific actions suggested by the blunt term massive retaliation in a slightly different form from that offered in Europe, where since 1954 NATO's shield forces had acted as a kind of tripwire which, in the event of a large-scale Soviet offensive, would trigger the retaliatory nuclear response that was designed to deter aggression in the first place. Over the chance of a revival of a Communist aggression in Korea, a direct move into Indochina, or any attempt to seize the offshore islands and Taiwan, the administration had been ready to assert it was prepared to use nuclear weapons, but that this would be in a selected and controlled manner and directed at military targets which were believed to be supporting the Communist forces engaged in the attack. As we have seen, the need for this important clarification had arisen at the Bermuda summit meeting of December 1953 and was increasingly expressed in public terms from March 1954 onwards, as Dulles's massive retaliation speech to the Council on Foreign Relations became the magnet for widespread criticism.

However, the efforts by the administration to convey the subtleties of its position were frequently undermined. One reason for this was the propensity of the American military authorities, whether they be the advocates of strategic air power at SAC, or the belligerent admirals who held commands in the Pacific, to maintain that any use of nuclear weapons should be of an overwhelming variety, and designed to destroy the power of the Chinese Communist Government to commit further aggression. Many military commentators also pointed to the inherent improbability of avoiding large-scale civilian casualties when nuclear strikes were directed at military installations which were also located near urban areas, making a fallacy of the administration's contention that nuclear use could be as discriminating as claimed. Besides this was the quite simple point that to

---

[3] See Gaddis, 'The Origins of Self-Deterrence', 117, 127–8.

the majority of publics around the world, there was a clear and sharp distinction to be drawn between the use and non-use of nuclear weapons, however low the yield of the latter might actually be. In this sense, the advocates of the New Look had singularly failed to convince a sceptical global and domestic audience that nuclear weapons could be regarded as in any sense conventional. The apotheosis of this position was probably reached when Lewis Strauss, in a statement issued in July 1956 which reviewed the results of the *Redwing* nuclear test series in the Pacific, maintained that the explosions were necessary to test methods of reducing fallout, and so the series had 'produced much of importance not only from a military point of view but from a humanitarian standpoint'.[4] This novel way of viewing the potential effects of nuclear weapons was widely derided in the United States and abroad, and seemed to confirm how out of touch was the AEC with popular views.

Coming at the beginning of a major crisis in Indochina, where the use of nuclear weapons was one of the options mooted, the *Bravo* test of March 1954 clearly stands as a major watershed. No sooner had Dulles begun to promulgate the idea of massive retaliation than an Asian and worldwide audience were offered a spectacle of what nuclear war might entail. The injuries sustained by the crew of the *Lucky Dragon* also gave new impetus to the anti-nuclear movement in Japan, with direct consequences for the planning of American nuclear deployments and the future of US nuclear strategy in the region. The fact that the victims of this particular nuclear accident were Asians provided an added dimension to *Bravo* and allowed contemporary commentators to make connections with the pictures of domestic US racism that had accumulated since the war, as well as rekindling the idea that there had been a racial side to the 1945 attacks. This all represented one further reason why the American authorities had a strong interest in spreading news about such legal breakthroughs for the cause of equality as the *Brown* decision on school desegregation in May 1954, though this soon came to be overshadowed by white 'massive resistance' to the practical implementation of the Supreme Court's ruling across the South.

With the world's attention increasingly drawn to the emerging civil rights struggle in the United States and the continuing evidence of endemic racism and the patterns of discrimination endured by African Americans, some officials (both American and British it is instructive to observe) could see Asians equating US nuclear plans and testing in the Far East with the attitudes associated with 'white superiority'. Americans

---

[4] Quoted in Divine, *Blowing*, 82.

during this period were acutely aware of their vulnerability to the accusation that US actions abroad were tainted with the same instances of white supremacy as could be discerned at home. As Harold Isaacs, writing in 1958, reminded his American readers:

In vast parts of the world that have suddenly become so important to us, there are people who have had experience of Western white racism, whose whole lives and personalities, indeed, were largely shaped by it. These people have ceased allowing themselves to be demeaned by white foreigners in their own countries and they are acutely sensitive to the race aspect of all their new relationships, especially with Americans, heirs to the declining power of Western white man.

According to one high official quoted by Isaacs, for the State Department and USIA, the race issue 'interlards almost everything we do', with very frequent reference made to its importance in the cable traffic coming in from overseas posts in Asia and Africa.[5] In the middle of the Little Rock school desegregation crisis of 1957, John Foster Dulles complained that the combustible issue of race was 'ruining our foreign policy. The effect of this in Asia and Africa will be worse for us than Hungary was for the Russians.'[6] Moreover, policy-makers such as Dulles also exhibited overblown fears that racial divisions could operate in the international context, so that exclusive 'white' and Asian groupings might emerge under the influence of such gatherings as the Bandung Conference of non-aligned states.

Nuclear issues, some State Department officials also came to believe, had the capacity to widen these kinds of cleavages and gave valuable ammunition to Communist allegations that the United States was planning to unleash atomic war across Asia. Plans to deploy atomic weapons in Asian countries, and to test them in the Pacific atmosphere, were seen as indicators that Americans were insensitive to local feeling, fixated by military solutions to the complex political problems, and ignorant of the economic and social injustices faced by an Asia emerging from the era of Western dominance. Dulles seems to have become especially alert to this problem by 1957, objecting to nuclear deployment in South Korea, for example, because of the 'very serious repercussions' it would raise 'throughout Asia' as the weapons were 'identified with the West and with the hated doctrine of white supremacy'. The initial proponent of massive retaliation seems to have come to the conclusion that American defence and foreign policy were frequently at odds when it came to nuclear questions, and Dulles began to argue for the 'political importance

---

[5] Isaacs, 'World Affairs and U.S. Race Relations', 365.
[6] Quoted in Dudziak, *Cold War Civil Rights*, 131.

of flexible military strength', as he put it to one conference of Pentagon officials. In a setting where the American cultural imagination conjured up alarming images of being overwhelmed by a faceless 'yellow' Asiatic horde, it was a temptation to see US technological prowess in the nuclear field as the natural method of offsetting Western weaknesses in manpower. The Communist side could riposte, however, with the line that the Americans were once again planning to use weapons of mass destruction against Asians. The result, US officials imagined, would be the wholesale alienation of Asian states and peoples then uncommitted in the Cold War, and even, around the time of Bandung, pan-Asian solidarity against the West in a revival of the wartime Japanese programme of 'Asia for the Asians'.[7]

This appraisal of the impact of nuclear use on Asian governments and peoples opened up a bureaucratic rift between the positions of the State Department and the JCS. When the subject of 'Asian opinion' was raised, the military tended to think of American allies such as South Vietnam, the Nationalist regime on Taiwan, and Thailand. For the anti-Communist political leadership of these states, American nuclear power was not conceived of in menacing terms, but as the best way to respond to the overwhelming military strength of the PRC if ever Beijing decided on overt aggression. Hence American military leaders were driven by a concern to reassure existing allies that Washington would not waver when coming to their defence in the most decisive fashion possible. By contrast, the State Department located the fulcrum of Asian opinion in the non-aligned states of the region, and above all in India, where anti-nuclear sentiment tended to be voluble, and also where much attention was given to racial discrimination within the United States. Officials in the Department were also anxious about anti-nuclear feelings in Japan, whose alliance with the United States was conceived of as so central to the whole balance of power in Asia, and whose post-occupation political orientation was by no means settled. The issue of the use of American bases in Japan for nuclear operations ran like a constant background thread in relations between Washington and Tokyo from the mid-1950s onwards, and played a key part in the still-sensitive negotiations over a new security treaty. For these kinds of reasons, the Americans searched for co-operative and willing partners in the ruling LDP and were not averse to intervening in the Japanese domestic political scene. Support for authoritarian figures in Asia led many observers to doubt

---

[7] For the deep cultural and historical roots of this version of the domino theory, see Richard Drinnon, *Facing West: The Metaphysics of Indian Hating and Empire Building* (Minneapolis, 1980), 403–4.

Washington's genuine attachment to democratic forms of government when its vital interests were at stake. In the opinion of one seasoned British diplomat based at the Washington Embassy, writing in 1958, the right-wing triumvirate of Chiang, Diem and Syngman Rhee were actually the preferred and natural candidates for an American policy that could not accommodate opposition:

> The State Department talk about the desirability of some form of effective parliamentary democracy in Japan, but the fact is that they are afraid to support democracy in Japan as elsewhere in Asia because they think it is likely to deviate towards the left. It is I know using rather loose terminology to speak of 'democracy' anywhere in Asia but the fact is that the Americans prefer to deal with authoritarian regimes. In the nature of things the authoritarian regimes which they support in Asia must be right wing – Chiang Kai-shek, Syngman Rhee and Diem. It is of course true that in these cases the Americans really had no alternatives, but the point I am making is that if there were an alternative they would not like it.[8]

This line-up of unsavoury figures, very much anchored to the United States through defence agreements and ties, and standing on the immediate periphery of Communist China, were also liabilities when it came to the task of convincing that segment of Asian opinion centred in the non-aligned world of American good intentions. This latter preoccupation gained in significance across the decade, as American officials discerned a new Soviet challenge appearing in the developing states of the region, a perception of Moscow's malign intent to gain Third World adherents that was to find its fullest expression in reactions to Khrushchev's wars of national liberation speech in early 1961.

Estimates of the political consequences of nuclear use in Asia, alongside the possibilities of escalation to general war, helped to make the Eisenhower administration far more cautious during the nuclear crises it faced with China than its public rhetoric would have indicated. There were many signs of this during the first two offshore islands crises of 1955 and 1958, where concerns over Japanese reactions were especially pronounced. Eisenhower wanted to see a conventional defence tried first before considering nuclear options, while Dulles began to have a better appreciation of the horrendously destructive effects of even the smaller-yield tactical nuclear weapons that might be employed against targets on the Chinese mainland. The outcome was often a shifting rather than consistent pattern of thinking during these fast-moving episodes, with ambiguity often seen as conferring advantages to the American position by the President. Gerard Smith later recalled that we 'muddled through

---

[8] Arthur J. de la Mare to Peter Dalton, 6 December 1958, FJ 1052/1, FO 371/133599, TNA.

the 1958 Quemoy crisis without any clear understanding as to whether and in what circumstances we would use nuclear weapons'.[9] During the Radford era, the apparent indecisions of the administration over the kind of force posture and response that was required in order to contain the Chinese regime was the cause of underlying tension and frustration. Having met both Radford and Admiral Stump, the US Commander-in-Chief Pacific, one British general wrote in September 1955 that they

> held that they should have been allowed to use the atom bomb at the time of Dien Bien Phu, and that had they done so the problem of the expansion of Chinese Communism would have been solved then and there, once and for all. They make no secret of having given this advice to the U.S. Administration, and it appears to be a matter of personal prestige to them to attempt to show that all present difficulties in Asia lie in [the] failure of the Administration to accept their advice. For all this they blame both their own politicians and the British, claiming that the latter were largely instrumental in leading the U.S. Government in (in their view) the wrong direction.[10]

The experiences of the State Department's political adviser to CINCPAC at Honolulu, appointed over Stump's opposition in 1957, was illustrative of some of these problems at a local level, as was the concern evidenced in Washington over the ideas coming from CINCPAC's staff for staging a so-called 'mousetrap' operation off the China coast, designed to lure the Communists into an engagement from which they might suffer a bloody nose. By the time of the second offshore islands crisis, some State Department officials were thoroughly alive to the possibility that elements in the military might see this as an opportunity to deliver the decisive blow against Beijing's regional ambitions that many had yearned for since the Korean War.

Emerging during the latter half of the 1950s was also the contention that the development of the Sino-Soviet split made it far less likely that the alliance would come into operation if the United States used nuclear weapons against mainland targets in a discriminating manner. American analysts never discounted the idea that the Russians would intervene on Beijing's behalf in the event of a full-scale Sino-American war (and, in fact, were still entertaining the notion in the mid-1960s), but there were fewer signs that Moscow would risk its own destruction for the sake of the increasingly unpredictable and errant Chinese Communists. It was in this

---

[9] See Smith comments in memorandum for the record of State–Defense meeting on military paragraphs of NSC 5906, 30 June 1959, *FRUS, 1958–1960, III, Microfiche Supplement*, fiche 168.

[10] Loewen note for Templer, 'United States Far East Policy and Inner Circle Planning', DO/CIC/64A, 30 September 1955, WO 216/902, TNA.

strategic context that State Department officials and members of the intelligence community, however, put forward with greater consistency and force the argument that any further use of nuclear weapons, even if only of a low-yield and targeted at military installations, would hold disastrous political ramifications for the overall US position in the Far East, cementing further the notion of the atomic bomb as a 'white man's weapon'. Predictions that key allies such as Japan would swing in a neutralist or even Communist direction were accompanied by the belief that crucial non-aligned states like India would turn their backs on the West. In the Asian dimension to the limited war debate of the later 1950s, it was this kind of analysis that helped to discredit massive retaliation, and where the issue of race played a demonstrable role.

By the end of the 1950s, indeed, despite Eisenhower's own refusal to be swayed by the arguments, the bureaucratic environment was ripe for acceptance of the new strategic posture of flexible response. With the advent of the Kennedy administration, and having gone through the chastening experience of the Laos crisis in early 1961, nuclear options were increasingly pushed to the fringes of the range of responses available to meet Communist aggression in South East Asia, with a corresponding effort made to enhance US conventional limited war capabilities under McNamara's firm hand at the Pentagon. When ideas to reduce American ground forces deployed in Korea were discussed in 1962–3 in what could be construed as a reversal of the policy then being adopted in Western Europe, they were ultimately rejected, with State Department officials arguing that this might be seen as a 'racist strategy' (at the very time when civil rights protests in the United States were again fixing international attention on inequality at home). Over the growing insurgency in South Vietnam, the use of nuclear weapons was, of course, wholly inappropriate in military terms but was also discounted as a way to destroy the power of the North to prosecute the war. In fact, the only Vietnam scenario where the use of nuclear weapons would have been given serious consideration in Washington – and had been an aspect of SEATO military planning since the mid-1950s – was in the event of a large-scale Chinese intervention in the fighting. It was to forestall any possibility of this unwelcome eventuality being presented to him that Lyndon Johnson, along with his senior advisers, resolved to keep sharp limits on the escalatory steps that would be considered in Vietnam. Behind some of these responses to the prospect of using tactical nuclear weapons to counter Chinese intervention was once again the notion that this would be seen in racial terms by much of Asia, with all the resulting negative political consequences that the State Department had consistently predicted throughout the 1950s. In 1964–5, as the Johnson administration became embroiled in Vietnam, one can still see surfacing in the consciousness of American policy-makers such as Rusk and Ball thoughts connected with the racial implications of using nuclear weapons in the Far East.[11] In December 1965, Arthur J. Goldberg, the US Ambassador to the UN, was moved to declare at a news conference summarizing the twentieth session of the General Assembly that the use of atomic weapons in Vietnam 'has not been contemplated and is not conceivable'. Goldberg's response had come after a pointed question from an Asian correspondent 'who said "non-white" observers feared that with the escalation of the war, heavy bombing attacks and the use of napalm and non-poisonous gases, the United States would not hesitate to use the atomic bomb'.[12]

In January 1946, the African-American leader W. E. B. Du Bois had prophesied that American development of the atomic bomb did not necessarily mean they would 'remain the undisputed masters of mankind' for it was not possible to keep the atomic secret as a 'monopoly of white folk. Can we hope that Japanese and Chinese brains, the intelligence of India and the rising intelligence of pan-Africa all over the world, will never be able to unlock the atom?' If such 'colored people' ever do, Du Bois foretold, 'it will be the people with massed cities, with sky-scrapers and factories, with piled material wealth, which will suffer all the more easily before desperate men in forest and on steppe, with nothing to lose but their chains'.[13] In October 1964, with the explosion of its first test device, China broke the Western and white monopoly on the atomic bomb, an event which was as symbolic of the changes that had occurred in the international politics of Asia as the American use of the bomb against Japan almost twenty years before. The arrival of a nuclear-armed China served to complicate the strategic picture in the Far East. Though the theoretical protection offered by Moscow's nuclear umbrella was looking increasingly threadbare by the early 1960s, if the PRC were ever subject to US nuclear attack, the Chinese could now conceivably retaliate with their own nuclear weapons against American bases or allies in Asia. This new

[11] As it was, the beginning of the US air campaign against North Vietnam in early 1965 opened up the United States (as before in the Korean War) to the charge that it was willing to bomb Asians with the resultant large-scale loss of innocent civilian lives. One CIA report of June 1965 noted that Asian diplomats at the UN were 'disgusted' with US military policy in Vietnam, which seemed to 'foster the indiscriminate killing of Asians … regardless of their politics. These same Asian diplomats are currently saying that it seems rather paradoxical that the first atomic bomb was dropped on Japan rather than Germany, and are asking whether this was done because Japan is an Asian nation.' CIA Intelligence Information Cable, No. 95979, 22 June 1965, DDRS/CK3100099714.
[12] 'United States Shuns A-Arms for Viet War', WP, 23 December 1965.
[13] W. E. B. Du Bois, 'Atom Bomb and the Colored World', Chicago Defender, 12 January 1946.

ability could, in the worst case envisaged by American policy-makers, give the Chinese greater confidence in using force to achieve regional hegemony. Yet as long as the Chinese stockpile of bombs remained small, and the means to deliver them rudimentary, overwhelming US nuclear superiority made this kind of outcome very unlikely. In fact, most American analysts saw the acquisition of nuclear status as inducing a greater caution in the Chinese leadership. Beijing was seen as being unlikely to provoke a strike by the United States against its developing nuclear capabilities, and there seemed no reason to suppose that the Chinese would depart from the calculated support being leant to revolutionary groups in other parts of Asia, while avoiding situations which might give Washington a clear-cut instance where the pressures to use nuclear weapons became compelling.

Although there were few worries over the impact of a nuclear-armed China on the military balance in Asia, there was, however, a widespread belief that Chinese stature would be raised quite dramatically by its entrance into the occidental nuclear club. This might then both increase its attractiveness to revolutionary groups and generate political problems, as China's neighbours came to feel intimidated and even coerced by the new strategic environment. This made it all the more important, so the reasoning went, that the United States show it was not inhibited from employing its own military force when required, and that Washington demonstrate its ability to stand by its Asian allies using conventional strength, rather than expose them to possible Chinese nuclear attack. The place where the immediate challenge was being made by China was in Vietnam, where Chinese support for Hanoi was considered fundamental to the North's war effort (and when Hanoi itself had, since June 1963, adopted a generally pro-Chinese line in the polemics of the Sino-Soviet dispute). The need for the United States to counter the political weight and prestige that it was assumed Beijing would gain when it acquired nuclear status was a common feature of American views of the Far Eastern scene during 1964, and formed an essential part of the background to the escalation of the war in Vietnam.

Supporting the regime in Saigon against the indigenous Communist insurgency had to be complemented with a willingness to place direct pressure on North Vietnam through military action, in order to both avert defeat in the South and show that the United States had the resolve to stand by its commitments, however difficult they might be to fulfil. The alternative, a reunified Vietnam under Communist control, would, for American policy-makers, represent humiliation and loss of credibility, just as Chinese power appeared to be dramatically enhanced. It was fear of this consequence that drove forward much of the fateful decision-making of the Johnson administration in late 1964 and early 1965, as bombing of the North was initiated in the aftermath of the Chinese test. Some of this kind of thinking was evident from notes composed by McGeorge Bundy for a Vietnam speech in March 1965: 'Vietnam – what is our interest there and our object? Cardinal: *not* to be a Paper Tiger. Not to have it thought that when we commit ourselves we really mean no high risks. This means, essentially, a willingness to fight China *if* necessary.'[14] When facing George Ball's arguments against substantial increases in the US troop presence in South Vietnam in July 1965, where Ball proposed that Washington cut its losses and adopt a 'neutralist' solution, Lyndon Johnson retorted of America's Asian allies such as Thailand and South Korea, 'wouldn't all those countries say Uncle Sam was a paper tiger – wouldn't we lose credibility breaking the word of three presidents – if we set it up as you proposed?'[15] Such appropriation of the language used by Mao to describe the essential weakness of Western imperialism, and the nuclear weapons brandished by the United States, is especially instructive. The United States embarked on war on the Asian mainland in part to demonstrate that even with China's acquisition of nuclear weapons, Washington was ready and able to employ military force in the region, making the eventuality which for much of the 1950s it had been considered so important to avoid now an urgent reality.

Alongside its more familiar strategic aspects, American nuclear history in Asia across the two decades that followed the use of the bomb against Japan in 1945 possessed a racial dimension, constituting one extra element making for tension in post-war US relations with the peoples and states of the developing world. The legacies of the Far Eastern War of 1941–5, which to contemporaries had in many respects pitted Occident against Orient, and the manner in which the conflict had been ended, were far reaching, helping to explain some of the ways the United States considered it would have to use force when confronted once more with an Asian enemy. By the end of the 1950s, the New Look's assumption that nuclear means could be used to counter Communist aggression in Asia was held doubtful from within the Eisenhower administration, and subject to outside criticism from the Democratic Party's foreign policy establishment. This was not simply because the dangers of escalation had increased with the growth of the Soviet Union's nuclear arsenal, but was also due to the increasingly vocal perspective of the State Department that any nuclear use in limited war would antagonize Asian opinion to an

---

[14] Bundy notes, 22 March 1965, 'Vietnam Speeches (2)', Files of McGeorge Bundy, box 17, NSF, LBJL.
[15] Notes of meeting, 21 July 1965, *FRUS, 1964–1968, III*, 195.

overwhelming extent. The United States had to have the ability to fight on the ground without recourse to the early use of nuclear weapons. But this assembling of the capacity and will to conduct extended conventional military operations contained its own perils, making the decision to inter-vene in some senses easier, for the initial stakes seemed lower and the chances of local success more tangible. The pioneer nuclear strategist Bernard Brodie wrote later that one of the most overworked terms of the McNamara era was the word 'options': 'By the end of his term in office Robert McNamara was very likely of the opinion that it had been far better that some options had not been so sedulously developed. One effective way of keeping out of trouble is to lack the means of getting into it.'[16] In 1945, when MacArthur had taken the Japanese surrender on the foredeck of the battleship USS *Missouri*, nuclear weapons had seemed the embodiment of American ascendancy in Asia, but by the mid-1960s, with a past pattern of Asian–American estrangement in the background, they had become in many respects a political encumbrance, symbolic of a destructive imperial hubris. It was the United States which was now widely portrayed as carrying the mentalities associated with the older European colonial presence – or as Isaacs put it, 'heirs to the declining power of Western white man' – and the practitioner of a hi-tech war, where Western technological superiority was assumed to equate with moral virtue, and arrayed in a small corner of South East Asia against an elusive, locally drawn enemy.[17] Twenty years had passed since the first use of nuclear weapons against Japan, but the shadow of Hiroshima still cast itself over the American conduct of war in Asia.

---

[16] Bernard Brodie, *War and Politics* (New York, 1973), 126.
[17] On this point see Loren Baritz, *Backfire: A History of How American Culture Led Us into Vietnam and Made Us Fight the Way We Did* (Baltimore, 1985), 44–9.

Bibliography

ARCHIVAL SOURCES

UNITED STATES

National Archives and Records Administration, Archives II, College Park, Maryland
RG 59, Records of the Department of State
    Central Decimal Files
    Subject Numeric Files
    Office (Lot) Files: records of the Bureau of Far East Affairs; records of the Bureau of Intelligence and Research; records of the Bureau of Politico-Military Affairs; Conference Files; records of State–JCS meetings; records relating to State Department participation in the OCB and NSC; records of the Special Assistant to the Secretary of State for Atomic Energy and Outer Space; records of the Deputy Assistant Secretary for Politico-Military Affairs; records of the Deputy Under-Secretary for Political Affairs; records of the Policy Planning Staff; records of the Policy Planning Council; subject files relating to National Security Policy; Secretary's memoranda of conversations; Secretary's staff meetings
RG 218, Records of the Joint Chiefs of Staff
    Chairman's Files
    Geographic Files
    Central Decimal Files
RG 306, Records of the United States Information Agency
    Office of Research
RG 341, Headquarters records of the United States Air Force
    Air Force Plans, Geographic Files

Harry S. Truman Library, Independence, Missouri
Harry S. Truman papers
President's Secretary's File
White House Central Files: Official File; Confidential File
Staff Member and Office Files: Korean War File; National Security Council Files; Naval Aide to the President Files; Psychological Strategy Board Files
Dean Acheson papers
George M. Elsey papers

Oral Histories: R. Gordon Arneson; Eben A. Ayers; Clark M. Clifford; George M. Elsey; Loy W. Henderson; Walter H. Judd; Elbert G. Mathews; John F. Melby; Paul H. Nitze; Evan M. Wilson

Dwight D. Eisenhower Library, Abilene, Kansas
Ann Whitman File
White House Central Files
White House Office, Office of the Special Assistant for National Security Affairs
White House Office, Office of the Staff Secretary
White House Office, National Security Council staff papers
John Foster Dulles papers
James C. Hagerty papers
Christian A. Herter papers
C. D. Jackson papers
Gerard C. Smith papers
Oral Histories: Andrew J. Goodpaster; Gordon Gray; John A. McCone; Gerard C. Smith

John F. Kennedy Library, Boston, Massachusetts
National Security File
President's Office File
Roswell L. Gilpatric papers
Roger Hilsman papers
Arthur Schlesinger Jr. papers
James C. Thomson papers
Oral Histories: George W. Ball; Roswell L. Gilpatric; Robert S. McNamara; Dean Rusk; Maxwell D. Taylor

Lyndon B. Johnson Library, Austin, Texas
National Security File
White House Central Files
White House Confidential File
Office Files of White House Aides
Cabinet Papers
Meeting Notes File
Vice-Presidential Papers, 1961–3
Vice-Presidential Security Files
George W. Ball papers
Francis M. Bator papers
Glenn T. Seaborg papers
Oral Histories: Chester Bowles; William P. Bundy; Roswell L. Gilpatric; W. Averell Harriman; U. Alexis Johnson; John A. McCone; Robert S. McNamara; Walt W. Rostow; Dean Rusk; Gerard C. Smith; Maxwell D. Taylor; James C. Thomson

Library of Congress
W. Averell Harriman papers
Curtis E. LeMay papers
Reinhold Niebuhr papers

Paul M. Nitze papers
Robert A. Taft papers
Nathan F. Twining papers
Thomas C. White papers

Butler Library, Columbia University
Pearl S. Buck papers
Institute of Pacific Relations office files
Oral Histories: Dean Acheson; George V. Allen; Lucius D. Battle; Chester
   Bowles; Gordon Gray; W. Averell Harriman; Roger Hilsman; Philip Jessup;
   Livingston Merchant; Kenneth D. Nichols; Edward Rice; Matthew
   B. Ridgway; Walter S. Robertson; Dean Rusk; H. Alexander Smith; Henry
   L. Stimson; Nathan F. Twining; Abbott Washburn

Georgetown University Library, Washington, DC
J. Graham Parsons papers

Seeley G. Mudd Library, Princeton University
Council on Foreign Relations records of meetings
Hamilton Fish Armstrong papers
Allen Dulles papers
John Foster Dulles papers
James V. Forrestal papers
Arthur Krock papers
H. Alexander Smith papers
John Foster Dulles Oral History collection: George V. Allen; John M. Allison;
   Joseph and Stewart Alsop; Dillon Anderson; Thomas Gates; Gordon Gray;
   John Irwin; U. Alexis Johnson; Walter H. Judd; Nosobuke Kishi; Henry Luce;
   Douglas MacArthur II; Neil McElroy; Arthur W. Radford; G. Frederick
   Reinhardt; Walter S. Robertson; Carlos Romulo; Gerard C. Smith; Felix
   Stump

Sterling Memorial Library, Yale University
Dean Acheson papers
Chester Bowles papers

UNITED KINGDOM

The National Archives, Kew
AIR 75, Air Ministry, private office papers and private collections, papers of
   Marshal of the Royal Air Force, Sir John Slessor
CAB 21, Cabinet Office, registered files
CAB 126, Cabinet Office, Tube Alloys Consultative Council and Combined
   Policy Committee (Atomic Energy): Minutes and Papers
CAB 128, Cabinet minutes
CAB 129, Cabinet memoranda
CAB 130, Miscellaneous Committees, minutes and papers (GEN and MISC series)

CAB 131, Cabinet, Defence Committee, minutes and papers
CAB 133, Commonwealth and international conferences
CAB 134, Miscellaneous Committees, minutes and papers (General series)
CAB 158, Joint Intelligence Committee, memoranda
CAB 195, Cabinet Secretary's notebooks
DEFE 4, Chiefs of Staff Committee, minutes
DEFE 5, Chiefs of Staff Committee, memoranda
DEFE 6, Joint Planning Staff papers
DEFE 7, Ministry of Defence, registered files
DEFE 11, Chiefs of Staff Committee, registered files
DEFE 13, Ministry of Defence, minister's office files
DEFE 32, Chiefs of Staff Committee, Secretary's Standard File
DO 35, Commonwealth Relations Office, Far East and Pacific Department files
DO 182, Commonwealth Relations Office, Western and Middle East Department files
FO 115, Foreign Office, Embassy and Consulates, United States of America: general correspondence
FO 371, Foreign Office, general political correspondence
FO 800, Foreign Office, private collections, ministers and officials
FO 953, Foreign Office, Planning Staff papers
FO 1110, Foreign Office, Information Research Department papers
PREM 8, Prime Minister's Office, 1945–51
PREM 11, Prime Minister's Office, 1951–64
WO 216, War Office, Office of the Chief of the Imperial General Staff, papers

Birmingham University Library
Avon papers

Bodleian Library, Oxford
Harold Macmillan papers

British Library
India Office records

NEWSPAPER AND MAGAZINE SOURCES

Amrita Bazar Patrika (Calcutta); *Bangkok Post*; *Ceylon Daily News*; *Chicago Daily Tribune*; *Chicago Defender*; *The Hindu* (Madras); *Hindustan Standard*; *Life*; *Manila Times*; *The Nation* (Rangoon); *New Straits Times* (Singapore); *New York Times*; *Newsweek*; *The Times*; *Times of India*; *Washington Post*.

PRINTED PRIMARY SOURCES

CANADA

Donaghy, Greg (ed.), *Documents on Canadian External Relations, Volume 16, 1950* (Ottawa, 1996).
  Documents on Canadian External Relations, Volume 21, 1955 (Ottawa, 1999).

INDIA

The Collected Works of Mahatma Gandhi, Vols. 89–94 (New Delhi, 2001).
Jawaharlal Nehru's Speeches, Vol. II: *August 1949–February 1953* (Delhi, 1967).

INTERNATIONAL

Cordier, Andrew W., and Harrelson, Max (eds.), *Public Papers of the Secretaries General of the United Nations*, Vol. VI: *U Thant, 1961–1964* (New York, 1976).
Roling, B. V. A., and Ruter, C. F. (eds.), *The Tokyo Judgement: The International Military Tribunal for the Far East, 29 April 1946–12 November 1948*, Vol. II (Amsterdam, 1977).
Royal Institute for International Affairs, *Documents on International Affairs, 1955* (Oxford, 1958).

UNITED KINGDOM

Foreign Office: Weekly Political Intelligence Summaries, Vol. XII: *July–December 1945* (London, 1983).
Yasamee, H. J., and Hamilton, K. A. (eds.), *Documents on British Policy Overseas*, Series II, Vol. IV: *Korea, June 1950–April 1951* (London, 1991).

UNITED STATES

Foreign Relations of the United States series
1942, I: General; The British Commonwealth; The Far East (Washington, DC, 1960).
1945, I: General: The United Nations (Washington, DC, 1967).
1945, VI: The British Commonwealth; The Far East (Washington, DC, 1969).
1948, I: General; The United Nations, Part 2 (Washington, DC, 1976).
1948, VI: The Far East and Australia (Washington, DC, 1974).
1950, I: National Security Affairs; Foreign Economic Policy (Washington, DC, 1977).
1950, V: Near East; South Asia; Africa (Washington, DC, 1978).
1950, VI: East Asia and the Pacific (Washington, DC, 1976).
1950, VII: Korea (Washington, DC, 1976).
1951, I: National Security Affairs; Foreign Economic Policy (Washington, DC, 1979).
1951, VI: Asia and the Pacific, Parts 1 and 2 (Washington, DC, 1977).
1951, VII: Korea and China, Parts 1 and 2 (Washington, DC, 1983).
1952–1954, I: General: Economic and Political Matters, Part 1 (Washington, DC, 1983).
1952–1954, II: National Security Affairs, Parts 1 and 2 (Washington, DC, 1984).
1952–1954, V: Western European Security, Part 1 (Washington, DC, 1983).
1952–1954, VI: Western Europe and Canada, Part 1 (Washington, DC, 1983).
1952–1954, XII: East Asia and the Pacific, Parts 1 and 2 (Washington, DC, 1984).
1952–1954, XIII: Indochina, Parts 1 and 2 (Washington, DC, 1982).
1952–1954, XIV: China and Japan, Parts 1 and 2 (Washington, DC, 1985).
1952–1954, XV: Korea, Parts 1 and 2 (Washington, DC, 1984).
1955–1957, I: Vietnam (Washington, DC, 1985).
1955–1957, II: China (Washington, DC, 1986).

1955–1957, III: China (Washington, DC, 1986).
1955–1957, IX: Foreign Economic Policy; Foreign Information Program (Washington, DC, 1987).
1955–1957, X: Foreign Aid and Economic Defense Policy (Washington, DC, 1989).
1955–1957, XIX: National Security Policy (Washington, DC, 1990).
1955–1957, XX: Regulation of Armaments; Atomic Energy (Washington, DC, 1990).
1955–1957, XXI: East Asian Security; Cambodia; Laos (Washington, DC, 1990).
1955–1957, XXIII, Part 1: *Japan* (Washington, DC, 1991).
1955–1957, XXIII, Part 2: *Korea* (Washington, DC, 1993).
1958–1960, III: National Security Policy; Arms Control and Disarmament (Washington, DC, 1996); and *Microfiche Supplement* (Washington, DC, 1998).
1958–1960, XVIII: Japan; Korea (Washington, DC, 1994).
1958–1960, XIX: China (Washington, DC, 1996); and *Microfiche Supplement* (Washington, DC, 1998).
1961–1963, V: Soviet Union (Washington, DC, 1998).
1961–1963, VIII: National Security Policy and *Microfiche Supplement* (Washington, DC, 1996).
1961–1963, XIX: South Asia (Washington, DC, 1996).
1961–1963, XXII: Northeast Asia (Washington, DC, 1996).
1961–1963, XXIV: Laos Crisis (Washington, DC, 1994).
1964–1968, I: Vietnam, 1964 (Washington, DC, 1992).
1964–1968, II: Vietnam, January–June 1965 (Washington, DC, 1996).
1964–1968, III: Vietnam, June–December 1965 (Washington, DC, 1996).
1964–1968, XXIX, Part 1: *Korea* (Washington, DC, 2000).
1964–1968, XXX: China (Washington, DC, 1998).

The Public Papers of the Presidents series
Harry S. Truman, 1950 (Washington, DC, 1965).
Harry S. Truman, 1952–53 (Washington, DC, 1966).
Dwight D. Eisenhower, 1953 (Washington, DC, 1955).
Dwight D. Eisenhower, 1954 (Washington, DC, 1960).
Dwight D. Eisenhower, 1957 (Washington, DC, 1958).
John F. Kennedy, 1961 (Washington, DC, 1962).
John F. Kennedy, 1962 (Washington, DC, 1963).
John F. Kennedy, 1963 (Washington, DC, 1964).
Lyndon B. Johnson, 1965 (Washington, DC, 1966).

Declassified Documents Reference System (online version).
Executive Sessions of the Senate Foreign Relations Committee (Historical Series), Vol. VII: *84th Congress, 1st Session, 1955* (Washington, DC, 1978).
The Pentagon Papers: The Defense Department History of United States Decision-Making on Vietnam, Senator Gravel edition, Vol. III (Boston, 1971).

DIARIES, MEMOIRS AND AUTOBIOGRAPHIES

Abell, Tyler (ed.), *Drew Pearson Diaries, 1949–1959* (New York, 1974).
Acheson, Dean, *Present at the Creation: My Years in the State Department* (New York, 1969).

Adams, Sherman, *First Hand Report: The Story of the Eisenhower Administration* (New York, 1961).

Anders, Roger M. (ed.), *Forging the Atomic Shield: Excerpts from the Office Diary of Gordon E. Dean* (Chapel Hill, 1987).

Ba Maw, *Breakthrough in Burma: Memoirs of a Revolution* (London, 1968).

Ball, George, *The Past Has Another Pattern: Memoirs* (New York, 1982).

Ball, Stuart (ed.), *Parliament and Politics in the Age of Churchill and Attlee: The Headlam Diaries, 1935–1951* (Cambridge, 1999).

Berle, Beatrice B., and Jacobs, Travis B. (eds.), *Navigating the Rapids, 1918–1971: From the Papers of Adolf A. Berle* (New York, 1973).

Blum, John M. (ed.), *The Price of Vision: The Diary of Henry A. Wallace, 1941–1946* (Boston, 1973).

Bowles, Chester, *Ambassador's Report* (London, 1954).

  Promises to Keep: My Years in Public Life, 1941–1969 (New York, 1971).

Burchett, Wilfred, *Shadows of Hiroshima* (London, 1983).

Collins, J. Lawton, *War in Peacetime: The History and Lessons of Korea* (Boston, 1969).

Douglas, William O., *Beyond the High Himalayas* (New York, 1953).

Eisenhower, Dwight D., *The White House Years: Mandate for Change, 1953–1956* (New York, 1963).

  Waging Peace, 1956–1961 (New York, 1965).

Ellsberg, Daniel, *Secrets: A Memoir of Vietnam and the Pentagon Papers* (New York, 2002).

Ferrell, Robert H. (ed.), *The Eisenhower Diaries* (New York, 1981).

  (ed.), *The Diary of James C. Hagerty: Eisenhower in Mid-Course, 1954–1955* (Bloomington, 1983).

Galbraith, John K., *Ambassador's Journal* (Boston, 1969).

Garthoff, Raymond L., *A Journey through the Cold War: A Memoir of Containment and Coexistence* (Washington, DC, 2001).

Hughes, Emmet John, *The Ordeal of Power: A Political Memoir of the Eisenhower Years* (London, 1963).

Jurika, Stephen, Jr (ed.), *From Pearl Harbor to Vietnam: The Memoirs of Admiral Arthur W. Radford* (Stanford, 1980).

Kistiakowsky, George B., *A Scientist at the White House: The Private Diary of President Eisenhower's Special Assistant for Science and Technology* (Cambridge, MA, 1976).

Krock, Arthur, *Memoirs: Sixty Years on the Firing Line* (New York, 1968).

LeMay, Curtis E., with Kantor, MacKinlay, *Mission with LeMay* (New York, 1965).

Lilienthal, David E., *The Journals of David E. Lilienthal*, Vol. II: *The Atomic Energy Years, 1945–1950* (New York, 1964).

  The Journals of David E. Lilienthal, Vol. III: *Venturesome Years, 1950–1955* (New York, 1966).

MacArthur, Douglas, *Reminiscences* (London, 1964).

McNamara, Robert S., *In Retrospect: The Tragedy and Lessons of Vietnam* (New York, 1995).

Miller, T. B. (ed.), *Australian Foreign Minister: The Diaries of R. G. Casey, 1951–60* (London, 1972).

Millis, Walter (ed.), *The Forrestal Diaries* (New York, 1951).

Moon, Penderel (ed.), *Wavell: The Viceroy's Journal* (London, 1973).

Nichols, K. D., *The Road to Trinity* (New York, 1987).

Nitze, Paul H., *From Hiroshima to Glasnost: At the Centre of Decision: A Memoir* (London, 1989).

Nixon, Richard M., *RN: The Memoirs of Richard Nixon* (New York, 1978).

Ridgway, Matthew B., *Soldier: The Memoirs of Matthew B. Ridgway* (New York, 1956).

Roosevelt, Eleanor, *India and the Awakening East* (London, 1954).

Rostow, Walt W., *The Diffusion of Power: An Essay on Recent History* (New York, 1972).

Rusk, Dean, *As I Saw It* (New York, 1990).

Shuckburgh, Evelyn, *Descent to Suez: Diaries, 1951–1956* (London, 1986).

Smith, Gerard C., *Disarming Diplomat: The Memoirs of Gerard C. Smith, Arms Control Negotiator* (Lanham, MD, 1996).

Strauss, Lewis L., *Men and Decisions* (New York, 1962).

Sulzberger, C. L., *A Long Row of Candles: Memoirs and Diaries, 1934–1954* (London, 1969).

The Last of the Giants (New York, 1970).

Taylor, Maxwell D., *Swords and Plowshares: A Memoir* (New York, 1972).

Twining, Nathan F., *Neither Liberty Nor Safety: A Hard Look at U.S. Military Policy and Strategy* (New York, 1966).

White, Theodore, *In Search of History: A Personal Adventure* (London, 1978).

Willkie, Wendell L., *One World* (New York, 1943).

Wright, Richard, *The Color Curtain: A Report on the Bandung Conference* (London, 1956).

Young, Kenneth (ed.), *The Diaries of Sir Robert Bruce Lockhart, 1939–1965* (London, 1980).

SECONDARY WORKS: BOOKS

Adas, Michael, *Machines as the Measure of Men: Science, Technology, and Ideologies of Western Dominance* (Ithaca, 1989).

Alexander, Charles C., *Holding the Line: The Eisenhower Era, 1952–1961* (Bloomington, 1975).

Aliano, Richard A., *American Defense Policy from Eisenhower to Kennedy: The Politics of Changing Military Requirements, 1957–1961* (Athens, GA, 1975).

Alperovitz, Gar, *The Decision to Use the Atomic Bomb* (New York, 1995).

Ambrose, Stephen, *Eisenhower: The President* (London, 1984).

Anderson, Carol, *Eyes Off the Prize: The United Nations and the African American Struggle for Human Rights, 1944–1955* (Cambridge, 2003).

Anderson, Stuart, *Race and Rapprochement: Anglo-Saxonism and Anglo-American Relations, 1895–1904* (London, 1981).

Bacevich, Andrew J., *The Pentomic Era: The U.S. Army between Korea and Vietnam* (Washington, DC, 1986).

Baldwin, Hanson W., *Great Mistakes of the War* (London, 1950).

Baritz, Loren, *Backfire: A History of How American Culture Led Us into Vietnam and Made Us Fight the Way We Did* (Baltimore, 1985).

Barker, Rodney, *The Hiroshima Maidens* (New York, 1985).

Barkin, Elazar, *The Retreat of Scientific Racism: Changing Concepts of Race in Britain and the United States between the World Wars* (Cambridge, 1992).

Baylis, John, and Garnett, John (eds.), *Makers of Nuclear Strategy* (London, 1991).

Beisner, Robert L., *Dean Acheson: A Life in the Cold War* (New York, 2006).

Bernstein, Barton J. (ed.), *The Atomic Bomb: The Critical Issues* (New York, 1976).

Betts, Richard K., *Soldiers, Statesmen, and Cold War Crises* (Cambridge, MA, 1977).

    Nuclear Blackmail and Nuclear Balance (Washington, DC, 1987).

Bills, Scott L., *Empire and Cold War: The Roots of US–Third World Antagonism, 1945–1947* (London, 1990).

Bird, Kai, and Lifschultz, Lawrence (eds.), *Hiroshima's Shadow* (Stony Creek, VA, 1998).

Blum, John M., *V Was for Victory: Politics and American Culture during World War Two* (New York, 1976).

Blum, Robert M., *Drawing the Line: The Origin of American Containment Policy in East Asia* (New York, 1982).

Bobbitt, Philip, Freedman, Lawrence and Treverton, Gregory F. (eds.), *US Nuclear Strategy: A Reader* (London, 1989).

Borg, Dorothy, and Heinrichs, Waldo H. (eds.), *Uncertain Years: Chinese–American Relations, 1947–1950* (New York, 1980).

Borstelmann, Thomas, *The Cold War and the Color Line: American Race Relations in the Global Arena* (London, 2001).

Botti, Timothy J., *Ace in the Hole: Why the United States Did Not Use Nuclear Weapons in the Cold War, 1945 to 1965* (Westport, CT, 1996).

Bowie, Robert R., and Immerman, Richard H., *Waging Peace: How Eisenhower Shaped an Enduring Cold War Strategy* (New York, 1998).

Bowles, Chester, *The New Dimensions of Peace* (New York, 1955).

Boyer, Paul, *By the Bomb's Early Light: American Thought and Culture at the Dawn of the Atomic Age* (New York, 1985).

    Fallout: A Historian Reflects on America's Half-Century Encounter with Nuclear Weapons (Columbus, OH, 1998).

Boyle, Peter (ed.), *The Churchill–Eisenhower Correspondence, 1953–1955* (Chapel Hill, 1990).

Brands, H. W., *The Specter of Neutralism: The United States and the Emergence of the Third World, 1947–1960* (New York, 1989).

    India and the United States: The Cold Peace (Farmington Hills, MI, 1990).

    Inside the Cold War: Loy Henderson and the Rise of the American Empire, 1918–1961 (New York, 1991).

Braw, Monica, *The Atomic Bomb Suppressed: American Censorship in Occupied Japan* (Armonk, NY, 1991).

Brinkley, Alan, *Liberalism and Its Discontents* (Cambridge, MA, 1998).

Brinkley, Douglas, *Dean Acheson: The Cold War Years, 1953–71* (New Haven, 1992).

    (ed.), *Dean Acheson and the Making of U.S. Foreign Policy* (New York, 1993).

Brodie, Bernard, *Strategy in the Missile Age* (Princeton, 1959).

    War and Politics (New York, 1973).

    (ed.), *The Absolute Weapon: Atomic Power and World Order* (New York, 1946).

Buck, Pearl S., *American Unity and Asia* (New York, 1942).

Buckley, Roger, *US–Japan Alliance Diplomacy, 1945–1990* (Cambridge, 1992).

Bullock, Alan, *Ernest Bevin: Foreign Secretary, 1945–1951* (Oxford, 1983).

Bundy, McGeorge, *Danger and Survival: Choices about the Bomb in the First Fifty Years* (New York, 1988).

Buszynski, Leszek, *SEATO: The Failure of an Alliance Strategy* (Singapore, 1983).

Cable, James, *The Geneva Conference of 1954 on Indochina* (London, 1986).

Caridi, Ronald J., *The Korean War and American Politics: The Republican Party as a Test Case* (Philadelphia, 1968).

Casey, Steven, *Selling the Korean War: Propaganda, Politics, and Public Opinion in the United States, 1950–53* (New York, 2008).

Chace, James, *Acheson: The Secretary of State Who Created the American World* (Cambridge, 1998).

Chang, Gordon H., *Friends and Enemies: The United States, China, and the Soviet Union, 1948–1972* (Stanford, 1990).

Chernus, Ira, *Eisenhower's Atoms for Peace* (College Station, TX, 2002).

Childs, Marquis, *Eisenhower: Captive Hero* (London, 1959).

Christensen, Thomas J., *Useful Adversaries: Grand Strategy, Domestic Mobilization, and Sino-American Conflict, 1947–1958* (Princeton, 1996).

Clodfelter, Mark, *The Limits of Air Power: The American Bombing of North Vietnam* (New York, 1989).

Cohen, Samuel, *The Truth About the Neutron Bomb* (New York, 1983).

Cohen, Warren I., *Dean Rusk* (Totowa, NJ, 1980).

  America's Response to China: A History of Sino-American Relations, 4th edn (New York, 2000).

Cohen, Warren I., and Iriye, Akira (eds.), *The Great Powers in East Asia, 1953–1960* (New York, 1990).

Colbert, Evelyn, *Southeast Asia in International Politics, 1941–1956* (Ithaca, 1977).

Committee for the Compilation of Materials on Damage Caused by the Atomic Bombs in Hiroshima and Nagasaki, *Hiroshima and Nagasaki: The Physical, Medical, and Social Effects of the Atomic Bombings*, translated by Eisei Ishikawa and David L. Swain (New York, 1981; originally published 1979).

Condit, Doris M., *History of the Office of the Secretary of Defense*, Vol. II: *The Test of War, 1950–1953* (Washington, DC, 1988).

Condit, Kenneth W., *History of the Joint Chiefs of Staff*, Vol. VI: *The Joint Chiefs of Staff and National Policy, 1955–1956* (Washington, DC, 1992).

Connelly, Matthew, *A Diplomatic Revolution: Algeria's Fight for Independence and the Origins of the Post-Cold War Era* (New York, 2002).

Craig, Campbell, *Destroying the Village: Eisenhower and Thermonuclear War* (New York, 1998).

Cullather, Nick, *Illusions of Influence: The Political Economy of United States–Philippines Relations, 1942–1960* (Stanford, 1994).

Cumings, Bruce, *The Origins of the Korean War*, Vol. II: *The Roaring of the Cataract, 1947–1950* (Princeton, 1990).

Dallek, Robert, *Franklin D. Roosevelt and American Foreign Policy, 1932–1945* (New York, 1979).

  The American Style of Foreign Policy: Cultural Politics and Foreign Affairs (New York, 1983).

Danchev, Alex, *Oliver Franks: Founding Father* (Oxford, 1993).

Daniels, Roger, *Prisoners without Trial: Japanese Americans in World War Two* (New York, 1993).

Defty, Andrew, *Britain, America and Anti-Communist Propaganda, 1945–53* (London, 2004).

DeGroot, Gerard, *The Bomb: A History of Hell on Earth* (London, 2004).

Dibblin, Jane, *Day of Two Suns: US Nuclear Testing and the Pacific Islanders* (London, 1988).

Divine, Robert A., *Second Chance: The Triumph of Internationalism in America during World War Two* (New York, 1967).

    Blowing On the Wind: The Nuclear Test Ban Debate, 1954–1960 (New York, 1978).

    Eisenhower and the Cold War (New York, 1981).

    The Sputnik Challenge: Eisenhower's Response to the Soviet Satellite (New York, 1993).

Dockrill, Saki, *Eisenhower's New-Look National Security Policy, 1953–61* (New York, 1996).

Donovan, Robert J., *Conflict and Crisis: The Presidency of Harry S Truman, 1945–1948* (New York, 1977).

Dower, John W., *War without Mercy: Race and Power in the Pacific War* (London, 1986).

    Japan in War and Peace: Essays on History, Race and Culture (London, 1993).

    Embracing Defeat: Japan in the Wake of World War Two (New York, 1999).

Drinnon, Richard, *Facing West: The Metaphysics of Indian Hating and Empire Building* (Minneapolis, 1980).

Dudziak, Mary L., *Cold War Civil Rights: Race and the Image of American Democracy* (Princeton, 2000).

Dulles, John Foster, *War or Peace* (New York, 1950).

Etzold, Thomas H. (ed.), *Aspects of Sino-American Relations since 1784* (New York, 1978).

Etzold, Thomas H., and Gaddis, John L. (eds.), *Containment: Documents on American Policy and Strategy, 1945–1950* (New York, 1978).

Fairchild, Bryon R., and Poole, Walter S., *History of the Joint Chiefs of Staff*, Vol. VII: *The Joint Chiefs of Staff and National Policy, 1957–1960* (Washington, DC, 2000).

Feis, Herbert, *Japan Subdued* (Princeton, 1961).

Finletter, Thomas K., *Power and Policy: U.S. Foreign Policy and Military Power in the Hydrogen Age* (New York, 1954).

Firth, Stewart, *Nuclear Playground* (Sydney, 1987).

Foot, Rosemary, *The Wrong War: American Policy and the Dimensions of the Korean Conflict* (Ithaca, 1985).

    A Substitute for Victory: The Politics of Peacemaking at the Korean Armistice Talks (Ithaca, 1990).

    The Practice of Power: U.S. Relations with China since 1949 (New York, 1995).

Frank, Richard B., *Downfall: The End of the Imperial Japanese Empire* (New York, 1999).

Freedman, Lawrence, *The Evolution of Nuclear Strategy*, 2nd edn (London, 1988).

    Kennedy's Wars: Berlin, Cuba, Laos, and Vietnam (New York, 2000).

Furedi, Frank, *The Silent War: Imperialism and the Changing Perception of Race* (London, 1998).

Fussell, Paul, *Thank God for the Atom Bomb and Other Essays* (London, 1988).

Gaddis, John L., *The United States and the Origins of the Cold War, 1941–1947* (New York, 1972).

The Long Peace: Inquiries into the History of the Cold War (New York, 1987).

The United States and the End of the Cold War: Implications, Reconsiderations, Provocations (New York, 1992).

Strategies of Containment: A Critical Appraisal of American National Security Policy during the Cold War (New York, 2005).

Gaddis, John L., Gordon, Philip H., May, Ernest R. and Rosenberg, Jonathan (eds.), *Cold War Statesmen Confront the Bomb: Nuclear Diplomacy since 1945* (Oxford, 1999).

Gallicchio, Marc, *The African American Encounter with Japan and China: Black Internationalism in Asia, 1895–1945* (Chapel Hill, 2000).

Gardner, Lloyd C., *Approaching Vietnam: From World War Two through Dienbienphu, 1941–1954* (New York, 1988).

Gelb, Lesley, with Betts, Richard K., *The Irony of Vietnam: The System Worked* (Washington, DC, 1979).

Gerstle, Gary, *American Crucible: Race and Nation in the Twentieth Century* (Princeton, 2001).

Gibbons, William Conrad, *The U.S. Government and the Vietnam War: Executive and Legislative Roles and Relationships: Part I: 1945–1960* (Princeton, 1986).

The U.S. Government and the Vietnam War: Executive and Legislative Roles and Relationships: Part II: 1961–1964 (Princeton, 1986).

Gopal, Sarvepalli, *Jawaharlal Nehru: A Biography*, Vol. II: *1947–1956* (London, 1979).

Jawaharlal Nehru: A Biography, Vol. III: *1956–1964* (Oxford, 1984).

Gossett, Thomas F., *Race: The History of an Idea in America* (New York, 1965).

Graebner, Norman A. (ed.), *The National Security: Its Theory and Practice, 1945–1960* (New York, 1986).

Guhin, Michael A., *John Foster Dulles: A Statesman and His Times* (New York, 1972).

Guttmann, Allen (ed.), *Korea and the Theory of Limited War* (Boston, 1967).

Halperin, Morton, *Limited War in the Nuclear Age* (New York, 1963).

China and the Bomb (London, 1965).

Harding, Harry, and Ming, Yuan (eds.), *Sino-American Relations, 1945–1955: A Joint Reassessment of a Critical Decade* (Wilmington, DE, 1989).

Hasegawa, Tsuyoshi, *Racing the Enemy: Stalin, Truman, and the Surrender of Japan* (Boston, 2005).

Hastings, Max, *The Korean War* (London, 1987).

Hay, Stephen N., *Asian Ideas of East and West: Tagore and His Critics* (Cambridge, MA, 1970).

Hayes, Peter, Zarsky, Lyuba and Bello, Walden, *American Lake: Nuclear Peril in the Pacific* (Ringwood, Victoria, 1986).

Hein, Laura, and Selden, Mark (eds.), *Living with the Bomb: American and Japanese Cultural Conflicts in the Nuclear Age* (Armonk, NY, 1997).

Herken, Gregg, *The Winning Weapon: The Atomic Bomb and the Cold War, 1945–1950* (New York, 1980).

Counsels of War (New York, 1987).

Hersey, John, *Hiroshima* (London, 1946; rev. edn, 1985).

Hershberg, James G., *James B. Conant: Harvard to Hiroshima and the Making of the Atomic Age* (Stanford, 1993).

Hewlett, Richard G., and Holl, Jack M., *Atoms for Peace and War, 1953–1961: Eisenhower and the Atomic Energy Commission* (Berkeley, 1989).

Hilsman, Roger, *To Move a Nation: The Politics of Foreign Policy in the Administration of John F. Kennedy* (New York, 1967).

Hitchcock, William I., *France Restored: Cold War Diplomacy and the Quest for Leadership in Europe, 1944–1954* (Chapel Hill, 1998).

Hixson, Walter L., *Parting the Curtain: Propaganda, Culture, and the Cold War, 1945–1961* (London, 1997).

Hogan, Michael J., *A Cross of Iron: Harry S. Truman and the Origins of the National Security State, 1945–1954* (Cambridge, 1998).

(ed.), *Hiroshima in History and Memory* (Cambridge, 1996).

Hoopes, Townsend, *The Devil and John Foster Dulles* (Boston, 1973).

Horne, Gerald, *Black and Red: W. E. B. Du Bois and the Afro-American Response to the Cold War, 1943–1963* (Albany, 1986).

Hunt, Michael H., *Ideology and U.S. Foreign Policy* (New Haven, 1987).

Immerman, Richard H. *John Foster Dulles: Piety, Pragmatism, and Power in U.S. Foreign Policy* (Wilmington, DE, 1999).

(ed.), *John Foster Dulles and the Diplomacy of the Cold War* (Princeton, 1990).

Iriye, Akira, *Across the Pacific: An Inner History of American–East Asian Relations* (New York, 1967).

Power and Culture: The Japanese–American War, 1941–1945 (Cambridge, MA, 1981).

Iriye, Akira, and Cohen, Warren I. (eds.), *The United States and Japan in the Postwar World* (Lexington, MA, 1989).

Isaacs, Harold, *No Peace for Asia* (New York, 1947).

Two-Thirds of the World: Problems of a New Approach to the Peoples of Asia, Africa, and Latin America (Washington, DC, 1950).

Scratches on Our Minds: American Views of China and India (New York, 1980; originally published 1958).

Jackson, Walter A., *Gunnar Myrdal and America's Conscience: Social Engineering as Racial Liberalism, 1938–1987* (Chapel Hill, 1990).

Jacobs, Seth, *America's Miracle Man in Vietnam: Ngo Dinh Diem, Religion, Race, and U.S. Intervention in Southeast Asia* (Durham, 2004).

Janis, Irving L., *Psychological Effects of the Atomic Attacks on Japan* (Santa Monica, 1950).

Jeffrey, Robin (ed.), *Asia: The Winning of Independence* (London, 1981).

Jespersen, T. Christopher, *American Images of China, 1931–1949* (Stanford, 1996).

Johnson, Sheila K., *American Attitudes Toward Japan, 1941–1975* (Washington, DC, 1975).

Kahin, George McT., *Nationalism and Revolution in Indonesia* (Ithaca, 1952).

The Asian–African Conference (Ithaca, 1956).

Intervention: How America Became Involved in Vietnam (New York, 1986).

Kaiser, David, *American Tragedy: Kennedy, Johnson, and the Origins of the Vietnam War* (Cambridge, MA, 2000).

Kalicki, J. H., *The Pattern of Sino-American Crises: Political and Military Interventions in the 1950s* (Cambridge, 1975).

Kaplan, Fred, *The Wizards of Armageddon* (New York, 1983).

Kaplan, Lawrence S., Artaud, Denise and Rubin, Mark R. (eds.), *Dien Bien Phu and the Crisis of Franco-American Relations, 1954–1955* (Wilmington, DE, 1990).

Kaplan, Lawrence S., Landa, Ronald D. and Drea, Edward J., *History of the Office of the Secretary of Defense*, Vol. V: *The McNamara Ascendancy, 1961–1965* (Washington, DC, 2006).

Karnow, Stanley, *In Our Image: America's Empire in the Philippines* (New York, 1989).

Kaufmann, William W. (ed.), *Military Policy and National Security* (Princeton, 1956).

Khong, Yuen Foong, *Analogies at War: Korea, Munich, Dien Bien Phu, and the Vietnam Decisions of 1965* (Princeton, 1992).

King, Richard H., *Race, Culture, and the Intellectuals, 1940–1970* (Washington, DC, 2004).

Kissinger, Henry, *Nuclear Weapons and Foreign Policy* (New York, 1957).

Klein, Christina, *Cold War Orientalism: Asia in the Middlebrow Imagination, 1945–1961* (Berkeley, 2003).

Knapp, Wilfrid, *A History of War and Peace, 1939–1965* (London, 1967).

Knebel, Fletcher, and Bailey, Charles, *No High Ground* (London, 1960).

Kochavi, Noam, *A Conflict Perpetuated: China Policy during the Kennedy Years* (Westport, CT, 2002).

Koshiro, Yukiko, *Trans-Pacific Racisms and the U.S. Occupation of Japan* (New York, 1999).

Kuklick, Bruce, *Blind Oracles: Intellectuals and War from Kennan to Kissinger* (Princeton, 2006).

Kushner, Tony, *The Holocaust and the Liberal Imagination* (Oxford, 1994).

LaFeber, Walter, *The Clash: U.S.–Japanese Relations throughout History* (New York, 1997).

Lapp, Ralph E., *The Voyage of the Lucky Dragon* (London, 1958).

Latham, Michael E., *Modernization as Ideology: American Social Science and 'Nation Building' in the Kennedy Era* (Chapel Hill, 2000).

Lauren, Paul Gordon, *Power and Prejudice: The Politics and Diplomacy of Racial Discrimination* (Boulder, CO, 1988).

Lawrence, Mark Atwood, *Assuming the Burden: Europe and the American Commitment to Vietnam* (Berkeley, 2005).

Layton, Azza Salama, *International Politics and Civil Rights Policies in the United States, 1941–1960* (Cambridge, 2000).

Leffler, Melvyn P., *A Preponderance of Power: National Security, the Truman Administration, and the Cold War* (Stanford, 1992).

Leighton, Richard M., *History of the Office of the Secretary of Defense*, Vol. III: *Strategy, Money, and the New Look, 1953–1956* (Washington, DC, 2001).

Lewis, David Levering, *W. E. B. Du Bois: The Fight for Equality and the American Century, 1919–1963* (New York, 2000).

Lewis, George, *The White South and the Red Menace: Segregationists, Anticommunism, and Massive Resistance, 1945–1965* (Gainesville, FL, 2004).

Lewis, John W., and Litai, Xue, *China Builds the Bomb* (Stanford, 1988).

Lifton, Robert Jay, and Mitchell, Greg, *Hiroshima in America: Fifty Years of Denial* (New York, 1995).

Lindee, M. Susan, *Suffering Made Real: American Science and the Survivors at Hiroshima* (Chicago, 1994).

Little, Robert D., *Building an Atomic Air Force, 1949–1953* (Washington, DC, Office of Air Force History, n.d.).

Logevall, Fredrik, *Choosing War: The Lost Chance for Peace and the Escalation of War in Vietnam* (Berkeley, 1999).

Mandelbaum, Michael, *The Nuclear Revolution: International Politics before and after Hiroshima* (Cambridge, 1981).

Marks III, Frederick W., *Power and Peace: The Diplomacy of John Foster Dulles* (Westport, CT, 1993).

Marr, David G., *Vietnam, 1945: The Quest for Power* (Berkeley, 1995).

Mayers, David Allan, *Cracking the Monolith: U.S. Policy against the Sino-Soviet Alliance, 1949–1955* (Baton Rouge, LA, 1986).

  George Kennan and the Dilemmas of US Foreign Policy (New York, 1988).

McGlothlen, Ronald, *Controlling the Waves: Dean Acheson and U.S. Foreign Policy in Asia* (New York, 1993).

McIntyre, W. David, *Background to the Anzus Pact: Policy-Making, Strategy and Diplomacy, 1945–55* (Christchurch, 1995).

McMahon, Robert J., *Colonialism and Cold War: The United States and the Struggle for Indonesian Independence, 1945–49* (Ithaca, 1981).

  The Cold War on the Periphery: The United States, India, and Pakistan (New York, 1994).

  The Limits of Empire: The United States and Southeast Asia since World War Two (New York, 1999).

McMaster, H. R., *Dereliction of Duty: Lyndon Johnson, Robert McNamara, the Joint Chiefs of Staff, and the Lies that Led to Vietnam* (New York, 1997).

Melanson, Richard A., and Mayers, David (eds.), *Reevaluating Eisenhower: American Foreign Policy in the Fifties* (Urbana, 1987).

Merrill, Dennis, *Bread and the Ballot: The United States and India's Economic Development, 1947–1963* (Chapel Hill, 1990).

Milne, David, *America's Rasputin: Walt Rostow and the Vietnam War* (New York, 2008).

Minear, Richard H., *Victor's Justice: The Tokyo War Crimes Trials* (Princeton, 1971).

Miscamble, Wilson D., *George F. Kennan and the Making of American Foreign Policy, 1947–1950* (Princeton, 1992).

Modelski, George (ed.), *SEATO: Six Studies* (Melbourne, 1962).

Mueller, John E., *War, Presidents and Public Opinion* (New York, 1973).

Naftali, Timothy, and Zelikow, Philip (eds.), *The Presidential Recordings: John F. Kennedy, The Great Crises*, Vol. II (New York, 2001).

Nevins, Allan (ed.), *The Strategy of Peace* (New York, 1960).

Ninkovich, Frank, *The Diplomacy of Ideas: U.S. Foreign Policy and Cultural Relations, 1938–1950* (Cambridge, 1981).

Offner, Arnold A., *Another Such Victory: President Truman and the Cold War, 1945–1953* (Stanford, 2002).

Okihiro, Gary Y., *Margins and Mainstreams: Asians in American History and Culture* (Seattle, 1994).

Oliver, Kendrick, *Kennedy, Macmillan and the Nuclear Test-Ban Debate, 1961–63* (London, 1998).

Osgood, Kenneth, *Total Cold War: Eisenhower's Secret Propaganda Battle at Home and Abroad* (Lawrence, KS, 2006).

Osgood, Robert E., *Limited War: The Challenge to American Security* (Chicago, 1957).

Panikkar, K. M., *Asia and Western Dominance* (London, 1953).

Parry-Giles, Shawn J., *The Rhetorical Presidency, Propaganda, and the Cold War, 1945–1955* (Westport, CT, 2002).

Paterson, Thomas G., *Meeting the Communist Threat: Truman to Reagan* (New York, 1988).

   (ed.), *Kennedy's Quest for Victory: American Foreign Policy, 1961–1963* (New York, 1989).

Paterson, Thomas G., and Merrill, Dennis (eds.), *Major Problems in American Foreign Relations*, Vol. II: *Since 1914*, 4th edn (Lexington, MA, 1995).

Peck, James, *Washington's China: The National Security World, the Cold War, and the Origins of Globalism* (Amherst, MA, 2006).

Plummer, Brenda Gayle, *Rising Wind: Black Americans and U.S. Foreign Affairs, 1935–1960* (Chapel Hill, 1996).

Pluvier, J. M., *South-East Asia from Colonialism to Independence* (Kuala Lumpur, 1974).

Polenberg, Richard, *One Nation Divisible: Class, Race, and Ethnicity in the United States since 1938* (New York, 1980).

Prados, John, *Operation Vulture* (New York, 2002).

Preble, Christopher A., *John F. Kennedy and the Missile Gap* (DeKalb, IL, 2004).

Preston, Andrew, *The War Council: McGeorge Bundy, the NSC and Vietnam* (Cambridge, MA, 2006).

Pruessen, Ronald, *John Foster Dulles: The Road to Power* (New York, 1982).

Rearden, Steven L., *History of the Office of the Secretary of Defense*, Vol. I: *The Formative Years, 1947–1950* (Washington, DC, 1984).

Richelson, Jeffrey T., *Spying on the Bomb: American Nuclear Intelligence from Nazi Germany to Iran and North Korea* (New York, 2006).

Roff, Rabbitt, *Hotspots: The Legacy of Hiroshima and Nagasaki* (London, 1995).

Roman, Peter J., *Eisenhower and the Missile Gap* (Ithaca, 1995).

Ross, Robert S., and Jiang Changbin (eds.), *Re-Examining the Cold War: US–China Diplomacy, 1954–1973* (Cambridge, MA, 2001).

Rostow, Walt W., *An American Policy in Asia* (New York, 1955).

Rotter, Andrew J., *The Path to Vietnam: The Origins of the American Commitment to Southeast Asia* (Ithaca, 1987).

   Comrades at Odds: The United States and India, 1947–1964 (Ithaca, 2000).

Ryan, Mark A., *Chinese Attitudes Toward Nuclear Weapons: China and the United States during the Korean War* (Armonk, NY, 1989).

SarDesai, D. R., *Indian Foreign Policy in Cambodia, Laos, and Vietnam, 1947–1964* (Berkeley, 1968).

Saunders, Francis Stoner, *Who Paid the Paper? The CIA and the Cultural Cold War* (London, 1999).

Schaller, Michael, *The American Occupation of Japan: The Origins of the Cold War in Asia* (New York, 1985).

  Douglas MacArthur: The Far Eastern General (New York, 1989).

  Altered States: The United States and Japan since the Occupation (New York, 1997).

Schlesinger Jr, Arthur M., *A Thousand Days: John F. Kennedy in the White House* (New York, 1965).

Schnabel, James F., and Watson, Robert J., *History of the Joint Chiefs of Staff: The Joint Chiefs of Staff and National Policy*, Vol. III: *The Korean War*, in 2 parts (Washington, DC, 1979).

Schoenbaum, Thomas J., *Waging Peace and War: Dean Rusk in the Truman, Kennedy, and Johnson Years* (New York, 1988).

Seaborg, Glenn T., with Loeb, Benjamin S., *Stemming the Tide: Arms Control in the Johnson Years* (Lexington, MA, 1987).

Shepherd Jr, George W., *Racial Influences on American Foreign Policy* (New York, 1970).

Sherry, Michael S., *The Rise of American Air Power: The Creation of Armageddon* (New York, 1987).

  In the Shadow of War: The United States since the 1930s (New Haven, 1995).

Sherwin, Martin J., *A World Destroyed: Hiroshima and Its Legacies*, 3rd edn (Stanford, 2003).

Singh, Anita Inder, *The Limits of British Influence: South Asia and the Anglo-American Relationship, 1947–1956* (London, 1993).

Sitkoff, Harvard, *The Struggle for Black Equality, 1954–1980* (New York, 1981).

Smith, R. B., *An International History of the Vietnam War*, Vol. I: *Revolution versus Containment, 1955–61* (London, 1983).

  An International History of the Vietnam War, Vol. II: *The Struggle for South-East Asia, 1961–65* (London, 1985).

Snead, David L., *The Gaither Committee, Eisenhower, and the Cold War* (Columbus, OH, 1999).

Soman, Appu K., *Double-Edged Sword: Nuclear Diplomacy in Unequal Conflicts: The United States and China, 1950–1958* (Westport, CT, 2000).

Southern, David W., *Gunnar Myrdal and Black–White Relations: The Use and Abuse of 'An American Dilemma', 1944–1969* (Baton Rouge, LA, 1987).

Spector, Ronald H., *Advice and Support: The Early Years of the U.S. Army in Vietnam, 1941–1960* (Washington, DC, 1983).

Statler, Kathryn C., *Replacing France: The Origins of American Intervention in Vietnam* (Lexington, MA, 2007).

Steel, Ronald, *Walter Lippmann and the American Century* (London, 1980).

Stoler, Mark A., *Allies and Adversaries: The Joint Chiefs of Staff, the Grand Alliance, and U.S. Strategy in World War Two* (Chapel Hill, 2000).

Storry, Richard, *Japan and the Decline of the West in Asia, 1894–1943* (London, 1979).

Stueck, William, *The Road to Confrontation: American Policy toward China and Korea, 1947–1950* (Chapel Hill, 1981).

  The Korean War: An International History (Princeton, 1995).

Rethinking the Korean War: A New Diplomatic and Strategic History (Princeton, 2002).

Swenson-Wright, John, *Unequal Allies? United States Security and Alliance Policy toward Japan, 1945–1960* (Stanford, 2005).

Takaki, Ronald, *Hiroshima: Why America Dropped the Atomic Bomb* (Boston, 1995).

Takemae, Eiji, *The Allied Occupation of Japan* (New York, 2002).

Tannenwald, Nina, *The Nuclear Taboo: The United States and the Non-Use of Nuclear Weapons since 1945* (Cambridge, 2007).

Taylor, Maxwell D., *The Uncertain Trumpet* (New York, 1959).

Thomson, James C., Stanley, Peter W. and Perry, John Curtis, *Sentimental Imperialists: The American Experience in East Asia* (New York, 1981).

Thorne, Christopher, *Allies of a Kind: The United States, Britain, and the War against Japan, 1941–1945* (London, 1978).

Racial Aspects of the Far Eastern War of 1941–1945 (London, 1982).

The Issue of War: States, Societies, and the Far Eastern Conflict of 1941–1945 (London, 1985).

Tinker, Hugh, *Race, Conflict and the International Order: From Empire to United Nations* (London, 1977).

Titus, A. Costandina, *Bombs in the Backyard: Atomic Testing and American Politics* (Reno, NA, 1986).

Toulouse, Mark G., *The Transformation of John Foster Dulles: From Prophet of Realism to Priest of Nationalism* (Macon, GA, 1985).

Toye, Hugh, *Laos: Buffer State or Battleground* (Oxford, 1968).

Trachtenberg, Marc, *History and Strategy* (Princeton, 1991).

A Constructed Peace: The Making of the European Settlement, 1945–1963 (Princeton, 1999).

Tucker, Nancy B., *Patterns in the Dust: Chinese–American Relations and the Recognition Controversy, 1949–1950* (New York, 1983).

(ed.), *China Confidential: American Diplomats and Sino-American Relations, 1945–1996* (New York, 2001).

Ungar, Sanford J. (ed.), *Estrangement: America and the World* (New York, 1985).

Von Eschen, Penny M., *Race against Empire: Black Americans and Anticolonialism, 1937–1957* (Ithaca, 1997).

Walker, J. Samuel, *Prompt and Utter Destruction: Truman and the Use of Atomic Bombs against Japan* (Chapel Hill, 1997).

Walzer, Michael, *Just and Unjust Wars: A Moral Argument with Historical Illustrations*, 4th edn (New York, 2006).

Watson, Robert J., *History of the Joint Chiefs of Staff*, Vol. V: *The Joint Chiefs of Staff and National Policy, 1953–1954* (Washington, DC, 1986).

History of the Office of the Secretary of Defense, Vol. IV: *Into the Missile Age, 1956–1960* (Washington, DC, 1997).

Weart, Spencer R., *Nuclear Fear: A History of Images* (Cambridge, MA, 1988).

Weinstein, Martin E., *Japan's Post War Defense Policy, 1947–1968* (New York, 1971).

Westad, Odd Arne, *The Global Cold War: Third World Interventions and the Making of Our Times* (Cambridge, 2005).

(ed.), *Brothers in Arms: The Rise and Fall of the Sino-Soviet Alliance, 1945–1963* (Washington, DC, 1998).

Whitfield, Stephen J., *The Culture of the Cold War*, 2nd edn (Baltimore, 1996).

Whiting, Allen S., *China Crosses the Yalu: The Decision to Enter the Korean War* (Stanford, 1960).

Williamson, Samuel R., and Rearden, Steven L., *The Origins of U.S. Nuclear Strategy, 1945–1953* (New York, 1993).

Winkler, Allen M., *Life under a Cloud: American Anxiety about the Atom* (New York, 1993).

Wittner, Lawrence S., *One World or None: A History of the World Nuclear Disarmament Movement Through 1953* (Stanford, 1993).

Resisting the Bomb: A History of the World Nuclear Disarmament Movement, 1954–1970 (Stanford, 1997).

Young, John W., *Winston Churchill's Last Campaign: Britain and the Cold War 1951–5* (Oxford, 1996).

Young, Marilyn B., *The Vietnam Wars, 1945–1990* (New York, 1991).

Zhai, Qiang, *The Dragon, the Lion, and the Eagle: Chinese–British–American Relations, 1949–1958* (Kent, OH, 1994).

China and the Vietnam Wars, 1950–1975 (Chapel Hill, 2000).

Zhang, Shu Guang, *Deterrence and Strategic Culture: Chinese–American Confrontations, 1949–1958* (Ithaca, 1992).

SECONDARY WORKS: ARTICLES AND CHAPTERS IN EDITED COLLECTIONS (FOR SPECIFIC PAGE NUMBERS SEE FOOTNOTES IN TEXT)

Anders, Roger M., 'The Atomic Bomb and the Korean War: Gordon Dean and the Issue of Civilian Control', *Military Affairs*, 52, 1, 1988.

Ball, George W., 'The Light that Failed', *Atlantic Monthly*, July 1972.

Beatty, John, 'Genetics in the Atomic Age: The Atomic Bomb Casualty Commission, 1947–1956', in Keith R. Benson, Jane Maienschein and Ronald Rainger (eds.), *The Expansion of American Biology* (New Brunswick, 1991).

Bernstein, Barton J., 'America in War and Peace: The Test of Liberalism', in Bernstein (ed.), *Towards a New Past: Dissenting Essays in American History* (New York, 1968).

'Ike and Hiroshima: Did He Oppose It?', *Journal of Strategic Studies*, 10, 1987.

'Seizing the Contested Terrain of Nuclear History: Stimson, Conant and Their Allies Explain the Decision to Use the Atomic Bomb', *Diplomatic History*, 17, 1, 1993.

'The Atomic Bombings Reconsidered', *Foreign Affairs*, 74, 1, Jan/Feb 1995.

Blackett, P. M. S. 'The Decision to Drop the Bomb', in Bird and Lifschultz (eds.), *Hiroshima's Shadow*.

Booth, Ken, 'Bernard Brodie', in Baylis and Garnett (eds.), *Makers of Nuclear Strategy*.

Bowles, Chester, 'A Fresh Look at Free Asia', *Foreign Affairs*, 33, 1, October 1954.

Brands, Hal, 'Rethinking Nonproliferation: LBJ, the Gilpatric Committee, and U.S. National Security Policy', *Journal of Cold War Studies*, 8, 2, Spring 2006.

Brands Jr, H. W., 'From ANZUS to SEATO: United States Strategic Policy towards Australia and New Zealand, 1952–1954', *International History Review*, 9, 2, 1987.

'Testing Massive Retaliation: Credibility and Crisis Management in the Taiwan Strait', *International Security*, 12, 4, Spring 1988.

'The Age of Vulnerability: Eisenhower and the National Insecurity State', *American Historical Review*, 94, 4, October 1989.

Braw, Monica, 'Hiroshima and Nagasaki: The Voluntary Silence', in Hein and Seldon (eds.), *Living with the Bomb*.

Brodie, Bernard, 'Nuclear Weapons: Strategic or Tactical?', *Foreign Affairs*, 32, 2, January 1954.

'More About Limited War', *World Politics*, 10, 1, October 1957.

'The Development of Nuclear Strategy', *International Security*, 2, 4, Spring 1978.

Broscious, S. David, 'Longing for International Control, Banking on American Superiority: Harry S. Truman's Approach to Nuclear Weapons', in Gaddis *et al.* (eds.), *Cold War Statesmen*.

Burr, William, and Richelson, Jeffrey T., 'Whether to "Strangle the Baby in the Cradle": The United States and the Chinese Nuclear Program, 1960–64', *International Security*, 25, 3, Winter 2000/1.

Chang, Gordon H., 'To the Nuclear Brink: Eisenhower, Dulles, and the Quemoy–Matsu Crisis', *International Security*, 12, 4, Spring 1988.

'JFK, China, and the Bomb', *Journal of American History*, 74, 4, March 1988.

Chang, Gordon H., and He, Di, 'The Absence of War in the US–China Confrontation over Quemoy and Matsu in 1954–1955: Contingency, Luck, Deterrence?', *American Historical Review*, 98, 5, December 1993.

Cohen, Warren I., 'Acheson, His Advisers, and China, 1949–1950', in Borg and Heinrichs (eds.), *Uncertain Years*.

Connelly, Matthew, 'Taking Off the Cold War Lens: Visions of North–South Conflict during the Algerian War for Independence', *American Historical Review*, 105, 3, June 2000.

Crane, Conrad C., 'To Avert Impending Disaster: American Military Plans to Use Atomic Weapons during the Korean War', *Journal of Strategic Studies*, 23, 2, June 2000.

Cumings, Bruce, 'On the Strategy and Morality of American Nuclear Policy in Korea, 1950 to the Present', *Social Science Japan Journal*, 1, 1, 1998.

Dalfiume, Richard M., 'The "Forgotten Years" of the Negro Revolution', *Journal of American History*, 55, 1, June 1968.

Dingman, Roger, 'Strategic Planning and the Policy Process: American Plans for War in East Asia, 1945–1950', *Naval War College Review*, 32, Nov–Dec 1979.

'Atomic Diplomacy and the Korean War', *International Security*, 13, 3, Winter 1988/9.

'John Foster Dulles and the Creation of the South-East Asian Treaty Organization in 1954', *International History Review*, 11, 3, August 1989.

'Alliance in Crisis: The Lucky Dragon Incident and Japanese–American Relations', in Cohen and Iriye (eds.), *The Great Powers in Asia*.

Dockrill, Michael, 'Britain and the First Chinese Offshore Islands Crisis, 1954–55', in Michael Dockrill and John W. Young (eds.), *British Foreign Policy, 1945–56* (London, 1989).

Dower, John W., '"NI" and "F": Japan's Wartime Atomic Bomb Research', in *Japan in War and Peace*.

'Yoshida in the Scales of History', in *Japan in War and Peace*.

'The Bombed: Hiroshimas and Nagasakis in Japanese Memory', in Hogan (ed.), *Hiroshima*.

Dudziak, Mary L. 'Desegregation as a Cold War Imperative', *Stanford Law Review*, 41, November 1988.

Dulles, John Foster, 'The Christian Citizen in a Changing World', in *The Church and the International Disorder: An Ecumenical Study Prepared under the Auspices of the World Council of Churches* (London, 1948).

'Security in the Pacific', *Foreign Affairs*, 30, 2, January 1952.

'Policy for Security and Peace', *Foreign Affairs*, 32, 3, April 1954.

'Challenge and Response in United States Policy', *Foreign Affairs*, 36, 1, October 1957.

Elliot, David C., 'Project Vista and Nuclear Weapons in Europe', *International Security*, 11, 1, 1986.

Engerman, David C., 'West Meets East: The Center for International Studies and Indian Economic Development', in David C. Engerman, Nils Gilman, Mark H. Haefele and Michael E. Latham (eds.), *Staging Growth: Modernization, Development, and the Global Cold War* (Amherst, MA, 2003).

Erskine, Hazel Gaudet, 'The Polls: Atomic Weapons and Nuclear Energy', *Public Opinion Quarterly*, 27, 2, Summer 1963.

Etzold, Thomas H., 'The Far East in American Strategy, 1948–1951', in Etzold (ed.), *Aspects of Sino-American Relations since 1784*.

Fetzer, James, 'Clinging to Containment: China Policy', in Paterson (ed.), *Kennedy's Quest for Victory*.

Foot, Rosemary, 'Nuclear Coercion and the Ending of the Korean Conflict', *International Security*, 13, 3, Winter 1988/9.

'Balancing against Threats: The Rise and Fall of the Sino-Soviet Alliance', in *Practice of Power*.

'China as the "Wave of the Future": The China Politico-Economic Model', in *Practice of Power*.

"We the People": U.S. Public Opinion and China Policy', in *Practice of Power*.

'Redefinitions: The Domestic Context of America's China Policy in the 1960s', in Ross and Changbin (eds.), *Re-Examining the Cold War*.

Fraser, Cary, 'An American Dilemma: Race and Realpolitik in the American Response to the Bandung Conference', in Brenda Gayle Plummer (ed.), *Window on Freedom: Race, Civil Rights, and Foreign Affairs, 1945–1988* (Chapel Hill, 2003).

Freedman, Lawrence, 'Kissinger', in Baylis and Garnett (eds.), *Makers of Nuclear Strategy*.

'Vietnam and the Disillusioned Strategist', *International Affairs*, 72, 1, 1996.

Gaddis, John L., 'The Unexpected John Foster Dulles', in *The United States and the End of the Cold War*.

'Drawing Lines: The Defensive Perimeter Strategy in East Asia, 1947–1951', in *The Long Peace*.

'The Insecurities of Victory: The United States and the Perception of the Soviet Threat after World War Two', in *The Long Peace*.

'The Origins of Self-Deterrence: The United States and the Non-Use of Nuclear Weapons, 1945–1958', in *The Long Peace*.

Gerstle, Gary, 'Race and the Myth of the Liberal Consensus', *Journal of American History*, 82, 2, September 1995.

Gizewski, Peter, 'From Winning Weapon to Destroyer of Worlds: The Nuclear Taboo in International Politics', *International Journal*, 51, Summer 1996.

Gleason, Philip, 'Americans All: World War Two and the Shaping of American Identity', *Review of Politics*, 43, October 1981.

Goldstein, Steven M., 'Chinese Communist Policy toward the United States: Opportunities and Constraints, 1944–1950', in Borg and Heinrichs (eds.), *Uncertain Years*.

Hart, Justin, 'Making Democracy Safe for the World: Race, Propaganda, and the Transformation of U.S. Foreign Policy during World War Two', *Pacific Historical Review*, 73, 1, 2004.

He, Di, 'The Evolution of the People's Republic of China's Policy toward the Offshore Islands', in Cohen and Iriye (eds.), *Great Powers in East Asia*.

Hess, Gary R., 'The First American Commitment to Indochina: The Acceptance of the "Bao Dai Solution", 1950', *Diplomatic History*, 2, 1978.

'The American Search for Stability in South East Asia: The SEATO Structure of Containment', in Cohen and Iriye (eds.), *The Great Powers in East Asia*.

Higuchi, Toshihiro, '"Clean" Bombs: Nuclear Technology and Strategy in the 1950s', *Journal of Strategic Studies*, 29, 1, February 2006.

Holsti, Ole, 'The Operational Code Approach to the Study of Political Leaders: John Foster Dulles' Philosophical and Instrumental Beliefs', *Canadian Journal of Political Science*, 3, 1, March 1970.

Herring, George C., and Immerman, Richard H., 'Eisenhower, Dulles and Dien Bien Phu: "The Day We Didn't Go to War" Revisited', in Kaplan, Artaud and Rubin (eds.), *Dien Bien Phu and the Crisis of Franco-American Relations*.

Hook, Glenn D., 'Roots of Nuclearism: Censorship and Reportage of Atomic Damage in Hiroshima and Nagasaki', *Multilingua*, 7, 1/2, 1988.

Hunt, Michael H., 'The Decolonization Puzzle in U.S. Foreign Policy: Promise versus Performance', in David Ryan and Victor Pungong (eds.), *The United States and Decolonization: Power and Freedom* (London, 2000).

Igarashi, Takeshi, 'Dean Acheson and the Japanese Peace Treaty', in Brinkley (ed.), *Dean Acheson*.

Immerman, Richard H., 'Eisenhower and Dulles: Who Made the Decisions?', *Political Psychology*, 1, Autumn 1979.

'Confessions of an Eisenhower Revisionist: An Agonizing Reappraisal', *Diplomatic History*, 14, 1990.

Isaacs, Harold R., 'World Affairs and U.S. Race Relations: A Note on Little Rock', *Public Opinion Quarterly*, 22, 3, Autumn 1958.

'Race and Color in World Affairs', *Foreign Affairs*, 47, 2, January 1969.

Jack, Homer, 'The Afro-Asian Conference', *Bulletin of the Atomic Scientists*, 11, 6, June 1955.

Jackson, Michael Gordon, 'Beyond Brinkmanship: Eisenhower, Nuclear War Fighting, and Korea, 1953–1968', *Presidential Studies Quarterly*, 33, 1, March 2005.

Jones, Matthew, 'The Radford Bombshell: Anglo-American-Australian Relations, Nuclear Weapons and the Defence of South East Asia, 1954–57', *Journal of Strategic Studies*, 27, 4, December 2004.

'A "Segregated" Asia? Race, the Bandung Conference, and Pan-Asianist Fears in American Thought and Policy, 1954–1955', *Diplomatic History*, 29, 5, November 2005.

'Targeting China: U.S. Nuclear Planning and "Massive Retaliation" in East Asia, 1953–1955', *Journal of Cold War Studies*, 10, 4, Fall 2008.

Kahin, George McT., 'The United States and the Anticolonial Revolutions in Southeast Asia', in Yonosuke Nagai and Akira Iriye (eds.), *The Origins of the Cold War in Asia* (Oxford, 1977).

Kaufman, Burton I., 'The U.S. Response to the Soviet Economic Offensive of the 1950s', *Diplomatic History*, 2, 2, Spring 1978.

Keefer, Edward C., 'President Dwight D. Eisenhower and the End of the Korean War', *Diplomatic History*, 10, 3, Summer 1986.

Luft, Joseph, and Wheeler, W. M., 'Reaction to John Hersey's "Hiroshima"', *Journal of Social Psychology*, 28, August 1948.

McHenry, Donald F., 'Confronting a Revolutionary Legacy', in Sanford J. Ungar (ed.), *Estrangement: America and the World* (New York, 1985).

McMahon, Robert J., 'Eisenhower and Third World Nationalism: A Critique of the Revisionists', *Political Science Quarterly*, 101, 1986.

'The Illusion of Vulnerability: American Reassessments of the Soviet Threat, 1955–1956', *International History Review*, 18, 3, August 1996.

McNamara, Robert S., 'The Military Role of Nuclear Weapons: Perceptions and Misperceptions', *Foreign Affairs*, 62, 1, Fall 1983.

Miles Jr, Rufus E., 'Hiroshima: The Strange Myth of Half a Million American Lives Saved', *International Security*, 10, 2, Autumn 1985.

Miyasato, Seigen, 'John Foster Dulles and the Peace Settlement with Japan', in Immerman (ed.), *John Foster Dulles*.

Nagayo, Homma, 'America in the Mind of the Japanese', In Iriye and Cohen (eds.), *The United States and Japan in the Postwar World*.

Nash, Philip, 'Bear Any Burden? John F. Kennedy and Nuclear Weapons', in Gaddis *et al.* (eds.), *Cold War Statesmen*.

Nitze, Paul H., 'Atoms, Strategy, and Policy', *Foreign Affairs*, 34, 2, January 1956.

Parker, Jason C., 'Small Victory, Missed Chance: The Eisenhower Administration, the Bandung Conference, and the Cold War', in Kathryn C. Statler and Andrew L. Johns (eds.), *The Eisenhower Administration, the Third World, and the Globalization of the Cold War* (Lanham, MD, 2006).

Passin, Herbert, 'Japan and the H-Bomb', *Bulletin of the Atomic Scientists*, 11, 8, October 1955.

Pruessen, Ronald W., 'Over the Volcano: The United States and the Taiwan Strait Crisis, 1954–1955', in Ross and Changbin (eds.), *Re-Examining the Cold War*.

Reichard, Gary R., 'Divisions and Dissent: Democrats and Foreign Policy, 1952–1956', *Political Science Quarterly*, 93, 1, Spring 1978.

Remme, Tilman, 'Britain, the 1947 Asian Relations Conference, and Regional Co-Operation in South-East Asia', in Anthony Gorst, Lewis Johnmann and W. Scott Lucas (eds.), *Postwar Britain, 1945–1964: Themes and Perspectives* (London, 1989).

Roman, Peter J., 'Ike's Hair Trigger: U.S. Nuclear Predelegation, 1953–60', *Security Studies*, 7, 4, Summer 1998.

Rosenberg, David Alan, 'American Atomic Strategy and the Hydrogen Bomb Decision', *Journal of American History*, 66, 1, June 1979.

    '"A Smoking Radiating Ruin at the End of Two Hours": Documents on American Plans for Nuclear War with the Soviet Union, 1954–1955', *International Security*, 6, 3, Winter 1981/2.

    'The Origins of Overkill: Nuclear Weapons and American Strategy, 1945–60', *International Security*, 7, 4, Spring 1983.

    'Reality and Responsibility: Power and Process in the Making of United States Nuclear Strategy, 1945–68', *Journal of Strategic Studies*, 9, 1, March 1986.

Rosendorf, Neal, 'John Foster Dulles' Nuclear Schizophrenia', in Gaddis *et al.* (eds.), *Cold War Statesmen*.

Ruane, Kevin, '"Containing America": Aspects of British Foreign Policy and the Cold War in East Asia, 1951–54', *Diplomacy and Statecraft*, 7, 1, March 1996.

Rushkoff, Bennett C., 'Eisenhower, Dulles and the Quemoy–Matsu Crisis, 1954–1955', *Political Science Quarterly*, 96, 3, 1981.

Schaller, Michael, 'Securing the Great Crescent: Occupied Japan and the Origins of Containment in Southeast Asia', *Journal of American History*, 69, 2, 1982.

Schulzinger, Robert D., 'The Johnson Administration, China, and the Vietnam War', in Ross and Changbin (eds.), *Re-Examining the Cold War*.

Sitkoff, Harvard, 'Harry Truman and the Election of 1948: The Coming of Age of Civil Rights in American Politics', *Journal of Southern History*, 37, 4, November 1971.

    'Racial Militancy and Inter-Racial Violence in the Second World War', *Journal of American History*, 58, 3, December 1971.

Smith-Norris, Martha, '"Only as Dust in the Face of the Wind": An Analysis of the BRAVO Nuclear Incident in the Pacific, 1954', *Journal of American–East Asian Relations*, 6, 1, Spring 1997.

Tadashi, Aruga, 'The Security Treaty Revision of 1960', in Iriye and Cohen (eds.), *The United States and Japan in the Postwar World*.

Tannenwald, Nina, 'The Nuclear Taboo: The United States and the Normative Bases of Nuclear Non-Use', *International Organization*, 53, Summer 1999.

    'Nuclear Weapons and the Vietnam War', *Journal of Strategic Studies*, 29, 4, August 2006.

Thayer, James R., 'Japanese Opinion on the Far Eastern Conflict', *The Public Opinion Quarterly*, 15, 1, Spring 1951.

    'The Quarter's Polls', *Public Opinion Quarterly*, 9, 3, Autumn 1945.

    'The Quarter's Polls', *Public Opinion Quarterly*, 15, 1, Spring 1951.

Thorne, Christopher, 'Racial Aspects of the Far Eastern War of 1941–1945', *Proceedings of the British Academy*, 66, 1980.

Trachtenberg, Marc, 'A "Wasting Asset": American Strategy and the Shifting Nuclear Balance, 1949–1954', in *History and Strategy*.

Tucker, Nancy B., 'A House Divided: The United States, the Department of State, and China', in Cohen and Iriye (eds.), *The Great Powers in East Asia*.

Vincent, R. J., 'Racial Equality', in Hedley Bull and Adam Watson (eds.), *The Expansion of International Society* (Oxford, 1984).

Warner, Geoffrey, 'Britain and the Crisis over Dien Bien Phu, April 1954: The Failure of United Action', in Kaplan, Artaud and Rubin (eds.), *Dien Bien Phu and the Crisis of Franco-American Relations*.

Watt, Donald Cameron, 'Restraints on War in the Air before 1945', in Michael Howard (ed.), *Restraints on War: Studies in the Limitation of Armed Conflict* (Oxford, 1979).

Wells, Samuel F., 'The Origins of Massive Retaliation', *Political Science Quarterly*, 96, 1, Spring 1981.

Woods, Randall B., 'The Politics of Idealism: Lyndon Johnson, Civil Rights, and Vietnam', *Diplomatic History*, 31, 1, January 2007.

Wynn, Neil A., 'The Impact of the Second World War on the American Negro', *Journal of Contemporary History*, 6, 2, May 1971.

Yavendentti, Michael, 'John Hersey and the American Conscience: The Reception of "Hiroshima"', *Pacific Historical Review*, 43, 1, February 1974.

Yi, Kil J., 'The U.S.–Korean Alliance in the Vietnam War', in Lloyd C. Gardner and Ted Gittinger (eds.), *International Perspectives on Vietnam* (College Station, TX, 2000).

Index